THIRD EDITION

lying AND deception *in*
HUMAN INTERACTION

MARK L. KNAPP
UNIVERSITY OF TEXAS–AUSTIN

WILLIAM EARNEST
ST. EDWARD'S UNIVERSITY

DARRIN J. GRIFFIN
UNIVERSITY OF ALABAMA

MATTHEW S. MCGLONE
UNIVERSITY OF TEXAS–AUSTIN

Kendall Hunt
publishing company

BOOK TEAM

Chairman and Chief Executive Officer **Mark C. Falb**
President and Chief Operating Officer **Chad M. Chandlee**
Vice President, Higher Education **David L. Tart**
Director of Publishing Partnerships **Paul B. Carty**
Senior Development Editor Angela **Willenbring**
Vice President, Operations **Timothy J. Beitzel**
Permissions Editor **Tammy Hunt**
Cover Designer **Suzanne Millius**

Cover image © Shutterstock.com

Kendall Hunt
publishing company

www.kendallhunt.com
Send all inquiries to:
4050 Westmark Drive
Dubuque, IA 52004-1840

BRIEF CONTENTS

PART IV – LYING AND DECEPTION FOR THE MASSES

CONTENTS

PART II: Deceptive Behavior 93

Chapter 4

NONHUMAN DECEPTION 95

Chapter 5

CHILDREN AS LIARS AND TARGETS OF LIES 127

Contents

PREFACE

Fall 2019

Every page of every chapter has been updated for this third edition. New references, new examples, even new technology—all have been brought to bear. Now fully a product of the Digital Age, embedded QR codes in the text bring examples to life, and journal articles in the reference lists are clickable thanks to the addition of permanent hyperlinks that use digital object identification.

A new prologue traces the evolution of a subject that is even more relevant now than when the first edition was published in 2007. A lot has happened in a dozen years. The emergence of social media, the digital revolution, and the Trump phenomenon have all brought renewed attention to deception as a uniquely complex aspect of human communication. Some things never change, of course. Lies in close relationships still operate under their own special rules, and detecting deception remains an elusive proposition that popular culture continues to prop up with stereotypes. Whether old or new, every topic in the book has been bolstered with updated research and current examples (did we mention the QR codes?).

As before, this book surveys the subject of deception from a variety of perspectives. The three chapters in **Part I** examine the nature of lying and deception, the nature of truth, and various ethical systems that address such matters. **Part II** looks at the broad spectrum of deceptive behaviors, from that of plants and animals, to children (the human sort), to the self. We consider both general deception encountered when dealing with others in everyday life (Chapter 7), but we also look at how the "specialists" do it—i.e., when habitual lying is enacted by those with personality disorders, as well as the behaviors and tactics of imposters, scammers, con artists, and hoaxers (Chapter 8). The two chapters in **Part III** address what is perhaps the most common subject of research on deception—lie detection. They do so by considering how it works based on human observation alone (Chapter 9) as well as surveying the various machines, drugs, and tests that have been employed to try to improve lie-detection accuracy (Chapter 10). **Part IV** concludes the book with a look at mendacity on a mass scale, from politics (Chapter 11) to the written word (Chapter 12) to the rapidly changing world of visual deception (Chapter 13).

More collaborators have joined the authors on this edition, and we are grateful for their assistance. Dr. Carolyn Conn, clinical professor of accounting at Texas State University and a certified fraud examiner, lent her considerable expertise to the revision of Chapter 9. Dr. Roger Gans, assistant professor of communication at The University of Texas at Arlington, suggested helpful updates to Chapters 7 and 8. A host of communication undergraduates at St. Edward's University in Austin, led by the inimitable Kelsey Ford, proofed both draft and final versions of various chapters. She was joined by Shannon Lowry, Patricia Medina, E.J. Jolly, Kailyn Hayes, Joseph Kulbeth, Patrick Richardson, Mary Elizabeth Buckel, Jake Painter, and Valentin Vial.

Dr. Jeanetta Sims, Dean of the Jackson College of Graduate Studies at the University of Central Oklahoma, was an early adopter of this text. She attended the first two short courses we offered at NCA, then joined us as a co-presenter for the third. Dr. Jen Hallett at Young Harris College was another early and enthusiastic adopter, as was Dr. Dennis Wignall at Dixie State University, Dr. Norah Dunbar at UC Santa Barbara, and Tony Docan-Morgan at Wisconsin-La Crosse. Dr. Tim Levine at the University of Alabama at Birmingham, whose research contributions to the field are as prolific as ever, is a regular part of our ongoing conversations. Dr. Joe Cutbirth at The University of Texas at Austin has become a valued part of the conversation as well. He brings vast experience in journalism and politics to the students in his deception course. Our colleagues as well as our chairs at Texas, Alabama, and St. Edward's—Dr. Barry Brummett, Dr. Beth Bennett, and Dr. Stephen King—buoyed us with their enthusiasm and encouragement throughout a two-year revision process. And Prometheus Williams at Trace in Austin buoyed one of the authors with cappuccino on Sunday mornings and bourbon and Diet Coke on Sunday afternoons. Finally, this new edition simply wouldn't exist were it not for the incredible support of the entire Kendall Hunt team, especially Angela Willenbring, Paul Carty, Ryan Brown, Deb Roth, and Tiffany Cue. In our opinion, no academic publisher does more to help authors bring their projects to fruition. We are also grateful for their regular sponsorship of the National Communication Association's Day of Service.

This book was, is, and always will be the brainchild of Dr. Mark Knapp. At 81, he somehow grows younger and fitter (or at least better looking) each year. His co-authors, to all of whom he is both mentor and friend, are uncertain as to how he does it, but suspect it involves a powerful, as yet little-understood form of deception. But of this much they are sure—it is their honor to dedicate this book to him.

And that's the truth.

ABOUT THE AUTHORS

Mark L. Knapp (PhD, Pennsylvania State University) is the Jesse H. Jones Centennial Professor Emeritus in Communication and Distinguished Teaching Professor Emeritus at The University of Texas at Austin. He co-edited the *Handbook of Interpersonal Communication* and *The Interplay of Truth and Deception*. In addition to authoring and then co-authoring *Lying and Deception in Human Interaction*, he co-authored *Nonverbal Communication in Human Interaction* and *Interpersonal Communication in Human Relationships*. He is past president and fellow of the International Communication Association and past president and distinguished scholar of the National Communication Association.

William J. Earnest (PhD, The University of Texas at Austin) is Assistant Professor of Communication at St. Edward's University in Austin. In graduate school at UT-Austin, he was Mark Knapp's teaching assistant when Lying and Deception was first taught as an undergraduate course (circa 1998). He is also the author of Kendall Hunt's *Save Our Slides: Presentation Design That Works*, now in its fourth edition. He has taught the Lying and Deception course every year since joining the faculty of St. Edward's in 2005. He was previously a lecturer in business communication at the McCombs School of Business at UT-Austin. Before beginning his academic career, he was a business analyst, technical writer, and trainer for Electronic Data Systems in Atlanta.

Darrin J. Griffin (PhD, University at Buffalo-SUNY) is Assistant Professor in the Department of Communication Studies at The University of Alabama and is Director of the Human Communication Research Lab at the College of Communication & Information Sciences. He recently published a chapter in the *Palgrave Macmillan Handbook on Deceptive Communication* that explores cultural influences on truth-telling and dishonesty. A child of Deaf adults, he is bilingual and bicultural and passionately advocates on behalf of Deaf communities for improved communication in a wide variety of settings. He has served as a research assistant at the FBI's Training Academy in Quantico, Virginia and the Buffalo, New York field office. While there, he studied how deception detection is implemented in real-world law enforcement contexts.

Matthew S. McGlone (PhD, Princeton University) is Professor of Communication Studies at The University of Texas at Austin (UT). His research and teaching focus on deception, persuasion, and stereotyping in human interaction. He co-edited *The Interplay of Truth and Deception* and *Work Pressures*. He is Associate Director of UT's Center for Health Communication and Program Director for UT in New York. He previously served as chair of the National Communication Association's Communication and Social Cognition Division. He directs research at UT's Center for Identity, focusing on the deceptive tactics of identity thieves; his research is the basis for developing widely accepted best practices when it comes to educating consumers and businesses about protecting themselves.

PROLOGUE The Emergence of the Post-Truth Era

Acts of lying and deception have been part of the human condition since our earliest primate ancestors began to socialize. Some of these acts of deception have played a pivotal role in the history of our species and have been well-documented elsewhere (Campbell, 2001; Denery, 2015; Harrington, 2009; Rue, 1994; Sullivan, 2001). Here, a few examples will suffice to illustrate the long-standing association our species has with falsehoods. At the same time, they will serve as a preview of what is to come in the chapters that follow.

ANCIENT HISTORY

The notion of "fake" news (or false news) that dominates current headlines is nothing new. Pharaohs and monarchs in antiquity communicated false information to the people they governed to win admiration and maintain power over them. Roman leaders famously dispatched couriers spreading false stories about rival Marc Antony to seize control of the republic. False news stories have also been used to paint negative pictures of entire groups of people. One commonly recurring myth in the antebellum South, for example, concerned African Americans who spontaneously turned white (Soll, 2016).

© pne/Shutterstock.com

Even the founders of the United States weren't above spreading false stories to accomplish their purposes. Ben Franklin created one to defame Native Americans, claiming that it came from a Boston newspaper (it did, sort of—in a pretend issue he created himself). The story maintained that bags containing scalps and other gifts had been discovered together with a letter to the King of England. The chilling implication was that Native Americans were murderous enemy agents loyal to King George III. Not unlike a false story on social media or online forums today, Franklin sent it to his friends, who read the story and sent it to their friends and eventually it got republished in real newspapers. As might be expected, the article created a lingering public animosity toward Native Americans (Parkinson, 2016).

In 1835, the *New York Sun* ran a series of articles supposedly based on telescopic observations of the moon by the country's leading astronomer. Among other things, the articles described a variety of *inhabitants* on the moon—bipedal beavers with no tails, unicorns, and bat-like winged humanoids. None of it was true (of course), nor was it meant to be as the author intended it as satire, entertainment, and a circulation builder for the newspaper—in other words, a hoax. Circulation did increase and eventually the newspaper revealed the ruse for what it was. But even after the newspaper's admission that the story was false, some people continued to believe it (Young, 2017).

Such is the life cycle of false stories people want to be true or seem just true enough to accept uncritically. Orson Welles and the American public found this out the hard way the night of the infamous "War of the Worlds" radio dramatization in 1938, intended as a piece of performance art for Halloween. The book had existed for 40 years and was well known, but that didn't stop a significant number of people from believing a real attack was underway, especially those who tuned in after the beginning of the performance.

The nature of the false news story is largely the same whether we're talking about the 1800s, 1938, or 2020. In the modern era, it is not unusual for satirical news sites to publish articles that get taken out of context and end up being reposted or shared as fact by users unaware of the original source. Even legitimate news sources are sometimes fooled by such stories (typically because of their own failure to verify information and confirm sources). At multiple points in the 2010s, for example, Chinese media outlets have misinterpreted satirical pieces published in *The Onion* or *The New Yorker* as authentic and reported them as real news (Hernández, 2017).

Documents central to the teachings of all major religions address matters of truthfulness, deception, and morality as they pertain to the lives of their devotees. In the Hebrew scriptures, sometimes the message was clear, as when the Ninth Commandment declared, "Thou shalt not bear false witness against thy neighbor." But at other times it was more complicated, as when Jacob, with his mother's help, deceived his father Isaac to get the blessing that should have rightfully gone to his older brother. And the Old Testament book of Joshua tells a story in which God spares the life of the Canaanite prostitute Rahab as a reward for lying and misleading to protect the lives of the Israelite spies. Judaism and Christianity include matters of truth and deception at the heart of their narratives about the human condition. Like its Abrahamic cousins, honesty is strongly advocated in Islam as well. According to some interpretations, however, the Quran may allow for prevarication in a very limited set of circumstances. And none other than the founder of Protestantism, Martin Luther, agreed that there could be exceptions. "A good strong lie for the sake of the good and for the Christian church ... a lie out of necessity, a useful lie, a helpful lie, such lies would not be against God, he would accept them" (Bok, 1978, p. 47).

Martin Luther notwithstanding, allowing for exceptions was not the position taken by other well-known Christian theologians, many of whom declared that no lie was permitted in any situation. Believers were flatly forbidden from lying (despite the example of Jesus himself deliberately deceiving two of his followers in Luke 24). In his treatise *De Mendacio* ("On Lying"), St. Augustine (d. 430) famously argued that lying infects personality and destroys integrity (Muldowney, 2002). Many subsequent and influential theologians embraced Augustine's absolutist stance, including St. Thomas Aquinas (d. 1274) and John Wesley (d. 1791), as well as moral philosopher Immanuel Kant (d. 1804). But congregants often found it difficult, if not impossible, to comply with decrees that forbade lying under *any* circumstances, so official "loopholes" were developed (see Chapter 3).

During the Renaissance (1300–1700) ambitious courtiers seeking fortune and power had to maintain a difficult balance, slandering competitors on the one hand while flattering superiors on the other. In an environment where any seemingly friendly face might conceal a plot, conspiracy, or coup, most courtiers thought lying was an appropriate and rational response. In other words, it was the norm, and everyone was doing it. This was the position of John of Salisbury, whose writing became very influential during the Renaissance. He claimed that the "virtuous few" had to deceive on occasion to protect themselves from the evil schemers surrounding them (1159/1990, Book III, p. 166). In *The Prince* (1513/1992), Niccolò Machiavelli famously cautioned monarchs to "never attempt to win by force what can be won by deception" (p. 128). Acknowledging that monarchs, must operate under the *public expectation* that they will be virtuous and true, Machiavelli promoted a decidedly more pragmatic mode of operation when one was out of the public eye:

> *Everyone admits how praiseworthy it is in a prince to keep his word, and to behave with integrity rather than cunning. Nevertheless, our experience has been that those princes who have done great things have considered keeping their word of little account and have known how to beguile men's minds by shrewdness and cunning. In the end, these princes have overcome those who have relied on keeping their word. (p. 69)*

Given the fact that human history is replete with acts of lying, it is not surprising to learn that efforts to detect lies also have a long history. Some of the earliest recorded thoughts about detecting deception are found in the sacred Hindu *Yajurveda*, written around 1000 BCE. In this text, clues are given for spotting spies, cleverly disguised as servants, who were intent on poisoning the food:

> *He does not answer questions, or they are evasive answers; he speaks nonsense, rubs the [big] toe along the ground, and shivers; his face is discolored; he rubs the roots of the hair with his fingers; and he tries by every means to leave the house. (Chand, 1980, p. 54)*

In ancient China, food itself was used as a detection tool. People suspected of lying were sometimes forced to chew dry rice while listening to the accusations against them. Afterwards, the chewed-up rice was examined, and if deemed too dry it was considered evidence of guilt (Ford, 1996). Greek biographer Plutarch relates an episode in which celebrated anatomist and physician Erasistratus (d. 250 BCE) treated food aversion as a deception cue.

© Anton Starikov/Shutterstock.com

In these ancient examples, the strategy for detecting deception was often predicated on an assumption that the *bodily expression of anxiety* (shifting posture, dry mouth, loss of appetite, heightened pulse, etc.) serves as evidence of deceptive intent. Similar beliefs led to the invention of the polygraph in the 20th century, which purportedly identifies liars by measuring blood pressure, heart rate, pulse, respiration, and skin conductivity (Alder, 2007; Trovillo, 1939). Despite numerous conceptual and empirical challenges to this assumption, it has continued to dominate public perception and influence deception research and theory in the modern era (see Chapters 9 and 10).

Another method our ancestors used for uncovering truth is known as "trial by ordeal," although it was often more like torture. Its origins date back some three or four thousand years, but it was widely practiced in medieval Europe and was very much a part of witch hunts in the 17th century. In a trial by ordeal, people suspected of lying about their criminal activity would be subjected to an extreme (if not impossible) physical challenge, the results of which were believed to reflect the will and judgment of God. That is, God would intervene and protect innocent truth tellers from harm but let guilty liars fail. There were at least three versions of these ordeals:

- **Trials by fire** required the accused to walk over molten coals, touch their tongues to red-hot pokers, or remove a stone from a boiling cauldron. If they couldn't complete the challenge or if God had not healed their burns within a prescribed time frame, they were guilty.

- **Trials by water** threw suspects who were rope-bound in the fetal position into a cold body of water. Those who sank were presumed innocent; those who floated were guilty—a standard clearly biased against those who had more fatty tissue, smaller bones, and flexible, lighter-weight muscles (physiologically, this may help explain why women accused of witchcraft and subjected to the water ordeal so often failed).

- **Trials by poison** forced defendants to swallow a toxic plant and survive the fever that followed to be proclaimed innocent or truthful.

While religious trials by ordeal may have served a different purpose, modern methods of torture like waterboarding are still believed by some to bring out the truth (see Chapter 9). But the idea that inflicting severe pain might inadvertently result in *false* confessions as well as truthful ones was recognized by public officials as early as the Renaissance (Langbein, 1977).

Not surprisingly, those who established the rules for detecting lies often exempted themselves from the detection methods they imposed on others. For example, the clergy who ordered trials by ordeal for others managed to sidestep such trials by adopting a much less difficult trial-by-light-snack approach for suspected liars among their own ranks (officially called a *corsned* and typically consisting of an ounce of bread and cheese). Shockingly, no priest was ever found guilty (Mackay, 1852). A modern example of these "good for you, but not good for me" double standards occurred when members of Congress rushed to polygraph 15,000 scientists in order to discover a security leak but wouldn't submit to taking such an examination themselves (Zelicoff, 2002, p. A23) (see Chapter 10).

RECENT HISTORY

In the early 20th century, Edward Bernays recognized the impact of advertising, promotion, spin, and propaganda on the American public (Tye, 2002). Widely regarded as the inventor of public relations, in his seminal work, *Propaganda* (1928), he said:

> *The conscious and intelligent manipulation of the organized habits and opinions of the masses is an important element in democratic society. Those who manipulate this unseen mechanism of society constitute an invisible government which is the true ruling power of our country. We are governed, our minds are molded, our tastes formed, and our ideas suggested, largely by men we have never heard of. (p. 37)*

So, by the time Daniel Boorstin wrote his book, *The Image: A Guide to Pseudo-Events in America* (1961), public relations was well-established. Pseudo-events are media vehicles that take the place of reality and are arranged for the sake of publicity or entertainment. For example, a movie studio leaks a story that a popular actor has died. Once that news is widely publicized, the studio calls a news conference to deny the death and, while they're at it, blame the false story on a competitor—then announce a new movie starring the very actor in question.

Boorstin felt that the variety of false and misleading events often associated with public relations had reached a critical point—one in which American culture was on the verge of creating a new reality for itself. Little did he know he was only looking at the tip of a huge iceberg that would be increasingly revealed over the next 60 years. He maintained that U.S. citizens live in a world:

> *where fantasy is more real than reality, where the image has more dignity than its original . . . . The pseudo-events that flood our consciousness are neither true nor false in the old familiar senses. The very same advances which have made them possible have also made the images—however planned, contrived, or distorted—more vivid, more attractive, more impressive, and more persuasive than reality itself. (p. 37)*

While Boorstin rarely used the terms *lying* or *deception*, the concept of pseudo-events clearly stands as a representative example of those categories and served as a forerunner for the many versions of public prevarication that would follow.

The theme of creating false realities initiated by Boorstin was subsequently taken up by numerous authors and researchers, who examined it from a variety of perspectives. In 1973, Herzog published a book called *The B.S. Factor: The Theory and Technique of Faking It in America* and each of the following four decades has seen more popular books about lying and deception than the previous one. Scholarly publications in research journals followed a similar pattern. Numerous academic disciplines contributed books on the subject, including:

- **Anthropology** (Bailey, 1991)
- **Art** (Gombrich, 2000; Honeycutt, 2014)
- **Biology** (Fujinami & Cunningham, 2000; Oldstone, 2005)
- **Botany** (Alcock, 2005)
- **Communication** (Knapp, 2008; Levine, 2014; McGlone & Knapp, 2010)
- **Economics** (Akerlof & Shiller, 2015)
- **Entomology** (Lloyd, 1986)
- **History** (Fernández-Armesto, 1997)
- **Journalism** (Paterno, 1997; Campbell, 2017)
- **Law** (Perlmutter, 1998)
- **Management** (Kihn, 2005)
- **Mathematics and statistics** (Mauro, 1992; Seife, 2011)
- **Media studies** (Mitchell, 1992)
- **Medicine and psychiatry** (Dubovsky, 1997; Ford, 1996; Kucharski, 2014)
- **Philosophy** (Nyberg, 1993)
- **Physics** (Park, 2000)
- **Psychology** (Ekman, 2001)
- **Political science and government** (Campbell, 2017; Cliffe, Ramsay, & Bartlett, 2000; Paterno, 1997)
- **Public policy** (Pfiffner, 2003)
- **Public relations and advertising** (Boush, Friestad, & Wright, 2009; Richards, 1990)
- **Religion** (Denery, 2015)
- **Sociology** (Barnes, 1994)
- **Zoology** (Cloudsley-Thompson, 1980; Stevens, 2016)

Since the late 1990s, an increasing number of colleges have added entire courses devoted solely to the subject of lying and deception while many existing courses now include dedicated units that explore the topic.

THE "POST-TRUTH" ERA

We are currently living in a time when public attention and concern for lying and deception may be at an all-time high. In 2004, Keyes said we were living in a "post-truth era"—a time when the lines between truth and lies, honesty and dishonesty, fiction and nonfiction are thoroughly blurred. In 2005, comedian Stephen Colbert introduced the term "truthiness" to

describe what he believed was an increasing tendency for people to claim as truth something that they only knew intuitively or because it feels right rather than something based on facts, evidence, and/or reasoning. In that same year, Frankfurt (2005) and Penny (2005) depicted America as a society where "bullshit" was rampant. Bullshit, according to Frankfurt, "is unavoidable whenever circumstances require someone to talk without knowing what he is talking about" (p. 63). Penny goes a little further:

> I am even tempted to make the case that lying is less dangerous than bullshit-ting . . . . The liar still cares about the truth. The bullshitter is unburdened by such concerns . . . . Bullshit is forever putting the rosiest of spins on rotten political and economic decisions. (pp. 4–5)

Manjoo (2008) was guided by these same perceptions when describing what he called a "post-fact era"—a society overrun with the tendency to believe whatever outlandish thing you wanted to believe without any regard for facts. It is exemplified by politicians who endlessly repeat talking points while ignoring factual rebuttals. While most people who behave this way are reluctant to admit their disdain for facts, Jeffrey Lord, CNN analyst and former associate political director for President Reagan, had no reservations when he said, "I honestly don't think this fact-checking business…is anything more than, you know, one more sort of out-of-touch, elitist, media-type thing. I don't think people out here in America care. What they care about are what the candidates say" (Borchers, 2016). Yet this nonsense simply echoed what Neil Newhouse, pollster for Mitt Romney, said the week of the Republican National Convention in 2012: "We're not going to let our campaign be dictated by fact-checkers" (Stein, 2012). Somewhat ironically, Krugman (2011) confirmed the truth of Newhouse's statement by documenting numerous factual omissions and misrepresentations in the Romney campaign.

"Post-truth" was named the 2016 Word of the Year by Oxford Dictionaries, defined as relating to or denoting circumstances in which objective facts are less influential in shaping public opinion than appeals to emotion and personal belief. That same year, PolitiFact chose "fake news" as the winner of their annual Lie of the Year award, calling it fabricated information, manipulated to look like credible reports, then easily spread online. Often driven by conspiracy theorists, prominent fake news items have included stories as seemingly ridiculous as Hillary Clinton running a child sex ring out of a pizza shop in suburban DC. But to believers like Edgar Welch it made sense. So much sense, in fact, that a month after the 2016 presidential election, the 28-year-old drove up from North Carolina to "self-investigate" the story—with an assault rifle, a shotgun, a .38 caliber handgun, and a knife. He pointed a weapon at a restaurant employee but, fortunately, the place emptied out before he managed to fire any shots (Siddiqui & Svriuga, 2016).

Other fake news headlines that were popular during the 2016 campaign season included "POPE BACKS TRUMP," "HILLARY SOLD WEAPONS TO ISIS," and "FBI AGENT SUSPECTED IN HILLARY EMAIL LEAKS FOUND DEAD." All went viral on Facebook during the 2016 campaign, gaining such high engagement that BuzzFeed published an analysis showing how they had *outperformed real news* in terms of posts, shares, and comments (Silverman, 2016). Separately, an Oxford University study found that Twitter users in swing states got more fake news than real news in the days leading up to the 2016 presidential election (Howard, Kollanyi, Bradshaw, & Neudert, 2017).

The most prolific source of these fake news stories appears to have been the Russian government and its agents, which already have a long history of meddling in other countries' elections (Priest & Birnbaum, 2017). But the sophistication of their fake news tactics in the 2016 presidential election created a major challenge for Facebook and Google, which, in the face of mounting public pressure, have begun to crack down on fake news (O'Sulllivan & Herb, 2018; Timberg, 2016). So it might be unsurprising to learn that PolitiFact's 2017 Lie of the Year winner was the demonstrably false idea that Russian election interference was a "made-up story" (Holan, 2017).

Exposing Fake News

Deception detection is always a close companion to deceptive behavior. Therefore, given the perception that we had entered a post-truth/post-fact era—replete with bullshit and what Jackson and Jamieson (2007) called a "world of disinformation"—it is instructive to trace the rising number of efforts to detect falsehoods and to publicize facts in response to undocumented claims and assertions confronting the public:

- One of the first groups to undertake the task of identifying and disseminating instances of public deception was the National Council of Teachers of English. During the Watergate scandal in 1971, the NCTE established the Committee on Public Doublespeak. Its purpose was to analyze, record, and publicize the way public officials, advertisers, and others use language to distort, mislead, and manipulate. The organization's *Doublespeak Award*, presented annually since 1974, is given to a public spokesperson or advertisement in which the language is grossly deceptive, confusing, or evasive. Lutz (1989) argued the most disturbing linguistic distortions of reality are those used by people in power to mislead others for their own purposes which, if not exposed, will structure the way we construe and experience reality.

- In 1995, Snopes.com was established to track down and clarify rumors, scams, urban legends, and other stories of unknown or questionable origin circulating on the Internet.

- In 2003, the Public Policy Center at the University of Pennsylvania's Annenberg School of Communication launched FactCheck. The non-partisan, non-profit site focuses primarily on political rhetoric and seeks to determine the validity of statements made by political candidates, office holders, and other public officials.

- Mentioned previously, PolitiFact, established in 2007 by the *Tampa Bay Times*, has similar goals. Since 2009 it has named a Lie of the Year, and its *Truth-O-Meter* has become a fixture on the pages of many U.S. newspapers, rating the accuracy of public statements from "True" all the way down to "Pants on Fire!"

- The stated goals of WikiLeaks, founded in 2006, are not to expose the deception in what is said as much as it is to expose secret and/or classified information that might be the basis of what is being left unsaid. They do not identify the names of their sources nor the means by which they obtain information. While there are individuals who, because of their "insider" status, try to expose the lies of corporations and public entities, these "whistleblowers" do not always fare well if they are identified. As a result, people with knowledge of individual or organizational deception may hesitate to go public (Alford, 2001; Glazer & Glazer, 1989) (see Chapter 9).

- Glenn Kessler's column, "The Fact Checker," began as a feature during the 2008 U.S. presidential campaign, but the *Washington Post* made it a permanent column in 2011. Its purpose is to "truth-squad" public statements having to do with matters of great importance, be they international, national, or local. About half of Fact Checker's stories begin as inquiries raised by readers (Kessler, 2013).

Some efforts have been made at the federal level to protect the consumer from deceptive messages, but free speech rights, poorly written laws, the difficulty in proving intent, and the lack of enforcement personnel often neutralize the effects of such legislation. Libel laws, designed to protect a person from lies that damage his or her reputation, have been in existence as long as the country itself. The Fair Packaging and Labeling Act of 1968 was designed to encourage honesty in product labeling. The Truth in Lending Act in the same year aimed at eliminating deceptive practices related to the costs and terms associated with borrowing money.

One of the primary jobs of the Federal Trade Commission is to protect the public from deceptive advertising. Congress even introduced a bill that was intended to protect the public from photoshopped images. In 2014 and again in 2016, a Truth in Advertising Act was proposed that would give the FTC the power to examine potential harm arising out of any media images in ads that were deliberately altered to materially change the appearance and physical characteristics of models' faces, bodies, skin color, weight, signs of aging, etc.

The problems with enforcement alone are likely to stifle such legislation, at least in the United States. In 2013, however, Israel's so-called "Photoshop Law" went into effect. Among other things, it requires advertisers to label any photos that have been retouched. As one commentator put it, now the general public can be assured that "even the models don't look like the models" (Horwath, 2016). France followed suit in 2017, enacting legislation that requires the label "Retouched Photo" be applied whenever models appearing in ads have been digitally altered. The law applies to online and in-print ads equally and carries a potential fine of €37,500 (Daldorph, 2017).

Of course, not everyone believes that government regulation is necessary, arguing that the marketplace is capable of self-regulation when it comes to such matters (Max, 2018). U.S. mega-retailer CVS has pledged to stop "materially altering" any images associated with their beauty products and is asking its suppliers to do the same, or at least use a "Retouched" label. Critics skeptical of the move, however, point out that the word "materially" is unnecessary and gives the company the ability to interpret it as they see fit (Friedman, 2018). Regardless, such efforts, whether public or private, are significant in that they represent an effort to deal with a potentially deceptive tool that is unique to the 21st Century and available to virtually anyone with a computer.

Here it's worth stepping back and asking just how it is that we got to this point. What led to the belief that we are being overrun with bullshit, living in a post-truth society, and badly in need of fact-checking organizations as a counterbalance? Like other subjects that dominate the public and academic mindset, our current concern with lying and deception was fertilized by and grew out of various social, political, and technological forces during the past half century.

Highly Publicized Acts of Lying

Most people tell the truth most of the time—the maintenance of social cohesion demands it. But some people lie a lot and some lies are more visible and affect more people. These lies, often by public figures in positions of power, are responsible for creating a widespread awareness of deception and its effects. Examples of this from the recent past are plentiful.

That U.S. presidents and candidates have engaged in willful deception is well documented (Alterman, 2004; Pfiffner, 1999). The vast volume of confirmed presidential lies prohibits detailed documentation here (entire books have been written), but confirmed or not, every past president seems likely to have lied to the public at some point during his tenure in office (see Chapter 11). Donald Trump, however, seems to have surpassed the deceit of his predecessors in both quantity and audacity. His track record of untruths during his first year in office was a scandal of epic proportions. Fact checkers for the *Washington Post* identified 2,140 false or misleading claims by President Trump during his first year in office—an average of nearly 5.9 per day (Kessler & Kelly, 2018). This figure almost doubled to 4,229 during

© egorkeon/Shutterstock.com

the next six months, upping his average to 7.6 false or misleading claims per day (Kessler, Rizzo, & Kelly, 2018). Reporters David Leonhardt and Stuart Thompson of the *New York Times* artfully expressed the shock and dismay many White House observers felt while monitoring the current president's conduct:

> *There is simply no precedent for an American president to spend so much time telling untruths. Every president has shaded the truth or told occasional whoppers. No other president—of either party—has behaved as Trump is behaving. He is trying to create an atmosphere in which reality is irrelevant. (2017)*

There is no federal law that prevents politicians from lying in public statements or advertisements, and while some states have laws prohibiting political lies, free speech rights and the difficulty in proving intent make them all but impossible to enforce. As Rue pointed out almost 25 years ago:

> *There are many honest and truthful ways to elicit positive responses from voters, but it has long been recognized that they are less effective than deceptive means. Exaggeration, distortion, quoting out of context, innuendo, false*

promises, pandering, scare tactics, and flat-out-lies have become the standard
fare of political campaigns. (1994, p. 246)

Little, it would seem, has changed in that time. From that same vantage point in the first half of the 1990s, Miller and Stiff expressed great alarm that the long-term effects of such behavior could have on citizens, warning that:

> *Many are becoming more permissive, or at least more fatalistically accepting, of*
> *deceptive tactics. Certainly, cynicism about the veracity of politicians is a ven-*
> *erable characteristic of the American voter, but this cynicism has typically been*
> *coupled with belief in the moral culpability and responsibility of the offending*
> *party. During recent campaigns, many political commentators and voters*
> *alike seem to have become resigned to the fact that deceptive communication*
> *is merely part of the 'getting elected' game. This tone of resignation surfaces in*
> *statements justifying deceit on the grounds that 'it was just something that was*
> *said during the campaign,' the implication being that campaign pledges can be*
> *expected to become inoperative on inauguration day. To the extent that citizens*
> *accept a shift from a norm of honesty to a norm of deceit, traditional democrat-*
> *ic values relating to the need for an informed populace and debate about the*
> *substance of issues will be seriously threatened. (1993, p. 5)*

But politicians haven't been the only ones producing deception for public consumption during the last half-century. During the 1980s, the testimony of children about incredibly fanciful, dangerous, and unhealthy events at the McMartin daycare grabbed national headlines and led to the imprisonment of innocent providers (not to mention the destruction of their livelihoods and the besmirching of the entire daycare industry). After many years and millions of dollars, the legal system found the stories told by these children to be false, but this case and others like it prompted researchers to look closely at the lying and truth telling behavior of children (Ceci & Bruck, 1995; Eberle & Eberle, 1993) (see Chapter 5). Among other findings, researchers have observed a "promise effect," in which children as young as five years old are substantially less likely to lie if, ahead of time, they make a verbal commitment not to do so (Heyman, Fu, Lin, Qian, & Lee, 2015).

As Chapter 12 discusses, memoirs are autobiographical life stories and, like any autobiographical work, are expected to be truthful. Sometimes memoirists are guilty of a faulty memory, but outright lies have characterized several nationally well-known memoirs:

- *I, Rigoberto Menchú* (1983)
- *Fragments: Memories of a Wartime Childhood* (Wilkomirski, 1996)
- *A Million Little Pieces* (Frey, 2003)
- *Angel at the Fence: The True Story of a Love That Survived* (Rosenblat, 2009)

Professional journalists who made up stories, plagiarized, invented sources, quotes, and events, or combined elements of several stories also received national media exposure. As a result, reporters from the *Washington Post, USA Today,* the *New York Times,* and the *New Republic,* among others, were publicly and often spectacularly discredited. Chief among these was the most popular television news anchor in the United States, Brian Williams of the *NBC Nightly News.* In 2014, Williams got called out for more than a decade of fibbing about his experiences as an embedded journalist in a combat zone during the Iraq War (Farhi, 2015). And when the Governor of New Mexico, the Notre Dame football coach, the Poet Laureate of California, executives from Oracle, Radio Shack, Bausch & Lomb, and the U.S. Olympic Committee, among others, fabricated information on their résumés, the public took notice.

A list that is probably even longer than the ones above would be of celebrities and others who have been caught lying about having served in the military (or, in some cases, lying about the details of their service, such as rank, medals earned, and whether or not they saw combat). The situation grew bad enough that Congress felt compelled to act—twice. The first version, the Stolen Valor Act of 2005, was struck down by the Supreme Court several years later as a violation of free speech. The updated 2013 version of the law was careful to target only people who benefit in some tangible way from their deception (Ford, 2018).

Popular Books, TV Shows, and Movies

Self-help books like Lieberman's *Never Be Lied to Again* (1998) and best-sellers like Harvard philosopher Sissela Bok's *Lying: Moral Choice in Public and Private Life* (1978) helped to illumine the subject of deception for the masses during the run-up to our current post-truth era. William Bennett served as Secretary of Education under Ronald Reagan and Drug Czar under George H.W. Bush. Later he would become an informal "Values Czar" as well, publishing not one but two volumes that included honesty as a virtue to be admired and practiced and lying as villainous. *The Book of Virtues: A Treasury of Great Moral Stories* (1993) and its successor *The Children's Book of Virtues* (1995) both spent months on national best-seller lists, and the latter became the basis of an animated series that ran on PBS from 1996 to 2000. But as has often been the case with moral crusaders, Bennett's advice seemed to be based on more of a "do as I *say*, not as I *do*" model. In 2003 it came to light that he was a high-stakes casino gambler who had lost at least $8 million in the 10 years since the first book was published. To be fair, Bennett had never crusaded against gambling or identified it as a vice. "I've made a lot of money and I've won a lot of money," he said when defending himself to reporters. "You don't see what I walk away with" (Seelye, 2003).

Beginning in the late 1960s, CBS debuted *60 Minutes* and it quickly built a worldwide reputation. It used investigative journalism primarily focused on the lies of various individuals, celebrities, governments, non-profits, and corporations. The interest in lying has, from the beginning, been a big part of television entertainment. As of 2016, the game show *To Tell the Truth* was one of only two game shows to have aired at least one new episode in each of the past seven decades. Some TV series have devoted a single episode of a drama or comedy to the subject of lying, but in recent years it has become the theme around which to base an entire series. From 2009 to 2011, the show *Lie to Me* featured a character (loosely based on deception researcher Paul Ekman) who could detect lies by carefully observing a person's nonverbal behavior. Showtime's dark comedy series *House of Lies* (2012–2016) was based on Martin Kihn's (2005) account of the manipulative practices he witnessed and performed as a management consultant for Booz Allen Hamilton. ABC's mystery detective series *Secrets and Lies* was launched in 2015. A movie by that same name (unrelated to the television series) was released in 1996 to great critical and commercial success, garnering five Oscar nominations.

Disney's animated film, *Pinocchio*, was a critical success but a box office disaster in 1940. But in 1994, the Library of Congress admitted it into the National Film Registry. The now-famous tale of a boy whose nose grows when he lies has become a cultural icon—inspiring dozens of books, movies, and sculptures and countless memes. The biggest box office success in movie history for any month of March was the 1997 film *Liar, Liar*, a comedy about a lawyer magically constrained from lying (and forced to speak the absolute truth) for 24 hours. *Catch Me if You Can*, based on the exploits of 1960s con artist Frank Abagnale, was both a critical and box office smash in 2002. Ricky Gervais' movie *The Invention of Lying* (2009) tells the story of a man living in an alternate universe in which it has never occurred to anyone else but him that the truth can be twisted.

These are just a few examples out of many. Lying and deception have proven to be reliable (and bankable) themes for media outlets and movie studios.

Computer-Mediated Communication

In less than 30 years' time, our society has undergone a bigger technological transformation than even the original personal computing revolution of the 1980s. All of the following developed in rapid succession beginning in the early 1990s and in the years since have grown so ubiquitous as to become a regular feature of everyday life—the Internet, e-mail, online chatting, photo editing software, mobile phones, texting, smartphones, blogs, apps, social media, and online dating sites. This new revolution in communication technology brought with it the ability of an individual liar (or group) to spread deceit faster and to more people than ever before—often anonymously. Corporations, whose reputation and profits could suffer from online disinformation, employed people to monitor what is being said about them on blogs, newsgroups, and social media so they can act quickly to counteract it. They use these same platforms to push information as they manage their online presence, necessary tools in any modern public image campaign.

After Photoshop was made available to the general public, virtually anyone with a computer could alter a visual image (see Chapter 13). Sometimes these alterations were done for purely aesthetic or comedic purposes, but a growing number are produced with the express goals of damaging someone's reputation (cyberbullying, revenge porn), misleading others about one's appearance and accomplishments, or reinventing a discredited idea (like Bigfoot or alien abduction). Software improvements and the increasing skill of users often make it difficult to identify the faked visual images. Using complex algorithms, tech companies and enterprising individuals are currently developing increasingly lifelike avatars (Pierson, 2018).

The increasing believability of a realistic person in a fake video will soon far exceed the believability of a fake photo and require even better methods of detection. The effort to develop viewer detection skills and visual literacy has been addressed in several books, but the speed with which new methods of faking visual reality are developed often outpaces the knowledge in books that try to address the issue (Barry, 1997; Brugioni, 1999; Messaris 1994; Mitchell, 1992). And any effort to sensitize us to the increasing number of visual hoaxes must also account for the possibility that as we scrutinize more false images and video, we may inadvertently ignore or question the authenticity of accurate ones.

Highly customizable smartphone applications now provide a mechanism for users to selectively disengage from any news or information they don't want or from people (including friends and family) whose beliefs differ from their own (*unfriending* didn't become a verb until 2007 but is now commonplace). And even as they cement divisions between people and groups, these applications also provide welcoming outlets for disinformation. This sophisticated (and often all-too-easy) filtering system means that users can select and/or manufacture their own evidence and, in that sense, create their own reality. Scientist and Internet critic David Helfand (2016) described it this way:

> *Today, the climate change denier, homeopathic practitioner, or presidential candidate can easily, quickly, and cheaply raise armies of the uninformed, the gullible, and the disenchanted by providing their echo chambers with an endless diet of self-reinforcing nonsense. (p. 56)*

Many disenchanted Americans gorged themselves during the wave of fake news that characterized the 2016 presidential campaign. Distributing these false stories via social media enabled the lies to spread faster, farther, and more frequently than ever before.

In addition, the availability and easy use of online publishing platforms and software allowed fakers to create professional-looking digital distribution sites for their stories.

If we are to withstand fake news epidemics in the future, we will have to sharpen our sense of skepticism and ask pertinent questions about the veracity of what we view and share. At a time when nearly 70% of Americans get their news primarily through social media (Matsa & Shearer, 2018), spreading false information requires only some web space and a receptive audience willing to share it with their online communities. The old saying (mistakenly attributed to both Twain and Churchill) has never seemed more apt: "A lie can travel halfway around the world while the truth is putting on its shoes."

Personal Relationships, Communication, and Nonverbal Behavior

In the '60s and '70s in the United States, numerous statements by officials, especially on social and political issues, were perceived by the public as intentionally secretive, deliberately deceptive, or outright manipulative. This situation not only led to a distrust of the people delivering the messages, but also of the mass media over which these messages were delivered. The social unrest that was generated probably reached its height during the Vietnam War. As a result, there developed a widespread yearning for a more transparent society where message truth was more reliable and where the quality of one's life was anchored more in personal relationships.

Given the perceived lack of reliability associated with verbal messages emanating from the mass media, many believed that *nonverbal* signals constituted a less easily manipulated source of information. Nonverbal behavior, it was incorrectly believed, was performed with little or no awareness by the communicator and therefore not subject to manipulation. Thus, learning how to "read" behaviors that a person had little or no control over seemed like a useful skill to acquire. So, the idea that these subtle cues might reveal unspoken prejudices and deceptive intent got traction. This was especially true in the academic community, which added more and more studies designed to shed light on the nature of nonverbal behavior and the role it played in lying and deception.

The academic interest in nonverbal behavior mirrored the growth of interest in studying communication in personal relationships (see Chapter 7). Sensitivity or "encounter" groups were fashionable in the 1970s. Participants in these small groups gained insights into the nuances of their interaction with others via unrestrained feedback and other techniques. The pros and cons of openness and "total honesty" was a common theme and prompted some to mistakenly think that "letting it all hang out"—or what later came to be known as "radical honesty"—was the secret to quality relationships, especially at a time when the divorce rate was climbing toward 50% (Blanton, 2005).

In the field of Communication Studies, interpersonal communication research was coming of age in the 1970s and two areas central to an understanding of honesty and deception were dominating the scholarship—*self-disclosure* and the *credibility of speakers* delivering persuasive messages. By the 1980s, the academic study of personal relationships was well-established in college courses and the *Journal of Social and Personal Relationships* was launched in 1984. Another academic journal, *Personal Relationships*, followed in 1994 and self-help books specifically focused on deception in romantic relationships appeared at the turn of the century, including *When Your Lover Is a Liar* by Forward (1999) and *Romantic Deception: The Six Signs He's Lying* by Campbell (2000).

The emergence of our post-truth era was dependent on many factors, but the preceding discussion highlighted four major contributors:

1. Lies of politicians, business leaders, authors, children, and others were widely publicized

2. Movies, television shows, and popular books added to the prominence of the deception theme and left little doubt it was a sign of the times

3. Widespread availability of technologies that could be used to produce deceptive messages (and visuals) coupled with platforms that could spread these messages faster and to more people than ever before

4. The increasing attention given by the academic community to the study of communication in personal relationships began to focus more attention on the nature of deceptive processes

CONCLUSION

This historical overview sets the stage for developing more in-depth knowledge about an increasingly pervasive communication phenomenon. The chapters in this book provide an up-to-date review of what is known (and not known) about lying, deception, and truth. They examine the full range of its manifestations from non-human deception to children's fantasies to the ploys of professional con artists and much more. Within these chapters, lies and truths are exposed as complex, nuanced phenomena that are too often treated simplistically and unrealistically—e.g., "lies are bad and truth is good, so always tell the truth and never lie."

We now live in an era that is so fraught with deception, it is especially important that citizens fully understand the nature of the beast. With that in mind, we invite you to read on.

REFERENCES

Akerlof, G. A., & Shiller, R. J. (2015). *Phishing for fools: The economics of manipulation and deception*. Princeton, NJ: Princeton University Press. https://dx.doi.org/10.1515/9781400873265

Alder, K. (2007). *The lie detectors: The history of an American obsession*. New York, NY: Free Press.

Alcock, J. (2005). *An enthusiasm for orchids: Sex and deception in plant evolution*. Oxford, England: Oxford University Press. https://dx.doi.org/10.1093/acprof:oso/9780195182743.001.0001

Alford, C. F. (2001). *Whistleblowers: Broken lives and organizational power*. Ithaca, NY: Cornell University Press. https://dx.doi.org/10.7591/9781501712937

Alterman, E. (2004). *When presidents lie: A history of official deception and its consequences*. New York, NY: Viking. http://dx.doi.org/10.1163/2468-1733_shafr_SIM010070007

Bailey, F. G. (1991). *The prevalence of deceit*. Ithaca, NY: Cornell University Press.

Barnes, J. A. (1994). *A pack of lies*. New York, NY: Cambridge University Press.

Barry, A. M. S. (1997). *Visual intelligence: Perception, image, and manipulation in visual communication*. Albany, NY: SUNY Press.

Bennett, W. J. (Ed.). (1993). *The book of virtues*. New York, NY: Simon & Schuster.

Bennett, W. J. (Ed.). (1995). *The children's book of virtues*. New York, NY: Simon & Schuster.

Blanton, B. (2005). *Radical honesty: How to transform your life by telling the truth* (Rev. ed.). New York, NY: Dell.

Bok, S. (1978). *Lying: Moral choice in public and private life*. New York, NY: Pantheon Books.

Boorstin, D. J. (1992). *The image: A guide to pseudo-events in America*. New York, NY: Vintage Books.

Borchers, C. (2016, June 27). Jeffrey Lord's absurd claim that media fact-checking is "elitist." *The Washington Post*. Retrieved from http://www.washingtonpost.com

Boush, D. M., Friestad, M., & Wright, P. (2009). *Deception in the marketplace: The psychology of deceptive persuasion and consumer self-protection*. New York, NY: Routledge. https://dx.doi.org/10.4324/9780203805527

Brugioni, D. A. (1999). *Photo fakery*. Dulles, VA: Brassey's.

Campbell, J. (2001). *The liar's tale: A history of falsehood*. NY: Norton.

Campbell, S. (2000). *Romantic deception: The six signs he's lying*. Holbrook, MA: Adams Media.

Campbell, W. J. (2017). *Getting it wrong: Debunking the greatest myths in American journalism*. Oakland, CA: University of California Press.

Ceci, S. J., & Bruck, M. (1995). *Jeopardy in the courtroom: A scientific analysis of children's testimony.* Washington, DC: American Psychological Association. https://doi.org/10.1037/10180-000

Chand, D. (1980). *The Yajurveda, Sanskrit text with English translation* (3rd ed.). Delhi, India: VVRI Press.

Cliffe, L., Ramsay, M., & Bartlett, D. (2000). *The politics of lying: Implications for democracy.* New York, NY: St. Martin's Press.

Cloudsley-Thompson, J. L. (1980). *Tooth and claw: Defensive strategies in the animal world.* London, England: J.M. Dent & Sons.

Daldorph, B. (2017, October 2). New French law says airbrushed or photoshopped images must be labelled. *France24.* Retrieved from http://www.france24.com

Denery, D. (2015). *The devil wins: A history of lying from the Garden of Eden to the Enlightenment.* Princeton, NJ: Princeton University Press. https://dx.doi.org/10.1515/9781400852079

Dubovsky, S. L. (1997). *Mind-Body Deceptions: The psychosomatics of everyday life.* New York, NY: W. W. Norton & Co.

Eberle, P., & Eberle, S. (1993). *The abuse of innocence: The McMartin preschool trial.* Amherst, NY: Prometheus Books.

Ekman, P. (2001). *Telling lies: Clues to deceit in the marketplace, politics, and marriage.* New York, NY: Norton.

Farhi, P. (2015, February 4). Brian Williams admits that his story of coming under fire while in Iraq was false. *The Washington Post.* Retrieved from http://www.washingtonpost.com

Fernández-Armesto, F. (1997). *Truth: A history and guide for the perplexed.* New York, NY: St. Martin's Press.

Ford, C. V. (1996). *Lies! Lies!! Lies!!! The psychology of deceit.* Washington, DC: American Psychiatric Press.

Ford, M. (2018, July 27). Is lying about an election free speech or fraud? *The New Republic.* Retrieved from http://newrepublic.com

Forward, S. (1999). *When your lover is a liar.* New York, NY: HarperCollins.

Frankfurt, H. G. (2005). *On bullshit.* Princeton, NJ: Princeton University Press.

Friedman, V. (2018, January 15). Airbrushing meets the #metoo movement. Guess who wins. *The New York Times.* Retrieved from http://www.nytimes.com

Frey, J. (2003). *A million little pieces.* New York, NY: Doubleday.

Fujinami, M., & Cunningham, R. S. (2000). *Molecular mimicry, microbes, and autoimmunity.* Washington, DC: American Society for Microbiology.

Glazer, M. P., & Glazer, P. M. (1989). *The whistleblowers*. New York, NY: Basic Books.

Gombrich, E. H. (2000). *Art and illusion: A study in the psychology of pictorial representation*. Princeton, NJ: Princeton University Press.

Harrington, B. (Ed.). (2009). *Deception: From ancient empires to internet dating*. Stanford, CA: Stanford University Press.

Helfand, D. J. (September/October 2016). The better angels of our nature vs. the Internet. *Skeptical Inquirer, 40*, 55–56.

Hernández, J. C. (2017, March 8). Chinese mistake satire on Trump for real news. *The New York Times*. Retrieved from http://www.nytimes.com

Herzog, A. (1973). *The B.S. factor: The theory and technique of faking it in America*. New York, NY: Penguin Books.

Heyman, G. D., Fu, G., Lin, J., Qian, M. K., & Lee, K. (2015). Eliciting promises from children reduces cheating. *Journal of Experimental Child Psychology, 139*, 242–248. http://dx.doi.org/10.1016/j.jecp.2015.04.013

Holan, A. D. (2017, December 12). PolitiFact's 2017 Lie of the Year: Russian election interference is a "made-up story." *Miami Herald*. Retrieved from http://www.miamiherald.com

Honeycutt, B. (2014). *The art of deception: Illusions to challenge the eye and the mind*. Watertown, MA: Imagine.

Horwath, A. (2016, April 9). Photoshop, models, and the law: How far is too far? *Pixelz*. Retrieved from http://www.pixelz.com/blog/

Howard, P. N., Kollanyi, B., Bradshaw, S., & Neudert, L-M. (2017). Social media, news and political information during the US election: Was polarizing content concentrated in swing states? *Data Memo 2017.8*. Oxford, England: Project on Computational Propaganda. Retrieved from http://comprop.oii.ox.ac.uk

Jackson, B., & Jamieson, K. H. (2007). *UnSpun: Finding facts in a world of disinformation*. New York, NY: Random House.

John of Salisbury. (1990). *Politicraticus* (C. J. Nederman, trans.). Cambridge, England: Cambridge University Press. (Original work published 1159).

Kessler, G. (2013, September 11). About the Fact Checker. *The Washington Post*. Retrieved from http://www.washingtonpost.com

Kessler, G., & Kelly, M. (2018, January 20). President Trump has made 2,140 false or misleading claims in his first year. *The Washington Post*. Retrieved from http://www.washingtonpost.com

Kessler, G., Rizzo, S., & Kelly, M. (2018, August 1). President Trump has made 4,229 false or misleading statements in 558 days. *The Washington Post*. Retrieved from http://www.washingtonpost.com

Keyes, R. (2004). *The post-truth era: Dishonesty and deception in contemporary life*. New York, NY: St. Martin's Press.

Kihn, M. (2005). *House of lies: How management consultants steal your watch and then tell you the time*. New York, NY: Grand Central Publishing.

Knapp, M. L. (2008). *Lying and deception in human interaction*. Boston, MA: Pearson/Allyn & Bacon.

Krugman, P. (2011, December 23). The post-truth campaign. *The New York Times*, A31.

Kucharski, A. J. (2014). Immunity's illusion. *Scientific American, 311*, 80–85. https://dx.doi.org/10.1038/scientificamerican1214-80

Langbein, J. H. (1977). *Torture and the law of proof: Europe and England in the ancient regime*. Chicago, IL: The University of Chicago Press.

Leonhardt, D., & Thompson, S. A. (2017, June 23). Trump's lies. *The New York Times*. Retrieved from http://www.nytimes.com

Levine, T. R. (2014). Truth-default theory (TDT): A theory of human deception and deception detection. *Journal of Language and Social Psychology, 33*, 378–392. https://dx.doi.org/10.1177/0261927x14535916

Lieberman, D. J. (1998). *Never be lied to again*. New York, NY: St. Martin's Press.

Lloyd, J. E. (1986). Firefly communication and deception: "Oh, what a tangled web." In R.W. Mitchell & N.S. Thompson (Eds.), *Deception: Perspectives on human and nonhuman deceit* (pp. 113–128). New York, NY: State University of New York Press.

Lutz, W. (1989). *Doublespeak*. New York, NY: Harper & Row.

Machiavelli, N. (1992). *The prince* (N. H. Thomson, Trans.). Mineola, NY: Dover Publications. (Original work published 1513).

Mackay, C. (1852). *Memoir of extraordinary popular delusions and the madness of crowds*. London, England: Office of the National Illustrated Library. https://dx.doi.org/10.1037/14716-000

Manjoo, F. (2008). *True enough*. Hoboken, NJ: John Wiley.

Mauro, J. (1992). *Statistical deception at work*. New York, NY: Routledge.

Matsa, K. E., & Shearer, E. (2018, September 10). News use across social media platforms. *Pew Research Center*. Retrieved from http://www.journalism.org

Max, T. (2018, February 20). Do we need a Truth in Advertising Act? The industry and retailers self-regulate photoshopping ads. *SheppardMullin*. Retrieved from http://www.fashionapparel-lawblog.com

McGlone, M. S., & Knapp, M. L. (Eds.). (2010). *The interplay of truth and deception*. New York, NY: Routledge. https://dx.doi.org/10.4324/9780203887851

Menchú, R. (1983). *I, Rigoberta Menchú: An Indian woman in Guatemala*. London, England: Verso.

Messaris, P. (1994). *Visual literacy: Image, mind, and reality*. Boulder, CO: Westview.

Miller, G. R., & Stiff, J. B. (1993). *Deceptive communication*. Newbury Park, CA: Sage.

Mitchell, W. J. (1992). *The reconfigured eye: Visual truth in the post-photographic era*. Cambridge, MA: MIT Press.

Muldowney, M. S. (2002). *Augustine's treatises on various subjects*. New York, NY: Catholic University of America Press.

Nyberg, D. (1993). *The varnished truth: Truth telling and deceiving in ordinary life*. Chicago, IL: University of Chicago Press.

Oldstone, M. B. A. (2005). *Molecular mimicry*. New York, NY: Springer.

O'Sullivan, D., & Herb, J. (2018, July 31). Facebook takes down suspected Russian network of pages. *CNN Money*. Retrieved from http://money.cnn.com

Park, R. (2000). *Voodoo science: The road from foolishness to fraud*. New York, NY: Oxford University Press.

Parkinson, R. G. (2016, November 25). Fake news? That's a very old story. *The Washington Post*. Retrieved from http://www.washingtonpost.com

Paterno, S. (1997). The lying game. *American Journalism Review*, *19*, 40–45.

Penny, L. (2005). *Your call is important to us: The truth about bullshit*. New York, NY: Crown.

Perlmutter, M. (1998). *Why lawyers (and the rest of us) lie and engage in other repugnant behavior*. Austin, TX: Bright Books.

Pfiffner, J. P. (1999). The contemporary presidency: Presidential lies. *Presidential Studies Quarterly*, *29*, 903–917.

Pfiffner, J. P. (2003). *The character factor: How we judge America's presidents*. College Station, TX: Texas A & M Press.

Pierson, D. (2018, February 19). Fake videos are on the rise. As they become more realistic, seeing shouldn't always be believing. *Los Angeles Times*. Retrieved from http://www.latimes.com

Priest, D., & Birnbaum, M. (2017, June 26). In Europe fake news from Russia is old news. *The Washington Post*. Retrieved from http://www.washingtonpost.com

Richards, J.I. (1990). *Deceptive advertising*. Hillsdale, NJ: Lawrence Erlbaum.

Rue, L. (1994). *By the grace of guile: The role of deception in natural history and human affairs*. Oxford, England: Oxford University Press.

Rosenblat, H. (2009). *Angel at the fence: The true story of a love that survived*. New York, NY: Berkley Books.

Seelye, K. Q. (2003, May 3) Relentless moral crusader is relentless gambler, too. *The New York Times*. Retrieved from http://nytimes.com

Seife, C. (2010). *Proofiness: The dark arts of mathematical deception*. New York, NY: Penguin.

Siddiqui, F., & Svriuga, S. (2016, December 5). N.C. man told police he went to D.C. pizzeria with gun to investigate conspiracy theory. *The Washington Post*. Retrieved from http://www.washingtonpost.com

Silverman, C. (2016, November 16). This analysis shows how viral fake election news stories outperformed real news on Facebook. *Buzzfeed*. Retrieved from http://www.buzzfeed.com

Soll, J. (2016, December 18). The long and brutal history of fake news. *Politico Magazine*. Retrieved from http://politico.com/magazine/

Stein, S. (2012, August 8). Mitt Romney campaign: We will not be "dictated by fact-checkers." *The Huffington Post*. Retrieved from http://www.huffingtonpost.com

Stevens, M. (2016). *Cheats and deceits: How plants and animals mislead*. Oxford, England: Oxford University Press.

Sullivan, E. (2001). *The concise book of lying*. New York, NY: Farrar, Straus & Giroux.

Timberg, C. (2016, November 24). Russian propaganda effort helped spread "fake news" during election, experts say. *The Washington Post*. Retrieved from http://www.washingtonpost.com

Trovillo, P. (1939). A history of lie detection (concluded). *American Journal of Police Science, 30*(1), 104–119. https://dx.doi.org/10.2307/1136392

Tye, L. (2002). *The father of spin: Edward L. Bernays and the birth of public relations*. New York, NY: Picador.

Wilkomirski, B. (1996). *Fragments: Memories of a wartime childhood*. New York, NY: Schocken Books.

Young, K. (2017). *Bunk: The rise of hoaxes, humbug, plagiarists, phonies, post-facts, and fake news*. Minneapolis, MN: Graywolf Press.

Zelicoff, A. P. (2002, August 9). Polygraph hypocrisy. *The Washington Post*, p. A23.

PART I

the nature of the phenomenon

PART I the nature of the phenomena

The first three chapters focus on fundamental questions associated with the study of lying, deception, and communication: Exploring the answers to such questions helps to establish a framework for ways of thinking about honesty and deception. Why is it important to understand lying and deception? Do lies have any distinguishing features? If a lie means a person isn't telling the truth, how do we identify truth? What ethical criteria do we associate with lies and truth telling?

Chapter 1: Perspectives on Lying and Deception

Chapter 2: Perspectives on Truth

Chapter 3: Ethical Perspectives

CHAPTER 1 Perspectives on Lying and Deception

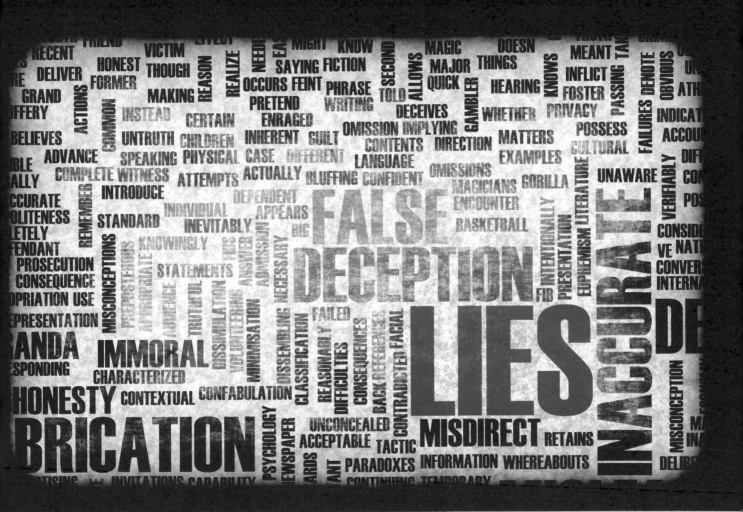

"Nothing is more common on earth than to deceive and be deceived."
– *Johann G. Seume, 19th-century German philosopher*

"If you do not wish to be lied to, do not ask questions. If there were no questions, there would be no lies."
– *B. Traven, 20th-century novelist (whose true identity remains the subject of debate)*

If you're reading this sentence, you've probably lied before, which is simply another way of saying that you're human. The ability to deceive and the desire to detect deception have been a part of the human story since the beginning. The contexts may have changed a bit—smartphones in place of spears and identity politics instead of hunting parties—but the idea is the same.

The first humans weren't the biggest or strongest species on the planet, but they just may have been the smartest. Using their wits, they developed language in order to work effectively in groups. Doing so not only helped them live until their next meal, it *transformed* them—from a band of struggling nomads into *us* (population 7 billion and counting).

The languages of the first human beings were probably simple signaling systems like those of other animals in their midst—clicks and noises used for alarm calls. Words and sounds were linked more closely to their referents in the physical world. But as our language grew more sophisticated, it began to relate to more abstract notions like *love* and *courage*—or *honesty, truth,* and *deception*. Whereas our ancestors millennia ago used language primarily to describe reality, Campbell says modern humans employ it "not just to reflect reality, but to transform it radically" (2001, p. 230).

> ... this cooperative form of social organization helped our ancestors survive, it is also easy to see how individuals who wanted to game the system for personal benefit might have been tempted to do so.

Social life and the language choices we use to manage it are considerably more complex today than for our earliest ancestors, who were primarily concerned about just living from one season to the next. When dealing with modern concepts as vague as religion, politics, economics, and social media, there are more opportunities to use language in abstract ways, to reflect reality or to transform it, and to serve the needs of others or only serve one's own needs.

Cooperating as a team required our ancestors to build a social system based on trust, honesty, reliability, and mutual aid, a process biologist Robert Trivers and anthropologist Richard Leakey called "reciprocal altruism" (Leakey & Lewin, 1978; Trivers, 1971). While this cooperative form of social organization helped our ancestors survive, it is also easy to see how individuals who wanted to game the system for personal benefit might have been tempted to do so. Undoubtedly, some did just that, but there was a catch—*they had to be good at it*. If you got caught trying to fool people who put their trust in you, the group punished you in some way. Depending on the scope of your specific violation, you might have been publicly shamed (minor), banished (serious), or turned into fertilizer (severe).

Against such a backdrop of mutual trust and cooperation, only the wisest deceivers could have preserved the trust of their groups and thus lived long enough to reproduce. In all likelihood, these skilled ancestors of ours:

- learned how to avoid detection
- lied infrequently rather than often
- resisted the urge to tell only self-serving lies
- occasionally used deception to benefit the group as a whole

When used in these strategic, calculated ways, deception likely helped our ancestors survive—even as the ability to *detect deception* developed into a highly desirable skill.

According to this view, lying and deception can best be understood as one aspect of learning how to communicate effectively. After all, effective communicators put themselves in the position of their audience—and the practical benefit of taking the audience's perspective is to produce messages that have the best chance of accomplishing one's communicative goals.

This kind of audience analysis requires us to ask a series of questions, all of which have the potential to be answered in ways that may be less than the complete, absolute truth. For example:

- What information does the audience seek?
- What will make them believe what I want them to believe?
- How are they likely to respond to a particular message?

Truthtellers and deceivers engage in a similar process. Both must ask themselves, "Out of all I *could* say, what do I *want* to say?" Both are manipulating information in some way—selecting what to include and what to leave out, choosing which words to use, deciding what kind of tone to strike, etc. In this way, matters relevant to deception and truth telling are central to every message we construct.

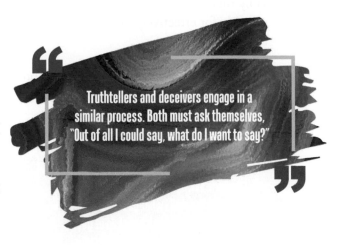

"Truthtellers and deceivers engage in a similar process. Both must ask themselves, "Out of all I could say, what do I want to say?"

As counterintuitive as it may seem, part of being an effective communicator involves discreetly employing deception. For example, in a study by Feldman, Forrest, and Happ (2002):

- While being filmed, college students were asked to engage another student (a stranger) in conversation with the goal of getting to know them.

- Ahead of time, some students were told to appear *likable*, others to appear *competent*, and some were not given any directives.

- After the conversation, the students watched the videos and counted the instances in which they had deceived the other person.

- Overall, students instructed to appear likable and competent told *significantly more* lies than those not asked to present themselves in a particular way.

Hundreds of millennia after the first humans, we still live in a world where many find it acceptable to sometimes deceive competitors and enemies. Yet, outside of certain specialized arenas, we continue to advocate (or at least give lip service to) an ethical/social system of reciprocal altruism, based on transparency, honesty, and trust. Being tricked, lied to, or otherwise deceived can still produce profound shock and severe consequences. The themes of American popular culture reflect this continuing fascination with all things deceptive—from television (*Big Little Lies*, *Lie to Me*, *Dexter*) to the box office (*Liar Liar*, *Gone Girl*, *The Invention of Lying*) and in songs both old and new (Fleetwood Mac's "Little Lies" and Eminem's "Love the Way You Lie"). And of course we'll always have Pinocchio.

Why then do we commonly engage in various forms of deception? Probably because it is valuable for effectively maintaining our *social lives*. Two thought experiments may help illustrate this point:

1. If lying and deception were strictly prohibited (or simply didn't exist), life would certainly be very different than it is now, but that's not to say it would be better. Imagine having to always say exactly (and in complete detail) what you think and feel in response to any question asked of you.

Imagine having to always say exactly (and in complete detail) what you think and feel in response to any question asked of you.

2. It would be equally futile to go too far in the other direction and promote the full acceptance of lying and deception as a social norm. Imagine you had to assume that almost everything you learned about was potentially false or misleading.

Most of us quietly accept this paradox, perpetuating a social system that keeps deception from becoming too dominant, but understanding that it is a common and inextinguishable part of human communication. We regularly embrace this paradox by engaging in behaviors that include the following:

- Valuing the truth yet not feeling compelled to hear or speak it all the time. No matter how much we believe it would be bad for us to publicly endorse lying and deception as a cultural norm, we also know that we live in a culture where people, ourselves included, sometimes mislead and lie.

- Entering into our daily encounters with the expectation that people will adhere to the cultural guideline of not deceiving others and will endeavor to tell us the truth as they know it.

- Recognizing the possibility that there may be more to the truth than we are told and that certain conditions may sometimes give rise to duplicity, whether benign or harmful.

A system in which people advocate truth telling while simultaneously recognizing that violations sometimes occur seems preferable to other options. Such a system is also more productive than one in which people naively believe everyone will always tell the truth. And it is certainly preferable to a dystopian world where deceiving others is condoned to the point that people must assume others are constantly lying (think *Game of Thrones* or *Mad Max*). A society that favors lying over telling the truth would be dysfunctional, but so would a society devoid of any deception at all (or, at the very least, it wouldn't be much fun).

But in some cultural groups around the world, deceptive practices are more central to daily life and are therefore more accepted (Slackman, 2006; Pitt-Rivers, 1954). These tactics include:

- false praise
- insincere promises
- giving reasons for hope when there is none
- professing agreement in order to avoid argument

For societies like that of the Guna on the San Blas Islands of Panama, trickery and deception are viewed as a natural part of the culture's discourse (Howe & Sherzer, 1986). Despite exceptions like the Guna, in many societies—particularly large and complex ones like the United States—the cultural relationship with the human tendency to mislead remains an uneasy one. Philosophers like Sissela Bok (1978) argue that accepting virtually any form of deceit without severe sanctions will lead to an increasing disregard for the truth and the eventual collapse of civilization.

LYING & DECEPTION AS COMMUNICATION

In recent decades, numerous studies have shown lies to be a common part of our daily discourse:

- Turner, Edgley, and Olmstead (1975) asked 130 people to record and analyze the honesty of their own statements in an important conversation. They rated only 38.5% of their statements as "completely honest."

- In a sample of college students, 92% admitted they had lied to a romantic partner (Knox, Schacht, Holt, & Turner, 1993).

- Surveys consistently show that thousands of high school students admit lying to their parents and teachers (see Bruggeman & Hart, 1996; Jensen, Arnett, Feldman, & Cauffman, 2004; Josephson Institute of Ethics, 2012; Lahey, 2013; Levine, Serota, Carey, & Messer, 2013).

- In an online survey, Kalish (2004) asked 3,000 adults if they'd ever engaged in any of 13 different acts of dishonesty. Some of the results are as follows:

    - 71% lied to spare the feelings of friends or family members
    - 63% had called into work pretending to be sick
    - 32% reported lying to their spouse about a purchase
    - 28% lied to their spouse about their relationship with another person
    - 13% shifted the blame to a co worker for something they did

In short, finding people who admit that lying and deception are common features of their everyday behavior is not difficult. Nor is it hard to find those who perceive lies all around them—in the media, in science reports, in history textbooks, in the rhetoric of our political leaders, etc. (Kick, 2001). For example, George Packer (2013) claims that the public's distrust of government and business over the last 30 years has prompted an "unwinding" of Americans' sense of community and has made lying more acceptable for people in all walks of life. One common explanation for the ubiquitous nature of lying and deception is that we are a society *in decay*—that duplicity is characteristic of a moral and ethical vacuum (hence terms like Packer's "unwinding").

Such arguments might be more convincing were it not for the fact that the frequency of lying and deception is not a recent phenomenon, nor has it been limited to societies in decay. Philosophers like Nyberg (1993) believe deception is omnipresent not because of a moral crisis,

... deception is omnipresent not because of a moral crisis, but because it is simply one of the tools we use to conduct our everyday affairs ...

but because it is simply one of the tools we use to conduct our everyday affairs—in other words, it is an inherent part of the way we communicate. Just like telling the truth, says Nyberg, deception is "a means for accomplishing purposes" (p. 53). Solomon (1996) echoes this view: "Some deception is harmful and even immoral, but some of it is neither" (p. 109).

It appears that the value of social harmony can, and often does, take precedence over the value of telling the truth. Being polite and trying not to hurt another person's feelings are commonly associated with effective communicators (and decent people generally), but each may require telling something other than what one believes to be the *whole* truth.

Consider the following examples from everyday life of being polite-but-not-completely-honest. Researchers refer to these as **prosocial** lies (i.e., lies told for someone else's benefit):

- *This kale-quinoa souffle is delicious but I can't eat another bite*
- *Your hair looks just fine*
- *You don't look a day over 30*
- *Leaving in 5 mins*
- *Nobody thinks you're stupid*

It may be hard for some to admit, but lies (or, at least, not telling the whole truth) can even help us maintain healthy relationships, cope with fear, tolerate stress, and gain a sense of control over uncertain or negative aspects of our lives. Consider the following examples:

- The ability to tell a vivid, interesting, and enjoyable story may involve adding and/or subtracting some information from what one recalls happening.

- Highlighting one's strengths and minimizing one's weaknesses are usually considered good advice on a job interview (and a first date).

- Not telling everything you know can protect your friendships and private life.

- Delicate negotiations often hinge on decisions about what to reveal, when to reveal it, and to whom.

- Sometimes loved ones ask us to help them perpetuate a lie, which obligates us to lie in order to succeed in preserving the relationship.

- When a young child with terminal cancer asks whether he or she is going to die, effective communicators ask themselves how they can best adapt a response to this child in this situation rather than simply and directly reporting the truth as they understand it.

And just because something is true doesn't make it automatically better than the alternatives. Like acts of deception, statements of truth that are considered effective communication in one situation may be ineffective or even unethical in another. Someone who speaks the plain truth in the wrong setting may get into just as much trouble as someone who spouts bald-faced lies—our social system holds both communicators accountable for their choices. When someone tells the truth without regard for another person's feelings, tells selective truth in order to mislead, or tells the truth to someone who doesn't want to hear it, they may be treated as harshly as someone who was deceptive in those same situations. Decisions about truth telling and deception are inextricably woven into our pursuit of communicating effectively—and of living meaningful, productive lives.

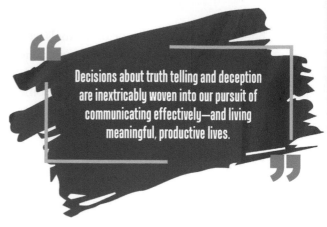

Decisions about truth telling and deception are inextricably woven into our pursuit of communicating effectively—and living meaningful, productive lives.

Even the very language we use to communicate can help explain why lying and deception are so much a part of our social world. Words are arbitrary labels for things, often lacking any intrinsic connection to what they represent. Nor are they complete—all words are abstractions that capture some qualities of the things they stand for but inevitably omit others. When we use language to represent something, we are automatically engaging in an act of omission—and deliberate omission of information is widely considered in courts, religion, and elsewhere to be a form of lying.

Because of the imprecise nature of language, truth and fiction can often be accomplished simultaneously using the same words. For example:

- "Crime is down from last year" could be a true statement about some types of crime, but it may not accurately represent all types. It could also be the case that some of the categories measured previously were not reported this year.

- Saying "I had a good day" may not mean everything that happened to you was good. In fact, you may only be thinking about one good thing that happened or how you feel in the moment when you are asked. Moreover, the person you're saying this to may interpret the words in other ways—thinking that because you said *good* instead of *great* you had an uneventful (but not wonderful) day or that *good* means nothing bad or negative happened to you at all that day.

- Referents for words are also subject to dramatic change as time passes (as when "bad" really means "good" and "sick" means "unbelievably good").

CONCEIVING OF DECEIVING

Up to this point in the chapter, the words *lying* and *deception* have been used almost interchangeably. The only clear distinction between them is that deception is a superordinate term that encompasses various fraudulent, tricky, and/or misleading behaviors—including verbally spoken or written lies. Beyond that, the distinctions are not as clear:

- Many argue that deception can be communicated in many ways, but lies are limited to *verbal* behavior.

- However, we know that accusations of lying are sometimes heavily rooted in perceptions of *nonverbal* behavior—e.g., avoiding eye contact, shrugging one's shoulders, using a particular tone of voice, or even maintaining silence.

- Hopper and Bell (1984) categorized many types of deceptions but reserved the label "lie" for a *false statement used with intent to deceive.*

- Deception can also be enacted by what is not said, or what is implied via the use of certain words, actions, and use of pausing/timing. Hopper and Bell labeled these types of misrepresentations as "unlies."

Dictionaries aren't particularly helpful in making useful distinctions either; they define words by telling us how people have historically used a word, not what it must or always mean. Terms like *lying* and *deception* are no different. They are abstractions that exist only as they are perceived by people in specific situations.

In most research, including an early study by the lead author of this text (see Knapp & Comadena, 1979), it has been common practice for social scientists to use definitions of lying that involve Person A (the liar) consciously altering information to significantly change the perceptions of Person B (the target). Fair enough, but what about the following factors?

- Should lies be defined from the standpoint of what the *liar* does rather than what the *target* experiences—who should get to decide if something is deceptive or not?

- Can the alteration of information only be conscious rather than subconscious?

- What if the liar didn't consider the information conveyed as significantly different from what she believed to be true in the first place?

- What if the liar mistakenly thought the target believed something was true when in fact the target did not? Is it still a lie?

- Some people believe (quite sincerely) that if they have a *good reason* for telling a lie then it isn't really a lie. But their targets may not be likely to see it that way.

These loopholes show just how difficult it can be to establish the domain of deception with a single, standard definition. One thing is certain, however: the perceptual worlds of liars and their targets are usually quite different (Gordon & Miller, 2000) as these examples illustrate:

- In 1978, former president Richard Nixon famously spinned Watergate by declaring "I was not lying. I said things that later on seemed to be untrue."

- Colonel Oliver North, testifying before Congress in 1987 during the Iran-Contra hearings, famously told the American public that he hadn't lied, but had instead based his actions on a "different version of the facts." North later became a regular contributor to Fox News and, in 2018, became the president of the National Rifle Association.

Lies and deception are defined by the contexts in which people experience them. If the behavior in question does not meet the contextual criteria for a lie, it may be considered something else, like an honest mistake (e.g., accidentally putting an incorrect number on your tax return).

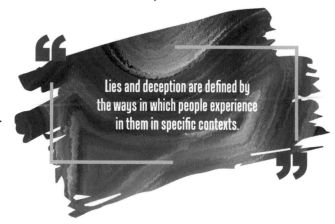

Lies and deception are defined by the ways in which people experience in them in specific contexts.

Sometimes there will be considerable agreement on whether or not a lie has occurred and other times there will be little agreement. More often than not, the extent to which we do/don't believe a person has lied (and therefore does or does not need to be sanctioned) hinges on how people perceive the following contextual features of the behavior in question:

1. Was the communicator **aware** of what he or she was doing?

2. Did the communicator **alter information** he or she knew to be true?

3. What was the **intent** or motive behind the communicator's message?

4. Was there anything about this **situation** that would encourage lying or even authorize it?

5. What **consequences** resulted from the communicator's behavior?

Awareness Level

Did the person knowingly and consciously perform the falsehood in question? Was it planned? The answers to such questions matter because, in most cases, *lying is perceived as something done with a high degree of awareness.* This is why accused liars will sometimes feign incompetence: "What? I said that? No way. If I did, I must have been completely out of my mind." If this person's defense is believed, the attribution of outright lying is less likely and any accompanying sanctions much less severe.

Consider actor Kevin Spacey's (photo at right) "apology" tweet following accusations that he had sexually assaulted fellow actor Anthony Rapp (in 1986, when Rapp was 14). He claimed that he wouldn't be able to remember such an encounter given that more than 30 years had passed, but also implied that if he did behave that way he must have been drunk at the time (and would certainly owe Rapp an apology). In Spacey's situation, the public didn't seem to accept his claimed lack of awareness as a valid excuse, particularly when more than a dozen other people went public with similar accusations in the weeks that followed.

Politics is another arena in which the "I don't recall" defense is often treated with great suspicion. When an elected officeholder claims not to remember key details of a controversial situation they were involved in, questioners sometimes react skeptically. This conversational dynamic was aptly illustrated by an exchange between New Jersey Senator Cory Booker (D) and Homeland Security Secretary Kirstjen Nielsen in January 2018. Testifying under oath, Nielsen claimed she "didn't hear" President Trump refer to Haiti and African states as "shithole countries" during an Oval Office meeting about immigration reform. Booker simply didn't believe her: "I've got a president of the United States whose office I respect, who talks about the country's origins of my fellow citizens in the most despicable manner. You don't remember?" he asked sternly. "You can't remember the words of your commander in chief? I find that unacceptable."

Another Trump cabinet official, former Attorney General Jeff Sessions, quickly gained a reputation for having one of the poorest memories in Washington. In sworn testimony before various House and Senate committees, Sessions used some version of the *I don't recall* defense in response to at least 47 distinct lines of questioning. His November 2017 appearance before the House Judiciary Committee, which was investigating Russian tampering in the 2016 election, drew particular scrutiny—so much, in fact, that *Saturday Night Live* spoofed him that weekend.

In general, how self-aware we think deceivers are depends greatly on our perceptions of their cognitive ability. This connection between cognition and awareness level is especially true for two social groups in particular—children and the elderly. When their level of awareness or understanding about something they did or said is in question, the very young and the very old are frequently given the benefit of the doubt (a "pass"). We often (and often incorrectly) attribute decreased cognitive skills to

these groups simply on the basis of widely held stereotypes about age. Knowing this perception exists, people who fit into these categories may use it to their advantage.

We also tend to give people we like or love (regardless of age) a pass when judging the truth of their questionable statements or actions—while we may just as quickly find someone we dislike "guilty" for doing the very same thing. Finally, we make allowances for people who are experiencing stress, trauma, or a serious medical condition because of our expectations about how these situations might affect their ability to process information and communicate.

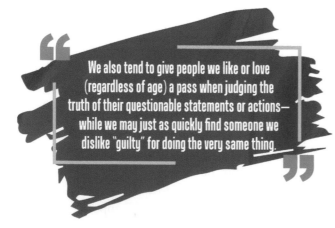

"We also tend to give people we like or love (regardless of age) a pass when judging the truth of their questionable statements or actions—while we may just as quickly find someone we dislike "guilty" for doing the very same thing."

Information Alteration

Awareness level is closely related to a second key context for evaluating deception—whether or not the message contained *altered information*. When deceivers who *deliberately altered* information are questioned, we are generally accusing them of that most straightforward of lies—the lie of commission. Lies of *omission* may be judged just as harshly, but because the liar *deliberately left out* some critical, game-changing detail rather than altering any facts. Whether commission or omission, our perception is that the information was conveyed in a less-than-straightforward way, and, above all, with the will to deceive.

Perceptions of Intent

The question of whether or not someone *intentionally* deceived us is often the key factor in determining if we were or were not lied to. At some level, intent trumps everything else, as in these scenarios:

© Shutterstock.com

- Someone may have remained *intentionally* unaware of a situation so that they could technically claim ignorance (the "plausible deniability" defense). If so, then we may still consider them culpable in the sense that they chose to shirk their responsibility, like the proverbial ostrich hiding its head in the sand (which is a myth, by the way; as far as we know, avoiding difficult realities by pre-emptively ignoring them is a strictly human phenomenon).

- It's possible for us to feel deceived despite the fact that the sender neither altered nor omitted important information. In other words, someone could communicate the complete, unvarnished truth to us, but still intend to deceive. For example, suppose you want to prank your friend with an exploding golf ball. Before they take their swing, you say to your friend, "Be careful. That's an exploding golf ball." While you have made a perfectly true statement, the context was such that your friend thought you were kidding and later may accuse you of lying—because he or she perceives that the actual intent of your technically true statement was to mislead.

- True statements are also used with deceptive intent when people are caught doing something they don't want to admit doing. For example, when a drugstore employee accuses a man who has just walked out of the store without paying for a candy bar of stealing it, the man replies (either wryly or with feigned anger): "Sure. Even though that's my new Mercedes in the parking lot and I make $250,000 a year, I wasn't willing to drop $1.50 on a candy bar. Okay, Sherlock. You got me. I'm your thief."

Of course, someone may say nothing at all—but that doesn't mean we'll let them off the hook. If we *expect* that they *should* have something to say, then we're likely to consider deception as a possibility. Such **lies of omission** are often evaluated on the basis of perceived intent—especially if the consequences are serious (Levine, Asada, & Lindsey, 2003). The ambiguities involved often provide ample opportunities for arguing about the extent to which the intent was to mislead.

Indirect responses, for example, imply a particular intent and run the risk of being judged as deceptive (Washburne, 1969). For example, when asked if you're going to join the regular gang at the neighborhood bar tonight, you reply: "It's a good night to celebrate." Your friends will assume you're coming and are likely to feel misled when you don't show. You may, of course, argue that it's unfair of them to feel that way because you didn't explicitly say that you would or wouldn't be at the bar that night. Your argument is unlikely to be successful because you'll be judged on the basis of your perceived intentions. On the other hand, if you say, "I have to take an important test tomorrow morning," they assume you mean *no* and will not expect to see you (Bowers, Elliott, & Desmond, 1977; Nofsinger, 1976).

Ironically, it is possible to intentionally present false or misleading information yet *not* be judged a liar. Such scenarios happen frequently, as when we are teasing, playing a joke, or planning a surprise for someone. The motive for any falsehoods in the pursuit of such goals is *meant to be uncovered* and is excused because the "lies" told were *clearly for the target's benefit* (unless of course the teasing or joking is viewed as having gone too far). Once again, intent is the deciding factor.

Part of the process of judging deceptive intent is asking yourself whether the person has *reason* to lie—whether in general or to you specifically. You may consider your relationship and history with him or her, their personality, and the particular demands of the topic being discussed in order to assess the likelihood a lie has been told.

Perceptions of the Situation

Regardless of other factors, sometimes we ask ourselves if there is anything about the particular *situation* that makes deception more likely:

- Is there any pressure to lie about this topic to this audience?

- Has lying occurred frequently in similar situations before?

- Are the rewards for telling a lie greater than those for telling the truth?

Asking such questions helps us form perceptions about the circumstances within which lying may take place. Sometimes lies occur so often in a particular situation that they become well known throughout the culture:

... it is possible to *intentionally present false or misleading information* yet *not* be overtly accused of lying or deception.

- When the receptionist says, "The doctor will call you right back."

- When the person who already owes you money says, "I promise to pay you back as soon as I get paid at the end of the week."

Similarly, we are not surprised to find lies occurring between people who intensely dislike or fear each other. Moreover, the conditions associated with the acts of some politicians and sales representatives (think about the expectations associated with buying a new or used car) create a climate in which lying is more or less expected. We generally are more accepting of the less-than-completely-honest communication used by people who work in contexts that require them to withhold or distort facts as part of their job or performance.

A few situations exempt people from attributions of lying and deception because such behavior is expected. Examples include politeness rituals ("I really had a great time tonight"), the behavior of poker players—even the subterfuge of secret agents. It's worth noting that even though our interactions with spies are often through fiction, it is interesting that our culture often portrays these professional liars as heroes (from Bourne to Bond). Lying—and doing it well—can be perceived as a critical job requirement when the situational conditions demand it.

Actors, comedians, magicians, and other performers have our consent to lie as long as their lying is clearly tied to these roles. For example, as long as comedian Andy Kaufman was standing on stage and it was clear he was performing his act, audiences expected and accepted exaggerations and falsehoods. Deception was authorized as a vehicle for creating humor; his performances were not intended to be taken literally or personally. However, when he began heckling other performers as an audience member and seemed to take too seriously his wrestling matches with women, his fans weren't always sure what behavior was the "real" Andy Kaufman and what behavior was the performer Andy Kaufman. Not knowing whether he was *performing* made it difficult to know whether

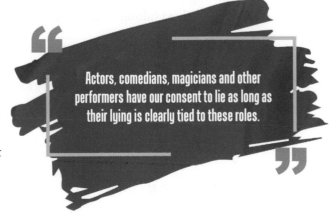

Actors, comedians, magicians and other performers have our consent to lie as long as their lying is clearly tied to these roles.

deception was occurring and whether it was appropriate in that situation or not. Such uncertainty made a lot of people uneasy (of course, it didn't help that sometimes even other cast and crew members weren't told ahead of time what Kaufman would be doing).

More than 30 years after his death, Kaufman's is-he-or-isn't-he legacy continues. At an awards show in 2013, his brother Michael claimed Andy was still alive, having faked his death in 1984, and introduced the comedian's now 24-year-old "daughter" to the audience. *The Smoking Gun* later revealed that the woman was an actress hired by the brother, although the latter claims he was duped. But it appears to have been a convincing, if unsettling, traditional Kaufman hoax (McCleod, 2013).

Perceptions of Effects/Consequences

If we suspect a lie has occurred, part of our assessment is focused on the effects or consequences of the behavior. Who was affected and in what ways? The answers to these questions may alter the extent to which we perceive the behavior as a lie and greatly affect our perceptions of the kind of sanctioning deserved. We don't like or trust a person who tells us a lot of lies. At the same time, not all lies are perceived as equally harmful (Tyler, Feldman, & Reichert, 2006). We attribute *less* harm to (and reduce sanctions for) lies we perceive as:

- benefitting another person (not the liar)
- resulting in positive consequences
- producing effects that were trivial rather than consequential
- producing short- rather than long-term effects
- affecting few rather than many
- occurring (along with any consequences) a long time ago
- acknowledged (along with the consequences) by the liar

Sometimes lies have multiple audiences with effects that are different for each audience. For example, a journalist writes a newspaper story about breast cancer. But the fact that he or she used a gripping, yet fictional, case study to make the story vivid comes to light. When this occurs, the consequences for the author and newspaper may be perceived by readers in very different ways (see Chapter 12). Lies directed to a large audience can be complicated, and the ways in which they are perceived by audiences can be equally as complex.

CONCLUSION

While the preceding perceptual categories have been presented in the context of assessing the deceptive behavior of any given individual, it is worth remembering that lies can be jointly created as well. This means perceptions of the preceding five categories are relevant to as many participants as there are in the exchange. How are lies jointly constructed? Let us count the ways:

- One interaction partner makes it easy for the other to lie by providing a fraudulent rationale for suspect behavior, to which the partner assents.

- One partner encourages lying by making it clear that they don't want to hear the truth.

- Parties in a relationship will collaborate in creating and perpetuating a lie to help keep it afloat.

- Parties will cooperate in what both know to be a lie in order to adhere to a politeness ritual or cultural expectations.

- Organizations may dictate that members be less than honest or forthcoming with information; while the individuals in the group may not use these types of deceptive behavior in their personal lives, they may go along for the purposes of their job.

Are there specific behaviors that are *clearly* (and always) lies—independent of what is perceived—or is the determination of lying and deception always dependent on perceptions of a particular act in a particular situation? Certainly there are behaviors that, based on a long history of perceptions in a variety of situations, almost everyone would count as lying. But even then, when such "clear-cut" behaviors are viewed by the demands of a particular context, the attributions of deception (and the types of sanctions) may be called into question.

SUMMARY

- Lying and deception evolved as a part of the social system established by the earliest human beings. Those who were skilled at lying and deception did so in ways that didn't always benefit themselves solely.

- Studies show that lying and deception are both widely practiced *and* widely condemned in today's society. While we advocate truth telling, we also recognize that lying and deception will occur and that sometimes they may even be appropriate responses to a situation. We seem to realize that a society that favors lying and deception over truth telling would be dysfunctional, as would a society devoid of any lying and deception.

- Lying and deception occur with regularity in daily discourse because they are a way of obtaining the responses we desire from others, of accomplishing our goals—just like truth telling. Someone wishing to tell the truth and someone wishing to deceive must both ask themselves, "Out of all I *could* say, what do I *want* to say?"

- Sometimes lying and deception are harmful, unethical, and immoral; sometimes they aren't. And there are times when telling the absolute truth can be just as hurtful. In addition, the incomplete and abstract nature of language itself provides a ready vehicle for duplicity. Truth and fiction aren't necessarily tied to the words we use, because in the modern era our language has grown to include incredibly abstract concepts. Millennia ago our ancestors used language to describe their world whereas we often use it to transform and manipulate ours (for better or worse).

- Answering the question "What is a lie?" or "What is deception?" is best done without the use of a standard definition. Generally, *lying* is considered a more specific behavior (often spoken or written) done with some intent, whereas *deception* encompasses a wide range of possibilities where the perception of the truth or reality is altered in less obvious ways. In practical terms, the best way to determine whether something is a lie or otherwise deceptive is to evaluate each occurrence in its context. How we perceive the answers to the following questions will help us arrive at an answer, but even then there is no guarantee that everyone, or even most, will agree:

  1. Was the communicator aware of what he or she was doing?
  2. Did the communicator alter information he or she knew to be true?
  3. What was the intent or motive behind the communicator's message?
  4. Was there anything about this situation that would encourage lying or even authorize it?
  5. What consequences resulted from the communicator's behavior?

  How we interpret the answers to these questions leads us to make attributions about whether lying or deception has occurred, whether it is serious or not, and to what extent it can or should be sanctioned.

EXERCISES

1. Identify one or two things in each of the following categories. For each item listed, explain <u>why</u> you feel the way you do. Try to avoid easy answers like "nothing" or "everything."

    o I never want to be lied to or deceived about.
    o I don't mind being lied to or deceived about.
    o Things I might lie or deceive about include.
    o Things I never lie or deceive about include.

2. Describe three of your close relationships. Now imagine and describe how these relationships would be if all the parties shared everything each person thought or believed to be true.

3. Describe two recent situations of deception in your life, one where omission played a crucial part and another where a lie of commission was utilized.

OF INTEREST

The trailer for the Netflix documentary *Jim & Andy: The Great Beyond*. Jim Carrey reveals that portraying Andy Kaufman in *The Man in the Moon* (1999) took a heavy psychological toll on him, blurring the distinction between reality and art.

From the NPR series *Hidden Brain*, an episode entitled: "Everybody Lies, and That's Not Always a Bad Thing." Features an interview with Dan Ariely, author of *The Honest Truth About Dishonesty* (2013).

Using iPods as if they were playing cards, illusionist Marco Tempest weaves an artful, 5-minute meditation on truth, lies, and human emotion. Delivered from the stage at TEDGlobal in 2011: "<u>The magic of truth and lies (and iPods)</u>."

REFERENCES

Bok, S. (1978). *Lying: Moral choice in public and private life*. New York, NY: Pantheon Books.

Bowers, J.W., Elliott, N.D., & Desmond, R.J. (1977). Exploiting pragmatic rules: Devious messages. *Human Communication Research, 3*(3), 235–242. https://doi.org/10.1111/j.1468-2958.1977.tb00521.x

Bruggeman, E.L., & Hart, K.J. (1996). Cheating, lying, and moral reasoning by religious and secular high school students. *The Journal of Educational Research, 89*(6), 340–344. https://doi.org/10.1080/00220671.1996.9941337

Campbell, J. (2001). *The liar's tale: A history of falsehood*. New York, NY: Norton.

Feldman, R.S., Forrest, J.A., & Happ, B.R. (2002). Self-presentation and verbal deception: Do self-presenters lie more? *Basic and Applied Social Psychology, 24*(2), 163–170. http://psycnet.apa.org/doi/10.1207/153248302753674848

Gordon, A.K., & Miller, A.G. (2000). Perspective differences in the construal of lies: Is deception in the eye of the beholder? *Personality and Social Psychology Bulletin, 26*(1), 46–55. https://doi.org/10.1177/0146167200261005

Hopper, R., & Bell, R. A. (1984). Broadening the deception construct. *Quarterly Journal of Speech, 70*(3), 288–302. https://doi.org/10.1080/00335638409383698

Howe, J., & Sherzer, J. (1986). Friend Hairyfish and Friend Rattlesnake, or keeping anthropologists in their place. *Man, 21*(4), new series, 680–696. doi: 10.2307/2802903

Jensen, L.A., Arnett, J.J., Feldman, S.S., & Cauffman, E. (2004). The right to do wrong: Lying to parents among adolescents and emerging adults. *Journal of Youth and Adolescence, 33*(2), 101–112. https://doi.org/10.1023/B:JOYO.0000013422.48100.5a

Josephson Institute of Ethics (2012). *2012 report card on the ethics of American youth*. Playa del Rey, CA: Josephson Institute.

Kalish, N. (2004, January). How honest are you? *Reader's Digest*, 114–119.

Kick, R. (2001). *You are being lied to: The disinformation guide to media distortion, historical whitewashes and cultural myths*. New York, NY: The Disinformation Co., Ltd.

Knapp, M.L., & Comadena, M.E. (1979). Telling it like it isn't: A review of theory and research on deceptive communications. *Human Communication Research, 5*(3), 270–285. https://doi.org/10.1111/j.1468-2958.1979.tb00640.x

Knox, D., Schacht, C., Holt, J., & Turner, J. (1993). Sexual lies among university students. *College Student Journal, 27*(2), 269–272.

Lahey, J. (2013, December). 'I cheated all through high school'. *The Atlantic*. Retrieved from https://www.theatlantic.com/education/archive/2013/12/i-cheated-all-throughout-high-school/282566/

Leakey, R., & Lewin, R. (1978). *People of the lake*. New York, NY: Anchor Press/Doubleday.

Levine, T.R., Asada, K.J.K., & Lindsey, L.L.M. (2003). The relative impact of violation type and lie severity on judgments of message deceitfulness. *Communication Research Reports*, *20*(3), 208–218. https://doi.org/10.1080/08824090309388819

Levine, T.R., Serota, K.B., Carey, F., & Messer, D. (2013). Teenagers lie a lot: A further investigation into the prevalence of lying. *Communication Research Reports*, *30*(3), 211–220. https://doi.org/10.1080/08824096.2013.806254

McCleod, K. (2013, November). Andy Kaufman's best lies. *The Atlantic*. Retrieved from https://www.theatlantic.com/entertainment/archive/2013/11/andy-kaufmans-best-lies/281535/

Nofsinger, R.E., Jr. (1976). On answering questions indirectly: Some rules in the grammar of doing conversation. *Human Communication Research*, *2*(2), 172–181. https://doi.org/10.1111/j.1468-2958.1976.tb00709.x

Nyberg, D. (1993). *The varnished truth: Truth telling and deceiving in ordinary life*. Chicago, IL: University of Chicago Press.

Packer, G. (2013). *The unwinding: An inner history of the new America*. New York, NY: Farrar, Straus, & Giroux.

Pitt-Rivers, J.A. (1954). *The people of the Sierra*. New York, NY: Criterion Books.

Slackman, M. (2006, August 6). The fine art of hiding what you mean to say. *New York Times*. Retrieved from https://nytimes.com

Solomon, R.C. (1996). Self, deception, and self-deception in philosophy. In R.T. Ames and W. Dissanayake (Eds.), *Self and deception: A cross-cultural philosophical enquiry* (pp. 91–121). Albany, NY: SUNY Press.

Trivers, R.L. (1971). The evolution of reciprocal altruism. *The Quarterly Review of Biology*, *46*(1), 35–57.

Turner, R.E., Edgley, C., & Olmstead, G. (1975). Information control in conversations: Honesty is not always the best policy. *Kansas Journal of Sociology*, *11*(1), 69–89. https://doi.org/10.17161/STR.1808.6098

Tyler, J.J., Feldman, R.S., & Reichert, A. (2006). The price of deceptive behavior: Disliking and lying to people who lie to us. *Journal of Experimental Social Psychology*, *42*(1), 69–77. http://psycnet.apa.org/doi/10.1016/j.jesp.2005.02.003

Washburne, C. (1969). Retortmanship: How to avoid answering questions. *ETC: A Review of General Semantics*, *26*(1), 69–75. Retrieved from http://www.jstor.org/stable/42576329

CHAPTER 2 Perspectives on Truth

© Diego Schutman/Shutterstock.com

"The truth is rarely pure and never simple."
– *Oscar Wilde*

"The truth is always something that is told, not something that is known. If there were no speaking or writing, there would be no truth about anything. There would only be what is."
– *Susan Sontag*

"Truth isn't truth."
– *Rudy Giuliani*

How do we determine what is "true" in any given circumstance? It's an important question because without a sense of what is true, we have no basis (or even a reason to) label something as "false" or otherwise deceptive—or even to "doubt" something. In other words, lies can only exist to the extent they can be measured against something we consider true. Any serious attempt to understand the phenomenon of deception in human communication requires that we devote at least some time reflecting on the nature and functions of truth. For a more detailed exploration, you can probably find whole courses devoted to the subject in your institution's catalog, or just ask the next philosophy professor you happen to run into on campus.

According to philosopher David Nyberg (1993), we need the *idea* of truth as much as anything else. "Truth" in this sense acts as a symbol for certainty—and a belief in certainties comes in handy in an existence so full of question marks. Since we have the almost limitless capacity to imagine more than we are capable of understanding (including our own mortality), truth and its synonyms (e.g., reality, evidence, facts, accuracy) are often the things that make it possible for us to navigate the complexities of daily life. Entire intellectual disciplines depend on these concepts just as much as (if not more than) individuals do. Law, journalism, religion—even the sciences—would be hard-pressed to function without various standards for approximating certainty.

Fernández-Armesto (1997) suggests that people throughout history have sought and experienced truth in one or more of the following ways:

1. **Felt truth**, based on personal feelings/emotions
2. **Told truth**, received from other people or sources
3. **Reasoned truth**, arrived at through the use of logic
4. **Observed truth**, perceived via our senses

In this view, any given truth a person acquires is derived from one or more of these sources. And we often determine the truth of something in different ways as time passes. For example, we may initially believe something because we feel it, then later reinforce that belief by reading a book by someone else who has the same belief and, many years from now, recall that our belief came about through reasoning.

Each approach has enjoyed a special prominence during different human epochs (the Enlightenment, for example, was known as the Age of Reason [QR]). On a much smaller scale, these approaches provide a useful lens for helping us understand how people find the truths they use to cope with the uncertainties of daily life. We'll consider each in turn.

TRUTH WE FEEL

We often rely on emotions as a source of truth. These are visceral, instinctive, or intuitive responses arrived at without the use of reason or logic. When this is the case, we "know" something is true because it "feels" true, even though the specific causes of our feelings may be difficult to identify or explain. And it may have little to do with the available information or apparent facts (a phenomenon Steven Colbert sarcastically refers to as "truthiness" [QR]). When people observe and process the nonverbal behavior of others, for example, they sometimes accurately describe the messages being communicated but are unable to verbally articulate what cues they used or how they went about constructing inferences about the other person's behavior. They may say, for example, that their judgment was based on a "hunch" or "just a feeling" (Smith, Archer & Costanzo, 1991). Interestingly, Katkin, Wiens, and Öhman (2001) found in an experiment that some people are better at detecting their own internal visceral reactions to stimuli than others (i.e., there are people who have increased abilities to rely on their "gut feelings").

The truth we experience through feelings can occur in a variety of ways. They may be a source of truth for an abstract belief (such as religious faith) or something very tangible (believing your doggo is the best pup in the world). They may precede a thought or they might follow it. While considering solutions to a problem, for example, it is not uncommon for business executives to report that the intuition associated with particular alternatives helped them determine which one to choose (the correct one, presumably; Sadler-Smith & Shefy, 2004). Whatever the source or the process, the truth we feel, at least initially, is uniquely owned by the person experiencing it.

Evaluating truth through the use of feelings may not even be a conscious process, at least initially, according to some research (Myers, 2002). For example, read the story below and try to answer the questions it poses at the end before proceeding (from Haidt, 2001):

> *Julie and Mark are brother and sister. They are traveling together in France on summer vacation from college. One night they are staying alone in a cabin near the beach. They decide that it would be interesting and fun if they tried making love. At the very least it would be a new experience for each of them. Julie was already taking birth control pills, but Mark uses a condom too, just to be safe. They both enjoy making love, but they decide not to do it again. They keep that night as a special secret, which makes them feel even closer to each other. What do you think about that? Was it wrong for them to make love?*

When Haidt presented this scenario to participants in a psychological study, the vast majority quickly and emphatically agreed that it was wrong for the siblings to make love.

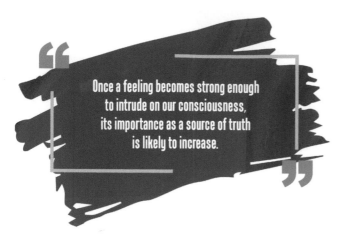

> Once a feeling becomes strong enough
> to intrude on our consciousness,
> its importance as a source of truth
> is likely to increase.

When asked to explain why it was wrong, they initially raised concerns about inbreeding, only to remember that the siblings used two types of birth control. They also argued that Julie and Mark would be hurt emotionally by the event, and then remembered that the story indicates that no harm befell them. Eventually, many participants explained their judgments by saying things like "I don't know, I can't explain it, I just know it's wrong." They seemed unable to consciously articulate their use of feelings in making their judgment, a phenomenon known as "moral dumbfounding" (Haidt, 2012).

Once a feeling becomes strong enough to intrude on our consciousness, its importance as a source of truth is likely to increase. Schwarz (2012) and others suggest that using feelings to assess the truth of something is more likely to occur under the following conditions:

- When making affective judgments
- When limited information is available
- When complex judgments are called for and/or time is constrained

When the judgment at hand is *affective* in nature (e.g., liking/disliking someone or a personal preference/taste), feelings are often the key source of information. This basic premise likely comes as no surprise—that we use *emotion* to make decisions about how to *feel*. Believing that your best friend is the "kindest person in the world," for example, is likely to result from the *feelings* you experience when in her presence.

Our mood at the time of such judgments may play a role as well (just ask any parent). Although generally vaguer and less well defined than most emotions, their presence may change the "polarity" (positive or negative) of any given emotion and help determine how we decide to feel. Your best friend's sunny disposition may normally be one of his most attractive traits. But if you're in a particularly foul mood one day, you may both be surprised when one of his Ned Flanders-like comments causes you to go all Homer Simpson on him and snap his head off. And in fact, there is research to support this idea. People who are in a good mood tend to see positive emotions in the faces of others, whereas those experiencing a bad mood tend to perceive negative emotions (Neidenthal, Halberstadt, Margolin, & Innes-Ker, 2000; Schiffenbauer, 1974).

We also rely on our feelings as a source of truth when there is very little information available about the object, person, or situation being judged. A similar condition arises when information is available but we are prevented from systematically using that information due to limited attentional resources (e.g., lacking the patience to read pages of terms and conditions for a piece of software we want to install).

A recent study offers an interesting twist on the use of available information. Schwikert and Curran (2014) found that if people are exposed to the same information repeatedly, it finds a place in their memory—even though it may not be at a high level of consciousness. Then, when they are asked to evaluate new information that is *similar* to the information that had already been repeated and stored, vague feelings of familiarity can result. Familiarity, in turn, enables people to process the new information more fluently, and people equate fluent processing with truth.

Other message features that boost fluent processing have also been shown to influence truth judgments. For example, McGlone and Tofighbakhsh (2000) asked people to judge the accuracy of unfamiliar proverbs as descriptions of human behavior. They found that people judged rhyming proverbs (e.g., *Woes unite foes*) to be more accurate than semantically equivalent non-rhyming versions (*Woes unite enemies* or *Sorrows unite foes*). Rhyme appears to afford a "ring of truth" to proverbs and poetry that they probably don't deserve (Haiman, 2018).

Anytime we are trying to make a particularly complex judgment, especially one based on incomplete fragments of information, feelings are more likely to act as our yardstick for measuring truth. Even when information is available and complex judgments are not required, time constraints or competing task demands may give priority to feelings as a way of assessing what is true. In such cases, feelings reflect a simplified decision-making strategy. Unfortunately, this simplified strategy may come at a cost. Research suggests that our accuracy when assessing the truth of something is reduced when we use feelings rather than more complex thought processes (Khazan, 2016).

Truth claims based on one's feelings, while valid and meaningful to the person experiencing them, may be difficult to defend to others under certain circumstances. For abstract claims to personal truth, like one's belief in the existence of God, the use of feelings is granted and normally goes uncontested. However, if an individual needs to have this kind of emotion-based truth accepted by others, they are well advised to look for corroborating sources—others with similar feelings, books, experts, logic, observations, etc. Some venues, like courtrooms, are especially resistant to truth claims based solely on feelings. When jurors hear courtroom evidence that features strong emotional content, for example, they are known to be less accurate in their judgments (Griffin, 2013).

TRUTH WE ARE TOLD

Very often we rely on other people as our source of truth. These may be the result of personal communication (face-to-face or electronic, such as e-mail or messaging), but are much more likely to be from various mediated sources, from television and radio to Internet sites and smartphone apps (and the occasional printed book, magazine, or newspaper). They become powerful sources of what we believe to be true—firmly anchored to the reality perceived by *other* people that we have chosen to believe. And because we do not have the time to personally investigate and verify the millions of bits of information we experience as the reality of our everyday existence, relying on truth from other sources is a pragmatic necessity as much as

> We take things on faith that what is told to us by others is usually correct, a natural human tendency known as the "truth bias".

it is a choice. Modern society is complex and the amount of information we are expected to process on a daily basis is huge. In fact, most of it is out of reach; by one estimate, more data are now being created every couple of years than existed in all of human history (Marr, 2015). We simply do not have the time or energy to investigate the truth of everything we hear or see. So we take things on faith that what is told to us by others is usually correct, a natural human tendency known as the "truth bias" (Levine, 2014).

These external sources of truth function as "opinion leaders" for us—designated authority figures, recognized experts in their fields (historians and journalists, for example), or celebrities we admire. But it is potentially anyone whose opinion we trust, who shares our worldview, or who happens to agree with us on a particular issue. For example, young children normally rely on their parents to determine what is true. As they grow older, however, other sources of truth such as friends, peers, or their college professors may come to be regarded as equally (or more) reliable.

As adults, we may develop expectations about the credibility and honesty of sources based on social categories such as occupation. For example, Gallup's 2017 Honesty and Ethics poll [QR] found that adults rate the honesty of nurses the highest of any group (82% approval), followed by military officers, grade school teachers, medical doctors, pharmacists, and police officers. The lowest ratings were given to lobbyists (8% approval), followed closely by car salespeople, members of Congress, and advertising practitioners. Day care providers, judges, and clergy fell roughly in the middle.

Throughout our lives, family and friends (our core social network) remain the most trusted of the various external sources of truth we rely on. Compared to others, lies are least expected from these two groups (Heyman, Luu, & Lee, 2009; Van Swol, Molhotra, & Braun, 2011). The trust we place in our friends as a source of truth is what some con artists depend on to make their scams work. For example, many victims of online "phishing" scams were lured in by an e-mail message they received from a friend or relative. In some cases, the message was forwarded to them by an acquaintance who didn't realize it was part of a scam; in others, it was sent by a scammer who hacked an acquaintance's e-mail account and then sent messages to all the contacts listed in the address book. In both situations, scammers tricked victims into sharing financial information or downloading malicious software by exploiting the trust they invest in their social network (Wang, Herath, Chen, Vishwanath, & Rao, 2012).

A lot of what we believe from other sources is dependent on inferences we make about their credibility. We expect people will generally tell us the truth (the truth bias) and we trust certain people (family and friends most of all) to be sources of valid information. But of course, not everyone always trusts the same sources. Noting the challenge this disagreement creates for combating the spread of fake news on various technological platforms, Internet pioneer Nathaniel Borenstein observed (in Anderson & Rainie, 2017):

> *Any attempt to improve the veracity of news must be done by some authority, and people don't trust the same authorities, so they will ultimately get the news that their preferred authority wants them to have. There is nothing to stop them choosing an insane person as their authority. (p. 46)*

As noted above, the truth we are told from others doesn't necessarily have to come from individuals. Sometimes we believe something is true based on the sheer number of other people who believe it. If 10 people believe the color of a shirt is dark blue, you too may see it as dark blue even though you would have said it was black if someone had asked you before you knew what others had perceived. "Social proof" of this sort is a common proxy for truth in the era of social media. Facebook users commonly judge the accuracy of a story in their news feed based on the number of likes or dislikes it receives from other users; credibility is given to Twitter users based on how many followers they have (MacCoun, 2012). Although social media users may believe there is "strength in numbers," computer programs that generate fake Facebook likes and phantom Twitter followers exploit the weakness of this herd mentality (Muscanell, Guadagno, & Murphy, 2014).

REASONING AS A SOURCE OF TRUTH

As a way of acquiring truth, reasoning and other types of systematic thinking stand in contrast to the use of feelings and emotions. This is the domain of logic, rules, standards, formulas, arguments, evidence, claims, and more. But as we will see, these formal systems of thought are only as good as the information on which they're based. In other words, the mere use of these approaches does not guarantee accurate results.

Some types of reasoning are highly formal, clearly defined, and well-known to others. When this is the case, what is true is what agrees with the rules, standards, or system being used. Consider the following:

$$(x + y)^2 = x^2 + 2xy + y^2$$

If you believe this equation to be true, you are saying it is consistent with a system of statements in the language called algebra. If someone says, "Today is September 6th," and you reply, "That's true," you are saying you accept the same system and rules for calculating dates. Many of the things we believe to be true are deeply ingrained in these widely accepted rules and formulas for thinking which usually go unchallenged. They are so taken for granted that people who do not accept them are labeled illogical, unable to reason, or not thinking straight. But we shouldn't forget that the truth of any claim deduced by its application to a known formula is only as strong as our *faith in the truth value of the formula itself.* As Fernández-Armesto (1997) says:

> We cannot get to the conclusion that Socrates is mortal without saying first, "If all men are mortal," or that spheres are round without first specifying roundness as a defining characteristic of a sphere. "You can only find truth with logic," as Chesterton said, "if you have already found truth without it." (p. 119)

There are also ways of reasoning in which the rules are less explicit and, as a result, the conclusions reached can show considerable variation. For example, we use reasoning to draw conclusions about numerous social issues, including:

© YKh/Shutterstock.com

- the extent to which guns should be controlled and how

- whether strict voter identification laws suppress voting by minorities

- whether sex education classes in schools reduce teenage pregnancy

- if government surveillance of citizens' phone calls and Internet usage is necessary to prevent terrorist attacks

- whether it is morally acceptable to spank children and the extent to which this helps make them better people or may negatively influence them psychologically

With complex (and often emotion-stirring) issues like these, people may reason differently and thereby draw different conclusions. Only information that supports one's beliefs is often the basis for reasoning. A belief in God is normally rooted in faith, but some people try to buttress their faith with what they feel is a reasoned argument to support God's existence. They reason that the world they know is so complex and inexplicable in so many ways that it could not have come about without the direction of God. However, a scientist may view this as an attempt to use reasoning to establish a scientific truth, and for the scientist a scientific truth is always subject to modification or refutation—typically not the case with the reasoning to support the existence of God (Shermer, 2003).

Some people also reason that if a person believes in the theory of evolution he or she must also be an agnostic or atheist. Even Charles Darwin, the scientist most credited with developing evolutionary theory, was a Christian until late in life. Many scientists use both religion and theories of science such as evolution in their truth-seeking journeys, including Gregor Mendel, the founder of genetics; Francis Collins, director of the National Institutes of Health; and theoretical physicist James Gates.

Reasoning in everyday life is always subject to questionable premises, biases, and incorrect inferential shortcuts (Kida, 2006). Incorrect inferences can be "reasoned" from accurate observations. For example, there is the story of a 6-year-old girl who flies on a plane for the first time. Having watched a number of airplanes take off, she knows how things are supposed to work. So, a few minutes after takeoff she turns to her parents and asks, "When do we start getting smaller?" Her reasoning followed logically from the flights she had seen from the ground, but her conclusion was wrong.

We also tend to discount the role of chance happenings in our life—preferring to reason that an event was *caused by* something. Most of us also tend to overestimate the number of deaths attributable to sensational accidents but underestimate the frequency of deaths due to diabetes, stroke, and asthma. This may be due to greater media coverage, but only a few vivid anecdotes

> We also tend to discount the role of chance happenings in our life—preferring to reason that an event was *caused by* something.

or stories can also greatly influence our reasoning. Judging the frequency and probability of things based on how easily they come to mind or whether you have experienced them are other ways we reason our way to incorrect conclusions. Despite the fact that several hundred people reported problems with air bags in the type of car you drive, you reason this is not a problem because you haven't experienced any trouble yourself. Or you may reason that because the names of 15 professional sports figures from your state come to mind, it has probably produced more professional athletes than any other state (Kahneman, 2011).

In everyday conversation as well as in courtroom proceedings, we often reason (incorrectly) that truthfulness is always associated with consistency and deception with inconsistency. There are two pitfalls associated with this premise:

1. First, human beings are not always highly consistent in the way they choose to report reality due to faulty memory and/or the different language choices they may make to describe a phenomenon across two or more different points in time.

2. Second, what may appear to be "inconsistent" to one person may be perfectly consistent to another. Consider the wife who says to her husband, "You spend too much money," and minutes later bemoans the fact that they don't ever go out and eat at nice restaurants anymore. To the husband, his wife is being inconsistent since she doesn't want him to spend money, but she wants to eat out at an expensive restaurant. The wife, however, sees no contradiction. Her husband spends too much money on himself, but she approves of spending money on something both of them can enjoy.

While the preceding examples illustrate some of the troublesome aspects that may accompany truth derived from reasoning, they should not be taken to mean that reasoning is a poor way to arrive at truth. On the contrary, truth derived from reasoned thinking has served humankind well for centuries. But these examples do remind us that reasoning, like other methods of seeking truth, is subject to the frailties and shortcomings that are part of being human.

THE TRUTH WE OBSERVE

Sometimes we find truth in what we observe. Unlike the three preceding ways of arriving at something we believe to be true, this approach requires sensory contact with the object in question. The senses serve as a way of certifying the truth. When someone says, "I saw it with my own eyes so it must be true," or "I know she said it because I heard her say it," they are testifying to their reliance on their own sensory observations as a source of truth.

The observers themselves are not the only ones who believe in the truth of their sensory observations. Jurors tend to believe eyewitnesses about 80% of the time, and this percentage increases if the witness shows confidence and/or includes more details in his or her testimony. The word of eyewitnesses has been given more credence in some court cases than fingerprint experts, polygraphs, handwriting experts, and, in at least one case, a DNA expert. The truth value of eyewitness (and earwitness) testimony in court is almost as good at getting a conviction as having the proverbial smoking gun, according to Loftus and Ketcham (1991):

> *Eyewitness identification is the most damning of all evidence that can be used against a defendant. When an eyewitness points a finger at a defendant and says, "I saw him do it," the case is "cast-iron, brass-bound, copper-riveted, and airtight" as one prosecutor proclaimed. For how can we disbelieve the sworn testimony of eyewitnesses to a crime when the witnesses are absolutely convinced that they are telling the truth? (p. 13)*

But research also tells us that eyewitnesses can and have been wrong. Neither the eyewitness's confident demeanor nor the inclusion of details has been linked to greater accuracy. In recent years, the analysis of DNA evidence has led to the release of numerous prisoners, some of whom were on death row, and most of whom were convicted solely or with the help of eyewitness testimony. Pezdek (2011) reports that of the first 292 prisoners exonerated by DNA evidence, approximately 75% were convicted based on eyewitness misidentification. One factor that contributes to these mistakes is that people tend to think their eyes work like a video camera, flawlessly recording what they see.

Scientific studies, however, tell a different story. Sometimes we do not observe large changes in objects and scenes (*change blindness*), and sometimes we do not even perceive certain highly visible objects in our visual field (*inattentional blindness*). For example, drivers may fail to notice another car when trying to turn or a person may fail to see a friend in a movie theater while looking for a seat, even though their friend is waving. Our brain is constantly trying to make sense out of an environment filled with a tremendous array of changing stimuli that vary in intensity. As a result, the brain tries to create a meaningful narrative and overlooks those stimuli that don't fit the narrative being created.

Our brain is constantly trying to make sense out of an environment filled with a tremendous array of changing stimuli that vary in intensity. As a result, the brain tries to create a meaningful narrative and overlooks those stimuli that don't fit the narrative being created.

Simons and Chabris (1999) demonstrated this phenomenon in an experiment. People were asked to watch a 1-minute video in which several people were dribbling and passing a basketball and told to count the number of times a pass was made from one player to another. Observers concentrated closely on the pass shots in order to determine the correct number. During the video, however, a person dressed in a gorilla suit slowly walked into the middle of the players, turned toward the camera and thumped his or her chest, and walked off (see it here [QR]). Surprisingly, *only 50% of viewers noticed the gorilla*. When we first heard of this experiment, we were skeptical of the results, but hundreds of our students have reacted in the same way when observing the video.

The Observer

Observations are affected by numerous long- and short-term characteristics of the observer—stress level, biases/prejudices, expectations, age, gender, interest in the object of observation, motivation to observe closely, etc. (Wells, Memon, & Penrod, 2006).

Both males and females, for example, can be accurate observers, but not necessarily with the same targets. Accuracy is often linked to one's interest in and experience with the thing being observed, and the interests and experiences of males and females may differ (Davis & Loftus, 2009). Accurate facial identification of people who have a different racial background can be negatively affected by the amount of experience and exposure one has had with that race (Scherf & Scott, 2012). Of course, too much familiarity with the object of observation may also make it difficult to accurately perceive things because we feel like we "know" the target and subconsciously relax our attention.

Observers also have biases. One common bias stems from people's desire to perceive the world *in a way that confirms their beliefs*. Sometimes this "confirmation bias" motivates them to see or hear things that others do not.

- A ufologist sees a fossil in a picture taken by one of NASA's Mars rovers.

- A devout Catholic sees the Virgin Mary on a tortilla.

- A paranormalist discerns the voices of dead people speaking in a grainy radio signal.

- A police officer in a crime-ridden neighborhood mistakes the cellphone a teenager is holding for a gun.

In other cases, confirmation bias motivates observers to not see or hear things that others do:

- Sports fans don't see why the referee called a foul against the team they are cheering on, but do when their opponents do the same thing.

lying and deception in HUMAN INTERACTION

36

- A woman smitten with a new boyfriend is baffled when her friends tell her it's obvious that "he's just not that into you."

- You witness your best friend having a tense interaction with a police officer, but fail to see him making threatening gestures toward and cursing at the officer.

Bias of this sort probably occurred when the twin daughters of accused murderer Robert Angleton were asked to listen to a garbled tape recording of two men plotting the murder of their mother—one of whom knew many details about how to enter the victim's house. With their mother dead and their father facing a murder charge, it is not surprising that they did not hear the voice on the tape as their father's. The consistency with which people hear and see things they want to believe and miss those they don't suggests that observations are to some degree influenced by motives (Shermer, 2011).

Observers are also influenced by the extent to which they are motivated to observe something for details or not. We are rarely asked to provide the same level of detail about our experiences in daily social interaction that we would be expected to recount in a court of law. Suppose you went horseback riding last year when you were vacationing at Lake Tahoe. Some or all of the following may be things you didn't think were important to observe and remember. What was the name of the horse you rode? How many miles did you ride? What were you wearing?

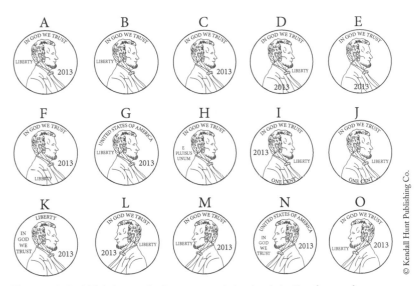

© Kendall Hunt Publishing Co.

Figure 2.1: Which rendering accurately depicts the face of an actual penny? (Answer at end of chapter).

What color was the saddle blanket? How many other people were in your party? A familiar test of how closely we observe an object we have seen many times is the identification of the correct penny face. How accurate are you? Choose one of the options in Figure 2.1, then find a real penny to compare it to (Nickerson & Adams, 1979).

Observers also make observations during times of heightened emotions, moods, and stress. While a certain amount of stress may be optimal for accurate observations, too much or too little may adversely affect what is observed and what is remembered. Observers under high stress focus on some details but not on others (Kensinger, 2009). For example, when an observer is threatened by someone brandishing a lethal weapon, their perception of the situation (and hence their recall of it) is likely to be narrowed to that of the weapon rather than the person holding it.

The Observation Conditions

Certain conditions under which the observation was made will affect what is observed. These include such things as viewing angle, lighting, distance, competing stimuli, and length of time observing. Consider the wildly differing observations of hundreds of people who reported seeing Flight 587 fall from the sky over New York, just two months after 9/11 ("Different Views," 2002):

- 52% saw a fire while the plane was in the air (22% said there was no fire)

- 8% said there was an explosion

- 22% saw smoke (20% said they saw no smoke)

- 18% saw the plane turn right (18% saw the plane turn left while 13% saw it wobble, dip, or move side to side)

- 57% saw something separate from the airplane but disagreed on what it was (9% said nothing fell off the plane)

So, who was right? The plane made several hard turns right and left, then the tail fin assembly snapped off. Both engines eventually separated as the plane continued in uncontrolled flight (Garrison, 2005). There was no in-air explosion or fire (National Transportation Safety Board, 2002).

Thus far we've focused on unaided human sensory perception. But observations are also made with devices that enhance and/or extend our senses. Microscopes and telescopes help us see what is prohibited by normal visual acuity, and sound wave analyzers measure acoustic signals we are unable to hear. We also rely on speedometers, stethoscopes, polygraphs, and seismographs to make observations our senses cannot. These devices further add to the possibility of multiple truths, depending on the type of observation used. For example, depending on the degree of measurement precision, one might say a

table length is 30 inches high, using an ordinary yard stick, or 30.11 inches with a more precise measuring instrument. Both are "true" measures, but the standard of measurement was different. Some people believe polygraphs detect deception, but they don't. They measure changes in breathing, heart rate, perspiration, blood pressure, and sometimes body movement. These measures are then observed by human beings who make inferences about whether certain patterns are likely to be associated with lying (for more on polygraphs, see Chapter 10).

Memory

The truth of any observation we make is partly in how we perceive it and partly in how we remember our perceptions. Memory, then, is a key factor in the truth we observe. Many people believe that their memories operate like a digital camera, recording the events of their lives just as they occurred and storing them as "files" for future reference. These people think that all of the details of an event are "in storage," and if not readily accessed, the use of hypnosis and other enhancement techniques can eventually recover them. Memory research, however,

does not support such a view (Winter, 2012). Although our brains do record some aspects of past experiences, remembering them is a reconstructive process in which we blend the aspects we did record with information from other events we experienced in the past and our ongoing experience in the present. As a result, our memories are not precise and permanent, but rather messy and changeable.

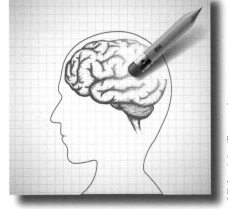

©Trifonenkolvan/Shutterstock.com

When our memory fails us, then, it can be because we never stored the information in the first place or if we have, it has been forgotten; false memories can be implanted by our suggestibility to outside sources or through our own biases that prompt us to rewrite history based on our present beliefs (Schacter, 2001).

Sometimes visual memories can be hindered simply because we try to verbally describe what we saw prior to visually identifying it, a phenomenon known as "verbal overshadowing" (McGlone, Kobrynowicz, & Alexander, 2005; Schooler, 2013). This is most likely to occur when the stimulus is complex and/or abstract and the perceiver does not have the specialized knowledge or vocabulary to adequately describe it. For example, when an eyewitness is asked to verbally describe the face of a person seen committing a crime before he or she is asked to identify the perpetrator's face in a photo lineup, a linguistically awkward and uncertain verbal description may create a memory that interferes with the visual memory.

The idea that we can and do permanently change remembered events (and create new ones) opens up the possibility that what we earnestly believe may not necessarily be what happened—not necessarily the truth. Since memories are altered in line with our own needs and interpretations, there is no reason for us to doubt them. They are beliefs that make sense to us and our sincerity in those beliefs is genuine.

Much of the information we lose or forget about an event occurs soon after our experience and then gradually continues thereafter. Some variations in this pattern will occur depending on the type of information involved, but immediately writing or talking about the event may aid in retaining details associated with it. Talking about the event, however, introduces the possibility that the remarks of the person or persons you talk to may somehow become blended into your memory of the event.

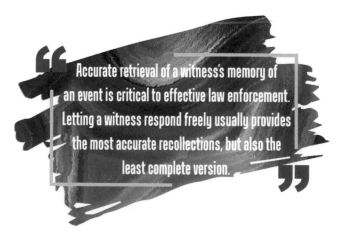

Accurate retrieval of a witness's memory of an event is critical to effective law enforcement. Letting a witness respond freely usually provides the most accurate recollections, but also the least complete version.

So how other people "help" us remember things may also be a part of the truth we observe. Accurate retrieval of a witness's memory of an event is critical to effective law enforcement. Letting a witness respond freely usually provides the most accurate recollections, but also the least complete version. Since our memory of an event is often incomplete and has gaps to be filled in, others can help us fill in those gaps:

- The "filling in" may take place immediately when you witness an event with another person and he or she turns to you and says, "Hey, could you believe the size of that guy's biceps?!" That one verbal comment may be enough to add big arm muscles to the mental image you recollect from your observation.

- Questioning subsequent to an event can also act as filler for memory gaps. For example, the question "Did you see *the* broken headlight?" could make a witness believe there was a broken headlight and incorporate it into his or her story. "Did you see *a* broken headlight?" or better "Was there a broken headlight?" is less likely to imply that there was a broken headlight. Better than all of these, however, would be to ask, "Did you notice anything about the car?"

The methods used in identifying a criminal from a photo lineup can also have a profound effect on memory retrieval. As a result of this growing awareness, some police departments have begun to modify their procedures.

- For example, 30% to 40% of witnesses who view a photo lineup will identify one of the photos as the perpetrator of the crime even though the suspect is *not* in the lineup. To offset the assumption that the suspect is there and they just need to find him or her, witnesses should be told by the administrator of the lineup that the suspect may or may not be in the lineup and that it is okay to say you don't know or aren't sure.

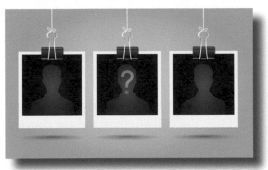

© enjoy your life/Shutterstock.com

- When all the photos are shown at the same time, witnesses tend to compare the photos and select the one that most closely resembles the face they remember. Showing the photos sequentially can reduce false identifications by 10% without affecting the percentage of accurate identifications.

- It is also important to select a person to administer the photo lineup who does not know the identity of the suspect. Unconscious movements or statements like "Be sure you look at all of the photos before you select one" (when the witness has selected someone other than the suspect known to the administrator) essentially tell the witness that his or her memory needs to be altered (Malpass, Tredoux, & McQuiston-Surrett, 2009; Wells & Olson, 2003). Once a witness has received implicit or explicit confirmation for his or her identification, it is very difficult to change his or her mind.

In contrast to the assumptions associated with several nationally publicized child abuse cases purported to have occurred in day care facilities in the 1980s, children are no longer

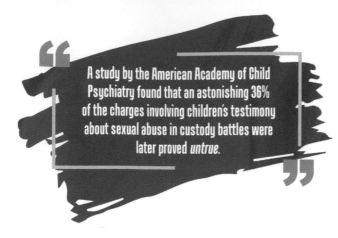

A study by the American Academy of Child Psychiatry found that an astonishing 36% of the charges involving children's testimony about sexual abuse in custody battles were later proved *untrue*.

uncritically accepted as totally credible sources of information (Eberle & Eberle, 1993) (see Chapter 5). We now know:

- Children engage in behavior adults would label a lie.

- Children's memories are just as fallible as an adult's.

- Children may modify their memories and tell stories they think adults *want them to tell.*

A study by the American Academy of Child Psychiatry found that an astonishing 36% of the charges involving children's testimony about sexual abuse in custody battles were later proved *untrue* (Green, 1986). Courts in many states do not allow children under 10 years of age to testify. When they do, the tests for competency generally seek to answer questions, such as:

1. Can the child recall and accurately report an event?
2. Can the child distinguish lies from truth?
3. Does the child understand the concept of one's duty to tell the truth?

Sometimes children will "lie" without prompting from adults, but most of the research in this area focuses on how children may be persuaded to tell a story by adults who have personal agendas (although such agendas are not always conscious). Generally, young children are more susceptible to suggestive techniques than adults, but getting a child to accept a suggestion is not always easy and may take repeated efforts over a period of time.

TRUTH AND CERTAINTY

We started this chapter by saying that people seek truth because they seek certainty in their lives. But not all of the things we believe to be true are held with the same degree of certainty—the same strength of belief. Instead, we think about things in terms of their probability of being true. Those with the highest probability of being true provide us with the greatest certainty. But truth is always in process. Something we are very certain about, something that has a high probability of being true for us, may or may not remain so; something with a lower probability of being true may, in time, become more certain for us.

What is true for many individuals or an entire society is also composed of beliefs that vary in their probability of being certain. Even if 17 million people in a society composed of 317 million people believe something is true, it may still be an improbable truth for society as a whole. For example, Gallup conducted polls in the 1990s that showed 6% of Americans had doubts that U.S. astronauts landed and walked on the moon, which the organization put into context this way:

> *Although, if taken literally, 6% translates into millions of individuals, it is not unusual to find about that many people in the typical poll agreeing with almost any question that is asked of them—so the best interpretation is that this particular conspiracy theory is not widespread.*

As if to confirm this phenomenon, in 2002 polls indicated 7% of the population believed Elvis may still be alive. Of course, sometimes a belief shared by most people and which represents the prevailing truth can change. Experts, people in positions of power, loud and persistent advocates who begin without a power base, new information, or conditions that change with time and make a belief more palatable—all are capable of changing societal truths. Hitler's notion of the "big lie" features some of these elements—say something so colossally absurd and keep repeating it long enough and eventually people will come to believe it (Dreyfuss, 2017).

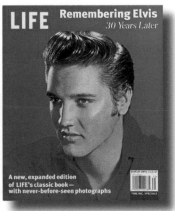

© Dan Kosmayer/Shutterstock.com

And when Copernicus first put forth the idea that the sun, not the earth, was at the heart of our solar system, most astronomers and natural philosophers did not believe it. Over a hundred years later, Galileo's support for Copernicus's ideas was denounced by leaders of the Roman Catholic Church as heresy because such ideas were believed to be contrary to doctrines of that branch of Christianity. Today, the idea that the earth, moon, and other planets in our solar system revolve around the sun is an astronomical truth that is not questioned by physicists. Yet some astronomical truths do change. In 1930, astronomers named Pluto the ninth planet in our solar system, but in 2006 poor Pluto was reclassified as a "dwarf planet" (following the 2005 discovery of a larger body, Eris). In the span of less than two years, our solar system went from having nine planets to eight (Rincon, 2015).

But even more "fundamental" truths like the speed of light are not immune to change. Scientists observing gas clouds as far away as 12 billion light years from the earth have presented data indicating that there is a strong possibility that the speed of light and other universal principles of physics may change with the passage of time (Urban, Couchot, Sarazin, & Djannati-Atai, 2013).

While the preceding examples have focused on new information and observations, what is true for the general public can sometimes be changed by simply mandating that something be classified in a different way. Before 1948, the harmonica was classified as a toy. As a result, not even the most accomplished players could join the Musician's Union because they did not play a musical instrument. After 1948, when the organization changed its mind, the harmonica became a musical instrument and those who played it were considered musicians (Krampert, 2002).

TELLING THE TRUTH

Up to this point we have focused on the ways people determine what they believe to be true and the degree of certainty with which those truths are held. In this section, we focus on the process of talking about what we believe to be true. Two crucial decisions face every truth teller: (a) what to say and (b) how to say it.

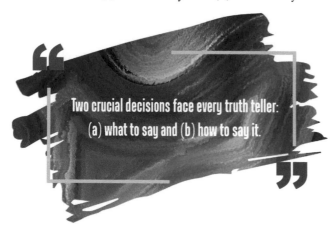

Two crucial decisions face every truth teller: (a) what to say and (b) how to say it.

At first, deciding what to say seems obvious. After all, aren't we just going to tell "the truth?" "The" truth makes it sound like there is only one thing to be said (and that it's clear what it is). While we may end up saying only one thing, there may be a lot of other associated truths we don't say. We can't ever say everything about anything. So from the standpoint of the courtroom oath, we are not likely to tell "the *whole* truth" even though we can tell what we believe to be "the truth and nothing but the truth." Part of the truth teller's task, then, is to select from all that he or she believes to be true about a particular issue, that which should be said.

For those who subscribe to the tenets of "radical honesty" (Blanton, 2005), this decision is an easy one because it is based more on the need to express oneself than on what the recipient should hear and what effects it might have. Adherents of radical honesty encourage you to tell:

- neighbors you'd rather watch TV than go to their house for dinner
- a prospective employer you left your previous job because you didn't like the supervisor
- your romantic partner that he or she looks fat

From this perspective, catharsis (emotional relief) is the motivation for telling the truth and for some people at some points in their life this may indeed be liberating, if not costly in some ways.

But just because you say it doesn't make it true, and even if it is true, it doesn't mean that saying it out loud was a good idea. As Nyberg notes: "It is a great distortion to believe you are speaking the truth simply because you say what you think. It is possible to be sincere and wrong. It is also possible to be sincere, right, and dumb" (1993, p. 17). When one is considering how to most effectively tell the truth, it is important to decide what parts of the truth one holds about a particular issue should be said and how those parts should be put into words.

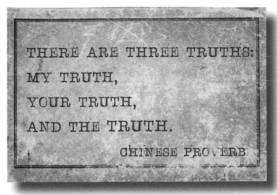

THERE ARE THREE TRUTHS:
MY TRUTH,
YOUR TRUTH,
AND THE TRUTH.

CHINESE PROVERB

© Yury Zap/Shutterstock.com

Knowing how to put the truth into words is greatly facilitated by understanding how we determine truth in the first place. Throughout this chapter, we have emphasized the potentially inexact nature of our perceptions and memory; the ongoing changes in the objects of our perceptions; the prevalent role of inferences in what we "know" to be true; that what we "know" as true can change over time; and that most, if not all, of what we know as true is based on probability rather than absolute certainty. On top of this, the language we use to describe our realities inevitably *abstracts* the things we're referring to. That is, when describing something, we are always selecting some aspects and ignoring others rather than perfectly reproducing the thing.

If one agrees with the preceding and strives to more accurately tell the truth, then language that is more circumspect and qualified is in order. Hayakawa and Hayakawa (1990, p. 209) said, "Knowledge is power, but effective knowledge is that which includes knowledge of the limitations of one's knowledge." Within this framework, truth tellers would strive to link their telling of truths to:

- their own perceptions ("It seems to me. . ." or "The way I see things. . .")
- the perceptions of others ("I believe what the article in *The New York Times* said. . .")
- anchor their claims to the here-and-now rather than imply that their claim is not subject to change over time

For example, saying "In my view, it was unethical of you to refuse to pay Chris after you said you would" is a very different basis for relating to your perceptions of what is true than flatly declaring "You are an unethical person." And, of course, the two statements are not likely to be processed by their recipients in the same ways. You might also consider qualifying truth statements that you have less confidence in with words like "might be" or "seems to be" or "could be." Fernández-Armesto (1997, p.105) reports that among India's Jain philosophers, "no statement is considered true unless it contains such qualifiers as 'perhaps' and 'as it were.'"

While being circumspect in the way you tell the truth may appropriately account for the often uncertain ways we come to know truths, it is not always the best way to accomplish communicative goals. Not everyone accepts the tentative nature of truth claims—especially their own. So even though you may understand and accept your truth claims as something short of certain, in some situations you may appropriately *choose to act as if* you had no doubts. For example, politicians who publicly acknowledge the uncertainties associated with what they believe to be true are likely to have trouble getting elected. Likewise, lovers who tell their partners they aren't sure what they feel is love may be accurate but suddenly single. As noted in Chapter 1, *effective* communication may involve some forms of lying and/or deception.

IS EVERYONE'S TRUTH EQUALLY VALID?

Given what has been discussed up to this point in the chapter, one might legitimately conclude that there is no truth apart from each person's own reality and therefore one person's truth is just as good and just as true as another's. While some academicians embrace the philosophical idea that "there is no truth," this rather depressing and unrealistic way to experience the world is not widely practiced by everyday people in everyday situations. Imagine if your plumber told you, "I don't see any point in following the installation instructions that came with your new toilet because there is no truth." Discussions of subjective truth fit better in college classrooms and, ironically, it is not unusual for the professors who support the idea that everyone's truth is equally valid to dismiss other points of view as incorrect (Kristof, 2016). Note also how this same idea undermines the study of lying and deception: If there is no such thing as truth, how could any statement be labeled a "lie" or otherwise "deceptive?"

In daily life, we find some areas where more truths are accepted and tolerated than others, but it is hard to think of any area where everyone's truth is treated as equally valid. In the United States, those who have found religious truth in Christianity and Judaism may get a sense that their truths are being treated as more culturally valid than those who find their truth in atheism, pagan witchcraft, shamanism, or religions that sacrifice animals in their rituals. Truth in such circumstances is often a matter of which view has the most cultural power. As an illustration, consider the following news story that occurred in Romania (adapted from Schofield, 2004):

> *Toma Petre died. After he was buried, his brother-in-law, Gheorghe Marinescu dug him up, ripped his heart out, burned it, mixed the ashes with water, and had Toma's son, daughter-in-law, and granddaughter drink it. Why? Because Gheorge (and a number of other villagers) believed Toma was a vampire. Vampires, according to some people in Marotinu De Sus, Romania, rise from their grave at night and feed on their loved ones, draining their blood. Thus, when relatives get sick following the*

death of a family member, a vampire is suspected. When Gheorghe unearthed Toma, it was clear to him that Toma was a vampire. He reported that Toma was on his side with blood around his mouth even though he was originally placed in his coffin on his back without any blood present. After drinking the mixture of water and heart ashes, the members of Toma's family, some who had been sick for weeks, recovered. Costel, Toma's son, said it was a miracle and that they had been saved from a vampire (his father). When asked by a reporter how he could be sure his illness was the result of a vampire, he replied: "What other explanation is possible?"

This story is about real people who earnestly believe in the existence of vampires—that certain dead people rise from their coffins at night to feed on the blood of family members. They also believe vampires can be stopped by ripping out their hearts and burning them.

To many people, such stories are pure superstition, have no basis in fact, and cannot be true. But many of the same people who see no truth value in vampires rising from the dead do believe it is true that a man was born to a virgin mother, walked on water, brought a dead man back to life, turned water into wine, and rose from the dead. The latter set of beliefs is widespread throughout the world. Why is one truth so widely accepted and not the other? The juxtaposition of these stories illustrates how some religious practices tend to be welcomed as truth while others are seen as bizarre or antisocial.

Differing standards of truth seem to apply in politics too. Even though the Republican and Democratic parties in the United States argue with each other, most would probably agree that the truths espoused by these parties are not the same as the truths espoused by other political parties in the United States, such as the Tea Party, the Libertarian Party, the U.S. Socialist Party, the Green Party, and Stormfront (a white supremacist party).

Are the people who believe they have been abducted by aliens, examined, and released telling the truth? As they perceive it, yes. Is this truth as valid as the truth of those who do not believe that the earth has been visited by a species from another planet? No more so than:

- those whose religious truth denies medical help to a dying child
- those who deny their children vaccines
- people who believe mental illness is caused by demonic possession curable by exorcism

Unlike many of the preceding examples, sometimes the number of people who believe in conflicting truths is comparable (e.g., when life begins). Instead of helping to see the other's truth as equally valid, advocates on each side are likely to work even harder to make sure their truth prevails. When truths come into conflict with one another, how does one prevail? Some venues have rules of evidence and standards for truth that are tailored to their particular situation (e.g., the courtroom), but in the public sphere, the following factors often account for what is accepted as true:

- Support by many people. What is considered true is often a function of how many people believe it is true. This belief may or may not be linked to a belief in an objective reality.

- Support by those who have the power to make decisions for many others

- Support by people whose knowledge of the issue in question is respected by many others and is considered expert

- Repeated arguments that convincingly appeal to what many others believe is reasonable or arguments that elicit a strong emotional response from many others

- The preference for truths linked to human survival and well-being is also a standard that may be applied

All of this suggests that there could be times when it's valuable to at least act like you've arrived at a given truth. At the same time, though, it is important to recognize that the quest for truth is an ongoing process. With this perspective, *even people who advocate a particular truth will continue to seek input from a variety of sources*:

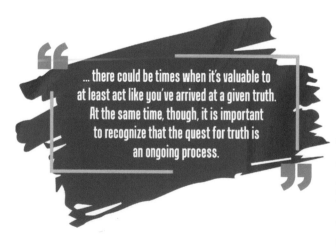

... there could be times when it's valuable to at least act like you've arrived at a given truth. At the same time, though, it is important to recognize that the quest for truth is an ongoing process.

- talking to people with different backgrounds and experiences

- reading a wide spectrum of what people write

- involving themselves in a variety of life's experiences

They will also struggle to maintain the truth-seeking process by testing, analyzing, and pitting their intuition, their emotional reactions, their reasoning, their observations, and what other people tell them against one another—especially when it doesn't seem necessary to do so.

SUMMARY

This chapter began with the assumption that in order to properly understand lying and deception, we need to understand how people determine truth. People want certainty in their lives, which prompts them to seek truth. Four common methods for determining truth were examined:

1. Truth we feel
2. Truth we are told
3. Truth we figure out through reasoning
4. Truth we observe

Some important factors that affect the nature of our truths, no matter how they are determined, include:

1. We don't perceive things exactly like anyone else.
2. Most of what we know is based on inferences.
3. Even what we know from observation is based on probabilities.
4. What we know today as true may not be known as truth tomorrow.
5. When we decide something is true, we label it but abstract it in the process.
6. Human memory, including eyewitness observations, is fallible.

Regarding memory in particular, not all events (nor all parts of a given event) are stored in the brain. What does manage to get stored can be forgotten over time, altered by other people/events, or altered by one's own changing needs and mindset.

When we tell the truth, we need to determine, out of all we know, *what* to tell and *how* to tell it. Given the often tenuous nature of truth, linguistic choices that are qualified and circumspect seem appropriate, but these linguistic choices may not be helpful in accomplishing various communicative goals. While it is theoretically possible to see how the process of determining truth might mean that everyone's truth is equally valid, certain truths tend to prevail in everyday life. Particular truths prevail because they have one or more of the following:

1. Many people believe it.
2. Powerful people and decision-makers believe it.
3. Experts believe it.
4. Arguments based on reason and/or emotion appeal to many people.
5. The truth appeals to human survival and/or well-being.

The chapter concluded by saying that even though truth-seeking is more journey than destination, communicators may sometimes have to act as if they have reached their destination in order to get the responses they desire.

By the way, the one (and only) accurate rendering of a U.S. penny in Figure 2.1 is choice A. If you didn't get it right, don't worry. As is so often the case with everyday objects, most people don't.

EXERCISES

1. Find an educator who has a graduate degree in a given field (if you're on a college campus, this should be easy). Ask them to reflect on the following questions: (a) How do scholars in your field determine what is true? (b) Describe some "truths" in your field that have changed over time. (c) How would you advise students to go about seeking truth?

2. Interview someone who is familiar with the following New Testament verse: "And ye shall know the truth, and the truth shall make you free" (John 8:32). Ask them the following questions: (a) What does it mean to you personally? (b) How does it relate to other forms of truth?

3. Choose a significant memory from your childhood. Independently ask multiple family members to describe the event in as much detail as possible. In all likelihood, their memories of it will differ dramatically. How do you explain these differing truths?

OF INTEREST

Do we see the world as it really is? That is the fundamental question explored by Donald Hoffman, a cognitive scientist who studies visual perception, in this TED Talk [QR]. He begins by suggesting that our brains are constructing the things we see. He then goes on to argue that *not* seeing the world in perfectly accurate terms actually gives us a survival advantage.

There are a lot of persistent scientific myths that just won't die. Antioxidants are good and free radicals are bad, right? Screening for cancer always saves lives, right? Here, the prestigious journal *Nature* sets out to bust five of the more resilient myths [QR] in fields such as medicine, education, and sociology.

The sciences are not alone when it comes to widely held beliefs that just aren't true. *TIME* magazine interviewed seven historians to find out what misconceptions Americans frequently cling to when it comes to understanding their own history [QR]. This list makes myths like the one about Betsy Ross and the flag seem like child's play.

REFERENCES

Anderson, J., & Rainie, L. (2017). The future of truth and misinformation online. *Pew Research Center*. Retrieved from http://www.pewinternet.org

Blanton, B. (2005). *Radical honesty: How to transform your life by telling the truth* (Rev. ed.) New York, NY: Dell.

Davis, D., & Loftus, E. F. (2009). Expectancies, emotion, and memory reports of visual events. In J. R. Brockmole (Ed.), *The visual world in memory* (pp. 178–214). New York, NY: Psychology Press.

Different Views of the Same Disaster. (2002, June 9). *Austin American Statesman*, p. E-1.

Dreyfuss, E. (2017, February 11). Want to make a lie seem true? Say it again. And again. And again. *Wired*. Retrieved from http://www.wired.com

Eberle, P., & Eberle, S. (1993). *The abuse of innocence: The McMartin preschool trial.* Buffalo, NY: Prometheus Books.

Fernández-Armesto, F. (1997). *Truth: A history and guide for the perplexed*. New York, NY: St. Martin's Press.

Garrison, P. (2005). AA587: The perils of flying by the book. *Flying Magazine*. Retrieved from http://www.flyingmag.com

Green, A. H. (1986). True and false allegations of sexual abuse in child custody disputes. *Journal of the American Academy of Child Psychiatry, 25*(4), 449–456. https://dx.doi.org/10.1016/S0002-7138(10)60001-5

Griffin, L. K. (2013). Narrative, truth, and trial. *Georgetown Law Journal, 101*(2), 281–335.

Haidt, J. (2001). The emotional dog and its rational tail: A social intuitionist approach to moral judgment. *Psychological Review, 108*(4), 814–834. https://dx.doi.org/10.1037//0033-295x.108.4.814

Haidt, J. (2012). *The righteous mind: Why good people are divided by politics and religion*. New York, NY: Pantheon.

Haiman, J. (2018). *Ideophones and the evolution of language*. Cambridge, England: Cambridge University Press.

Hayakawa, S. I., & Hayakawa, A. R. (1990). *Language in thought and action* (5th ed.). New York, NY: Harcourt, Brace, Jovanovich.

Heyman, G. D., Luu, D. H., & Lee, K. (2009). Parenting by lying. *Journal of Moral Education, 38*(3), 353–369. https://dx.doi.org/10.1080/03057240903101630

Kahneman, D. (2011). *Thinking, fast and slow*. New York, NY: Farrar, Straus, and Giroux.

Katkin, E. S., Wiens, S., & Öhman, A. (2001). Nonconscious fear conditioning, visceral perception, and the development of gut feelings. *Psychological Science, 12*(5), 366–370. https://dx.doi.org/10.1111/1467-9280.00368

Kensinger, E. A. (2009). Remembering the details: Effects of emotion. *Emotion Review, 1*(2), 99–113. http://dx.doi.org/10.1177/1754073908100432

Khazan, O. (2016, September). The best headspace for making decisions. *The Atlantic.* Retrieved from https://theatlantic.com

Kida, T. (2006). *Don't believe everything you think: The 6 basic mistakes we make in thinking.* Amherst, NY: Prometheus Books.

Krampert, P. (2002). *The encyclopedia of the harmonica.* Pacific, MO: Mel Bay Publications.

Kristof, N. (2016, May 7). A confession of liberal intolerance. *The New York Times.* Retrieved from http://www.nytimes.com

Lester, P. M. (2010). The sin in sincere: Deception and cheating in the visual media. In M. S. McGlone & M. L. Knapp (Eds.), *The interplay of truth and deception* (pp. 89–103). New York, NY: Routledge.

Levine, T. R. (2014). Truth-default theory (TDT): A theory of human deception and deception detection. *Journal of Language and Social Psychology, 33*(4), 378–392. https://dx.doi.org/10.1177/0261927x14535916

Loftus, E., & Ketcham, K. (1991). *Witness for the defense.* New York, NY: St. Martin's Press.

MacCoun, R. J. (2012). The burden of social proof: Shared thresholds and social influence. *Psychological Review, 119*(2), 345–372. https://dx.doi.org/10.1037/a0027790

Malpass, R. S., Tredoux, C. G., & McQuiston-Surrett, D. (2009). Public policy and sequential lineups. *Legal and Criminological Psychology, 14*(1), 1–12. https://dx.doi.org/10.1348/135532508x384102

Marr, B. (2015, September 30). Big data: 20 mind-boggling facts everyone must read. *Forbes.* Retrieved from https://www.forbes.com

McGlone, M. S., Kobrynowicz, D., & Alexander, R. B. (2005). A certain *je ne sais quoi*: Verbalization bias in evaluation. *Human Communication Research, 31*(2), 241–267. https://dx.doi.org/10.1111/j.1468-2958.2005.tb00871.x

McGlone, M. S., & Tofighbakhsh, J. (2000). Birds of a feather flock conjointly (?): Rhyme as reason in aphorisms. *Psychological Science, 11*(5), 424–428. https://dx.doi.org/10.1111/1467-9280.00282

Messaris, P. (1994). *Visual literacy: Image, mind & reality.* Boulder, CO: Westview Press.

Messaris, P. (2012). Visual "literacy" in the digital age. *The Review of Communication, 12*(2), 101–117. https://dx.doi.org/10.1080/15358593.2011.653508

Muscanell, N. L., Guadagno, R. E., & Murphy, S. (2014). Weapons of influence misused: A social influence analysis of why people fall prey to internet scams. *Social and Personality Psychology Compass, 8*(7), 388–396. https://dx.doi.org/10.1111/spc3.12115

Myers, D. G. (2002). *Intuition: Its powers and perils.* New Haven, CT: Yale University Press.

National Transportation Safety Board. (2002, January 15). *Fourth update on NTSB investigation into crash of American Airlines Flight 587* [Press release]. Retrieved from https://www.ntsb.gov/news/press-releases

Neidenthal, P., Halberstadt, J. B., Margolin, J., & Innes-Ker, A. H. (2000). Emotional state and the detection of change in facial expression of emotion. *European Journal of Social Psychology, 30*(2), 211–222. https://dx.doi.org/10.1002/(sici)1099-0992(200003/04)30:2%3C211::aid-ejsp988%3E3.0.co;2-3

Nickerson, R. S., & Adams, M. J. (1979). Long-term memory for a common object. *Cognitive Psychology, 11*(3), 287–307. https://dx.doi.org/10.1016/0010-0285(79)90013-6

Nyberg, D. (1993). *The varnished truth: Truth telling and deceiving in ordinary life.* Chicago, IL: University of Chicago Press.

Pezdek, K. (2011). Fallible eyewitness memory and identification. In B. Cutler (Ed.), *Conviction of the innocent: Lessons from psychological research* (pp. 202–231). Washington, DC: APA Press. https://dx.doi.org/10.1037/13085-005

Rincon, P. (2015, July 13). Why is Pluto no longer a planet? *BBC News.* Retrieved from http://www.bbc.com/news

Sadler-Smith, E., & Shefy, E. (2004). The intuitive executive: Understanding and applying "gut feel" in decision-making. *Academy of Management Perspectives, 18*(4), 76–91. https://dx.doi.org/10.5465/ame.2004.15268692

Schacter, D. L. (2001). *The seven sins of memory: How the mind forgets and remembers.* Boston, MA: Houghton-Mifflin.

Scherf, K. S., & Scott, L. S. (2012). Connecting developmental trajectories: Biases in face processing from infancy to adulthood. *Developmental Psychobiology, 54*(6), 643–663. https://dx.doi.org/10.1002/dev.21013

Schiffenbauer, A. (1974). Effect of observer's emotional state on judgments of emotional state of others. *Journal of Personality and Social Psychology, 30,* 31–35. https://dx.doi.org/10.1037/h0036643

Schofield, M. (2004, March 31). Romanian villagers decry police investigation into vampire slaying. *McClatchy Newspapers.* Retrieved from http://www.mcclatchydc.com

Schooler, J. W. (2013). The costs and benefits of verbally rehearsing memory for faces. In D.J. Herrmann, C. Hertzog, C. McEvoy, & P. Hertel (Eds.), *Basic and applied memory research, Volume 1: Theory in context.* New York, NY: Psychology Press.

Schwarz, N. (2012). Feelings-as-information theory. In P. A. M. Van Lange, A. W. Kruglanski, & E. T. Higgins (Eds.), *Handbook of theories in social psychology, Vol. 1* (pp. 289–308). Thousand Oaks, CA: Sage. http://dx.doi.org/10.4135/9781446249215.n15

Shermer, M. (2003). *How we believe* (2nd ed.). New York, NY: Henry Holt & Co.

Shermer, M. (2011). *The believing brain: From ghosts to gods to politics and conspiracies—how we construct beliefs and reinforce them as truths.* New York, NY: Times Books.

Schwikert, S. R., & Curran, T. (2014). Familiarity and recollection in heuristic decision making. *Journal of Experimental Psychology: General, 143*(6), 2341–2365. https://dx.doi.org/10.1037/xge0000024

Simons, D. J., & Chabris, C. F. (1999). Gorillas in our midst: Sustained inattentional blindness for dynamic events. *Perception, 28*(9), 1059–1074. https://dx.doi.org/10.1068/p281059

Smith, H. J., Archer, D., & Costanzo, M. (1991). "Just a hunch": Accuracy and awareness in person perception. *Journal of Nonverbal Behavior, 15*(1), 3–18. https://dx.doi.org/10.1007/bf00997764

Urban, M., Couchot, F., Sarazin, X., & Djannati-Atai, A. (2013). The quantum vacuum as the origin of the speed of light. *European Physical Journal, 67*(3), 58. https://dx.doi.org/10.1140/epjd/e2013-30578-7

Van Swol, L. M., Molhotra, D., & Braun, M. T. (2011). Deception and its detection: Effects of monetary incentives on personal relationship history. *Communication Research, 39*(2), 217–238. https://dx.doi.org/10.1177/0093650210396868

Wang, J., Herath, T., Chen, R., Vishwanath, A., & Rao, H. R. (2012). Phishing susceptibility: An investigation into the processing of a targeted spear phishing email. *IEEE Transactions on Professional Communication, 55,* 345–362. https://dx.doi.org/10.1109/tpc.2012.2208392

Wells, G. L., & Olson, E. A. (2003). Eyewitness testimony. *Annual Review of Psychology, 54,* 277–295.

Wells, G. L., Memon, A., & Penrod, S. D. (2006). Eyewitness evidence: Improving its probative value. *Psychological Science in the Public Interest, 7,* 45–75. https://dx.doi.org/10.1111/j.1529-1006.2006.00027.x

Winter, A. (2012). *Memory: Fragments of a modern history.* Chicago, IL: University of Chicago Press. https://dx.doi.org/10.7208/chicago/9780226902609.001.0001

CHAPTER 3 Ethical Perspectives

© Trifi/Shutterstock.com

"Whatever matters to human beings, trust is the atmosphere in which it thrives."
– *Sissela Bok*

"Helping others is often more important than honesty."
– *Emma Levine*

In the preceding chapters, we noted that effective communication (in terms of getting the response you desire) may sometimes be accomplished by behaviors associated with lying and deception. But just because lying and/or deception may help you succeed in accomplishing your communicative goals doesn't necessarily mean it is the right thing to do. Is it ever right for communicators to lie to and/or deceive their fellow human beings? What standards or criteria can be used to help us determine the rightness or wrongness of lying and other forms of deception? These are the primary questions explored in this chapter.

WHY CONCERN OURSELVES WITH ETHICS?

How to feel about the appropriateness of deceptive behavior is one of many ethical landscapes we must navigate. Almost daily, we are confronted with complex issues at work, in our family, and in other relationships that challenge us to assess our commitment to what we think is right, fair, respectful, good, responsible, etc. These values not only guide our own behavior but serve as standards we use to evaluate the behavior of others. Giving them serious thought is intrinsically important to each of us personally and to all of us collectively and should be an ongoing subject of personal reflection and public discussion.

There are those who argue that we should be especially attuned to ethical issues today because they believe we are living in an era of moral decay (with an abundance of lying as only one manifestation of it). In a 2017 Gallup poll, 81% of Americans described the overall status of moral values in the country as "fair" or "poor," and almost as many (77%) believed moral values are "getting worse." Although social conservatives have traditionally been more critical of society's morals than liberals, survey respondents from both groups expressed comparable degrees of pessimism. Former U.S. Representative Scott Raecker concluded that America is in a "moral recession" after observing "a continual parade of headline-grabbing incidents of dishonest and unethical behavior from political leaders, business executives, and prominent athletes" (Raecker, 2014).

There are many well-publicized examples used by those who see U.S. society as one on the brink of moral bankruptcy:

- There have been numerous award-winning journalists, historians, and novelists who have plagiarized or made up facts to fit their stories (see Chapter 12).

- The abandonment of business ethics for greed and selfishness is exemplified by Bernie Madoff's billion-dollar Ponzi scheme and scandals involving Volkswagen (falsifying vehicle emissions tests), Enron (accounting fraud), FIFA (taking bribes), News International (wiretapping), Samsung (making bribes), and Theranos (falsifying research data and financial records).

- By the end of 2007, corrupt practices at major banks (Bank of America, Citigroup, JPMorgan Chase, etc.) triggered the worst recession of modern times.

- Presidents have regularly lied to the American people over the last 60 years:

  - **Eisenhower**: U-2 spy planes
  - **Kennedy**: Invasion of Cuba
  - **Johnson**: Gulf of Tonkin attacks
  - **Nixon**: Watergate
  - **Reagan**: Iran–Contra affair
  - **George H. W. Bush**: Tax increases
  - **Clinton**: Lewinsky affair
  - **George W. Bush**: WMDs in Iraq
  - **Obama**: NSA wiretapping
  - **Trump**: Extramarital affairs, Russian meddling in the 2016 election, and more

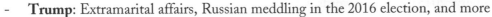

- Widespread cynicism is further fueled by the low frequency with which white-collar liars are punished. Despite public outrage over their transgressions, few are ever fired or prosecuted (see Chapter 11). Stevenson and Wolfers (2011) argued that the absence of repercussions for congressional and corporate deceivers has produced a "historic sharp decline in the confidence the American public has in their government, financial, and business sectors, and to a lesser extent their media and courts." National Book Award winner George Packer (2014) claimed that the public's distrust of government and business has prompted an "unwinding" of Americans' sense of community, which in turn makes lying and deception more acceptable for people in all walks of life.

Furthermore, middle and high school students admit to a lot of lying and cheating. Consider the findings of a recent survey of 23,000 high school students about the frequency with which they behave unethically (Josephson Institute of Ethics, 2012). Lying was the focus of several questions:

- **76%** of the students said they had lied about something significant once or more

- **55%** said they had lied to a teacher once or more

- **52%** said they had cheated on a test

- **74%** said they had copied someone else's homework

While many people lament that we are facing an unprecedented ethical crisis, others are convinced this is just business as usual. They argue that behaviors like lying and cheating have always existed and it isn't clear whether things really are worse now. Other arguments to support this position include:

- Illbruck's (2012) attribution of many current anxieties about the state of society to collective memory failure caused by the "unenlightened disease" we call *nostalgia* (see also *The Way We Never Were* by Stephanie Coontz).

- According to the Judeo-Christian-Islamic tradition, lying has plagued the affairs of humans as long as they have existed (beginning with Adam and Eve). Moses, Jesus, and Mohammed all criticized the prevalence of deceit in human society and recommended honesty and faith as the way return to God's grace.

- Theologians of all faiths over the centuries have perennially interpreted natural disasters and other calamities as divine retribution for widespread wickedness and treachery (Denery, 2015). In other words, what else is new?

- In 19th-century America, lies were central features of transactions involving child labor, African slaves, treaties made with native Americans, etc.

- In the 1920s, a study of 11,000 school children also found cheating and dishonesty to be widespread (Hartshorne & May, 1928).

- Today's population is far larger than in previous generations *and* ethical transgressions are more likely to be made public *and* the dissemination of such information to large groups of people is more efficient than ever before.

- The perception that "everybody's doing it" may lead to more people admitting to lying than in previous generations. And what does it mean when a lot of people say they have lied? Is the sheer number of lies people report a sign we are living in a moral wasteland? It may be that we're simply paying more attention to it than ever before.

- The same modern polls that seem to point to an ethical crisis contain other data that present a somewhat different picture. In the aforementioned 2012 survey of high school students, fully **99%** said it was *important for people to trust them and to be a person of good character,* **98%** said *honesty and trust are essential in personal relationships,* and **86%** said it was *not worth it to lie and cheat because it hurts your character.*

- There are more and more institutions in place to prevent and sanction unethical behavior. Ethics courses are offered (and often required) by colleges and universities worldwide, and there are more institutes and centers for the study of ethics than ever before.

New discoveries in genetics, technology, and other fields also keep ethical questions on the front page and serve as encouragement for testing our values. Alder (2007) believes a society is not best defined by its levels of deceit, but how it *deals with* such deceit: "There has never been, nor ever will be, an honest society . . . what distinguishes a culture is how it copes with deceit: the sorts of lies it denounces, the sorts of institutions it fashions to expose them" (p. 270).

Thus, the answer to the question of whether or not we are collectively experiencing a moral crisis may be far less important than each individual recognizing that our world is complex and demands that we have as clear a sense of our own values as possible. Why? Because we often don't have the luxury of thinking long and hard about something before we have to make a decision. We live in an era when complicated ethical issues face everyone, not just leaders. It is increasingly difficult to get away with simply giving lip service to values and reciting moral platitudes. More and more of us are personally involved in circumstances that require us to test and possibly modify our ethical principles as we apply them to real-life situations.

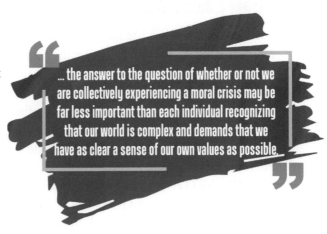

... the answer to the question of whether or not we are collectively experiencing a moral crisis may be far less important than each individual recognizing that our world is complex and demands that we have as clear a sense of our own values as possible.

Determining whether or not to tell the truth is especially important in this age of information when:

- each of us is confronted with many opportunities and channels to lie and to disguise our lies.

- each individual, not just public figures or institutions, is now capable of lying to the masses with a computer or smartphone.

- when every piece of information we communicate is processed and reacted to by numerous individuals and special interest groups.

It is an age that demands an ongoing reflection about the ethics of dishonesty as well as honesty.

IS IT EVER RIGHT TO LIE?

The answers to this question can be grouped into four categories. They range from the absolutist position that no lie is ever acceptable to a Machiavellian attitude that lies are neither right nor wrong, just tools for accomplishing goals. Between these two opposite and extreme positions are two others that vary by how they look at the role circumstances play in determining the rightness or wrongness of lying. Let's look more closely at each of the four answers.

Answer 1: No, It Is Never Right to Lie

Augustine

This "never" position has no exceptions—lying is always wrong. Good intentions or the absence of harm don't matter either. Even lying to save an innocent life is wrong. Aside from the practitioners of "radical honesty" (Blanton, 2005) it is difficult to find people today who are willing to publicly advocate this position, but several well-known figures from world history did. Augustine (345–430), Thomas Aquinas (1225–1274), John Wesley (1703–1791), and Immanuel Kant (1724–1804) all believed it was never right to lie (Bok, 1978). It should be noted, however, that even though Augustine and Aquinas believed that lying was always wrong and never justified, some lies could still be forgiven by God (BBC, n.d.).

For these absolutist theologians and philosophers, the justification for believing it is never right to lie rests primarily on three arguments:

1. Lies, by their very nature, *disrespect humanity* and, like a disease, infect the liar's character and ruin his or her integrity.

2. Lying violates religious precepts. It is a sin to lie.

3. Lying begets lying. If you lie about something, you'll be tempted to lie about it again and you'll have to tell additional lies to avoid detection. These lies, in turn, lead you to lie about other things. Others will match your lies with their own and eventually society will become utterly dysfunctional.

In reality, this absolute prohibition has never been one that people could follow without provisions that excused or redefined their behaviors, as a closer look at its three supporting arguments will show.

Lying Disrespects Humanity and Negatively Affects Character

The underlying assumption here is that *lies are always harmful and telling the truth is always beneficial*. But the truth can be harmful as well—even fatal. Judas Iscariot, arguably the worst villain in the New Testament, betrayed Jesus by identifying him to the Roman soldiers—an act of treacherous honesty. A lie told to protect people from someone whose stated intent was to kill them would also seem to be respecting humanity and a testament to the liar's character. For example, Amsterdam businessman Victor Kugler won Israel's Yad Vashem Medal for his efforts to conceal Anne Frank and her family from the Nazis in the early 1940s (Kardonne, 2008). Positive interpretations could also be given to "noble lies" that promote social harmony rather than truth that creates social discord.

Difficult choices are sure to follow those who try to live by the principle that lies of any kind are always wrong and truth telling of any kind is always right. It won't take long before a person is confronted with a situation that requires a choice between the sacred belief in telling the truth and some other deeply-cherished and another treasured value. As Nyberg (1993) says:

Difficult choices are sure to follow those who try to live by the principle that lies of any kind are always wrong and truth telling of any kind is always right.

> *Human beings live in a world of competing genuine values, and this pluralism of values is as much a part of each individual consciousness as it is of society . . . Such conflict of values between peoples, or within one's own moral universe, should not always lead to a forced choice of the right one, the wrong one, the only true or false one. Truth telling is a value that is likely to exist in conflict with many others—kindness, compassion, self-regard, privacy, survival, and so on. (pp. 198–199)*

Lying Is a Transgression Against Divine Law

Augustine, Thomas Aquinas, and John Wesley were Christians who believed the Bible prohibited all forms of deception. Kant was not a theologian, but his writings on moral behavior were strongly influenced by his Christian beliefs. But their interpretation is seen as extreme by Christians who do not believe the Bible says that all deception is wrong. They point to biblical examples of deceit that did not provoke God's wrath (e.g., the story of Rahab as told in the book of Joshua). And while Buddhist prayers and Jewish texts also condemn lying, they also allow for exceptions (Bok, 1978). The Quran does grant permission for Muslims to conceal their faith from non-believers (the "taqiya" doctrine), but only to avoid religious persecution (Stewart, 2013).

Needless to say, those who tried to follow Augustine's prohibition against all lies found themselves sinning a lot. As a result, he conveniently developed a list of eight types of lies. All were considered sins, but some were greater sins than others. Later, Thomas Aquinas boiled the list down to three: (1) lies told in jest, (2) lies told to be helpful, and (3) malicious lies. Again, telling a lie in any category was considered a sin, but only malicious lies were considered a "major" sin. In short, they recognized that their position was problematic, but instead of changing the principle, they created loopholes. Bok (1978) explains:

> *Many ways were tried to soften the prohibition, to work around it, and to allow at least a few lies. Three different paths were taken: to allow for pardoning of some lies; to claim that some deceptive statements are not falsehoods, merely misinterpreted by the listener; and finally to claim that certain falsehoods do not count as lies. (p. 34)*

Two ancient but ingenious inventions for helping people who believed in not lying (but needed to lie) were the concepts of **mental reservation** and **equivocation**. The first allowed a person to make a misleading statement to someone else (e.g., "I have never cheated on an exam . . .) and silently add the qualification in his or her mind to make it true (e.g., ". . . until the one you gave last week"). As long as the person used the mental reservation, there was no lie and no sin. *Equivocation* took advantage of words' multiple meanings to mislead without technically lying. For example, when asked by persecutors whether a man they intended to kill passed this way, the equivocator might reply "He did not pass here" with "here" signifying the precise spot on which the speaker stands and not the other spots the man actually did walk through (Denery, 2015).

Such controversial methods to make the "never lie" principle more compatible with normal human experience (where some deception is common) only served to highlight why such complete prohibitions don't work.

If You Lie About One Thing, You'll Lie About Another

Absolutists believe that authorizing any deception will cause lies to spread throughout society, eventually destroying it. This is called the "slippery slope" argument or the "domino effect." Many critics have made such an argument about Donald Trump. His political rise began with a lie about his predecessor's birthplace (i.e., that Barack Obama was born in Kenya, not Hawaii, as indicated by his birth certificate). In his first 40 days in office, Trump made at least one misleading public statement every day, ranging from exaggerated claims about how many people attended his inauguration and the number of times he appeared on the cover of *Time* magazine to outright fabrications about his original stance on the invasion of Iraq and a nonexistent terrorism attack in Sweden (Leonhardt, Philbrick, & Thompson, 2017). Almost a year into Trump's term, Jimmy Kimmel (using *Washington Post* data) marked the occasion of the President telling his 2,000th lie since taking office in a mini-documentary (QR).

At the time of this writing, he continues to publicly deny having had extramarital affairs with two different women, despite the existence of nondisclosure agreements that included $280,000 in apparent hush money. His opponents have raised questions based on the domino effect: How can we trust this President not to lie to the American public about important matters when he lies about his popularity, his previous political stances,

© Frederic Legrand – COMEO/Shutterstock.com

or about having sex with women other than his wife? His supporters (like Bill Clinton's defenders in the 1990s) contend that misleading statements about his private life have little to do with how he responds to matters affecting the health and welfare of the country. When a person lies about one thing, can we assume that lies in other areas of this person's life will naturally follow? Obviously, this can and does happen, but it would be a mistake to assume this will normally be the case. A careful analysis of the person and the factors associated with each situation where lying might occur would be a more prudent approach.

Lying, like other forms of behavior, is influenced by many personal and contextual factors. The assumption that dishonesty in one area of your life will automatically lead to it happening in another ignores a host of mitigating variables. How important is it to lie about the issue at hand? Who is the target of the lie and what is your relationship to the target? What are the risks if caught? Are lies often performed or even expected in this situation?

In a massive study of 11,000 school children, ages 8 to 16, Hartshorne and May (1928, 1971) provided persuasive evidence on the powerful effect of *context* on dishonesty. They concluded that the likelihood of a child practicing deceit in any given situation was partly due to factors like his or her age, intelligence,

"The assumption that dishonesty in one area of your life will automatically lead to it happening in another ignores a host of mitigating variables."

and home background and partly due to the student's response to situational demands. Over the course of several months, these researchers gave students dozens of tests (both academic and physical) designed to measure honesty, but varied the context/conditions greatly:

- Sometimes cheating was prohibited by close monitoring on the part of test administrators.

- Sometimes the monitoring was deliberately lax.

- In other instances, students were given an answer key and allowed to grade their own tests.

- Sometimes the students did the work at home.

- In one test, students were unobtrusively observed, but asked to provide self-reports of how many chin-ups they did and how far they were able to broad jump.

Student scores under all conditions were then compared. No simple, reliable patterns of honesty or dishonesty in the students' behavior could be found. The findings led these researchers to advance the "doctrine of specificity" about children's moral compasses: *Honesty and dishonesty are not unified traits but specific functions of life situations, and the consistency across situations is due to what those situations have in common* (see also Lee, 2013). A child may cheat on a word completion test, but not on a test of his or her physical performance. On the other hand, if you gave the same test in the same way to the same group of children six months apart, the same kids were likely to cheat in the same way on both tests.

As we've seen, prohibiting all forms of lying is a moral principle that often requires nuanced interpretations. This is consistent with a 2006 Associated Press poll of adults in which:

- **52%** said lying was never justified, but two-thirds of this group also said it was sometimes okay to lie to avoid hurting someone's feelings.

- **40%** said it was okay to exaggerate a story to make it more interesting.

- **33%** said it was okay to lie about your age.

If there are situations in which lies aren't "as bad" as other lies, could it be that lying in those situations might even be the "right" thing to do?

Answer 2: It Is Not Right to Lie Except as a Last Resort

Sissela Bok's *Lying: Moral Choice in Public and Private Life* (1978), provides an extended discussion of this position. Although Bok believes there are circumstances under which lying could be justified, she also agrees with the basic tenets of the "lying is never justified" position:

- lying is generally bad for the liar and for society in general

- people today lie too often and too easily

- unless something is done, the frequency of lies will continue to grow

- the more lies that are told, the more trust is destroyed and the more dysfunctional society becomes.

For Bok, deception of any kind is a virus that attacks human social life, a position that stands in sharp contrast to fellow philosopher David Nyberg's, who believes that "social life without deception to keep it going is a fantasy" (1993, p. 25).

Bok's position is grounded in what she calls the veracity principle, the claim that "truthful statements are preferable to lies in the absence of special consideration" (p. 30). Like the absolutists, her position gives lies an inherently negative value. But despite her philosophical kinship to them, Bok's ethical solution does differ from theirs. Instead of prohibiting all deception, she says certain positive lies may be acceptable—provided they pass a stringent set of tests. Our main concern with these standards is the assumption that, in any given situation, "the truth" and what it means to tell it are perfectly clear (they are often not). Related to this is the equally troubling notion that a person never has to justify telling the truth. Regardless, her three tests are summarized below. We encourage you to research them further and determine for yourself what value they hold. While problematic in respects, her overall position seems light-years ahead of the fantasy world of the "never lie" absolutists.

1. First, no lie is permissible if the same goal can be achieved by using the truth. She argues that observing this restriction will eliminate many lies that are told too easily and without careful examination. Even if a lie saves a life, it is not acceptable if there is a way to save the life by telling the truth:

   If lies and truthful statements appear to achieve the same result or appear to be as desirable to the person contemplating lying the lies should be ruled out. And only where a lie is a last resort can one even begin to consider whether or not it is morally justified. (p. 31)

   Asking liars to consider truthful alternatives is admirable, but how is the prospective liar supposed to find (and be drawn to) them? In the next step, perhaps?

2. In this step, the would-be liar is expected to weigh the morality of the reasons for and against the anticipated lie. This evaluation can be accomplished in a number of ways, including:

    *   mentally assuming the place of the deceived and considering your reaction

    *   understanding how the lie might affect the deceived as well as others

    *   asking friends/colleagues how they would react

    One of the results of such a thorough moral investigation should be to brainstorm a list of truthful (and desirable) alternatives to the planned deception—in theory at least. But note that Bok is not asking us to find excuses to lie. Excuses, she says, can be used to forgive deception but not to justify it.

    So, what acceptable deceptive options remain at this point? Few, if any, but if they do exist they will still have to pass the third test.

3. This final step in Bok's approval process requires the would-be liar to seek the approval of an imaginary audience of "reasonable" people who subscribe to a shared moral code (religious, legal, etc.). It's a "publicity test" of sorts, designed to counter the biases and hastily-drawn conclusions that often cloud the perspective of liars. Beyond the specific person(s) you're intending to deceive, how would the general public respond (or an audience of millions on social media)? "Only those deceptive practices which can be openly debated and consented to in advance are justifiable in a democracy," she says (p. 181). This doesn't necessarily mean you have to tell the target the specific lie you are going to tell—only that the target be forewarned that a lie might be told. Since most people expect enemies to lie to each other and since one might get the consent of reasonable people to lie to an enemy, lying to enemies is justified—but only when there is no truth telling alternative; there is a crisis; and there are open, lawfully declared hostilities.

Bok's position begins with the premise that lying is inherently wrong and that exceptions should be exceedingly rare. But how "reasonable" a public is and whether ethical decisions should always be determined by majority perceptions remain unresolved (and critical) issues. Considering how politically polarized the world's major democracies are at the moment, a truly shared moral code across a general public may not even be possible.

The antithesis of this perspective views lying as functional—with its goodness or badness being determined by how well it helps or doesn't help in accomplishing one's goals.

Answer 3: It Is Right to Lie When It Serves Your Purposes

This ethical stance is the polar opposite of the previous ones. Nevertheless, it has been used by enough people that it should be part of any journey to explore ethical perspectives on lying and deception.

Since it prohibits nothing, this perspective has the advantage of being totally flexible—if you're the liar, that is. If you're the target, then it's totally forced. For the liar, the rightness or wrongness of deception (or of truth) is an irrelevant measure. Unlike Bok's tests, the only question these would-be liars must ask is, "Does this behavior help me or hinder me from accomplishing my goal?" The liar is the sole moral arbiter and what is "right" is whatever serves the liar best.

© Ilia Baksheev/Shutterstock.com

Machiavelli

The best known advocate of this position is Niccolò Machiavelli, an Italian statesman and political philosopher who lived 500 years ago. His book *The Prince* (1532/2010) was designed as a leader's guide to effective governance. In Chapter 18 of his book, Machiavelli argues that a prince should know how to be deceitful when it suits his purpose. However, he cautions, the prince must not appear deceitful. Instead, he must seem to manifest mercy, honesty, humaneness, uprightness, and religiousness. By emphasizing the strategic manipulation of others for one's own benefit, Machiavelli's name is now used by many people to signify things like deceit, treachery, and opportunism in human relations.

Most people think there are certain occasions where "the end justifies the means"—e.g., lying to survive or to protect national security. Almost 2,000 years ago, the Roman rhetorician Quintilian said there was "no disgrace" in "making use of vices" to accomplish your goals and speaking "the thing that is not" (1922, Chapter II, xvii, 26). Quintilian, however, was assuming that the speaker's goals were noble ones and therefore justified the use of deception. But for the highly Machiavellian person (or "high

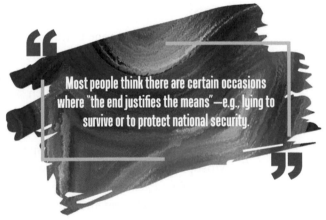

"Most people think there are certain occasions where "the end justifies the means"—e.g., lying to survive or to protect national security."

Machs"), lying is a justified means to accomplish any particular end or goal. To his credit (or not), Machiavelli practiced what he preached. In a letter to a friend he wrote:

> *For a long time I have not said what I believed, nor do I ever believe what I say, and if indeed sometimes I do happen to tell the truth, I hide it among so many lies that it is hard to find. (R. Greene, 2002, p. 321)*

To more fully appreciate the Machiavellian belief system (and your relationship to it), try answering the questions in Figure 3.1 below.

How Machiavellian Are You?

Those who subscribe to the Machiavellian belief system will **agree** with the following statements:

1. The best way to handle people is to tell them what they want to hear.
2. Anyone who completely trusts anyone else is asking for trouble.
3. It is hard to get ahead without cutting corners here and there.
4. It is safest to assume that all people have a vicious streak and it will come out when they are given a chance.
5. Never tell anyone the real reason you did something unless it is useful to do so.
6. It is wise to flatter important people.
7. People suffering from incurable diseases should have the choice of being painlessly to death.
8. Most people forget more easily the death of their father than the loss of their property.
9. Generally speaking, people won't work hard unless they're forced to.
10. The biggest difference between most criminals and other people is that criminals are stupid enough to get caught.

Those who subscribe to the Machiavellian belief system will **disagree** with the following statements:

1. When you ask someone to do something for you, it is best to give the real reasons for wanting it rather than giving reasons that might carry more weight.
2. Honesty is the best policy in all cases.
3. One should take action only when sure it is morally right.
4. All in all, it is better to be humble and honest than important and dishonest.
5. Barnum was very wrong when he said there's a sucker born every minute.
6. It is possible to be good in all respects.
7. Most people are basically good and kind.
8. There is no excuse for lying to someone else.
9. Most people who get ahead in the world lead clean, moral lives.
10. Most people are brave.

Figure 3.1: Inventory of Machiavellian characteristics (adapted from Christie & Geis, 1970)

People who are strongly Machiavellian in their beliefs cannot afford to be very emotionally involved with others. Empathy and affective attachments only make it harder for the Machiavellian to dispassionately manipulate and deceive others for his or her own purposes. Another reason why high Machs are emotionally detached from others is that they have little respect for most people, seeing them as inherently gullible, weak, easily persuaded, and not trustworthy.

Machiavelli is often portrayed as a teacher of evil, but in *The Prince*, he never urged evil for evil's sake. The proper aim of a prince, he argues, is to maintain power over the state. Politics is a delicate arena in which following a virtue can ruin a state and pursuing what appears to be a vice may promote security and well-being. Leaders are called upon to make difficult choices, and prudence sometimes involves recognizing the good that can be engineered from bad options. These themes are explored in a BBC documentary that reflects on the legacy of *The Prince* five centuries after it was written (QR).

In his bestseller, *The 48 Laws of Power*, Robert Greene (2002) reiterated many of Machiavelli's principles for gaining and keeping power. He begins his book by noting that, in today's world:

> *Everything must appear to be democratic, civilized, and fair . . . . but if we play by those rules too strictly, if we take them too literally, we are crushed by those around us who are not so foolish . . . . Power requires the ability to play with appearances. To this end you must learn to wear many masks and keep a bag full of deceptive tricks. Deception and masquerades should not be seen as ugly or immoral . . . . Deception is a developed art of civilization and the most potent weapon in the game of power. (p. xvii)*

Deception is central to most of Greene's laws and especially evident in the four described in Figure 3.2.

Many of us have either used or been the target of one or more of the deceptive strategies in the Machiavellian playbook. But the specific tactics used aren't even the issue. Instead, the ethical judgment rests squarely on whether or not power-seekers should be guided solely by self-interest. A few of the questions (out of many) to consider include:

- Is it right for people to lie simply because it helps them meet their goals?

- What happens to virtues that value others, like fairness, justice, and compassion?

- Can the greater good still exist in a world where goodness is not a shared value but, rather, and individual one?

The last of the four answers to the question of whether or not it is ever right to lie combines the acceptance of some deceptive strategies with moral standards that go beyond any given individual's preferences.

Robert Greene's Laws

LAW THREE
Conceal Your Intentions

Keep people off balance and in the dark by never revealing the purpose behind your actions. If they have no clue what you are up to, they cannot prepare a defense. (p. 16)

LAW FOUR
Always Say Less Than Necessary

When you are trying to impress people with words, the more you say, the more common you appear, and the less in control . . . . Powerful people impress and intimidate by saying less. The more you say, the more likely you are to say something foolish. (p. 32)

LAW TWELVE
Use Selective Honesty and Generosity to Disarm Your Victim

One sincere and honest move will cover over dozens of dishonest ones. Honest moves bring down the guard of even the most suspicious people. Once your selective honesty opens a hole in their armor, you can deceive and manipulate them at will. (p. 89)

LAW TWENTY-ONE
Play a Sucker to Catch a Sucker: Seem Dumber Than Your Mark

No one likes feeling stupider than the next person. The trick, then, is to make your victims feel smart—and not just smart, but smarter than you are. Once convinced of this, they will never suspect that you may have ulterior motives. (p. 156)

Figure 3.2: A sampling of the Laws of Power (adapted from R. Greene, 2002)

Answer 4: Sometimes Lying Is Right, Sometimes It Isn't

From this perspective, the extent to which lying is morally right or wrong is largely determined by taking into account the special circumstances of a particular situation within which the lie occurred. Ethical judgments, then, may vary depending on whether (Seiter, Bruschke, & Bai, 2002):

- the target is a child or an adult
- the target is a stranger or a loved one
- the lie impacts many people or a few
- constructive or destructive intentions are perceived

- lies are expected in this situation
- cultural sanctions exist for this particular lie and if so, whether they are strong or weak

General principles aren't excluded from this perspective. "Don't be an asshole" and "give people the benefit of the doubt whenever possible" are good guidelines. But the "rightness" (or the "wrongness") of such guidelines isn't a foregone conclusion. The final moral arbiter of any decision to deceive is found in the context of any particular situation. For example, "malicious lies which hurt people are immoral" may be usefully applied to most situations, but may not be applicable to lies directed to an enemy in a declared war.

History also teaches us that the climate of the times affects ethical judgments. Stories about President Clinton's extramarital sexual behavior were front page news at the turn of the 21st century and his public denial of such behavior was considered scandalous by many Americans—including his congressional colleagues who impeached (then later acquitted) him. But most reporters who knew about the extramarital affairs of President Roosevelt in the 1930s and 1940s or President Kennedy's affairs in the early 1960s chose not to make these transgressions headline news. Given the many factors that can affect a moral judgment about lying, Nyberg concludes: "the idea of adjusting the principle of truth telling to fit the circumstances is a sound moral position just as surely as is adherence to the ideal of honesty itself" (1993, p. 201).

In theory, everything relevant to a given situation has the potential to influence whether a lie is morally justified or not. In practice, though, it is usually the liar's motive or intent and the consequences of the lie that get the most attention and are often weighted more heavily than other factors in determining the acceptability of the lie. In one study, the liar's motive accounted for three and a half times more of the variance in determining the acceptability of the lie than the liar's culture or the liar's relationship to the target (Seiter et al., 2002).

Needless to say, "good motives" and/or "good consequences" from the liar's perspective may not always be viewed as "good" by the target of the lie or even an outside observer. This is only one of the difficulties involved in evaluating the motives and consequences used to justify a lie.

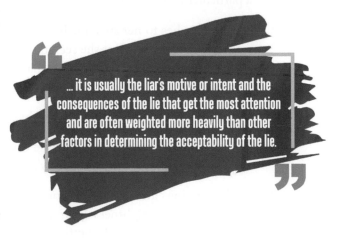

… it is usually the liar's motive or intent and the consequences of the lie that get the most attention and are often weighted more heavily than other factors in determining the acceptability of the lie.

Motives

We often equate deception with self-serving motives—cheating on taxes to avoid payment, padding a resume to get a job interview, inflating one's salary to impress friends and first dates, etc. But people often try to justify a lie by *linking it to prosocial motives*:

- Isn't it okay to lie, they might argue, if you were trying to avoid harm, to produce benefits, to promote or preserve fairness, or to protect a larger truth (Bok, 1978)?

- What about lying because an authority figure (parents, boss) expected you to?

- Or, lying in order to prevent being disloyal or breaking a confidentiality agreement?

- And what's wrong with a lie to someone who makes it clear they don't want to hear the truth (Johnson, 2001)?

Depending on the circumstances, any of the preceding reasons may suffice to successfully defend a deceptive act. When school children falsely accuse their teachers of molestation and sexual abuse, for example, we would expect widespread agreement that these lies are malicious and wrong (Bowles, 2000). Politeness routines in which people thank other people for things they aren't all that thankful for are generally agreed to benefit social relations (McGlone & Giles, 2011).

But some situations might be far more complicated and, as a result, the moral choices less clear-cut. When this occurs, the decision to lie may mean choosing between two (or more) equally desirable, revered values. Thus the question is not why the liar was motivated by something nasty like greed or malice, but why, for example, they chose compassion over justice in a given situation. Consider the following scenarios:

- A husband has told his wife that he will never lie to her and will never hurt her. But circumstances lead him to believe that a person promised never to lie to his/her partner—but also never to let any harm come to them. But circumstances lead this person to believe that a particular lie would be far less damaging to the partner than the truth would be.

- A professor lies to her students by telling them that she is treating them all the same (the principle of fairness). But she secretly makes an exception for a student who missed an assignment because of circumstances that were beyond his control. Without this exception, he would be disadvantaged relative to the rest of the class (the principle of compassion).

- What about being loyal to one friend by lying to another?

- What about the government employee who covers up wrongdoing by his/her colleagues because he/she believes that the country's national security could be harmed by the revelations?

The liar's conscious awareness of his or her motives is another potentially complicating factor in trying to assess the rightness or wrongness of a lie. In the pursuit of self-defense (avoiding tension or harm) or self-needs (getting something you want), liars may not spend a lot of time reflecting on their motives. But as soon as they are suspected of lying or discovered lying, they often work hard to find more acceptable motives for their behavior:

- *"I thought it was an open-book test."*
- *"I must have made a math error in my tax return."*
- *"I meant that I drove a Tesla once, not that I owned one."*

Under these circumstances, a skilled (or Machiavellian) communicator might still be able to convince their target that, despite appearances, the lie was not meant to be self-serving (Chance & Norton, 2011).

Consequences

English philosopher Jeremy Bentham (1748–1832) is normally credited with initiating a philosophical position called *utilitarianism*—that decisions are moral to the extent they promote happiness and immoral to the extent they do the reverse. Within this framework, moral decisions about lies would be based on the consequences of telling them. Utilitarianism favors those things that benefit the most people and those outcomes in which the advantages outweigh the disadvantages (Gorovitz, 1971; Hearn, 1971; Robinson, 1994; Smart & Williams, 1973). It would be "right" to tell a lie, then, that resulted in benefits that outweighed the problems or that benefited the most people. As a result, a utilitarian might determine that the telling of a lie in a particular situation was justified even though they simultaneously maintained the belief that lying usually causes more harm than good and should be avoided.

One widely used form of deception that is justified on utilitarian grounds is the placebo. When testing a new drug or surgical technique, medical researchers try to distinguish its direct benefit to patients' health from the psychological benefit that comes from believing that it will heal them. To do this, clinical studies are conducted in which the actual drug or surgery is administered to some patients while others receive a placebo (a pill containing sugar or gelatin instead of the active drug ingredient or "sham surgery" in which incisions are made in the skin and sewn up, but no invasive procedures are performed; etc.).

One widely used form of deception that is justified on utilitarian grounds is the placebo.

Placebos in medical research are controversial, whether the deception is authorized or not. However, their use is rationalized in utilitarian terms. According to Miller and colleagues, "in placebo research, participants are not deceived for their own benefit. Rather, they are deceived for the benefit of science and society in general, through the development of generalizable knowledge" (2005, p. 262). Hundreds of studies in the medical research literature document such "placebo effects"—cases when placebos benefit patients' health, sometimes as much as the real drug or surgery helps them (Kirsch, 2013). "Authorized deception" was used in some of these studies, in that patients were told beforehand they could receive the actual medical procedure or the placebo, but weren't told which until after their health outcomes were assessed; in other studies, the use of placebos wasn't revealed to patients until the assessment phase (Miller, Wendler, & Swartzman, 2005).

The goal of seeking consequences with more benefit than harm is not one many would disagree with but there are potential complications:

- Consequences of lies are not always easy to predict (ahead of time) or determine (after the fact).

- When (before or after) should consequences be measured, and how do you decide which consequences should be given more weight?

- Are short-term effects fundamentally different than long-term consequences in terms of their moral justifiability?

- Who should be allowed to say what the consequences are—the liar, the target, or outside observers? Understandably, liars tend to view their own lies as good while targets tend to see those same lies as bad.

- What happens if lie targets multiple audiences, each with potentially different consequences? Using a single score to assess multiple effects may not be a realistic expectation.

- Deceptive acts often have unintended consequences.

Consider the following commonplace situation in light of the above issues: You decide to lie to your father about the seriousness of your hospitalized mother's (his wife's) illness. While doing so may help him stay focused and unharmed by worry, he may also be prevented from making important decisions relevant to his wife's life and their future together.

ETHICAL GUIDELINES

To this point, we've examined multiple answers to the question of whether lying can ever be ethically justified. Without a doubt, each reader of this book will have his/her own preferences, which is why ethics gets so messy so quickly.

At the very least, we can try to agree on the premise that learning how to deal ethically with subjects like honesty and dishonesty is an ongoing process. If possible, we might also agree that no single set of rules can be expected to apply equally to all situations at all times. One ethicist put it this way: "As we practice resolving dilemmas we find ethics to be less a goal than a pathway, less a destination than a trip, less an inoculation than a process" (Kidder, 1995). This doesn't mean that at some point in life we might not need (or find useful) certain principles to effectively guide our behavior in certain situations. They may serve us well, for example, when we don't have time to analyze various aspects of a situation.

But the idea that practicing ethical behavior is a journey rather than a destination means that if life reveals a situation in which broad principles do not seem to be useful, we are willing

to consider alternative behaviors. It is not that a person taking this approach doesn't have a moral stance—only that he or she recognizes that their current stance may be improved. Because we are human beings we should not expect to live a mistake-free life. But if we can "learn to learn" from our mistakes, then we might at times manage to become better versions of ourselves. We don't need to be good all the time to be a good person, but we need to struggle toward that goal. What follows are some tips to help guide that struggle.

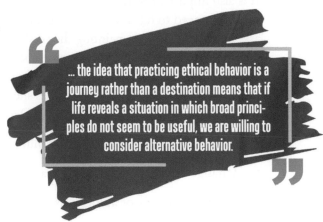

… the idea that practicing ethical behavior is a journey rather than a destination means that if life reveals a situation in which broad principles do not seem to be useful, we are willing to consider alternative behavior.

1. Tell the Truth Most of the Time

Start with goal of telling the truth as you understand it in most situations, as doing so recognizes that:

- telling the truth is a good idea even if you don't do it all the time

- telling the truth is a general principle that serves both the individual and his/her communities well

- even though we will deceive others in various ways at various times, lying is not considered the norm or default

- in certain situations, telling the complete and unabridged truth (or saying everything you think you know) might not be the most ethical thing to do

Still this guideline asks us to give priority to what we believe to be the truth. An important personal benefit of this approach is that it helps to establish a track record, a history, an image of you as a communicator—a history and image that may serve you well if one of your lies is used to impugn your character.

2. Explore Alternatives to Lying

Lying isn't always something people think a lot about before they do it. Too often we quickly think things like, "Uh oh, I'm gonna get in trouble," or "I don't want to deal with this," followed by a lie. There are no doubt situations that require quick, spontaneous reactions, but we would do well to think more strategically when we face the possibility of lying. It is, after all, a communication decision. In some cases, we can anticipate situations where we might lie and we can plan accordingly, including finding truthful alternatives to deception.

It is also important to remember that just because you decide not to tell the truth it doesn't mean you need to tell a falsehood. People in Bell and DePaulo's study (1996), for example, were asked to comment on a painting they disliked to a person they were led to believe was the artist. These creative individuals talked more about positive than negative features of the painting, but did not come right out and say they liked or disliked it. As DePaulo considered the possibility of reducing the number of altruistic lies she told, she reported: "I tried to figure out how to tell tactful truths instead of reassuring lies" (DePaulo, 2004, p. 319). Other methods to explore:

- Delay responding (perhaps indefinitely)

- Change the subject (but don't make it obvious)

- Respond vaguely or ambiguously

- When doing any of the above, do so in a confident, self-assured style

- Listen very carefully to what other people say as they may be asking for less than you know, thereby allowing you to tell what you believe to be the truth (but not every facet of it)

Why is this important? Because, as Hosmer (2008) has observed, ethical decisions need not always be framed as a dichotomy—i.e., that something is either right or wrong. Instead we may think in terms of degrees—that a particular way of responding to a situation is either highly ethical, moderately ethical, slightly ethical, slightly unethical, moderately unethical, or highly unethical. Targets of lies or other observers may not be inclined to think in terms of gradations, but "not telling the truth" can be performed in different ways and may, in turn, be evaluated differently.

3. Lie Selectively

Another issue bearing on the question of the rightness or wrongness of lying concerns what you choose to lie about. Not all lies are created equal:

- Is it about something trivial?

- Are you lying to save another person from harm, particularly someone who has done nothing wrong?

- Does your lie benefit others and not just you?

- Does your lie have the potential to harm other people?

Concepts may not be easy to sort out, but it is important that we know that all dishonest acts are not evaluated similarly so we may want to lie selectively. Other people are always saying things we don't agree with, but much of the time we let things go. Only on certain occasions do we choose to engage another person in conflict. Ethically, we might do well to think about lying in the same way.

4. Anticipate Discovery

Seriously considering issues related to the discovery of a lie will surely affect the telling of it. Assume all your lies will be discovered—especially if someone else knows about them. Don't ever say to a friend, "Don't tell anyone" without assuming they will. What is the worst thing that is likely to happen if your lie is discovered—to you and others? Are you willing to live with those consequences? Will you admit and be accountable for your lie? How will you defend it? For some lies, the consequences of discovery will be minimal, but liars often put such issues out of their mind. As a result, liars often imagine "things will work out fine" even with lies that have huge consequences. The bigger the lie (the greater impact, the more important the issue, the more reprehensible the lie, the more people involved, etc.), the more the liar has at stake and the more work he or she will put into keeping the lie from being discovered. But we also know that big lies are often detected. This may be a result of the correspondingly greater desire to detect such lies, the greater guilt experienced by the teller, or both (Seiter & Brushke, 2007).

© Robert Adrian Hillman/Shutterstock.com

5. Consider the Golden Rule

Confucius, Aristotle, Jesus, Mohammed, and others have said we should behave toward others as we would like them to behave toward us. Doing what you'd expect others to do were they in your position doesn't, however, guarantee that your behavior is ethical. After all, it's possible that you and your target each consider yourselves unethical, but the other even more-so. But you've at least taken the time to consider another person's perspective, which may be the minimum necessary investment for behaving ethically.

In a letter to one of the authors of this textbook, David Nyberg suggested that a more productive rephrasing of the Golden Rule would be: *Do unto others as if you were the others*. Imagining that we are the other person(s) affected by our behavior might not be the easiest thing to do, but Nyberg believes the new wording accomplishes two important goals:

1. It changes the authority to decide what the right thing is from the doer to the other

2. It highlights the need for empathetic understanding that is not explicit in the traditional wording. Empathy, Nyberg believes, plays a key role in most ethical and moral decisions.

There is no completely adequate way to summarize the ethical guidelines discussed above, but Nilsen (1966) may capture their essence as well as anyone, suggesting that we should approach "truth telling [and lying] with benevolence and justice as our moral commitments, and then apply knowledge and reason to the best of our ability" (p. 34).

ETHICS AND SELF-DECEPTION

Do you think it's wrong to lie to yourself? Is there anything wrong, for example, in pretending that a problem doesn't exist, avoiding or ignoring unpleasant information, or telling yourself an illegal act is justified because the law that was broken is unjust? Just as there are those who believe lies directed toward other human beings are always wrong, there are those who believe lies directed toward ourselves are always wrong. Those who believe we should all be trying to develop an "authentic self" regard any type of self-deception as a betrayal of that goal. Regardless, self-understanding is certainly a worthwhile goal—one that self-deception can sometimes hinder (Zahavi, 2005). A general commitment to being honest with ourselves is no doubt helpful in coping with obstacles to self-understanding. But it is also possible that a less-than-perfect understanding of ourselves is part of a worthy life, helping us keep hope alive, restore our self-esteem, or maintain productive relationships (see Chapter 6).

ETHICS OF LIE DETECTION

Is the act of *detecting* deception also subject to questions of right and wrong? There are two issues here, having to do with the decision to initiate detection and the methods used to carry out that detection. In daily social interaction, we normally initiate detection only when the target is suspected of having lied—a story doesn't fit other known facts, a third person makes an accusation, etc. Prosecutors and other law enforcement agencies, too, need to have reasons to justify detection deception through interrogation or wiretaps.

Ethical behavior is breached, however, when detection is undertaken without probable cause (Gordon, 2018).

In 2013, a breach of epic proportions by the U.S. National Security Agency (NSA) was exposed. Former NSA contractor Edward Snowden leaked classified documents to journalists revealing that the agency had been recording nearly every phone call placed in the United States for years. These documents contradicted assurances from President Barack Obama and senior intelligence officials to the American public that their privacy was protected from the NSA's dragnet surveillance programs (Greenwald, 2014). The agency was originally granted the power to monitor citizens' phone and e-mail communication by the USA PATRIOT Act passed by Congress in 2001 after the September 11th attacks.

The name of the Act is an acronym for "Uniting and Strengthening America by Providing Appropriate Tools Required to Intercept and Obstruct Terrorism." NSA officials interpreted vague wording in the Act as allowing them to collect communication of all U.S. citizens to identify terrorists among them and to do so without a warrant. When the "bulk data collection" program was exposed, government officials initially denied its existence and charged Snowden, who had already fled the country, with espionage. Two years later, it was declared unlawful by the courts and was disowned by Congress and President Obama. In an op-ed marking the program's termination, Snowden (2015) urged Americans not to assume that their privacy had been restored. Although chastened, the NSA continues to spy on the communication of U.S. citizens for whom there is no probable cause to believe they are concealing their identities as terrorists. In Snowden's words: "Though we have come a long way, the right to privacy—the foundation of the freedoms enshrined in the United States Bill of Rights—remains under threat."

Snowden went on to allege that:

- the U.S. government has taken measures to undermine the security of the Internet in an effort to examine the private lives of its citizens.

- governments around the world are pressuring technology companies to place the interests of the government above those of their customers by taking part in massive surveillance operations.

- cell phone data and Internet use is being monitored and recorded by the U.S. government regardless of who people are and what they're doing.

The *methods used to carry out the detection* of deception comprise the second ethical issue, one that has grown in importance since the September 11th attacks. Machines have always had a special credibility for the American public when it comes to lie detection, but the polygraph is not portable and requires training to administer and interpret. New technology has elimi-nated these barriers to public usage and has resulted in the sale of thousands of small, portable devices that claim to accurately measure micro-tremors in a person's voice. These consumers then surreptitiously use them to detect lying spouses, job applicants, employees, and insur-ance claimants, among others. Many of these devices, which range from 20 dollars to several thousand, claim the ability to distinguish vocalized statements by the suspected deceiver that are false, inaccurate, uncertain, or true. In our experience, all are a waste of money.

Despite the lack of research supporting the validity of these devices, people continue to buy, use, and, too often, trust them. A number of studies conducted by the U.S. Department of Defense concluded these devices were not a scientifically reliable method of detecting decep-tion (Hopkins, Ratley, Benincasa, & Grieco, 2005). They are, however, a reliable method of invading a person's privacy and in states with laws that forbid recording a person's communi-cation without their knowledge, they are against the law Beam (2011). It is also illegal to use the readings from these devices as justification for denying a job applicant employment. There is, however, no restriction on using the results of devices that analyze the voice to flag certain responses by a job applicant, which then become the basis for seeking additional information.

CREATING HONEST CITIZENS

No matter how difficult it is to say exactly what it means to be honest, no matter how often we are reminded that honesty can be dysfunctional sometimes, and no matter how many surveys tell us we frequently tell lies, citizens of the United States still consider honesty a prized virtue and a core characteristic of an ethical person. We want our children to be honest and we want them to grow up to be honest citizens. Can we teach people to be honest? If we can't, it certainly isn't for lack of trying. We try to legislate honesty, we teach it at home and in our schools, and it is a standard theme in our books, movies, and television shows (Mazur & Kalbfleisch, 2003).

Legislating Honesty

Various approaches are used to formally specify the desirability of truthful behavior. We have libel laws that are designed to keep people from disseminating false information about a person that would damage his or her reputation. The Federal Trade Commission (FTC) oversees various forms of consumer protection, including the enforcement of honesty in product labeling, lending contracts, and advertising. However, the FTC division enforcing truth-in-advertising standards has a small staff and must grant accused deceivers due process of law, with the result that false ads can air for months before any legal action takes effect (Williams, 2015).

Although the public has some legal protection against false advertising of products, they have none when it comes to politics. There is no federal law preventing a candidate for office from making a false political claim. Not only can they legally lie, but the Federal Communication Act requires broadcasters to show their ads uncensored, even if the broadcaster finds evidence that the ad content is false. Truth-in-political-advertising laws have been enacted in three states but have had little practical success. Courts in Minnesota and Washington struck down their state laws as abridgements of a candidate's Constitutional right to free speech. Ohio's law has survived court challenges, but is so weak that most violators receive only a letter of reprimand, not a fine or forfeit of the office they lied to get (Jackson, 2009).

In October of 2017, a bipartisan group of U.S. senators proposed the Honest Ads Act to close a loophole that has existed since politicians started advertising on the Internet (Bertrand, 2017). Introduced as Congress investigated how the Russian government used tech companies to influence the 2016 U.S. Presidential election, it was considered by many in Washington to be the bare minimum lawmakers could do to address the problem. The Act introduces disclosure and disclaimer rules to online political advertising. Tech companies would have to keep copies of election ads and make them available to the public. The ads would also have to contain disclaimers similar to those appearing in TV or print political ads, informing voters who paid for the ad and how much, and whom they targeted.

At the time of this writing, the bill has the support of many senators, but has yet to be voted on. Facebook had initially opposed such legislation, but in a surprise move—just days before his highly publicized (and widely memed) testimony before Congress—CEO Mark Zuckerberg decided to endorse it after all (Wang & Dennis, 2018). Behind the scenes, the company's lobbyists had initially argued that Facebook and other social media companies were already "voluntarily complying" with most of what the proposed

© Frederick Legrand – COMEO/Shutterstock.com

Mark Zuckerberg

Act requests, so such bills are unnecessary (Timmons & Kozlowska, 2018). The company's sudden approval of the bill was likely a public relations attempt at damage control, but the lobbying campaign that preceded it is just one example of the major hurdles lawmakers face in legislating honesty in the political domain.

Organizations that serve various professional groups like physicians, lawyers, engineers, and journalists also develop ethical codes that are designed to illustrate membership standards for right and wrong behavior. Expected behavior relative to appropriate disclosure and confidentiality is often an important part of these codes. For more information on current practices, do an online search for reports like the National Business Ethics Survey, which is typically published every two years.

Educational institutions also try to legislate honesty through the use of honor codes. Even though the students themselves are often instrumental in creating these honor codes and they are printed in student handbooks, it is not unusual for students to be unfamiliar with them. The Honor Code at The University of Texas at Austin's McCombs Business School says lying is a violation of the honor code and explains:

> *Lying is any deliberate attempt to deceive another by stating an untruth, or by any direct form of communication to include the telling of a partial truth. Lying includes the use or omission of any information with the intent to deceive or mislead. Examples of lying include, but are not limited to, providing a false excuse for why a test was missed or presenting false information to a recruiter.*

The academic honor codes at U.S. military academies are well known not only to the students but also to the American public. Cheating scandals that have occurred at these institutions have received national coverage in the press and resulted in the expulsion of numerous cadets.

People will follow laws, regulations, and codes of conduct that prescribe honest behavior if they are fairly and consistently enforced. They work best when they are well known, supported by the membership, and firmly entrenched as a part of the institutional culture. They are far less effective when they are viewed as largely symbolic and enforcement is weak and/or irregular.

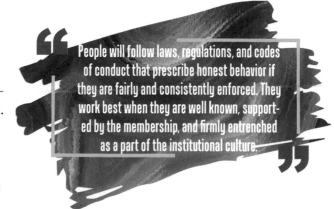

People will follow laws, regulations, and codes of conduct that prescribe honest behavior if they are fairly and consistently enforced. They work best when they are well known, supported by the membership, and firmly entrenched as a part of the institutional culture.

Teaching Honesty

Children learn about honesty and lying from their parents, their school teachers, and their peers. As these children become adults, their exposure to these lessons takes the form of books, television shows, movies, the rhetoric of public leaders, and press accounts of noteworthy liars and truth tellers. The teaching that parents do is the child's first exposure to the culture's expectations concerning lying and truth telling. Parents are usually the child's primary role models. During early childhood, it is common for parents to be emphatic about their desire for children not to lie. At the same time, however, the child is picking up clues that this prohibition against dishonesty doesn't always apply:

- A child may overhear a parent saying to someone on the phone that they aren't feeling well and need to stay home in bed, only to see the parent spending the day working on the computer.

- A child with a younger sibling might observe a parent telling that sibling that her scribbled drawing is "absolutely beautiful," then later hear the parent tell someone else that the remark was made simply to avoid hurting the child's feelings.

- Children also take in elaborate rituals put forth by their parents that confirm the existence of the Tooth Fairy and Santa Claus.

- Children believe their parents when they say storks bring babies and that Granny Mia left for a really long vacation.

But kids aren't dumb. They witness all of this, learning sooner or later that none of it is true. What's more, they may also find out that telling the truth isn't always valuable behavior:

- When they get scolded for blurting out the truth at the wrong time.

- As the child gets older, he or she learns that in order to win certain games, activities, or sports, deceiving one's opponents is an important skill.

- Once the child is old enough to be held accountable for being polite, he or she may be punished for not lying.

So the message kids seem to get is that adults want them to be honest, but that there are times when lying and deception may be acceptable. Parents may feel comfortable throughout early childhood because either their kids don't raise the tough questions about honesty and dishonesty or they readily accept whatever assertion a parent makes in order to shut down further discussion of the topic. Later, when the child asks tough questions and they are accompanied by examples of the parent's behavior, parent teaching gets significantly more difficult and it may be time for implementing different teaching methods. Instead of portraying life's decisions as clear, uncomplicated, and bound by certain rules that will apply to every situation, parents may want to reveal more about how they sometimes struggle with making the "right" decisions in certain situations involving honesty and how they go about trying to "do the right thing"—even though they aren't always sure if they are.

In some school districts, parents have been influential in supporting "character education" in which various "values" and "virtues" (including honesty) are taught. These parents believe there is a close connection between character and academic achievement. In elementary and secondary schools, this may be done through the reading of stories that exemplify the behavior to be modeled. For example, elementary school teachers may read stories like "George Washington and the Cherry Tree," "The Boy Who Cried 'Wolf,'" or tales about truth telling in Cortlett's *E Is for Ethics* (2009). An animated television show based on stories from Bennett's *The Children's Book of Virtues* (1995) has been broadcast numerous times.

At some elementary and secondary schools, students are rewarded for acts that conform to any of the statements that make up the school's code of ethics. These acts include honesty (e.g., "I tell the truth to myself and others") as well as integrity, promise-keeping, loyalty, fairness, concern for others, respect for others, civic duty, pursuit of excellence, and accountability. Colleges and universities provide additional formal learning experiences in courses focused on honesty issues—in contexts that are applied (e.g., public relations, management) as well as theoretical (e.g., philosophy, religion, ethics).

As adults we are regularly confronted with experiences that cause us to examine and reflect on our beliefs about honesty and dishonesty. Adults also continue their learning about truth telling and deceit by reading books. Bennett's *The Book of Virtues* (1993) was on the *New York Times* Bestseller List for 88 weeks. Berger's *Raising Kids With Character* (2006) and Josephson's *Making Ethical Decisions* (2002) are two of many books that provide guidance to parents on how to instill honest and ethical behavior in children.

Learning by Doing

Each of the preceding sources of information makes a contribution to what we know and what we believe about honesty and deception. But it is one thing to pontificate about what is right and wrong after you read a newspaper story or see a television show and another thing to be responsible for making hard choices about honest and dishonest behavior in real-life situations. Active learning is a powerful teacher. We can learn a lot about honesty by being honest and a lot about deceit by being deceptive. By being active in the affairs of our family, neighborhood, and community, we not only increase the chances that we will face difficult challenges involving honesty and deception, but we also increase the chances of having meaningful (though not necessarily pleasant) learning experiences. Having had such experiences, in turn, puts us in a better position to pass on useful knowledge to others.

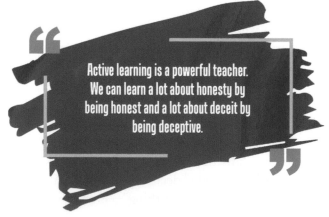

Active learning is a powerful teacher. We can learn a lot about honesty by being honest and a lot about deceit by being deceptive.

HARD-WIRED MORALITY

Despite all the efforts to nurture honesty in this culture, it appears that nature may also play an important role in our moral development. This was first brought to the attention of the medical community in 1848 when Phineas Gage (QR) suffered a terrible accident in which an explosion hurled an iron bar through his eye, brain, and skull. His speech and other cognitive abilities remained intact and he recovered his health rather quickly. But his personality was irreparably damaged: This pleasant, responsible person who had been popular with his coworkers was transformed into a jackass. After his accident, he had no respect for social conventions, no sense of responsibility, could not be trusted to honor his commitments, and would lie and curse uncontrollably (Macmillan, 2000).

More recent cases of damage to the ventromedial prefrontal cortex of the brain in childhood also show a severe and negative effect on social and moral behavior—including the tendency to lie frequently. Neuroscientists theorize that this brain area connects emotional experience to decision-making processes, such as the anxiety most people experience when they consider doing something that might harm someone else (J. Greene, 2013). People who incur damage to this area apparently never develop a moral compass to distinguish right from wrong and interventions are generally ineffective (Cushman, 2014).

Honesty, then, is not only something we can learn, but is also firmly grounded in neurobiology to the extent that one part of our brain seems hard-wired to specialize in internalizing norms/rules, getting along, and other social/moral functions that interface with our communicative choices that we subsequently label as "lying" and "truth telling" (Haidt, 2012).

SUMMARY

- Ethics addresses matters of right and wrong. Whether our nation is currently experiencing a moral crisis or not, it is important for citizens to regularly engage themselves and others on how they feel about the rightness and wrongness of the many faces of honesty and deceit. The bulk of this chapter focused on the right and wrong of lying to another person, but issues associated with the ethics of self-deception and lie detection were also examined.

- Four answers were given to the question, "Is it ever right to lie?" The first two subscribed to the general principle that lying is, in principle, wrong. The absolutists say it is always wrong to lie and the almost-absolutists say there are rare occasions when it is right to lie but only as a last resort and only after you are satisfied that the general public would approve. These positions sharply contrast with a Machiavellian approach that views lying, not in terms of rightness or wrongness, but in terms of whether it will help a person accomplish his or her goals. The situational approach believes matters of right and wrong are best determined by examining the circumstances surrounding the telling of a lie (or the truth) to determine its degree of rightness or wrongness. Of particular importance to this approach are the communicator's intentions and the consequences of his or her message.

- Some practical guidelines were proposed for ethical behavior relative to lying that included the following:

  1. Tell the truth most of the time.
  2. If you lie, be creative about it. There are many ways to lie and some are considered worse than others.
  3. If you lie, lie selectively—i.e., when you feel it is absolutely necessary and it is done with "good" intentions.
  4. If you lie, consider discovery—i.e., what it will mean to you if the lie is revealed.
  5. Consider the Golden Rule or whether your behavior is what you'd want from the target of your lie—given similar circumstances.

- Because some lies create a lot of personal and social damage, and frequent lying poses a potential threat to a society held together by the belief that people will generally tell them the truth, we have implemented various measures to create an honest citizenry. We legislate honesty through laws, regulations, and honor codes. We also encourage the teaching of honesty by parents, schools, public leaders, books, movies, and the press. Whatever is gleaned from all these lessons about honesty and deception is fused with what appears to be a section of the brain devoted to moral behavior.

1. Recall a lie you told in which you had to choose between being dishonest and being one of the following: compassionate, loyal, courageous, dependable, or fair. Why did you make the decision you did? Make your story into a case study. Identify all the people and conditions involved, but don't use your own name and don't identify that you chose dishonesty over another value. Write your case as objectively as possible, providing only the necessary facts, relationships, hard choices, and circumstances leading up to the main character's decision about how to act. Conclude your case by asking, "What would you do?" Have someone you don't know read your case and identify how they think they would respond in such a situation and why. With your partner, discuss honesty, deception, and other values as they relate to your case.

2. This chapter spent a lot of time addressing the question of whether it was ever "right" to lie. Examine the other side of that question: Is it ever "wrong" to tell the "truth"? Make a list of as many different types of situations where you think telling the truth would be wrong. Indicate why you believe this. Exchange lists with another person and discuss your answers.

OF INTEREST

"Is Every Lie a 'Sin'? Maybe not." In this video and accompanying interview produced by the University of Pennsylvania's Wharton School, researchers Maurice Schweitzer and Emma Levine revisit Augustine's prohibition against all lying. They argue that the modern moral standard shouldn't be "Don't lie to me," but "Don't be selfish" instead.

"How the Golden Rule Makes Us Dumb." Not everyone is convinced that the Golden Rule is inherently useful. In this iconoclastic column for *Psychology Today*, author and lecturer Jeremy Sherman pulls back the curtain and explains why he's not a fan.

REFERENCES

Alder, K. (2007). *The lie detectors: The history of an American obsession*. New York, NY: Free Press.

Associated Press (2006, July 11). It's the truth: Americans conflicted about lying. *NBC News*. Retrieved from http://www.nbcnews.com

BBC (n.d.). *BBC ethics guide: Lying*. Retrieved from http://www.bbc.co.uk/ethics/guide/

Beam, C. (2011, March 10). Broken record laws: Why do 12 states still make it illegal to tape people without their knowledge? Slate. Retrieved from http://www.slate.com

Bell, K. L., & DePaulo, B. M. (1996). Liking and lying. *Basic and Applied Social Psychology, 18*(3), 243–266. https://dx.doi.org/10.1207/s15324834basp1803_1

Bennett, W. J. (1993). *The book of virtues*. New York, NY: Simon & Schuster.

Bennett, W. J. (1995). *The children's book of virtues*. New York, NY: Simon & Schuster.

Berger, J. (2006). *Raising kids with character*. New York, NY: Jason Aronson, Inc.

Bertrand, N. (2017, October 19). Senators have a new plan to fix a major loophole that let Russia take advantage of Facebook and tech giants. Business Insider. Retrieved from http://www.businessinsider.com

Bok, S. (1978). *Lying: Moral choice in public and private life*. New York, NY: Pantheon.

Bowles, S. (2000, March 21). Misconduct reports against teachers changing classrooms. *USA Today*, p. 4A.

Blanton, B. (2005). *Radical honesty: How to transform your life by telling the truth* (Rev. ed.) New York, NY: Dell.

Chance, Z., & Norton, M. I. (2011). "I read Playboy for the articles": Justifying and rationalizing questionable preferences. In M. S. McGlone & M. L. Knapp (Eds.), *The interplay of truth and deception* (pp. 136–148). New York, NY: Routledge.

Christie, R., & Geis, F. L. (1970) *Studies in Machiavellianism*. New York, NY: Academic Press.

Cortlett, I. (2009). *E is for ethics: Read-aloud stories about morals, values, and what matters most*. New York, NY: Atria.

Cushman, F. (2014). The neural basis of morality: Not just where, but when. *Brain, 137*(4), 974–980. https://dx.doi.org/10.1093/brain/awu049

DePaulo, B. M. (2004). The many faces of lies. In A. G. Miller (Ed.), *The social psychology of good and evil* (pp. 303–326). New York, NY: Guilford.

Denery, D. (2015). *The devil wins: A history of lying from the Garden of Eden to the Enlightenment*. Princeton, NJ: Princeton University Press.

Gordon, N. (2018, January 24). Misconduct and punishment: State disciplinary authorities investigate prosecutors accused of misconduct. The Center for Public Integrity. Retrieved from http://www.publicintegrity.org

Gorovitz, S. (Ed.). (1971). *Utilitarianism: Text and critical essays.* Indianapolis, IN: Bobbs-Merrill.

Greene, R. (2002). *The 48 laws of power* (Rev. ed.). New York, NY: Penguin Books.

Greene, J. (2013). *Moral tribes.* New York, NY: Penguin.

Greenwald, G. (2014). *No place to hide: Edward Snowden, the NSA, and the U.S. surveillance state.* New York, NY: Metropolitan Books.

Haidt, J. (2012). *The righteous mind: Why good people are divided by politics and religion.* New York, NY: Pantheon.

Hartshorne, H., & May, M. A. (1928) *Studies in the nature of character: Studies in deceit* (Vol. 1). New York, NY: MacMillan. http://dx.doi.org/10.1037/13386-000

Hartshorne, H., & May, M. A. (1971). Studies in the organization of character. In H. Munsinger (Ed.), *Readings in child development* (pp. 190–197). New York, NY: Holt, Rinehart & Winston.

Hearn, T. K., Jr. (Ed.) (1971). *Studies in utilitarianism.* New York, NY: Meredith.

Hopkins, C. S., Ratley, R. J., Benincasa, D. S., & Grieco, J. J.. (2005). Evaluation of voice stress analysis technology. Proceedings of the 38th Annual Hawaii International Conference on System Sciences (p. 20b). http://dx.doi.org/10.1109/HICSS.2005.254

Hosmer, L. T. (2008). *Ethics of management.* New York, NY: McGraw-Hill.

Illbruck, H. (2012). *Nostalgia: Origins and ends of an unenlightened disease.* Evanston, IL: Northwestern University Press.

Jackson, B. (2009). Finding the weasel word in "literally true." In M. S. McGlone & M.L. Knapp (Eds.), *The interplay of truth and deception* (pp. 1–15). New York, NY: Routledge.

Johnson, C. E. (2001). *Meeting the ethical challenges of leadership.* Thousand Oaks, CA: Sage.

Josephson, M. S. (2002). *Making ethical decisions.* Marina del Rey, CA: Josephson Institute of Ethics.

Josephson Institute of Ethics. (2012). *2012 report card on the ethics of American youth.* Los Angeles, CA: Josephson Institute of Ethics.

Kardonne, R. (2008). *Victor Kugler: The man who hid Anne Frank.* Jerusalem, Israel: Gefen Publishing House.

Kidder, R.M. (1995). How good people make tough choices. New York, NY: William Morrow.

Kirsch, I. (2013). The placebo effect revisited: Lessons learned to date. *Complementary Therapies in Medicine, 21*(2), 102–104. https://dx.doi.org/10.1016/j.ctim.2012.12.003

Lee, K. (2013). Little liars: Development of verbal deception in children. *Child Development Perspectives, 7*(2), 91–96. https://dx.doi.org/10.1111/cdep.12023

Leonhardt, D., Philbrick, I. P., & Thompson, S. A. (2017, December 14). Trump's lies vs. Obama's. *The New York Times*. Retrieved from https://www.nytimes.com

Machiavelli, N. (2010). *The prince*. New York, NY: Capstone. (Original work published 1532).

Macmillan, M. (2000). *An odd kind of fame*. Cambridge, MA: MIT Press.

Mazur, M. A., & Kalbfleisch, P. J. (2003). Lying and deception detection in television families. *Communication Research Reports, 20*(3), 200–207. https://dx.doi.org/10.1080/08824090309388818

McGlone, M. S., & Giles, H. (2011). Language and interpersonal communication. In M. L. Knapp & J. A. Daly (Eds.), *The SAGE handbook of interpersonal communication* (4th ed.) (pp. 201–237). Thousand Oaks, CA: Sage.

Miller, F. G., Wendler, D., & Swartzman, L. C. (2005). Deception in research on the placebo effect. *PLoS Medicine, 2*(9), 853–859. https://dx.doi.org/10.1371/journal.pmed.0020262

Nilsen, T. R. (1966). *Ethics of speech communication*. Indianapolis, IN: Bobbs-Merrill.

Nyberg, D. (1993). *The varnished truth: Truth telling and deceiving in ordinary life*. Chicago, IL: University of Chicago Press.

Packer, G. (2014). *The unwinding: An inner history of the new America*. New York, NY: Farrar, Straus, & Giroux.

Plante, T. G. (2004). *Do the right thing: Living ethically in an unethical world*. Oakland, CA: New Harbinger.

Raecker, S. (2014). Strengthening a culture of ethics. Presentation to the U. S. Senate Legislative Ethics Committee.

Quintilian, M. F. (1922). *The institutio oratoria, Book I*. H. E. Butler (Trans.). Cambridge, MA: Harvard University Press. (Original work published ca. 90 CE).

Robinson, W. P. (1994). Reactions to falsifications in public and interpersonal contexts. *Journal of Language and Social Psychology, 13*(4), 497–513. https://dx.doi.org/10.1177/0261927x94134007

Seiter, J. S., & Brushke, J. (2007). Deception and emotion: The effects of motivation, relationship type, and sex on expected feelings of guilt and shame following acts of deception in United States and Chinese samples. *Communication Studies, 58*(1), 1–16. https://dx.doi.org/10.1080/10510970601168624

Seiter, J. S., Bruschke, J. & Bai, C. (2002). The acceptability of deception as a function of perceivers' culture, deceiver's intention, and deceiver-deceived relationship. *Western Journal of Communication, 66*(2), 158–180. https://dx.doi.org/10.1080/10570310209374731

Smart, J. J. C., & Williams, B. (1973). *Utilitarianism for and against*. London, England: Cambridge University Press.

Snowden, E. (2015, June 4). The world says no to surveillance. *The New York Times*. Retrieved from http://www.nytimes.com

Stevenson, B., & Wolfers, J. (2011). *Trust in public institutions over the business cycle*. Cambridge, MA: National Bureau of Economic Research. https://dx.doi.org/10.3386/w16891

Stewart, D. (2013). Dissimulation in Sunni Islam and Morisco Taqiyya. *Al-Qanṭara, 34*(2), 439–490. https://dx.doi.org/10.3989/alqantara.2013.016

Timmons, H., & Kozlowska, H. (2018, March 22). Facebook's quiet battle to kill the first transparency law for online political ads. *Quartz*. Retrieved from https://qz.com

U.S. Department of the Treasury. Internal Revenue Service. (2014) *IRS Oversight Board taxpayer attitude survey, 2014*. Retrieved from https://www. treasury.gov/IRSOB/

Wang, S., & Dennis, S. T. (2018, April 10). Twitter follows Facebook in endorsing the Honest Ads Act. *AdAge*. Retrieved from http://www.adage.com

Williams, T. M. (2015). *False advertising and the Lanham Act*. Albany, NY: LexisNexis/Matthew Bender.

Zahavi, D. (2005). *Subjectivity and selfhood: Investigating the first-person perspective*. Cambridge, MA: MIT Press.

PART II

deceptive behavior

PART II deceptive behavior

There are many ways to deceive, so the following five chapters focus on the science (and art) of lying and deception. First, we explore the manifestations of deception among various nonhuman species, as it provides a fascinating beginning and a useful backdrop for understanding how humans deceive. In the same way, an examination of how the developing child learns the skills needed to lie effectively is a useful antecedent to learning about adult deceivers. Then, two types of adult behavior are examined: self-deception and interpersonal deception. Finally, we conclude with an examination of people for whom lying is a prominent part of life—pathological liars, con artists, and hoaxers.

Chapter 4: Nonhuman Deception

Chapter 5: Children as Liars and Targets of Lies

Chapter 6: Self-Deception

Chapter 7: Performing Lies and Deceit

Chapter 8: Specialists in Lying and Deception

CHAPTER 4 Nonhuman Deception

"Even if a snake is not poisonous, it should pretend to be venomous."
– *Chanakya*

"Liar, liar, plants for hire!"
– *Patrick, passing judgment on SpongeBob*

Figure 4.1: That's no snake. Pupa of *Dynastor darius*, a species of butterfly native to Trinidad.

If at first glance you thought that the butterfly cocoon in Figure 4.1 was a snake, you're not alone. Predators of this caterpillar native to Trinidad avoid it during the pupal stage because of its striking resemblance to a viper.

It turns out that nature tends to reward organisms of all kinds (not just humans) who practice deception effectively and/or detect it effectively. Why? Because the purpose of natural selection is to develop traits that promote survival, including adaptations that enable trickery and deceit, as well as detection of the same.

Deception and its detection are just as important in the nonhuman world as they are in ours. Predator or prey, friend or enemy, in any communication system, there are senders who create messages, channels to carry those messages, and receivers who interpret them.

More so than in our world, perhaps, the nonhuman communication process uses not just visual and auditory information, but also olfactory (smell) and tactile (touch). Skilled nonhuman communicators know how to distort the ways other organisms perceive this information. In doing so, they survive and reproduce.

Everything is a trade-off, of course. Deceptive communication in the animal kingdom has benefits and costs, just as it does in human communication. Blue Jays, for example, have developed a perceptual system that recognizes colors and patterns specific to monarch butterflies—because monarchs are toxic to them. At the same time, however, Blue Jays also needlessly avoid tasty, non-toxic butterflies like queens (Fig. 4.2) who have cleverly learned to mimic the monarch's

Figure 4.2: This queen butterfly is perfectly happy being mistaken for a monarch. In fact, it's counting on it.

appearance. All in all, being deceived in this way is a small price for Blue Jays to pay get a perceptual system that otherwise keeps them alive and flourishing. By the way, when harmless organisms like queen butterflies masquerade as a harmful species, the process is known as Batesian mimicry, a phenomenon we will discuss in more detail later in the chapter.

Occasionally, however, changes in the physical environment may render an organism's existing perceptual systems inadequate. When this happens, it's time for an upgrade. Let's assume, for example, that all sources of Blue Jay food disappeared from their habitat except

lying and deception in **HUMAN INTERACTION**

the toxic monarchs and their non-toxic lookalikes. Under these new conditions, some Blue Jays would have to develop a refined perceptual system capable of finally distinguishing the safe butterflies from the toxic ones—else the species would go extinct.

Deception functions in the animal kingdom not only to protect organisms from being eaten, but also to lure prey (as we will discuss later). For example, the spider-tailed horned viper (QR) has a tail that appears to be an insect or spider, which it moves in a fashion intended to attract birds (Fathinia, Rastegar-Pouyani, Rastegar-Pouyani, Todehdehghan, & Amiri, 2015).

Such examples abound. Given the important roles deception and its detection play in the survival of any given organism, it is not difficult to find it present in the lives of insects, fish, birds, amphibians, reptiles, and mammals. But first, we'll begin our tour of nonhuman deception where we might least expect to find it—among microscopic organisms within the human body.

DECEPTION AT THE MOLECULAR LEVEL

Despite the best efforts of the human immune system to target and destroy harmful or unwanted viruses and bacteria, many evade detection through the use of deception. Sometimes the disease-producing organism (i.e., the pathogen) is relatively harmless. When this is the case, Goodenough (1991) says, its deception of our immune system is "a lie we can live with."

The immune system's first task is not to amass a huge army, but to develop effective techniques for detecting foreign presences. For relatively harmless pathogens, "winning" simply means surviving by avoiding detection. More harmful pathogens like viruses are more like embedded agents, parasites that are unable to replicate and survive without a host cell. Their goal is to find a way to survive undetected behind enemy lines where they can create havoc. Harmful or not, how do pathogens use deception to evade detection by the immune system? We'll look at three strategies: mimicry, camouflage, and illusion.

Mimicry

One common way pathogens deceptively enter a host cell is by resembling something that is regularly permitted into the cell—taking on the appearance of a protein or hormone (Damian, 1989; Yoshino & Coustau, 2011). Examples of such mimics include the rabies and Epstein-Barr viruses. A similar type of mimicry is used by several types of bacteria that have evolved a coating of sialic acid, a cue the immune system uses to distinguish benign cells from parasites. Bacteria that cause food poisoning often rely on this type of molecular mimicry (Louwen et al., 2013).

Camouflage

Camouflage, like mimicry, is a form of concealment/disguise designed to avoid detection. However, camouflaged pathogens *blend into the background* rather than proactively exhibiting characteristics of benign organisms. The primary agent of the common cold, the rhinovirus, hides in "canyons" on the host cell that are too narrow for an antibody molecule to enter, and thereby is able to gain access to the host (Goodenough, 1991). Many viruses, bacteria, and parasites rely on camouflage to avoid detection by the immune system—making it difficult to develop vaccines for many illnesses (De Groot et al., 2014). Identifying and understanding camouflage at the molecular level is an important step in the field of immunobiology when it comes to creating cures and effective vaccines.

Illusion

The key to many a good magic trick is illusion—for example, one thing appears to be happening when in fact something else is actually occurring. Viruses also use this technique. The African trypanosome virus is transmitted by the tsetse fly and causes a form of sleeping sickness. This virus does not invade cells, but circulates in the blood, which gives it access to tissue and organs (Wu, Liu, & Shi, 2017). Since the antibodies generated to fight this virus are also circulating in the blood, most trypanosomes are destroyed—but there are always survivors.

Some of those survivors manage to change their physical characteristics, so they are not recognized by the existing antibodies. These trypanosomes have evolved a built-in system that quickly swaps out the specific type of antigen they are using—and which the body's immune system has produced customized antibodies for. This is called *antigenic variation.* Each time the immune system identifies the antigen the virus appears to be using, targets it, and sends out the correct antibodies to combat it, the pesky virus switches to a new variant of the antigen. The African trypanosome virus is believed to be capable of presenting as many as a thousand antigenic variations, or as Ooi and Rudenko (2017) put it, "a coat for all seasons." Chronic infections may be caused by viruses that are constantly able to elude the attacks of the immune system by relying on this form of trickery.

Each year the Centers for Disease Control and Prevention (CDC) urges people to get shots designed to combat the current form of the flu virus, in hopes of preventing an epidemic. But these viruses are also capable of changing their identity, which is why the CDC's plea is accompanied by the disclaimer (QR, see "Vaccine Match") that flu shots may not be effective in combating *new* strains of the influenza virus that have mutated, or "drifted" (Centers for Disease Control and Prevention, 2018).

This trick of the ever-changing virus can cause problems as we age. As adults, our bodies create fewer antibodies that are used to detect new pathogens, thus making adults more susceptible to the flu than children (Kucharski, 2014). The immune system is under the impression that past experiences with the flu have created the correct recognition program to fight off future attacks, but new strains of the changing virus go undetected when the body is in this relaxed, "default" state of defense.

DECEPTION AMONG PLANTS AND FUNGI

To further illustrate the omnipresence of deception among organisms, we need look no further than the weeds, grasses, and flowers that surround us. Plants, algae, and fungi rely on deception to obtain food, reproduce, and to form symbiotic relationships between species. You likely know about the famed Venus flytrap. To supplement the nutrients it gets from the soil and air, it has developed a flower-like structure that attracts insects. As the unsuspecting creature begins to explore the "flower," it might trip one of the short, stiff hairs lining its opening. The plant's mechanism is quite developed, however, because it could be a false alarm. So, a *second* hair must be touched within 20 seconds to activate the trap. Activating two of the trigger hairs will snap the plant shut, trapping the insect, and creating a meal the plant has procured through deception (Fig. 4.3).

Figure 4.3: A Venus flytrap eating dinner.

As a species, orchids are masters of deception and trickery (QR). Many orchid plants pretend to offer food in order to attract insect pollinators (e.g., the appearance of having nectar attracts bees), but in fact there is no such reward. In addition, some orchids rely on deception as a means to *reproduce* (Gaskett, 2011):

- The bee orchid, for example, uses a variety of tricks to entice male bees to attempt copulation with it. This versatile flower has not only developed the visual appearance of a female bee, but also feels and smells like one (Fig. 4.4). As the male is mounting what he thinks is a female of his own species, pollen sacs on the orchid become attached to the male bee's head. When the male bee visits another bee orchid, he brings along the attached sacs and thereby completes the pollination process for the orchid.

- Another species of orchid attracts male wasps and the deception is successful enough to cause the wasp to ejaculate into the flower—these orchids have the highest pollination rates (Gaskett, Winnick, & Herberstein, 2008).

Figure 4.4: The bee orchid is aptly named.

Figure 4.5: *Hydnora africana.* A rose by any other name would smell as sweet, but only to a dung beetle.

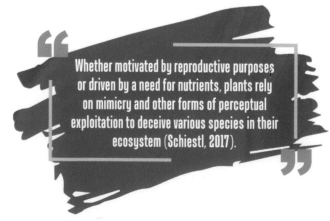

Whether motivated by reproductive purposes or driven by a need for nutrients, plants rely on mimicry and other forms of perceptual exploitation to deceive various species in their ecosystem (Schiestl, 2017).

Some plants have developed features and odors similar to feces. They accomplish their pollination goals by attracting insects looking for food or a place to lay their eggs. While something that has the odor or appearance of feces may not be appealing to humans, it is irresistible to a dung beetle. The flower of the *Hydnora africana* (Bolin, Maass, & Musselman, 2009) emits a dung-like odor that encourages beetles to enter the flower (Fig. 4.5). The opening to the flower has hairs that prevent the beetle from exiting. In this case, the insects are only temporarily imprisoned—the flower opens up after a few days and releases the captive beetles after coating them in pollen. Other plants that rely on similar deceptions are not as friendly and contain fluids that digest insects entering their flowers.

Smells (i.e., chemical mimicry) are but one of the mechanisms used to attract pollinators—the color of a flower and even the ability of the plant to *heat up* their flowers are others. Whether motivated by reproductive purposes or driven by a need for nutrients, plants rely on mimicry and other forms of perceptual exploitation to deceive various species in their ecosystem (Schiestl, 2017).

But some plants are as interested in keeping other species away from them as others are in luring them. Plants that seek to stay out of harm's way have evolved an appearance that does not portend a good meal—examples include living plants that, from all outward appearances, are dead, resemble bird droppings, or even look like rocks (as does *lithops*, Fig. 4.6).

The aptly named passion flower (Fig. 4.7) is the furthest thing from boring, but such good looks come with a price. It needs *Heliconius* butterflies to help with pollination, and the butterflies are attracted to the beautiful passion flower so they want to leave eggs there. Technically, that's fine, but if there are *too many* eggs, they turn into a whole lot of larvae. Too many larvae will eat the passion flower leaves and potentially kill it.

Figure 4.6: *Lithops otzeniana* doing its best impersonation of a box of rocks.

Figure 4.7: The beautiful passion flower doesn't want too many *Heliconius* butterflies knocking on its door.

So what does the passion flower do? It uses multiple deceptive strategies, including (Williams & Gilbert, 1981):

- varying leaf shapes, starting when it's young, to discourage some of the butterflies from dropping off their eggs (the butterflies use leaf shape as a decision guide)

- having young passion flowers give off unpleasant odors to drive the butterflies away

- growing structures that resemble the butterfly's eggs, to give the impression that the flower has already been occupied and there's no room left (the butterflies have a built-in rule that prevents them from laying too many eggs in one place)

- producing a nectar on its stems and leaves to attract ants that will destroy the larvae

Other green species rely on the nurturing drive of other species to ensure their survival, as in the case of the cuckoo fungus. Termites are known for their abilities to be carpenters, miners, and builders. However, one fungus has tapped into the child-rearing skill of termites for its own survival. The fungus exists in balls that are so similar in shape, size, and smell to termite eggs that the workers bring them back to their nests where, unbeknownst to the termites, they germinate safely (Ahmad, Dawah, & Khan, 2018).

Comrade Vavilov and his rye.

Plants also evolve to mimic other plants around them that animals are known not to eat. However, when humans get involved there can be unpredicted outcomes. Such is the case with the history of the rye plant, which was originally a weed, but resembled and grew alongside the domesticated wheat crop.

A process of artificial selection allowed rye weeds to become a crop over time because farmers identified and removed rye weed from their crops by eye. Thus, the rye weeds that most closely resembled wheat went undetected, survived, and evolved to be so similar to wheat that it became a viable crop (Zohary, Hopf, & Weiss, 2012). This unintentional culling process in crops is referred to as Vavilovian mimicry (and important enough to earn its discoverer his own commemorative stamp). It's similar in outcome to the strategies used by farmers and animal breeders to select mates based on genetically driven characteristics of their stock.

The preceding examples of deception in viruses and plants appropriately set the stage for examining deception among other creatures. The following model will help us understand and organize such behavior. Before doing so, however, it's worth stepping back for a moment and offering the following observation: Since most of the deceptive displays in the nonhuman world are not subject to conscious processing or awareness by the organism, references to deception as a goal are based on our human observations, not the intentions of the organism itself. This realization has led some evolutionary biologists to study nonhuman deception by focusing on the *cost and benefits* for the organism rather than relying on any sense of conscious motive or intention (Searcy & Nowicki, 2005).

STRATEGIES OF NONHUMAN DECEPTION: RUE'S TYPOLOGY

All organisms, says Rue (1994), are perceivers—predators perceive their prey and prey perceive their predators. Whether playing offense or defense, defeating the other organism's perceptual system confers a distinct advantage. In the natural world, how does deception help to accomplish this? Rue suggests the following typology. Any strategy of deception aimed at defeating the opponent's perception, he says, can be understood as a combination of the following three factors:

1. The **purpose**, or objective, of the deception: offense or defense
2. The **strategy** used to deceive: evasive or "perversive" (manipulative)
3. The **means** of deception: morphological (physical) or behavioral

We'll define each of these categories and then apply them to examples from the natural world. Throughout, the term *dupe* will be used to refer to the target of the deception.

Purpose: Offense or Defense

In short, organisms use deception, as they do all the skills available to them, either to survive or to reproduce. Life is a complicated, uncertain thing, and if an organism needs to be swift (but isn't), needs to be strong (but isn't), or needs to have protective armor (but doesn't), deception is the next best thing. Like any tool, when deception is needed, it serves one of two purposes—either to act defensively or to go on the offensive.

Strategy: Evasive or Perversive

The extent to which a deceptive act is successful is the extent to which it manages to defeat the perceptual system of the dupe (Thompson, 1986). This can be accomplished in two ways:

- **Evasively**: The deceiver uses a strategy of masking/hiding, allowing it to escape the perceptual system of the dupe completely. Camouflage, for example, works this way.

- **Perversively**: The deceiver uses a strategy that confuses, deludes, or otherwise "perverts" the dupe's perceptual system into misidentifying the deceiver. Using a decoy of some kind is a type of perversive strategy.

In this context, a "perversive" strategy is one that *manipulates* the dupe's perceptual system rather than simply bypassing it.

Means: Morphology or Behavior

The specific method, or means, by which the deception occurs constitutes the third component in Rue's deception typology. The means may be physical (or what Rue calls *morphological*) or it may have to do with *behavior*, that is, the actions taken by the organism to bring about the deception. If the means is morphological, then some physical aspect of the organism—its color, shape, appearance, size, or smell—is responsible for the deception.

Even though they are separate categories for purposes of understanding the process, morphology and behavior often work together in nature. For example, a moth's coloration may be indistinguishable from a leaf, but deception based on that morphology may not be effective unless the moth behaves appropriately—e.g., landing on the right leaf and remaining motionless (Barber & Kawahara, 2013).

Putting It All Together

Rue notes that the components of the deceptive process can be combined in a variety of ways. For example, an organism's coloration (**morphology**) may enable it to effectively **evade** the perceptual system of a predator for the purpose of resisting a threat (**defensive**).

How many of the components of Rue's typology can you identify in the life cycle of swallowtail butterflies?

- **Fig. 4.8** – Like a number of other species, some swallowtail larvae are "shit mimics." Birds looking for food are likely to mistake them for their own droppings and, needless to say, leave the larvae alone.

- **Fig. 4.9** – In the caterpillar stage, the swallowtail's coloring helps it blend in with its surroundings. Also, the caterpillars tend to have eye spots or "false eyes." The markings on their heads may also look enough like a snake to keep some hungry birds at bay.

- **Fig. 4.10** – In its next stage, the pupa takes on the coloring of the tree or twig to which it is attached.

- **Fig. 4.11** – Once the butterfly has emerged, it continues its deceptive ways. When upright, the wingtips of these species often give the appearance of a prominent head. Birds that attack this part of the butterfly may damage the swallowtail's wing, but the assault will not be lethal.

Figure 4.8: "You look like crap!" is a compliment for a swallowtail larvae.

Figure 4.9: Eye spots passing for real (and really scary) eyes on a swallowtail caterpillar.

Figure 4.10: Somewhere in here is a swallowtail pupa hiding in plain sight. Would you have spotted it?

Figure 4.11: A swallowtail butterfly with an imitation head on its wing tips.

The following are some specific examples of how the different components in Rue's typology are manifested in the lives of deceptive insects, fish, reptiles, amphibians, birds, and mammals.

I. Offensive Purpose, Evasive Strategy, Morphological Means

The coloring and shape of some insects are so much like the flowers they inhabit that they simply lie in wait until an unsuspecting victim approaches, thinking it has found a flower to pollinate. The last thing some poor bees and butterflies ever do is search for nectar near what turns out to be the orchid mantis (Fig. 4.12; Tormoen, 2013).

II. Offensive Purpose, Perversive Strategy, Morphological Means

Cleaner fish, as their name suggests, "clean" other fish by removing (feeding on) unwanted bacteria, parasites, and damaged tissue. It's a win-win relationship that benefits both species of fish. But some fish with more sinister motives *mimic* the appearance of the cleaner to tag along and gain access to some fresh fish flesh. One such mimic is the bluestriped fang-blenny, which can change its color to blend in with several different types of cleaner fish.

Figure 4.12: Thinking this is an actual orchid might be the last mistake a bee or butterfly ever makes.

But as its name suggests, its ample teeth allow it to attack and feed on the healthy tissue of the host fish, who was deceived by its color-changing disguise into believing it was a harmless, friendly cleaner fish (Côté & Cheney, 2005). The bluestriped fangblenny is no novice. In addition to tricking its way in by looking like a harmless cleaner fish, when it takes a yummy bite out of the host fish, it uses an opioid-based venom that numbs the site. By the time the host fish realizes it's been wounded, the fangblenny is long gone (de Witt, 2017).

Brood parasitism is an intriguing, opportunistic act that uses deception to "outsource" the raising of one's young to someone else. The female cuckoo, for example, lays her eggs in the nests of other birds, as do nearly 100 bird species. Greenspan (2016) summarized a three-step strategy that cuckoos and other parasitic birds commonly use:

- **Step 1 – Invade the nest:** The cuckoo puts only one egg into the nests of as many as 25 different hosts. Waiting patiently for the real parents to leave isn't always necessary, however, as some cuckoos have evolved to look like raptors and can just scare them away instead.

- **Step 2 – Disguise the eggs:** To fool the foster parents, the cuckoo's eggs are produced with almost exactly the same coloring as those of the host species (see Fig. 4.13). Some birds, however, can detect when one of the eggs is a forgery and will push it out of the nest, refuse to incubate it, or even abandon the nest altogether. When this happens, though, Hoover and Robinson (2007) found that some cuckoos employ a mafia-like strategy. After paying a visit to observe the status of her egg, if the mother cuckoo finds that a host bird has rejected it, then she will destroy the host's nest.

- **Step 3 – Murder the siblings:** After about 12 days, the cuckoo egg hatches (often before the real chicks) and the nesting mother bird feeds it as her own. Newly hatched cuckoos aren't especially interested in sharing the nest or their foster mother's food, so they shove any remaining eggs (even hatchlings) out of the nest (QR). In other cases, such as that of the greater African honeyguide, though the chick is still blind and featherless, it will immediately proceed to use its hooked beak to stab and kill the host's chicks. Once the competition is eliminated, some cuckoo babies will even simulate the sounds of an entire brood in order to triple the amount of food they get.

III. Defensive Purpose, Evasive Strategy, Morphological Means

The ability to assume the coloration, textures, and even forms existing in one's habitat is a feature shared by many species. As far as predators are concerned, these animals don't exist; in other words, they are indistinguishable from the environment itself. Many amphibians (toads, frogs) and reptiles (turtles, lizards, snakes), for example, are capable of rapid color changes that conform to their surroundings. The mimic octopus, discovered by Norman and Hochberg (2005), takes on the shape of many other creatures, such as a poisonous flatfish swimming across the sandy bottom, and these octopuses change colors instantly to take on the appearance of seemingly any background to evade predators (Fig. 4.14).

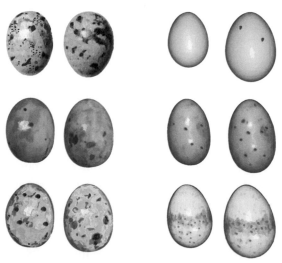

Figure 4.13: European cuckoo eggs (right) compared with regular bird eggs.

IV. Defensive Purpose, Perversive Strategy, Morphological Means

Normally, the appearance of the frilled lizard (Fig. 4.15) is not particularly distinctive.

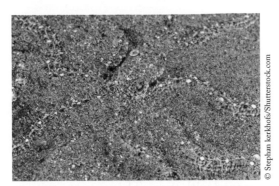

Figure 4.14: Octopus? What octopus? A mimic octo hiding in the Red Sea.

Figure 4.15: Welcome to Jurassic Park. The frilled lizard.

When frightened, however, it opens its mouth, bares its teeth, and simultaneously unfurls an umbrella-like collar, with bright orange and red scales, around its neck. To a predator, this display may make the frilled lizard seem like a far more formidable foe.

The "alligator bug" (or lanternfly) in the Brazilian rainforest has a long, hollow, nose-like protrusion from its head that looks very much like an alligator's head, complete with a row of menacing "teeth." In this environment, monkeys regularly prey on large insects like cicadas, but they tend to steer clear of the alligator bug. Anything that appears to have a lot of visible teeth or looks like an alligator or caiman (no matter how small) is likely to briefly activate the monkey's "steer clear" program, providing time for the alligator bug to escape. It is a process similar to a human being who frantically dances away from a rope, which at first glance looks like a snake (DeLoache & LoBue, 2009)—or, better yet, a rubber snake used to prank coworkers (QR).

American avocets are birds that usually build their nests along the shores and nearby flat lands of sparsely vegetated lakes and sloughs. The lack of cover allows hungry predators (looking for newborn avocets who cannot fly) to spot them at a distance. Even though the newborns will not learn to fly until they are about 5 weeks old, they develop the plumage of an adult after only 2 weeks—thereby giving the appearance of a full-grown (and flying) adult (Sordahl, 1988).

V. Offensive Purpose, Evasive Strategy, Behavioral Means

The West African assassin bug seems like the stuff of horror movies. In order to enter a yummy ant colony undetected, these bugs first capture and kill some ants—by liquefying their insides and drinking them like a milkshake (Masterson, 2018). Then they *glue* the ant corpses to their bodies (QR) and make their way undetected into the colony proper (Brandt and Mahsberg, 2002). The bug moving around doesn't seem to tip off the ants. In fact, because the assassin bug *smells* like their comrades, the unsuspecting colony is lured into a false sense of security.

VI. Offensive Purpose, Perversive Strategy, Behavioral Means

Unlike vultures, zone-tailed hawks prefer to dine on fresh kill rather than dead and decaying animals they happen upon. Small critters aren't afraid of vultures and don't go scurrying when they see them flying overhead. The clever zone-tailed hawk takes full advantage of this situation, creating the illusion that it's a vulture by flying around with them. Then as soon as it sees a worthy prey, the hawk drops away from the vulture pack and dive bombs its target.

Some female fireflies (*Photuris*) obtain a needed part of their diet by giving males of another firefly species (*Photinus*) the idea that they have found one of their own to mate with. The *Photuris* female sends out a flashing courtship signal specific to *Photinus*, leading the male to believe there is another *Photinus* female who wants to have sex. When the male *Photinus* comes calling, however, he is promptly eaten (QR) by the *Photuris* female (Lloyd, 1986).

By devouring *Photinus* males, *Photuris* females (and their offspring) are able to acquire a defensive chemical they aren't able to produce themselves. The higher the concentration of this chemical in fireflies, the less desirable they are to predators like spiders and birds; so in this case, the offensive deception also plays an important defensive role for the *Photuris* firefly (Eisner, Goetz, Hill, Smedley, & Meinwald, 1997).

VII. Defensive Purpose, Evasive Strategy, Behavioral Means

The bittern is a bird with a long neck, similar to a heron or stork. It lives in aquatic areas. When it is threatened, it points its beak toward the sky and remains motionless. This act makes it look like one of the many reeds in its habitat (Fig. 4.16).

Tiger beetles have a long list of enemies who find them delicious—spiders, robber flies, lizards, bats, and birds. With such a variety of foes, they've developed an extensive repertoire of evasive maneuvers, including running away, flying away, and communal roosting (Schultz, 2001).

VIII. Defensive Purpose, Perversive Strategy, Behavioral Means

One way the eastern hognose snake (*Heterodon platyrhinos*) misleads predators is to play dead by opening its mouth, writhing as if in pain, and then rolling onto its back and going

Figure 4.16: Just one of the reeds. The bittern bird blending in.

Figure 4.17: And the Oscar for Best Performance in a Death Scene goes to . . . the eastern hognose snake.

limp, with mouth still agape and tongue hanging out (Fig. 4.17). It has even been known to continue playing dead and remaining limp when picked up (QR); however, we can't recommend that readers try this for themselves.

When a person "plays possum," it's a deliberate behavior, such as when a child pretends to be asleep. But many who use the expression don't realize that in actual opossums, playing dead is an involuntary response—they've basically fainted, in other words. The phenomenon, which can last up to 4 hours, even includes the excretion of smelly anal gland fluid to add even more credence to the guise of death (Kennedy, 2018). Like the hognose snake, its little tongue even hangs out.

DeWaal (1986) observed chimpanzees at the Arnhem Zoo in the Netherlands. One male chimp sustained a minor injury to his hand in a fight with another chimp, and for about a week after the fight the chimp limped—but only if he could be seen by the chimp he had been fighting with. Otherwise, he would walk normally. In this case, limping in the presence of a dominant male may have prevented further aggression.

... for about a week after the fight the chimp limped—but only if he could be seen by the chimp he had been fighting with.

THE ABILITY TO DECEIVE: FOUR LEVELS

As the preceding examples demonstrate, Rue's typology provides a useful way to classify different types of nonhuman deception. Mitchell's (1986; 1993) classification system goes into more detail on the way deception is enacted, particularly the "programs" driving the behavior:

- **Level I** is *physical appearance* (roughly the same as *morphology* in the section above)

The subsequent levels all deal with *behavior*:

- **Level II** is coordination of perception and action
- **Level III** is learning
- **Level IV** is planning

As you continue reading through this book, we challenge you to consider how these levels of nonhuman deception might apply to the acts of human deceit you will be learning about.

Level I—Physical Appearance

Deceptive acts at this level are not adaptable. The "deceiver" looks or acts in a particular way because it cannot do otherwise. Sometimes predators will avoid killing organisms that resemble (in appearance or behavior) other organisms that are distasteful or noxious to them. This, then, is their deception: They survive and multiply because they resemble an organism that predators have learned to avoid. In this case, survival of the fittest means survival of the look-alikes—a phenomenon known as *mimicry*. There are at least 18 different types of mimicry with multiple subtypes (Pasteur, 1982), but here we will focus on two types: Batesian and Müllerian.

Batesian Mimicry

In the mid-19th century, Henry Walter Bates spent time in the Brazilian Amazon observing and collecting thousands of insects and butterflies. He noticed that palatable butterflies—which should have been easily captured by predators because of their brightly colors and slow speed—were instead surviving quite well. He concluded that palatable butterflies that most resembled the unpalatable ones survived because predators mistakenly perceived them as unpalatable (O'Hara, 1995).

Such mimicry works best when the unpalatable organisms outnumber the palatable ones. Why? Because the predators experience mostly toxic meals from the butterflies they sample, and will more quickly learn the general lesson that "all butterflies with these markings shouldn't be eaten."

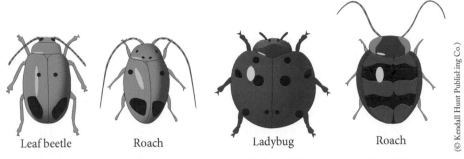

Leaf beetle   Roach   Ladybug   Roach

(© Kendall Hunt Publishing Co.)

Figure 4.18: Two examples of Batesian mimicry. These perfectly edible roaches survive by mimicking their unpalatable counterparts

Batesian mimicry is not limited to butterflies or even members of the same species or family. Figure 4.18 shows mimicry of unpalatable beetles by palatable roaches, but beetles are also mimicked by grasshoppers. Some ants survive by mimicking spiders. Even harmless flies can convincingly look like poisonous wasps and bees (like this adorable little guy) (QR).

While mimicry is plentiful among insects, it is far less common among vertebrates. One such rare example among mammals is the striking visual similarity between the shy, inoffensive aardwolf (Fig. 4.19) and the striped hyena. The similarity is no accident, however, and stems from the fact that the two creatures are closely related.

Another instance of Batesian mimicry among mammals involves the tree shrew in Borneo (Fig. 4.20). Predators find the flesh of the tree shrew repulsive and tend to leave it alone. Palatable squirrels in the area look so much like the tree shrew that it is nearly impossible to tell them apart (Parrish, 2014). So much so, in fact, that mammalogist Louise Emmons (who has studied them extensively) believes they should have been called "squirrelshrews" from the beginning (Naish, 2015).

© Joe McDonald/Shutterstock.com

Figure 4.19: The aardwolf benefits from looking like its much meaner cousin, the hyena.

© Mr. Meijer/Shutterstock.com

Figure 4.20: The "treeshrew." Not exactly a squirrel, but close enough for Müllerian mimicry to do its job.

Müllerian Mimicry

In 1878, Fritz Müller discovered that mimicry also occurs between organisms where *both* are distasteful or noxious to predators (unlike Batesian mimicry, where only one is). Predators have to learn that an organism is unpalatable or harmful by killing it (or trying to). Therefore, even if a species is noxious, a number of organisms will be killed before all the predators learn the lesson to avoid that species. But if those kills affect both of the noxious species, then neither has to sacrifice as many of their members in this process of "predator education" (Ruxton, Sherratt, & Speed, 2004). Among numerous other species, certain wasps, bees, and butterflies are capable of this type of mimicry.

By the way, for a very long time it was assumed that viceroy butterflies were Batesian (i.e., palatable) mimics of monarch butterflies. But research published in the early 1990s revealed that viceroys are in fact unpalatable, making their mimicry of monarchs a case of Müllerian rather than Batesian mimicry (Ritland & Brower, 1991).

Level II—Coordination of Perception and Action

At this level, the deceiver has some control of the deceptive act, unlike Level I. The deceiver's act is triggered *in response to* something the target either needs or does. A Level II deceiver hasn't necessarily *learned* (as in Level III) that its deception will get a particular response, only that *the target is doing X,* so behavior Y is triggered. Examples of Level II deceptive behavior include scare tactics, such as when butterflies display eyespots on their wings in response to threat (Fig. 4.21). Another popular threat response is to play dead, something that opossums are famous for of course, but which is also used by squirrels, birds and insects, and snakes.

The anglerfish is another good example of deception at Level II. When prey are nearby, the anglerfish dangles its own tasty-looking lure (from a rod built into its head).

Figure 4.21: The grayling butterfly hides its eyespots when resting, but reveals them to predators when it feels threatened.

A shrimp or a fish (even a fish twice the anglerfish's size) hoping to make a meal out of the dummy lure may discover only too late that it is both the dummy and the meal (QR, starting at 1:15).

The killdeer is a type of plover, a species of bird that feigns injury (QR) in the presence of a formidable predator (e.g., a fox) in order to keep it away from its eggs or young. Because plovers make nests on the ground, it is vital to lead approaching predators away from the nest. So the bird makes a distress call, limps, and drags a wing as if it were injured (Ristau, 2014a). The predator, giving no thought to the nest, follows what it thinks is an injured

bird and moves in for the kill. At that point, the bird takes flight. Feigning an injured wing is only one of many diversionary responses these birds manifest (Gómez-Serrano & López-López, 2017).

Fire ants have a very effective nestmate recognition system, but some myrmecophilous (literally, "ant-loving") beetles manage to convince the ants that they are one of them (Vander Meer & Wojcik, 1982). The beetle passively acquires species- and colony-specific odors from its hosts, which give it the smell of a dues-paying member of the colony. Such strategies give the beetle permission not only to move about the colony unchecked, but also to feed on ants as it pleases (Mathis & Tsutsui, 2016).

In similar fashion, a parasitic mite that makes its home on honeybees also uses chemical mimicry to remain undetected on the bees (Kather, Drijfhout, Shemilt, & Martin, 2015). The mite acquires the host's odor to remain chemically camouflaged so that it can feed on the hemolymph (the invertebrate equivalent of blood). As the parasite matures, it shifts its attention from the hive's adult bees to its younger members. The young bees smell different, of course, but the parasite is able to adjust to smell like the baby bees.

Level III—Learning

Deceptive behavior at this level can be either repeated or else modified by the deceiver on the basis of the actions and observations of the target. Mitchell (1986) says these deceptive tactics are based on "trial-and-error, instrumental, and/or observational learning" (p. 25). The deceiver's control over its deceptive actions and the extent to which the deceiver takes the target into account are both greater than at either of the two previous levels. Deceivers at this level have learned that certain actions they perform will or will not result in a particular consequence.

But acting (or not acting) because it believes its behavior will have a particular effect does not mean the organism recognizes how the target is processing and interpreting the deceptive

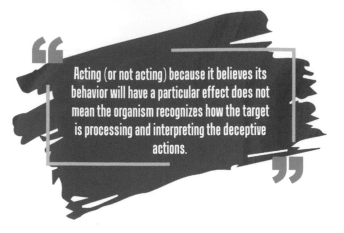

> Acting (or not acting) because it believes its behavior will have a particular effect does not mean the organism recognizes how the target is processing and interpreting the deceptive actions.

actions. Deceivers at this level are not able to take the mental perspective of the target in order to know they are behaving deceptively (that's Level IV).

Healthy dogs and chimpanzees that have received attention and comfort from humans as a result of past injury will sometimes feign an injury (e.g., begin limping) in order to elicit the same human response again (Byrne & Stokes, 2003; de Waal, 1986). Dogs and cats that are interested in removing the human occupant of a comfortable chair have also been observed to paw at the front door or otherwise make noise. Then when the human gets up to see why, the pet runs and jumps into the chair (the late, great Minnie Kuhl, a flat-coated retriever mix (Fig. 4.22), once did this very thing to her uncle, who happens to be one of the authors of this book). Once they're in the desired chair, some dogs, like YouTube star Remy the Siberian Husky, will pretend to throw a temper tantrum (QR) when told to get down.

People sometimes fake-toss a ball, but hide it and laugh while the duped dog runs off in pursuit of it. A few dogs, however, have been known to answer this deception on occasion. They'll bring back a fetched ball but divert it away when the thrower reaches for it (Goode, 2007).

Just as animals learn to perform behaviors that elicit certain responses, they also learn to suppress or avoid behaviors that produce undesired responses. Chimpanzees, for example, learn to suppress vocal expressions of emotion in order to keep from alerting prey and to keep other chimps from knowing they have acquired some prized food (Goodall, 1986). Tanner and Byrne (1993) observed a gorilla that repeatedly inhibited its "play face" by covering it with one or both hands. The exact motive was not clear, but the act of concealing the face had the effect of delaying play activity and showed that the gorilla was aware that spontaneous facial expressions affect the behavior of others.

Figure 4.22: Excuse me, but is that seat taken? Minnie the chair-thief.

Level IV—Planning

Deception at Level IV is not only intentional (like Level III), but is intentionally deceptive. In other words, deception at this level

lying and deception in HUMAN INTERACTION

means that the deceiver is *aware that his or her actions will be misleading to the target*. Consider the additional implications of this state:

- It means the deceiver can, to some extent, understand what he or she is doing from the perspective of the other.

- It means the deceiver recognizes that the target is not just a target, but also a potential deception detector and deceiver.

- It means the deceptive act or acts must be planned and altered if things don't go as expected.

In short, it is the *kind of behavior typical of most adult human liars*. Bryne and Corp (2004) found that the larger the neocortex of the brain, the more often nonhuman primates will engage in deceptive tactics. Byrne (1995) suggested several ways nonhuman primates show us they are attributing intentions to others, including the use of counter-deception and by displaying indignation over having been deceived by another.

A male chimp named Santino at a Swedish zoo shows how nonhuman primates can exhibit mindfulness and awareness. He would find rocks or break off pieces of concrete in his enclosure and hurl them at zoo visitors. Santino would hide these projectiles in various locations prior to the arrival of any visitors and conducted his planning in a calm, deliberate, and nonagitated manner so as to not alert the zoo keepers. Once visitors came to observe his area, he would unmask his aggression and start hurling projectiles (Osvath & Karvonen, 2012). Santino's example reveals not only the presence of deceptive plans, but also an understanding of how others might perceive and react to a particular behavior. For what it's worth, Santino is also an artist (QR).

An earlier study (Hare, Call, & Tomasello, 2006) also supports the idea of intentional deception on the part of chimpanzees. In this experiment, chimps were competing for food with human researchers. When a solid barrier wall was in place, they approached the food source from behind the wall. This strategy indicated knowledge that the experimenter couldn't see them through the wall, so they used it to hide their intentions. When the solid wall was replaced by a translucent one, the chimps approached from further away and used a much more circuitous route to the food. This modified strategy indicated they understood the experimenter could see through the wall—making it useless as an instrument of deception. Their behaviors suggested full awareness of what the human researchers could see and not see.

Jane Goodall (1986) reported an incident in which a chimp knew it had been duped—*and resented it*. A researcher who was working with Goodall and observing chimpanzees in their natural habitat became the object of grooming by a female chimp. Close contact between the researchers and the chimps was discouraged, so he considered ways to extract himself from this situation. He did not want to push the chimp away for fear its mother, who was nearby, would see it as an act of aggression. Instead, he looked at a bush in an alert and expectant manner, as if he had noticed something. The chimp stopped grooming in order to find out what the researcher seemed to be looking at in the bush. After finding nothing, the chimp returned to the researcher, hit him over the head with her hand, and ignored him the rest of the day.

"Most examples of counter-deception involve primates, but it has also been observed in birds—specifically in ravens, which are widely considered to be among the smartest animals."

Most examples of counter-deception involve primates, but the phenomenon has also been observed in birds—specifically in ravens, which are widely considered to be among the smartest animals (Stymacks, 2018). Several ravens were searching for food in film canisters that they could pry open. When a subordinate male was successful in finding food, the dominant male took over—but the subordinate male then pretended to find food in empty canisters. When the dominant male came over to investigate, the subordinate male quickly ran to the real food that had been left unattended. In time, the dominant male learned not to follow the subordinate male and started searching for food canisters without depending on the actions of the subordinate (Bugnyar & Kotrschal, 2004).

SIGNING APES

Since the late 1960s, researchers have taught chimpanzees, gorillas, and orangutans to communicate with gestural signs that represent words or ideas. It's important to note that researchers did not teach them how to use the signs deceptively—they learned to do that on their own.

Miles (1986) offers the example of Chantek, an orangutan who learned to use gestures adapted from American Sign Language. Chantek used the sign for "dirty" in order to keep from working on an assigned task that he didn't feel like doing. "Dirty" meant he had to go to the bathroom, so it was the perfect sign to get him out of the unwanted work assignment. But after allowed to take a break, he showed no interest in actually going to the bathroom. This pattern is very similar to the Level III behavior discussed earlier, where animals learn that by doing *X* they can get *Y*. But Chantek also manifested more complex acts of deception. For example, anticipating he would be denied an opportunity to play with certain tools, he asked to go see a monkey (who happened to be in the room with the tools). Once in the room, of course, he ignored the monkey and went straight for the tools. Still more complex behavior (similar to Level IV) occurred when Chantek hid an eraser, then signed that he had eaten it. He hadn't, but he wanted his trainer to think he had. In that instance, Chantek was using deception in an attempt to get the trainer to acquire a new belief. For more about Chantek, see the TEDx Talk given by his human foster mom, Dr. Lyn Miles (QR, with examples of lies beginning at 5:00). Like Santino the chimp, Chantek was also an artist.

Koko, perhaps the most famous of the signing primates, was once asked by her handler how a steel sink got ripped from the wall. In a deceptive reply not unlike one a child might use, Koko signed "cat did it" and pointed to her pet kitten (Green, 2005). Koko lived until 2018, passing away at the age of 46. Online magazine *The Cut* offered this remembrance (QR), including some of her "greatest hits."

There are several other nonhuman primates who have been taught signing vocabulary in an effort to explore their capacity for language use. While deception research was not specifically a motive for teaching sign language to apes, all illustrated they could use it to employ tricks to obtain food or some other reward, or even make jokes. However, Miles (1986) cautions that many of the documented uses of "deception" may have been due to verbal mistakes (such as those made by children) or perceptual biases of their caretakers, who may desire for the apes to know or perform at a level higher than may be actually occurring.

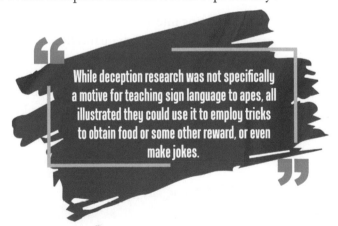

> " While deception research was not specifically a motive for teaching sign language to apes, all illustrated they could use it to employ tricks to obtain food or some other reward, or even make jokes. "

NONHUMAN DECEPTION DETECTION

This chapter has presented a variety of nonhuman deceptive acts, but we shouldn't lose sight of the fact these attempts aren't always successful. Sometimes the deception is performed poorly or at the wrong time; sometimes a skilled detector (perceiver) sees through the deceptive act; sometimes the deceptive act works for a while, but eventually detectors catch on.

Figure 4.23: Fool me once . . . A young arctic fox.

The ongoing struggle between deceiver and deception detector is as alive and well in the nonhuman world as it is among human beings, as these examples make clear:

• Batesian mimicry is only beneficial to non-toxic butterflies if there are enough toxic ones around to ensure that attacking predators can learn that butterflies with this particular appearance are not ever tasty.

• Wickler (1968) points out that older, more experienced "customers" of the cleaner fish mimics can distinguish the mimic from the real thing. As a result, the deception of these mimics is more likely to be successful if it is practiced on younger fish.

• Rüppell (1986) noted that a young Arctic fox had driven its parent away from some food. The parent fox, in turn, gave a warning call when no apparent danger could be observed. The worried young fox ran away and the parent took its food. But after a few days, the young fox realized there was no danger and refused to leave its food despite the parent's warning call. A case, we suppose, of the fox who cried wolf.

When humans interface with the nonhuman world, the effects of nonhuman deception and perception may change dramatically:

• Non-poisonous snakes that mimic poisonous ones may profit from their deception when human beings are not around, but when people are determined to eliminate poisonous snakes in an area they are not likely to look for subtle differences. A burrowing owl, which nests in a hole in the ground, might scare a person with its vocalizations that imitate the rattlesnake's tail, but after the initial scare the human is not likely to kill the owl (Wickler, 2013). However, the non-poisonous gopher snake acts and looks so much like a rattlesnake that humans often kill it by mistake.

Figure 4.24: Most people aren't going to take the time to notice that this non-poisonous gopher snake isn't a rattlesnake.

• There are situations where humans must learn to identify animal deception and to interact with the animals accordingly. Those who work with chimps learn that certain displays of affection may not guarantee a chimp will be friendly. Humans who fall for these ruses may be bitten, spat on (Ristau, 2014b), or even mauled (Harmon, 2009), as these graphic examples illustrate (QR).

When needed, however, humans can be adept at deceiving animals. Those who work with wolves have learned that wolves sense fear (which triggers an attack) by the smoothness and coordination of movement they *see*, not by smell (Ginsburg, 1987). As a consequence, people who work closely with wolves have learned how to defeat the animal's perceptual system by walking and moving purposefully and confidently no matter how much fear they actually feel. Recent research has shown that wolves who have been socialized to interact with humans exhibit reductions in stress after training (da Silva Vasconcellos et al., 2016). This finding suggests that nonhuman species can learn how to cope with us, but it is the exception rather than the rule.

SUMMARY

- This chapter demonstrated the omnipresence of deception in our world—from the deception and deception detection battles fought within our body by pathogens and our immune system to the complex deceptions performed by nonhuman primates with each other and with the humans who come into contact with them. If performed effectively and adapted to the circumstances, deceptive acts contribute toward an organism being selected by nature for survival; in turn, deceptive signaling is passed on genetically to offspring (Searcy & Nowicki, 2005). Deceptive communication is part of the exchanges that take place in small and large ecosystems.

- Following a discussion of deception at the molecular and plant level, Rue's (1994) typology of deceptive strategies provided the framework for presenting examples of deception among insects, fish, reptiles, amphibians, birds, and mammals. These examples were classified according to their ostensible purpose for deceiving (offensive or defensive), the effects of the deception on the dupe (evasive or perversive), and the means of deception (morphology or behavior). Further detail on the way deception is enacted by nonhuman species and the processes driving their deceptive acts was based on Mitchell's (1986) work. He identified four levels of deception that increase in complexity with each level. Level I is enacted mainly by appearance, Level II involves the coordination of perception and action, learning characterizes deception at Level III, and Level IV requires planning and awareness.

- The increasing skill and ability to deceive that is characteristic of Mitchell's four levels provides a useful bridge to the next chapter, which describes the increasingly complex developmental stages associated with a growing child's ability to deceive others effectively. Throughout the rest of the book, there are parallels to the various forms of human deception enacted for a variety of motives.

EXERCISES

1. Have a group of people write down the name of any insect, fish, reptile, amphibian, or mammal *not mentioned in this chapter* on a small piece of paper. Put them all in a box and mix them up. Each person then draws one piece of paper from the box and researches information about any forms of deception used by the organism they chose.

2. What are some similarities and differences in human and nonhuman deception?

3. Can you think of any examples of morphology (physical appearance) as a means of deception in human interaction?

4. Can you think of any nonhuman organisms that do not employ deception? If you answer "yes," identify the organism and explain why deception is not used. If you answer "no," explain why deception seems so pervasive.

5. Try to think of occasions when an animal deceived you. What happened? How did you discover the deception?

OF INTEREST

This clip (QR), part of a longer documentary about reef life in the Andaman Sea (in the Bay of Bengal, west of Burma and Thailand), focuses on deceptive strategies that include camouflage and mimicry. The full documentary is *Reef Life of the Andaman* (2012, 116 mins).

Orcas, otters, and owls—oh my! NATURE, the award-winning PBS documentary series, spotlights animal deception in their three-part special: "Natural Born Hustlers" (QR). This link goes to the summary page on the NATURE website. The complete series is available on Netflix.

In biology, macromolecules (QR) are complex structures, such as proteins, carbohydrates, and lipids. They have a lot of information that needs to be shared, so they communicate—and not always honestly, as it turns out. Our bodies, it seems, are chock full of little liars. Free PDF available on full web site.

REFERENCES

Ahmad S. K., Dawah H. A., & Khan M.A. (2018). Ecology of termites. In M. A. Khan & W. Ahmad (Eds.), *Termites and sustainable management* (Vol. 1) (pp. 47–68). Cham, Switzerland: Springer International Publishing AG. https://dx.doi.org/10.1007/978-3-319-72110-1_3

Barber J. R., & Kawahara A. Y. (2013). Hawkmoths produce anti-bat ultrasound. *Biology Letters, 9*, 20130161. https://dx.doi.org/10.1098/rsbl.2013.0161

Bolin, J. F., Maass, E., & Musselman, L. J. (2009). Pollination biology of *Hydnora africana* Thunb. (*Hydnoraceae*) in Namibia: Brood-site mimicry with insect imprisonment. *International Journal of Plant Sciences, 170*(2), 157–163. https://dx.doi.org/10.1086/593047

Bugnyar, T., & Kotrschal, K. (2004). Leading a conspecific away from food in ravens (*Corvus corax*)? *Animal Cognition, 7*(2), 69–76. https://dx.doi.org/10.1007/s10071-003-0189-4

Brandt, M., & Mahsberg, D. (2002). Bugs with a backpack: The function of nymphal camouflage in the West African assassin bugs *Paredocla* and *Acanthaspis* spp. *Animal Behaviour, 63*, 277–284. https://dx.doi.org/10.1006/anbe.2001.1910

Byrne, R. (1995). *The thinking ape: Evolutionary origins of intelligence.* New York, NY: Oxford University Press.

Byrne, R. W., & Corp, N. (2004). Neocortex size predicts deception rate in primates. *Proceedings of the Royal Society B: Biological Sciences, 271*, 1693–1699. https://dx.doi.org/10.1098/rspb.2004.2780

Byrne, R., & Stokes, E. (2003). Can monkeys malinger? In P. W. Halligan, C. Bass, & D. A. Oakley (Eds.), *Malingering and illness deception* (pp. 54–67). New York, NY: Oxford University Press.

Centers for Disease Control and Prevention (2018). *Key facts about seasonal flu vaccine.* Retrieved from https://www.cdc.gov/flu/protect/keyfacts.htm

Côté, I. M., & Cheney, K. L. (2005). Choosing when to be a cleaner fish mimic. *Nature, 433*, 211–212. https://dx.doi.org/10.1038/433211a

Damian, R. T. (1989). Molecular mimicry: Parasite evasion and host defense. In M. B. A. Oldstone (Ed.), *Molecular mimicry: Cross-reactivity between microbes and host proteins as a cause of autoimmunity* (pp. 101–115). Berlin, Germany: Springer-Verlag.

da Silva Vasconcellos, A., Virányi, Z., Range, F., Ades, C., Scheidegger, J. K., Möstl, E., & Kotrschal, K. (2016). Training reduces stress in human-socialised wolves to the same degree as in dogs. *PloS one, 11*(9): e0162389. https://dx.doi.org/10.1371/journal.pone.0162389

De Groot, A. S., Moise, L., Liu, R., Gutierrez, A. H., Tassone, R., Bailey-Kellogg, C., & Martin, W. (2014). Immune camouflage: Relevance to vaccines and human immunology. *Human Vaccines & Immunotherapeutic, 10*, 3570–3575. https://dx.doi.org/10.4161/hv.36134

de Witt, D. (2017, November 13). The fish's dilemma: A mimic takes advantage of a symbiotic relationship [Blog post]. Retrieved from https://naturestories.org/the-fishs-dilemma-2143b6a8e55c

DeLoache, J. S., & LoBue, V. (2009). The narrow fellow in the grass: Human infants associate snakes and fear. *Developmental science, 12*, 201–207. https://dx.doi.org/10.1111/j.1467-7687.2008.00753.x

de Waal, F. (1986). Deception in the natural communication of chimpanzees. In R. W. Mitchell & N. S. Thompson (Eds.), *Deception: Perspectives on human and nonhuman deceit* (pp. 221–244). New York, NY: State University of New York Press.

Eisner, T., Goetz, M. A., Hill, D. E., Smedley, S. R., & Meinwald, J. (1997). Firefly "femmes fatales" acquire defensive steroids (lucibufagins) from their firefly prey. *Proceedings of the National Academy of Sciences, 94*, 9723–9728. https://dx.doi.org/10.1073/pnas.94.18.9723

Fathinia, B., Rastegar-Pouyani, N., Rastegar-Pouyani, E., Todehdehghan, F., & Amiri, F. (2015). Avian deception using an elaborate caudal lure in Pseudocerastes urarachnoides (Serpentes: Viperidae). *Amphibia-Reptilia, 36*, 223–231. https://dx.doi.org/10.1163/15685381-00002997

Gaskett, A. C. (2011). Orchid pollination by sexual deception: pollinator perspectives. *Biological Reviews, 86*(1), 33–75. https://dx.doi.org/10.1111/j.1469-185X.2010.00134.x

Gaskett, A. C., Winnick, C. G., & Herberstein, M. E. (2008). Orchid sexual deceit provokes ejaculation. *The American Naturalist, 171*(6), 206–212. https://dx.doi.org/10.1086/587532

Ginsburg, B. E. (1987). The wolf-pack as a socio-genetic unit. In H. Frank (Ed.), *Man and wolf: Advances, issues, and problems in captive wolf research* (pp. 401–424). Dordrecht, Netherlands: Dr. W. Junk Publishers.

Gómez-Serrano, M.-Ý, & López-López, P. (2017). Deceiving predators: Linking distraction behavior with nest survival in a ground-nesting bird. *Behavioral Ecology, 28*(1), 260–269, https://dx.doi.org/10.1093/beheco/arw157

Goode, D. (2007). *Playing with my dog Katie: An ethnomethodological study of dog–human interaction.* West Lafayette, IN: Purdue University Press.

Goodenough, U. W. (1991). Deception by pathogens. *American Scientist, 79*(4), 344–355. https://www.jstor.org/stable/29774426

Goodall, J. (1986). *The chimpanzees of Gombe: Patterns of behavior.* Cambridge, MA: Harvard University Press.

Green, M. (2005). *Book of lies.* Kansas City, MO: Andrews McMeel Publishing.

Greenspan, J. (2016, February 25). The brilliant ways parasitic birds terrorize their victims. *Audubon.* Retrieved from http:www.audubon.org/news

Hare, B., Call, J., & Tomasello, M. (2006). Chimpanzees deceive a human competitor by hiding. *Cognition, 101*, 495–514. https://dx.doi.org/10.1016/j.cognition.2005.01.011

Harmon, K. (2009, February 19). Why would a chimpanzee attack a human? *Scientific American*. Retrieved from http://www.scientificamerican.com

Hoover, J. P., & Robinson, S. K. (2007). Retaliatory mafia behavior by a parasitic cowbird favors host acceptance of parasitic eggs. *Proceedings of the National Academy of Sciences, 104*, 4479–4483. https://dx.doi.org/10.1073/pnas.0609710104

Kather, R., Drijfhout, F. P., Shemilt, S., & Martin, S. J. (2015). Evidence for passive chemical camouflage in the parasitic mite *Varroa* destructor. *Journal of chemical ecology, 41*(2), 178–186. https://dx.doi.org/10.1007/s10886-015-0548-z

Kennedy, R. (2018, March 27). We're not playing: Here's how possums can help your household. *Atlanta Journal-Constitution*. Retrieved from http://www.ajc.com

Kucharski, A. J. (2014). Immunity's illusion. *Scientific American, 311*(6), 80–85. https://dx.doi.org/10.1038/scientificamerican1214-80

Lloyd, J. E. (1986). Firefly communication and deception: "Oh, what a tangled web." In R. W. Mitchell & N. S. Thompson (Eds.), *Deception: Perspectives on human and nonhuman deceit* (pp. 113–128). New York, NY: State University of New York Press.

Louwen, R., Horst-Kreft, D., de Boerl, A. G., van der Graaf, L., de Knegt, G., Hamersma, M., . . . van Belkum, A. (2013). A novel link between *Campylobacter jejuni* bacteriophage defence, virulence and Guillain–Barré syndrome. *European journal of clinical microbiology & infectious diseases, 32*, 207–226. https://dx.doi.org/10.1007/s10096-012-1733-4

Masterson, A. (2018, February 26). When it comes to venom, assassin bugs are double trouble. *Cosmos*. Retrieved from https://cosmosmagazine.com

Mathis, K. A., & Tsutsui, N. D. (2016). Dead ant walking: A myrmecophilous beetle predator uses parasitoid host location cues to selectively prey on parasitized ants. *Proceedings of the Royal Society B: Biological Sciences, 283*(1836), 20161281. http://dx.doi.org/10.1098/rspb.2016.1281

Miles, H. L. (1986). How can I tell a lie? Apes, language, and the problem of deception. In R. W. Mitchell & N. S. Thompson (Eds.), *Deception: Perspectives on human and nonhuman deceit* (pp. 245–266). New York, NY: State University of New York Press.

Mitchell, R. W. (1986). A framework for discussing deception. In R. W. Mitchell & N. S. Thompson (Eds.), *Deception: Perspectives on human and nonhuman deceit* (pp. 3–40). New York, NY: State University of New York Press.

Mitchell, R. W. (1993). Animals as liars: The human face of nonhuman duplicity. In M. Lewis & C. Saarni (Eds.), *Lying and deception in everyday life* (pp. 59–89). New York, NY: Guilford.

Naish, D (2015, December 4). Introducing the treeshrews: They don't all live in trees and they aren't close to shrews. *Scientific American*. Retrieved from http://www.blogs.scientificamerican.com

Norman, M. D., & Hochberg, F. G. (2005). The "Mimic Octopus" (Thaumoctopus mimicus n. gen. et sp.), a new octopus from the tropical Indo-West Pacific (Cephalopoda: Octopodidae). *Molluscan Research, 25*(2), 57–70. http://www.mapress.com/mr/content/v25/2005f/n2p070.htm

O'Hara, J. E. (1995). Henry Walter Bates—his life and contributions to biology. *Archives of Natural History, 22*(2), 195–219. https://dx.doi.org/10.3366/anh.1995.22.2.195

Ooi, C.-P., & Rudenko, G. (2017). How to create coats for all seasons: Elucidating antigenic variation in African trypanosomes. *Emerging Topics in Life Sciences, 1*(6), 593–600. https://dx.doi.org/10.1042/ETLS20170105

Osvath, M., & Karvonen, E. (2012). Spontaneous innovation for future deception in a male chimpanzee. *PloS one, 7*(5), 1–8. https://dx.doi.org/10.1371/journal.pone.0036782

Parrish, A. C. (2014). *Adaptive rhetoric: Evolution, culture, and the art of persuasion*. New York, NY: Routledge.

Pasteur, G. (1982). A classificatory review of mimicry systems. *Annual Review of Ecology and Systematics, 13*,(1) 169–199. https://dx.doi.org/10.1146/annurev.es.13.110182.001125

Ristau, C. A. (2014a). Cognitive ethology of an injury-feigning bird, the piping plover. In C. A. Ristau (Ed.), *Cognitive ethology: The minds of other animals* (pp. 91–125). New York, NY: Psychology Press.

Ristau, C. A. (2014b). Conscious chimpanzees? A review of recent literature. In C. A. Ristau (Ed.), *Cognitive ethology: The minds of other animals* (pp. 231–250). New York, NY: Psychology Press.

Ritland D. B., & Brower, L. P. (1991). The viceroy butterfly is not a Batesian mimic. *Nature, 350*, 497–498. https://dx.doi.org/10.1038/350497a0

Rue, L. (1994). *By the grace of guile: The role of deception in natural history and human affairs*. Oxford, England: Oxford University Press.

Rüppell, V. G. (1986). A "lie" as directed message of the arctic fox (*Alopex lagopus* L.). In R. W. Mitchell & N. S. Thompson (Eds.), *Deception: Perspectives on human and nonhuman deceit* (pp. 177–181). New York, NY: State University of New York Press.

Ruxton, G. D., Sherratt, T. N., & Speed, M. P. (2004). *Avoiding attack: The evolutionary ecology of crypsis, warning signals, and mimicry*. Oxford, England: Oxford University Press.

Schiestl, F. P. (2017). Innate receiver bias: Its role in the ecology and evolution of plant–animal interactions. *Annual Review of Ecology, Evolution, and Systematics, 48*, 585–603. https://dx.doi.org/10.1146/annurev-ecolsys-110316-023039

Schultz, T. D. (2001). Tiger beetle defenses revisited: Alternative defense strategies and colorations of two neotropical tiger beetles, *Odontocheila nicaraguensis* Bates and *Pseudoxycheila tarsalis* Bates (Carabidae: Cicindelinae). *The Coleopterists Bulletin, 55*(2), 153–163. https://dx.doi.org/10.1649/00 10-065x(2001)055[0153:tbdrad]2.0.co;2

Searcy, W. A., & Nowicki, S. (2005). *The evolution of animal communication: Reliability and deception in signaling systems.* Princeton, NJ: Princeton University Press.

Sordahl, T. A. (1988). The American avocet (*Recurvirostra americana*) as a paradigm for adult auto-mimicry. *Evolutionary Ecology, 2*(3), 189–196. https://dx.doi.org/10.1007/bf02214282

Stymacks. A. (2018, March 15). Why ravens and crows are earth's smartest birds. *National Geographic.* Retrieved from http://www.news.nationalgeographic.com

Tanner, J. E., & Byrne, R. W. (1993). Concealing facial evidence of mood: Perspective-taking in a captive gorilla? *Primates, 34,* 451–457. https://dx.doi.org/10.1007/bf02382654

Thompson, N. S. (1986). Deception and the concept of behavioral design. In R. W. Mitchell & N. S. Thompson (Eds.), *Deception: Perspectives on human and nonhuman deceit* (pp. 53–65). New York, NY: State University of New York Press.

Tormoen, E. (2013, December 5). Orchid mantis lures prey with beauty. *Outside.* Retrieved from http://www.outsideonline.com

Vander Meer, R. W., & Wojcik, D. P. (1982). Chemical mimicry in the *Myrmecophilous* beetle *Myrmecaphodius excavaticollis. Science, 218,* 806–808. https://doi.org/10.1126/science.218.4574.806

Wickler, W. (1968). *Mimicry in plants and animals.* New York, NY: World University Library.

Wickler, W. (2013). Understanding mimicry—with special reference to vocal mimicry. *Ethology, 119*(4), 259–269. https://dx.doi.org/10.1111/eth.12061

Williams, K. S., & Gilbert, L. E. (1981). Insects as selective agents on plant vegetative morphology: Egg mimicry reduces egg laying by butterflies. *Science, 212,* 467–469. https://dx.doi.org/10.1126/science.212.4493.467

Wu, H., Liu, G., & Shi, M. (2017). Interferon gamma in African trypanosome infections: Friends or foes? *Frontiers in Immunology, 7,* 1105. https://dx.doi.org/10.3389/fimmu.2017.01105

Yoshino, T. P., & Coustau, C. (2011). Immunobiology of *Biomphalaria*–trematode interactions. In R. Toledo & B. Fried (Eds.), *Biomphalaria snails and larval trematodes* (pp. 159–189). New York, NY: Springer.

Zohary, D., Hopf, M., & Weiss, E. (2012). *Domestication of plants in the Old World: The origin and spread of domesticated plants in Southwest Asia, Europe, and the Mediterranean Basin.* Oxford, England: Oxford University Press.

"I grew up Catholic. I don't go to church anymore, but I went on Christmas Eve with my parents—because you know how you lie to your parents?"
– *John Mulaney*

"Can we get a dog? I promise I'll take care of it."
– *Every kid in history*

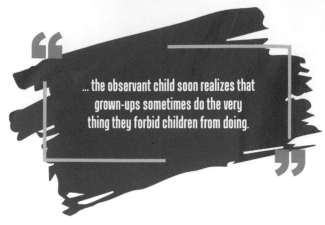
It's fortunate that kids are good problem solvers. Otherwise, they might really be confused by adult messages concerning lying and deception. Early on, children are told loud and clear: "Do not lie. Lying is wrong. You will be punished if you lie." But they eventually learn that some lies are perceived as worse than others and the ability to lie in certain situations can be a valuable part of their budding social competence (Feldman, Tomasian, & Coats, 1999). They even discover that they can be punished for telling the truth as well as for lying (telling a family secret, for example, or repeating gossip). And the observant child soon realizes that grown-ups sometimes do the very thing they forbid children from doing. While it's true that children who observe adults lying are more likely to lie themselves (Hays & Carver, 2014), fewer become chronic liars in adulthood (Serota & Levine, 2014; Stouthamer-Loeber, 1986). Most kids eventually figure it all out. They somehow manage to learn the importance of telling the truth and the necessity of having a moral compass.

How does all this come about? Let's begin by chronologically plotting the development of deceptive behavior. Along the way, we'll consider the kinds of cognitive and behavioral skills that children of various ages employ whenever they attempt to engage in deliberately deceptive acts.

LYING IN CHILDHOOD: A GROWING REPERTOIRE OF DECEPTION

Observations of deceit-like behavior are rare prior to age 2, although there have been examples noted in the context of playfulness (see, for example, Chevalier-Skolnikoff, 1986; Ford, 1996). By age 2, however, and certainly by age 3 (when language skills are exploding), the occurrence of deceitful behavior becomes much more common and its range more varied. It is not possible to establish the exact ages when children acquire certain skills because learning environments and genetic pre-wiring vary from child to child. Nevertheless, the general developmental pattern is as follows:

© noBorders–Brayden Howie/Shutterstock.com

Ages 2 to 3

Between the ages of 2 and 3, children will often make *false statements*, but it's important to recognize that these utterances bear little resemblance to the teenage or adult versions. The following qualifiers are key to understanding the differences:

- Perhaps the most common form of false statements at this age involves *denials of wrong-doing*. These denials usually serve one of two purposes:

  1. **To avoid punishment**: "Billy did it. Not me."
  2. **To get rewarded for good behavior**: "I cleaned my plate. I get a cookie now."

- They seem to have very little understanding of the *effects* their behavior might have on their intended target(s).

- Some false statements are simply *mistakes* based on a limited knowledge of the language they are learning (and experimenting with) during this period of development.

- Some of these false statements are simply the result of *poor memory*.

- Sometimes a child's everyday reality is enriched by his or her *fantasy life* (having an imaginary friend, for example).

- At this age, some false statements are the result of wishful thinking—e.g., saying "My Mom is going to take me to Disneyland" when Mom has never mentioned this possibility.

In most kids, the skills typical of adult lying ability (perspective-taking, intentionality, behavioral control, etc.) have yet to develop significantly. Nevertheless, a few youngsters may be running slightly ahead of the pack, as these examples illustrate:

- An experiment by Chandler, Fritz, and Hala (1989) found evidence that some children between 2 and 3 did perform acts intended to mislead others into believing something that was false. A puppet hid a "treasure" in one of several containers and children were told the purpose of the game was to hide the treasure from adults who were searching for it. Some of these children not only erased the tracks left by the puppet to the container holding the treasure, but made new tracks leading to an empty container.

- Sodian, Taylor, Harris, and Perner (1991) also found a few children under 3 years who understood the idea of creating a false belief, but even these children needed prompting and rarely anticipated the effects of their deception on the target's beliefs.

Even the presence of older siblings does not seem to help a great deal in facilitating the understanding of false beliefs for 2- and 3-year-olds, but it can speed up such learning with children over the age of three-and-a-half (Ruffman, Perner, Naito, Parkin, & Clements, 1998).

Ages 3–6

Children develop a **theory of mind** and thereby acquire **perspective-taking** ability typically between the ages of 3 and 6. The combination of this ability and their expanding knowledge of intentionality and social norms leads children in this age range to lie with increasing frequency and skill. A number of studies support this conclusion.

One of the first forms of deception employed by children in this age range is of the "I didn't do it" variety, in which they violate orders issued by adults and then attempt to conceal it:

- Researchers have studied this phenomenon in "temptation resistance" experiments. A version of this test (QR) was recently featured on the British TV series *What Would Your Kid Do?* In the original scientific versions of these studies, a child is seated in a room and a toy is placed behind her. An adult experimenter then instructs the child not to peek at or play with the toy for several minutes while the adult leaves the room. The child is covertly monitored while alone in the room and, when the experimenter returns, is asked whether she followed the instructions. Many children don't obey the order, so researchers are watching to see if they confess the transgression or lie about it (Lewis, 1993; Lewis, Stanger, & Sullivan, 1989). In numerous studies using this procedure (reviewed in Lee, 2013), most children between 3 and 5 lie in this situation, but the youngest ones aren't especially convincing. For example:

  o When 3-year-olds lie about peeking at the toy and then are later asked by the experimenter to "guess" what the toy might be, many blurt out its name without hesitation, revealing that they both violated the instructions and lied.

  o A 5-year-old girl who lied about peeking later said, "I didn't peek at it. I touched it and it felt purple. So, I think it is Barney."

  o Many 6-year-old peekers subsequently feign complete ignorance of the toy's properties (Evans, Xu, & Lee, 2011).

Leekam (1992) says that by age 4 or 5, children "understand the effects of a false message on a listener's mind, recognizing that the listener will interpret and evaluate a statement in the light of their existing knowledge." In support of this, Sodian et al. (1991) say that by age 4 most kids have developed an understanding of **false beliefs**. These children have a lot to learn about how complex the other person's perspective really is and how many different ways it can be tapped, but the basic mechanism for developing this knowledge is now beginning to function.

As they get older, children incrementally learn to avoid such blatant inconsistencies. Moreover, somewhere in this age range, children begin to tell white lies in situations for which social norms dictate that they not convey awkward truths:

- Talwar and Lee (2002) asked 3- to 6-year-olds to take a photograph of an adult who had a large red mark on his nose. Most children lied to this adult when he asked "Do I look okay for the photo?" but later told someone else that he did not look okay.

- In a similar study, children in this age range were given an undesirable present (a bar of soap) but told the giver that they liked it, even though their behavior while opening it clearly indicated disappointment (Talwar, Murphy, & Lee, 2007). In this wildly popular Vine (QR), for example, Henry does his best to politely feign enthusiasm for the birthday avocado he's just unwrapped.

Despite their sometimes imperfect manifestations of it, this is also a time when we can see a child's early efforts at behavioral control to conceal a lie:

- In-depth analyses of children's nonverbal behaviors by Talwar and Lee (2002) reveal that those in the act of telling a lie mimic the behaviors of people who tell the truth (e.g., making direct eye contact with the listener).

- When the situation calls for children to avert their gaze when telling the truth (because they have to ponder the answer to a question), they also deliberately avert their gaze when lying (McCarthy & Lee, 2009).

- By the age of 6, a child's nonverbal concealment behaviors are coordinated and natural enough to convince many adults that they are telling the truth, including their parents, teachers, social workers, police officers, and judges (Crossman & Lewis, 2006).

Beyond age 6, the deception phenomenon in children begins to evolve dramatically.

Ages 6–9

Beyond age 6, the deception phenomenon in children begins to evolve dramatically. When a young child begins spending time with other children in school, new developmental challenges arise. The process of developing and managing new interpersonal relationships and undertaking new tasks may create new conditions for lying. Ford (1996) says some children experience what he calls "double bookkeeping"—keeping family secrets that might be embarrassing or espousing beliefs that fit one's peer group, but not one's family.

In addition, many children in this age range are spending a lot of time playing board, card, and sports games that highlight the need for deceptive skills in order to win the game. Vasek (1986, p. 288) puts it this way: "Games, then, provide a situation in which children can practice deception and its detection, learn about its functions, and become acquainted with the social implications of its use."

During this period, children are facing a variety of conditions that may prompt them to lie and an increasing variety of situations provide ample opportunities to practice, elicit feedback, and refine their deceptive skills. The teenagers Ekman (1989) interviewed recalled that their first experience in "getting away with" a lie was when they were between 5 and 7 years old. Whereas some young communicators will gain confidence in their deceptive ability, others will be reminded that they still have a lot to learn, as the following classic dialogue illustrates (Krout, 1931, p. 23):

> "Hello Miss Brown, my son is very ill and, I am sorry to say, cannot come to school today."
>
> "Who is talking?" asked the teacher.
>
> "My father," the boy answered.

This is also a time when adults start pressing children to learn **politeness norms** (which often require deception). Saarni (1984) promised an attractive toy to groups of 6-, 8-, and 10-year-old children if they performed a particular task for her. After completing the task, the children were given a less attractive toy than had been promised and their facial expressions were observed. Analysis of the expressions showed that as the child gets older, *less* disappointment is shown in the face. The girls in Saarni's study manifested this ability to facially mask their disappointment in the name of politeness earlier than the boys.

Ten-year-olds with more Machiavellian tendencies may be especially adroit at deception ...

Ages 10–12

By the end of this period, most children have developed adult-like deception skills. This doesn't mean that these kids have nothing more to learn—only that many 10–12-year-old children are able to (and do) lie without being detected. Ten-year-olds with more Machiavellian tendencies may be especially adroit at deception, capable of using bribery, two-sided arguments, transferal of blame to others, and lies of commission and omission.

By about age 11 they also think about lying and truth telling differently. Their views are in sharp contrast to 5-year-olds. For example, most no longer believe it is always wrong to lie and fewer are willing to say they've never lied (Peterson, Peterson, & Seeto, 1983). Adults, in turn, hold these pre-teens responsible for knowing what they are doing.

Along with their increasing verbal skills, children in this age range also show a greater sophistication in their ability to manage their nonverbal behavior as well (DePaulo & Jordan, 1982; Talwar & Crossman, 2011). Notably, the encoding skills of 11- and 12-year-old girls are likely to be superior to their male counterparts.

Ages 13–18

With adult-like deception ability in place by the beginning of adolescence, children practice their skills in an ever-expanding range of social interactions. In this period, teens not only hone their skills, but also develop more sophisticated reasoning about whether and when lying serves their interests. The decision to lie or not depends in part on a consideration of whether it will assist in the attainment of a goal and at what cost.

The weighing of various facts in this cost-benefit analysis becomes more complicated with age. In particular, adolescents give more thought to *probabilities* than younger children, considering not merely the punishment for getting caught but also the different *likelihoods* of getting caught in various circumstances. They also consider consequences of getting caught that extend beyond the immediate context, such as disappointment in the eyes of friends, parents, and teachers. In particular, parental disappointment is a consequence that could hinder the expansion of autonomy children crave in their teens. Thus if getting caught seems like more than a remote possibility, a teen might be hesitant to risk this anticipated cost regardless of a lie's immediate benefit (Perkins & Turiel, 2007).

" ... adolescents give more thought to *probabilities* than younger children, considering not merely the punishment for getting caught but also the different *likelihoods* of getting caught ... "

As the first generation to grow up immersed in an online world, teens today have opportunities to deceive via technological channels that their parents didn't have at their age. What's more, teens often exploit their parents' lack of experience and technical limitations to engage in digital deception that can be risky, rude, and sometimes illegal. Consider the results of this survey of over a thousand teenagers and their parents about online behavior (McAfee, 2013):

- About half of the teenagers admitted searching the Internet for material they believed their parents would not approve of (pornography, simulated or real violence, etc.). When asked, 86% of the parents didn't believe their children would do these things.

- About 70% of teens overall reported hiding their online behavior from their parents. The frequency with which the young respondents reported digital deception was clearly fueled by their parents' complacency and cluelessness.

- 62% of parents reported believing their kids cannot get in serious trouble online.

- Only 40% of parents reported using software to monitor or restrict their children's online behavior. More than half of the children of these parents claimed to know how to bypass it.

Another way to look at how children's capacity for deception evolves into its adult form is to step back and consider it as a series of critical developmental leaps.

COGNITIVE DEVELOPMENT

In order to truly engage in the kind of behavior adults would consider lies, children have to master skills in five key areas (Lee, 2013; Vasek, 1986):

1. Perspective-taking ("theory of mind")
2. Executive functions
3. Intentionality
4. Social norms
5. Communicating

Because of their fundamental importance in human development, each of these areas deserves a closer look.

Perspective-Taking and "Theory of Mind"

As adults, we take for granted that people have differing needs, beliefs, attitudes, interests, and priorities. But we were not born knowing these things. Somewhere along the way, we had to develop this sense of perspective. Human infants are profoundly "egocentric"—i.e., unable to comprehend that someone else may have a different mental experience from their own and consequently unable to take another person's perspective (Piaget, 1954). As young children develop, they not only learn that other perspectives exist, but also learn how to take those

© Jordan mclenan/Shutterstock.com

perspectives and use them. Children who can recognize that other people are independent entities who can think on their own are thus said to have developed a "theory of mind" (QR) (McHugh & Stewart, 2012).

A coherent theory of mind typically emerges between ages 3 and 5 (although rudiments of this skill, such as following another person's gaze to understand what he or she is looking at, appear earlier). Failure to acquire a theory of mind and perspective-taking skills is a hallmark symptom of autism, a developmental disorder that usually appears early in life (Korkmaz, 2011).

But even for adult humans, perspective-taking can be challenging. Its accuracy is hindered by the "other minds problem," which occurs because we can never know from a first-person perspective exactly how things are experienced in another person's mind.

Some scholars argue that a true understanding of theory of mind is unique to the human species (e.g., Penn & Povinelli, 2007). Regardless, perspective-taking has important social implications:

- In both children and adults, it is often associated with greater empathy, prosocial behavior, and more favorable treatment of the person (or group) whose perspective is taken.

- Instructing people to take the perspective of a person in need often increases feelings of compassion and leads to offers of help (Malle & Hodges, 2005; Vasek, 1986).

- Taking the perspective of another is also essential for someone to engage in deception. Ceci, Leichtman, and Putnick (1992) explain it as the ability to "substitute belief for disbelief, in accepting the stance of the other."

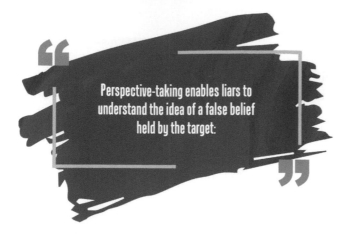

Perspective-taking enables liars to understand the idea of a false belief held by the target:

Perspective-taking enables liars to understand the idea of a false belief held by the target:

- Knowledge gained through perspective-taking is also invaluable to deceivers in determining what messages are likely to create that false belief.

- Some lies can become terribly complex and the liar's ability to anticipate the target's behavior is the difference between a successful and a failed lie.

Executive Functions

What psychologists call "executive functions" (QR) are higher order cognitive skills that emerge in late infancy and continue developing throughout childhood. Three of these functions are critical to the development of deceptive ability:

- **Inhibitory control** is the ability to suppress interfering thoughts or actions (Carlson, Moses, & Breton, 2002). To successfully mislead someone, children must not only utter false information that differs from reality but also conceal the true information it contradicts. To maintain the lie, they must inhibit thoughts and statements contrary to the lie and remember the contents of the lie, at least in the short term.

- **Working memory** is a system for temporarily holding and processing information, for whatever purposes or tasks are at hand.

- **Planning** is also required to maintain a lie in that liars must prepare the contents of a lie prior to uttering it in order to appear convincing to their audience.

Carlson, Moses, and Hix (1998) found that preschool children who experience difficulty with learning tasks that require a high level of inhibitory control, working memory, and planning also have difficulty with deception tasks. Clemens et al. (2010) argue that individual differences in deceptive skill are strongly related to one's ability to regulate behavior and handle the increase in cognitive load a lie creates. Thus, children's maturing executive functions seem to facilitate their increasing success at lie-telling.

Intentionality

As discussed in Chapter 1, lies are not just "mistakes." They are designed to deliberately mislead others. Like any communicative act, lying is governed by considerations of intentionality and conventionality (Lee, 2013). The former concerns various mental states (e.g., intentions, beliefs) involved in communication, whereas the latter concerns the social norms governing conversation (e.g., being polite when receiving a gift). To lie successfully, children must:

- differentiate between their mental state and that of their target

- make statements that effectively conceal the truth while simultaneously inducing false beliefs in the target's mind (the intentionality component)

- understand whether the specific social context they're in prohibits or permits deception (the conventionality component)

Much of the evidence on intentionality comes from studies of children's attempts to conceal their transgressions, which typically use the "temptation resistance" technique mentioned earlier. When children are told to not peek at or play with a toy when the adult leaves the room, many violate the instructions, allowing researchers to examine whether the children will admit or deny their transgression when directly asked about it. In studies conducted in a variety of cultures, most 2- and 3-year-olds confess their transgression, but after 4–5 years of age, most children lie and continue to do so (Lewis et al., 1989; Polak & Harris, 1999; Talwar & Lee, 2002). The importance of intentionality in children's lying also manifests itself in *how* children lie, which has been examined by comparing the nonverbal behaviors of liars with those of non-liars. Such behaviors cannot be distinguished accurately by naïve adults (Crossman & Lewis, 2006; Leach, Talwar, Lee, Bala, & Lindsay, 2004; Talwar & Lee, 2002), including parents, child protection lawyers, social workers, police, customs officers, and judges.

Social Norms

Successful liars must also be aware of the specific social-cultural contexts in which lying is prohibited or permissible. For example, most societies disapprove of lying to conceal transgressions for personal gain, but condone white lies designed to spare others' feelings. Most children over 3 years of age understand that lying to conceal a transgression is inappropriate and that telling the truth is preferred (Lyon & Dorado, 2008). Not surprisingly, however, their knowledge of this social norm doesn't necessarily dictate their actual behavior:

- Children often report believing that lying is morally wrong, but lie anyway.

- In contrast, their knowledge of norms about promises does seem to affect their decisions to lie or not. Children asked to promise to tell the truth about a transgression are less likely to lie than others who are not (Evans & Lee, 2010).

- But they are more likely to lie in situations in which social norms (such as politeness) direct them to refrain from being completely honest (Talwar & Lee, 2008).

When deciding whether to lie or not, children must learn to effectively assess the social context in which the truth or a lie is called for, as well as the specific social norm that motivates it.

Communicating

The preceding list of cognitive abilities must work in concert with certain communication behavior in order for the deceiver to lie effectively:

- Deceivers must have a verbal repertoire from which language choices and persuasive strategies can be implemented as needed. Ideally, these decisions are based on effectively anticipating needs as well as information obtained from monitoring the target's reactions.

- Deceivers also need the ability to effectively manage their own behavior—to mask or hide their true feelings and to avoid enacting any behavior that might make the target suspicious that "something just doesn't seem right"—e.g., too little or too much eye gaze, speech that is too hesitant or too rapid, too many nervous mannerisms or too little movement, or too much vocal uncertainty.

- Effective deceivers not only have to avoid showing some behaviors, they have to enact others. And some of these behaviors will be effective at one age and not another. A pleasant smile on a very young child, for example, may be a very effective cover for deceptive behavior, but the same behavior shown by an adult may arouse suspicion.

The growing child gradually acquires each of these cognitive and behavioral skills and learns how to coordinate them for maximum effectiveness. These are the basic skills necessary to effectively deceive others, but they are also skills that are fundamental to *social competence*. A person with greater social competence is also likely to be the better liar (Feldman et al., 1999; Lee, 2013).

WHY CHILDREN LIE

The motivation for lying during childhood is affected by a variety of factors, including the tasks they face, the kind of relationship they have with their parents, and their own changing cognitive and physical abilities. Scholars who have addressed the question of why children lie have focused primarily on two life stages—early childhood and adolescence.

Lies in Early Childhood

There is widespread agreement that the most fundamental and common reason for lying (at all ages) is the *desire to avoid punishment* for a misdeed (DePaulo & Jordan, 1982; Vasek, 1986). Paul Ekman (1989, p. 19) calls it "one of the most consistent findings" from deception studies.

Although young children lie most frequently to conceal misdeeds, they also tell *prosocial* lies intended to benefit others out of politeness or altruism. Prosocial lies bring two social norms of communication into conflict—the expectations that (a) speakers should be truthful and (b) they should be considerate of others. To tell a prosocial lie, children must have an empathetic understanding of another's mental state and the desire to manipulate that state (e.g., *Dad is embarrassed about his weight, so I will tell him he looks nice*).

Children may be motivated to tell such a lie not only to benefit someone else but also to benefit themselves, in that it enables them to avoid an awkward interaction or be positively regarded by the target of the lie. However, a truly altruistic lie is told solely for the benefit of another and perhaps at a personal cost (e.g., taking the blame for a friend's misdeed). Altruistic lies emerge later than polite white lies as children learn social norms regarding loyalty in friendship and groups (Talwar & Crossman, 2011).

Early childhood is a time when children are learning about words and body movements and how they are used to effectively communicate with those around them. When lies, deceptions, misrepresentations, and false statements take place, they can be understood as part of this process of learning what is acceptable and what isn't, what works and what doesn't. These rules are primarily learned within the confines of the child's immediate family. But family guidelines are put to the test as the child grows older, forms new relationships, and develops his or her own standards for what is appropriate and inappropriate behavior. Peer groups, teachers, and a steadily increasing appetite for autonomy provide additional contexts and reasons for lying.

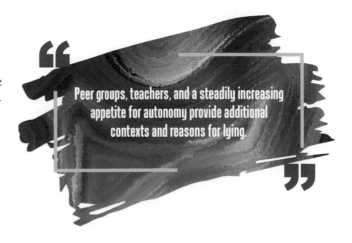

"Peer groups, teachers, and a steadily increasing appetite for autonomy provide additional contexts and reasons for lying."

Lies in Adolescence

Finding a reason to lie during adolescence is about as difficult as finding a reason to be happy when you've won the lottery. The only reason for some adolescent lies is that the adolescent just wants to see if he or she can pull it off and/or the enjoyment derived from the manipulation. Ekman (1989) interviewed adolescents who identified a number of different reasons for lying. Some of these reasons were basically the same as reasons given by young children—e.g., lying to avoid punishment and lying to get something that couldn't be obtained in other ways.

But adolescents also mentioned other reasons for lying that reflected matters especially pertinent to their life stage:

1. Peer group relations
2. Authority figures
3. Increasing independence

Before proceeding, it should be noted that *malingering* (e.g., feigning illness to avoid work) is a separate phenomenon with more intense psychological roots. These and other patterns of deception are discussed in Chapter 8.

Peer Group Relations

Some teenagers want to be "popular" with their peers; most just want to be accepted. The process of learning how to be accepted by one's peers presents teens with a number of situations that inevitably involve decisions about whether and/or how to tell the truth. Some common situations include:

• making themselves look good to others by magnifying or inventing experiences

• the invention of negative stories about others in an effort to clearly distinguish oneself from those in the "out-group"

• keeping secrets for friends—even taking the blame for something their friend(s) did. Ekman (1989) found many teenagers willing to lie for a friend. Less than a third of the teens he interviewed said they would snitch on their friend.

Authority Figures

People who are in charge of various aspects of an adolescent's life can expect there will be some efforts to challenge their power. Unquestioningly obeying the directives of authority figures is linked to a developmental stage adolescents believe is behind them. Secrecy and deception are commonly used by adolescents to level the playing field with authority figures. Recognizing that knowledge gives power, lies of omission (e.g., "Nobody asked, so I didn't say anything!") are not unusual. It is, of course, more likely when authority figures expect teens to follow orders as if they were young children, do not reward truth telling, hypocritically hold teenagers to

> Secrecy and deception are commonly used by adolescents to level the playing field with authority figures.

standards of truth telling they do not adhere to, and act infallible. Holt (1982, p. 254) says, "We present ourselves to children as if we were gods, all-knowing, all-powerful, always rational, always just, always right. This is worse than any lie we could tell about ourselves."

Increasing Independence

During adolescence, children gain an increased sense of autonomy within the family. In the course of their teens, they typically are granted decision-making responsibility for an expanding range of behaviors, including choice of dress, friends, and recreational activities. But what happens when adolescents disagree with their parents about the appropriate limits of their autonomy?

- In some cases, they truthfully express their difference of opinion and deal with the conflict it creates.

- In other cases, they lie to avoid a clash. In particular, when parents try to exert influence on an issue that young teens believe to be none of their business (e.g., a dating partner), teens may feel justified in lying to avoid what they perceive as a wrongful encroachment on their privacy (Jensen, Arnett, Feldman, & Cauffman, 2004).

- They may also justify lying in terms of adult social norms about deception they are learning—e.g., acting sorry when you aren't, acting like something somebody said didn't hurt when it did, etc.

But the apparent ease and frequency with which some adolescents lie may taper off as they become young adults. Even though adolescents and young adults both lie to their parents about such things as friends, dates, and money, Jensen et al. (2004) found emerging adults were less accepting of lying and reported lying less frequently than adolescents. Whether we should believe them is anybody's guess.

CAN CHILDREN DETECT DECEPTION?

Even though kids can detect deception more accurately with increasing age, they are not likely to exceed the adult norm of detecting deceptive behavior of strangers at slightly better than chance accuracy (see Chapter 9). At all ages, children who are better able to put themselves in the position of the communicator being judged (role-taking) are likely to

© Ollyy/Shutterstock.com

be capable of better detection. In one classic study, the child's detection task involved judging adults who were lying about whether they liked or disliked someone (DePaulo, Jordan, Irvine, & Laser, 1982). Groups of students from grades 6, 8, 10, 12, and college were tested. The ability to identify dishonest messages as more deceptive than honest ones did not begin to exceed chance to a significant degree until 12th grade. In short, good deception detection skills may not kick in until about age 17.

As kids grow up, they also come to appreciate the fact that it may not always be socially (or personally) desirable to accurately detect deception in others. Male and female high school students who were skilled at reading covert behavior but did not politely ignore these "leaky" behaviors were rated by their teachers as less popular and less socially sensitive. DePaulo and Jordan (1982) found indications that even though girls are capable of detecting deception more accurately than boys, they will sometimes refrain from stealing cues they believe senders do not want read.

THE ROLE OF PARENTS

Parents play an important role in determining how often their children lie, what they lie about, and the ethical framework within which lying is viewed. One way parents teach their children about lying and deception is by the way they respond (QR) to their child's deceitful behavior. Since "not telling the truth" may occur for many reasons and have numerous consequences, this underscores the need for a variety of responses.

When adults *vary* their responses to a young child (according to the way the child misrepresents reality, the context in which it is done, how often it has occurred, how much harm it causes, and the apparent motive for doing it) the child learns what behavior is permissible and what isn't. This learning process is ongoing and adult reactions may vary considerably to the same behavior performed by a 4-year-old versus a 14-year-old.

Parents are role models for their children and when children are regularly disappointed in their parents' behavior, receive ineffective supervision, or can't establish a warm parental bond, the probability of their lying increases (Stouthamer-Loeber, 1986; Stouthamer-Loeber & Loeber, 1986; Touhey, 1973). This process works in both directions. Parents who think their adolescent children are engaging in a lot of concealment and lying seem to exhibit more withdrawal from their children. They are less accepting, less involved, less responsive, and know less about their child's activities and whereabouts (Finkenauer, Frijns, Engels, & Kerkhof, 2005).

Needless to say, the way parents respond to lying (their own and their children's) will go a long way in determining how their kids behave. Experts say parents should consider the following guidelines:

1. Adapt responses to the life stage of the child

2. Consider the effects of double standards

3. Try to "struggle visibly"

4. Practice reciprocity

5. Avoid extreme emotional reactions

Adapt Responses to the Life Stage of the Child

Parents should understand, for example, that the unambiguous certainty that "you should never lie" may be more palatable to younger children than older ones. Furthermore, the extent to which parents hold their children accountable for their lies will probably increase as the child learns what behavior is acceptable and what isn't. Although the way it is done may vary by age, parents may want to practice accountability with their child early and often. For example, the extent to which an adolescent feels comfortable telling the truth to his or her parents is often the extent to which that comfort has been established throughout his or her development. It means children must have some positive experiences in which they told an unpleasant truth if parents expect that behavior to continue.

Consider the Effects of Double Standards

Some parents don't like to admit it, but others freely acknowledge the fact that they lie to their children and lie to others in front of their children even while admonishing their children not to lie. One survey of several thousand parents found 59% of them saying they regularly lied to their kids (Patterson & Kim, 1991). Most parental lies are designed to ease their young child's fears, enrich their fantasy world, or control their behavior. Some appear to be told simply because the parent delights in tricking a very gullible child. A delightful collection of these parental lies includes the following (Connolley, 2004):

• When the ice cream trucks play music, it means they've run out of ice cream.

• There are special factories where bananas are bent before being sold.

• If you pee in the pool, it will rise to the top and spell out your name.

Young children may be more accepting of the paradox that it's okay for their parents to be deceptive even if they themselves are forbidden from doing so. But as children get older, they increasingly scrutinize this disparity. Parents who say they lie to their very young children "for their own sake" may find that their children increasingly see such lies as serving the parents' needs—e.g., to maintain power and/or control over their child or to avoid discussing a difficult topic. As children get older, they increasingly expect to be treated like other adults—especially their own parents.

Try to "Struggle Visibly"

The Josephson Institute of Ethics recommends this behavior to parents. All parents are bound to make mistakes and face difficult dilemmas when it comes to communicating and acting on values—like honesty. But instead of blaming others or denying a problem when problems occur, Josephson says, parents might effectively use such occasions to teach children and serve as a role model by talking about the various factors that prompted the particular deception or lie and reflecting on why it occurred and how similar situations are likely to be handled in the future.

Practice Reciprocity

In the area of human behavior, we often *reap what we sow*, and parenting is no exception. Parental modeling of honesty will in many cases have the effect of encouraging children to behave in honest ways themselves (LoBue, 2017). Trust and respect are likely to beget trust and respect, just as dishonesty, suspicion, and distrust are likely to reproduce themselves.

Avoid Extreme Emotional Reactions

Ekman (1989) says the fear of a parent's intense anger is one of the prime reasons children lie. This doesn't mean parents can't implement punishment for lying nor does it mean they

... fear of a parent's intense anger is one of the prime reasons children lie.

shouldn't act upset. But *extreme* emotional reactions to unpleasant truths may establish a level of fear that causes the child to do anything to avoid it. The child may feel that *telling the truth results in the same punishment* as getting discovered does. Under such conditions, telling the truth has no inherent appeal for children, so it's worth taking the chance that the lie won't be discovered. The parental goal should be to understand what led to the child's deceptive behavior and, if necessary, work with them on ways to avoid the same outcome in the future. A 2017 study by Smith and Rizzo mapped the emotional expectations of 4- to 9-year-old children as it related to either lying or confessing. Not surprisingly, they found that children who expected a more positive emotional reaction from parents were more likely to confess. Talwar, Arruda, and Yachison (2015) found similar results.

DETECTING CHILDREN'S DECEPTION

There will always be a few kids (in all age groups) whose lies are difficult to accurately detect.

As a general rule, though, how effective adults are at detecting deception by children varies according to the child's age. Not surprisingly, adults and children alike are more successful at detecting lies told by very young children. That accuracy gradually *decreases* as the detection targets get older. Key findings in this particular area of research include:

- In general, adults are better able to detect younger than older children's lies (e.g., Feldman et al., 1999; Feldman & White, 1980; Morency & Krauss, 1982). This could be explained by younger children's lies being particularly transparent. Children only gradually acquire the cognitive and behavioral sophistication necessary to conceal through control of non-verbal behaviors. Indeed, Talwar and Lee (2008) found that children's ability to manage verbal behavior associated with successful lying (in temptation resistance experiments, at least) increased with age.

- However, some studies have found that adults were more accurate in judging the lies of older children rather than younger. These researchers speculate that the older children were more cognizant of the negative consequences of lying than the younger ones, which made them more anxious and thus less able to conceal their lies:

  o When Newcombe and Bransgrove (2007) asked adults to rate the accuracy of two conflicting retellings of a children's story from same-aged pairs—one accurate and one inaccurate—they were more accurate in judging older pairs (i.e., 9-year-olds or adults) than younger pairs (4-year-olds).

  o Similarly, a study by Nysse-Carris, Bottoms, and Salerno (2011) found that lay adults and "expert" detectors (prosecutors, police officers, and clinical social workers) were more accurate in detecting lies told by 6-year-olds than those told by 3-year-olds. Their study used a simulated "high stakes" situation (doing something that children were told could get their parents in trouble).

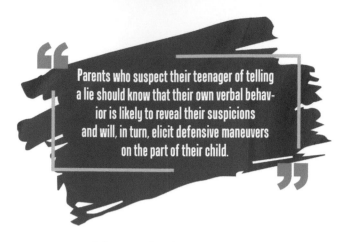

> Parents who suspect their teenager of telling a lie should know that their own verbal behavior is likely to reveal their suspicions and will, in turn, elicit defensive maneuvers on the part of their child.

At any age, most of us are not particularly good at detecting deceptive behavior in face-to-face contexts—with the best accuracy rates typically between 50% and 60% (see Chapter 9). As children age, they become better liars, but they also become better detectors and use more sophisticated detection strategies. Parents who suspect their teenager of telling a lie should know that their own verbal behavior is likely to reveal their suspicions and will, in turn, elicit defensive maneuvers on the part of their child. In other words, let the games begin.

CHILDREN TESTIFYING IN COURT

The legal arena is its own unique environment when it comes to the detection of deception in children. Judges, social workers, and mental health professionals are *sometimes* able to judge the veracity of children based on their experience with certain traumatic experiences like sexual abuse. When a child involved in a child custody case freely and unemotionally gives details of the abuse and occasionally uses adult terminology, the professional may suspect that the child is repeating a story that his parent wants him or her to tell. *Actual* incest victims are more likely to be secretive, manifest depression, and retract the allegations before restating them (Ekman, 1989).

Despite a reservoir of experience and knowledge like the preceding example, studies show that experts often find it difficult to distinguish true from false testimony in sex abuse cases (Ceci & Bruck, 1994; Lyon & Dorado, 2008). The story of the McMartin daycare scandal illustrates the unique challenges such cases present.

In 1983, the mother of a two-and-a-half-year-old child called police to report that her son had been sodomized at the McMartin preschool in Manhattan Beach, California. As a result, police and social workers began interviewing hundreds of children who were or had been enrolled in the McMartin preschool. Stories of sexual abuse and satanic rituals were commonly reported. In addition to accounts of child rape and sodomy, children reported such things as the killing of a horse, being taken on an airplane to Palm Springs, being lured into underground tunnels where day care workers dressed up like witches and flew in the air, the drinking of blood and eating of feces, and the exhumation and mutilation of bodies from a cemetery. One child said they had been regularly beaten with a 10-foot-long bullwhip and taken to the Episcopal Church where they were slapped by a priest if they did not pray to three or four gods.

Sounds hard to believe, doesn't it? Not for the prosecutors, who were so sure of their case that they charged seven people. The multi-year trials that captured national headlines involved a series of acquittals, mistrials, and deadlocked juries. During this time, Peggy McMartin Buckey and her son spent several years in jail and their life savings on legal fees. In 1990, all defendants were acquitted (Eberle & Eberle, 1993; Nathan & Snedeker, 1995).

The mother who made the original complaint was later determined to be a paranoid schizophrenic. Neighbors and parents who stopped by the day care facility during the day could not corroborate these bizarre happenings and the police were not able to find *any* physical evidence (e.g., tunnels, witch costumes, and horse bones) to support the allegations. Instead of shutting down the investigation, however, the lack of evidence and corroboration forced prosecutors to make the testimony of the children paramount to the outcome of their case. Were these children telling the truth? It turned out of course that they were not—but why? Videotapes of the initial interviews with children were revealing:

- It was not uncommon for adult interviewers to use leading questions and show children dolls with shockingly realistic genitalia ("He did touch you there, didn't he?").

- Outright coercion was also used—e.g., praising kids who confirmed the offenses and bizarre happenings and telling those who didn't that they were "dumb."

- Sometimes the answers children gave to court-appointed interviewers were the result of first being "coached" (intentionally or not) in discussions with their parents.

As an adult many years later, one of the children admitted he lied in order to please the people who were questioning him (Zirpolo, 2005).

Even though the McMartin case was perhaps the most widely publicized in the United States, there were several similar cases here and abroad during the 1980s. In addition, the allegations of sexual abuse in child custody cases were increasing at this time (indications suggest that between 36% and 50% were later proved to be untrue; Benedek & Schetky, 1985; Cramer, 1991; Ekman, 1989; Green, 1986). Given the obvious importance of determining the truthfulness of children in situations like this, researchers have closely examined issues surrounding a child's competency to tell the truth in court and the extent to which they are subject to adult influence or "suggestion."

Children's Competency to Tell the Truth

In *Wheeler v. United States* (1895), the court determined that age alone was insufficient for determining whether or not a person is likely to tell the truth. Instead, competency is usually based on the answers to some variation of the three questions shown below.

Sometimes the competency exam is done in the courtroom and sometimes it is done solely by the judge in chambers. While there are very young children capable of meeting these criteria, in many jurisdictions they are not likely to be allowed to testify. The standards are:

1. Can the child witness recall and describe past events?
2. Does the child witness know the difference between a truthful statement and a lie?
3. Does the child witness understand his or her obligation to tell the truth in court?

The last of these was often interpreted as determining whether or not the child understands what it means to take an oath. As children age, many will come to realize that while lying isn't always bad, there are certain contexts in which truth telling is paramount. Peterson (1991) found a majority of 6- to 9-year-olds thought it was worse to have a memory lapse in court than at home and worse to tell a self-protective lie in court than at home. (For what it's worth, a slightly higher percentage of undergraduate college students felt the same way).

In the years since McMartin, the trend has been to avoid having children take an oath and instead asking them to promise to tell the truth or in some other way demonstrate that they understand the importance of being truthful in a courtroom setting (see Evans & Lyon, 2012). Empirical studies have demonstrated that explicitly asking children to make this same kind of promise significantly decreases children's deception. For example, Talwar, Lee, Bala, and Lindsay (2004) found that children between 3 and 11 who had made a promise to tell the truth were less likely to tell a lie concealing a transgression their parents had committed. Interestingly, making children promise to tell the truth in court seems to deter lie telling more than discussing the morality of truth telling with a judge, as is required in moral competency examinations in U.S. courts (Evans & Lee, 2010).

... making children promise to tell the truth in court seems to deter lie telling more than discussing the morality of truth telling ...

As for the first of the three standards listed above, the ability to recall and describe the central facts of past events is normally not a problem for most children, even the very young. However, we also know that this ability can be constrained in the following ways:

- Compared to adults, children typically do not report events as fully, coherently, or in the same amount of detail.

- If the event is stressful or associated with one's "private" parts, the reliability of children's reports can be affected in several different ways (see Saywitz, Goodman, Nicholas, & Moan, 1991).

The second of the three standards tests whether children know the difference between truthful statements and lies. A number of studies provide support for such claims. By age 5, most children (though not all) are able to:

- distinguish lies from truth (Bussey, 1992a; Bussey, 1992b)

- distinguish between pretending and lying (Taylor, Lussier, & Maring, 2003)

- understand that it would be a lie if their parent asked them to say something happened that didn't or to make an inaccurate statement to protect a friend (Haugaard & Reppucci, 1992)

These studies also point out that the way children conceive of a lie changes as they grow older. More specifically:

- Young children are prone to see lies as deviations from what they perceive as factual reality, but beginning around age 8 the communicator's *intent* is increasingly used as a key distinguishing factor.

- Because their repertoire of experience is more limited, younger children are more likely to make accurate distinctions between lying and truth telling if they are asked to judge examples they are familiar with.

- The reliability of children distinguishing mistakes and lies is likely to reach adult standards around the age of 12. But it is important to remember that even adults are sometimes far from perfect in their ability to make such distinctions: Peterson et al., (1983) found half of the adults they tested labeled an exaggeration as a lie and 30% of them labeled an act of admitted guessing as a lie.

The difficulty in determining a young child's ability to distinguish between truthful statements and lies makes it critical that the adults involved adapt their language use to the level of the child and to clarify responses.

Suggestibility and Children's Testimony

As the McMartin case tragically illustrated, a primary reason child witnesses give false testimony is that they are coerced or misled by adults. Some believe that, given the right conditions, an adult can get a child to agree with virtually anything they are told—despite the child's recollections to the contrary. While anything is possible, here's what we know with some confidence based on the studies:

- It is true that children between the ages of 3 and 5, as a group, are more suggestible than older children and adults.

- But we also know that children who are highly resistant to adult suggestions are found in all age groups.

- In addition, the same child may be highly suggestible in some situations and not others (Eisen, Goodman, Qin, & Davis, 1998; Doris, 1991).

The following are common ways that adult interviewers exert influence over the recollections of children (Bruck & Ceci, 1999; Ceci & Bruck, 1995):

- **Interviewer biases**: Adult professionals who normally interview children in abuse cases likely come with preconceptions of what happened. Children may detect these expectations and biases and allow them to enter into their memory of an event. A common way this is done is through the use of leading questions. Adults, as well as children, are subject to the effects of leading questions, but very young children are especially susceptible. Another way interviewers can convey their biases is by mentioning inferred traits (positive or negative) of the people involved in an event—e.g., "Did you see the bad man hit the woman?" (Leichtman & Ceci, 1995).

- **Selective reinforcement of information provided**: Let's assume a child is being interviewed and the interviewer suspects sexual abuse. Whenever the child mentions anything that fits the interviewer's expectations, the interviewer becomes attentive—encouraging the child to talk and telling the child how good they are to talk about this with the interviewer.

- **Peer pressure**: Young interviewees may be told that other children have already said that a particular act or event occurred. This can be a powerful force in leading the young child to an altered recollection. Principe and Ceci (2002) found that leading questions combined with either the presence of peers or a discussion of the event with peers led to inaccurate reports and the addition of information that was not experienced by these young children.

- **Dolls with realistic genitalia**: Because virtually all the dolls children play with do not have realistic genitals, this feature will draw their attention in a leading manner. First introduced in the 1970s, such anatomically detailed dolls were widely believed to be helpful in interviews with children suspected of being sexually abused. The research, however, does not indicate that anatomically detailed dolls add any validity beyond a child's responses to verbal questioning alone (Ceci & Bruck, 1993; Poole & Bruck, 2012).

Young children are most suggestible on matters they don't care a lot about, such as issues or events that:

- are unfamiliar to them
- lack personal meaning for them
- pertain to details they see as peripheral or irrelevant

But some children may be more suggestible in various situations—particularly those who have negative or unreliable life experiences and perceive they have little power (Bugental, Shennum, Frank, & Ekman, 2001).

The legal system in the United States has recognized that the testimony of young children can also be altered by the presence of a perceived threat (Talwar et al., 2004). This recognition has resulted in the establishment of two related precedents:

1. The U.S. Supreme Court allowed child abuse victims to testify over closed-circuit television when the presence of the accused will create "serious emotional distress" (*Maryland v. Craig*, 1990).

2. In 1999, the same court extended this privilege to children who *witness* a traumatic event like sexual abuse and can prove serious emotional distress will occur in the presence of the person they are accusing.

In both cases, there is an opportunity for the defendant's lawyer to cross-examine the witness. These decisions were designed to protect the child witness and ensure truthful testimony, but critics suggest they violate the Sixth Amendment to the United States Constitution, which gives the accused the right to confront their accusers. Some also believe that the use of closed-circuit testimony tells the jury that the defendant is a person whom children fear for a good reason—because he or she is guilty. Orcutt (1998) did not find this to be true, but her experiment did not involve a defendant accused of rape or assault.

Obtaining Accurate Child Testimony

Very young children can produce fairly accurate accounts of their experiences when they are interviewed in a non-suggestive and neutral manner (QR). However, as we noted earlier, there are a variety of possible pitfalls associated with interviewing child witnesses. As a result, the following guidelines have been proposed (Davies, 2004; Saywitz & Geiselman, 1998):

- Establish pleasant surroundings for the child.

- Begin the interview with rapport-building small talk that is unrelated to the testimony. Tell the child that he or she knows what happened and the interviewer doesn't so the child is just being asked to tell the truth about everything he or she remembers. The child is instructed that it is okay to say, "I don't know" or "I don't understand," but the child is also asked to make a promise to tell the truth. During this phase, the interviewer may also want to demystify the legal context and allay fears associated with it.

- Begin by asking the child an open-ended question about what is remembered about the incident in question. Let them talk uninterrupted.

- Children often respond without much elaboration so questioning is the next step. Interviewers should understand that even though probing is likely to elicit more information, it may also increase the chances that the child will provide more incorrect information. Interviewers should do everything they can to avoid leading questions; to use appropriate age-adapted language; to avoid condescension, accusation, or intimidation; and to be open to more than one explanation of what happened.

- Conclude the interview on a positive note and with a brief summary of how the child's testimony is understood.

Even skilled interviewers who try to follow the preceding guidelines may sometimes find themselves using imprecise language, making incorrect assumptions, and unintentionally leading a child witness to false testimony. Consider, for example, the child in the following interview who has *not* been to his or her grandmother's house on the day in question.

Adult Q1:	*Where have you been today?*
Child:	*(No answer)*
Adult Q2:	***Did you visit Grandma perhaps, have you been to her house?***
Child:	*(Child makes a head nod)*
Adult Q3:	*OK, that is nice, did you like it at grandma's place?*
Child:	*(Child makes another head nod)*

The interviewer's second question (in bold) could easily be misinterpreted by the child as "Have I *ever* been to Grandma's house?" (Vrij, 2000, p. 115).

SUMMARY

- There are certain cognitive and behavioral abilities that children need in order to engage in what most adults in this culture call lying. The child must be able to understand that other people see things in different ways than they do and that they can mentally make contact with some of the other person's reality through a *theory of mind* and *perspective-taking*. Lying also requires children to have executive functions like inhibitory control so that they can conceal the truth they are trying to mislead others about. They also must understand *intentionality* and the *social norms* operating in different contexts where they might consider lying. A lie is intentionally performed to change another person's reality. In addition, children must learn that the other person has intentions, too, and may be trying to detect deception. In many contexts, social norms dictate that it is wrong to lie (e.g., lying for personal gain), but in others the norms encourage deception (e.g., expressing gratitude for an undesirable gift). Children must be able to distinguish between these contexts in order to weigh the costs and benefits of lying in a particular situation. They also need to have the communication skills to perform the deceptive act. This requires a linguistic repertoire, an understanding of situational norms and expectations, and the ability to manage/control their own behavior in a manner consistent with the lie being told.

- Before the age of 4, children engage in some "deceit-like" behaviors, but most of these children do not have the necessary cognitive and behavioral skills for lying as it is understood by most adults. By age 4 or 5, many children seem to have installed the basic deception program. From this point on, we see a gradual refinement of their cognitive and behavioral skills necessary for lying. Going to school provides an expanding number of relationships and opportunities for testing these skills. By the time they are 11 or 12, their skills are well-developed and lies are difficult to detect even though there is still room for considerable refinement. Lies are most easily detected with very young children, even though there are some kids who lie without being detected at all ages.

- Children lie for a variety of reasons, but avoiding punishment seems to be the primary one. Dealing with popularity, status, and influence in peer groups; learning to deal with authorities; and seeking greater independence/autonomy are tasks that gain importance during adolescence and provide additional occasions for lying and deception.

- An important part of understanding childhood lies is found in the behavior of their parents. Parents may lie to the very children from whom they are demanding the truth. Parents will sometimes argue that they lie to their children to protect them, but these lies are often performed to protect the parents themselves—to avoid having to talk about a difficult topic, to maintain power or control over their child, etc. Experts say parents need to adapt their teachings on honesty and lying to the developmental stage of the child; to be careful of asking older children to adhere to rules the parents break; to avoid pretending that they know all the right answers in front of their children, but show them how they continue to struggle to do better; to recognize that they are a model for their children and their children may behave as they do; and to make sure the punishment for children who tell the truth isn't just as severe as the punishment for lying.

• The extent to which children can and will tell the truth in a court of law became a major issue after several cases involving charges of widespread sexual abuse in day care facilities in the 1980s and simultaneously increasing charges of sexual abuse in child custody cases. Even though young children do not often testify, those who do must pass a competency exam that tries to determine if the child is capable and willing to tell the truth. Children are capable of reporting the basic facts of an event, but details are often obtained through interviewing. Suggestibility through these interviews has been a major focus of social scientists. Some children are generally more suggestible than others, but suggestibility can be induced in most children through intimidation, accusation, leading questions, selective reinforcement, peer pressure, and dolls with realistic genitals.

EXERCISES

1. Note similarities and differences between the four levels of nonhuman deception (Chapter 4) and the developmental stages of human deception abilities described in this chapter.

2. Interview one parent who has a child who is either age 4, 5, or 6; interview another parent with a child who is either age 11, 12, or 13. Neither parent should be your own. Compare their answers and indicate what you learned. Use follow-up questions as needed, but ask these basic questions:

   a. Has your child ever lied to you?
   b. If so, about what? If not, why not?
   c. If your child has lied to you, how did you deal with it?
   d. Did you ever lie to your child?
   e. If so, about what? If not, explain what counts as a lie for you.
   f. What is the most important thing to teach children about honesty? What is the best way to teach children about honesty?

3. Interview one child who is either age 4, 5, or 6; interview another child who is either age 11, 12, or 13. Neither child should be a sibling. Compare their answers and

indicate what you learned. You may also want to comment on your own interviewing behavior. Use follow-up questions as needed, but ask these basic questions:

a. Did you ever lie to your parents? If so, about what? If not, why not?
b. Did you ever get caught in a lie to your parents? What happened? How did they react?
c. Has either of your parents ever lied to you? If so, about what? If not, how do you know?
d. What is the most important thing for parents to teach their children about honesty?
e. What is the best way for parents to teach children about honesty?

OF INTEREST

In this popular TED Talk, psychologist Kang Lee, a renowned expert on deception in childhood, summarizes key findings from 20 years of research. Among other topics, he addresses three common misconceptions about children and lying: (1) Children only begin to lie after entering elementary school; (2) children are poor liars that adults can easily catch; and (3) if children lie at a very young age, it must be the result of a character flaw.

A child's testimony is often the only evidence of alleged abuse. It is therefore critical to make sure that forensic interviews are free from bias in order to reduce the possibility of a false report. In this paper, the authors make recommendations based on their summary of the latest research. They begin by noting that the suggestibility of a child does not always decrease with age.

REFERENCES

Benedek, E., and Schetky, D. (1985). Allegations of sexual abuse in child custody cases. In E. Benedek & D. Schetky (Eds.), *Emerging issues in child psychiatry and the law* (pp. 145–156). New York, NY: Brunner Mazel.

Bruck, M., & Ceci, S. J. (1999). The suggestibility of children's memory. *Annual Review of Psychology*, *50*(1), 419–439. https://dx.doi.org/10.1146/annurev.psych.50.1.419

Bugental, D. B., Shennum, W., Frank, M., & Ekman, P. (2001). "True lies": Children's abuse history and power attributions as influences on deception detection. In V. Manusov & J.H. Harvey (Eds.), *Attribution, communication behavior, and close relationships* (pp. 248–265). New York, NY: Cambridge University Press.

Bussey, K. (1992a). Children's lying and truthfulness: Implications for children's testimony. In S.J. Ceci, M.D. Leichtman, and M.E. Putnick (Eds.), *Cognitive and social factors in early deception* (pp. 89–109). Hillsdale, NJ: Erlbaum.

Bussey, K. (1992b). Lying and truthfulness: Children's definitions, standards, and evaluative reactions. *Child Development*, *63*(1), 129–137. https://dx.doi.org/10.2307/1130907

Carlson, S. M., Moses, L. J., & Breton, C. (2002). How specific is the relationship between executive functioning and theory of mind? Contribution of inhibitory control and working memory. *Infant and Child Development*, *11*(2), 73–92. https://dx.doi.org/10.1002/icd.298

Carlson, S. M., Moses, L. J., & Hix, H. R. (1998). The role of inhibitory control in young children's difficulties with deception and false belief. *Child Development*, *69*(3), 672–691. https://dx.doi.org/10.2307/1132197

Ceci, S. J., & Bruck, M. (1993). The suggestibility of the child witness. *Psychological Bulletin*, *113*(3), 403–439. https://dx.doi.org/10.1037//0033-2909.113.3.403

Ceci, S. J., & Bruck, M. (1994). How reliable are children's statements?… It depends. *Family Relations*, *43*(3), 255–257. https://dx.doi.org/10.2307/585411

Ceci, S. J., & Bruck, M. (1995). *Jeopardy in the courtroom: A scientific analysis of children's testimony*. Washington, DC: American Psychological Association. https://dx.doi.org/10.1037/10180-000

Ceci, S. J., Leichtman, M. D., & Putnick, M. E. (Eds.) (1992). *Cognitive and social factors in early deception*. Hillsdale, NJ: Erlbaum.

Chandler, M., Fritz, A. S., & Hala, S. (1989). Small-scale deceit: Deception as a marker of two-, three-, and four-year olds' early theories of mind. *Child Development*, *60*(6), 1263–1277. https://dx.doi.org/10.2307/1130919

Chevalier-Skolnikoff, S. (1986). An exploration of the ontogeny of deception in human beings and nonhuman primates. In R. W. Mitchell & N. S. Thompson (Eds.), *Deception perspectives on human and nonhuman deceit* (pp. 205–220). Albany, NY: SUNY Press.

Clemens, F., Granhag, P. A., Strömwall, L. A., Vrij, A., Landström, S., Hjelmsater, E. R. A., & Hartwig, M. (2010). Skulking around the dinosaur: Eliciting cues to children's deception via strategic disclosure of evidence. *Applied Cognitive Psychology, 24*(7), 925–940. https://dx.doi.org/10.1002/acp.1597

Connolley, M. (2004). *Butter comes from butterflies*. San Francisco, CA: Chronicle Books.

Cramer, J. (March 4, 1991). Why children lie in court. *Time*, 76.

Crossman, A. M., & Lewis, M. (2006). Adults' ability to detect children's lying. *Behavioral Sciences and the Law, 24*(5), 703–715. https://dx.doi.org/10.1002/bsl.731

Davies, G. (2004). Coping with suggestion and deception in children's accounts. In P. A. Granhag & L. A. Strömwall (Eds.), *The detection of deception in forensic contexts* (pp. 148–171). New York, NY: Cambridge University Press. https://dx.doi.org/10.1017/cbo9780511490071.007

DePaulo, B. M., & Jordan, A. (1982). Age changes in deceiving and detecting deceit. In R. S. Feldman (Ed.), *Development of nonverbal behavior in children* (pp. 151–180). New York, NY: Springer-Verlag. https://dx.doi.org/10.1007/978-1-4757-1761-7_6

DePaulo, B. M., Jordan, A., Irvine, A., & Laser, P. S. (1982). Age changes in the detection of deception. *Child Development, 53*(3), 701–709. https://dx.doi.org/10.2307/1129383

Doris, J. (Ed.). (1991). *The suggestibility of children's recollections*. Washington, DC: American Psychological Association.

Eberle, P., & Eberle, S. (1993). *The abuse of innocence: The McMartin preschool trial*. Amherst, NY: Prometheus Books.

Eisen, M. L., Goodman, G. S., Qin, J., & Davis, S. L. (1998). Memory and suggestibility in maltreated children: New research relevant to evaluating allegations of abuse. In S. J. Lynn & K. M. McConkey (Eds.), *Truth in memory* (pp. 163–189). New York, NY: Guilford.

Ekman, P., with Ekman, M. A. M., & Ekman, T. (1989). *Why kids lie: How parents can encourage truthfulness*. New York, NY: Penguin Books.

Evans, A. D., & Lee, K. (2010). Promising to tell the truth makes 8- to 16-year olds more honest. *Behavioral Sciences and the Law, 28*(6), 801–811. https://dx.doi.org/10.1002/bsl.960

Evans, A. D., & Lyon, T. D. (2012). Assessing children's competency to take the oath in court: The influence of question type on children's accuracy. *Law and Human Behavior, 36*(3), 195–205. http://dx.doi.org/10.1037/h0093957

Evans, A.D., Xu, F., &, Lee, K. (2011). When all signs point to you: Lies told in the face of evidence. *Developmental Psychology, 47*(1) 39–49. http://dx.doi.org/10.1037/a0020787

Feldman, R. S., & White, J. B. (1980). Detecting deception in children. *Journal of Communication, 30*(2), 121–129. https://dx.doi.org/10.1111/j.1460-2466.1980.tb01974.x

Feldman, R. S., Tomasian, J. E., & Coats, E. J. (1999). Nonverbal deception abilities and adolescents' social competence: Adolescents with higher social skills are better liars. *Journal of Nonverbal Behavior, 23*(3) 237–249. https://dx.doi.org/10.1023/A:1021369327584

Finkenauer, C., Frijns, T., Engels, R. C. M. E., Kerkhof, P. (2005). Perceiving concealment in relationships between parents and adolescents: Links with parental behavior. *Personal Relationships, 12*(1), 387-406. https://dx.doi.org/10.1111/j.1475-6811.2005.00122.x

Ford, C. V. (1996). *Lies! Lies!! Lies!!! The psychology of deceit*. Washington, DC: American Psychiatric Press.

Green, A. (1986). True and false allegations of child sexual abuse in child custody disputes. *Journal of the American Academy of Child Psychiatry, 25*(4), 449–456. https://dx.doi.org/10.1016/s0002-7138(10)60001-5

Haugaard, J. J., & Reppucci, N. D. (1992). Children and the truth. In S. J. Ceci, M. D. Leichtman, & M. Putnick (Eds.), *Cognitive and social factors in early deception* (pp. 29–45). Hillsdale, NJ: Lawrence Erlbaum Associates.

Hays, C., & Carver, L. J. (2014). Follow the liar: The effects of adult lies on children's honesty. *Developmental Science, 17*(6), 977–983. https://dx.doi.org/10.1111/desc.12171

Holt, J. C. (1982). *How children fail* (Rev. ed.). New York, NY: Dell.

Jensen, L. A., Arnett, J. J., Feldman, S. S., & Cauffman, E. (2004). The right to do wrong: Lying to parents among adolescents and emerging adults. *Youth and Adolescence, 33*(2), 101–112. https://dx.doi.org/10.1023/b:joyo.0000013422.48100.5a

Korkmaz, B. (2011). Theory of mind and neurodevelopmental disorders of childhood. *Pediatric Research, 69*, 101R–108R. https://dx.doi.org/10.1203/PDR.0b013e318212c177

Krout, M. H. (1931). The psychology of children's lies. *Journal of Abnormal Psychology, 26*(1), 1–27. https://dx.doi.org/10.1037/h0070324

Leach, A.-M., Talwar, V., Lee, K., Bala, N., & Lindsay, R. C. L. (2004). "Intuitive" lie detection of children's deception by law enforcement officials and university students. *Law and Human Behavior, 28*(6), 661-685. http://dx.doi.org/10.1007/s10979-004-0793-0

Lee, K. (2013). Little liars: Development of verbal deception in children. *Child Development Perspectives, 7*(2), 91–96. https://dx.doi.org/10.1111/cdep.12023

Leekam, S. R. (1992). Believing and deceiving: Steps to becoming a good liar. In S. J. Ceci, M. S. Leichtman, & M. E. Putnick (Eds.), *Cognitive and social factors in early deception* (pp. 47–62). Hillsdale, NJ: Lawrence Erlbaum Associates.

Leichtman, M. D., & Ceci, S. J. (1995). The effects of stereotypes and suggestions on preschoolers' reports. *Developmental Psychology*, *31*(5), 567–578. https://dx.doi.org/10.1037/0012-1649.31.5.758

Lewis, M., Stanger, C., & Sullivan, M. W. (1989). Deception in 3-year-olds. *Developmental Psychology*, *25*(3), 439–443. https://dx.doi.org/10.1037/0012-1649.25.3.439

Lewis, M. (1993). The development of deception. In M. Lewis & C. Saarni (Eds.), *Lying and deception in everyday life* (pp. 90–105). New York, NY: Guilford.

LoBue, V. (2017, April 10). On raising an honest child. *Psychology Today*. Retrieved from http://www.psychologytoday.com

Lyon, T. D., & Dorado, J. S. (2008). Truth induction in young maltreated children: The effects of oath-taking and reassurance on true and false disclosures. *Child Abuse and Neglect*, *32*(7), 738–748. https://dx.doi.org/10.1016/j.chiabu.2007.08.008

Malle, B. F., & Hodges, S. D. (Eds.). (2005). *Other minds: How humans bridge the divide between self and other*. New York, NY: Guilford Press.

Maryland v. Craig, 497 U.S. 836 (1990).

McAfee. (2013). *McAfee digital deception study: Exploring the online disconnect between parents and pre-teens, teens, and young adults*. Retrieved from http://www.mcafee.com

McCarthy, A., & Lee, K. (2009). Children's knowledge of deceptive gaze cues and its relation to their actual lying behavior. *Journal of Experimental Child Psychology*, *103*(2), 117–134. https://dx.doi.org/10.1016/j.jecp.2008.06.005

McHugh, L., & Stewart, I. (2012). *The self and perspective-taking: Contributions and applications from modern behavioral science*. Oakland, CA: New Harbinger.

Morency, N., & Krauss, R. (1982). Children's nonverbal encoding and decoding of affect. In R.S. Feldman (Ed.), Development of nonverbal behavior in children (pp. 181–199). New York, NY: Springer-Verlag. https://dx.doi.org/10.1007/978-1-4757-1761-7_7

Nathan, D., & Snedeker, M. (1995). *Satan's silence: Ritual abuse and the making of a modern American witch hunt*. New York, NY: Basic Books.

Newcombe, P. A., & Bransgrove, J. (2007). Perceptions of witness credibility: Variations across age. *Journal of Applied Developmental Psychology*, *28*(4), 318–331. http://dx.doi.org/10.1016/j.appdev.2007.04.003

Nysse-Carris, K. L., Bottoms, B. L., & Salerno, J. M. (2011). Experts' and novices' abilities to detect children's high-stakes lies of omission. *Psychology, Public Policy, and Law*, *17*(1), 76–98. https://dx.doi.org/10.1037/a0022136

Orcutt, H. K. (1998). Detecting deception: *Factfinders' abilities to assess the truth*. Unpublished Ph.D. dissertation, SUNY-Buffalo.

Patterson, J., & Kim, P. (1991). *The day America told the truth: What people really believe about everything that really matters*. New York, NY: Prentice Hall.

Perkins, S. A., & Turiel, E. (2007). To lie or not to lie: To whom and under what circumstances. *Child Development*, 78(2), 609–621. https://dx.doi.org/10.1111/j.1467-8624.2007.01017.x

Peterson, C. C. (1991). What is a lie? Children's use of intentions and consequences in lexical definitions and moral evaluations of lying. In K. J. Rotenberg (Ed.), *Children's interpersonal trust: Sensitivity to lying, deception, and promise violations* (pp. 5–19). New York, NY: Springer-Verlag. https://dx.doi.org/10.1007/978-1-4612-3134-9_2

Peterson, C. C., Peterson, J. L., & Seeto, D. (1983). Developmental changes in ideas about lying. *Child Development*, 54(6), 1529–1535. https://dx.doi.org/10.2307/1129816

Piaget, J. (1954). *The construction of reality in the child* (M. Cook, Trans.). New York, NY: Basic Books. https://dx.doi.org/10.1037/11168-000

Polak, A., & Harris, P. L. (1999). Deception by young children following noncompliance. *Developmental Psychology*, 35(2), 561–568. https://dx.doi.org/10.1037//0012-1649.35.2.561

Penn, D. C., & Povinelli, D. J. (2007). On the lack of evidence that non-human animals possess anything remotely resembling a 'theory of mind'. *Philosophical Transactions of the Royal Society B: Biological Sciences*, 362(1480), 731–744. https://dx.doi.org/10.1098/rstb.2006.2023

Poole, D. A., & Bruck, M. (2012). Divining testimony? The impact of interviewing props on children's reports of touching. *Developmental Review*, 32(3), 165–180. http://dx.doi.org/10.1016/j.dr.2012.06.007

Principe, G. F., & Ceci, S. J. (2002). "I saw it with my own ears": The effects of peer conversations on preschoolers' reports of nonexperienced events. *Journal of Experimental Child Psychology*, 83(1), 1–25. https://dx.doi.org/10.1016/s0022-0965(02)00120-0

Ruffman, T., Perner, J., Naito, M., Parkin, L., & Clements, W. A. (1998). Older (but not younger) siblings facilitate false belief understanding. *Developmental Psychology*, 34(1), 161–174. https://dx.doi.org/10.1037//0012-1649.34.1.161

Saarni, C. (1984). An observational study of children's attempts to monitor their expressive behavior. *Child Development*, 55(4), 1504–1513. https://dx.doi.org/10.2307/1130020

Saywitz, K. J., & Geiselman, R. E. (1998). Interviewing the child witness. In S. J. Lynn & K. M. McConkey (Eds.), *Truth in memory* (pp. 190–223). New York, NY: Guilford.

Saywitz, K. J., Goodman, G. S., Nicholas, E., & Moan, S. F. (1991). Children's memories of a physical exam involving genital touch: Implications for reports of child sexual abuse. *Journal of Consulting and Clinical Psychology*, 59(5), 682–691. https://dx.doi.org/10.1037/0022-006x.59.5.682

Serota, K. B., & Levine, T. R. (2014). A few prolific liars: Variation in the prevalence of lying. *Journal of Language and Social Psychology, 34*(2), 138–157.

Smith, C. E., & Rizzo, M. T. (2017). Children's confession- and lying-related emotion expectancies: Developmental differences and connections to parent-reported confession behavior. *Journal of Experimental Child Psychology, 156*, 113–128. https://dx.doi.org/10.1016/j.jecp.2016.12.002

Sodian, B., Taylor, C., Harris, P. L., & Perner, J. (1991). Early deception and the child's theory of mind: False trails and genuine markers. *Child Development, 62*(3), 468–483. https://dx.doi.org/10.2307/1131124

Stouthamer-Loeber, M. (1986). Lying as a problem behavior in children: A review. *Clinical Psychology Review, 6*(4), 267–289. https://dx.doi.org/10.1016/0272-7358(86)90002-4

Stouthamer-Loeber, M., & Loeber, R. (1986). Boys who lie. *Journal of Abnormal Child Psychology, 14*,(4), 551–564. https://dx.doi.org/10.1007/bf01260523

Talwar, V., Arruda, C., & Yachison, S. (2015). The effects of punishment and appeals for honesty on children's truth-telling behavior. *Journal of Experimental Child Psychology, 130*, 209–217. https://dx.doi.org/10.1016/j.jecp.2014.09.011

Talwar, V., & Crossman, A. (2011). From little white lies to filthy liars: the evolution of honesty and deception in young children. *Advances in Childhood Development and Behavior, 40*, 139–79. https://dx.doi.org/10.1016/B978-0-12-386491-8.00004-9

Talwar, V., & Lee, K. (2002). Development of lying to conceal a transgression: Children's control of expressive behavior during verbal deception. *International Journal of Behavioral Development, 26*(5), 436–444. https://dx.doi.org/10.1080/01650250143000373

Talwar, V., & Lee, K. (2008). Social and cognitive correlates of children's lying behavior. *Child Development, 79*(4), 866–881. https://dx.doi.org/10.1111/j.1467-8624.2008.01164.x

Talwar, V., Lee, K., Bala, N., & Lindsay, R. C. L. (2004). Children's lie-telling to conceal a parent's transgression: Legal implications. *Law and Human Behavior, 28*(4), 411–435. https://dx.doi.org/10.1023/b:lahu.0000039333.51399.f6

Talwar, V., Murphy, S. M., & Lee, K. (2007). White lie-telling in children for politeness purposes. *International Journal of Behavioral Development, 31*(1),1–11. https://dx.doi.org/10.1177/0165025406073530

Taylor, M., Lussier, G. L., & Maring, B. L. (2003). The distinction between lying and pretending. *Journal of Cognition & Development, 4*(3), 299–323. https://dx.doi.org/10.1207/s15327647jcd0403_04

Touhey, J. E. (1973). Child-rearing antecedents and the emergence of Machiavellianism. *Sociometry, 36*(2), 194–206. https://dx.doi.org/10.2307/2786566

Vasek, M. E. (1986). Lying as a skill: The development of deception in children. In R. W. Mitchell & N. S. Thompson (Eds.), *Deception perspectives on human and nonhuman deceit* (pp.271–292). Albany, NY: SUNY Press.

Vrij, A. (2000). *Detecting lies and deceit: The psychology of lying and the implications for professional practice.* New York, NY: Wiley.

Wheeler v. United States, 159 U.S. 523 (1895).

Zirpolo, K. (October 30, 2005). I'm sorry. *Los Angeles Times Magazine*, 10–13, 29.

CHAPTER 6 Self-Deception

"I did that, says my memory. I could not have done that, says my pride, and remains inexorable. Eventually—the memory yields."
– *Friedrich Nietzsche*

"You can fool yourself, you know. You'd think it's impossible, but it turns out it's the easiest thing of all."
– *Jodi Picoult*

Most people admit to having some first-hand experience with "self-deception." The problem is that the experiences people call self-deception include many different psychological and social processes, and so the essence of the phenomenon is elusive (Patten, 2003). Rather than looking for something that characterizes all cases of perceived self-deception, Sanford (1988) says we would do well to think of them as simply sharing a "family resemblance." Self-deception, then, like so many other things in the human experience, may be a "many-splendored thing." Consider the similarities and differences in the following scenarios:

- Rick is a college student who is taking a basic communication course, because he wants to be a communication major. He made a D on the first two tests and a C on the term paper. He believes that the material is easy and that he understands it completely, but also that his grades do not reflect what he knows. He points out that he makes a B in "most of his classes." He also believes he is smarter than other students who are getting higher grades, but his grade is a result of "tricky" test questions and a professor whose lectures are boring.

- Cassar and Craig (2009) asked entrepreneurs in the early stages of building start-up companies to estimate the chances that their start-ups would eventually become operating businesses. Later, the entrepreneurs whose start-ups had failed were asked to recall their estimates. Although they had actually estimated their chances of success as 80% on average, they recalled generating more pessimistic estimates, around 50%. Similarly, researchers asked investment bankers to forecast the values of several financial variables (stock prices, currency exchange rates, etc.) one week in advance (Biais & Weber, 2009). After the week had passed, the bankers recalled their predictions as being far more accurate than they really were. Surprisingly, experienced bankers were no less prone to this type of "hindsight bias" than the novices.

- In 2015, NBC reporter Brian Williams (QR) found himself under extreme public scrutiny for lying. A respected news anchor for decades, Williams had publicly claimed he had come under enemy fire while aboard a military helicopter in Iraq in 2003. Others on board with him challenged his account, saying the helicopter they were following had been fired on, not the one they were in. Williams eventually admitted that he "made a mistake," saying "I don't know what screwed up in my mind that caused me to conflate one aircraft with another" (Farhi, 2015).

What do these examples have in common? How are they different? What do they tell us about the needs of human beings and how their minds work? Although they don't always agree on the answers, scholars from many fields of study have tackled these and other questions as they relate to self-deception (Ames & Dissanayake, 1996; Fingarette, 1969; Lockhard & Paulhus,

1988; Martin, 1985; McLaughlin & Rorty, 1988; Mele, 2001; Trivers, 2011). Drawing on these and other resources, this chapter will seek answers to the following questions:

1. What is self-deception?

2. Why do we deceive ourselves?

3. How do we deceive ourselves?

4. What are the effects of self-deception?

WHAT IS SELF-DECEPTION?

A good way to begin exploring the nature of self-deception is to take a closer look at the words themselves: *self* and *deception*.

Self

There are fewer things that seem more certain to us than our sense of self. Most of us don't reflect on it very often, but philosophers such as Descartes (1641/2010) have explored the question for ages. It seems that there are at least three assumptions underlying the sense of self:

- We regard ourselves as **continuous in time and space**. That is, there is something that remains constant so that the "I" at work is the same person at home or on vacation, and the "I" of now is the same person I was last year and will be next year.

- The self is **unified**. The world may enter our consciousness as distinct sights, sounds, smells, tastes, and tactile experiences, but they are assumed to represent a single reality that is integrated and experienced by a single self.

- The self is an **independent agent** that acts in the world based on conscious choices and judgments.

We take these assumptions for granted, but they unravel when scrutinized (QR) (Westerhoff, 2011). Consider the following challenges to these assumptions, which represent just a few out of hundreds of such examples:

- During the time when people live, they undergo significant changes in their bodies, thoughts, and emotions.

- Most of the things we think of as defining ourselves—skills, social roles, beliefs, preferences, etc.—are things that change over time.

- When we observe someone speaking to us, we perceive her lips as moving simultaneously as we hear her voice. However, physicists have established that light travels much faster than sound, so this simultaneity is an illusion that supports a comforting but ultimately misleading sense of perceptual unity (Keetels & Vroomen, 2011).

- Psychological research has demonstrated that conscious consideration of the reasons for making a decision sometimes happens after the decision has already occurred, and thus couldn't have produced the decision in the first place (Hood, 2012; Wegner, 2003).

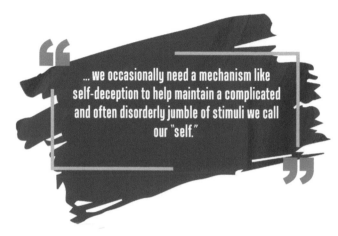

... we occasionally need a mechanism like self-deception to help maintain a complicated and often disorderly jumble of stimuli we call our "self."

The idea of having a unitary self that houses a vast array of thoughts, feelings, and perceptions (some of which are bound to be incompatible and inharmonious) creates an intense *pressure for consistency*, which explains why certain kinds of self-deception occur. In other words, we occasionally need a mechanism like self-deception to help maintain a complicated and often disorderly jumble of stimuli we call our "self." As a result, this self is more recognizable to us and easier to live with. The inconsistencies that self-deceivers wrestle with, according to Chanowitz and Langer (1985), stem from the fact that we are actually composed of many social selves—each of which seeks coherence according to the standards appropriate to its context. Our work self, our school self, and our home self, for example, have separate qualities and sometimes we let them operate independently. But we also have the capacity to relate our various social selves together as sub-units or as a whole. Each of us struggles with the social and psychological demands associated with these processes.

Deception

The idea of deceiving one's self seems sufficiently illogical to some people that they maintain it cannot occur. Self-deception, they argue, is a paradox: You can't have one person *know* that something is a lie and simultaneously *not know* it is a lie. From this perspective, you can't be unaware of something that you are aware of doing.

Deceiving others can occur in a variety of ways, and some of these are similar to the ways self-deception can occur (Nyberg, 1993). Consider these examples of traditional deception:

- Sometimes people deceive others by giving support to a false belief already held by the other person.

- Sometimes people deceive others by hiding the truth or distracting attention away from information that would lead to the truth.

- Sometimes people deceive others by intimating, but not actually saying, that the other person's truthful belief may be fallacious.

Self-deception, too, as we will learn, can be accomplished through similar processes, including:

- **selective information searches** to support preferred ideas
- **hiding ideas** through repression or dissociation
- **distracting attention** away from unpleasant ideas
- **discounting** the value of unwanted information

Deceiving others and self-deception may also produce similar *effects*. For example, sometimes we:

- may be completely unaware that we have deceived ourselves

- suspect we're deceiving ourselves but are far from certain (there's just an uneasy feeling that "something isn't right")

- are pretty sure we're deceiving ourselves, but go along with it anyway

Self-deception does have some qualities that make it unique from traditional deception, and we will explore those throughout the remainder of this chapter.

Self-Deception

There are multiple formal definitions of self-deception (Gur & Sackeim, 1979; Sackeim, 1988), but the one put forth by Starek and Keating (1991, p. 146) effectively identifies the key elements:

> *Self-deception is a motivated unawareness of conflicting knowledge in which threatening knowledge is selectively filtered from consciousness as a psychological defense, thereby reducing anxiety and inducing a positive self-bias.*

It will be easier to understand self-deception if we further examine two key terms in this definition: *motivated* and *unawareness*.

Levels of Awareness

We live in a culture that reveres the idea that we are fully aware of everything we think and do. This belief provides a feeling of self-assurance and control. In turn, it makes us fully responsible for what we do. There's only one problem. There is a vast amount of mental activity that takes place without conscious awareness (Lynch, 2014; Wegner, 2003). In fact, this ability to deal with thoughts at different levels of awareness can be quite functional. We often manage life's trials and tribulations by striving not to know certain things. It enables us to cope with uncertainty, anxiety, fear, confusion, and powerlessness.

© Bruce Rolff/Shutterstock.com

> Self-deception requires a mental environment in which thoughts move among varying states of consciousness.

And it facilitates self-deception. Awareness should be conceptualized as a series of gradations, from fully conscious to completely unconscious. The more aware we are of something, the harder it is to self-deceive about it, and vice-versa. In this sense, self-deception is the flip-side of self-awareness. If we were fully conscious of everything in our mind, different forms of self-deception would be difficult, if not impossible, to enact. Self-deception requires a mental environment in which thoughts move among varying states of consciousness. Our ability to access thoughts and memories can change over time; some thoughts are further removed from our consciousness and those that are well hidden are less accessible to us, though they remain in our consciousness.

We may, for example, be highly critical of some behavior exhibited by another person while being blissfully unaware that we exhibit the same behavior. Over time, however, we may develop an awareness that we, too, act the same way. Self-deception and self-awareness often occur gradually (Rorty, 1996). For example, spouses may continue having sex with partners they no longer love if they themselves are having difficulty admitting how they feel. A religious person who has gradually lost his or her faith over time may continue to attend services.

Intentional vs. Motivated

Intentional self-deception begins knowingly. Such "brazen" self-deception as Newman (1999) calls it, may occur when we need to convince ourselves of something (e.g., that our bad relationship is okay, or that we will survive the semester). But for it to become actual self-deception, the belief in question *cannot remain at its initial level of high awareness*. Through a number of processes, the amount of conscious attention needed to sustain the false belief has to decrease so that the belief becomes more "automatic" and operates outside of our awareness (Lynch, 2014; Wegner, 2003).

Much self-deception, however, occurs without conscious intent. Sackeim (1988, p. 156) explains it this way:

> *It may well be that our success in creating and maintaining self-deception often depends on our lack of awareness of the process. Particularly when what we lie to ourselves about are issues that are highly affectively-charged and critical to our self-esteem.*

In other words, with unintentional deception, emotion is in the driver's seat. When they guide our judgment, emotions can induce biases such as *motivated reasoning*—the tendency to draw conclusions from one's experiences and other data that are emotionally preferable, regardless of their objective accuracy. In Hastorf and Cantril's (1954) classic study of motivated reasoning, students from rival colleges watched film of a football game between their teams and were asked to assess the accuracy of the referees' penalty calls. Students from both schools reported the referees had assessed more unwarranted penalties against *their* team than against the rival. The emotional stake the students had in experiencing solidarity with their colleges and fellow students unconsciously motivated them to "see" different things when they viewed the game.

Motivated reasoning helps explain why political conservatives and liberals in the United States can review the same facts yet draw radically different conclusions about issues such as climate change, income inequality, voter fraud, vaccine safety, homeland security, or the truthfulness of politicians. Their deliberations about these issues tend to make the facts fit their attitudes, not vice versa. Motivated reasoning also reflects a key insight of modern neuroscience—that our thinking is suffused with emotion. Not only are the two difficult to separate, but our feelings come to the surface more quickly than our thoughts (Haidt, 2012). Many scientists have argued that emotions evolved to promote self-protective action in the wild, prompting us to push threatening stimuli away and pull comforting ones close. Our fight-or-flight reflexes thus appear to apply to *information* as well as to physical predators.

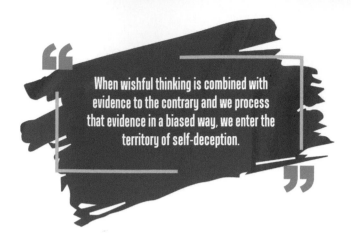

> When wishful thinking is combined with evidence to the contrary and we process that evidence in a biased way, we enter the territory of self-deception.

The Content of Self-Deception

Instances of self-deception are mostly about things we want to be true (or false) but aren't. This is distinct from wishful thinking, which on its own does not meet the content requirements for self-deception. Whereas wishful thinking is wanting something to be true (or false) that is highly unlikely to be, self-deception requires the coexistence of two or more incongruous or contradictory beliefs. When wishful thinking is combined with evidence to the contrary and we process that evidence in a biased way, then we've entered the realm of self-deception.

Another important characteristic of self-deception is that it typically involves beliefs and other matters that *allow some latitude* in determining the truth (Baumeister, 1993). It would be much more difficult, for example, to deceive yourself about an automobile accident you were actually in than to deceive yourself about who caused the accident (people engage in the latter version quite frequently). Some would argue that self-deception involving what others would consider incontrovertible facts (like believing you were not involved in the automobile accident) so radically violates agreed standards for measuring reality that psychological counseling is warranted.

Nevertheless, these beliefs can sometimes be induced in perfectly sane, otherwise rational people under the right circumstances. In *coerced-internalized* false confessions, for example, innocent suspects who are tired, confused, and subjected to highly suggestive interrogation techniques (often lasting many hours) may eventually believe they did commit a crime and sometimes create a false memory to back it up (Kassin, 2005). Thus, even seemingly unquestionable facts or events can become mentally ambiguous under the right conditions—and thereby subject to the domain of self-deception.

Self-Deception: A Social as Well as a Psychological Process

Up to this point, we've focused on the internal mental activities involved in self-deception. But deception of one's self also involves dealing with input from other people:

- Sometimes it is interaction with other people that encourages a person to self-deceive. People who are already deceiving themselves about something will at times present themselves to others in ways that seek confirmation for their self-deception. If they are successful, the reactions of other people help them obtain even greater psychological distance from their self-deception (Gilbert & Cooper, 1985). Self-deceivers are often so hungry for support they will eagerly embrace the slightest endorsement of their belief (Ford, 1996). What happens when a person's self-deception is known to their interaction partner? Sometimes the interaction partner will "play along" and support the self-deception. But sometimes they will try to expose the self-deception, which may be why self-deceivers are not always anxious to discuss their self-deception. Once the subject matter has been made public, self-deceivers no longer have exclusive control over it and run the risk of having to consciously confront a belief they wish to avoid.

> Once the subject matter has been made public, self-deceivers no longer have exclusive control over it and run the risk of having to consciously confront a belief they wish to avoid.

- But even when they are confronted with their self-deception, self-deceivers are not always easily swayed. Kruger and Dunning (1999) conducted several studies of people who scored in the 12th percentile on tests of humor, grammar, and logic. They believed, however, that they were in the 62nd percentile. There are a number of different reasons why these people dramatically overestimated their abilities. One reason is that these unskilled and unaware individuals may have received accurate feedback about their lack of competence but, for some reason, chose not to believe it.

- Another type of "social fallout" was noted by journalist Michael Kinsey. When people avoid talking to others about the subject of a self-deception, they may also have to learn to live with the other lies this subterfuge generates.

- Self-deception may also be fostered by group membership. Intense identification with the values and policies associated with labels like "progressive," "evangelical," and "Wiccan" becomes integral to the self-concept of those who consider themselves to belong to such tribes. The group label creates a filter for processing information in a way that confirms the associated beliefs while contradictory facts are put away, ignored, or reinterpreted (Welles, 1988). Thus, when there is evidence that threatens the beliefs of a primary group, it is a threat to one's own self and self-deception becomes an option. For example, fervently patriotic Americans may find reports of U.S. military members engaging in the torture of prisoners at Guantanamo Bay or border guards separating migrant children from their parents to be so inconsistent with American values that they must be denied, rationalized, or interpreted in some other way. The label "fake news" is often employed in this way; President Trump, for example, frequently uses the term to describe news stories that are factually accurate but nevertheless unflattering to him (Sullivan, 2018).

Interaction with a group can also lead to self-deception on the part of *all* members of the group. Janis (1983) famously called this phenomenon *groupthink*. Groupthink occurs when the members are so intent on preserving agreement that:

- they fail to seriously consider alternative courses of action
- dissent and controversy are unwelcome
- assertions associated with group goals go unchallenged
- critical thinking is replaced by "right" thinking

All this is facilitated when the leader makes an early declaration of what he or she prefers. Janis points out that even when groups are confronted with evidence demonstrating that their policy isn't working or is too risky, they tend to persist in following their original course of action.

Groupthink is more likely to occur within certain types of policy-making groups, within certain types of organizational structures, and within certain situational constraints ('t Hart, Stern, & Sundelius, 1997). In every case, it is more likely when group members all share the same strong group identification:

1. **The group overestimates its power and morality**. It believes it is invulnerable and this belief leads to excessive optimism and extreme risk-taking. The group's inherent morality is never questioned.

2. **The group exhibits closed-mindedness**. Information that challenges the group's goals and decisions is collectively discounted or rationalized. Enemy leaders are stereotyped as too evil, weak, or stupid to deal with.

"What was the decision making process that led to hiring a cat?"

© Cartoon Resource/Shutterstock.com

lying and deception in **HUMAN INTERACTION**

3. **The group exerts various kinds of pressure to ensure uniformity**. Individual members censor (i.e., remain quiet about) their own counter-arguments, leading others to assume that silence means consent. When a member does voice a strong counter-argument, other members make it clear that this behavior is not consistent with a loyal group member.

WHY DO WE DECEIVE OURSELVES?

People deceive themselves for a variety of reasons. Self-deception serves as a way to feel better, to enhance one's abilities, and to more effectively manage the day-to-day stresses of everyday life. This is not to suggest that successful adaptation to life doesn't also involve facing and dealing with unwanted stressors and unpleasant facts. But it does mean that self-deception works effectively alongside self-confrontation and self-knowledge in coping with everyday life. Sullivan (2001) dramatizes the point when she says:

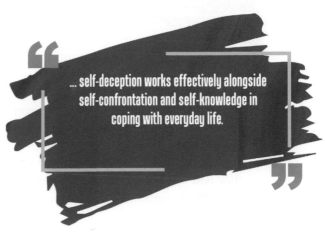

" ... self-deception works effectively alongside self-confrontation and self-knowledge in coping with everyday life.

> *Only by believing, against the evidence, that our lives have meaning and that there is hope for the future do we keep having children, or washing the windows, or spending twelve hours a day designing software that will be obsolete six months after it hits the shelves. Take away the thousand and one delusions we weave and we will be paralyzed by apathy, or run screaming for the hills, or turn to stone while staring into the unblinking void of a Godless, purposeless, blind universe. (p. 180)*

Though Sullivan's prose may be a tad melodramatic, it helps us think about the value of using a radically different perspective at times. Accordingly, the primary reasons for engaging in self-deception are to:

1. enhance self-esteem and protect one's self-concept

2. reduce cognitive dissonance

3. enhance deception skills

4. preserve physical and/or mental health; and

5. enhance competitive performance

Self-deception may occur for other reasons, too, but this list will account for most instances.

... the ability to think of ourselves as more decent, generous, competent, smart, respected, loved, in control, etc. than we really are is probably an indispensable part of effectively negotiating everyday life.

To Enhance Self-Esteem and Protect One's Self-Concept

The need to think well of ourselves is strongly embedded in all of us. In fact, the ability to think of ourselves as more decent, generous, competent, smart, respected, loved, in control, etc. than we really are is probably an indispensable part of effectively negotiating everyday life (Sullivan, 2001).

Very few people think of themselves as having low self-esteem or being "below average" (Baumeister, 1998). In fact, almost everyone reports being better than average across a wide range of personality characteristics and in the fashioning of their own personal narratives:

- In a survey of a million high school seniors, all thought they had above average ability to get along with others and 70% thought they had better than average leadership skills.

- Another survey found 93% of college professors saying they were better than average at their work (Gilovich, 1991). We often deceive ourselves about what we know or knew by using **hindsight bias** (Fischhoff, 1975). When your friend tells you his girlfriend discovered a lie he had told her, it is easy for you to say, "I knew that would happen" (and to explain the reasons why you knew it would happen) when, in fact, you would have been far less certain if asked to make a prediction about what would happen beforehand. We all become a lot smarter after we know how things have turned out.

- People also use self-deception to rewrite the past as a way to feel better about the present:

  - Lewis (2004) says most adults derogate their past and see themselves as having undergone considerable positive change during adulthood—e.g., "I'm more stable than I used to be." In some cases, these comparisons may be valid, but others may be a function of self-deception. Offer, Kaiz, Howard, and Bennett (2000) studied the same people at age 14 and again at age 48. At age 48, the participants in this research tended to recall their family life and the emotional climate at age 14 as a lot more negative than they actually did when surveyed at age 14. Thus, we can boost our self-esteem by believing we have overcome a past that was more difficult than it actually was, by

thinking more positively of our current selves than reality can confirm, and by anticipating a more positive future self than the data would justify (Taylor & Brown, 1988).

- Alternatively, we can distort the past by selectively recalling positive experiences and forgetting negative ones. The memory phenomenon of "nostalgia" induces a sentimentality
for positive past events and periods of significance both to individuals (senior prom, the
college years, "my bachelor days in New York City," "our first date," etc.) and to the public (the "Swinging '60s," the "Tech Boom," "when the Sox won the World Series," etc.).
Nostalgic recollections can provide existential meaning to people by reminding them of
their lived experience during historic events and connections to others who share this
experience (e.g., ask anyone over age 65 where they were, who they were with, and what
they were doing when John F. Kennedy was assassinated).

- Routledge et al. (2011) found that people's propensity for nostalgia correlates positively with their sense of purpose in life and with their resilience in the face of existential threats. Importantly, the therapeutic power of nostalgia comes at the expense
of recall accuracy. For example, when people become nostalgic about positive events
during the "Reagan Era" (booms on Wall Street, the decline of the Soviet Union, the
return of "family values"), they selectively disregard the negative ones (the savings and
loan scandal, the Iran-Contra Affair, the AIDS pandemic, etc.).

To Reduce Cognitive Dissonance

Most of us want (or need) to think of ourselves as reasonable, moral, and smart. When we are
confronted with information implying that we may have acted unreasonably, immorally, or
stupidly, we experience discomfort. The discomfort caused by performing an action that runs
counter to one's positive self-conception was popularized as "cognitive dissonance" by Festinger
(1957), who developed the concept into one of social psychology's most powerful and provocative
theories. According to Festinger, when we experience cognitive dissonance, we work to reduce it
just as we would hunger by eating or thirst by drinking.

But unlike these other drives, the path to reducing dissonance is not so simple or obvious. There
are three basic ways we reduce dissonance. To illustrate, suppose you developed a behavioral habit
that you know is unhealthy—smoking, drinking alcohol to excess, eating junk food, etc. (let's call
it your "nasty habit"). Knowing these behaviors can harm your health and other aspects of your life
will cause dissonance as you observe yourself performing them. So, what do you do?

1. One way to reduce the dissonance is by stopping the behavior altogether, but that can be
difficult, especially if the habit is established or has become a biological addiction.

2. In this case, you might opt for the second dissonance-reducing strategy: justifying your
behavior by changing one of the dissonant thoughts. For example, you might justify

continuing your nasty habit by questioning the scientific evidence purporting to show these things are bad for your health.

3. But even if you are convinced the behavior really is bad, you can still opt for the third reduction strategy of adding new thoughts about your behavior that dampen the dissonance created by existing thoughts. You might say to yourself, "Sure, my nasty habit can be bad for my health, but it helps me cope with the stress of work and life, so there are benefits as well as costs." Or you might put all your faith in a rare exception to the rule: "My uncle Mykel had the same nasty habit for years and still lived into his 90s, so maybe I'll beat the odds too."

These justifications might sound silly to health enthusiasts, which is precisely the point—people experiencing dissonance will self-deceive, sometimes in spectacular ways, to reduce it:

- Dieters who try but fail to lose weight may misremember themselves as being heavier when they started their diets, thereby distorting a big failure into a slight success.

- Executives in fossil fuel industries question the contribution of humans to climate change, despite universal agreement among climatologists that this is the case (Anderegg, Prall, Harold, & Schneider, 2010).

- Environmentalists who embrace the scientific evidence of humans' role in climate change deny that reducing fossil fuel consumption will slow or stall financial growth worldwide, despite a wealth of economic evidence to the contrary (Norgaard, 2010).

- The effect of cognitive dissonance is so strong that even knowing about it doesn't help us avoid it. In fact, Festinger himself was an inveterate smoker who continued the habit up until his death—from liver cancer. On his deathbed he said, "make sure everyone knows that it wasn't lung cancer!" (Gilovich & Ross, 2016).

Occasionally, dissonance-reducing self-deception can actually be helpful. For example, Taylor et al. (1992) found that men who had tested positive for HIV/AIDS, but had unrealistically positive illusions about surviving the illness, lived longer than those who were more "realistic."

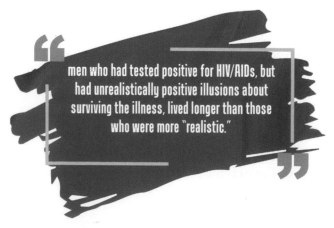

men who had tested positive for HIV/AIDs, but had unrealistically positive illusions about surviving the illness, lived longer than those who were more "realistic."

Most people think of themselves as rational and are indeed capable of rational thought. However, the drive to reduce dissonance can lead to thinking that is not rational but *rationalizing*. People who are in the midst of reducing dissonance get so caught up in convincing themselves they are right as to induce irrational and maladaptive behavior (Aronson, 1997).

To Enhance Deception Skills

... we engage in self-deception in part to make ourselves more adept at deceiving others.

According to evolutionary theorist Robert Trivers (2011), "we hide reality from our conscious minds the better to hide it from onlookers" (p.16). That is, we engage in self-deception in part to make ourselves more adept at deceiving others. Liars who are aware of their lies are more likely to be caught. Liars who are *less* aware of their lies are more likely to project believable sincerity in their communications. Or, as *Seinfeld* character George Costanza (QR) put it, "It's not a lie if you believe it." Trivers argues the desire to more effectively fool our fellow human beings was the primary reason we acquired the ability to self-deceive in the first place.

Essock, McGuire, and Hooper (1988) believes that humans are genetically wired to act in their own self-interests, but they find themselves having to make friends, mate, and manage resources in a society that views altruism and selflessness as an important virtue. Therefore, in order to be seen as a person who is motivated by a concern for others, one may have to engage in self-deception in order to pursue self-interests.

To Enhance Physical and Mental Health

Through self-deception a person may develop a sense of optimism and control over his or her pain or illness. This feeling of control (despite being an illusion) may activate certain neurochemical reactions and behaviors that, in turn, positively affect one's health. Taylor (1989) points out that the "placebo effect" is strong testimony to the power of unrealistic optimism in healing. *Adam Ruins Everything* addressed the topic in a 2017 episode (QR).

Placebos begin as lies. Patients are led to believe that some treatment (e.g., sugar pills or even fake surgery) will improve their health. The administrator, however, expects the placebo to have little or no effect on the person's condition. However, many who have been administered placebos report substantial positive effects, such as reduced pain, less discomfort, and even the disappearance of symptoms related to their illness (for a little while at least).

Self-deception may also be needed as one adjusts to a severe disability. An unjustified sense of optimism and control is often called for as these individuals reframe their quality of life. In what they call the "*disability paradox*," Albrecht and Devlieger (1999) studied 150 people who had serious disabilities and found over 50% of them saying that they had an excellent or good quality of life. For a particularly astonishing example of this phenomenon, you may wish to explore the case of Kaylee Muthart (QR). After gouging out her eyes while high on crystal meth, she says life is "more beautiful now" because the experience served as the turning point that finally got her into rehab.

Self-deception can yield psychological benefits even when it is induced in the moment. Chance, Norton, Gino, and Ariely (2011) conducted an experiment in which participants had an opportunity to cheat on a test by looking at an answer key. Participants then systematically overpredicted their performance on future tests: Rather than attributing their prior achievement to the presence of the answers, they convinced themselves they would do well even without the answer key.

To Enhance Competitive Performance

Self-deception can even enhance performance during athletic competition. Starek and Keating (1991) studied highly skilled swimmers at a national competition and found that the more successful ones engaged in more self-deception.

In the 2016 championship series of the National Basketball Association, the Golden State Warriors competed against the Cleveland Cavaliers. The Warriors held a home court advantage for the series by earning an astounding 72–3 win/loss record during the regular season, the best ever in NBA history and far better than the 57–25 record of the Cavaliers. Playing on their home court, the Warriors handily won the first two games by a combined margin of victory of 48 points, the largest in finals history. When the series moved to Cleveland, the Cavaliers won the third game but lost the fourth. To win the championship, the Cavaliers would have to overcome their 1–3 deficit by winning the next three games, a feat no NBA team had ever accomplished in the finals, let alone one playing against a squad being touted as the greatest of all time. To make matters worse, only one of the three games would be played on their home court; worse still was the widespread belief in the "Cleveland Curse," stemming from the failure of any professional sports team in the city to win a championship since 1964.

All signs pointed to a decisive victory for the Warriors. But Cavaliers captain Lebron James strongly believed in his team's preparation for the challenge, declaring he had "full faith" they could pull it off. This led many sportswriters to call him "delusional" in light of the long odds (Lynch, 2016). But Lebron's faith was ultimately fulfilled—the Cavaliers won the next three games, becoming the first team in NBA history to come back from such a steep deficit and the first professional sports team in Cleveland to win a championship in over

50 years. It should be noted in this case and others like it that self-deception on the part of one's opponent could also be an active ingredient in the outcome—e.g., perhaps the Warriors were so certain they would be victorious that they did not prepare as rigorously as they should have.

HOW DO WE DECEIVE OURSELVES?

Nyberg (1993, p. 81) astutely observed that human self-deception is one of the most impressive software programs ever devised. Briefly, here's how it seems to work:

1. Humans have a general "confirmation bias" to seek out and interpret information that supports their prior beliefs or goals.

2. In particular, our biases toward self-enhancement and self-consistency are especially relevant to self-deception.

3. When the self is threatened with negative information—information deemed potentially harmful to the self—one or more of these biases will be implemented to deal with the threat.

4. However, if the threat persists and promises to do serious damage to the self, arousal occurs and one or more psychological defense mechanisms are activated—e.g., denial, rationalization, and repression.

5. The use of biased thought processes coupled with psychological defense mechanisms affects the selection, treatment, and retrieval of information about the issue in question and leads to a state of self-deception.

Let's look more closely at each of these processes.

Confirmation Bias and Patternicity

There is an obvious difference between the way scientists and attorneys think about and use "evidence." A research scientist is supposed to impartially evaluate the available evidence to draw an unbiased conclusion about the phenomenon (physical, biological, chemical, psychological, etc.) under study. In contrast, an attorney's job is to seek out and use evidence to build a case for one side or the other in a legal dispute. Attorneys are not required to unbiasedly weight the evidence at hand. Instead, they are motivated to weigh heavily only the evidence confirming their legal position. Although professional attorneys engage in this "confirmation bias" consciously and methodically in court cases, laypeople do so unwittingly when they process information in light of their beliefs and attitudes.

Our tendency to seek out and interpret new information in a way that confirms our prior beliefs is a form of the "motivated reasoning" phenomenon described earlier in the chapter. This bias is exacerbated by the human tendency to search for meaningful patterns, or "patternicity" (Shermer, 2012). Finding meaningful patterns can be a very good thing if there is actually something systematic, intentional, and/or intelligent causing the patterns to occur, such as:

- hearing a radio distress signal being broadcast by a sinking ship
- correctly guessing the region where someone grew up based on her accent
- identifying a killer based on clues left at a crime scene, etc.

But people also find what they believe to be meaningful patterns in meaningless noise:

- the Virgin Mary on a piece of toast
- extraterrestrial spacecraft in fuzzy pictures of a night sky
- satanic messages in rock music played backward

Shermer argues that we make these perceptual "errors" because of their relative cost. In our evolutionary history, if our ancestors mistakenly thought a rustle in the grass was a predator when it was really just the wind, it was no big deal. However, if they interpreted the sound as just the wind when it really had been a dangerous predator, this error could be deadly. We lose little or nothing if we think we see or hear something that really isn't there (a false positive), but if we miss something that is there, we might get ambushed or killed.

Self-Enhancement Bias

People have biased thought processes that help them create and maintain a favorable view of themselves (Steele, 1988). These predispositions toward self-flattery are extremely useful when self-deception is in play, effectively countering and holding at bay any contrary or contradictory views of the self. In a review of the relevant research in social psychology, Baumeister (1998, pp. 690–691) identified the following ways we distort data in the pursuit of a favorable view of the self:

1. **Dealing with positive and negative feedback**

    - We tend to attribute successes to our own abilities and blame our failures on external factors.

    - We tend to think that evidence depicting us unfavorably is flawed while viewing positive feedback uncritically. Such criticism is seen as having been motivated by prejudice or similar attributions designed to discredit it.

- We tend to spend little time processing negative information—thereby reducing the chances it is encoded into memory. On the other hand, we dwell on praise.

- We selectively forget feedback about failure and recall feedback of a positive nature.

2. **Comparing ourselves to others**

- We tend to compare ourselves to others who will make us look good.

- We tend to view our group membership positively while viewing "out-group" members as less worthy, less responsible for their successes, and more responsible for their misfortunes.

- We tend to overestimate how many people have opinions similar to our own and underestimate how many people have abilities similar to our own.

3. **Trait identification**

- We tend to sort through our memory in a biased way—finding traits deemed desirable. For example, when people are led to believe that introversion is a desired trait and characteristic of success, they tend to recall instances when they were introverted; when led to believe that extroversion is related to success, people tend to remember times when they were extroverted. When people believe conflict is good for relationships, they recall a lot more conflict episodes than when they are told it is harmful to relationships.

We tend to think our good traits are unusual while our faults are common.

- We tend to think our good traits are unusual while our faults are common.

- We tend to associate what *we* do as a mark of success when the standards for success are ambiguous—e.g., if people don't spank their kids, then they tend to view the practice as a sign of good parenting.

Self-Consistency Bias and Self-Persuasion

The self-enhancement bias is accompanied by a self-consistency bias. After all, if you think well of yourself, you'd like to maintain that state. When you feel good about yourself, stability is comforting. But sometimes we say or do something that throws into question something we believe about ourselves. One way we restore consistency in such situations is through *self-persuasion*. That is, we focus on the positive aspects of something or convince ourselves that something was better (a bad movie), more interesting (a first date), or more worthwhile (an expensive seminar) than it really was (Aronson & Mills, 1959).

The effectiveness of self-persuasion requires that the target of the persuasive message feels he or she is making a change because they want to—not because of a request from someone else.

The Role of Psychological Threat

Psychological threat plays an important role in self-deception because threat increases emotional arousal that, in turn, affects information processing. According to Paulhus and Suedfeld (1988), psychological threat and emotional arousal prompt us to reduce the complexity of our message processing to only the most salient elements—e.g., Am I going to be helped or hurt? Using an interpersonal analogy, one would not expect combatants who saw conflict as imminent to be reflecting on the complexity of the many intersecting issues involved and the multi-dimensional nature of their opponent. Instead, simple evaluative judgments like "friend or foe," "profitable or unprofitable," and "good or bad" are processed.

As noted earlier, this does not necessarily mean such processing is done on a highly conscious level. When self-deception is used to protect the self, there are numerous psychological defense mechanisms available to us (Ford, 1996; Goleman, 1985; Paulhus & Suedfeld, 1988; Smith, 2004; Sullivan, 2001).

Self-Defense Mechanisms

As noted, psychological defense mechanisms for self-protection and self-deception are plentiful. However, we do not need to examine all of them to understand the way they work. Six processes will be examined:

1. Denial
2. Rationalization and excuses

3. Repression and suppression
4. Dissociation
5. Projection
6. Civilization

In daily life, these processes often work in conjunction with one another and serve overlapping functions, so it is not always clear which ones are at work. By examining them separately, though, one can see the range of mental gymnastics that can be employed in the pursuit of self-deception.

Denial

Denial is the refusal to attend to something. Even though the self-deceiver may be initially conscious of the thing being denied, the ultimate goal of denial is to keep the disagreeable information out of awareness in order to enhance or protect self-esteem. This is largely accomplished by selectively giving attention to confirming data and giving little attention to that which is disconfirming. With selective attention, unpleasant truths may be avoided all together or simply passed over quickly in order to focus more intently on other things.

> the ultimate goal of denial is to keep the disagreeable information out of awareness in order to enhance or protect self-esteem.

Sometimes we can spot the possibility of potentially threatening information and preemptively ignore it. This can be done in conversation by changing the topic or by *"willful ignorance"*—i.e., making it clear to others you do not want to know something.

Through denial one may be able to reject an unpleasant reality, but it may be obvious to others. For example:

© igor kisselev/Shutterstock.com

- excessive alcohol consumption by the person who refuses to recognize it
- a person who has a terminal illness and refuses to face his or her mortality
- lovers who refuse to see the signs that their partners are no longer in love with them

Rationalization and Excuses

Rationalizing goes hand in hand with self-deception. We "rationalize" inconsistent acts, beliefs, and feelings to our self in order to justify self-deception. Often this intrapersonal justification is done at a subconscious level and the self-deceiver may not know exactly how he or she has rationalized a particular behavior unless he or she is forced to overtly confront it in a social context.

> We learn from an early age that we are better off when we can give an acceptable reason to explain why we did something—even if we really don't know why we did it.

Excuses may also be a vehicle for "making sense" out of irrational and/or inconsistent behavior when talking to others. It wouldn't be surprising if stating an excuse out loud was the first time a self-deceiver had consciously justified their belief or behavior even to themselves. We learn from an early age that we are better off when we can give an acceptable reason to explain why we did something—even if we really don't know why we did it.

Sanford (1988) says the "thirst for rationality" is a major source of lies and he maintains that self-deception could not exist without it. When excuses are used to rationalize behavior, they are designed to minimize the fault of the actor—i.e., masking "I have acted improperly and am guilty" with "I have done nothing wrong and am not responsible." According to Snyder (1985) excuses may:

- dismiss or deny the problem
- diminish the degree of harm done
- downplay one's responsibility for the problem

The following are examples of rationalization used as a self-defense mechanism:

- During the Holocaust, German physicians participated in gruesome and inhumane experiments on prisoners in concentration camps (Roelcke, 2004). Some viewed their work as a "duty to their country" and others saw it as "furthering scientific knowledge."

- A business executive goes to his hometown on business and visits his mother. To show her he is doing well, he takes her to a fancy restaurant. When he seeks reimbursement for the trip from his employer, he lists the high bill as a travel expense. He tells himself, "The rules in such situations aren't clear. After all, my mother always has good business advice."

In this manner, he frames the rules in the situation as ambiguous, avoids a moral dilemma, acts as he wishes, and does not feel bad about it.

- Georgina is an alcoholic. She attends weekly meetings of Alcoholics Anonymous (AA) and this makes it harder for her to start drinking again. But recently she stopped attending these meetings. The reason she stopped attending, she said, was because her day job at a rehabilitation center involved working with addicts all day long and she felt like another hour in the evening with addicts was more than she could handle.

Rationalization is sometimes facilitated by relationship partners. A wife, for example, may construct excuses and rationalize her husband's misdeeds, make his faults look like virtues, and downplay the significance of his shortcomings. Her behavior is based on the hypothesis that if her husband feels good about himself, the relationship will be better for her. And, indeed, Murray and Holmes (1996) found that people in satisfying relationships do exhibit these "positive illusions."

"Rationalization is sometimes facilitated by relationship partners.

Repression and Suppression

Repression describes what happens when a person mentally blocks ideas and feelings from reaching consciousness. They are ideas and feelings that are likely to cause pain, anxiety, or threat. It is a motivated amnesia or an unwillingness to recall. In Goleman's (1985, p. 117) words, it is "forgetting and forgetting we have forgotten." Traumatic events may trigger repression. For example, a sexual assault survivor may not recall information about the rape or a soldier can't recall killing people. In situations like this, an effort to retrieve the repressed information can create enough anxiety so that the accuracy of the memory may suffer a great deal.

Suppression differs from repression in that it puts information or feelings away for a short time. The memories that have been set aside can then be retrieved and dealt with at a more appropriate or desirable time. One way we can suppress mental content is through a process Wegner (1989) calls "*self-distraction*." Self-distraction involves thinking about things that will cover and replace the things we don't want to think about—our fears, worries, secrets, or even itches. The distraction occurs because we become immersed in some activity and/or in some thoughts that blot out the unwanted ones. Many have found success in suppressing the feelings and thoughts associated with mild pain through self-distraction (exercise, for example, or binge-watching a favorite show).

Dissociation

Dissociation is a psychological process involving the separation and isolation of mental content—psychologically removing the links, connections, or associations to related content. We may be quite aware of our troubling behavior, belief, or emotion, but not willing to acknowledge its relevance to other parts of ourselves with which it is incompatible. When the associations between contrary and inconsistent content are mentally removed, it also removes the need to explain the behavior.

© Lightspring/Shutterstock.com

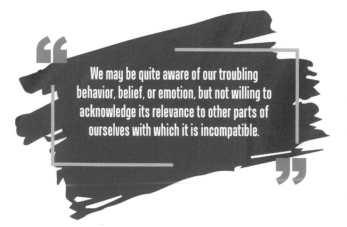

We may be quite aware of our troubling behavior, belief, or emotion, but not willing to acknowledge its relevance to other parts of ourselves with which it is incompatible.

People sometimes justify their immoral acts after the fact by pointing to others' immoral deeds. Recent research indicates that when people cannot deny, confess, or compensate for their wrongdoings, they psychologically "distance" themselves from these transgressions, use stricter ethical criteria, and judge other people's immoral behavior more harshly (Barkan, Ayal, Gino, & Ariely, 2012). Distancing the self from evil and demonizing others allow people to view themselves as "ultra-moral" and lessen the tension elicited by a "one-time" slip.

Projection

Projection is a self-defense mechanism that deals with unpleasant and unacknowledged realities by misattributing them to others—e.g., a manager who is unwilling to admit his own incompetence blames his failures on the fact that his employees are incompetent. When the problem is not your own, there is no need to make any changes. Projection can occur in other ways as well. People may misperceive the behavior of another person and project that misperception onto themselves. For example, someone who can't face her own angry outbursts might perceive the angry outbursts of another person as a "controlled response" that makes her feel better about her own behavior.

Projection relies on our ability to selectively search for information. If we start with a preferred conclusion ("I am a good manager."), we can often find the little evidence needed to support it in a very short period of time. To reject the preferred conclusion, however, normally requires a lot of evidence and takes much longer.

Civilization

There is another variation on mechanisms like denial and rationalization, but in this version it isn't a single person or any one group that's experiencing it. Instead, it's all of humanity, and rather than calling it rationalization or denial, we know it by a much more common name: *civilization*.

In his Pulitzer Prize-winning work *The Denial of Death*, anthropologist Ernest Becker (1973) argued humans are so frightened by awareness of their own mortality that they have created an elaborate and collective defense mechanism to buffer them from the fear: the notion of "civilization" or culture. We are able to transcend the fear of death through the noble work of "civilization" (the arts, philosophy and religion, law, government, etc.). By focusing our attention and efforts on the "immortality project" of civilization, our symbolic selves may enjoy a sense of eternal life our physical selves cannot. This in turn gives people the feeling that their lives have meaning, a purpose, and significance in the grand scheme of things.

© Timofeev Vladimir/Shutterstock.com

> " By focusing our attention and efforts on the "immortality project" of civilization, our symbolic selves may enjoy a sense of eternal life our physical selves cannot. "

Although critically acclaimed, Becker's book has been controversial for many reasons, not the least of which is his claim that culture in general and religion in particular are mechanisms of mass self-deception. Moreover, Becker asserts that humans will need new "illusions" to replace these mechanisms as advances in science and engineering rob them of their capacity to distract us from death thoughts. He does not speculate about what these new illusions might be, instead recommending that people come to grips with their own mortality and thereby reduce its power to make them self-deceive.

The Interplay of Self-defense Mechanisms

In any given situation, numerous self-defense mechanisms come into play in order to sustain self-deception. Twerski's (1997) analysis of substance abusers' "addictive thinking" points to the prominence of denial, rationalization, and projection in rationalizing self-destructive behavior. Their function is to protect the addict from intolerable awarenesses—e.g., the imagined stigma of being perceived as an addict, the fear of not being able to use drugs or alcohol again, the worry that they'll have to face and deal with their personal and social weaknesses.

However, Twerski points out that it is only after the distortions that these self-defense mechanisms cause are decreased or eliminated that the addict's recovery can begin. Multiple self-defense mechanisms can be seen in the following example as well. A mother's son has committed a horrible crime. The evidence supporting his guilt is plentiful, but:

- the mother is unable to acknowledge his guilt (denial)

- she believes the "crowd he hangs with" is responsible (projection)

- she believes she is a good mother who raised a good boy and good boys don't commit crimes like this (dissociation)

- she hides evidence because "it isn't relevant," and is evasive with investigators "because they are rude" (rationalization)

WHAT ARE THE EFFECTS OF SELF-DECEPTION?

Like so many human abilities and creations, self-deception is capable of producing effects that range from great good to great harm. There are times when seeing things as they are *not* can be rewarding. But when our view of reality is radically different from what our social groups perceive or when we regularly refuse to cope with the problems of everyday life, self-deception becomes a liability. Even though his advice assumes a degree of conscious control that is not often present in self-deception, Rorty (1975, p. 22) sums up the ideal balance nicely: "What we need is not the wholesale substitution of self-knowledge for self-deception, but the gifts of timing and tact required to emphasize the right one in the appropriate place." Some of the major advantages and disadvantages of self-deception can be thought of as a question of good vs. bad:

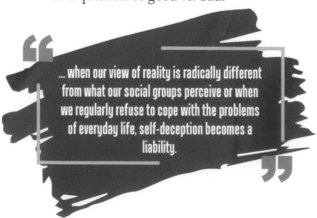

... when our view of reality is radically different from what our social groups perceive or when we regularly refuse to cope with the problems of everyday life, self-deception becomes a liability.

- Mental health vs. mental illness
- Physical well-being vs. physical affliction
- Fooling others vs. fooling one's self
- Performance gain vs. performance loss
- Courageous decisions vs. reckless decisions

We'll examine each of these balancing acts in the following sections.

Mental Health vs. Mental Illness

After reviewing numerous scientific studies involving self-deception, Taylor and Brown (1988, p. 204) concluded that "the mentally healthy person appears to have the enviable capacity to distort reality in a direction that enhances self-esteem, maintains beliefs in personal efficacy, and promotes an optimistic view of the future." They go on to say that these illusions "appear to foster traditional criteria for mental health, including the ability to care about the self and others, the ability to be happy or contented, and the ability to engage in productive or creative work."

In short, it can be a useful way to adapt and cope with everyday life. In fact, Alloy and Abramson (1979) discovered that people experiencing depression engaged in less self-deception than those who weren't depressed. Baumeister (1993, p. 178) maintains that:

> it may be necessary to deceive oneself in order to have a realistic chance at some of life's peak experiences . . . . Grand ambition, romantic passion, and religious faith all require some heavy doses of faith and optimism beyond what is strictly warranted by the facts.

As Vahinger (1925) noted long ago, we often act contrary to certain central realities of life—e.g., acting "as-if" we are fully in control of and/or responsible for what we're doing; making plans "as-if" we are going to live forever.

On the other hand, self-deception that prohibits coping with issues that demand attention is not a sign of successful, adaptive living. Not being able to face certain realities or creating a reality that *impedes* normal everyday living may require therapy and can lead to disaster if left untreated (Baumeister & Scher, 1988). These negative forms of self-deception are often a defining characteristic of mental illness, including substance abuse and impulse control disorders like gambling, kleptomania, compulsive eating, and compulsive shopping.

In these situations, therapists often look for ways their clients may be lying to themselves. They also try to determine how their clients will react if they are forced to face the intolerable reality they have been avoiding and, ultimately, help them find strategies for coming to terms with it.

Physical Well-Being vs. Physical Affliction

Self-deception is credited with overcoming pain and triggering bodily responses that assist in conquering some conditions. Unfortunately, it is also responsible for facilitating serious illness and death. People sometimes ignore or dismiss symptoms of a disease because they don't want to learn that they have it in the first place. Patients sometimes fail to take medications as prescribed

> In one study, students expressed a high degree of confidence that they could determine whether someone was lying to them about risk-related sexual behavior. Despite their confidence, the students turned out to be poor lie detectors.

because they want to believe they don't need it, that they're well, or that their doctor doesn't know as much about their body as they themselves do. Physical harm also stems from an "it can't happen to me" attitude—e.g., not wearing a helmet while riding a motorcycle or not taking steps to prevent contracting sexually transmitted diseases. In one study, students expressed a high degree of confidence that they could determine whether someone was lying to them about risk-related sexual behavior. Despite their confidence, the students turned out to be poor lie detectors (Swann, Silvera, & Proske, 1995).

Fooling Others vs. Fooling One's Self

Earlier we noted that one's skill at deceiving others is greatly enhanced by convincing one's self that a lie is not being told. Self-deception, then, has evolved as a support system for the many goals of lying—ranging from taking advantage of others to strengthening social bonds. But some scholars believe that the more we engage in self-deception with the specific purpose of fooling others, the more damage we are likely to do to ourselves (Baron, 1988; Kipp, 1985). The fallout could include:

- a corrosion of one's sense of responsibility for one's own beliefs
- a deteriorating tendency to question and scrutinize one's own beliefs
- preventing the conscious mind from processing useful information

Performance Gain vs. Performance Loss

Sometimes performers (athletes, artists, entertainers, etc.) find it advantageous to develop a belief in their abilities that is not warranted by an objective assessment. They overestimate what they can accomplish in order to develop the confidence required to do it. Sometimes, however, this type of self-deception can backfire. For example, when performers expect to accomplish feats that are too far beyond their capabilities, they fail. This failure may then lead to self-doubts about one's abilities—doubts that were not there before. In addition, performers sometimes use a public forum to boast about their talent in an effort to convince themselves as well as others. When their subsequent performance doesn't match this boasting, they become less credible to others and, in many cases, to themselves.

Courageous vs. Reckless Decisions

People sometimes end up doing extraordinary things despite not calculating (or miscalculating) the risks involved. Some brave and courageous actions would not occur if the actor(s) actually took the time to calculate the risks involved. Charging an armed airplane hijacker, for example, or defending a military position against 50–1 odds instead of retreating depends on misreading the reality of one's actual vulnerability.

But the difference between a courageous decision and a reckless decision is not always easy to see. Trivers (2000, p. 124) concluded his analysis of human disasters by saying: "There can be little doubt that self-deception makes a disproportionate contribution to human disasters, especially in the form of misguided social policies, wars, being perhaps the most costly example." An analysis of the cockpit conversation prior to the crash of Air Florida Flight 90 (QR), which killed 78 people in a Washington, DC, snowstorm, revealed what Trivers and Newton (1983) said was a clear pattern of self-deception involving denial and rationalization by the pilot about instrument readings and other warnings (the pilot kept overruling the co-pilot's objections).

Wrangham (1999) says military incompetence is often the result of self-deception associated with overconfidence, ignoring or downplaying intelligence reports, and wasting manpower. In her analysis of how leaders and governments have needlessly gone to war throughout history, Tuchman (1984) says "woodenheadedness" is the source of this self-deception, which she defines as assessing a situation in terms of rigid, preconceived notions while ignoring or rejecting any contrary signs. Decisions are based on what is wished for rather than what is, and contrary facts can't deflect or change these wishes.

The essays in Sternberg's *Why Smart People Can Be So Stupid* (2002) remind us that intelligence does not make us immune to reckless decisions associated with self-deception. Smart people, for example, may believe so strongly in their own intelligence that they find ways to immunize or isolate themselves from "less informed" versions of the truth or surround themselves with people willing to tell them only what they want to hear. Self-inflated beliefs about one's own knowledge can also lead to feelings of invulnerability that, in turn, may lead to reckless decisions. Because there are different kinds of intelligence, a person may be smart in some areas of life and foolish in others. Presidents Clinton and Trump, for example, actors Kevin Spacey and Bill Cosby, and media icons Bill O'Reilly and Harvey Weinstein all demonstrated intelligence in many of life's domains, but not when it came to the conduct of their personal lives.

SUMMARY

- Self-deception develops in a number of different ways and involves a variety of mental processes. With an expanded view of interpersonal deception, it is possible to see similar processes at work in self-deception. If, however, one's view of interpersonal deception is limited to a conscious, intentional effort to tell someone a "truth" that you know to be false, the analogy to self-deception becomes problematic. To understand self-deception, we need to imagine information that can be housed at different levels of mental awareness and to acknowledge that human beings can deceive themselves without conscious intent—often with the help of emotions. The condition that prompts self-deception is the presence of two contrary beliefs that invite biased processing. Self-deception is a social as well as psychological process because the responses of other people can greatly affect an individual's need to self-deceive and his or her ability to maintain it. Groupthink is a process in which the nature of social deliberations of group members facilitates self-deception among them.

- We engage in self-deception to:

  1. feel better by enhancing and/or protecting our self-concept
  2. reduce cognitive dissonance
  3. improve our ability to persuade and deceive others
  4. withstand pain and to generally enhance our physical and mental health
  5. improve our chances in winning competitive contests

- Human beings tend to be biased toward self-enhancement and self-consistency. When negative information is perceived as a threat to the self, one or more of these biases are activated to deal with the threat. If the threat persists and promises to do serious harm to one's self, arousal occurs and one or more self-defense mechanism is implemented. There are many self-defense mechanisms, but denial, rationalization, repression, dissociation, distancing, and projection are commonly associated with self-deception. The notion of "civilization" has been described as a collective defense mechanism against the realities of our morality and the meaning of life, but this claim is controversial.

- This chapter concluded with an examination of several areas in which self-deception is both advantageous and disadvantageous—depending on how often self-deception occurs, what problems are being masked, and the extent to which the self-deception is within the bounds of what society would call "normal." Thus, self-deception can lead to mental health or mental illness, physical well-being or physical affliction, improved skill in fooling others or improved skill in fooling one's self, performance gain or performance loss, and courageous decisions or reckless decisions.

1. In face-to-face interaction, the word "suspicious" can be used to reflect one person's doubts or uncertainty about the truthfulness of another person. Once a person becomes suspicious, his or her behavior relative to the potential liar changes—e.g., increased attentiveness, less trust, etc. If the liar perceives suspicion on the part of the target, the liar will try to counteract it. Does suspicion play a role in *self*-deception? If so, how? If not, why not?

2. The focus of this chapter has been primarily limited to understanding self-deception in the context of intrapersonal and interpersonal communication. Is self-deception a concept that may also be applicable to large segments of society or society as a whole? Amélie Rorty (1996, p. 82) seems to think so. Read her statement and decide whether you agree or disagree with her. Use examples to support your position.

   It is virtually impossible to imagine any society that does not systematically and actively promote the self-deception of its members, particularly when the requirements of social continuity and cohesion are subtly at odds with one another . . . . Socially induced self-deception is an instrument in the preservation of social cooperation and cohesion.

OF INTEREST

In this TEDx Talk, former University of Nevada, Las Vegas psychology professor Cortney Warren takes a hard look at self-deception. She suggests we aren't doing ourselves any favors by relying on it more than we need to, especially when it comes to managing our relationships. The key, she says, is to begin practicing greater self-awareness.

Jon Taffer's *Don't Bullsh*t Yourself! Crush the Excuses That Are Holding You Back* tackles our tendency to rationalize. It's every bit as in-your-face as his popular show, *Bar Rescue*, is.

REFERENCES

Albrecht, G. L., & Devlieger, P. J. (1999). The disability paradox: High quality of life against all the odds. *Social Science & Medicine, 48*(8), 977–988. https://dx.doi.org/10.1016/s0277-9536(98)00411-0

Alloy, L. B., & Abramson, L. Y. (1979). Judgment of contingency in depressed and nondepressed students: Sadder but wiser? *Journal of Experimental Psychology: General, 108*(4), 441–485. https://dx.doi.org/10.1037/0096-3445.108.4.441

Ames, R. T., & Dissanayake, W. (Eds.) (1996). *Self and deception: A cross-cultural philosophical enquiry.* Albany, NY: State University of New York Press.

Anderegg, W. R. L., Prall, J. W., Harold, J., & Schneider, S. H. (2010). Expert credibility in climate change. *Proceedings of the National Academy of Sciences, 107*, 12107–12109. https://dx.doi.org/10.1073/pnas.1003187107

Aronson, E. (1997). The theory of cognitive dissonance: The evolution and vicissitudes of an idea. In C. McGarty & S. A. Haslam (Eds.), *The message of social psychology: Perspective on mind in society* (pp. 20–35). Oxford, England: Blackwell.

Aronson, E., & Mills, J. (1959). The effect of severity of initiation on liking for a group. *Journal of Abnormal and Social Psychology, 59*(2), 177–181. https://dx.doi.org/10.1037/h0047195

Baron, M. (1988). What is wrong with self-deception. In B. P. McLaughlin & A. O. Rorty (Eds.), *Perspectives on self-deception* (pp. 431–449). Berkeley, CA: University of California Press.

Baumeister, R. F. (1993). Lying to yourself: The enigma of self-deception. In M. Lewis & C. Saarni (Eds.), *Lying and deception in everyday life* (pp. 166–183). New York, NY: Guilford.

Baumeister, R. F. (1998). The self. In D. T. Gilbert, S. T. Fiske, & G. Lindzey (Eds.), *The handbook of social psychology, Vol. 1* (4th ed.) (pp. 680–740). New York, NY: McGraw-Hill.

Baumeister, R. F., & Scher, S. J. (1988). Self-defeating behavior patterns among normal individuals: Review and analysis of common self-destructive tendencies. *Psychological Bulletin, 104*(1), 3–22. https://dx.doi.org/10.1037//0033-2909.104.1.3

Barkan, R., Ayal, S., Gino, F., & Ariely, D. (2012). The pot calling the kettle black: Distancing response to ethical dissonance. *Journal of Experimental Psychology: General, 141*, 757–773. https://dx.doi.org/10.1037/a0027588

Becker, E. (1973). *The denial of death.* New York, NY: Free Press.

Biais, B., & Weber, M. (2009). Hindsight bias, risk perception, and investment performance. *Management Science, 55*(6), 1018–1029. https://dx.doi.org/10.1287/mnsc.1090.1000

Cassar, G., & Craig, J. (2009). An investigation of hindsight bias in nascent venture activity. *Journal of Business Venturing, 24*(2), 149–164. https://dx.doi.org/10.1016/j.jbusvent.2008.02.003

Chance, Z., Norton, M. I., Gino, F., & Ariely, D. (2011). Temporal view of the costs and benefits of self-deception. *Proceedings of the National Academy of Sciences, 108*, 15655–15659. https://dx.doi.org/10.1073/pnas.1010658108

Chanowitz, B., & Langer, E. J. (1985). Self-protection and self-inception. In M. Martin (Ed.), *Self-deception and self-understanding* (pp. 117–135). Lawrence, KS: University Press of Kansas.

Descartes, R. (2010). *Meditations on first philosophy* (7th ed.). New York, NY: Watchmaker Publishing. (Original work published 1641).

Essock, S. M., McGuire, M. T., & Hooper, B. (1988). Self-deception in social-support networks. In J. S. Lockard & D. L. Paulhus (Eds.), *Self-deception: An adaptive mechanism?* (pp. 200–211). Englewood Cliffs, NJ: Prentice-Hall.

Farhi, P. (2015, Feb. 4). Brian Williams admits that his story of coming under fire while in Iraq was false. *The Washington Post*. Retrieved from http://www.washingtonpost.com

Festinger, L. (1957). *A theory of cognitive dissonance*. Evanston, IL: Row, Peterson.

Fingarette, H. (1969). *Self-deception*. New York, NY: Humanities Press.

Fischhoff, B. (1975). Hindsight does not equal foresight: The effect of outcome knowledge on judgement under uncertainty. *Journal of Experimental Psychology: Human Perception and Performance, 1*(3), 288–299. https://dx.doi.org/10.1037//0096-1523.1.3.288

Ford, C. V. (1996). *Lies! Lies!! Lies!!! The psychology of deceit*. Washington, DC: American Psychiatric Press.

Gilbert, D. T., & Cooper, J. (1985). Social psychological strategies of self-deception. In M. Martin (Ed.), *Self-deception and self-understanding* (pp. 75–94). Lawrence, KS: University Press of Kansas.

Gilovich, T. (1991). *How we know what isn't so*. New York, NY: Macmillan.

Gilovich, T., & Ross, L. (2016). The wisest one in the room. New York, NY: Free Press.

Goleman, D. (1985). *Vital lies, simple truths: The psychology of self-deception*. New York, NY: Simon & Schuster.

Gur, R. C., & Sackeim, H. A. (1979). Self-deception: A concept in search of a phenomenon. *Journal of Personality and Social Psychology, 37*(2), 147–169. https://dx.doi.org/10.1037/0022-3514.37.2.147

Haidt, J. (2012). *The righteous mind: Why good people are divided by politics and religion*. New York, NY: Pantheon Books.

Hastorf, A. H., & Cantril, H. (1954). They saw a game: A case study. *The Journal of Abnormal and Social Psychology, 49*(1), 129–134. https://dx.doi.org/10.1037/h0057880

Hood, B. (2012). *The self illusion: Why there is no you inside your head*. New York, NY: Oxford University Press.

Janis, I. L. (1983). *Groupthink: Psychological studies of policy decisions and fiascoes* (2nd ed.). Boston, MA: Houghton Mifflin.

Kassin, S. M. (2005). On the psychology of confessions: Does innocence put innocents at risk? *American Psychologist, 60*(3), 215–228. https://dx.doi.org/10.1037/0003-066x.60.3.215

Keetels, M., & Vroomen, J. (2011). Perception of synchrony between the senses. In M. M. Murray and M. T. Wallace (Eds.), *The neural bases of multisensory processes* (pp. 147–178). London, England: Taylor & Francis Group. https://dx.doi.org/10.1201/b11092-12

Kinsley, M. (December 17, 2001). In defense of denial. *Time*, 72–73.

Kipp, D. (1985). Self-deception, inauthenticity, and weakness of will. In M. Martin (Ed.), *Self-deception and self-understanding* (pp. 261–283). Lawrence, KS: University Press of Kansas.

Kruger, J., & Dunning, D. (1999). Unskilled and unaware of it: How difficulties in recognizing one's own incompetence lead to inflated self-assessments. *Journal of Personality and Social Psychology, 77*(6), 1121–1134. https://dx.doi.org/10.1037//0022-3514.77.6.1121

Lewis, J. M. (2004, July). How much self-deception helps? *Psychiatric Times, 21*(8), 35–37.

Lockard, J. S., & Paulhus, D. L. (Eds.) (1988). *Self-deception: An adaptive mechanism?* Englewood Cliffs, NJ: Prentice-Hall.

Lynch, A. (2016, June 15). Why history suggests the Cavaliers' finals comeback is doomed to fail. *Fox Sports*. Retrieved from http://www.foxsports.com

Lynch, K. (2014). Self-deception and shifts of attention. *Philosophical Explorations, 17*(1), 63–75. https://dx.doi.org/10.1080/13869795.2013.824109

Martin, M. W. (Ed.) (1985). *Self-deception and self-understanding*. Lawrence, KS: University Press of Kansas.

McLaughlin, B. P., & Rorty, A. O. (Eds.), (1988). *Perspectives on self-deception*. Berkeley, CA: University of California Press.

Mele, A. R. (2001). *Self-deception unmasked*. Princeton, NJ: Princeton University Press.

Murray, S. L., & Holmes, J. G. (1996). The construction of relationship realities. In G. J. O. Fletcher & J. Fitness (Eds.), *Knowledge structures in close relationships: A social psychological approach* (pp. 91–120). Mahwah, NJ: Erlbaum.

Newman, L. S. (1999). Motivated cognition and self-deception. *Psychological Inquiry, 10*(1), 59–63. https://dx.doi.org/10.1207/s15327965pli1001_9

Nyberg, D. (1993). *The varnished truth: Truth telling and deceiving in ordinary life.* Chicago, IL: University of Chicago Press.

Norgaard, K. M. (2010). *Cognitive and behavioral challenges in responding to climate change.* The World Bank Development Economics and World Development Report Team. https://dx.doi.org/10.1037/e595792012-001

Offer, D., Kaiz, M., Howard, K. I., & Bennett, E. S. (2000). The altering of reported experiences. *Journal of the American Academy of Child & Adolescent Psychiatry, 39*(6), 735–742. https://dx.doi.org/10.1097/00004583-200006000-00012

Patten, D. (2003). How do we deceive ourselves? *Philosophical Psychology, 16*(2), 229–246. https://dx.doi.org/10.1080/09515080307767

Paulhus, D. L., & Suedfeld, P. (1988). A dynamic complexity model of self-deception. In J. S. Lockard & D. L. Paulhus (Eds.), *Self-deception: An adaptive mechanism?* (pp. 132–145). Albany, NY: State University of New York Press.

Roelcke, V. (2004, December). Nazi medicine and research on human beings. *The Lancet, 364,* 6–7. https://dx.doi.org/10.1016/S0140-6736(04)17619-8

Rorty, A. O. (1975). Adaptivity and self-knowledge. *Inquiry, 18*(1), 1–22. https://dx.doi.org/10.1080/00201747508601747

Rorty, A. O. (1996). User-friendly self-deception: A traveler's manual. In R. T. Ames & W. Dissanayake (Eds.), *Self and deception: A cross-cultural philosophical enquiry* (pp. 73–89). Albany, NY: State University of New York Press.

Routledge, C., Arndt, J., Wildschut, T., Sedikides, C., Hart, C. M., Juhl, J., … Schlotz, W. (2011). The past makes the present meaningful: Nostalgia as an existential resource. *Journal of Personality and Social Psychology, 101*(3), 638–652. https://dx.doi.org/10.1037/a0024292

Sackeim, H. A. (1988). Self-deception: A synthesis. In J. S. Lockard & D. L. Paulhus (Eds.), *Self-deception: An adaptive mechanism?* (pp. 146–165). Englewood Cliffs, NJ: Prentice-Hall.

Sanford, D. H. (1988). Self-deception as rationalization. In B. P. McLaughlin & A. O. Rorty (Eds.), *Perspectives on self-deception* (pp. 157–169). Berkeley, CA: University of California Press.

Shermer, M. (2012). *The believing brain: From ghosts and gods to politics and conspiracies—How we construct beliefs and reinforce them as truths.* New York, NY: St. Martin's Griffin.

Smith, D. L. (2004). *Why we lie: The evolutionary roots of deception and the unconscious mind.* New York, NY: St. Martin's Press.

Snyder, C. R. (1985). Collaborative companions: The relationship of self-deception and excuse making. In M. Martin (Ed.), *Self-deception and self-understanding* (pp. 35–51). Lawrence, KS: University Press of Kansas.

Starek, J. E., & Keating, C. F. (1991). Self-deception and its relationship to success in competition. *Basic and Applied Social Psychology, 12*(2), 145–155. https://dx.doi.org/10.1207/s15324834basp1202_2

Steele, C. M. (1988). The psychology of self-affirmation: Sustaining the integrity of the self. In L. Berkowitz (Ed.), *Advances in experimental psychology, Vol. 21* (pp. 261–302). New York, NY: Academic Press. https://dx.doi.org/10.1016/s0065-2601(08)60229-4

Sternberg, R. J. (Ed.). (2002). *Why smart people can be so stupid*. New Haven, CT: Yale University Press.

Sullivan, E. (2001). *The concise book of lying*. New York, NY: Farrar, Straus and Giroux.

Sullivan, M. (2018, April 4). The term "fake news" has lost all meaning. *The Washington Post*. Retrieved from http://washingtonpost.com

Swann, W. B., Jr., Silvera, D. H., & Proske, C. U. (1995). On "knowing your partner": Dangerous illusions in the age of AIDS? *Personal Relationships, 2*(3), 173–186. https://dx.doi.org/10.1111/j.1475-6811.1995.tb00084.x

't Hart, P., Stern, E. K., & Sundelius, B. (Eds.). (1997). *Beyond groupthink: Political group dynamics and foreign policy-making*. Ann Arbor, MI: University of Michigan Press. https://dx.doi.org/10.3998/mpub.11178

Taylor, S. E. (1989). *Positive illusions: Creative self-deception and the healthy mind*. New York, NY: Basic Books.

Taylor, S. E., & Brown, J. D. (1988). Illusion and well-being: A social psychological perspective on mental health. *Psychological Bulletin, 103*(2), 193–210. https://dx.doi.org/10.1037//0033-2909.103.2.193

Taylor, S. E., Kemeny, M. E., Aspinwall, L. G., Schneider, S. G., Rodriguez, R., & Herbert, M. (1992). Optimism, coping, psychological distress, and high-risk sexual behavior among men at risk for acquired immunodeficiency syndrome (AIDS). *Journal of Personality and Social Psychology, 63*, 460–473.

Trivers, R. (2000). The elements of a scientific theory of self-deception. *Annals of the New York Academy of Sciences, 907*(1), 114–131. https://dx.doi.org/10.1111/nyas.2000.907.issue-1

Trivers, R. (2011). *The folly of fools: The logic of deceit and self-deception in human life*. New York, NY: Basic Books.

Trivers, R., & Newton, H. P. (1983, November). The crash of flight 90: Doomed by self-deception? *Science Digest, 90*(11), 66–67, 111.

Tuchman, B. W. (1984). *The march of folly: From Troy to Vietnam*. New York, NY: Knopf.

Twerski, A. J. (1997). *Addictive thinking: Understanding self-deception* (2nd ed.). Center City, MN: Hazelden.

Vahinger, H. (1925). *The philosophy of "as-if," a system of the theoretical, practical, and religious fictions of mankind*. New York, NY: Harcourt Brace.

Wegner, D. M. (1989). *White bears and other unwanted thoughts: Suppression, obsession, and the psychology of mental control*. New York, NY: Penguin Books.

Wegner, D. M. (2003). *The illusion of conscious will*. Cambridge, MA: MIT Press.

Welles, J. F. (1988). Societal roles in self-deception. In J. S. Lockard & D. L. Paulhus (Eds.), *Self-deception: An adaptive mechanism?* (pp. 54–70). Englewood Cliffs, NJ: Prentice-Hall.

Westerhoff, J. C. (2011). *Reality: A very short introduction.* Oxford, England: Oxford University Press. https://dx.doi.org/10.1093/actrade/9780199594412.001.0001

Wrangham, R. (1999). Is military incompetence adaptive? *Evolution and Human Behavior, 20*(1), 3–12. https://dx.doi.org/10.1016/s1090-5138(98)00040-3

Chapter 7 Performing Lies and Deceit

© nuvolanevicata/Shutterstock.com

"The behavioral clues in face, body, voice, and manner of speaking are not signs of lying per se . . . . They are flags marking areas which need to be explored."
– Paul Ekman

"Anyone can spin a victory, it's a total loss that demands creativity."
– Josh Stern

Not everyone wants to know if trustworthy signals of deception exist. They point out that our burning need to reliably catch other liars cools off considerably if it also means (as it would) that we will be unable to hide our own fabrications. Nevertheless, lots of people wish they could know *with certainty* what behavior or behaviors people exhibit when they are not telling the truth. This wish (and the focus of this chapter) has been increasingly scrutinized by scientists over the last 50 years. Their research has revealed some important things about the way liars behave, but it has also made one thing abundantly clear: **There is no simple answer to the question of what behaviors betray a liar.** If there were, then books like this one probably wouldn't exist (and neither would liars).

In this chapter, we will identify:

- some commonly manifested liar behaviors
- behaviors of liars that occur under certain circumstances

Above all, we will find that there is no definitive list of behaviors that can expose all liars in all situations. Anyone who says otherwise is probably trying to sell you something.

DIFFICULTIES IN IDENTIFYING LIAR BEHAVIOR

The following challenges must be recognized in any search for observable behaviors that reliably occur during acts of lying and/or deception:

1. Determining what the observed behavior really means
2. Stereotypes about how liars behave
3. Competent liars alter their behavior
4. Liar behavior can vary by circumstance
5. Liars' motives can affect their behavior
6. The type of lie told may influence liar behavior

Determining What the Observed Behavior Really Means

The central problem is this: The behaviors people exhibit when they are lying are not behaviors solely associated with lying. Ekman (2001, p. 80), who has studied the question more than anyone, puts it this way: "There is no sign of deceit itself—no gesture, facial expression, or muscle twitch that in and of itself means that a person is lying." He goes on to say that many behavioral clues to deceit are signs of more than one emotion and may even be a sign that someone is telling the truth. This interview with Ekman (QR) on gesture, emotion, and deception is worth viewing as a general backdrop for the material presented throughout the chapter.

So, the following list of behaviors may indeed mean someone is lying, or it *might* mean they are definitely not lying:

- Liars may manifest various **nervous mannerisms**, but such behaviors are also a sign of anxiety—an emotion that both liars and truth tellers experience. For example, liars may sweat and swallow frequently due to fear or guilt, but truth tellers may also exhibit these behaviors if they are distressed and/or angry at being unfairly accused of lying.

- Some truth tellers, like some liars, are **uncomfortable in social situations** and, as we expect liars to do, they may also tend to:

  - use longer response latency
  - rely on indirect speech or stumble on their words
  - and/or give brief replies to questions

- We also need to remember that the *absence* of some particular behavior doesn't mean that we're being told the truth. Some liars are just really good at what they do (the primary focus of Chapter 8).

Stereotypes About How Liars Behave

Despite the glaring lack of scientific evidence for a list of behaviors unique to deception, popular stereotypes about liar behavior abound. These stereotypes show up consistently worldwide, regardless of one's age, profession, or culture (Castillo & Mallard, 2012; Global Deception Research Team, 2006; Granhag, Andersson, Strömwall, & Hartwig, 2004; Hurley, Griffin, & Stefanone, 2014; Vrij, Akehurst, & Knight, 2006).

If these stereotypes do not reflect the way liars really behave, how do they arise in the first place? There are several different sources for people's false beliefs about deception:

1. The stereotypes reflect social norms about lying that are more traditional than factual (Bond & DePaulo, 2006). Across cultures, people are socialized to believe lying is generally the wrong thing to do and to feel shame when they do it. As a result, the cultural undesirability of lying is equated with communication behaviors perceived as undesirable or flawed (reduced eye contact, stuttering, nervous demeanor, inconsistent stories, etc.).

2. The stereotypes are communicated to us and reinforced by family members, friends, and others in our networks, all of whom were socialized to believe these stereotypes too.

3. Mass media messages about deception disseminated by popular TV shows, news reports, and Internet commentary are permeated with these stereotypes, leading consumers to put faith in false deception clues (Hurley et al., 2014).

4. Another source is *confirmation bias*—i.e., the human tendency to seek out and interpret new information that confirms our prior beliefs (see Chapter 6). Many people who believe stereotypes about lying behavior claim they are consistent with their past experience in successfully spotting liars (Castillo & Mallard, 2012). In all likelihood, they are selectively remembering a time or two when the stereotypes were confirmed but forgetting the majority of instances when they were not. Confirmation bias is the chief mechanism by which stereotypes of many kinds become entrenched in people's beliefs and attitudes (Aronson & McGlone, 2008).

"Confirmation bias is the chief mechanism by which stereotypes of many kinds become entrenched in people's beliefs and attitudes."

Competent Liars Alter Their Behavior

If scientists ever uncover certain behaviors that reliably identify liars, this information will quickly become public knowledge. As a result, competent liars are likely to avoid the behavior in question, mask it, or create distractions so it won't be seen (recall from Chapter 1 that lying probably developed as a survival skill). Good liars already do this when it comes to certain stereotypes about lying:

• The long-standing belief in the United States that a liar "will not look you in the eyes" is not a behavior *typically* manifested by liars (DePaulo et al., 2003).

• When people want to control their behavior, some are capable of doing so to a remarkable degree:

  – After polygraph examinations in which liars were correctly spotted **88%** of the time, Corcoran, Lewis, and Garver (1978) taught people how to control their bodily responses through biofeedback and relaxation training. Subsequent polygraph examinations detected lies told by these same people at a rate of only **24%**.

- Vallacher and Wegner (1985) say that people who are practiced at impressing others can coordinate numerous individual behaviors by relying on a broader (and truer) *goal* like "I intend to make a good impression." Instilling such a goal appears to have the power to psychologically bring together the coordination of numerous individual behaviors (smile, nod, shake hands, etc.). This remarkable strategy removes the need to consciously attend to each separate behavior and facilitates a fluid performance. It is, in effect, the way someone learns to master riding a bike or throw a baseball. They achieve their goal, at least in part, by no longer having to pay attention to all the particulars.

But some human behaviors are far less subject to voluntary control than others, and these largely involuntary behaviors may provide some clues to deception—especially with novice liars and in situations where the stakes are perceived to be high. Liars can't always control the many behaviors they wish to control.

Without practice, communicators may be as inept as the person first learning to do something new, like ride a hoverboard for the first time—awkwardly trying to control and coordinate a variety of individual behaviors while also trying to avoid embarrassment or injury. There are a few other things to consider related to the alteration of behavior:

- **Long and complex messages** and/or **intense interrogations** can make complete and undetectable control even more difficult (Wegner & Bargh, 1998).

- When liars are not able to effectively control their behavior, they communicate what Ekman and Friesen (1969) call **leakage clues** (behavior that unintentionally "leaks" the truth) or **deception clues** (behavior that may be associated with lying). Both of these concepts are discussed in more detail in Chapter 9.

- Of course, people try to exert control over their behavior for reasons other than to deceive (e.g., to control their temper), so deception should only become an issue when you suspect the controlled behavior is being done with the *intent to deceive*.

Liar Behavior Can Vary by Circumstance

The specific circumstances of any given attempt to deceive can have significant effects on the kind of behavior the deceiver exhibits. Examples of these include:

- the extent to which deception is *expected* or not
- the perceived *consequences* of deceptive success and failure
- the *relationship* and involvement of the deceiver with the target of the deception
- the *medium* by which the liar communicates with the target

Expectations

Situations vary with regard to whether lies are expected or not. Misleading signals given by poker players or athletes are *expected* and considered to just be "part of the game." Likewise, many people are on guard for deceptive behavior during the process of purchasing a car (especially a used one)—and if they are not, they certainly should be because negotiation and sales are contexts where we should expect others to use various facets of deception (e.g., *bluffing*, *exaggeration*, *false promises*, *omission of key details*).

On the other hand, it is typically quite *unexpected* when friends and lovers lie to you—especially about *important things*. In these situations, lies are not normally expected, so when they occur it is genuinely shocking. Some lies in relationships are expected, but these are generally harmless, or at least *low-stakes*, so their occurrence is not a bombshell. Different expectations have the power to influence how liars feel about their lies, how they enact them, and how their targets react. If your significant other fibs about

Pancakes? I loooooove your pancakes!

liking your ugly outfit or how delicious your awful pancakes are, it's more or less expected because the situation is essentially a matter of being polite, so it's not likely to be a big deal (in fact, you may even be grateful for it). But if they lie about still loving you when in fact they don't—a deception that strikes at the very fabric of the relationship—then you're in for one hell of an unpleasant shock (Cole, 2001).

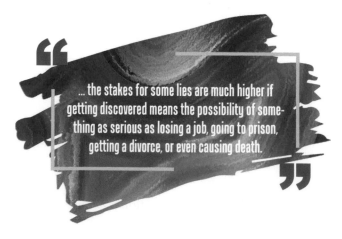

… the stakes for some lies are much higher if getting discovered means the possibility of something as serious as losing a job, going to prison, getting a divorce, or even causing death.

Consequences

Most lies we tell during the course of our daily activities do not have major consequences. The stakes are low in most of our polite little social lies. At times in everyday life, you may not even care what happens if your lie is discovered by a person whom you already dislike, or someone who you barely know and will not likely interact with again. These common place lies include being less than fully accurate about how we feel, saying less than we know, or pretending to know more than we do.

But the stakes for some lies are much higher if getting discovered means the possibility of something as serious as losing a job, going to prison, getting a divorce, or even causing death. You would not expect to observe the same type of behavior when a person tells lies to a friend that he had a nice time at a party versus when an spy tells an enemy that she is not a U.S. citizen.

While unconsequential lies are one thing, the research suggests that we tend to tell fewer completely false statements, or what McCornack, Morrison, Paik, Wisner, and Zhu (2014) refer to as **bald-faced lies**. Recent research has found that most people do not tell such lies on a daily basis, suggesting that a few prolific liars skew and inflate statistics about how often people tell lies (Serota & Levine, 2015).

Relationship and Involvement with Target

Liars may display one cluster of verbal and nonverbal behavior with people who do *not* know them and another cluster with those who know them better. Creating a false message for a relational partner who shares a lot of inside information requires entirely different skills and maneuvers.

Bond, Thomas, and Paulson (2004) wanted to find out how communicators behaved when confronted by two different targets to whom they had previously told two different stories. The researchers repeated this same scenario multiple times, with different student participants: They would ask a student to describe, in front of two peers, how he or she felt about a teacher they all knew. Some of the students were told to lie about their feelings and some were told to tell the truth. Prior to this meeting, however, the student had privately (and separately) told each of the peers *opposite* stories, one true and one not.

So what happened back in the presence of both of these peers? Did the student's behavior change based on whether he or she was telling the truth or lying? It didn't seem to matter. When confronted by their peers in this awkward situation (one of whom, remember, believed they were being lied to), the now-uncomfortable student was perceived as deceptive regardless of whether he or she told the truth or not. Why? Because of their *discomfort with the situation,* *truth tellers and liars both* displayed speech that was equivocal (i.e., perceived as having multiple meanings), vague, and dysfluent.

The experiment just described evaluated the *liar's* behavior. But the behavior exhibited by the *target* of a lie is also a factor that may influence a liar's behavior. For example, White and Burgoon (2001) found that deceivers were less responsive than truth tellers when their interaction partner became either *more* or *less* involved in the conversation.

Sometimes interaction partners can inadvertently facilitate the performance of a liar—e.g., finishing his or her sentence when the liar seems to be having trouble finding the right words or attributing their partner's anxious behavior to some past event. On other occasions, though, an interaction partner can make lying (or truth telling) more difficult. For example, a liar or truth teller may change his or her behavior when a partner acts suspiciously. Sometimes the result of this changed behavior is to make speakers appear more deceptive—whether they are or not (Bond & Fahey, 1987; Burgoon, Buller, Ebesu, White, & Rockwell, 1996).

Different manifestations of suspicion (e.g., a furrowed brow vs. intense and persistent questioning) are also likely to elicit different responses. Needless to say, the demands for adaptation and the effects of mutual influence that occur in ongoing interactions are bound to affect the nature of a liar's behavioral profile (Buller & Burgoon, 1996).

Communication Medium

One of the most striking cultural and social changes in recent decades has been the revolution in the ways people communicate. Until the 1990s, humans were confined to communicating face to face, through letters, and traditional landline telephones. In the last 30 years, first computers, then cell phones, then smartphones, and eventually social media have dramatically expanded the ways we communicate. Despite the appearance of new technologies, the original question scholars and laypeople alike have been asking for a very long time remains the same: Does the communication medium people are using affect how and when they lie?

Hancock, Thom-Santelli, and Ritchie (2004) identified three features that can moderate the incidence of deception in different media:

1. The "distribution" of the message's sender and receiver allowed by the medium in physical space. Only face-to-face communication requires close physical proximity; other media allow the sender and receiver to be distant or "distributed."

2. The "synchronicity" of the interaction—i.e., the degree to which messages are exchanged instantaneously and in real time. Face-to-face communication is always synchronous and phone communication often is (except for the exchange of voice mail messages), but texting and e-mail are asynchronous because people read and reply to them after a time delay.

3. The "recordability" of the medium, the degree to which the interaction is automatically documented. Texting and e-mail are automatically recorded during the exchange of messages, but face-to-face and phone communication are not recorded unless the sender or receiver takes the extra effort to do so.

Hancock and colleagues hypothesized that *different combinations* of these features affect the *frequency* with which people lie in different media. Specifically, they predicted that lying should occur *most frequently* when the medium meets these three criteria:

- *distributed* (because there are fewer nonverbal clues to reveal a liar's deceit)
- *synchronous* (because most lies emerge spontaneously from conversation)
- *less recordable* (because liars are hesitant to leave a record of their deceit)

It is increasingly more common for people to meet, interact, and conduct business through online tools. Does this mean that deception is more common? Things aren't quite that simple. While the increase in online communication may seem to be a hotbed for deception, there are many variables that influence mendacity online. Caspi and Gorsky (2006) found that age, frequency of use, technological competency, and privacy concerns all influenced uses of deception online.

Not surprisingly, they found that participants in their study perceived that deception was much *more prevalent* than was actually reported, a finding supported by other research (Toma, Jiang, & Hancock, 2016). Culture, world views, and nationality also play a role in how people bend the truth online (Marett, George, Lewis, Gupta, & Giordano, 2017).

As might be expected, deceptions employed online typically include sharing information that does not accurately represent users' attractiveness (e.g., curbing one's weight, changing one's height, distorting age, exaggerating experiences, or lying about one's occupation). Toma (2017) suggests that deception online is akin to those lies told in traditional face-to-face interactions and also observes:

> *Online dating deception, while facilitated by the disembodied nature of online dating, where users get to construct their self-presentation in the absence of corporeal presence and through highly editable photographic and textual means, is, nonetheless, kept in check by the anticipation of face-to-face interaction with romantic partners. Since deception tends to be a relational deal-breaker, online daters who are motivated to pursue serious relationships tend to minimize it. (p. 425)*

The bottom line is this—different communication channels influence the ways in which lies are told and the degree to which deception occurs. However, we must remember that there are many variables that influence lying, and these matter when considered across various media. In the case of online deception, research continues to show us that **media literacy** is important in curbing and detecting deception.

Liars' Motives Can Affect Their Behavior

Sometimes liars are especially concerned about "getting away with" their lie. As a result, they may think a lot about how to succeed and how to fool the target. These liars are highly motivated and are determined not to get caught. This heightened motivation may be of particular help to at least three types of people who are keen to lie without emitting any obvious signs of deception:

- The socially skilled
- Those who are experienced liars
- Those who have fewer qualms about lying

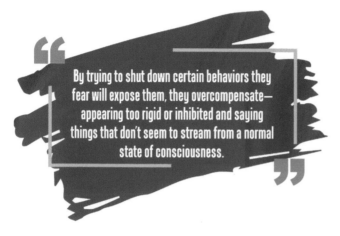

> By trying to shut down certain behaviors they fear will expose them, they overcompensate—appearing too rigid or inhibited and saying things that don't seem to stream from a normal state of consciousness.

Burgoon and Floyd (2000) found that such motivation sometimes enhances performance of verbal and nonverbal behavior. In other words, a strong desire to succeed may help these liars control their verbal and nonverbal behavior. On the other hand, many liars experience what DePaulo and Kirkendol (1989) call a "motivational impairment"—i.e., trying *very hard to manage their behavior* and *worrying* about how they are perceived. As a result, they are especially likely to reveal their deception through various verbal and nonverbal signals, including facial expressions and use of words that betray their intentions. By trying to shut down certain behaviors they fear will expose them, they overcompensate—appearing too rigid or inhibited and saying things that don't seem to stream from a normal state of consciousness.

For example, a person who doesn't want to signal deception by looking away or avoiding too much eye contact may end up staring at their partner. In this case, too much eye gaze is just as much a sign to the target that "something's not right" as too little eye gaze would be. They may say things to their target that are too formal or rehearsed—saying more than they should know or less than they would be expected to in a particular situation.

It is also the case that different people lie for different reasons. Any given motive for lying may be more or less troubling to the liar, easier or more difficult to accomplish, or in some other way able to affect the verbal and

nonverbal behavior that accompanies it. Most lies are told for the sole benefit of the liar, but motives are complex. There may be several reasons why a person lies and the liar may not even be fully aware of all the reasons. For example, a person who lies to their partner about an affair may think the primary reason for doing so is to save their relationship and avoid embarrassing the partner. At the same time, they may let themselves be only faintly aware that they are also lying to avoid being scorned by the partner and/or the possible fallout of losing kids, a house, money, pets, and mutual friends (Guthrie & Kunkel, 2013). In general terms, the main reasons adults lie are:

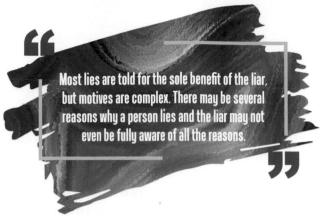

Most lies are told for the sole benefit of the liar, but motives are complex. There may be several reasons why a person lies and the liar may not even be fully aware of all the reasons.

- **To avoid punishment**
  - High-stakes lies are often told to avoid being punished for a misdeed. Lying is *especially* likely to occur when the liar perceives that the punishment for telling the truth will be as great as the punishment for lying.

- **To protect oneself from harm**
  - This reason is not the same as lying to avoid any punishment that might result from getting caught. Instead, these types of lies are meant to prevent situations where people anticipate actual harm.

- **To protect or help others**
  - Lies told to help others are more likely when the lie will also help (or at least not hurt) the liar.

- **To obtain a reward**
  - A few of the many things people regularly try to acquire through deceit include jobs, sex, money, and good grades in school.

- **To win admiration**
  - The desire to make a positive impression on others is a common motive for lying. It may be especially strong for individuals who generally place a high value on the opinions of others, or for most people in situations where the opinion of highly influential individuals could help achieve a desired goal.

- **To avoid an awkward or embarrassing social situation**
  - Here, lies are told to avoid conflict or as excuses for behaviors/activities the liar likes to engage in. While not expected, such lies are certainly understandable and often

viewed as benign. In these cases, the target of the lie may not be interested in sanctioning the liar even if the lie is later exposed (thinking, perhaps, that they themselves would have done the same thing were the roles reversed).

- **To maintain privacy**
  - No surprise here. Some lies are told in order to keep a part of one's personal identity from being known to others.

- **To exercise power over others**
  - Oppressors and their victims both know the value of controlling information as a way of gaining or maintaining power. Guards and their prisoners as well as children and their parents tell lies for this reason.

- **To fulfill social expectations**
  - These everyday lies involve politeness routines, compliments, and other "socially authorized" lies.

- **To have fun**
  - Some lies are undertaken as a game. Many of these scenarios (like planning a surprise party or other put-ons) are temporary in nature and require the liar to be exposed in the end (Stebbins, 1975). Hence they are sufficiently different from actual lying that their status as a real lie is questionable. April Fool's Day pranks and practical jokes are also in this category. The feeling  of enjoyment associated with these lies can be intensified when the target is hard to fool or when there is an audience to the deceptive performance. Facial expressions will sometimes reveal the fun these liars are having. Ekman (2001) calls such expressions "duping delight."

Although any of the aforementioned reasons might prompt adults to lie, it is important to note that none of these motives are *unique to deception*. For example, someone motivated to maintain their privacy in a social setting could accomplish this goal either through *deception* (giving a fake name and phone number to a stranger) or through the use of *honesty* (telling the stranger you don't want to share your contact information).

Deception is best thought of as a strategy for fulfilling motives such as these rather than a desired end in itself (Levine & Kim, 2008). In general, research suggests people will not resort to deception to fulfill a motive unless the truth poses an obstacle. Levine, Kim, and Hamel (2010) asked participants in their study how they would respond to a dinner host who had just served a meal and then asked if they liked the food. When participants were further told to imagine they had really enjoyed the meal, 100% of them said they would give their honest opinion to the host. But when they were asked to imagine that the food was not enjoyable, the clear majority (62.5%) opted to deceive rather than convey a truth that might hurt the host's feelings.

Levine, Ali, Dean, Abdulla, and Garcia-Ruano (2016) examined lie motives across five distinct national cultures. They found further support for the notion that people typically choose to deceive only when telling the truth would create a problem. Across various cultures, general motives for deception resemble those previously listed.

The Type of Lie Told May Affect Liar Behavior

There are two primary types of lies, plus a third type that's something of a gray area. (Note that these have to do with how the lie is constructed, not the underlying motivation for the deception):

- **Falsifying**
  - Falsification means the liar is *actively* trying to *create a false belief* in the target or *support a false belief* the target already holds. Because they involve action on the part of the deceiver, these are generally referred to as *lies of commission*.

- **Concealing**
  - Here the liar is *hiding or withholding* true information or feelings—what is referred to as a *lie of omission*. These lies can occur when a person decides not to correct another person's false belief.

- **Misleading**
  - Attributions of lying or deception may also be due to *misleading* behavior, but this type of lie is not as "pure" as the others. Misleading behavior can occur without any deceptive intent on the part of the communicator. Because creating or maintaining a false belief isn't always an inherent goal of such behavior, it is not considered as fundamental a form of deception as falsifying and concealing. Nevertheless—and regardless of the communicator's intention—when people feel they have been misled by such things as half-truths, indirect speech, equivocation, or distortion, they won't hesitate to label the instigator a flat-out liar.

Often people oversimplify the truth-lie dichotomy and see acts of communication as either inherently true or completely false. McCornack and colleagues (2014) refer to each end of this spectrum as **bald-faced truths** and **bald-faced lies**. While these terms may not be used frequently in everyday conversation, the point is that most communicative exchanges do not swing to the extreme ends of this hypothetical pendulum. The real world is far more complex, and statements and behaviors of liars tend to be blends of truth and lies.

When considering the three types—falsifying, concealing, and misleading—there appear to be some behaviors that characterize each type of lie, but none that characterize all three (Buller & Burgoon, 1996; Buller, Burgoon, Buslig, & Roiger, 1994; Ebesu & Miller, 1994). For example, Frank and Ekman (2004) found consistent facial, body, and paralinguistic behaviors with two different types of high-stakes *falsifications*. In one, the liars were giving a false opinion and in the other they were lying about taking money.

Not surprisingly, lies in everyday life often borrow elements from more than one of the three types. For example, a lie in the form of a conversation may be made up of some information that is falsified, some that is misleading, and some that is concealed. In such cases, the behaviors exhibited by the liar might combine information in unexpected ways and vary depending on whether the lie:

- happens spontaneously or is premeditated
- has a subject matter that is simple or complex
- requires short or long responses
- needs to be repeated in different contexts or is limited to a single performance

Mimicking these real-life conditions in research studies is not always easy, but it's an important issue because it has a direct bearing on what we claim to know about liar behavior. DePaulo et al. (2003) reviewed approximately 120 deception studies, and their findings are worth noting. The studies they reviewed were set up in ways that would seem to differ dramatically from lying in the real world:

- 86% of the studies involved liars and targets who were strangers
- 84% involved students
- 57% provided no motivation to liars to tell a successful lie
- About an equal number involved prepared versus spontaneous messages
- 60 involved lies about attitudes, facts, or perceptions of visual materials
- 21 involved lies about transgressions

It would seem, then, that the most-researched kind of lie is one that:

- does not deal with an actual transgression,
- is short in duration and only told once,
- by an undergraduate student,
- who has no real motivation to succeed in distorting the truth.

Researchers might do well to consider Levine's (2018) advice. He argues that we must design deception studies that more accurately replicate how lies and truth work beyond the walls of sterile laboratory settings. Communication is complex, lies can be spontaneous, and contexts range from simple statements between friends to those told to law enforcement during high-stakes security situations.

This does not mean that the existing data we have from deception experiments and studies is not informative or useful. But it does mean we should resist the temptation to generalize what we know about deception. Too often, people want to take the findings from a single study conducted under a very particular set of conditions and draw some sweeping conclusion about lying behavior in general, such as "Liars do X" or "You can catch a liar because they do Y." Be skeptical when you listen to people on television or online giving advice about how to detect when someone is lying. It is likely they're oversimplifying the results of the research. Liars do lots of different things for lots of different reasons.

... we should resist the temptation to generalize what we know about deception.

LOW-STAKES LIES

Most of the lies we tell do not have serious consequences. These are called low-stakes lies because there isn't much to be gained if the lie is successful and there isn't much to be lost if the lie fails. Here's what we know about these types of lies:

- Some low-stakes lies are an expected part of everyday conversation (polite remarks, for example).

- It is true, however, that almost any lie, no matter how trivial it may seem, will offend some people.

- In addition, any lie that was initially treated as trivial can be transformed into a lie of great consequence when a positive relationship turns sour.

- Low-stakes lies are mostly told for one's personal benefit—to improve one's image, to feel better, to protect oneself from embarrassment, hurt, or disapproval, etc.

- We tell such lies to everyone, but more often to people we don't know all that well.

- These lies occur frequently. In one study, students reported telling these lies once in every three interactions (DePaulo & Kashy, 1998).

- Low-stakes lies are often communicated via technology or online because this eliminates some difficulties liars feel when telling the lie in person. Phone calls eliminate visual cues and texting, e-mail, and social media reduce the presence of the other person while also providing more control over the verbal message. Lying online or through social media (see Tsikerdekis & Zeadally, 2014) may be easier to enact, and it may even make the liar feel less responsible for the lie (Hancock et al., 2004).

> Low-stakes lies are often communicated via technology or online because this eliminates some difficulties liars feel when the target is in his or her presence.

Low-stakes lies occur in a wide variety of contexts, each of which is worth examining in more detail:

- everyday conversation
- self-presentation
- attracting a romantic partner
- flattery and ingratiation
- sports, games, and magic
- the workplace

With most low-stakes lies, the behavioral differences between liars and truth tellers are barely discernible, if at all. The primary explanation is simple: Such lies involve little stress, little emotion, and the amount of thought involved is minimal. DePaulo et al. (2003) stated, ". . . ordinary people are so practiced, so proficient, and so emotionally unfazed by the telling of untruths that they can be regarded as professional liars" (p. 81). Ekman (2001) echoed this sentiment when he said, "Most liars can fool most people most of the time" (p. 162).

Everyday Conversation

Low-stakes lies infiltrate our compliments, invitations, requests, excuses, complaints, offers, and assessments (Rodriguez & Ryave, 1990). This type of lie includes everything from the faking of listening—also referred to as pseudo-listening—to the faking of, well, *other things*. To illustrate, consider some of the following examples that may seem familiar:

- You tell someone you feel fine when you don't, or that you feel sick when you don't.

- You text "Omw" to a friend who is already waiting when you haven't left the house yet.

- A stranger approaches you to tell you to vote, and you tell them that you already did (but you haven't).

- You tell someone, "It's the perfect gift and I love it," when it isn't and you don't.

- You tell someone you are with, "I was *not* looking at her/him," when you totally were.

- You say, "I'll call you tomorrow," when you have no (or only a vague) intention of doing so.

- You like someone's post on Facebook when you really don't.

- You tell your date, "I never felt comfortable enough with anyone before to do what we just did," when it isn't true. Or perhaps you play innocent by declaring ahead of time, "I've never done this before," when, in fact, it is far from your first rodeo.

- You play the "mark-down" game, saying a recent purchase cost far less than it really did.

- You play the "mark-up" game, telling someone your purchase cost far more than the bargain-basement price your cheap self actually paid.

- You automatically say "I love you, too," when a family member says it to you, even when you don't and it feels unnatural and inauthentic (after a conflict, for example).

- You tell a group of people, "When he said that, I told him what I really thought of him," but you didn't.

- You nod and say things that lead another person to believe you *agree* with what they are saying, but you don't.

- You say you were studying over the weekend when you were not. Or you say you have homework to avoid going to a reception (or something else boring).

Sometimes when people embellish their stories, listeners consider such lies to be of little consequence, accepting and sometimes even encouraging them. There are even times when someone's narrative or storyline is more important than an otherwise complete and utterly boring version of the truth. A common expression shared about these types of storytellers is that they "never let the truth get in the way of a good story." Their exaggerations stretch the truth in ways that tend to be acceptable and within the boundaries of what we expect.

© Nadia Snopek/Shutterstock.com

Self-Presentation

According to DePaulo and her colleagues (1992; 2003), low-stakes lies are most accepted when they're an aspect of self-presentation, which is the process of managing the impression we make on others. We sometimes resort to low-stakes lies to enhance that impression in-person or online (Guadagno, Okdie, & Kruse, 2012). Among other things, these types of low-stakes lies are used to:

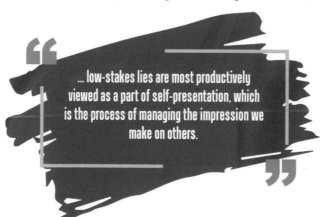

... low-stakes lies are most productively viewed as a part of self-presentation, which is the process of managing the impression we make on others.

- make us look better than we really are

- hide things we consider detrimental to our image

- shield ourselves from disapproval

Meeting new people is often seen as an opportunity to present a new self. Feldman, Forrest, and Happ (2002) demonstrated how such "self-presentation" lies can be triggered and how often they occur. Students were asked to have a 10-minute conversation with another student they didn't know. Some were told to make their partner think they were competent; some were told to try to make the other person like them; some weren't told anything. The researchers found the following:

- 60% of students reported having lied.

- Students who were told to seem competent and likeable lied twice as much as those who were not given any specific instructions.

- On average, there were two lies in each conversation, but the totals ranged from none all the way up to 12.

Attracting a Romantic Partner

Dating is another self-presentation context where people use low-stakes lies to make the best possible first impression. In this context, deception is plentiful and may even be expected (at least to a degree). In bars or at a party, for example, where one of the main goals is to meet other people, the validity of one's personal details is open to question. How many of the following tidbits have you ever modified in some way or strategically omitted? Remember, you have three basic strategies available—to fabricate (completely falsify), to conceal/omit, or to mislead (half-truths, distortions, etc.):

- Name, phone number, or address
- Causes you care about
- People you like (or hate)
- Skills, interests, hobbies, or athleticism
- Sexual interests and history
- Major, classification, scholarships, or grades
- Jobs/internships

But things don't necessarily end there—even your *personality traits* are up for grabs. And this is especially true in the arena of dating (how "chill" are you, really?).

Suppose it goes well at the party or in the bar. You meet someone and begin to date him/her. The research suggests that the prevalence of low-stakes, self-presentation lies is likely to continue, at least in the early stages of your relationship. Deception may be more prevalent during dating than in more established relationships for a variety of reasons:

1. As potential partners are just getting to know one another and decide whether or not to pursue something more serious, the scrutiny with which they evaluate one another is particularly high. This in turn can increase the occurrence of falsifications (or concealments) as daters make great effort to come across as desirable and worth the time and effort invested (Vangelisti, 2012).

2. The dating environment may highlight people's insecurities about their attractiveness and stoke a fear of rejection, both of which may prompt daters to lie.

3. Deception may also be a response to a sense of competitiveness with other potential partners (Toma & Hancock, 2010).

Anyone who has been on a first date (even if you're just "hanging out" as a group) will remember putting their best foot forward:

- taking extra time to prepare their physical appearance

- dressing with great contemplation, ensuring their clothes are color-coordinated, clean, and wrinkle-free

- rehearsing lines (compliments, for example) and topics of conversation

- camouflaging behavioral quirks with polite talk (see previous bullet) and at times show impeccable manners

> It is unlikely anyone will later call you a liar because you were on your best behavior during a first encounter, first date, or while making a first impression.

These extra steps are taken to make a first impression that is more favorable than it is accurate. But for the most part, deceptions of this kind are considered normal, socially acceptable, and are widely encouraged. It is unlikely anyone will later call you a liar because you were on your best behavior during a first encounter, first date, or while making a first impression.

Speaking of dating, *sexual issues* are another particularly common subject for low-stakes deceit. In her research focused on the dating lives of heterosexual college students, Luchetti (1999) found the following results:

- 20% of college students misrepresented their sexual history to their sexual partners

- 33% avoided disclosing their sexual history to at least one partner

- Around other men, men tend to exaggerate the number of sexual partners and the specifics of their sexual activities

- Women tend to say they've had fewer sexual partners and experiences than they actually have, especially with a potential long-term male partner

Both men and women also tell lies about possible sexual competitors. For example, a man may tell someone he is interested in that another man (his competition) is only interested in using them for sex. He, on the other hand, is way more interested in the fun they have together.

While this may be sincere, the strategy he is using is one often used by men who want to hide their intent to have sex. In other words, the mere *simulation* of commitment (a type of falsification) can be effective in attracting a partner (Buss, 1994).

Tooke and Camire (1991) found **88** distinct ways that university men and women deceive each other as they try to attract a partner. Some of these included:

- misleading statements about their career goals
- sucking in their stomachs when walking near a desirable target
- giving the appearance of being more trusting and considerate than they actually were
- acting uninterested in having sex

Because they play an important role in attracting a romantic partner, men are particularly prone to use the following deceptive behaviors:

- exaggerate their accomplishments at work and the money they make

- act more confident, masculine, or assertive than they really feel

- sell themselves as honest, vulnerable, and considerate (they may even reveal a "painful secret" that is neither painful nor secret—or even real for that matter)

More and more people meet prospective partners online, via any of the 2,500 online dating services (in the United States alone), including location-based dating apps such as Bumble. However, these services also provide a platform for would-be daters to deceive before they even speak or meet prospective partners in person. Consider the information daters post about themselves in their online profiles. Toma, Hancock, and Ellison (2008) surveyed 80 people who submitted online profiles on various dating websites. Here's what they found:

- The vast majority (81%) lied about one or more of their physical attributes, such as height, weight, and age.

- As a general rule, women tended to lie about their weight and men about their height.

- The more a woman's actual weight was higher than average, the more she was likely to exaggerate her thinness.

- Similarly, men whose height was lower than average were more likely to exaggerate their height.

In a follow-up study, Hancock and Toma (2009) focused on the role of photographs and found:

- about one third of the online photographs users post of themselves were not representative

- overall, women's photographs appeared to be less accurate than men's photographs

- women were more likely to be older than they were portrayed in their photographs

- female photographs were also more likely to be retouched or taken from an angle that deceptively portrayed them as thinner or taller

- even though people frequently distorted pictures and other information in their online profiles, they typically kept their alterations *within believable parameters* knowing that they might subsequently meet their correspondents face-to-face.

... in the 21st century, an online profile has become, in a sense, the equivalent of a first date.

The magnitude of deception in online profiles that Hancock and colleagues observed should not come as a surprise. After all, in the 21st century, an online profile has become, in a sense, the equivalent of a first date. More recently, Markowitz and Hancock (2018) conducted a study of messages sent on dating apps during the discovery phase and found that 7% of messages exchanged were deceptive and that two thirds of the lies were constructed for self-presentation and impression management purposes.

Flattery/Ingratiation

Low-stakes lies are also used for **false praise**. We sometimes give compliments we don't think are deserved in order to make the target feel good. This goodwill, in turn, may make them feel obligated to help us in the future, something that Jones (1964) calls a "subversive masquerade," and its fundamental insidiousness is apparent when one considers the basic goals of the ingratiator:

1. Locate a target who can provide benefits (self-serving)
2. Identify what the target needs/wants to hear (scheming)
3. Determine how to satisfy the target's wants/needs in ways that will be believed (deception) or prompt the target to act in ways that benefit the ingratiator (manipulation).

Forms of false praise like flattery and ingratiation are widely condemned (think of terms like *ass-kisser* and *brown-noser*). Why, then, is it so common? Gordon (1996) suggests that the main reason is simple—*it works*. False praise (especially giving undeserved compliments and appearing to agree with another person's opinion) can be very effective. This is because we tend to like (and thus be inclined favorably toward) people who:

- appear to like us
- seem to agree with us
- say they see good things in our behavior and/or thinking
- who ask our opinion and advice

These acts are usually initiated by the deceiver, but occasionally the target will provide the setup—e.g., "Do you think I'm smart?" If the truth is likely to hurt (or get you fired), deception may be called for as a response to such questions. It may even be *expected* (as when someone is "fishing" for a compliment or other validation).

But to be maximally effective, it has to be done well (which means that it shouldn't be obvious). Some of the issues at play for the effective performance of deceptive compliments and opinion agreement are identified by Stengel (2000) and Jones (1964). They are basically recommendations for how to do it in ways that will yield results:

- Consider the benefits of praising someone behind their back. If your positive comments eventually reach the target, your intent to obligate the target to you is less likely to be perceived. In other words, avoid the perception that your compliment is given strictly because you want some benefit in return.

- Make the compliment one that addresses a characteristic of the target that cuts across situations, so that it can't be automatically linked to the situation you're gaming.

- Ingratiation is especially difficult with people who have authority over the complimenter because his or her motives are immediately called into question. In such cases, subtlety is key. Compliment or agree with a supervisor while simultaneously communicating a lack of dependence on him or her. In other words, the message is that the ingratiator's behavior is being performed without any desire for benefits in return. Oddly enough, even if the ingratiator's motive for complimenting or opinion agreement is crystal clear to the target, it may still have the desired effect.

- Don't make a habit of always agreeing with the target (in other words, don't be a brown-nosing "yes"-person). Disagree on minor things, especially things that are a matter of opinion or that are entirely unrelated to work (although we recommend not joking about their alma mater, even if it is A&M). When you want to pretend to agree, pick issues that are both important to the target AND where your true opinion can't be easily determined (so be careful what you've posted on Facebook).

- Allow the target to see you disagreeing with others from time to time. And occasionally show resistance to the target's opinion, then slowly "come around" to their point of view.

- When possible, anticipate the target's opinion and state it as your opinion before he or she does.

Sports and Games

To play and win at various sports, effective deception skills are required (Mawby & Mitchell, 1986). Here are but a few illustrations:

- Basketball players use their eyes and shifting body positions to provide misleading information to those guarding them, including direction of movement, where the ball will be passed, and whether they intend to shoot.

- A boxer's left hook may only be effective if the opponent is defending against an expected right jab.

- Offensive linemen in football mislead their opponents about the direction of a running play by the way they block.

- A pass receiver in football may run the same route at the same speed several times in order to establish an expected routine for the pass defender. Then the receiver will exploit the defender's expectations by changing speed and running a different route.

- In baseball, players use subtlety to steal a base, or use the "hidden ball" trick to catch an offensive player not touching the base.

Whether in football, boxing, basketball—even table games like chess and poker—winning often depends on misleading one's opponent.

- Hockey has "dekes" and soccer has all types of sly maneuvers and fake shots.

- Check out ESPN's "Top 10 Deception Plays" (QR), beginning at 0:40.

Whether in football, boxing, basketball—even table games like chess and poker—winning often depends on misleading one's opponent. As long as it remains within the rules of the game, this type of deception is not only tolerated but encouraged (even taught). In fact, the stakes can be high for professional athletes who could lose their livelihood if their ability to deceive is lacking.

Does deceitful skill in game-playing transfer to everyday life? Obviously the game of life and games played for sport are different in many ways. But there may be some lessons that carry over, such as learning:

- to anticipate a person's reaction to a deceptive maneuver
- various ways to mask one's real intentions
- the importance of preparation and practice for effective execution of deception
- the value of setting up a deceptive move by preceding it with truthful behavior
- not to overuse any particular type of deception or disguise

Deception in the context of sporting events, like deception in everyday life, has to be *adapted to the circumstances*. In sporting events, like daily life, deceivers learn to develop effective maneuvers that undermine what others anticipate, expect, or consider normal. A basketball player who fakes a shot too far from the basket is not likely to fool many opponents but a player who uses deceptive maneuvers strategically (and in non-obvious ways) is likely to enjoy some success.

Effective deceivers in these contexts not only learn how to deceive opponents (offense), but also to detect when their opponents are attempting to deceive them (defense). Sebanz and Shiffrar (2009) asked basketball players to view videos of other players preparing to perform *deceptive* moves (such as faking a pass or a jump shot). The videos ended right before the deceptive moves were executed. Participants were then shown an additional video in which players were preparing to make *real* passes or jump shots. Finally, they were asked to distinguish between the fake and real attempts, with results as follows: Expert players performed *somewhat* better than novices (60% vs. 54%) in detecting fake moves from the videos. The researchers speculated that the experts likely drew on *their own experience in performing the fake moves* to distinguish real from fake moves made by other players. While that 6% improvement might not seem like a lot, it could mean the difference between going pro or remaining in the amateurs, or between a career player and a hall-of-famer.

Like many card games, deception is critical to the success of poker players. Good players know that opponents are closely watching their behavior in order to determine whether they have a strong hand or not. Poker is usually played for money, so competitors are continually scanning each other for "tells" (short for *telegraph*). Tells are unintended verbal and/or nonverbal signals that may indicate any number of important details, such as the quality of opponents' hands, their intention to bet, and whether the wager will be large or small (Caro, 2003). Accurate reading (QR) of such information can confer a huge competitive advantage.

Therefore, like deceivers in other contexts, poker players try to mask their feelings and intentions. A common way of masking their behavior is to use a *poker face* to neutralize the display of emotion:

- use an unchanging, typically neutral, facial expression
- minimal hand, body (posture), and head movement
- little or no verbal behavior

Some players even wear sunglasses to keep competitors from observing any dilation of their pupils that might occur when they are dealt a strong hand (our pupils tend to dilate when we get excited or anxious, and it happens outside our conscious control).

Instead of masking, some poker players try to *confuse or mislead* their opponents which occurs when players (Hayano, 1980):

- deliberately change moods—sometimes engaging in relaxed chatter and a happy facial expression when they have a poor hand and sometimes when they have a good hand (so that no consistent relationship can be discerned)

- are quiet and deliberate with a good hand on one occasion and performing the same behavior with a poor hand on another occasion

Good poker players also use misleading signals. For example, they may set a trap using a *false tell*—e.g., pressing one's lips tightly together when bluffing. Later, when there is a lot of money at stake and they actually have a good hand, they again press their lips together. The other players are misled by the false tell, so they continue to bet more money thinking they're about to beat a bluffer.

New and inexperienced poker players may not be good deceivers. Common rookie mistakes include:

- straightening posture and looking attentive when they have good cards, and doing the opposite (or at least remaining unchanged) on good hands.

lying and deception in **HUMAN INTERACTION**

- quickly grasping chips to bet when they have good cards but reaching slowly when they have bad cards. Sometimes novice poker players, like inexperienced liars, will "oversell" their lie—e.g., dramatizing the weakness or strength of their cards to such an extent that their affectations are not believable.

Remember, expert players do these things too, but do so *deliberately*. In addition, they are intentionally switching up the associations between bad and good so that no predictable pattern can be discerned.

Magic

The magician Karl Germain is credited with saying, "Magic is the only honest profession. A magician promises to deceive you and he does." It's a unique way of thinking about deception because magicians are *expected* to be deceitful. Just as curiously, the targets of this deceit (audience members) *want* to be fooled. In fact, if they can figure out how the trick was done, then they may feel it wasn't a good act.

Magician Peter the Adequate readily admits to being a professional deceiver. From his comments, it is not hard to see how some of the same skills he uses as an entertainer are also used by deceivers of all kinds in everyday life:

- "I rely on audience assumptions about how they think things work and how a trick is done."

- "Misdirection is the key. Audiences follow movement, gaze direction, things that are higher, and things that are closer. Misdirection can be accomplished with props, speech, hands, or an assistant."

- "I give the audience reasons to believe what I want them to believe."

- "I convince myself the ball is in my hand (when it isn't)."

- "I practice so much I can often think five or six steps ahead."

- "I tell the audience some truths with some lies."

The Fitzkee Trilogy (1945) is a series of books detailing the activities of magicians. In one volume, the author provided some tips for deception that complement those made by Peter the Adequate:

1. Deliberate repetition of what appears (to the audience) to be the same action will eventually become monotonous and commonplace. When that occurs, it ceases to attract close attention and clears the way for the magician to engage in secret maneuvers.

2. The control of one's voice, especially during the time of the deception, is necessary for the trick to succeed. Avoid hesitations, slower speech, stammering, and pitch change—all are giveaways to the audience that something important is happening.

3. Provide the audience with familiar things and let them assume they know what you are dealing with.

4. Do not explain what should be obvious as doing so leads to suspicion. If you cut the bottom out of a tomato can and show the cylinder to the audience, they will assume it is like other tomato cans and is empty. If you *say* it is empty, however, they may wonder if it really is.

The Workplace

According to Shulman (2007), lying and deception are part of the infrastructure of most places of work. The consequences for much of the deception that takes place there are not usually serious (in other words, low-stakes), including:

- politeness rituals enacted when dealing with rude customers
- professing adherence to an official set of rules but acting in ways that are at odds with them
- falsely complimenting a person who can help you get ahead (discussed previously)
- telling a supervisor only what you believe they want to hear
- pretending to accomplish more than you have or work harder than you did

Of course, given the right circumstances, these and other forms of deception can become high-stakes lies, but behaviors like the ones in the above list are a far cry from obviously high-stakes (and potentially criminal) actions like cheating customers, fraudulently acquiring or spending money, and hiding flaws in products. When companies rely on deception to advertise a product or use it for financial gain, they are expected to do so within the boundaries allowed by federal law.

When they go too far with their use of deception, their lies become high-stakes (the subject of the next section). One example of this is how Southwest Airlines was fined in 2014 after advertising a very low airfare ($59 one way) for flights between certain large cities—but no such fares were available online. The company claimed this was due to a programming error and had pulled the ads as soon as they discovered the problem. However, a strikingly similar error had occurred the previous year, which led skeptical industry regulators to slap the company with a $200,000 fine this time (Peterson, 2014).

HIGH-STAKES LIES

With low-stakes lies, you risk little if caught but also gain little if successful. Not so with high-stakes lies, which are likely to have strong negative consequences if uncovered, but carry the potential for considerable gain if they remain undetected. Because the stakes are high, many researchers believe the liar's observable behavior and language are more likely to manifest the cognitive and emotional strain that often accompanies these forms of deception.

Cognitive and Emotional Processes

Deceivers may be more likely to manifest emotional signs associated with things like *fear*, *apprehension*, and *general arousal* when:

- they are very afraid of getting caught in their lie
- the target of the lie is perceived as being difficult to fool
- the target is suspicious
- the liar has had little experience with deception

Other emotional signs of deceit might be associated with a liar's *guilt*, *anger*, or even *happiness* (if experiencing duping delight). When these emotions are the drivers, the expectation is that, in attempting to cover them up, liars will display affective states that *do not fit* (or are otherwise inappropriate to) the situation at hand (Ekman, 2001).

High-stakes lies require more thinking than low-stakes lies, as they are presumed to be much more cognitively complex (Vrij, Fisher, & Blank, 2017). When cognition is stressed in this way, we may see (and hear) liars telling stories that are inconsistent and delivered with hesitation, or that seem too rehearsed or overly awkward (Blair, Reimer, & Levine, 2018; Zuckerman, DePaulo, & Rosenthal, 1981). The underlying belief regarding these signs of deception based on cognitive difficulty and inappropriate emotions is that they will distinguish liars from truth tellers *when the stakes are high*. In order to determine the validity of such a critical assumption, researchers have endeavored to match real-world, high-stakes conditions in controlled laboratory settings and then compare the behaviors of people who are telling the truth with the behaviors of those who are lying. It's not a particularly easy thing to do, so it's worth examining approaches to this type of research.

Generating High-Stakes Lies for Research

Even though these studies are not plentiful, several different methods have been used to successfully generate high-stakes lies under controlled conditions:

- Horvath and colleagues (1973; 1994) compared the interrogations of actual criminal suspects who subsequently had been determined to be telling truths or telling lies.

- Other researchers put people in stealing, false opinion, and cheating situations. These formats created conditions that made the cognitive and emotional demands of the participants similar to those they would experience in a real criminal investigation. A study by Frank and Ekman (2004) illustrated the stealing and false opinion formats:

  - In both conditions, there was a cash reward for a successful deception and punishment for an unsuccessful one. Unsuccessful liars were shown demonstrations of the punishment ahead of time and made to believe they would have to endure these fairly unpleasant physical conditions (for obvious ethical reasons, none were actually punished, but it was critical that they believed they would be).

  - In the false opinion format, participants were given a list of social issues like "Should convicted, cold-blooded murderers be executed?" and asked to indicate how strongly they agreed or disagreed with each issue. The issues they felt most strongly about were the ones they were expected to *support* in front of interviewers. For some, this professed support was the truth, but others were asked to fake it. The reward–punishment system for the false opinion scenario was the same as for the theft scenario.

The general framework for the cheating format is similar, with a modest but attractive cash prize as a reward counterbalanced by the threat of severe punishment. If you're interested in the details, review the research designs used by Exline, Thibaut, Hickey, and Gumpert (1970); Shulman (1973); and Feeley and deTurck (1998). In short, the approach is this:

1. A researcher gives an unsuspecting participant (a university student) a task that cannot possibly be solved in the 5 minutes allotted. The person with him or her is given the same task to share but is secretly a confederate working for the researcher.

2. Soon, the researcher is called out of the room for "an important phone call." The confederate then pretends to find that the answer to the task was left on the researcher's desk. The participant then has the choice to join the confederate in cheating or remain honest. Either way, the confederate writes down an answer that is startlingly close to the correct number and submits it when the interviewer returns (even if one of the honest participants disagreed with doing so).

3. The interviewer first interviews the pair together, then separately:

  – The interrogation strategy is to gradually increase the pressure on the participant during the interview (concluding with a veiled threat of expulsion), whether they cheated or remained honest.

  – When interviewed *together*, the majority of cheaters did *not* confess.

  – When interviewed *alone*, the majority of cheaters *did* confess.

4. The taped interviews are then viewed to see how the behaviors of those not involved in cheating (the truth tellers) compared with those who cheated.

THE BEHAVIOR OF LIARS

Given the expectation that liars are trying to control any behavior that might reveal their deception, early research efforts to isolate liar behavior looked closely at *nonverbal* behavior (starting with the work of Ekman and Friesen in 1969). It was assumed that liars knew how to control their verbal behavior, but nonverbal behavior could not be controlled consciously, or at least not as much. Polygraphs, and more recent attempts to study the brain activity of liars, are also based on the belief that there are some aspects of the liar's behavior that they cannot control.

But the more researchers learned about nonverbal behavior, particularly those behaviors that get regular social commentary and feedback, the more they realized that some nonverbal behavior is *far more controllable* than originally believed (including the possibility of managing physiological responses so as to fool the polygraph). However, it turned out that some extremely subtle (and hard to spot) nonverbal behaviors are typically outside of the liar's control. False smiles, micro-momentary, and poorly timed facial expressions are examples (Ekman, 2001).

" ... some extremely subtle (and hard to spot) *nonverbal* behaviors are typically outside of the liar's control. False smiles, micro-momentary, and poorly timed facial expressions are examples. "

Researchers have also learned that some *verbal* behavior is not as controllable as was first believed. Pennebaker (2011), for example, found that liars use words in ways that won't betray them or their message. More specifically, liars tend to use fewer first person singular pronouns (e.g., *I, me, my, mine*) in their speech. We also know that some liars don't always choose to control behaviors that could be controlled, which includes their language and word selection.

Put all of this together and we find that the profile of liar behavior may not be limited to a few hard-to-control behaviors as originally thought. Instead, it is likely to be a combination of verbal, vocal, nonverbal, and physiological signals that—*when evaluated as a group—tend to be associated with lying.* A holistic approach for detecting deception has been used to examine constellations of behaviors that correlate during deception (Burgoon, Schuetzler, & Wilson, 2015; Hartwig & Bond, 2014). Various scholars have summarized the research that distinguishes behavioral patterns in liars versus those found in truth tellers (Knapp & Comadena, 1979; Vrij, 2000; Zuckerman et al., 1981). These research summaries examined all types of lying (except pathological) in an effort to look for common features:

- Knapp, Hart, and Dennis (1974) predicted that deceivers would manifest verbal and nonverbal behaviors *signaling uncertainty, vagueness, nervousness, reticence, dependence on others,* and *negative affect* (emotion). Behaviors in these categories have been repeatedly found in research.

- DePaulo et al. (2003) examined 120 separate deception studies and 158 behaviors. Their findings supported the following general conclusions:

  - **Liars are less forthcoming than truth tellers**: They respond less (shorter responses and less elaboration), seem to be holding back, speak at a slower rate, and take longer before responding (however, when liars have *time to plan* their lie, this difference in response latency tends to decrease).

  - **Liars tell stories that are less plausible**: Their stories make less sense, contain more discrepancies, are less engaging (have more word and phrase repetitions), and liar behavior is:

    - less immediate (more indirect, fewer self-references)
    - more uncertain
    - less fluent (more hesitations, errors, pauses)
    - less active (fewer gestures)

  - **Liars, *unlike truth tellers,* seem to want their stories to be *without error:*** They make fewer spontaneous corrections during the telling of their stories, and they are *less likely* to admit they can't remember something.

- **Liars make a more negative impression:** They seem less cooperative, make more negative statements, use more words denoting anger and fear, use offensive language, complain more, smile less, and seem more defensive.

- **Liars are more tense:** They exhibit this through higher pitch in their voice, increased fidgeting, and their pupils tend to dilate for longer periods.

Even though many of the studies supporting the preceding findings have quantified the frequency and duration of multiple cues (40% of the studies observed *10 or more* behaviors), we still have a lot to learn about the organization and coordination of these behaviors when they do occur. We do know from years of research, however, that *multiple* cues tend to be more reliable for detecting deception than *single* cues (e.g., avoiding eye contact).

Lying in Close Relationships

Compared to relationships with strangers and acquaintances, close relationships create a context with expectations for lying that are likely to alter liar behavior dramatically. To begin, we tell *fewer* lies to those we identify as close relationship partners. But lies that *violate the basic understandings* of a close relationship are likely to be *explosive* ones (DePaulo & Kashy, 1998). What are those things that make liar behavior different in close relationships (Knapp, 2006)?

1. **In a close relationship, you interact and expect to influence your partner frequently:**

   - Each partner *learns how the other behaves* when telling the truth AND when lying.

   - Therefore, when a partner in a close relationship lies about something detrimental to the relationship, it will be in the context of someone who may be very finely attuned to non-normative behavior.

2. **Close relationship partners establish rules about how the partners should and should not act in a given context:**

   - Roloff and Miller (2006) characterize these rules as "prescriptions that, if obeyed, should reduce the destructive nature of interpersonal conflicts" (p. 105).

   - Among these prescriptions are idealized rules about communication that portray honesty as desirable at any cost and deception as unacceptable and malignant. However, when examined through the lens of a relationship, it *may not be obvious to either partner* when he or she has broken a "rule" about truth telling or deception.

– Thus, although the partners may agree that lying is wrong, they may enact and detect lies in very different ways. While one partner may adopt a stance requiring "full and complete" disclosure in the relationship, the other may believe only "important information" needs to be disclosed, perhaps in the interest of tact or avoiding conflict. Sometimes *not disclosing* something to the other partner is interpreted by that partner as deception (concealment), and has the potential to create an explosive conflict (Roggensack & Sillars, 2014).

3. **Each person in a close relationship is aware of the vulnerabilities of their partner and is expected to recognize and respect them:**

– Many lies in close relationships are designed to help one's partner—making them feel good, building up their self-esteem, turning their faults into virtues, constructing excuses for misdeeds, and selectively concealing negative feelings.

– Each partner trusts the other to tell *all the truth* that matters to the health and welfare of the relationship. Neither partner is expected to *harm* or *take unfair advantage* of the other.

4. **Relationship partners are emotionally (and sometimes sexually) invested in their relationship and expect it to continue:**

– The continuing, often long-term nature of these relationships means that the subject of any given lie may have a particularly long shelf-life (Remember that one thing you said at the picnic 17 years ago?).

– Thus, some piece of the story that doesn't fit the liar's earlier portrayal may come up months or years later and need explanation. For example, in Arthur Miller's play *All My Sons*, a slip by the female lead (saying her husband hadn't been sick in 15 years) reveals the family's big lie, causing everything to come crashing down.

– Williams (2001) found that lying about sex (behaviors and history) was decreased in close relationships, and that most of these lies were protective of others rather than self-serving in nature (e.g., "I'm still attracted to you," or "You're just as amazing as ever."). However, in what may be more representative of self-deception (Chapter 6), it seems that people who most want to know their partners' sexual history are actually less inclined to seek information about it in an effort to avoid psychological discomfort that the truth may create (Afifi & Weiner, 2006).

5. **Close relationship partners are a team:**

– As such, they will co-construct some lies. Barnes (1994) says that sometimes one partner in a close relationship knows that the other partner is lying, but pretends not to—thereby engaging in what he calls *connivance*.

- There may also be *denial* by one partner that the other is not a team player—e.g., "He lies to others, but not to me."

- A close relationship team may also *collaborate* in their lies. This can be done by literally asking one's partner *not to reveal* certain information or the pair may *agree to lie* to a third party.

- The idea that partners in a close relationship are a team also means that when one tells a lie to make their partner feel good, it is likely to serve them well. When a liar's partner feels good, the liar may also feel good (as the old expression goes, "If Mama's happy, everybody's happy").

IS IT THE SAME AS LYING?

Language, for better or worse, gives us a lot of options for communicating—and lying. However, we can also be clear or ambiguous, direct or indirect, precise or general, and accurate or inexact without intending to lie or mislead. Since linguistic constructions that leave room for interpretation are so much a part of our everyday interaction, the question of deception is often not an issue. We'll look at six of them here. You may not recognize them all by name, but you've experienced each many times (whether as the sender of the message or the receiver), because they are so common in everyday conversation and public discourse:

- equivocation
- contextomy
- paltering
- spin
- bullshit
- doublespeak

Unlike bald-faced lies, each of these acts can be performed without the conscious intent to create a false sense of reality in the target. But because it is not unusual for people to use them to intentionally create a false reality, deception is sometimes attributed to these acts even when that is not the speaker's intent. When this happens, it's typically because at least three things are going on from the receiver's perspective:

- They perceive important consequences associated with the message. In other words, it *matters* to them. If it didn't, they wouldn't have called something a *lie* that, on the surface at least, isn't.

- They have reason(s) to believe the message was consciously and intentionally designed to mislead or create some kind of false belief.

- They know the attribution of deception will be hard to prove. Outright falsehoods can be revealed by finding contrary factual evidence. But the proof that misleading messages are deliberate often hinges on interpretations of language use and the establishment of a motive to mislead.

Let the word games begin.

Equivocation

Some messages that are perceived as evasive, indirect, or ambiguous result from what Bavelas, Black, Chovil, and Mullett (1990) call an *avoidance-avoidance conflict*. It happens when people find themselves in situations where they want to avoid the negative reactions that *either* telling the truth or telling a lie might elicit (hence avoidance-avoidance). So they go *in between* linguistically, saying something that is neither the literal, outright truth nor an obvious falsehood. In other words, they *equivocate*, and in so doing leave room for doubt.

For example, let's assume you find some old e-mails that reveal that your partner had a brief affair. After this heart-wrenching reading session, you inform him/her of the discovery and say: "You must have really been in love." Your partner wants to avoid saying no because you can point to various sentences in the e-mails that offer clear evidence to the contrary and your partner will have been caught in an outright lie. On the other hand, you don't get a *yes* answer either, perhaps because your partner doesn't want to hurt you any further and wants your relationship to remain intact.

Your partner could equivocate a thousand different ways, but chooses to go with, "We hardly knew each other." The implication is that no matter what may be in the e-mails, the only kind of love you should find threatening would be one that involved knowing the other person well and this was not the case (remember, this was brief, in the past, and let's assume for the sake of argument that your currrent relationship has never been stronger than it is now).

You both know it wasn't a direct answer to your question (neither of you is an idiot). What happens next is up to you:

- Do you get angry, accuse him or her of giving an evasive answer, and keep asking tougher and tougher questions?

- Do you let it go? Deep down, are you secretly relieved you didn't get a straightforward, unequivocal response?

- Or do you [fill in the blank]? Just as there were a thousand equivocal answers you could have gotten, there are probably as many different responses/reactions on your part. In a way, it all hinges on the existing rules of your relationship. Depending on what they are, you can follow them, ignore them, or change them.

In other contexts, however, equivocation can result in charges of deceptive intent (i.e., the receiver will view it as no different from an outright lie). For example, let's assume a person has been previously convicted of driving under the influence (DUI). Months later, the person is pulled over for speeding and is asked by the officer, "Have you been convicted of driving under the influence of alcohol within the last year?" and the equivocal response is, "I still have my driver's license." In this potentially risky situation, the driver obviously doesn't want to *admit* to a previous DUI conviction, but really doesn't want to get caught lying to a police officer. In this case, however, the response is more likely to be perceived as deliberately misleading (particularly since officers can usually access driving and conviction records from their vehicles).

Contextomy

Although not a household word, "contextomy" is something you know very well. It's more than merely misquoting someone; misquotes are often accidental and many times we are still able to glean the gist of what was originally meant. Rather, contextomy is the act of deliberately altering the fundamental meaning of what someone said or wrote by taking their

... contextomy is the act of deliberately altering the fundamental meaning of what someone said or wrote by taking their quote out of context.

quote out of context (McGlone, 2005). Here, the deceiver's express purpose is to mislead the audience into believing that the author meant something that, in fact, they did not (it could even, and often is, the exact opposite of what they meant).

Sometimes these are harmless and fun, even entertaining. We are often willing to overlook contextomies when everyone is in on the game. For example, contextomy occurs frequently when critics are quoted in movie advertisements. We all know that these ads often select a word or phrase from a reviewer's comments, which makes it appear that the critic is endorsing the movie. "Tom Hanks gives a brilliant performance," says the ad, which happens to be an entirely accurate quote from a critic. But if you bothered to actually read the critic's review, you would find that, in context, the quote has an entirely different meaning: "The only redeeming part of this entire movie, and it is less than a minute in length, is when Tom Hanks gives a brilliant performance as a barista with attention deficit disorder." In such settings, no one is likely to sue, lodge a formal complaint, or take any other serious action. And if you're naïve enough to believe such advertising on its own to rush to the theater and drop money on a ticket, then buyer beware.

In other arenas, such as politics (McGlone & Baryshevtsev, 2015) and courts of law, contextomy has serious consequences and attributions of intentionally deceptive behavior are more likely. In the 2006 U.S. Senate race in Missouri, television ads (QR) sponsored by Republican Senator Jim Talent criticized opponent Claire McCaskill by featuring quotes like "spreading untruths," and "clearly violated ethical standards" attributed simply to the *Kansas City Star*. The *Star* did indeed publish those quotes, but they were words McCaskill's opponents had used and were simply being quoted in the article. The words were not the opinion of the newspaper editors, yet the clearly intended implication was that the *Star* itself was endorsing Talent and condemning McCaskill, which was not the case.

In another ad, Talent's campaign accurately quoted a 2004 *St. Louis Post-Dispatch* article about McCaskill, which said she "used this office (state auditor) transparently for political gain." What the ad *didn't* say was that the quote was taken from an otherwise positive endorsement of McCaskill by the *Dispatch*, which said she was a "promising and dynamic leader" (FactCheck.org, "Talent for Deception," October 21, 2006).

Paltering

As contextomy illustrates, a statement need not be patently false to be perceived (or intended) as deceptive. "Paltering" refers to the use of accurate statements or labels with the intention of conveying an inaccurate impression (Schauer & Zeckhauser, 2009). Unlike a lie of commission, paltering only involves truthful statements; and unlike a lie of omission, it entails actively misleading a target rather than merely omitting relevant information. Advertisers wishing to draw consumers' attention to the contents of an envelope sometimes put a government warning about tampering with the mail on the outside of the envelope while also omitting a return address, thus purposefully creating the false impression the envelope contains an official letter from a government agency.

Some PhDs may make restaurant or hotel reservations using the title "Dr.," hoping in the process to lead the establishment to believe they are (typically wealthy) physicians rather than (middle class) academics. Politicians routinely present extreme and unrepresentative examples of social problems with the intent of leading voters into making erroneous generalizations (for example, in reality, welfare fraud is relatively rare and unprofitable; Levin, 2013). For example, Linda Taylor, the woman Ronald Reagan decried for collecting excessive public assistance, became known as the "welfare queen." This atypical example nevertheless tapped into stereotypes about the welfare system that resonated with many voters who believed the system was corrupt.

Rogers, Zeckhauser, Gino, Schweitzer, and Norton (2014) investigated corporate executives' attitudes toward paltering in business negotiations. A sample of executives was presented with the following scenario:

> *Imagine that over the last 10 years your sales have grown consistently and that next year you expect sales to be flat. In order to convey the impression that sales will continue to grow, you might palter by saying 'over the last 10 years our sales have grown consistently' and not highlight your expectation that sales this coming year will be flat.*

After reading this definition and example of paltering, the executives were then asked about their paltering habits during business negotiations and their attitudes toward this behavior:

- A majority of executives reported paltering in some or most of their negotiations (66%).
- Only 34% said they had done so in only a few or none of their negotiations.
- 80% said they perceived their paltering as "acceptable and honest" communication.

These findings suggest paltering is an especially pernicious form of deception because, unlike lies of commission and omission, it allows the deceiver to preserve an honest self-image. However, a follow-up study indicated that the *targets* of paltering in negotiations generally perceive it as the ethical equivalent of making intentionally false statements.

… paltering is an especially pernicious form of deception because, unlike lies of commission and omission, it allows the deceiver to preserve an honest self-image.

Spin

The term "spin" originates from baseball. When the pitcher spins the ball as it is thrown, it curves, making it difficult for the batter to accurately predict where it will cross the plate. Putting a spin on a story simply means that the communicator finds a way to:

- make it look like something it isn't (e.g., a loss is recast as a win of some kind)

- redirect a target's attention to a particular part of a story to distract from the original narrative (e.g., the numerous ways in which members of the Trump administration sought to discredit the inquiry into Russian election meddling)

With spin, the communicator's overarching goal is to *redirect the target's thinking in a way that is favorable to his or her point of view* (Jackson & Jamieson, 2007). In its purest form, spin:

1. looks like it is addressing an issue directly (but isn't)
2. is hard to factually discredit
3. uses language that allows room for interpretation so that the spinner can deny lying

The spinner is a person who is predisposed to a particular point of view and perceives several possible interpretations of the information in question, so the spin on the story is not perceived as outright lying. Instead, it is seen as something closer to opinion or commentary (think of right-leaning Fox News and left-leaning MSNBC). Half-truths and refocusing/redirecting are two common ways to spin:

- *Half-truth*: In 1996, President Clinton said he had put 100,000 new police officers on American streets. He had signed a bill authorizing 100,000 new police officers, but at the time of his statement, only about 40,000 were funded and only about 21,000 of them were actually on duty.

- *Refocusing*: President George W. Bush justified the invasion of Iraq by claiming the regime had weapons of mass destruction. When none were found, the war was later justified on the grounds that the United States had removed a tyrant from power and brought democracy to Iraq.

Statistics can also be used to refocus and redirect thinking (Holmes, 1990; Huff, 1954). Notice how easy it is to argue that robberies in a particular city involving a weapon have increased either 5% or 100% from the following data.

	2017	2018
All Robberies	400	400
Robberies With Weapons	20	40

One person might argue that, "There has been a small increase of 5% in robberies with weapons. In 2017, it was 5% of all robberies and in 2018 it was 10% of all robberies." But another person might say, "There has been a shocking 100% increase in robberies with weapons. In 2017, there were 20 and in 2018 that figure doubled to 40." The data are the same, but the messages (and the agendas behind them) couldn't be more different. When visual graphs or charts showing statistics are distorted in ways that are misleading it is called **statistification**.

Bullshit

Liars are very concerned about the possible impact of a target learning the truth. As a result, they make a special effort to hide it or guide targets away from it. Bullshitters, on the other hand, *have little regard for the truth*—it just doesn't concern them. Frankfurt (2005, p. 55) put it this way: "It is impossible to lie unless you think you know the truth. Producing bullshit requires no such conviction." From this perspective:

Bullshitters are not concerned with where they find information or whether it is true as long as it supports their overall purpose.

- Bullshitters may say things that are accurate or they may say things that are inaccurate, but it doesn't matter either way as accuracy is not the issue for them. They are not trying to hide the truth.

- Instead, they are either trying to hide their lack of concern for the truth or just outright illustrating it through their banter.

- Bullshitters are not concerned with where they find information or whether it is true as long as it supports their overall purpose. They may sometimes be accused of outright lying, but reactions to bullshit are often benign.

© Arcady/Shutterstock.com

- People who participate in "bull sessions" typically suspend their concern for factual accuracy as well as their certainty that the speaker really believes what he or she is saying. Orators, politicians, and stand-up comedians frequently rely on this model, and most of the time audiences readily accept it. Bullshitting might be thought of as the original virtual reality—a way for people to share their imaginations with others.

Bullshitting is widely practiced (Penny, 2005). Frankfurt (2005) offers an explanation as to why:

> *Bullshit is unavoidable whenever circumstances require someone to talk without knowing what he is talking about. Thus the production of bullshit is stimulated whenever a person's obligations or opportunities to speak about some topic exceed his knowledge of the facts that are relevant to that topic. This discrepancy is common in public life, where people are frequently impelled—whether by their own propensities or by the demands of others—to speak extensively about matters of which they are to some degree ignorant. (p. 63)*

Larson's (2006) view of bullshit differs from Frankfurt's. He argues that bullshit often does hide or mask the truth, but it is done in such a way that it isn't a direct contradiction of something that others subscribe to as truth. Wakeham (2017) worries that bullshit interferes with everyday truth-seeking and the solving of social problems. The perfect example is the paradox you may experience as you are reading this chapter to prepare for class/an assignment while you are also simultaneously enjoying learning new information. Bullshit is woven heavily into our lives.

Doublespeak

The term *doublespeak* has been around since the 1950s, but it was popularized by an annual doublespeak award given by the National Council of Teachers of English and in the works of William Lutz (1989; 1996; 1999). Lutz uses the term to describe a broad spectrum of language used to deliberately misrepresent reality. The more disturbing ones, he argues, are those used by people in positions of power to mislead others for their own purposes. Rosen's (2003) observations concerning the labels given to programs in the Bush administration are compatible with Lutz' definition of doublespeak:

- The "healthy forests" program allows increased logging of protected wilderness.

- The "clear skies" program permits greater industrial pollution.

- The new "opt in" feature of the Head Start program is simply a way of telling states they will now share a greater portion of the costs of the program.

Our individual reactions to doublespeak are more likely rooted in our particular expectations, attitudes, and values than in the language form itself. Unless there is a clear factual and/or tangible referent, words and phrases that don't fit *our* view of reality are more likely to be seen as a deceptive distortion of reality. But tangible referents are subject to interpretation as well. It is possible that the same behavior could be seen as either the work of "terrorists" or the work of "freedom fighters," depending on whose side you're on.

Although the distinctions between them are not always sharp, Lutz illustrates doublespeak by discussing four ways in which language is used:

- *Euphemisms*: These are constructions that try to cover up what might otherwise be a painful reality. Lutz is particularly concerned about euphemisms used to soften realities he believes the public should face. One example is the use of the term "incontinent ordinance" to refer to military bombs and artillery shells that kill civilian non-combatants. He also points out that the subject of the book you are currently reading, lying and deception, is often discussed by people in ways that make it seem less onerous—e.g., "strategic manipulation," "reality augmentation," "disinformation," or "counterfactual proposition."

- *Jargon*: This is specialized language that people in a particular trade or profession understand, but when it is used with outside audiences (like the general public), it can be confusing or misleading. For example, a crack in a metal support beam might be described as a "discontinuity," or a tax increase as "revenue enhancement." And instead of saying in plain language that their rocket "blew up," SpaceX is apt to use "rapid unscheduled disassembly" (Hern, 2015).

- *Bureaucratese*: Lutz also calls this "gobbledygook." It is a way of confusing a target audience with technical terms, jargon, long sentences, etc.—i.e., the proverbial "word salad." Lutz (1989) gives the following example. During the investigation of the 1986 Challenger space shuttle explosion, Jesse Moore, NASA's associate administrator, was asked if the performance of the shuttle program had improved with each launch or if it had remained the same. His "answer" was:

  > *I think our performance in terms of liftoff performance and in terms of the orbital performance, we knew more about the envelope we were operating under, and we have been pretty accurately staying in that. And so I would say the performance has not by design drastically improved. I think we have been able to characterize the performance more as a function of our launch experience as opposed to it improving as a function of time. (pp. 5–6)*

- *Inflated language*: This occurs when language is specifically used to make things seem better than they really are—to "puff" them up. When the job title of a car mechanic is changed to an "automotive internist," most people don't care and the mechanic is happy. But when Chrysler Corporation "initiates a career alternative enhancement program", and it really means they are laying off 5,000 workers, people are more likely to feel that a deliberate attempt to mislead has taken place.

SUMMARY

- The possibility that we might be able to tell when a person is lying by simply observing certain tell-tale behaviors has been a matter of great interest to laypersons and scientists alike. There are, however, a number of reasons why an unerring profile of liar behavior may not be possible. For example, behaviors often signal emotions like anxiety or anger not lying per se. Truth tellers also experience anxiety and anger and the unlimited other things experienced by liars as they craft false messages. Furthermore, when the behavior of liars is made public, competent liars will try to behave differently. In addition, liars do not behave the same way all the time. The extent to which lies are expected; the perceived consequences of being discovered; the liar's relationship with the target; the liar's motives for lying; desire to succeed; and whether the lie involves falsification, concealment, misleading, or some combination of these, will all affect the kind of behavior the liar manifests.

- Low-stakes lies do not have serious consequences and, in some situations, are expected as part of daily interaction. Behavioral differences between liars telling low-stakes lies and truth tellers are extremely difficult to perceive. Several low-stakes lies are told daily by most people. They are often told to strangers and acquaintances, but they are also a staple for the maintenance of close relationships. Low-stakes lies are triggered when people want to present themselves in a positive way, when trying to impress and attract a romantic partner, when flattering or ingratiating oneself to others, in various sporting activities, and when performing magic or other entertainment in society.

- When serious consequences are associated with the telling of a lie, it is considered a high-stakes lie. Sometimes the high-stakes liar also perceives a substantial reward if the lie is not discovered. Researchers believe that we are more likely to develop a behavioral profile of high-stakes liars because they are likely experiencing more intense emotions and cognitive difficulties associated with lying (such as increased demands on memory).

- An analysis of more than a hundred studies comparing the behavior of liars and truth tellers found specific behaviors supporting the following conclusions. Compared with truth tellers, liars:

  - are less forthcoming
  - tell stories that are less plausible
  - make a more negative impression
  - are more tense

- Liars in close relationships are likely to behave differently than those communicating with strangers. They tell lies to support and protect their partner, they know their partner is likely to spot behavior that deviates from their normal patterns, they know the story associated with a lie can come up at any time during the length of the relationship, and they actively collaborate and conspire with their partner on some lies.

- The chapter concluded with a discussion of six acts that can be performed with the intention to create a false reality in the target (lying), but they are also acts that can and are often performed without deceptive intentions. When persons or groups perceive harm associated with these acts, they are likely to characterize them as intentionally deceptive. We discussed six of these acts: equivocation, contextomy, paltering, spin, bullshit, and doublespeak.

EXERCISES

1. Identify the circumstances when the conversational exchanges (i, ii, iii) below would:

   a) be accepted as a legitimate response without any concern for deceptive intent, or
   b) create suspicion as to why the question was answered in that fashion, or
   c) definitely be considered deliberately evasive with deceptive intent

   i. Q: Have you ever used illegal drugs?
      A: *I don't use illegal drugs.*

   ii. Q: Do you plan to attend the next meeting?
       A: *I think it's important—I've got a lot going on.*

   iii. Q: Did you read this chapter thoroughly for class discussion?
        A: *I looked through the book and I'm ready for the reading quiz (read chapter summary while watching Netflix).*

2. What is the difference between saying a particular behavior is a "behavior of liars" and saying a particular behavior is a "behavior of liars *when compared to* truth tellers?"

3. Do you think most people's attitude toward bullshit is more benign than toward lying? Why? Frankfurt (2005, p. 61) says ". . . bullshit is a greater enemy of truth than lies are because the bullshitter is not concerned with the truth and the liar is." Do you agree? Does bullshit help us get through our institutional lives? What about college; are there hoops you jump through that don't seem to make a lot of sense? Does that bother you?

4. Find at least one example of each of the variations of lying on p. 233 (equivocation, contextomy, paltering, spin, bullshit, and doublespeak) that have been communicated by a political party or movement *you support*. Analyze them in terms of their intent and consequences. Discuss this with another person who supports a different political party. If you do not identify with a political party, find another person like yourself and flip a coin to see who does research on Party A and who examines Party B. When you are finished, compare your findings with your partner. How difficult was this? Why? Does your partner agree with your analysis of the intent and consequences for each example?

OF INTEREST

For better or worse, some examples of **gobbledygook** stick around long enough that they become mainstream. *Mental Floss* unearths the forgotten history of 12 words that, quite possibly, we never needed in the first place.

As noted above, **paltering** is the use of factually accurate statements to mislead—in effect, using the truth to lie. This video by *Psychology Unlocked* uses research by Todd Rogers and colleagues to illustrate how this deceptive tactic works and why people commonly resort to it.

Kittenfishing is the use of little inaccuracies when describing ourselves in online profiles. *CBS Los Angeles* says it's nothing like the downright malicious act of catfishing. Nevertheless, when we kittenfish, we probably aren't doing ourselves any favors. Misrepresenting yourself even slightly may be the primary cause of the "no second date" phenomenon.

REFERENCES

Afifi, W. A., & Weiner, J. L. (2006). Seeking information about sexual health: Applying the theory of motivated information management. *Human Communication Research, 32*(1), 35–57. https://dx.doi.org/10.1111/j.1468-2958.2006.00002.x

Aronson, J., & McGlone, M. S. (2008). Social identity and stereotype threat. In T. Nelson (Ed.), *Handbook of stereotyping and discrimination* (pp. 153–178). New York, NY: Psychology Press.

Barnes, J. A. (1994). *A pack of lies: Towards a sociology of lying*. New York, NY: Cambridge University Press.

Bavelas, J. B., Black, A., Chovil, N. & Mullett, J. (1990). *Equivocal communication*. Newbury Park, CA: Sage.

Blair, J. P., Reimer, T. O., & Levine, T. R. (2018). The role of consistency in detecting deception: The superiority of correspondence over coherence. *Communication Studies*. Advance online publication. https://dx.doi.org/10.1080/10510974.2018.1447492

Bond, C. F., Jr., & DePaulo, B. M. (2006). Accuracy of deception judgments. *Personality and Social Psychology Review, 10*(3), 214–234. https://dx.doi.org/10.1207/s15327957pspr1003_2

Bond, C. F., Jr., & Fahey, W. E. (1987). False suspicion and the misperception of deceit. *British Journal of Social Psychology, 26*(1), 41–46. https://dx.doi.org/10.1111/j.2044-8309.1987.tb00759.x

Bond, C. F., Jr., Thomas, B. J., & Paulson, R. M. (2004). Maintaining lies: The multiple-audience problem. *Journal of Experimental Social Psychology, 40*(1), 29–40. https://dx.doi.org/10.1016/s0022-1031(03)00087-8

Buller, D. B., & Burgoon, J. K. (1996). Interpersonal deception theory. *Communication Theory, 6*(3), 203–242. https://dx.doi.org/10.1111/j.1468-2885.1996.tb00127.x

Buller, D. B., Burgoon, J. K., Buslig, A. S., & Roiger, J. F. (1994). Interpersonal deception VIII. Further analysis of nonverbal and verbal correlates of equivocation from the Bavelas et al. (1990) research. *Journal of Language and Social Psychology, 13*(4), 396–417. https://dx.doi.org/10.1177/0261927x94134003

Burgoon, J. K., & Floyd, K. (2000). Testing for the motivation impairment effect during deceptive and truthful interaction. *Western journal of Communication, 64*(3), 243–267. https://dx.doi.org/10.1080/10570310009374675

Burgoon, J. K., Buller, D. B., Ebesu, A. S., White, C. H., & Rockwell, P. A. (1996). Testing interpersonal deception theory: Effects of suspicion on communication behaviors and perceptions. *Communication Theory, 6*(3), 243–267. https://dx.doi.org/10.1111/j.1468-2885.1996.tb00128.x

Burgoon, J. K., Schuetzler, R., & Wilson, D. W. (2015). Kinesic patterning in deceptive and truthful interactions. *Journal of Nonverbal Behavior, 39*(1), 1–24. https://dx.doi.org/10.1007/s10919-014-0190-4

Buss, D. M. (1994). *The evolution of desire: Strategies of human mating.* New York, NY: Basic Books.

Caro, M. (2003). *Caro's book of poker tells: The psychology and body language of poker.* New York, NY: Cardoza Publishing.

Caspi, A., & Gorsky, P. (2006). Online deception: Prevalence, motivation, and emotion. *CyberPsychology & Behavior, 9,* 54–59. https://dx.doi.org/10.1089/cpb.2006.9.54

Castillo, P. A., & Mallard, D. (2012). Preventing cross-cultural bias in deception judgments: The role of expectancies about nonverbal behavior. *Journal of Cross-Cultural Psychology, 43*(6), 967–978. https://dx.doi.org/10.1177/0022022111415672

Cole, T. (2001). Lying to the one you love: The use of deception in romantic relationships. *Journal of Social and Personal Relationships, 18,* 107–129. https://dx.doi.org/10.1177/0265407501181005

Corcoran, J. F. T., Lewis, M. D., & Garver, R. B. (1978). Biofeedback-conditioned galvanic skin response and hypnotic suppression of arousal: A pilot study of their relation to deception. *Journal of Forensic Sciences, 23,* 155–162. https://dx.doi.org/10.1520/jfs10665j

DePaulo, B. M. (1992). Nonverbal behavior and self-presentation. *Psychological Bulletin, 111*(2), 203–243. https://dx.doi.org/10.1037//0033-2909.111.2.203

DePaulo, B. M., & Kashy, D. A. (1998). Everyday lies in close and casual relationships. *Journal of Personality and Social Psychology, 74,* 63–79. https://dx.doi.org/10.1037//0022-3514.74.1.63

DePaulo, B. M., Lindsay, J. J., Malone, B. E., Muhlenbruck, L., Charlton, K., & Cooper, H. (2003). Cues to deception. *Psychological Bulletin, 129,* 74–112. https://dx.doi.org/10.1037//0033-2909.129.1.74

Ebesu, A. S., & Miller, M. D. (1994). Verbal and nonverbal behaviors as a function of deception type. *Journal of Language and Social Psychology, 13*(4), 418–442. https://dx.doi.org/10.1177/0261927x94134004

Ekman, P. (2001). *Telling lies* (3rd ed.). New York, NY: Norton.

Ekman, P., & Friesen, W. V. (1969). Nonverbal leakage and clues to deception. *Psychiatry, 32*(1), 88–106. https://dx.doi.org/10.1080/00332747.1969.11023575

Exline, R. V., Thibaut, J., Hickey, C. B., & Gumpert, P. (1970). Visual interaction in relation to Machiavellianism and an unethical act. In P. Christie & F. Geis (Eds.), *Studies in Machiavellianism.* New York, NY: Academic Press.

Feeley, T. H., & deTurck, M. A. (1998). The behavioral correlates of sanctioned and unsanctioned deceptive communication. *Journal of Nonverbal Behavior, 22*(3), 189–204. https://dx.doi.org/10.1023/A:1022966505471

Feldman, R. S., Forrest, J. A., & Happ, B. R. (2002). Self-presentation and verbal deception: Do self-presenters lie more? *Basic and Applied Social Psychology, 24*(2), 163–170. https://dx.doi.org/10.1207/153248302753674848

Fitzkee, D. (1945). *Magic by misdirection.* San Rafael, CA: Saint Raphael House.

Frank, M. G., & Ekman, P. (2004). Appearing truthful generalizes across different deception situations. *Journal of Personality and Social Psychology, 86*(3), 486–495. https://dx.doi.org/10.1037/0022-3514.86.3.486

Frankfurt, H. G. (2005). *On bullshit.* Princeton, NJ: Princeton University Press.

Global Deception Research Team. (2006). A world of lies. *Journal of Cross-Cultural Psychology, 37*(1), 60–74. https://dx.doi.org/10.1177/0022022105282295

Gordon, R. A. (1996). Impact of ingratiation on judgments and evaluations: A meta-analytic investigation. *Journal of Personality and Social Psychology, 71*(1), 54–70. https://dx.doi.org/10.1037/0022-3514.71.1.54

Granhag, P. A., Andersson, L. O., Strömwall, L. A., & Hartwig, M. (2004). Imprisoned knowledge: Criminals beliefs about deception. *Legal and Criminological Psychology, 9,* 103–119.

Guadagno, R. E., Okdie, B. M., & Kruse, S. A. (2012). Dating deception: Gender, online dating, and exaggerated self-presentation. *Computers in Human Behavior, 28,* 642–647.

Guthrie, J., & Kunkel, A. (2013). Tell me sweet (and not-so-sweet) little lies: Deception in romantic relationships. *Communication Studies, 64*(2), 141–157. https://dx.doi.org/10.1080/10510974.2012.755637

Hancock, J. T., Thom-Santelli, J., & Ritchie, T. (2004). Deception and design: The impact of communication technology on lying behavior. *Proceedings of CHI 2004,* 24–29.

Hancock, J., & Toma, C. (2009). Putting your best face forward: The accuracy of online dating photographs. *Journal of Communication, 59,* 367–386.

Hartwig, M., & Bond, C. F. (2014). Lie detection from multiple cues: A meta-analysis. *Applied Cognitive Psychology, 28*(5), 661–676. https://dx.doi.org/10.1002/acp.3052

Hayano, D. M. (1980). Communicative competency among poker players. *Journal of Communication, 30,* 113–120.

Hern, A. (2015, January 16). This is what a 'rapid unscheduled disassembly' looks like. *The Guardian.* Retrieved from http://www.theguardian.com

Holmes, C. B. (1990). *The honest truth about lying with statistics.* Springfield, IL: Charles C. Thomas.

Horvath, F. S. (1973). Verbal and nonverbal clues to truth and deception during polygraph examinations. *Journal of Police Science and Administration, 1,* 1138–152.

Horvath, F. S., Jayne, B., & Buckley, J. (1994). Differentiation of truthful and deceptive criminal suspects in behavior analysis interviews. *Journal of Forensic Sciences, 39,* 793–807.

Huff, D. (1954). *How to lie with statistics.* New York, NY: Norton.

Hurley, C. M., Griffin, D. J., & Stefanone, M. A. (2014). Who told you that? Uncovering the source of believed cues to deception. *International Journal of Psychological Studies, 6,* 19–32.

Jackson, B., & Jamieson, K. H. (2007). *UnSpun: Finding facts in a world of disinformation.* New York, NY: Random House.

Jones, E. E. (1964). *Ingratiation: A social psychological analysis.* New York, NY: Appleton-Century-Crofts.

Knapp, M. L. (2006) Lying and deception in close relationships. In A. L. Vangelisti & D. Perlman [Eds.], *Cambridge handbook of personal relationships.* New York, NY: Cambridge University Press.

Knapp, M. L., & Comadena, M. E. (1979). Telling it like it isn't: A review of theory and research on deceptive communications. *Human Communication Research, 5,* 270–285.

Knapp, M. L., Hart, R. P., & Dennis, H. S. (1974). An exploration of deception as a communication construct. *Human Communication Research, 1,* 15–29.

Larson, T. (2006, August/September). On bovine excrement. *Free Inquiry, 26*(5), 64–65.

Levin, J. (2013, December 19). The welfare queen. *Slate.com.* Retrieved from http://www.slate.com

Levine, T. R. (2018). Ecological validity and deception detection research design. *Communication Methods and Measures, 12*(1), 45–54. https://dx.doi.org/10.1080/19312458.2017.1411471

Levine, T. R., Ali, M. V., Dean, M., Abdulla, R. A., & Garcia-Ruano, K. (2016). Toward a pancultural typology of deception motives. *Journal of Intercultural Communication Research, 45,* 1–12. https://dx.doi.org/10.1080/17475759.2015.1137079

Levine, T. R., & Kim, R. K. (2008). Some considerations for a new theory of deceptive communication. In M. S. McGlone & M. L. Knapp (Eds.), *The interplay of truth and deception* (pp. 16–34). New York, NY: Routledge.

Levine, T. R., Kim, R. K., & Hamel, L. M. (2010). People lie for a reason: Three experiments documenting the principle of veracity. *Communication Research Reports, 27*(4), 271–285. https://dx.doi.org/10.1080/08824096.2010.496334

Luchetti, A. E. (1999). Deception in disclosing one's sexual history: Safe-sex avoidance or ignorance? *Communication Quarterly, 47*(3), 300–314. https://dx.doi.org/10.1080/01463379909385561

Lutz, W. (1989). *Doublespeak.* New York, NY: Harper & Row.

Lutz, W. (1996). *The new doublespeak: Why no one knows what anyone's saying anymore.* New York, NY: HarperCollins.

Lutz, W. (1999). *Doublespeak defined: Cut through the bull**** and get the point.* New York, NY: HarperCollins.

Marett, K., George, J. F., Lewis, C. C., Gupta, M., & Giordano, G. (2017). Beware the dark side: Cultural preferences for lying online. *Computers in Human Behavior, 75,* 834–844. https://dx.doi.org/10.1016/j.chb.2017.06.021

Markowitz, D. M., & Hancock, J. T. (2018). Deception in mobile dating conversations. *Journal of Communication, 68*(3), 547–569. https://dx.doi.org/10.1093/joc/jqy019

Mawby, R., & Mitchell, R. W. (1986). Feints and ruses: An analysis of deception in sports. In R. W. Mitchell and N. S. Thompson (Eds.), *Deception: Perspectives on human and nonhuman deceit* (pp. 313–322). Albany, NY: State University of New York Press.

McCornack, S. A., Morrison, K., Paik, J. E., Wisner, A. M., & Zhu, X. (2014). Information Manipulation Theory 2 (IMT2): A propositional theory of deceptive discourse production. *Journal of Language and Social Psychology, 33*(4), 348–377. https://dx.doi.org/10.1177/0261927x14534656

McGlone, M. S. (2005). Quoted out of context: Contextomy and its consequences. *Journal of Communication, 55*(2), 330–346. https://dx.doi.org/10.1093/joc/55.2.330

McGlone, M. S., & Baryshevtsev, M. (2015). Deception by quotation. In J. Meibauer (Ed.), *The Oxford handbook of deception* (pp. 220–233). Oxford, England: Oxford University Press.

Pennebaker, J. W. (2011). *The secret life of pronouns: How our words reflect who we are.* New York, NY: Bloomsbury.

Penny, L. (2005). *Your call is important to us: The truth about bullshit.* New York, NY: Crown.

Peterson, B. (2014, May 30). Southwest Airlines fined $200K for misleading fare ads. *Condé Nast Traveler.* Retrieved from http://www.cntraveler.com

Rodriguez, N., & Ryave, A. (1990). Telling lies in everyday life: Motivational and organizational consequences of sequential preferences. *Qualitative Sociology, 13*(3), 195–210. https://dx.doi.org/10.1007/bf00989593

Rogers, T., Zeckhauser, R., Gino, F., Schweitzer, M., & Norton, M. (2014). *Artful paltering: The risks and rewards of using truthful statements to mislead others.* Faculty Research Working Paper Series, John F. Kennedy School of Government, Harvard University.

Roggensack, K. E., & Sillars, A. (2014). Agreement and understanding about honesty and deception rules in romantic relationships. *Journal of Personal and Social Relationships, 31*(2), 178–199. https://dx.doi.org/10.1177/0265407513489914

Roloff, M. E., & Miller, C. W. (2006). Social cognition approaches to understanding interpersonal conflict and communication. In J. G. Oetzel & S. Ting-Toomey (Eds.), *The SAGE handbook of conflict communication: Integrating theory, research, and practice* (pp. 97–128). Thousand Oaks, CA: Sage.

Rosen, R. (July 14, 2003). Bush doublespeak. *San Francisco Chronicle*, p. B7.

Schauer, F., & Zeckhauser, R. (2009). Paltering. In B. Harrington (Ed.), *Deception: From ancient empires to internet dating* (pp. 38–54). Stanford, CA: Stanford University Press.

Sebanz, N., & Shiffrar, M. (2009). Detecting deception in a bluffing body: The role of expertise. *Psychonomic Bulletin & Review, 16*(1), 170–175. https://dx.doi.org/10.3758/pbr.16.1.170

Serota, K. B., & Levine, T. R. (2015). A few prolific liars: Variation in the prevalence of lying. *Journal of Language and Social Psychology, 34*(2), 138–157. https://dx.doi.org/10.1177/0261927x14528804

Shulman, D. (2007). *From hire to liar: The role of deception in the workplace.* Ithaca, NY: Cornell University Press.

Shulman, G. M. (1973). *An experimental study of the effects of receiver sex, communicator sex, and warning on the ability of receivers to detect deceptive communicators.* Unpublished master's thesis, Purdue University.

Stebbins, R. A. (1975). Putting people on: Deception of our fellow-man in everyday life. *Sociology and Social Research, 69,* 189–200.

Stengel, R. (2000). *(You're too kind) A brief history of flattery.* New York, NY: Simon & Shuster.

Toma, C. L. (2017). Developing online deception literacy while looking for love. *Media, Culture & Society, 39*(3), 423–428. https://dx.doi.org/10.1177/0163443716681660

Toma, C. L., & Hancock, J. T. (2010). Lying for love in the modern age. In M. S. McGlone & M. L. Knapp (Eds.), *The interplay of truth and deception* (pp. 149–163). New York, NY: Routledge.

Toma, C. L., Hancock, J. T., & Ellison, N. (2008). Separating fact from fiction: An examination of deceptive self-presentation in online dating profiles. *Personality and Social Psychology Bulletin, 34*(8), 1023–1036. https://dx.doi.org/10.1177/0146167208318067

Toma, C. L., Jiang, L. C., & Hancock, J. T. (2016). Lies in the eye of the beholder: Asymmetric beliefs about one's own and others' deceptiveness in mediated and face-to-face communication. *Communication Research.* https://dx.doi.org/10.1177/0093650216631094

Tooke, J., & Camire, L. (1991). Patterns of deception in intersexual and intrasexual mating strategies. *Ethology and Sociobiology, 12*(5), 345–364. https://dx.doi.org/10.1016/0162-3095(91)90030-t

Tsikerdekis, M., & Zeadally, S. (2014). Online deception in social media. *Communications of the ACM, 57*(9), 72-80. https://dx.doi.org/10.1145/2629612

Vallacher, R. R., & Wegner, D. M. (1985). *A theory of action identification.* Hillsdale, NJ: Erlbaum.

Vangelisti, A. (2012). Interpersonal processes in romantic relationships. In M. L. Knapp & J. A. Daly (Eds.), *The SAGE handbook of interpersonal communication* (pp. 597–631). Thousand Oaks, CA: Sage.

Vrij, A. (2000). *Detecting lies and deceit.* Chichester, England: Wiley.

Vrij, A., Akehurst, L., & Knight, S. (2006). Police officers', social workers', teachers', and the general public's beliefs about deception in children, adolescents and adults. *Legal and Criminological Psychology, 11*(2), 297–312. https://dx.doi.org/10.1348/135532505x60816

Vrij, A., Fisher, R. P., & Blank, H. (2017). A cognitive approach to lie detection: A meta-analysis. *Legal and Criminological Psychology, 22*(1), 1–21. https://dx.doi.org/10.1111/lcrp.12088

Wakeham, J. (2017). Bullshit as a problem of social epistemology. *Sociological Theory, 35*(1), 15–38. https://dx.doi.org/10.1177/0735275117692835

Wegner, D. M., & Bargh, J. A. (1998). Control and automaticity in social life. In D. T. Gilbert, S. T. Fiske, & G. Lindzey (Eds.), *The handbook of social psychology, Vol. 1* (4th ed.) (pp. 446–496). New York, NY: McGraw-Hill.

White, C. H., & Burgoon, J. K. (2001). Adaptation and communicative design: Patterns of interaction in truthful and deceptive conversations. *Human Communication Research, 27*(1), 9–37. https://dx.doi.org/10.1111/j.1468-2958.2001.tb00774.x

Williams, S. S. (2001). Sexual lying among college students in close and casual relationships. *Journal of Applied Social Psychology, 31*(11), 2322–2338. https://dx.doi.org/10.1111/j.1559-1816.2001.tb00178.x

Zuckerman, M., DePaulo, B. M., & Rosenthal, R. (1981). Verbal and nonverbal communication of deception. In L. Berkowitz, (Ed.), *Advances in experimental social psychology, Vol. 14* (pp. 1–59). New York, NY: Academic Press.

CHAPTER 8 Specialists in Lying and Deception

HELLO
I AM...
AN EXPERT
© iQoncept/Shutterstock.com

"Who can I trust? You have to invest in somebody and chances are you're probably going to invest in somebody who's going to deceive you. I've been conned a couple of times, but now I'm a little more savvy."
– Maggie Gyllenhaal

"I think Bigfoot is blurry, that's the problem. It's not the photographer's fault. Bigfoot *is* blurry, and that's extra scary to me. There's a large, out-of-focus monster roaming the countryside."
– Mitch Hedberg

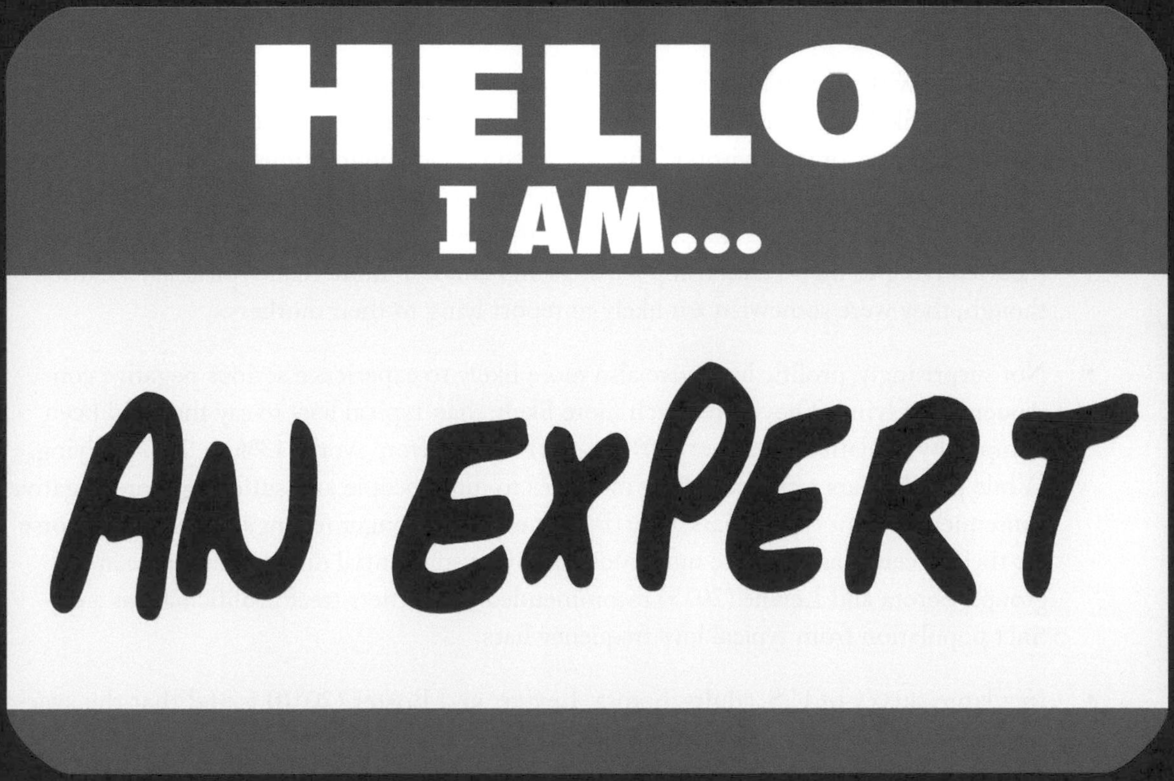

Everyone deceives from time to time, but some people do it a lot more than others. Consider these findings:

- In a U.K. survey, Serota and Levine (2015) examined the characteristics of "prolific liars," defined as people who reported lying five times or more per day (289 of 2,980 respondents, about 10% of the sample), in contrast to a majority of respondents who reported lying about twice per day.

- Compared with typical low-frequency liars, these "prolific" liars tended to be younger and were more likely to be male, work in technical occupations, and have higher occupational status (managers or supervisors). They reported telling about **6** times as many "little white lies" (e.g., saying you like a gift you really don't) per day as typical liars, and almost **20** times as many "big lies" (e.g., insincerely declaring "I love you" to someone). They also reported lying to their relationship partners and children more than typical liars. Curiously, though, they were somewhat *less* likely to report lying to their mothers.

- Not surprisingly, prolific liars were also more likely to experience serious negative consequences of lying. They were much more likely than typical liars to say they had been dumped by a relational partner (**20%** vs. **5%**) or fired from work (**13%** vs. **2%**) for lying. While prolific liars reported telling more lies to more people and suffering more negative consequences than typical liars, they did not express stronger feelings of guilt or remorse for their deceit. Based on the numerous and often substantial differences between the groups, Serota and Levine (2015) recommended researchers treat prolific liars as a distinct population from typical low-frequency liars.

- In a large survey of U.S. adults, Serota, Levine, and Boster (2010) found that the average number of lies per day reported by respondents was between 1 and 2 (specifically 1.65), *most* reported telling fewer or no lies, and a very small subset reported telling many lies.

MEET THE SPECIALISTS

Lying "specialists" can appear in a variety of roles: addicts, imposters, con artists, identity thieves, people with personality disorders, people who alter the history of their past accomplishments and activities (imposeurs), or people who perpetrate a hoax.

What does it take to qualify as a specialist? It basically comes down to experience. Lying specialists lie repeatedly and habitually; lying is an indelible part of their lifestyle. The distinction between a lie and the truth is often less important to them than communicating whatever is necessary to accomplish a desired goal.

Lies are so commonplace for specialists that they may even tell lies when there is no apparent benefit to lying. People addicted to drugs and/or alcohol often provide telling examples. Addicts initially use lies to deny or minimize their usage, to cover-up problems linked to their usage, or to create situations that would facilitate their usage. But as Twerski (1997) says:

> Sooner or later it [lying] takes on a life of its own. The addict manipulates just to manipulate and lies just to lie, even though there may be nothing to gain. Manipulation and lying, instead of being a means to an end, actually become ends in themselves. (p. 63)

Lying Specialists Manifest a Variety of Behaviors

Their goals may be to swindle others, to help others, to make themselves look and feel good, or to enjoy the deceptive performance itself. Some of these liars specialize in a particular content area (e.g., military service) while others use a broad knowledge base in order to be successful.

Despite the many ways lying specialists manifest themselves, some characteristics seem to be widely shared. Aside from those with certain personality disorders, lying specialists tend to be socially adept in that they are:

- familiar with situational/behavioral norms and expectations
- able to anticipate the reactions of others
- able to adapt accordingly for the manipulation of their targets

They are often outwardly self-confident and willing to take risks. Adhering to ethical and moral standards is often secondary (or non-existent) to getting what they want.

Mixed Public Reaction to Lying Specialists

Prolific liars may be resented and condemned for their disregard of truthfulness. Those who use lying to swindle others are sometimes sent to prison. Targets of lying specialists are not likely to have any kind words for them. Yet the public is often intrigued (even captivated) by certain charming scoundrels who specialize in lying. Popular culture is full of such characters, from *Catch Me If You Can* to *Dirty Rotten Scoundrels* to *Star Wars*, when Han Solo famously told Princess Leia, "You like me because I'm a scoundrel. There aren't enough scoundrels in your life." (QR)

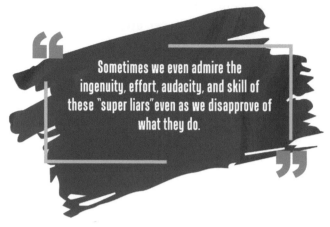

> Sometimes we even admire the ingenuity, effort, audacity, and skill of these "super liars" even as we disapprove of what they do.

In real life, as long as we aren't victimized by lying specialists, we may find a certain fascination with their brazen disregard for the truth and how they manage to carry out their duplicitous lives. We may also be curious about why they weren't uncovered sooner. People who treat lying like most people treat truth telling are an oddity, and oddities attract our attention. Sometimes we even admire the ingenuity, effort, audacity, and skill of these "super liars" even as we disapprove of what they do. It is similar to the admiration we have for the handiwork of a skilled magician. The big difference, of course, is that we give permission to magicians to fool us; lying specialists do not seek our consent.

To further understand these specialists in lying and deception, this chapter examines:

1. personality disorders that feature deception
2. imposeurs
3. imposters
4. con artists
5. hoaxers

These categories enable us to talk about various types of lying specialists, but it's important to keep in mind that the behavior of any given liar may encompass several of these categories—e.g., an imposter may be a con artist with a particular personality disorder.

PSYCHOLOGICAL DISORDERS

The German physician Anton Delbruck (1891) is credited with being the first to describe the concept of **pathological lying** in patient case studies. He observed that some of his patients told lies so abnormal and disproportionate as to deserve a special psychiatric category he described as *pseudologia fantastica* (not to be confused with the song (QR) by Foster the People). To date, however, there is no consensus among mental health professionals about the definition of pathological lying, although there is general agreement about its core elements (Dike, Baranoski, & Griffith, 2005).

Pathological lying is characterized by a long (perhaps lifelong) history of frequent and repeated lying for which no apparent psychological motive or external benefit can be discerned. Although ordinary lies are goal-directed and intended to obtain an external benefit or avoid punishment, pathological lies appear to be without purpose. In some cases, they may even be self-incriminating or damaging, which makes the behavior even more puzzling.

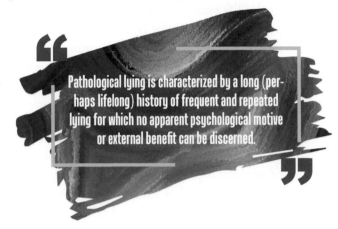

Pathological lying is characterized by a long (perhaps lifelong) history of frequent and repeated lying for which no apparent psychological motive or external benefit can be discerned.

It is a pattern of behavior familiar to psychotherapists—excessive lying, easily determined to be false, mostly unhelpful to the liar in any apparent way, and sometimes harmful to the liar, yet told repeatedly over time. Even prominent and successful individuals engage in this pattern. For example, California Superior Court Judge Patrick Couwenberg was removed from office not only for lying in his official capacity (claiming to have academic degrees and military experience he clearly did not have) but also for lying under oath to a commission investigating his behavior. A psychiatric expert witness diagnosed him with *pseudologia fantastica* and suggested the judge needed treatment (Winton, 2001).

Personality Disorders

Lenzenweger, Lane, Loranger, and Kessler (2007) estimate that about 9% of the people in the United States suffer from some kind of personality disorder. The *Diagnostic and Statistical Manual of Mental Disorders* (DSM-5; American Psychiatric Association, 2013) identifies five personality disorders that, in practice, psychiatric professionals often associate with pathological lying:

1. Antisocial
2. Borderline
3. Narcissistic
4. Histrionic
5. Obsessive-compulsive

Contrary to popular belief, pathological lying is not its own personality disorder, although some experts believe it may someday be classified as its own distinct diagnosis (Griffiths, 2013; Hausman, 2003). In the meantime, it remains best understood as commonly associated with other disorders.

Anyone may engage in habitual lying for a brief period of time or in conjunction with a particular life event. But lying in conjunction with a personality disorder means it is an enduring pattern of maladaptive behavior exhibited in a wide variety of situations. Many people diagnosed with these personality disorders tell a lot of lies that go undetected and become confident, skilled liars. Their ability to deceive themselves and the negligible amount of guilt or anxiety they feel about lying may help facilitate their ability to deceive others.

Individuals with any of these personality disorders are extremely self-oriented and use lies to get what they want, including a boost to their typically low self-esteem. Their low self-esteem may be the result of growing up in a dysfunctional family environment. Absent or neglectful parents, relatives who engage in physical abuse, and family members with a drug and/or alcohol addiction are not uncommon in the lives of these people. They are not likely to get the love and attention they need as children. As adults, they tend to avoid emotional ties and close relationships because it makes the lying and exploitation a lot easier.

Antisocial Personality Disorder: Sociopathy and Psychopathy

People diagnosed with this disorder have little, if any, regard for the needs of others. They have no remorse when they hurt others; they often show little affection or positive response when others are kind. They are almost devoid of empathy, emotional sensitivity, and ethical standards. Other people are useful only to the extent that they play a role in serving and gratifying the needs of the person with the antisocial personality disorder. When others are not serving the needs of this person, he or she is likely to get frustrated, irritable, and aggressive.

These personalities want what they want when they want it. As a result, people with this condition are often in conflict with authorities over unlawful behavior. Their relationships at home and at work are unstable, frequently changing, and filled with self-serving manipulations and cheating. However, they can be very persuasive, even charming, in efforts to establish relationships (Forward, 1999).

The *DSM-5* lists **sociopathy** and **psychopathy** as subtypes of antisocial personality disorder. Some mental health professionals use the terms interchangeably, but others argue there are important and significant distinctions between the types (e.g., Pemment, 2013). Sociopaths tend to be nervous and prone to emotional outbursts, including fits of rage. They also tend to be uneducated, living on the edge of society, and unable to hold a steady job. While they have difficulty forming attachments with individuals, sociopaths may form attachments to groups with an antisocial orientation (street gangs, white supremacists, etc.). If they commit crimes, they are typically spontaneous, haphazard, and disorganized.

In contrast, psychopaths often have disarming or charming personalities. While they, too, find it difficult to form emotional attachments to individuals, psychopaths find it easy to gain people's trust, which they then use for manipulation. Psychopaths are often well-educated and hold steady jobs. Some are so good at manipulation that they have families and other long-term relationships without those around them ever suspecting their true malignant nature. When they commit crimes, they tend to plan them out in a calm, cool,

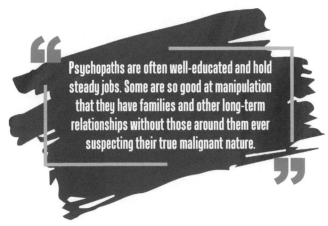

Psychopaths are often well-educated and hold steady jobs. Some are so good at manipulation that they have families and other long-term relationships without those around them ever suspecting their true malignant nature.

and meticulous manner. Many notorious and prolific serial killers such as Ted Bundy, Jeffrey Dahmer, John Wayne Gacy, and Dennis Rader have been diagnosed by forensic psychiatrists as psychopaths (Martens, 2014). If all this reminds you of Machiavellianism (discussed in Chapter 3), you see the same connections observed by McHoskey, Worzel, and Szyarto (1998). Based on their research, they maintain that psychopathy and Machiavellianism are essentially the same personality construct.

Lying is an addiction for both sociopaths and psychopaths. Lies are told frequently, effortlessly, and without much guilt or anxiety. These pathological liars may even find it difficult to understand why others value truth, especially when it hurts to tell it. Because they practice lying so often, they can respond effectively to the most challenging confrontations to their credibility with considerable aplomb. They may occasionally admit to a lie or promise to change their behavior, but be careful not to get fooled—normally this is a tactic to establish trust for a future lie (Cleckley, 1982).

The vast majority of those diagnosed with antisocial personality disorder are men.

Borderline Personality Disorder

Sudden (sometimes intense) mood swings are characteristic of the borderline personality disorder. A rational and efficient worker may, for no apparent reason, become unreasonable and irresponsible; an understanding and committed lover may become angry, close-minded, and absent. Their behavior is notoriously hard to predict.

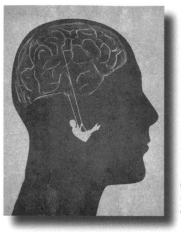

These mood swings are often linked to the person's idealization of a job or person that leads to euphoric feelings but also creates unrealistically high expectations. In time, there will be anxiety, frustration, and/or rejection associated with the object of idealization. Disproportionate disappointment and anger (at self and others) may lead to destructive behavior in the form of self-mutilation, substance abuse, or spending money excessively. Impulse control is often a problem for people with a borderline personality.

In addition to the types of deception that may be associated with various self-destructive behaviors, people with this disorder often use lies as a weapon to get even with people for not living up to expectations or for disappointments they are believed to have created. Spreading false rumors or filing a fraudulent lawsuit are ways people can use to get even with those who shattered their dreams.

The vast majority of those diagnosed with borderline personality disorder are women, although there is debate as to whether this is equivalent to saying it is more common in women than in men (Sansone & Sansone, 2011).

Narcissistic Personality Disorder

People with narcissistic personality disorder (NPD) are pathologically preoccupied with themselves. They exaggerate their achievements and expect this portrayal to be accepted by others. They require an excessive amount of admiration but have relatively little empathy for those who might provide the veneration they desire. They view themselves as "special" and entitled to special treatment. Ironically, this outwardly self-confident, even arrogant, behavior may mask a low sense of self-esteem.

People with NPD may use lies, exaggerations, and half-truths to support the grandiose personalities they have created. This can occur in self-presentations or in the exploitation of others for their own needs. To maintain the brilliant, skilled, attractive, and immeasurably successful selves they have created, narcissists are also skilled at self-deception. Unless they deceive themselves, narcissists aren't able to function very well.

Not surprisingly, people with NPD often seek and achieve positions of power and prestige. Rijsenbilt and Commandeur (2013) report evidence indicating an overrepresentation of narcissistic personalities among corporate CEOs who have been prosecuted for financial fraud. Although never formally diagnosed, several psychiatrists have suggested that former investment advisor Bernie Madoff, currently serving a life sentence for perpetrating the largest Ponzi scheme in history, has this disorder.

Dr. Gerald Bryant of the Forensic Psychology Group claimed Madoff's ability to conceal fraud on such a massive scale was driven in part by a narcissistic belief that no matter what he did, he was so much smarter than everyone else that he would never get caught. "Authorities looked at Madoff a number of times and didn't do anything," Bryant observed, "so his crimes became substantiated in his mind. He most likely felt no remorse over what he had done" (*International Business Times*, 2011). Paulhus (2014) characterized Madoff as possessing a "dark personality" common to many white-collar criminals that combines malignant narcissism with Machiavellianism.

Long before he became president, Donald Trump displayed classic characteristics of a narcissist, such as an all-consuming need for love and approval. In 2005, he described the celebrities and rich people who would flock to his Mar-a-Lago estate: "They all eat, they all love me, they all kiss my ass. And then they all leave and say, 'Isn't he horrible.' But I'm the king" (McAdams, 2016). As president, an Associated Press fact check suggests that Trump has elevated the half-truth, an NPD staple, to an art form (Yen & Woodward, 2018):

- On July 7, 2018, he tweeted that a lawsuit filed by the Democratic National Committee against the Trump Campaign had been dismissed, proving there had been no collusion with Russia. It's true the case had been thrown out, but in doing so, the judge actually wrote, "It bears emphasizing that this Court's ruling is not based on a finding that there was no collusion between defendants and Russia during the 2016 presidential election." Moreover, the suit was brought by Democratic partisans (or "crazies" as Trump called them), but not by the Democratic National Committee.

- Three days earlier, on July 4, 2018, he tweeted that OPEC was driving up oil prices. It's true that oil prices were climbing, but the claim glossed over the primary causes, including Venezuela's economic crisis and internal strife in Libya, both of which severely decreased the available supply of crude oil. Trump was also ignoring the fact that OPEC had very recently agreed to begin increasing production of crude to help stabilize global prices.

- That same week, Trump told a Montana rally, "We've become a nation that is exporting energy for the first time." His administration had previously announced this might happen by 2020, but the U.S. Energy Information Agency says that it's more likely to occur sometime before 2030. Either way, it hasn't happened yet. He also told rally-goers, "I won Montana by so many points I don't have to come here," and that he beat his opponent by 44 points. He won Montana by 21 points, not 44. Perhaps he was confusing it with nearby Wyoming. A state with a population smaller than many cities, Trump's Wyoming votes—all 174,419 of them—were 46 points higher than Clinton's 55,973.

Other famous NPD candidates include:

- Apple founder **Steve Jobs,** who purportedly cried when *Time* magazine not only failed to name him the 1982 Man of the Year but actually wrote an unflattering article about him instead (DeWitt, 2015). Because he believed he was doing the right thing, Jobs had no problem misleading the entire world when he debuted the first iPhone at the 2007 Macworld conference. A *working* iPhone didn't exist, but he needed everyone to believe it did. More a "premature version of the truth" than an outright lie, Jobs and his team (Marks, 2017; Vogelstein, 2013):

   - created a carefully scripted set of steps representing the only sequence that wouldn't cause the phone to crash, and which had to be followed exactly (without this "golden path" there was no way to make the phone look like it actually worked);
   - rigged the display to simulate five full bars of service rather than the spotty, unreliable coverage that was actually available;
   - surreptitiously switched between multiple iPhone units on stage to avoid the inevitable crash that would happen when the device's faulty memory ran low. As he switched from one iPhone to the next, team members would restart the previous device to reset the memory and make it ready for its next turn at bat (Knight, 2013).

The flawlessly executed presentation (QR) made history and arguably changed the world. Only after Jobs's death would it be revealed that the only thing real about that day was the iPhone's potential promise.

- **Kim Kardashian**, who admitted she took 6,000 selfies during a four-day vacation in Mexico—the equivalent of one selfie every minute (Kirkpatrick, 2016). It's no accident that Kardashian's statue at the Tussauds Wax Museum in London depicts her taking a selfie (Leon, 2015). On the occasion of her 36th birthday, Brooklyn-based news aggregator *Inquisitr* published "36 Kardashian Lies For Kim Kardashian's 36th Birthday" (QR) (Katherine, 2016).

- **Kanye West**, who famously earned the scorn of, well, almost everyone when he stole Taylor Swift's thunder at the MTV Video Music Awards in 2009. He left the country and went into a self-imposed exile after the incident. But like all true narcissists, he proved incredibly resilient in the face of what would have been a career-ending disaster for most people (Markson, 2017). Since his return to the spotlight, West's relationship with the truth has been called into question more than once:

  - In September 2018, he tweeted that he would be teaching a course at the Art Institute of Chicago, but the organization politely corrected him. In a statement, the Institute said it was flattered by his interest but that he wasn't currently teaching and there were no plans for him to do so. In other words, this was the first they'd heard of it (Johnson, 2018).

  - The same week, West told *Extra* that he and wife Kim Kardashian were focused on getting incarcerated African Americans out of prison by breaking down the country's class system ("Kanye West," 2018). So far, so good, but then he added a supporting detail that turned out not to be true: "My wife is in law school now," he said, "and it's extremely serious to us." Soon after, a representative for Kardashian attempted to clarify what West meant. Rather than actually being enrolled in law school, explained the rep, Kim "is so entrenched in the legal system with her activism that it is like going to law school" (Gonzales, 2018).

- **Lyndon Johnson**, who, like Trump, needed to have his name (or initials) on everything: his wife, **L**ady **B**ird **J**ohnson, daughters **L**ynda **B**ird **J**ohnson and **L**uci **B**aines **J**ohnson—even the family dog, **L**ittle **B**eagle **J**ohnson (Jones, 2016). While Trump has yet to be ranked, a 2013 study by *Psychological Science* declared Johnson the most narcissistic U.S. president (Morin, 2013). His habit of deceiving the public about the status of the Vietnam conflict led to the popularization of the term "credibility gap" (Lazarus, 2017).

Men are slightly more likely than women to have NPD (Whitbourne, 2015).

Histrionic Personality Disorder

The word "histrionic" is associated with excessively dramatic and emotion-laden behavior, like that of an actor. These affectations are designed to call attention to themselves. The speech of a person with this disorder may be theatrical; their appearance and dress may be flamboyant. They are not comfortable for long if not the center of attention.

Like all the preceding personality disorders, people with a histrionic personality disorder (HPD) are self-centered and demanding, but unlike antisocials, they are not violent. Histrionic individuals seek to: build their self-esteem by calling attention to themselves, use flattery to get others to meet their needs, engage in sexually seductive or predatory behavior, respond positively to suggestions by others, and refuse to dwell on frustrations and unpleasantries.

People with this disorder may engage in deception in order to garner and hold attention and to offset feelings of threat and rejection. A person with HPD might, for example, spontaneously make up a story for his or her co-workers that he or she was nearly run over by a circus clown riding a bicycle while returning from lunch. It is the kind of story sure to draw a crowd. And, like the narcissist, a person who depends on being the center of attention to boost his or her self-esteem is dependent on proficient self-deception.

All of this may help to explain why former Penn State assistant football coach Jerry Sandusky was diagnosed with HPD during his trial over the alleged sexual abuse of 10 boys. Exhibits at trial included "creepy love letters" Sandusky sent to one of his victims. In one of them, Sandusky wrote, "Yes, I am a 'Great Pretender.' I pretend that I can sing. I pretend about many things. However, I can't pretend about my feelings and want you to always remember that I care" (Cosentino, 2012).

To be sure, Sandusky's ill-advised phone interview (QR) with NBC's Bob Costas didn't help his case any. When Costas asked him, "Are you sexually attracted to young boys?" Sandusky prevaricated, saying that he was attracted to young people in the sense that he enjoyed being around them. It took him more than 16 seconds to get around to saying the word 'no' (Carmichael, 2011). "In retrospect," he said in response to another question, "I shouldn't have showered with those kids" (Greene, 2011). From prison, where he is serving 30 to 60 years, Sandusky has continued to deny all charges and maintain his innocence (Deppen, 2016).

Women are more likely to have histrionic personality disorder than men. It may be the case, however, that more women are diagnosed than men because societal norms about sexual forwardness and attention-seeking make such behavior seem less acceptable (and more aberrant) in women (Berman, 2012).

Obsessive-Compulsive Personality Disorder

Distinct from the anxiety disorder that we're more familiar with (OCD), obsessive-compulsive *personality* disorder (OCPD) is characterized by a state of mind that is preoccupied with orderliness, rules, matters of right and wrong, and interpersonal control at the expense of flexibility, openness, and efficiency (Bressert, 2017). Dogged perfectionists, the things that occupy these people's attention often keep them from seeing the big picture. Because emotions are held in check, personal relationships may lack the kind of closeness that free-flowing feelings may provide. This person's obsession with perfection may deter success in some occupations and facilitate it in others. However, the amount of time and effort dedicated to work may be at the expense of leisure-time activities and friendship maintenance.

Compared to the lies told by those with other personality disorders, those told by people with OCPD can seem fairly benign. If they resort to deceptive tactics, it is in an effort to protect their secrets, preserve their independence, maintain control of a situation, or perhaps to support their own self-deception. Persons with OCPD may be especially prone to lies of omission, wherein important information is never shared with others because "it's a secret" and "you never asked." As Sullivan (2001) notes, they consider themselves extremely

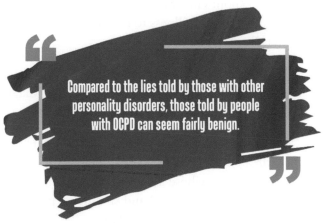

Compared to the lies told by those with other personality disorders, those told by people with OCPD can seem fairly benign.

honest simply because they rarely resort to bald-faced lies. This makes them true "masters at deception" and can confound the people around them (p. 155). Another possible source of deception for those with OCPD is their extreme difficulty in admitting fault, which stems from their overpowering need to always be in the right and in control (Hammond, 2017).

Men are twice as likely as women to be diagnosed with OCPD.

Other Mental Illness Disorders

Lying is also a key symptom of "factitious" or "dissociative" disorders, in which people deliberately act as if they are physically or mentally ill when they are not. Unlike people who feign illness to acquire drugs or avoid punishment (known as "malingerers" and described later in the chapter), those with a factitious disorder behave this way because of an inner need to be seen as ill or injured, not to achieve an external benefit. Factitious disorders are frequently comorbid (i.e., occurring) with personality disorders. We'll consider three of the more noteworthy disorders in this category: Ganser syndrome, factitious disorder imposed on self (Munchausen syndrome), and factitious disorder imposed on another (Munchausen syndrome by proxy).

Ganser Syndrome

Now classified as a dissociative disorder, and sometimes called "prison psychosis," Ganser syndrome was first observed in prisoners following their release from solitary confinement. People with this syndrome exhibit short-term episodes of bizarre behavior resembling schizophrenia.

Symptoms include confusion, repeated mimicking of vocalizations (echolalia) and movements (echopraxia) of other people, and bizarre conversational interaction. "Approximate" (though potentially absurd) answers are often given in response to straightforward questions (e.g., Question: How many legs does a dog have? Answer: Five). In fact, some consider the primary feature of this illness to be the tendency to give such "near-miss" answers to simple questions (Dieguez, 2018).

The subject of ongoing debate within the medical community, the disorder is exceedingly rare—with less than 100 cases officially diagnosed (of which about 75% have been male). Approximately 1 in 3 diagnosed with the syndrome had a prior history of mental illness.

The vast majority of Ganser sufferers (76%) exhibit no recollection of their symptoms after the episode. What appears to be common to almost all Ganser cases is an individual faced with stress whose ability to cope is compromised by chronic personal problems (alcohol abuse, drug use, etc.) and situational pressures, such as losing a job or being incarcerated (Mendis & Hodgson, 2012).

Factitious Disorder Imposed on Self

People exhibiting factitious disorder imposed on self (FDIS) are being deceptive about some aspect of an illness in order to encourage attention from medical providers, friends, or family members. The psychological motivations are complex, but are based on the need to relieve emotional distress by playing the role of a sick person (Savino & Fordtran, 2006). A severe personality disorder is often at the heart of this syndrome, but there can be other driving forces. Ford (1996) identified three possibilities:

1. A person who feels vulnerable and incompetent in other areas of life may feel clever, skillful, and powerful by fooling physicians and nurses.

2. For a person who needs a clear and well-defined identity, a "sick person," particularly one with a serious disease, satisfies that need while simultaneously generating attention and feelings of self-importance.

3. A person with an excessive and/or unmet need to be cared for and nurtured may also find satisfaction in being treated for a false disease.

Patients with FDIS may exaggerate the extent of actual symptoms, or they may make up symptoms they don't have. They could feign an illness altogether or, in extreme cases, purposely make themselves sick, engage in self-injury, or tamper with the results of medical tests (Mayo Clinic, 2018). In one documented case, a patient was admitted to over 400 hospitals (Boyd, 2014). The most extreme cases of factitious disorder were previously referred to as Munchausen syndrome (named after an 18th-century military officer known for extreme exaggeration).

Patients with factitious disorder may exaggerate the extent of actual symptoms, or they may make up symptoms they don't have.

Patients with FDIS are routinely examined by physicians. To be successful in their deception, therefore, they need to have an extensive knowledge of the diseases they are faking. But the ruse isn't always easy to get away with. Doctors may become suspicious when patients report symptoms that sound too much like descriptions in medical textbooks. Those who carry on their pretense even when they are not being scrutinized by a physician may also enhance their chances of deceiving others. Side note: Pretending to be sick once in a while to get out of a commitment or take a day off does not qualify as FDIS.

Factitious Disorder Imposed on Another

First identified by British pediatrician Roy Meadow (1977) and previously known as Munchausen syndrome by proxy, factitious disorder imposed on another (FDIA) is an often-misdiagnosed form of child abuse in which people induce symptoms of a disease in their own children (usually preverbal infants or toddlers) and then give false reports to medical caregivers (Talbot, 2004). The vast majority (95%) of people diagnosed with FDIA are women. Once the abused child is hospitalized, the perpetrator gets the attention she has been seeking. She will pretend to be grief-stricken by what has happened to the child she loves, and the physician and hospital staff provide a wealth of comfort and support. On occasion, FDIA can occur with adults as the victims. For example, a nurse may induce cardiac arrest in a patient to enjoy the exhilaration and excitement derived from being a member of the medical team seeking to remedy the problem.

Several methods used by FDIA patients to inflict factitious illness in children have been documented, including poisoning, drawing blood to induce anemia, rubbing dirt into wounds to cause infection, and choking to the point of asphyxiation (Criddle, 2010). In one case, a 6-year-old girl's mother put her own blood in her child's urine sample to make her appear ill. The child saw 16 doctors, underwent 12 separate hospitalizations, was catheterized, X-rayed, and given no less than 8 different antibiotics (Talbot, 2004). Fans of the blockbuster film *The Sixth Sense* may remember the scene in which Mrs. Collins is revealed to be responsible for murdering Kyra by slowly poisoning her (QR).

In real life, there is the shocking case of Gypsy Rose Blanchard and her mother Dee Dee. The subject of HBO's documentary, *Mommy Dead and Dearest* (QR), Dee Dee forced her daughter to be in a wheelchair and endure a host of maladies, many of them brought on by physical abuse. The situation continued until Gypsy Rose was in her mid-20s, fooling family and friends alike and earning Dee Dee and her daughter free trips to Disneyland and a house built by Habitat for Humanity (Morabito, 2017). All of it began to unravel one day in June of 2015 when Gypsy Rose posted on their joint account, "that Bitch is dead!" The post led authorities to Wisconsin, where they arrested Gypsy Rose and boyfriend Nicholas Godejohn, whom she'd met on a Christian dating site. He was charged with murdering Mrs. Blanchard at her daughter's request. For her part in the murder, Gypsy Rose was sentenced to 10 years in prison. She gave an exclusive interview (QR) to ABC News that was aired in 2018.

Imposeurs

A term coined by Keyes (2004), "imposeurs" are people who retain most of their own personal identity but fabricate key elements such as experiences they never had, skills they never learned, degrees they didn't earn, jobs they never had, and awards they never received. They may be done with selfish or altruistic motives but may also reflect the imposeur's "deepest yearnings and feelings of inadequacy" (p. 71). To be convincing, these falsehoods may require the use of forged/stolen documents or misleading props. Imposeurs probably occupy all domains of human life, but representative illustrations of their behavior can be seen in stories about relationships, the military, illness, and crime. Even though the deceptive ability of imposeurs is sometimes formida-

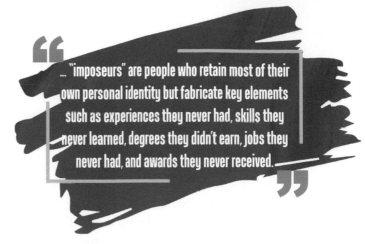

... "imposeurs" are people who retain most of their own personal identity but fabricate key elements such as experiences they never had, skills they never learned, degrees they didn't earn, jobs they never had, and awards they never received.

ble, they are amateurs when compared with full-blown imposters discussed later in this chapter. That's why they are classified separately even though the nature of their behavior is similar.

Like other skilled liars, the best imposeurs mix lies with related truths—e.g., "I was in the Army (true) where I flew helicopters (can fly a helicopter but did not fly one in the Army) in Iraq (false)." Another lie may be implicit in this statement if the person was not an Army officer since helicopter pilots are officers.

Imposeurs will also invent identities to control and/or defraud a romantic relationship partner (Campbell, 2000). People may claim, for example, that they are from a wealthy family or make a lot of money in order to develop a relationship with someone who actually is wealthy. They may try to increase the credibility of such claims by renting or borrowing an expensive car. A person who falsely claims to have an MBA in accounting or investment banking may be setting the stage for taking charge of his or her partner's money. In addition to greed, fabricated stories in close relationships can also be used to control and create dependence—e.g., "I'm a doctor, so you should come to me first when you have any questions about health matters."

Sometimes couples work together to make up or embellish aspects of their relationship history to impress friends, draw public attention, and even reap financial gain. A particularly notorious example is Herman and Roma Rosenblat's (2009) memoir *Angel at the Fence*. The book purports to tell how the couple met and later married under poignant circumstances. According to the story, they met in 1944, when he was a young Jewish man imprisoned in the infamous Buchenwald concentration camp in Nazi Germany, and she (also Jewish) was posing as a Christian with her family at a nearby farm. Rosenblat claimed she had tossed him apples and passed other food to him through an electrified camp fence for several months, until he was transferred to another location. He did not see her again until the war was over and the two had moved with their families to the United States. As the story went, they met in 1957 on a blind date in Coney Island, New York, discovered their "shared past," and married shortly thereafter.

In 2007, about a year before the book was to be released, Oprah Winfrey invited the couple to appear on her show (for the second time since 1996) to tell "the single greatest love story in 22 years of doing this show" (Zarrella & Kaye, 2008). Fueled in part by the public attention generated by the Rosenblats' 2007 appearance on her show, the film rights to the book were purchased from the publisher for $25 million.

The media coverage also drew attention to their story from several Holocaust scholars. Historian Ken Waltzer, who was familiar with the physical layout of the Buchenwald camp, publicly challenged the story on the grounds that it would have been impossible for civilians or prisoners to approach the perimeter fence without being detected by SS guards. Waltzer also determined that although Roma and her family did pose as Christians in the German countryside, in 1944 they resided in a town over 200 miles away from Buchenwald (Langer, 2015).

Several survivors who were in the camp at the same time as Herman were later interviewed and none could recall him ever mentioning a girl throwing apples over the fence (Sherman, 2008). Family members of the couple, including their son, also raised questions about the memoir's accuracy (Siemaszko, 2009). In light of these questions, the publisher canceled the book's release. Both the publisher and the movie studio demanded the Rosenblats return advances totaling $150,000. According to the *New York Times*, neither advance was ever repaid (Roberts, 2015).

Herman then admitted (sort of) in a statement that the story had been invented. "I wanted to bring happiness to people," he wrote. "In my dreams, Roma will always throw me an apple, but I now know it is only a dream" (Day, 2009). He remained astonishingly unrepentant: "It wasn't a lie," he told Good Morning America (QR). "It was my imagination," he argued. "In my imagination, it was true."

Military Imposeurs

There are always people who claim military experiences and medals but never served in the military. They do it for one or more of the following reasons:

- to make their résumé look better
- to make their life seem more significant, even heroic
- to gain respect and self-esteem
- to savor being associated with others who are admired

lying and deception in **HUMAN INTERACTION**

- to support a fantasy or wished-for life
- or to make them feel like they have accomplished something important for their country

It is also common for some who actually *did* serve in the military to fabricate their rank, where they served, what they did, and/or what medals they earned.

Stolen Valor

In a ruse that began in 1985 and lasted for 15 years, Edward Daily went to extraordinary lengths to create his make-believe military life. He did in fact serve during the Korean War, but spent all of his time well behind the front lines in a maintenance unit. After the war, however, he forged documents that praised him for commanding his troops under fire, bravely rescuing a fellow soldier, and spending time as a prisoner of war. These imaginary actions served as the basis for creating fraudulent Silver Star and Distinguished Service Cross citations.

When a 1973 fire destroyed some Army records, veterans were contacted and asked to provide the lost information. This prompted Daily to forge his name and photo on an original photo of soldiers from the Seventh Cavalry Regiment, a unit that had seen a lot of combat during the Korean War. In the ensuing years, he insinuated himself into reunions and trips (including one to South Korea), gathered up stories from men who'd actually served in the regiment, added his own, and published three books (Moss, 2000). By the time his sham was uncovered, he had convinced several men in that regiment that he had actually served in combat with them (Ellison, 2000). Over the years, he filed for benefits based on this false record of service, receiving almost $325,000 in compensation and $88,000 in medical benefits (Marquis, 2002). The *New York Times* archive contains a detailed account of the Edward Daily saga (QR).

Beginning with persons like Edward Daily, a rash of military imposeurs in the 2000s prompted the U.S. Congress to pass two versions of the Stolen Valor Act (2005 and 2013). This law makes it a crime for someone to falsely claim having received any of a series of military decorations or awards including the Purple Heart, Silver Star, and Medal of Honor. The penalty for violating this law is a fine of up to $100,000 and up to a year in prison (Yarnell, 2013).

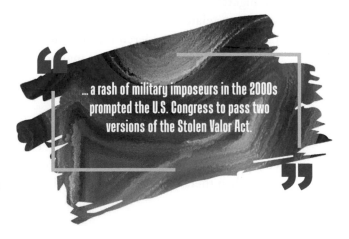

... a rash of military imposeurs in the 2000s prompted the U.S. Congress to pass two versions of the Stolen Valor Act.

Brian Williams lost his post as anchor and managing editor of the NBC Nightly News after falsely claiming for years that he had been aboard a military helicopter in Iraq in 2003 that drew enemy fire. In truth, he was riding in an aircraft behind the helicopter that had been fired upon. Further investigation revealed this was not the only time Williams misrepresented his experience in war zones (Farhi, 2015). He also falsely claimed to have flown into Baghdad with the Navy Seals (who do not "embed" journalists), to have been present at the Brandenburg Gate the night the Berlin Wall fell in 1989, and in Cairo's Tahrir Square during the "Arab Spring" protests of 2011 (Bancoff, 2015).

After Fox News host Bill O'Reilly publicly criticized Williams for these deceptions, it came to light that O'Reilly had fabricated stories of his own about being fired upon while covering the 1982 Falklands War in Argentina and being assaulted by protestors during the 1992 Los Angeles riots (Corn and Shulman, 2015). O'Reilly was not fired for his fabrications, however. In fact, the negative coverage created a huge ratings boost for his show from viewers convinced that the challenges to his recollections were just liberal propaganda. Many reporters who called for Williams to be fired did not recommend ousting O'Reilly on the grounds that he isn't a "journalist" in a strict sense.

"It's ridiculous to compare Bill O'Reilly to Brian Williams," said *Washington Post* reporter Sally Quinn. "O'Reilly is an entertainer and everything he does is totally subjective, including his memories" (Chariton, 2015).

Illness Stories

Unlike people with factitious disorders, *malingerers* feign illness symptoms for an external incentive—e.g., compensation from an insurance company, obtaining desired drugs, avoiding work, putting off an exam, dodging military service, or evading criminal prosecution.

Malingerers invent pain, sickness, and injury that never existed, but they may also report symptoms related to an illness long after recovery should have occurred. Some forms of malingering are considered less serious than others—e.g., feigning illness in order to avoid sex or a social commitment. But malingering may also be costly (e.g., people falsely reporting they are too sick to work) and/or illegal (e.g., scams designed to defraud insurance companies).

Because malingering can have serious social consequences, considerable effort has been put into effective methods of detection (Hall & Poirier, 2001; Halligan, Bass, & Oakley, 2003; McCann, 1998; Rogers, 1988). Sometimes malingerers can be extremely effective liars, especially when there is much to gain and they have time to prepare their story. They may benefit from the fact that most observers have a hard time distinguishing between real and faked expressions of pain (Craig & Hill, 2003). But faking mental illness to professionals is far more difficult, even when the malingerer has knowledge of the symptoms and behavior associated with a particular mental illness (Kropp & Rogers, 1993; Resnick & Knoll, 2005).

" ... malingerers can be extremely effective liars, especially when there is much to gain and they have time to prepare their story. "

The verbal behavior of malingerers may offer clues to deception—e.g., reporting obvious symptoms of an illness, but ignoring subtle ones that should also be present; or reporting too many symptoms, some of which are not likely to co-occur (Young, 2014). Nevertheless, some malingerers succeed in fooling psychiatrists. For example, Mafia boss Vincent "The Chin" Gigante deceived some of the most respected forensic psychiatrists for years by malingering schizophrenia—wearing a bathrobe out in public, muttering about voices in his head, slobbering while recounting frightening hallucinations, and engaging in other bizarre behaviors.

A Harvard psychiatrist, five former presidents of the American Academy for Psychiatry and Law—even the forensic expert who created the standard test for psychiatric malingering—all judged him as incompetent to stand trial at some point. Ultimately, he admitted to maintaining his charade from 1990 to 1997 during evaluations of his competency to stand trial for racketeering (Newman, 2003).

Crime Stories

The reputed victims of crimes are not always the actual victims. Some people go to great lengths to stage a crime to make it look like they are the victim. This is known as the *crying wolf* phenomenon. For instance:

- In 2004, a University of Wisconsin honors student was found tied up near a marsh in Madison, Wisconsin. She lied to the police, saying she'd been held captive at knife point by her abductor for four days.

- In 2003, a woman in Washington falsely reported she had been raped in a park while her 5-year-old daughter played nearby.

- That same year, a New York girl made up a story about being punched in the face by a man with a swastika tattoo after she refused to get into his car (Parmar, 2004).

At first glance, these stories and the people who tell them seem very credible. Initial attention is naturally focused on the perpetrator identified by the victim. In addition, many of those who "cry wolf" are often people who have no criminal record and no apparent reason for lying (O'Sullivan, 2003). Some confess when facts do not support their story. The Wisconsin student's deception (above) was revealed when detectives watched a store surveillance tape showing the girl purchasing the same rope and knife she said her abductor used to hold her captive.

Why do they do it? It appears to be the result of an intense desire for attention, sympathy, love, caring, and/or help. They believe that by becoming the victim of a serious crime their significant other, parents, or some other person close to them will no longer ignore and neglect them.

Others who fake crimes may be seeking attention not for themselves but for a cause. For example:

- A faculty member at a California college was believed to have slashed tires, smashed a car's windshield, and spray-painted it with racial slurs prior to giving a speech against campus hate crimes.

- A Mexican-American student at Northwestern University filed two false reports of hate crimes purportedly directed at his heritage in order to call attention to race relations on campus (Parmar, 2004).

Sometimes crime fakers are aided and abetted by reporters with an agenda. In 2015, *Rolling Stone* reporter Sabrina Rubin Erdely published a widely read article describing a horrific sexual assault of a University of Virginia freshman female in a fraternity house and how the school mishandled the incident. For several days after it was published, the article served a noble purpose: It sparked a national conversation about sexual violence on college campuses and the indifference with which campus administrators respond to these brutal crimes. However, an investigation by the Charlottesville Police found "no basis to conclude that any assault happened in the fraternity house" and "no substantive basis to support the account alleged in the *Rolling Stone* article" (Robinson & Stolberg, 2015).

It eventually came to light that not only did the alleged victim fabricate several characters and crucial episodes in the story, but author Erdely never even attempted to contact the fraternity members she had accused of perpetrating the assault (Coronel, Coll, & Kravitz, 2015). A review by the Columbia School of Journalism concluded Erdely had "failed to engage in basic, even routine journalistic practice" (Somaiya, 2015). *Rolling Stone* eventually retracted the article and Erdely publicly apologized, although her apology did not mention the fraternity members who were accused.

IMPOSTERS

Many of us feel like imposters, but we are not. The phenomenon known as *imposter's syndrome* is very different from the behavior of people we call imposters. People who experience imposter's syndrome *feel like* they are imposters, but they aren't. Instead, they are high-achieving individuals who unfairly see themselves as frauds. They believe their accomplishments have been obtained because they are physically attractive, likeable, lucky, or any reason other than their own talents. In fact, they often have a low self-concept and worry that someone will reveal the sham they've been carrying on. If you've ever felt like this, you're not alone. Even highly successful actors are especially prone to feeling as though they don't deserve their success, from Tom Hanks to Tina Fey to Meryl Streep (Simon, 2017).

Actual imposters also worry about whether they are fooling others, but it has nothing to do with an ill-gotten persona. It is because they have purposefully enacted a false persona designed to fool others, and they worry about getting caught. The behavior of an imposter is normally far more complex than that of an imposeur.

© James Steidl/Shutterstock.com

Imposters engage in longer, more elaborate deceptions. They assume different names and different identities. Deception for an imposter is a part of a lifestyle. The good ones are confident, quick learners, skilled communicators, and people who know how to effectively enact the roles they choose to play. As noted in the following cases of famous imposters, there may be many reasons behind their imposture, for example:

- The need to live a life other than the one they have
- The need to obtain something they want
- The need to prove something to themselves or someone else
- The need to gather information about an enemy

"The Great Impostor"

Whether you spell it *imposter* or *impostor*, Fred Demara Jr. was probably the most successful one of the 20th century (Crichton, 1959). In fact, a Hollywood version of his extraordinary life was portrayed in the movie, "The Great Impostor" (1961). He did not graduate from high school but would one day manage to convincingly pose as a PhD in Psychology. His work masquerades included teacher, deputy sheriff, college dean, monk, civil engineer, assistant prison warden, and a cancer biologist. At one point, he actually deserted the Army and then joined the Navy. He later deserted the U.S. military altogether and joined the Canadian Navy (where he successfully impersonated a ship's doctor, even performing surgery).

He reportedly performed the tasks associated with each role quite well, and his surgical skill was featured in newspaper articles. He spent time in prison, but he did not seem to be driven by the desire to take advantage of people for his personal financial gain. In fact, he liked helping people. But there was also a drive for identity and he seemed to enjoy the experience and challenge of living lives other than the one he had.

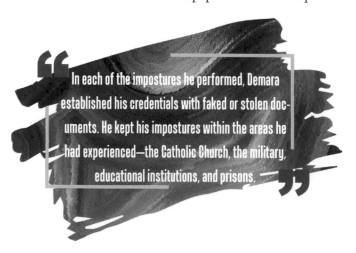

"In each of the impostures he performed, Demara established his credentials with faked or stolen documents. He kept his impostures within the areas he had experienced—the Catholic Church, the military, educational institutions, and prisons."

In each of the impostures he performed, Demara established his credentials with faked or stolen documents. He kept his impostures within the areas he had experienced—the Catholic Church, the military, educational institutions, and prisons. On the job, he sought ways to fulfill others' needs. He fostered feelings of affinity from others and with the aid of a little self-deception showed complete confidence in his ability to perform job-related tasks. He was able to learn things quickly. On one occasion, he managed to successfully extract an infected tooth from his ship's captain after reading about the procedure the night before.

Konnikova's 2016 best selling book, *The Confidence Game: Why We Fall for It … Every Time*, chronicles Demara's exploits in depth, revealing some unsavory details that Demara managed to slip past his own biographer (whom he later impersonated).

David Pecard

David Pecard had at least eight different names and posed as a lawyer, police officer, soldier, and emergency room technician (Mathur, 1999; Moya, 1999). He enlisted and deserted the Army at least seven different times under seven different identities. He conducted investigations for the FBI and arrested a wanted con man. As a lawyer, he obtained the early release of a prison inmate. So it came as a surprise to many when he was charged with sexual abuse and conning a couple out of $7,500.

One of the detectives who arrested him said, "He's got that air about him, that you will buy whatever he's selling." This was never truer than when Pecard prepared briefs and argued convincingly in court that the charges against him should be dismissed. Like Demara, Pecard knew the value of learning. He took courses in medicine and law and learned Chinese and Korean. If he needed credentials he didn't have, he forged them. To get a new Social Security number, he argued that he had been out of the country his entire life doing missionary work.

"Doors can be opened if you know how to open them," Pecard said. "I am a chameleon. I adapt. It's what I've been my whole life." Escaping from an unhappy home life, he developed his first new identity at age seven. When he was turned down for a paper route, he went to an office that managed a different route of the same paper, gave them a different name and age, and was hired. When he was 14, he posed as an 18-year-old to enlist in the Army. The Army discharged him when they learned his actual age, but a few months later he managed to enlist in the Army again, using a different name.

He explained his multiple impostures by saying, "When I reach a point where I can no longer safely be that person, then I have one focus. I must survive, and I must create a new person."

Frank Abagnale

Abagnale was another remarkably gifted imposter whose exploits also led to the Hollywood blockbuster *Catch Me If You Can* (2002). He masqueraded as an airline pilot, pediatrician, hospital administrator, and lawyer (Abagnale, 1980). He wrote about 2.5 million dollars in bad checks, and served time in prison in France, Sweden, and the United States.

© Featureflash Photo Agency/Shutterstock.com

Abagnale was smart enough to pass bar exams and to convince the United States government to cut his prison time from 12 years to 5. He did that by convincing law enforcement agencies that his knowledge and experience would greatly assist them in catching swindlers and preventing fraud.

Running away from an unhappy home life at 16, Abagnale learned various dishonest ways to survive. He needed to be older in order to get work, so he changed the date on his driver's license. He needed money, so he put his checking account number on other account holders' bank deposit slips. When people filled them out and turned them in, their money went to his account. He used his father's credit card to buy four tires for his car. Then, he told the seller that he would sell them back to him for half of what he just paid—as long as it was in cash.

For two years, he impersonated an airline pilot so he could catch free rides to places all over the world. He would stay in hotels where airline crews stayed and where the airlines picked up the bill. To carry out this imposture, he convinced an airline representative that dry cleaners had lost his uniform and he needed a new one. He was also able to get a fake identity card made by posing as a person wanting to do business with the company that made airline identity cards.

Gerald Barnbaum

Gerald Barnbaum, a.k.a. Gerald Barnes and other aliases, was a notorious imposter—but he differs from the aforementioned in important ways:

- First, people suffered as a result of his impostures. Unlike Demara, Barnes's medical knowledge and skill never merited recognition—far from it, in fact. One of his patients died while many others were likely misdiagnosed (Munoz, 1996).

- Second, unlike many imposters, he stuck with one basic role the entire time.

- Third, he was it in primarily for the money rather than adventure.

Barnbaum loved acting and appeared in plays during and after college. He earned a degree in Pharmacy from the University of Illinois and practiced until the clinic was caught defrauding Medicaid (Kohn, 2001). Relocating to California, he decided to put his acting skills to work and build the life he'd always wanted. He read medical texts and enrolled in continuing education courses for physicians. He even worked as an assistant to some doctors from India who had recently arrived in the United States.

Initially, Barnbaum obtained a job as a physician at a community clinic because no one checked any of the claims on his résumé. Then he saw a chance to get a permanent identity when he discovered there was an existing California physician named Gerald Barnes. He legally changed his name to Gerald Barnes, then wrote the California Medical Board and explained that his diploma and license had been lost when his ex-wife destroyed them in the midst of a bitter divorce (Noble, 1996). Copies of these documents were sent, which he then used to retrieve copies of the real Dr. Barnes's credentials going all the way back to medical school. He would use them again and again to re-establish his career after each of his first four arrests and subsequent prison terms. Over the course of his fraudulent career, he earned around $400,000. His various employers, meanwhile, had billed individuals, insurance companies, and Medicare for approximately five million dollars (Fernandez, 2001).

Frederic Bourdin

Frederic Bourdin was a serial imposter nicknamed "The Chameleon" by members of the U.S. media. Unlike those reviewed earlier, Bourdin rarely pretended to have an occupation he wasn't qualified for. In fact, during the height of his impersonating career he never admitted he was of legal working age.

Born and raised in France, Bourdin first drew the attention of the FBI in 1998, after a tip from a private investigator hired by the TV tabloid show *Hard Copy*. The P.I. had been hired to investigate the extraordinary story of Nicholas Barclay. At the age of 13, Barclay was reported missing by his family in San Antonio and had not been seen nor heard from in three years. In 1997, the family received a phone call from a youth shelter in Spain from someone claiming to be Nicholas. The caller explained that he had been kidnapped in the U.S. and then sold into a child prostitution ring in Europe. During his captivity, so he claimed, the kidnappers had injected his eyes with a chemical and did not allow him to speak English, thereby transforming the brown-eyed boy with a Texas accent into the blue-eyed, French-accented adolescent he had become. He convinced the family he was Nicholas and was flown to Texas, where he lived with them for several months.

The hired investigator did not find this story credible, however. After examining several old photos of Nicholas, he became convinced the person living with the Barclay family was not their son and notified the authorities. The FBI obtained a court order to take the young man's fingerprints and DNA, which were identified as belonging to 28-year-old Bourdin, not the 16-year-old missing boy he claimed to be.

Bourdin had nothing to do with Nicholas Barclay's disappearance, but had learned of the boy's identity and disappearance by calling the National Center for Missing and Exploited Children in Virginia from the youth shelter in Spain. In 1998, Bourdin pleaded guilty to passport fraud and perjury and was imprisoned for six years in the United States. After completing his sentence and returning to Europe, he continued to impersonate abused and abandoned adolescents, insinuating himself into youth shelters, orphanages, foster homes, and hospitals in 14 different countries over a two-year period.

When he was captured again in northern France, the authorities launched an investigation to determine why a 30-year-old man would pose as a teenage orphan. They found no evidence to suggest sexual or financial motives.

"In my twenty years on the job, I've never seen a case like it," prosecutor Eric Maurel said. "Usually people con for money. His profit seems to have been purely emotional" (Grann, 2008, p. 71). Bourdin has apparently ended his career as an imposter and now lives with his wife and four children in Le Mans, France. Bourdin's exploits have been the subject of a fictionalized film (*The Chameleon*, 2010) and a documentary (*The Imposter*, 2012).

Female Imposters

Although the imposters noted thus far have all been male, imposture is not exclusively a male activity. There have been women disguised as men in the military, one of whom achieved the rank of Lieutenant Colonel in the Civil War (Hall, 1993), and there have been female imposters and con artists (DeGrave, 1995).

> During the middle ages it was not unusual for a woman in a small village to try to escape a dismal future by posing as a male, leaving the village, and enjoying the benefits of a male-dominated culture.

Female imposters and spies face all the same challenges as men, but when female imposters assume the role of a male they face the additional challenges of looking and acting like a man as well as the role they are trying to portray.

During the Middle Ages, it was not unusual for a woman in a small village to try to escape a dismal future by posing as a male, leaving the village, and enjoying the benefits of a male-dominated culture. One such woman imposter may actually have become Pope, although scholars disagree on the authenticity of this story (Boreau, 2001; Stanford, 1999).

Figure 8.1: Pictures of Loreta Janeta Velazquez as Harry T. Buford (left) and as herself

lying and deception in HUMAN INTERACTION

The truth of Loreta Janeta Velazquez's (1876/2003) autobiography is also disputed, but she claims to have raised a battalion of men and fought at the U.S. Civil War's first battle of Bull Run, at Shiloh, and at Fort Donelson as Lieutenant Harry T. Buford. Later, as a female, she became a spy for the Confederacy in Washington, D.C.

In the introduction to Velazquez's 1876 memoir, editor C.J. Worthington said she was so adept at imitating male behavior that she could easily pass herself off as a man. Good thing, too, since she had to frequent saloons and walk, drink, smoke, spit, swear, and tell bawdy stories like a man. She was, in short, an entertaining conversationalist with a "fund of racy anecdotes" (Davis, 2016, p. 152).

Sarah Edmonds spent two years disguised as a male book salesman before she joined a Union regiment during the Civil War. She was a medical orderly and a mail courier, but her own claim that she was also a spy is disputed. After the war, she returned to her female identity, married, and became the only woman to receive a soldier's pension for her Civil War service (Gansler, 2005).

Norah Vincent (QR) spent a year and a half masquerading as a man (Ned) in order to find out how men behaved and what their life was like. She hired a voice coach, had a makeup artist alter her face and hair, worked out to add muscle and gain weight, and wore a "packable softie" to simulate bulging genitals. As a male, she participated with an all-male bowling team and a men's therapy group, went to strip clubs, dated women, and worked as a salesman. She had this to say about the experience:

> In the end, the biggest surprise in Ned was how powerfully psychological he turned out to be. The key to his success was not in his clothing or his beard or anything else physical that I did to make him seem real. It was in my mental projection of him, a projection that became over time undetectable even to me. People didn't see him with their eyes. They saw him in their mind's eye. (p. 282)

Her account of the experience, *Self-Made Man: One Woman's Journey into Manhood and Back Again*, from which the above quote is taken, was published as a memoir in 2006.

SPIES AND DOUBLE AGENTS

Some spies maintain their personal identity and secretly collect and pass classified information to another group or country. For example, FBI agent Robert Hanssen and CIA agent Aldrich Ames passed secret documents and the names of Russian citizens who were spying for the U.S. to the Russian KGB.

Although spies of this type are required to act like people they are not, spies who infiltrate and assume the role of the enemy are imposters who face additional, very special challenges. FBI agent Joe Pistone, who assumed the name of Donnie Brasco and infiltrated the New York Mafia for six years, is a good example of this type of spy (Pistone, 1987).

The first objective for spies who want to be accepted as a member of an enemy group is to gain entrance. This must be done slowly and without any hint that this is the goal. Whether the targeted group is the Mafia or an intelligence unit of the enemy, outsiders are viewed with suspicion and mistrust. Brasco, an Italian-American, hung around restaurants and bars frequented by members of the mob. He cut his hair and dressed like they did, used their type of language, showed respect to family members and avoided conversations that didn't involve him.

Like them, he adopted a way of interacting that demanded respect, showed indignation toward personal questions, and exhibited a willingness to settle disagreements by fighting. But unlike other imposters who assume the mannerisms and identity of their adopted group, infiltrators like Brasco face more intense scrutiny and wariness, and greater penalties for exposure.

Brasco said he tried not to tell many lies to avoid the possibility of inconsistent information raising suspicion. He said he'd been raised in an orphanage that burned down so his early history could not be checked. He also carried the phone number of an FBI agent who would portray a criminal and vouch for his competence as a jewel thief.

IDENTITY THIEVES

Although many of the imposeurs and imposters reviewed earlier could be described as "identity thieves," the term is typically used to describe criminals who use someone else's personally identifying information (name, Social Security number, credit card number, etc.) to commit fraud and other crimes.

The term was coined in 1964, but it did not enter common parlance until the 1990s with the rise of the Internet, the principal medium through which identity theft now occurs. Identity theft can both facilitate and be facilitated by other crimes. For example, possessing other people's Social Security numbers can make it possible to commit crimes such as bank fraud and espionage; crimes such as robbery and burglary can result in the misappropriation of

Social Security numbers. Identity theft victimizes both the people whose identifying information is stolen as well the various third parties defrauded (government, banks, insurance providers, etc.).

Identity theft became a federal crime in the U.S. in 1998 when Congress passed the Identity Theft Assumption Deterrence Act. The subsequent Identity Theft Penalty Enhancement Act established harsher penalties for thieves who use stolen credentials to commit another federal crime (e.g., Medicare fraud). Identity theft has been the most commonly reported consumer fraud complaint to the Federal Trade Commission since 2004. In 2013, about 12.6 million Americans were victims (most had credit card numbers stolen) and averaged $365 in direct costs as well as many hours spent filing reports and restoring their credit (Finklea, 2014).

Identity theft is a rapidly evolving criminal threat, with new forms developing on a regular basis. Six of the most common forms are described on the following pages.

Financial Identity Theft

Financial identity theft occurs when someone steals another person's personally identifiable information and commits a crime that results in financial injury to the victim. Information can include the name, bank account number, credit card numbers, Social Security number, and other personal financial data. It is the most common form of identity theft, accounting for approximately 28% of all cases (Federal Trade Commission, 2013). Once thieves have accessed victims' information, they have the tools necessary to counterfeit checks or ATM cards and wipe out accounts, open utility, cable, or cellular accounts in the victim's name, apply for car loans or mortgages, claim their tax refunds from the IRS, file for bankruptcy, and other activities, all potentially resulting in vast debts and destroyed credit.

Criminal Identity Theft

When criminals falsely identify themselves to police as other people at the point of arrest, they have committed "criminal identity theft" (Newman & McNally, 2005). In some cases, criminals have previously obtained state-issued identity documents using credentials stolen from others or have simply presented fake IDs.

When this subterfuge works, charges may be placed under the victim's name, getting the criminal off the hook. Victims might only learn of such incidents by chance—e.g., discovering a driver's license is suspended when stopped for a minor traffic violation, or through a background check performed by a potential employer.

It can be difficult for victims of criminal identity theft to clear their records. The steps required can differ dramatically depending on the jurisdiction in which the crime occurred and whether the true identity of the criminal can be determined. Victims may need to locate the original arresting officers and prove their own identity by some reliable means such as fingerprinting or DNA testing. Obtaining an expungement of court records may also be required. Authorities may permanently maintain the victim's name as an alias for the criminal's true identity in their criminal records databases.

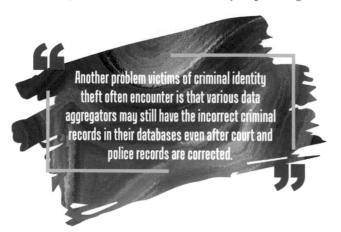

Another problem victims of criminal identity theft often encounter is that various data aggregators may still have the incorrect criminal records in their databases even after court and police records are corrected.

Another problem victims of criminal identity theft often encounter is that various data aggregators may still have the incorrect criminal records in their databases, even after court and police records are corrected. Thus, it is possible that a future background check will return the incorrect criminal records. This is just one example of the kinds of impact that may continue to affect the victims of identity theft for months or even years after the crime, on top of the psychological trauma that being "cloned" typically creates.

Medical Identity Theft

Medical identity theft occurs when someone seeks medical care under the identity of another person. In addition to risks of financial harm common to all forms of identity theft, the thief's medical history may be added to the victim's medical records. Inaccurate information in the victim's records is difficult to correct and may affect future insurability or cause doctors relying on the misinformation to deliver inappropriate medical care (Finklea, 2014).

Child Identity Theft

Child identity theft occurs when a minor's identity is used by another person for the impostor's personal gain (Power, 2011). The impostor can be a family member, a friend, or even a stranger who targets children. Children's Social Security numbers are valued because they do not have any other credentials associated with them. Thieves can establish lines of credit,

obtain driver's licenses, or even buy a house using a child's identity. This fraud can go undetected for years, as most children and their parents do not discover the problem until they
apply for a driver's license or a job. Child identity theft is one of the fastest-growing forms of
identity crime (FTC, 2013).

Synthetic Identity Theft

An increasingly prevalent new form of identity theft is *synthetic identity theft*, in which
identities are completely or partially fabricated. The most common technique involves combining a real Social Security number with a name and birthdate other than the ones associated with the number. Synthetic identity theft is difficult to track because it often doesn't
show up on the credit reports of any of the individuals whose credentials were grafted into
the synthetic identity. Rather, it is likely to appear as an entirely new person to a credit rating agency. Synthetic identity theft primarily harms the creditors who unwittingly grant the
fraudsters credit. Individual victims can be affected if their names become confused with
the synthetic identities.

Synthetic identity fraud first made major headlines in 2007 when two hackers were convicted
for managing approximately 500 fake personas in 200 residences in 14 states (Conkey, 2007).
In 2013, 18 people were prosecuted for running a $200 million credit card scam that created
7,000 new identities. These stories are clear examples of how synthetic identity fraud is growing as an area of concern.

Synthetic identities are used to obtain financial services, medical benefits, insurance, and rent-
al housing, among other things. In addition, organized crime and terrorist groups are realizing
the benefits that the anonymity of synthetic identities can bring to their operations (IBM
Analytics, 2015). Because children do not have public database records, their Social Security
numbers are ideal for creating synthetic identities (Power, 2011).

CONS AND CON ARTISTS

In 1849, the label "Confidence Man" was coined by the *New York Herald*
to describe William Thompson (QR) and his scheme for stealing watches.
Charismatic and well-dressed, Thompson would find a way to convince
upper-class New Yorkers he met on the street that they knew each other. Then he'd ask to briefly borrow the mark's (very valuable) timepiece,
saying, "Do you have enough confidence in me to trust me with your watch until tomorrow?" Most of the time, the answer was yes. The label struck a nerve with the public

> Con games are designed to take the target's money without a weapon, made possible because, in addition to inspiring confidence and trust, the con appeals to the target's needs, desires, or greed.

and quickly gained popularity. Within a few years, Herman Melville published his last novel, calling it *The Confidence-Man: His Masquerade* (1857) and featuring a Thompson-esque central character who sneaks aboard a passenger steamboat on the Mississippi (Redlitz, 2014).

Con games are designed to take the target's money without a weapon, made possible because, in addition to inspiring confidence and trust, the con appeals to the target's needs, desires, or greed. Luring targets in with the promise of easy money is common, but targets may also be conned because of their need to find a romantic partner, to grieve for a deceased loved one, to increase their sexual prowess, to improve their appearance, to catch a thief, or any number of other needs the con artist promises to fulfill. There are many well-known con artists (Larsen, 1966; Nash, 1976; Weil & Brannon, 1948/2004) and many types of cons. But George C. Parker remains the personal favorite of the authors. Parker famously "sold" the Brooklyn Bridge on numerous occasions, giving rise to the popular expression, "If you believe that, I've got a bridge to sell you" (Cohen, 2005).

Running a Con: The Fundamentals

There are cons that take place quickly and those that develop over time and involve several contacts, people, and locations. Cons focus on sales, investments, psychic readings, faith healings, gambling, romance, lottery or inheritance winnings, and many other topics. Each con has a distinct strategy, but cons often include the following elements (Faron, 1998; Hankiss, 1980; Langenderfer & Shimp, 2001; Maurer, 1940/1999):

- **Select a vulnerable victim or "mark."** Sometimes visual cues prompt selection, but marks may also self-select by answering an advertisement, phone call, or e-mail. Those who are most vulnerable are those who have little knowledge and/or experience with the subject of the con.

- **Make the "bait" for the con seem "authentic"**—i.e., linked to reliable sources, a happenstance occurrence, etc. At this point, the main goal for the con artist is to gain the victim's confidence and to set the stage for working together. This can be facilitated with verbal behavior, which establishes a positive feeling by the mark for the swindler.

- **Build on the needs of the mark.** At this point, the mark is told how he or she can make a lot of money, can be the recipient of a miracle cure, can win a valuable prize, etc. without any risk. It is usually a story that sounds too good to be true (and it is), but it is tempting to the mark because it taps into a powerful desire. Often, the story will have some true information that accompanies the scam to make it more convincing. Any doubts the mark has are anticipated ahead of time so that they can be talked through.

- **Provide a "convincer."** In many con games, the belief that the probabilities are overwhelmingly in the mark's favor is enough of a convincer. Or the mark may be given a strong reason to believe the con artist when he or she quickly receives a small amount of what is promised (usually money). Other cons steer the mark to a neutral person who is actually part of the scheme. This person may be a bystander, a reference for the con's identity, an expert, or any "outsider" who testifies to the legitimacy of the scam.

- **Extract money from the mark.** Payment normally precedes the promised rewards. Sometimes payment is made on the spot, but if it is determined the mark has more to give, the extortion may take place over a longer period of time. But no matter how long the con takes, there is always a sense of urgency for the mark to act immediately or the promised rewards may no longer be attainable. Any further consultation by the mark with anyone else is prohibited by the con artist.

- **Finish the job.** This may necessitate a trick or swap. Like a magician, the con artist uses distraction and misdirection, keeping the mark's focus on the rewards to be gained.

- **Blow off the mark.** This may involve both physical separation and reasons for the mark to keep quiet. Marks who are trying to obtain money in a manner they know is dishonest have a clear reason to keep quiet, but other victims may not report a scam because they feel embarrassed or mistakenly fear they are culpable in some way.

Types of Cons

The following types of cons, while far from being comprehensive, illustrate various ways they take place. Regardless of the particular type of con or scam being run, Konnikova (2016) cautions that, to the extent we already want to believe what people are telling us (or buy what they're selling us), we make the job of the confidence artist that much easier.

The Big Con

In 1992, three members of the Travelers, a group known nationwide for home-repair scams, nearly succeeded in getting a multi-million-dollar payoff for an elaborate con (QR) staged at a Disney World hotel (Faron, 1998).

Such big cons have a long and storied history. For a definitive account based on hundreds of interviews, see David Maurer's *The Big Con: The Story of the Confidence Man*. First published in 1940, it became the inspiration for 1973's Best Picture, *The Sting*, starring Paul Newman and Robert Redford.

Big cons promise big things and aim for big scores, which is why they often involve land and landmarks (see "Sales and Investments" below) and involve a number of players. Featured on a 2008 episode of *American Greed*, Reed Slatkin, co-founder of IT giant EarthLink, was also a minister in the Church of Scientology. What his wealthy Hollywood Scientologist pals didn't know, however, is that he was also a con artist, eventually bilking them and other investors out of nearly $600 million over the course of 15 years (Tkacik, 2002).

Big cons promise big things and aim for big scores, which is why they often involve land and landmarks and involve a number of players.

Internet Scams

Online scams cost people hundreds of millions of dollars each year. Thanks to the Internet, the bait for the con can reach tens of millions of people—and if only a small percentage of these recipients are conned, the financial profit can be substantial.

One well-known example, which surged in the early years of the Internet and e-mail, is the "Nigerian Letter Scam." The Federal Trade Commission received more than 55,000 complaints about this scam in 2005 (Zuckoff, 2006). The basic strategy of the con has been around since the 1920s when it was called the "Spanish Prisoner" and appeals were made via letters and fax machines until the advent of the e-mail era.

New types of online scams emerge on a regular basis. The following are several types that have become prevalent in recent years (FBI, 2014):

- **"Phishing" e-mails** are designed to look like they come from a financial institution or a shopping website. At first glance, the logo, graphics, and wording look authentic. If you don't have an account with *eBay* or *Barclay's Bank*, you may think a mistake has been made and ignore the request. But sooner or later an e-mail will arrive with a name and logo of a company with which you do business. The e-mail indicates that the security on your account may have been compromised and fraud may have occurred. In order to re-establish your account and safeguard it, you need to click on the site provided and input your personal account information, Social Security number, and passwords again. If you don't, your account will be canceled. The site provided, of course, is the phishing site, not the company you do business with.

- **Online love**. Millions of Americans use dating sites, social network sites like Facebook, and chat rooms to meet potential romantic partners. While many forge successful relationships, scammers also use these sites to meet potential victims. They create fake profiles to build online relationships and eventually convince people to send money in the name of love. Some even make wedding plans before disappearing with the money. An online love interest who asks for money is almost certainly a scam artist, or otherwise a person with baggage. In either case, run the other way.

- **Good news! You're 'pre-qualified!'** In an advance payment credit scam, you receive an e-mail with the "good" news that you've been "pre-qualified" to get a low-interest loan or credit card, or to repair your bad credit even though banks have turned you down. To take advantage of the offer, you have to ante up a processing fee of several hundred dollars. A "pre-qualified" offer simply means you've been selected to apply for a credit card or loan. You still have to complete an application and you can still be turned down. If you paid a fee in advance for the promise of a loan or credit card, you've been hustled. You might get a list of lenders, but there's unlikely to be any loan and the person you've paid has taken your money. You will be a sad panda.

- **Bad news! You have a virus!** In a recent twist, scam artists are using the phone to break into your computer. They call claiming to be computer techs associated with well-known companies like Microsoft. They say that they've detected viruses or other malware on your computer to trick you into giving them remote access or paying for software you don't need. These scammers take advantage of your reasonable concerns about viruses and other threats. They know that computer users have heard time and again that it's important to install security software, so scammers have been peddling bogus security software for years. They set up fake websites, offer free "security" scans, and send alarming messages to try to convince you that your computer is infected. Then, they try to sell you software to fix the problem. At best, the software is worthless or available elsewhere for free. At worst, it could be malware—i.e., software designed to give criminals access to your computer and your personal information.

- **Work-at-home scams** begin with an e-mail ad promising steady income for home-based work, typically in medical claims processing, online searching, international shipping, rebate processing, envelope-stuffing, or assembling crafts and other items. The ads use variations on these themes: "Be your own boss," "Earn thousands of dollars working at home," etc. What the ads don't say is that you will have to spend your own

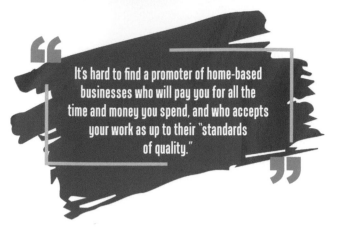

money to fulfill the terms of the assignment—placing newspaper ads, making copies of documents, and buying supplies, software, or equipment to do the job. They probably also won't say you will be paid for all the hours you put in, either. It's hard to find a promoter of home-based businesses who will pay you for all the time and money you spend, and who accepts your work as up to their "standards of quality."

- For an up-to-date list of the latest cons and scams, consult the "International Financial Scams" page maintained by the U.S. Department of State and the FBI's "Common Fraud Schemes" (which currently lists 23 broad categories). Despite its unassuming appearance, ScamBusters has been around since 1994 and earned a solid reputation with regular bulletins alerting consumers to the latest schemes. FraudAid, another decidedly low-tech website, is also a reliable clearinghouse for such information.

Street Cons

Street cons vary, but many involve "finding" things on the street—a diamond ring or a package full of money.

- In the "Indian Head Penny" scam, a mark and a con both come upon a bag of Indian head pennies in a place with high pedestrian traffic. The bag has a phone number on it. The con artist convinces the mark to call the number. The call is answered by the "owner" (also part of the con) who says he will pay a thousand dollars for the return of his coin collection. Then the con artist who discovered the collection with the mark says he is willing to let the mark have most of the reward because he has to go to another appointment. He will settle for $250 now and let  the mark make a $750 profit when he collects the reward. If the mark agrees, he will soon find out that the address given by the so-called owner of the coin collection does not exist and the phone number is no longer in service (Faron, 1998).

lying and deception in **HUMAN INTERACTION**

- With "Three Card Monte," one con shows three cards to bystanders and bets $20 that he can turn the cards over and move them so quickly that a person will not be able to select a specific card from among the three. The mark observes the other players winning more than they're losing, so he or she is seduced into getting in on the action and making a bet. What the mark doesn't know is that the "bystanders" are part of the con. Eventually the mark loses much more than he or she wins.

In the "Block Hustle," a mark is shown some brand-new television sets and other electronic equipment on the back of a truck.

- In the "Block Hustle," a mark is shown some brand-new television sets and other electronic equipment on the back of a truck. The mark is told he or she only has to pay about a quarter of what the retail price would be. The mark may suspect they are stolen but can't pass up such a good deal. The mark pays and a box with a "television" label is put in his or her car. The mark discovers later that there is no TV in the box and the cons are nowhere to be found (Faron, 1998).

Faith Healers

Pat Robertson, Oral Roberts, Peter Popoff, Ernest Angley, W. V. Grant, and Leroy Jenkins are among other evangelical preachers who have practiced faith-healing. They claim the ability to repair broken bones and eradicate tumors simply by touching the patient and invoking God's name.

There are, no doubt, some people who may experience some temporary pain suppression brought on by temporal lobe epilepsy or the release of endorphins during a heightened emotional state (Hines, 2003). Yet the fact remains that independent, verifiable records of people who have experienced long-term healing or cures at the hands of faith healers simply do not exist.

In addition, faith-healers engaging in fraud are commonly exposed (Randi, 1989). Sometimes the people who are healed are working with the faith-healer. People who don't need to be in a wheelchair can miraculously walk; "blind" people who still have some visual acuity can miraculously see. One man, who also posed as a woman, was healed by four different healers in six different cities of six different diseases under four different names.

Some of the scams performed by faith-healers are similar to those done by magicians. W. V. Grant's "leg stretching miracle" is an old carnival trick. Peter Popoff (QR)

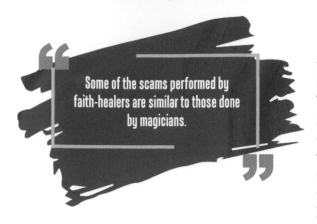

Some of the scams performed by faith-healers are similar to those done by magicians.

wore a receiver in his ear while his wife transmitted information to him about people and their illness. These people had previously filled out cards with this information and Popoff pretended to have divinely obtained this information. Unlike the faith-healers who use such tricks, magicians admit they are doing tricks rather than enacting spiritual powers. As a result, their audiences are likely to fill their pockets with far less money.

Sales and Investments

The most notorious con artists are exceptionally persuasive and able to sell virtually anything—even things that don't exist and things they don't own. Sales and investment scams are the bread and butter of con artists.

- Arthur Furguson sold the Admiral Nelson statue in London's Trafalgar Square, complete with fountains, to an American businessman. He later tried to sell the Statue of Liberty.

- Victor Lustig twice sold the Eiffel Tower as scrap iron and conned gangster Al Capone (Larsen, 1966).

- Oscar Hartzell sold the non-existent estate of Sir Francis Drake. He made hundreds of thousands of dollars from investors eager to help him establish his claim to the supposedly lucrative Sir Francis Drake estate (Rayner, 2002).

- During the 1920s and 1930s, "Dr." John Brinkley convinced many American men to have goat glands implanted in their testicles to restore their sexual prowess. At the height of his popularity, he was doing 50 of these bogus operations a month (Lee, 2002).

- Charles Ponzi made millions of dollars through his "pyramid scheme." Investors were told they could double the amount of their investment in 90 days. Investors flocked to Ponzi and as long as he kept getting new investors, he could pay earlier investors. Eventually, he was audited and arrested (Dunn, 1975).

- In 2008, Bernie Madoff was sentenced to 150 years in prison for running the biggest pyramid scheme in U.S. history. A well-respected financier, Madoff convinced thousands of investors to hand over their savings, falsely promising consistent profits in return. He conned investors out of almost $65 billion and went undetected for decades. Few of his victims have regained any of their substantial losses.

- Joseph R. "Yellow Kid" Weil, is considered by many to be the greatest con man in American history. He devised numerous phony deals, some with props and several accomplices. One of Weil's favorite scams involved horses. He got himself admitted to the American Turf Association and purchased several horses. Then he spread the word that he was secretly training a fast horse named Black Fonso. *But he told gamblers that he was racing a slow horse by the same name.* Marks were taken to his secret training track and shown a magnificent horse that ran a fast time. What they weren't told was that this horse only ran fast in the morning and that the fast and the slow Black Fonso were the same. On the day when the race was supposed to be fixed, the marks gave thousands of dollars to Weil that he was supposed to bet on Black Fonso to win. Weil kept the money and Black Fonso lost (Weil and Brannon, 1948/2004).

Psychics and Paranormal Phenomena

Psychics claim abilities that require a sixth sense—e.g., the ability to read people's minds, to move objects without touching them, to predict the future, to levitate, and to communicate with the dead. Despite the lack of scientific evidence for these amazing powers and the exposure of many psychics as frauds (Randi, 1982), Americans' belief in psychics and psychic phenomena continues to abound (Musella, 2005):

- **73%** believe in the paranormal
- **41%** believe in ESP
- **37%** believe in haunted houses
- **32%** believe in ghosts
- **31%** believe in telepathy
- **26%** believe in clairvoyance
- **25%** believe in astrology
- **21%** believe in communication with the dead
- **21%** believe in witches
- **20%** believe in reincarnation
- **9%** believe in channeling spiritual entities

Given these statistics, it is not surprising that psychics continue to flourish. Some probably believe they have these powers, but many know they are just playing out a scam.

Psychic surgery is a process that purportedly involves no cutting, pain, or scars. The psychic simply reaches into a person's body and removes a tumor or some other diseased material. To an untrained observer, it looks shockingly real. But instead, it is more like a magician's trick. Blood is concealed in a false finger. The patient's skin is folded in such a way that the psychic's hand appears to be going into the body when it is actually grabbing some hidden chicken entrails, which are then displayed as the patient's diseased material.

Wiseman (1997) says psychic frauds employ a variety of strategies. Initially, they do everything they can to show that they are unwilling, unable, and/or have no reason to engage in fraudulent behavior. Saying they don't accept payment for their services, for example, is one way to buttress their credibility. The believability of the psychic fraud's performance is certainly enhanced when it is linked to something the mark wants very much to believe—e.g., that a recently deceased spouse can be contacted.

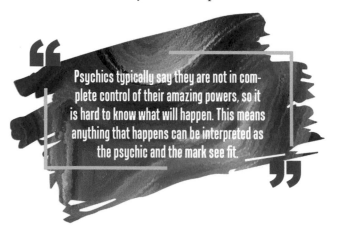

> Psychics typically say they are not in complete control of their amazing powers, so it is hard to know what will happen. This means anything that happens can be interpreted as the psychic and the mark see fit.

Psychics typically say they are not in complete control of their amazing powers, so it is hard to know what will happen. This means anything that happens can be interpreted as the psychic and the mark see fit. Like magicians, psychics learn to do tricks when the mark's attention is relaxed or diverted. They are most effective when they are in charge of establishing the conditions for their performance—e.g., "No video cameras. They send out bad electronic vibes." or "Darkness is essential." In séances, people may be asked to hold hands so they are less likely to touch a wire or an accomplice. Psychic frauds must also be prepared to explain things that seem to have logical explanations—e.g., "I couldn't do that alone," or "I'm not strong enough to do that," or "I can't talk like that."

Who Gets Scammed and Why?

As Faron (1998) points out, *any of us can be conned under the right circumstances*. Still, there are some people who are more likely to fall victim to a scam than others. Some of the most common include those who are:

- **Lonely**. *People who are socially isolated are often older.* They are less likely to be familiar with how scams operate and the signs typically associated with such traps (Brown, Feng, & Lee, 2018).

- **In a hurry**. *People who have important needs to satisfy and little hope of doing so.* They are ready to believe anything—e.g., the cancer patient who desperately wants to believe in the power of a faith healer; the lonely, dateless person who believes a con artist is actually a person who will provide romantic companionship. In general, people under time pressure to make important choices may be more easily manipulated by hustlers (Stajano & Wilson, 2011).

- **Emotional or greedy.** *People who have a strong visceral response to the subject of the scam.* Visceral responses can override a rational decision-making process. Common visceral responses activated by con artists include excitement, fear, greed, and sexual desire ("These are the 4," 2018). The overwhelming urge to quickly satisfy these needs is why cons often require the mark to respond immediately (Langenderfer & Shimp, 2001). Some people even have a feeling they may be entering into a scam, but the promised payoff is so attractive to them that they end up participating anyway ("Psychology of scams," 2017).

- **Egotistical.** *People who strongly believe they can't be conned because they are too smart.* Sometimes these "smart" people rely too heavily on stereotypes and general probabilities that con artists use to their advantage (Cohn, 2015). In addition, people who think they can't be conned may not feel the necessity to check out things they "know" are true. This breeds a false sense of trust, which is exactly what the con artist wants (Francavilla, 2018).

- **Unquestioning.** *People who, without questioning, easily attribute expertise to others and defer to their judgment.* This is not the same as being trustful, a character trait that is not only commendable but also necessary in most healthy relationships, be they personal or professional. Trust contributes greatly to our ability to succeed in life, but—like love and so many other things in human experience—it also makes us vulnerable (Hutson, 2016).

HOAXES

Like cons, hoaxes are meant to fool people. But hoaxes are usually designed for large audiences and the payoff is less likely to be financial. People create hoaxes to make a point, to gain notoriety for an idea, to further their reputation and career, or simply because they enjoy playing practical jokes. The revelation of numerous hoaxes associated with a particular phenomenon does not extinguish belief in the phenomenon—e.g., Bigfoot,

> People create hoaxes to make a point, to gain notoriety for an idea, to further their reputation and career, or simply because they enjoy playing practical jokes.

UFOs, and crop circles.

Hoaxes are a common cultural activity (Kominsky, 1970; *U.S. News & World Report*, 2002). There are so many hoaxes on the Internet that several websites are exclusively dedicated to checking the factuality of information, rumors, and urban legends. These include Snopes, TruthorFiction, and HoaxBusters.

Another site devoted to debunking myths and promoting a scientific approach to inexplicable phenomena is Skeptic.com. There are too many current and former hoaxes to thoroughly document here, but we offer some highlights in the following sections.

Aliens

Many humans believe Earth has been visited by beings from other worlds. Three commonly claimed sources of evidence for this include crop circles, a film of an alien autopsy, and the sighting of unidentified flying objects (UFOs).

Some people honestly believe they have been abducted and analyzed by aliens, although hypnopompic and hypnagogic hallucinations—mental states between sleep and wakefulness—may be an important factor in explaining this experience (Hines, 2003; Shermer, 1997/2002).

Crop Circles

In the 1970s, huge circles and later complex geometric figures were found impressed on fields of wheat, barley, and other crops in southern England (see Figure 8.3). Because some of these circles were surrounded by four smaller circles, it was easy for some to assume these were impressions made by the landing pods of alien spaceships. Later, as the designs became more complex, they were interpreted by some to be the way aliens chose to communicate with us. By the 1990s there were thousands of these crop circles in several countries.

In 1991, two Englishmen admitted they had been making crop circles for 15 years. They explained how they did it with planks and ropes. This inspired other hoaxers. Physicist Eltjo Haselhoff (2001) admits that humans could have made even the most complex designs, but he argues that certain characteristics of the grain found in some crop circles cannot be the result of the methods currently revealed by hoaxers. So, there is still more to learn.

The Alien Autopsy

In 1995, Fox aired a film that purportedly showed a 1947 autopsy of an alien who was found in the wreckage of a UFO in Roswell, New Mexico. The data to support the authenticity of the film was weak, at best:

- The wreckage housing the alien was never confirmed as an alien spaceship.

- The story of how the film was acquired was not consistent.

- The entire original film was not analyzed by Eastman Kodak for authenticity.

- Security marks on the film disappeared after they were labeled as phony by military experts.

- Special effects analysts said the film was flawed in some important ways.

Then, in 2006, British hoaxers confessed that the film was shot in England using 48-year-old film. The "alien" was filled with sheep brains and chicken entrails (Horne, 2006).

UFOs

Hoaxers have admitted the creation of visual phenomena that others have labeled as UFO sightings and many UFO photos have been faked. Some UFO sightings have simply been natural phenomena that were unfamiliar to the observer (Sagan, 1995). There are, of course, some visual phenomena that have yet to be explained, but observers who label them UFOs are subject to the many problems associated with eyewitness observations (see Chapter 2). Consequently, we need more than eyewitness testimony alone to conclude that alien space-ships have visited our planet.

Manufactured News

Long before news that people don't want to believe became "fake news," there was news that was *actually fake*. Joey Skaggs hoaxed the media (QR) for years (http://www.joeyskaggs.com/). His goal was to manufacture a story that he knows TV stations and newspapers will relish and often broadcast or publish without checking its validity. His hoaxes were designed to remind the media how vulnerable they are to false and misleading stories.

He created plausible stories he knew journalists would want to report. In addition to stories of general appeal, Skaggs says the media will predictably look for certain kinds of stories (on holidays, anniversaries of disasters, etc.), so he gave them what they want. After they run the story, he informs them it's a hoax. Generally, however, news organizations are not interested in reminding their readers and viewers that they fell for a hoax because they failed to check it out. Compared to the hoax itself, the retractions get little, if any, publicity.

It seems that not much has changed from the era of Skaggs's pre-Internet exploits. In 2009, Irish undergraduate Shane Fitzgerald decided to test the modern world's commitment to fact-checking. When French composer Maurice Jarre died, Fitzgerald added a fictitious quote to Jarre's Wikipedia entry: "When I die there will be a final waltz playing in my head, that only I can hear." The quote had no referenced sources, so the moderators of Wikipedia took it down almost immediately. He reposted it again and they took it down again. But he persisted and eventually it stayed up for more than 24 hours. That was long enough for the all-too-perfect quote to show up in obituaries around the world. He assumed it would spread quickly to blogs and other sites, but was surprised that it also got picked up by mainstream news sources, including the *Guardian* and *Daily Mail*. Weeks went by while he waited in vain for the news sites to discover their error. None did, nor would they have, he believes, if he hadn't contacted them to reveal the ruse (Carbery, 2009).

Readers of the BBC's website questioned the legitimacy of a story the site published in 2011. The BBC, Business Insider, CNN, and Mashable were among dozens of news organizations and tech sites fooled by ApTiquant. The fake research company, whose creation was meant to be a joke, announced findings from its "online IQ tests" (complete with data and charts), concluding that users of Internet Explorer had statistically lower IQs than people who used other browsers (Bott, 2011). Not everyone was fooled, though. GeekWire noticed that the company misused the word "faired" in their write-up and that its online contact form repeatedly returned an error message. "C'mon, we're not that dumb," was how GeekWire titled an article critical of the so-called "psychometric consulting" company's methodology (Bishop, 2011).

Religious Miracles

Miracles are integral to some religious beliefs, so it is not surprising that some hoaxers try to create their own miracles—e.g., a statue that cries real tears or bleeds real blood. Italian chemist Luigi Garlaschelli is one of a group of scientists who has weighed in on the Shroud of Turin, a cloth that purportedly covered Jesus after his crucifixion. Even though scientific tests have shown that the fabric is from the 14th century, some argued that the tests were inaccurate. Since the shroud was purportedly wrapped around the body and face, Garlaschelli reasoned that the facial image on the shroud should be distorted, like a Mercator map projection. It wasn't. To prove his point, Garlaschelli covered one of his students in paint and asked him to lie on a slab. Then he covered him with a shroud. When it was removed, the facial image was distorted, not in perfect proportion like the Shroud of Turin (Williams, 2005). Additional research by Garlaschelli revealed that the bloodstain patterns on various parts of the shroud were not consistent with how an actual corpse would leave them, suggesting they were applied by an artist (Choi, 2018).

Science and Medicine

Scientists are in the business of testing and retesting claims, so one might reasonably assume this would not be fertile ground for hoaxers. *Au contraire*. Park (2000) recounts numerous scientific hoaxes. In 2005, a South Korean scientist claimed to have cloned human cells and gained international celebrity. Subsequently, an investigation found the data for his claim to be fabricated. Four widely publicized scientific hoaxes include Piltdown Man, Bigfoot, the "Sokol hoax," and the MMR vaccine controversy.

Piltdown Man

In 1912, paleontologists in England believed they had found the "missing link" between humans and apes, but it wasn't until about 1950 that the hoax began to unravel (Russell, 2003). The hoaxer, still unknown, assembled an ape jaw and a woman's skull, remodeled the teeth, and stained them to make them look ancient. Even though later discoveries were at odds with the large brain cavity of Piltdown Man, skeptics were often ignored because there was such a strong desire to believe that an important find had been made. Eventually, chemical tests showed the bones weren't as old as originally thought and that the cranium and jaw were not the same age.

© Cactus Studio/Shutterstock.com

Bigfoot

Prankster Rant Mullens had been carving large feet out of wood and leaving tracks in the woods of northern California since 1930. But it wasn't until 1958 that similar oversized footprints made by Ray Wallace, a neighbor of Mullens, gained international notoriety and firmly established the reputation of a creature unknown to science. This large, ape-like primate who walks on two feet is known as Bigfoot. Sasquatch was the name given to a similar animal reportedly seen by Native Americans.

Since the "discovery" of the Wallace footprints, which he admitted he made, Bigfoot sightings continue to be reported and Bigfoot hunters continue their search. In 1967, Roger Patterson reportedly shot blurry footage of Bigfoot that has since been carefully scrutinized by experts (Daegling, 2004). These analyses have neither established the film's authenticity nor have they proven it to be a hoax.

The "Sokal Hoax"

Physicist Alan Sokal was apparently fed up with the articles published in *Social Text* (and other academic journals) that denied the existence of objective realities and supported the idea that reality is socially constructed. Sokal felt that the value, methods, and findings of science were under fire. He believed this kind of theorizing wasn't going to help people develop an anti-AIDS treatment or a solution to global warming. He believed it is important to be able to distinguish true and false ideas in both the sciences and humanities.

Instead of writing an article that directly stated his misgivings with these ideas, he undertook a hoax that he hoped would expose the lack of critical standards for judging the ideas he opposed. He wanted to find out how much scientific rigor was associated with the process of publishing in *Social Text*. He believed that an article that favored the views of the social constructionists could be published even though it was full of bogus claims—claims that Sokal said any math or physics student would immediately realize were bogus. The article was accepted by the editors of *Social Text* without being examined by knowledgeable experts who would have readily identified the invalid claims made by Sokal. After the editors of *Social Text* published his article, Sokal published an article in *Lingua Franca* that exposed his hoax (Editors of *Lingua Franca*, 2000).

The MMR Vaccine Controversy

In 1998, a team of British medical researchers led by physician Andrew Wakefield published an article in the respected medical journal *The Lancet*. The researchers described a set of endoscopy and biopsy findings they characterized as evidence for a novel syndrome linking children's development of autism with receiving the MMR (measles,

© BestStockFoto/Shutterstock.com

mumps, and rubella) vaccine. At a pre-publication press conference, Wakefield recommended parents forego the combined MMR in favor of single-disease vaccines in light of the findings. His recommendation was widely reported, causing vaccination rates in the United Kingdom and Ireland to drop sharply. Not surprisingly, what followed was an increase in measles and mumps cases in these countries, several of which resulted in deaths and permanent injury.

Investigative journalists later discovered that Wakefield and colleagues had published the article without declaring multiple conflicts of interests, including their financial stake in a pharmaceutical company developing new single-disease vaccines to compete with the MMR. An independent scientific panel reviewed the research reported in the article and concluded Wakefield and his team had fabricated evidence supporting the MMR/autism link while discarding other evidence showing no link.

The Lancet eventually retracted the article, and Wakefield was found guilty by the British General Medical Council of professional misconduct serious enough to strip him of his license to practice medicine. The scientific consensus continues to be that no evidence links MMR to the development of autism in children and the vaccine's benefits greatly outweigh its risks. In a review of the controversy and disease epidemic caused by Wakefield's actions, Flaherty (2011) described the episode as "the most damaging medical hoax of the last 100 years" (p. 1303).

That damage continues to resonate. Despite the absence of evidence and the formal re-traction, a significant portion of the public persists in holding to this false belief. In fact, its influence appears to be *growing* rather than subsiding. Consider the case of Travis County, Texas. Home to the state capital, a large research university, and a booming tech industry, Travis County is one of the most well-educated, politically progressive regions in the country. Given that profile, one would think that the MMR vaccine hoax would have little traction but, in fact, the opposite is true. Since 2008, the number of "conscientious exemptions" (i.e., parents refusing to vaccinate their children) has *quadrupled*. Officials place the blame for this increase squarely on the hoax and the anti-government sentiment it helped stoke. Meanwhile, infectious diseases are on the rise, with cases of mumps in Texas increasing tenfold from 2015 to 2016 (Chang, 2018).

Hoax Detection

Just as with scams, we are all subject to believing in hoaxes. But there are some things we can do to minimize the risk of being duped:

1. Pay attention to your beliefs.
2. Check the reliability of sources and veracity of the information.

3. Know the difference between science and pseudoscience.
4. Resist the temptation to explain everything.

Pay Attention to Your Beliefs

MacDougall (1958) observed that people often have incentives to believe certain things. Objectivity, therefore, requires that we test our beliefs by asking (and answering) some probing questions:

- On any particular issue, why do you believe the way you do?
- Can you admit your biases?
- What are those things you want desperately to be true?

Many people go through life without a lot of thought about questions like this. Instead, they focus on the weird, irrational, and biased beliefs *of others*. Once a belief is established, people commonly read and listen to information and people who support that belief and ignore the substance of the opposition. This is particularly true when the belief is strongly endorsed and the pressure of peers to hold the belief is high (Knowles & Linn, 2004).

Contrary to expectations, exposure to contrary beliefs does not necessarily weaken one's belief; it can strengthen it. If you do not examine the nature of your beliefs, much less question them, you are especially vulnerable to hoaxes that seem to support your beliefs and more likely to falsely label a counter-belief phenomena as a hoax.

Check the Reliability of Sources and Veracity of the Information

Make verification a habit. Valid information can be difficult to find. Sometimes we depend on sources like the press, the Internet, or our friends to validate information for us, and they report unverified claims and superstitions (MacDougall, 1983).

Despite these problems, an *investigative mindset* is a barrier to imposters, hoaxers, and cons who depend on your belief that they do not need to be checked out. When it comes to online sources, in particular, *Wired* recommends watching out for the following "red flags" as an indication that something might be amiss (Carmody, 2011):

- No footprint or history
- Lack of sound methodology; data and charts must be scrutinized
- No verifiable or mappable address
- Laughable or absurd claims
- Astonishing implications

If reliable checking can't be accomplished right away, it's always prudent to withhold judgment (and, of course, avoid monetary participation) until you've had a chance to do your homework.

Know the Difference between Science and Pseudoscience

Science is dedicated to confirming or not confirming hypotheses about phenomena that can be tested. These tests are conducted under conditions that are as objective as possible. Subsequent testing by others is expected. Scientists make mistakes, biases sometimes affect their results, and their conclusions may be limited by current knowledge and methods of measurement. The nature of science, however, is to admit these problems, try to correct them, and continue testing in the pursuit of valid findings.

THEORY OF FLAT EARTH

© Oleksandr Dulyakov/Shutterstock.com

On the other hand, hoaxes often rely on pseudoscience for their claims. People who make a claim based on pseudoscience are not likely to seek systematic, unbiased, and independent testing of their claim.

Some of the more common characteristics of pseudoscientific claims include (Kida, 2006; Sagan, 1995; Shermer, 2001; Shermer, 1997/2002):

- the use of scientific-sounding terms like "resonant vibrations" without any indication of what they mean and how they can be measured

- the exclusive use of anecdotal observations that cannot be verified in other ways to prove the validity of a claim

- the use of "mysterious forces" or "special powers" to explain the unlikely co-occurrence of two events (or, for that matter, any phenomenon)

- rationalizing or not reporting negative findings and/or failures

Resist the Temptation to Explain Everything

Embrace living in a world where there is much to learn and much we don't know about both natural phenomena and magic tricks. There is nothing wrong with suspending judgment

> ... instead of remaining in a state of uncertainty relative to some phenomenon, many people feel the need to immediately settle on an explanation.

until further data is available, but instead of remaining in a state of uncertainty relative to some phenomenon, many people feel the need to immediately settle on an explanation.

This may be a productive strategy on some occasions, but it also sets up the *confirmation bias* and makes it harder to objectively weigh new information that does not agree with the initial explanation (Nickerson, 1998). For example, when people experience a phenomenon that seems inexplicable based on what they know, they may immediately choose to understand it as something spiritual, demonic, or the result of alien beings.

Later, when the phenomenon is explained in terms of science, nature, or human nature, it can be very difficult to change the more mystical initial belief. It may be especially difficult if Shermer (2000) is correct in suggesting that human beings are inclined toward "magical thinking."

SUMMARY

Lying specialists are generally quite skilled at deception. They can be identified by examining various manifestations of their behavior. For example, there are five personality disorders associated with pathological liars:

- Antisocial
- Borderline
- Narcissistic
- Histrionic
- Obsessive-compulsive

Most of these personality disorders are associated with people who are very self-oriented, come from dysfunctional families, and didn't get needed love and attention as children. As adults, they use lies to exploit others to get what they want, including a boost in self-esteem.

Imposeurs are people who enhance certain aspects of their personal identity but usually do not try to change their entire identity. They may claim jobs, military experiences, awards, sports experiences, wealth, and relationships they never had. People with **factitious disorder imposed on self** simulate a disease they don't have in order to garner attention. When parents do the same thing with their children or to other adults it is known as **factitious disorder imposed on another**. When people fake an illness to get a tangible reward, it is known as *malingering*. Some people seek attention by claiming to be a victim of a crime when they aren't or pretending to be a victim of a crime in order to make a point.

When people have **imposter syndrome**, they feel like their success is ill-gained and that they don't have the talent others think they have. This is very different than an actual **imposter** who assumes a false persona or identity. Famous imposters reviewed in this chapter include Ferdinand Demara Jr., David Pecard, Frank Abagnale, Gerald Barnes, Frederic Bourdin, and spies who infiltrated an enemy organization. Most of the notorious imposters have been men, but there are some well-known examples of women spies. In the age of the Internet, imposters are proliferating through the practice of stealing people's personally identifiable information such as Social Security numbers and bank account passwords. **Identity thieves** use this information to impersonate the people they rob from in order to make purchases, take out loans, receive medical care, and apply for passports.

Con artists or **scammers** are also specialists in lying. They try to take a mark's money with nothing more than their communicative skills. Familiar cons occur on the Internet and the street; by faith-healers and psychics; and often involve buying or investing in something. The *"big con"* is a more elaborate scam involving several people, places, and props. Anyone can be conned, but the socially isolated and gullible are especially at risk. People who feel that the promised payoff of the con will satisfy strongly felt needs are also people who are easily conned. Trusting people do not seem to be more gullible than mistrustful people and they are likely to have a more satisfying life.

Cons are often directed at a single mark (or at least one at a time), but **hoaxes** tend to fool large numbers of people. The payoff for a con is monetary but that is not usually the case with hoaxes. Well-known hoaxes have involved aliens, the media, religious icons, and science. As with cons, anyone can be the victim of a hoax, but this risk can be lessened by analyzing one's own beliefs, learning to check the veracity of information, knowing the difference between science and pseudoscience, and learning to be comfortable without knowing why some phenomena occur.

EXERCISES

1. What kind of scam would you be most vulnerable to because of your expectations, needs, and beliefs? Indicate who would perpetrate the scam and how it would develop.

2. Indicate whether you do or do not believe alien spaceships have visited our planet. Then develop a persuasive speech, based on research, supporting the opposite view of the one you currently hold.

3. Design what you believe would be a successful hoax. Indicate how it would occur and what you expect to happen.

OF INTEREST

This episode of the popular YouTube series "Good Mythical Morning with Rhett and Link" spotlights some of the most interesting imposters (QR) in recent years. As good as Frank Abagnale was, suggest the hosts, these lesser-known perpetrators may have been even better.

In 2005, ABC News ran a *PrimeTime* segment exploring the Pope Joan (QR) legend. It should be noted that the piece was widely criticized as "tabloid-style" journalism. Timed with the publication of the Donna Cross novel, *Pope Joan*, it features an interview with the author.

The Internet of Things has the potential to provide technological solutions to almost every aspect of modern life, but it also represents a dangerous new world of opportunities for hackers (QR) and scammers. Warning: You might feel more than a little paranoid after watching this documentary.

lying and deception in HUMAN INTERACTION

REFERENCES

Abagnale, F. (1980). *Catch me if you can*. New York, NY: Grosset & Dunlap.

American Psychiatric Association (2013). *Diagnostic and statistical manual of mental disorders* (5th ed.). Washington, DC: Author.

Bankoff, C. (2015). Brian Williams might have also lied about Navy SEALs, the Pope, and the Berlin Wall. *New York Magazine*. Retrieved from http://nymag.com/daily/intelligencer

Berman, M. (2012, June 20). Jerry Sandusky and histrionic personality disorder. *MedPage Today*. Retrieved from http://www.medpagetoday.com

Bishop, T. (2011, July 31). The Internet Explorer IQ test: Come on, we're not that dumb. *GeekWire*. Retrieved from http://www.geekwire.com

Boreau, A. (2001). *The myth of Pope Joan* (L. G. Cochrane, Trans.). Chicago, IL: University of Chicago Press.

Bott, E. (2011). That Internet Explorer "IQ test" was a hoax [updated]. *ZDNet*. Retrieved from http://www.zdnet.com

Boyd, A. S. (2014). Cutaneous Munchausen syndrome: Clinical and histopathologic features. *Journal of Cutaneous Pathology*, *41*(4), 333–336. https://dx.doi.org/10.1111/cup.12320

Bressert, S. (2017). Obsessive compulsive personality disorder. *Psych Central*. Retrieved from https://psychcentral.com

Brown, K., Fenge, L., & Lee, S. (2018, July 18). Recognising the link between loneliness, social isolation and susceptibility to scam involvement. *HM Government*. Retrieved from https://industrialstrategy.dialogue-app.com/ageing-society/recognising-the-link-between-loneliness-social-isolation-and-susceptibility-to-scam-involvement

Campbell, S. (2000). *Romantic deception: The six signs he's lying*. Holbrook, MA: Adams Media Corp.

Carbery, G. (2009, May 6). Student's Wikipedia hoax quote used worldwide in newspaper obituaries. *The Irish Times*. Retrieved from http://www.irishtimes.com

Carmichael, E. (2011, November 14). "I enjoy young people": Sandusky thinks it over, tells Bob Costas he's not sexually attracted to young boys. *Deadspin*. Retrieved from http://www.deadspin.com

Carmody, T. (2011, August 3). "Internet Explorer users have lower IQs" study is a hoax: Here are some of the red flags. *Wired*. Retrieved from http://www.wired.com

Chang, J. (2018, September 1). Since 2008, rate of unvaccinated kids quadruples. *Austin American Statesman* (pp. A1, A14).

Chariton, J. (2015). Bill O'Reilly vs. Brian Williams: Why the media is treating them differently. *The Wrap*. Retrieved from http://www.thewrap.com

Choi, C. Q. (2018, July 18). Shroud of Turin is a fake, bloodstains suggest. *Live Science*. Retrieved from http://www.livescience.com

Cleckley, H. (1982). *The mask of sanity* (5th ed.). St. Louis, MO: Mosby.

Cohen, G. (2005, November 27). For you, half price. *The New York Times*. Retrieved from http://www.nytimes.com

Cohn, S. (2015, November 6). The greed report: American ego—the common thread in the biggest scams. *CNBC*. Retrieved from http://www.cnbc.com

Conkey, C. (2007). The borrower who never was: Synthetic identity fraud hits credit bureaus, Banks. *The Wall Street Journal*. Retrieved from http://www.wsj.com

Corn, D., & Schulman, D. (2015, February 15). Bill O'Reilly has his own Brian Williams problem. *Mother Jones*. http://www.motherjones.com

Coronel, S., Coll, S., & Kravitz, D. (2015, April 5). Rolling Stone and UVA: The Columbia University Graduate School of Journalism Report: An anatomy of a journalistic failure. Rolling Stone. Retrieved from http://www.rollingstone.com

Cosentino, D. (2012, June 22). "I have many Forrest Gump qualities": Read the 'creepy love letters' Jerry Sandusky wrote to one of his victims. *Deadspin*. Retrieved from http://www.deadspin.com

Craig, K. D., & Hill, M. L. (2003). Misrepresentation of pain and facial expression. In P. W. Halligan, C. Bass, & D. A. Oakley (Eds.), *Malingering and illness deception* (pp. 326–347). New York, NY: Oxford University Press.

Crichton, R. (1959). *The great impostor*. New York, NY: Random House.

Criddle, L. (2010). Monsters in the closet: Munchausen syndrome by proxy. *Critical Care Nurse*, *30(6)*, 46–55. https://dx.doi.org/10.4037/ccn2010737

Daegling, D. J. (2004). *Bigfoot exposed: An anthropologist examines America's enduring legend*. New York, NY: AltaMira Press.

Davis, W. C. (2016). *Inventing Loreta Velasquez: Confederate soldier impersonator, media celebrity, and con artist*. Carbondale, IL: SIU Press.

Day, E. (2009, February 14). When one extraordinary life story is not enough. *The Guardian*. Retrieved from http://www.theguardian.com

DeGrave, K. (1995). *Swindler, spy, rebel: The confidence woman in nineteenth-century America*. Columbia, MO: University of Missouri Press.

Delbruck, A. (1891). *Die pathologische lüge und die psychisch abnormen schwinder: Eine untersuchung uber den allmahlichen uebergang eines normalen psychologischen vorgangs in ein pathologisches symptom, fur aerzte und juristen.* Stuttgart, Germany: Enke.

Deppen, C. (2016, August 12). On stand for first time, Sandusky maintains innocence, blames lawyer for questionable TV spot. *Penn Live.* Retrieved from http://www.pennlive.com

DeWitt, P. E. (2015, November 10). How *Time* magazine made the real Steve Jobs cry. *Fortune.* Retrieved from http://www.fortune.com

Dieguez, S. (2018). Ganser syndrome. In J. Bogousslavsky (Ed.), *Frontiers of Neurology and Neuroscience, 42 [Neurologic-Psychiatric Syndromes in Focus, Part II: From Psychiatry to Neurology],* 1-22. Basel, Switzerland: Karger. https://dx.doi.org/10.1159/000475676

Dike, C. C., Baranoski, M., & Griffith, E. E. H. (2005). Pathological lying revisited. *The Journal of the American Academy of Psychiatry and the Law, 33*(3), 342–349. https://www.ncbi.nlm.nih.gov/pubmed/16186198

Dunn, D. H. (1975). *Ponzi: Boston swindler.* New York, NY: McGraw-Hill.

Ellison, M. (2000, May 31). Korean veteran's massacre claim proves false. *The Guardian.* Retrieved from http://www.theguardian.com

Farhi, P. (2015, February 4). Brian Williams admits that his story of coming under fire while in Iraq was false. *The Washington Post.* Retrieved from http://www.washingtonpost.com

Faron, F. (1998). *Rip-off: A writer's guide to crimes of deception.* Cincinnati, OH: Writer's Digest Books.

Federal Bureau of Investigation. (2014). *Internet Crime Complaint Center Annual Report.* Retrieved from https://www.fbi.gov/news

Federal Trade Commission. (2013). *Guide for assisting identity theft victims.* Retrieved from http://ftc.gov/idtheftresources

Fernandez, E. (February 18, 2001). Bizarre medical masquerade: Determined con man steals Stockton doctor's identity for 20 years. *San Francisco Chronicle,* A1.

Finklea, K. (2014). *Identity theft: Trends and issues.* Washington, DC: Congressional Research Service.

Flaherty, D. K. (2011). The vaccine-autism connection: A public health crisis caused by unethical medical practices and fraudulent science. *Annals of Pharmacotherapy, 45,* 1302–1304. https://dx.doi.org/10.1345/aph.1q318

Ford, C. V. (1996). *Lies! Lies!! Lies!!! The psychology of deceit.* Washington, DC: American Psychiatric Press.

Forward, S. (1999). *When your lover is a liar.* New York, NY: HarperCollins.

Francavilla, W. M. (2018, April 30). Of course you are way too 'smart' to be scammed. Think again. *CNBC*. Retrieved from http://www.cnbc.com

Gansler, L. L. (2005). *The mysterious private Thompson: The double life of Sarah Emma Edmonds, Civil War soldier*. New York, NY: Free Press.

Gonzales, E. (2018, September 10). Is Kim Kardashian actually studying at law school? *Harper's Bazaar*. Retrieved from http://www.harpersbazaar.com

Grann, D. (2008, August 11). The chameleon: The many lives of Frederic Bourdin. *The New Yorker*. Retrieved from http://www.newyorker.com

Greene, L. (2011, November 15). Penn State coach says "I shouldn't have showered with kids." *New York Post*. Retrieved from http://www.nypost.com

Griffiths, M. D. (2013, October 11). Fiddler of the truth: A brief look at pathological lying. Psychology Today. Retrieved from http://www.psychologytoday.com

Hall, R. (1993). *Patriots in disguise: Women warriors of the Civil War*. New York, NY: Paragon House.

Hall, H. V., & Poirier, J. G. (2001). *Detecting malingering and deception: Forensic distortion analysis* (2nd ed.). Boca Raton, FL: CRC Press.

Halligan, P. W., Bass, C., & Oakley, D. A. (Eds.) (2003). *Malingering and illness deception*. New York, NY: Oxford University Press.

Hammond, C. (2017). How OCPDs escape responsibility. *Psych Central*. Retrieved from https://pro.psychcentral.com

Hankiss, A. (1980). Games con men play: The semiosis of deceptive interaction. *Journal of Communication, 30*(2), 104–112. https://dx.doi.org/10.1111/j.1460-2466.1980.tb01972.x

Haselhoff, E. H. (2001). *The deepening complexity of crop circles: Scientific research and urban legends*. Berkeley, CA: Frog, Ltd.

Hausman, K. (January 3, 2003). Does pathological lying warrant inclusion in DSM? *Psychiatric News, 38*(1), 24. https://dx.doi.org/10.1176/pn.38.1.0024

Hines, T. (2003). *Pseudoscience and the paranormal* (2nd ed.). Amherst, NY: Prometheus Books.

Horne, M. (April 16, 2006). Max Headroom creator made Roswell alien. *The Sunday Times*. Retrieved from http://www.timesonline.co.uk/

Hutson, M. (2016, January 12). Why we all fall for con artists. *The Cut*. Retrieved from http://www.thecut.com

IBM Analytics (2015). *Synthetic identity fraud: Can I borrow your SSN?* Armonk, NY: IBM Corporation.

International Business Times (2011, February 4). Psychiatrist reveals how to spot another Bernie Madoff. http://www.ibtimes.com/

Johnson, S. (2018, September 10). No plans to have Kanye West teach, says School of the Art Institute of Chicago. *Chicago Tribune*. Retrieved from http://www.chicagotribune.com

Jones, J. B. (2016, May 25). Trump may be a grandiose narcissist, but he's no match for the Lyndon Johnson of All the Way. *Chicago Reader*. Retrieved from http://www.chicagoreader.com

Kanye West on Kim Kardashian's Legal Activism: "I Love It." (2018, September 9). *Extra*. Retrieved from http://www.extra.com

Katherine, A. (2016, October 21). 36 Kardashian lies For Kim Kardashian's 36th birthday. *Inquisitr*. Retrieved from http://www.inquisitr.com

Keyes, R. (2004). *The post-truth era: Dishonesty and deception in contemporary life*. New York, NY: St. Martin's Press.

Kida, T. (2006). *Don't believe everything you think: The 6 basic mistakes we make in thinking*. Amherst, NY: Prometheus Books.

Kirkpatrick, E. (2016, September 14). Kim Kardashian took 6,000 selfies on her 4 day trip to Mexico. *People*. Retrieved from http://www.people.com

Knight, S. (2013, October 5). Former Apple engineer reveals secrets behind Jobs' first iPhone presentation. *TechSpot*. Retrieved from http://www.techspot.com

Kohn, D. (Correspondent). (2001, October 26). Double life: The imposter [Television broadcast]. *48 Hours*. New York, NY: CBS. Retrieved from http://www.cbsnews.com

Kominsky, M. (1970). *The hoaxers: Plain liars, fancy liars, and damned liars*. Boston, MA: Branden Press.

Konnikova, M. (2016). *The confidence game: Why we fall for it … every time*. New York, NY: Penguin Books.

Knowles, E.S., & Linn, J.A. (Eds.) (2004). *Resistance and persuasion*. Mahwah, NJ: Lawrence Erlbaum Associates.

Kropp, P. R., & Rogers, R. (1993). Understanding malingering: Motivation, method, and detection. In M. Lewis & C. Saarni, *Lying and deception in everyday life* (pp. 201–216). New York, NY: Guilford.

Langenderfer, J., & Shimp, T. A. (2001). Consumer vulnerability to scams, swindles, and fraud: A new theory of visceral influences on persuasion. *Psychology & Marketing, 18*, 763–783. https://dx,doi.org/10.1002/mar.1029

Langer, E. (2015, February 25). Herman Rosenblat, whose Holocaust love story was beautiful but false, dies. *The Washington Post*. Retrieved from http://www.washingtonpost.com

Larsen, E. (1966). *The deceivers: Lives of great imposters*. New York, NY: Roy Publishers.

Lazarus, O. (2017, January 9). 50 years ago, Americans finally got a look across the line of the Vietnam War. *PRI*. Retrieved from http://www.pri.org

Lenzenweger, M. F., Lane, M. C., Loranger, A. W., & Kessler, R. C. (2007). DSM-IV personality disorders in the National Comorbidity Survey Replication. *Biological Psychiatry*, *62*, 553–564. https://dx.doi.org/10.1016/j.biopsych.2006.09.019

Lee, R. A. (2002). *The careers of John R. Brinkley*. Lexington, KY: University of Kentucky Press.

Leon, S. (2015, July 10). Take a selfie with Kim Kardashian. *W*. Retrieved from http://www.wmagazine.com

Lingua Franca (Eds.). (2000). *The Sokal hoax: The sham that shook the academy*. Lincoln, NE: University of Nebraska Press.

MacDougall, C. D. (1958). *Hoaxes*. New York, NY: Dover.

MacDougall, C. D. (1983). *Superstition and the press*. Buffalo, NY: Prometheus Books.

Marks, G. (2017, July 14). How Steve Jobs misled a room full of tech media and changed the world. *Entrepreneur*. Retrieved from http://www.entrepreneur.com

Markson, R. (2017, August 27). A little bit of narcissim can take you a long way. *The Daily Telegraph*. Retrieved from http://www.dailytelegraph.com

Marquis, C. (2002, February 9). Korea veteran is charged with fraud. *The New York Times*. Retrieved from http://www.nytimes.com

Martens, W. H. J. (2014). The hidden suffering of the psychopath. *Psychiatric Times*. http://www.psychiatrictimes.com/psychotic-affective-disorders/hidden-suffering-psychopath/

Mathur, A. (Correspondent). (1999, November 10). The impostor's early years [Television broadcast]. In D. Kohn (Producer), *48 Hours*. New York, NY: CBS. Retrieved from http://www.cbsnews.com

Maurer, D. W. (1999). *The big con: The story of the confidence man*. New York, NY: Anchor Books. (Original work published 1940).

Mayo Clinic. (2018, February 6). Factitious disorder. Retrieved from http://www.mayoclinic.org

McAdams, D. P. (2016, June). The mind of Donald Trump. *The Altantic*. Retrieved from http://www.theatlantic.com

McCann, J. T. (1998). *Malingering and deception in adolescents: Assessing credibility in clinical and forensic settings*. Washington, DC: American Psychological Association.

McHoskey, J. W., Worzel, W., & Szyarto, C. (1998). Machiavellianism and psychopathy. *Journal of Personality and Social Psychology*, *74*, 192–210. https://dx.doi.org/10.1037/0022-3514.74.1.192

Meadow, R. (1977). Munchausen syndrome by proxy: The hinterland of child abuse. *The Lancet*, *310*, 343–345. https://dx.doi.org/10.1016/s0140-6736(77)91497-0

Mendis, S., & Hodgson, R. E. (2012). Ganser syndrome: Examining the aetiological debate through a systematic case report review. *The European Journal of Psychiatry*, *26*, 96–106. https://dx.doi.org/10.4321/s0213-61632012000200003

Morabito, A. (2017, May 9). Mom pretended her kid was disabled—until the girl rebelled with murder. *New York Post*. Retrieved from http://www.nypost.com

Morin, R. (2013, November 14). The most narcissistic U.S. presidents. *Pew Research Center*. Retrieved from http://www.pewresearch.org

Moss, M. (June 1, 2000). A soldier's lie. *Austin American Statesman*, A2.

Moya, A. (Correspondent). (1999, November 10). The impostor: A master of disguise [Television broadcast]. In D. Kohn (Producer), *48 Hours*. New York, NY: CBS. Retrieved from http://www.cbsnews.com

Munoz, L. (1996, April 18). Man accused of posing as a physician. *Los Angeles Times*. Retrieved from http://www.latimes.com

Musella, D. P. (2005, September/October). Gallup poll shows that Americans' belief in the paranormal persists. *Skeptical Inquirer*, *29.5*. Retrieved from https://www.csicop.org/si/archive/category/volume_29.5

Nash, J. R. (1976). *Hustlers and con men: An anecdotal history of the confidence man and his games*. New York, NY: Evans.

Newman, A. (2003, April 13). Analyze this: Vincent Gigante, not crazy after all these years. *The New York Times*. Retrieved from http://www.nytimes.com

Newman, G. R., & McNally, M. M. (2005). *Identity theft literature review: Report for the National Institute of Justice Focus Group*. Washington, DC: U.S. Department of Justice.

Nickerson, R. S. (1998). Confirmation bias: A ubiquitous phenomenon in many guises. *Review of General Psychology*, *2*, 175–220. https://dx.doi.org/10.1037//1089-2680.2.2.175

Noble, K. B. (1996, April 17). Doctor's specialty turns out to be a masquerade. *The New York Times*. Retrieved from http://www.nytimes.come

O'Sullivan, M. (2003). The fundamental attribution error in detecting deception: The boy-who-cried-wolf effect. *Personality and Social Psychology Bulletin*, *29*, 1316–1327. https://dx.doi.org/10.1177/0146167203254610

Paulhus, D. L. (2014). Toward a taxonomy of dark personalities. *Current Directions in Psychological Science*, *23*, 421–426. https://dx.doi.org/10.1177/0963721414547737

Park, R. (2000). *Voodoo science: The road from foolishness to fraud*. New York, NY: Oxford University Press.

Parmar, N. (August, 2004). Crying wolf: Fabricated crimes. *Psychology Today*. Retrieved from https://www.psychologytoday.com

Pemment, J. (2013). Psychopathy versus sociopathy: Why the distinction has become crucial. *Aggression and Violent Behavior*, *18*, 458–461. https://dx.doi.org/10.1016/j.avb.2013.07.001

Pistone, J. D. (1987). *Donnie Brasco: My undercover life in the Mafia*. New York, NY: Penguin.

Power, R. (2011, April). "Child identity theft: A lot of questions need to be answered, but the most important one is 'Has it happened to your child?'" *CyBlog*. Carnegie Mellon University. Retrieved from http://www.cyblog.cylab.cmu.edu

Psychology of scams: The emotional traps to watch out for. (2017, February 27). *ABC*. Retrieved from https://search-beta.abc.net.au

Randi, J. (1989). *The faith healers*. Amherst, NY: Prometheus Books.

Randi, J. (1982). *Flim-flam!: Psychics, ESP, unicorns, and other delusions*. Amherst, NY: Prometheus Books.

Rayner, R. (2002). *Drake's fortune: The fabulous true story of the world's greatest confidence artist*. New York, NY: Doubleday.

Redlitz, H. (2014, July 15). 8 cons that seem too ridiculous to be true. *Mental Floss*. Retrieved from http://www.mentalfloss.com

Resnick, P. J., & Knoll, J. K. (2005). Faking it: How to detect malingered psychosis. *Current Psychiatry*, *4*(11), 12–25. Retrieved from https://www.mdedge.com

Rijsenbilt, A., & Commandeur, H. (2013). Narcissus enters the courtroom: CEO narcissism and fraud. *Journal of Business Ethics*, *117*, 413–429. https://dx.doi.org/10.1007/s10551-012-1528-7

Roberts, S. (2015, February 21). Herman Rosenblat, 85, dies; made up Holocaust love story. *The New York Times*. Retrieved from http://www.nytimes.com

Robinson, O., & Stolberg, S. (2015, March 23). Police find no evidence of rape at UVA fraternity. *The New York Times*. Retrieved from http://www.nytimes.com

Rogers, R. (Ed.) (1988). *Clinical assessment of malingering and deception*. New York, NY: Guilford.

Russell, M. (2003). *Piltdown man: The secret life of Charles Dawson & the world's greatest archaeological hoax*. Gloucestershire, England: Tempus.

Sagan, C. (1995). *The demon-haunted world*. New York, NY: Random House.

Sansone, R. A., & Sansone, L. A. (2011). Gender patterns in borderline personality disorder. Innovations in Clinical Neuroscience, 8, 16–20.

Savino, A. C., & Fordtran, J. S. (2006). Factitious disease: clinical lessons from case studies at Baylor University Medical Center. *Baylor University Medical Center Proceedings*, *19*(3), 195–208. https://dx.doi.org/10.1080/08998280.2006.11928162

Serota, K. B., Levine, T. R., & Boster, F. J. (2010). The prevalence of lying in America: Three studies of self-reported lies. *Human Communication Research*, *36*(1), 2–25. https://dx.doi.org/10.1111/j.1468-2958.2009.01366.x

Serota, K. B., & Levine, T. R. (2015). A few prolific liars: Variation in the prevalence of lying. *Journal of Language and Social Psychology*, *34*, 138–157. https://dx.doi.org/10.1177/0261927x14528804

Sherman, G. (2008, December 24). The greatest love story ever sold. *The New Republic*. Retrieved from http://www.newrepublic.com

Shermer, M. (2001). Baloney detection. *Scientific American*, *285*(5), 36. https://dx.doi.org/10.1038/scientificamerican1101-36

Shermer, M. (2000). *How we believe: Science, skepticism, and the search for god* (2nd ed). New York, NY: Henry Holt.

Shermer, M. (2002). *Why people believe weird things: Pseudoscience, superstition, and other confusions of our time* (Rev. ed.). New York, NY: Henry Holt.

Siemeszko, C. (2009, February 18). Herman Rosenblat, author of *Angel at the Fence*, defends faked Holocaust memoir. *Daily News*. Retrieved from http://www.nydailynews.com

Simon, S. (2017, December 8). 25 stars who suffer from imposter syndrome. *InStyle*. Retrieved from http://www.instyle.com

Somaiya, R. (2015, April 2015). Rolling Stone article on rape at University of Virginia failed all basics, report says. *The New York Times*. Retrieved from http://www.nytimes.com

Stajano, F., & Wilson, P. (2011). Understanding scam victims: Seven principles for systems security. *Communications of the ACM*, *54*(3), 70–75. https://dx.doi.org/10.1145/1897852.1897872

Stanford, P. (1999). *The legend of Pope Joan: In search of the truth*. New York, NY: Henry Holt & Co.

Sullivan, E. (2001). *The concise book of lying*. New York, NY: Farrar, Straus and Giroux.

Talbot, M. (2004, August 9). The bad mother. *The New Yorker*. Retrieved from http://www.newyorker.com

These are the 4 emotions scammers often prey on to trick us. (2018, March 9). *Irish Examiner*. Retrieved from http://www.irishexaminer.com

Tkacik, M. (2002, March 27). EarthLink co-founder Slatkin admits to fraud in Ponzi scheme. *The Wall Street Journal*. Retrieved from http://www.wsj.com

Twerski, A. J. (1997). *Addictive thinking* (2nd ed.). Center City, MN: Hazelden.

U. S. News & World Report. (2002, August 26). The art of the hoax, pp. 30–79.

Velazquez, L. J. (2003). *The woman in battle: A narrative of exploits, adventures, and travels of Madame Loreta Janeta Velazquez*. New York, NY: Arno Press. (Original work published 1876).

Vincent, N. (2006). *Self-made man: One woman's journey into manhood and back again*. New York, NY: Viking.

Vogelstein, F. (2013, October 4). And then Steve said, "Let there be an iPhone." *The New York Times*. Retrieved from http://wwwnytimes.com

Weil, J. R., & Brannon, W. T. (2004). *Con man: A master swindler's own story*. New York, NY: Broadway Books. (Original work published 1948)

Whitbourne, S. K. (2015, March 7). Which is the more narcissistic sex? Psychology Today. Retrieved from http://www.psychologytoday.com

Williams, D. (November 13, 2005). In Italy, chemist scrutinizes science of religious miracles. *Austin American Statesman*, A16.

Winton, R. (2001, August 16). Panel ousts judge for lying. Los Angeles Times. Retrieved from http://articles.latimes.com

Wiseman, R. (1997). *Deception and self-deception: Investigating psychics*. Amherst, NY: Prometheus Books.

Yarnell, E. C. (2013). Medals of dishonor? Military, free speech, and the Stolen Valor Act. *Veterans Law Review*, *5*, 56–135.

Yen, H., & Woodward, C. (2018, July 7). AP Fact Check: Trump's half-truths on court case, economy. *Boston Globe*. Retrieved from http://www.boston.com

Young, G. (2014). *Malingering, feigning, and response bias in psychiatric/psychological injury: Implications for practice and court*. Dordrecht, Netherlands: Springer-Verlag.

Zarrella, J., & Kaye, R. (2008, December 30). Holocaust "greatest" love story a hoax. *CNN*. Retrieved from http://www.cnn.com

Zuckoff, M. (2006, May 15). The perfect mark: How a Massachusetts psychotherapist fell for a Nigerian e-mail scam. *The New Yorker*. Retrieved from http://www.newyorker.com

PART III

lie detection

Is it possible to determine whether a person is lying? How accurate are methods for identifying when lies are being told? Is there any benefit to using equipment or other assistance to identify when people are lying? The next two chapters focus on questions such as these. Chapter 9 deals with lie detection during everyday encounters as well as the special context of law enforcement and military interrogations. Chapter 10 assesses the ability of various devices (including machines and drugs) to assist in the process of lie detection.

Chapter 9: Unassisted Lie Detection

Chapter 10: Assisted Lie Detection

"If you can't lie no better than that, you might as well tell the truth."
— *Delbert McClinton & Gary Nicholson*

"Why I should fear I know not, since guiltiness I know not; but yet, I feel, I fear."
— *Desdemona (Othello, Act V, Scene 2)*

As long as there have been liars, there have been people who wanted to catch them. Throughout most of history, these human detectors had to rely on strategies that did not involve machines. Such *unassisted* lie detection (i.e., strictly human, without the benefit of any tools) is still the only option available to most people, and its success or failure hinges upon:

- a person's skill in questioning a suspected liar
- observing the suspect's behavior
- gathering lie-relevant information
- making a decision about the suspect's truthfulness

Even though efforts to build an infallible lie detection machine are as popular as ever (see Chapter 10), unassisted lie detection is likely to continue for a long time to come. In this chapter, we will consider what techniques are available to the would-be human lie detector. Along the way, we'll bust a few myths and stereotypes.

WAYS PEOPLE DETECT LIES

In everyday life, people don't usually rely on a single approach when trying to determine whether another person is lying to or has otherwise deceived them. Instead, they likely use two or more of the following four methods identified by Park, Levine, McCornack, Morrison, and Ferrara (2002):

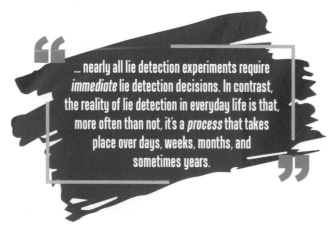

... nearly all lie detection experiments require *immediate* lie detection decisions. In contrast, the reality of lie detection in everyday life is that, more often than not, it's a *process* that takes place over days, weeks, months, and sometimes years.

1. Obtaining information from others
2. Finding physical evidence
3. Receiving a confession
4. Observing behavior and listening

It's important to note that nearly all lie detection experiments require *immediate* lie detection decisions. In contrast, the reality of lie detection in everyday life is that, more often than not, it's a *process* that takes place over days, weeks, months, and sometimes years.

Obtaining Information From Others

Consider this not-so-hypothetical example:

> *Katia and Rachel are classmates and live in the same residence hall. Katia missed the most recent exam, then lied to her professor about being ill. The professor allows*

her to make up the exam and she gets a perfect score. Rachel actually was sick but took the exam anyway and got a C. Seeing the whole situation as very unfair, she lets the professor know about Katia's lie.

In this scenario, Rachel could be considered a "whistleblower" because she reported a suspicious situation to someone in authority. This contemporary use of the term—someone who reports potential wrongdoing—began with Ralph Nader, a U.S. consumer activist who wanted to avoid the negative connotations of "rat" or "snitch" or "tattletale" (Barrera & Hughes, 2014).

Whistleblowers are usually members of public corporations, private companies, or government entities who report on misconduct in the organization for the purpose of serving the public good. Typically they are "blowing the whistle" on a cover-up, financial fraud, or some other egregious form of deception (Alford, 2001; Glazer & Glazer, 1989; Lacayo & Ripley, 2002). Whistleblowers have been at the center of many stories that made national news and some of their stories were produced as feature films. High-profile whistleblowers (QR) in the past 20 years have included:

- Jeffrey Wigand, a tobacco company executive, reported fellow executives at his company for lying about what they knew about the addictive levels of nicotine in their products (Carnegie Council, 2017). Wigand was portrayed by Russell Crowe in the movie, *The Insider* (1999).

- Mark Whitacre was president of the BioProducts division of Archer Daniels Midland when he began working with the FBI in the 1990s to expose his employer's involvement in price-fixing in agricultural markets. He later got into legal problems for his own actions associated with the scandal. His story was made into the movie *The Informant* (1999), starring Matt Damon.

- Cynthia Cooper, a VP at WorldCom, and Enron executive Sherron Watkins both reported fraudulent accounting practices that misrepresented the financial well-being of their respective employers, thereby misleading investors and the public. Several books and a movie, *The Smartest Guys in the Room,* have depicted the situation at Enron.

- FBI special agent Coleen Rowley revealed that the Bureau had received critical information about an al-Qaeda terrorist plot prior to the 9/11 attacks on the World Trade Center, but her superiors had been slow to take action.

- Edward Snowden famously exposed the secret surveillance practices of the NSA to the public and remains in exile as a result (MacAskill, 2018).

When seeking to obtain information from others about someone's deception, there may be a perception that the process will be easy or straightforward. Surely, individuals with knowledge of the deceit will also be eager to blow the whistle on the bad acts. As it turns out, that's not the case, because the costs for the whistleblower are often high:

- Many lose their jobs and have trouble finding other employment despite being exceptionally qualified. Enron's Sherron Watkins was a licensed certified public accountant (CPA) who graduated with honors from her master's program, but after leaving, she received no job offers that would have utilized her high-level experience with multinational corporations. In fact, she ultimately had to establish her own consulting firm and has remained self-employed since leaving Enron (Swartz, 2016). Potential employers may be reluctant to hire a person who views the value of truth telling over company loyalty.

- Some whistleblowers have had to declare bankruptcy and/or lose their homes. Snowden had to seek asylum in other countries to avoid federal prosecution. Employees of intelligence-gathering agencies are required by law to report wrongdoing to their own agency, which is often the target of their complaint. In so doing, they risk losing their security clearance and/or being transferred to a menial job (Carr, 2005).

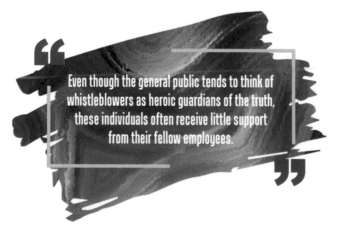

Even though the general public tends to think of whistleblowers as heroic guardians of the truth, these individuals often receive little support from their fellow employees.

Even though the general public tends to think of whistleblowers as heroic guardians of the truth, these individuals often receive little support from their fellow employees (Harper, 2012). Possibly, this is because they expect the whistleblower will be targeted by the organization's power structure and they don't want to be in the line of fire (or they may be reluctant to join an effort to ruin the reputation of the company responsible for their paycheck). It is not unlike a group of people standing idly by while a person gets mugged, famously known as the bystander effect (Fischer et al., 2011; Latané & Darley, 1970).

There are some federal laws designed to protect whistleblowers from retaliation or mistreatment by their employer, including the Whistleblower Protection Act of 1989 and the Whistleblower Protection Enhancement Act of 2012. Under these laws, employees of federal government agencies are theoretically protected from retaliation if they "blow the whistle" on dishonest or illegal actions. The actual effectiveness of such laws remains the subject of much debate, and many whistleblowers say they are reluctant to do it again (Peffer et al., 2015; Whyall, 2018).

In recent years, though, some whistleblowers have been recognized and rewarded financially for reporting misdeeds of their employers. Examples of these include the following:

© designer491/Shutterstock.com

- Dani Shemesh, a former employee of CA Software Israel LTD, was awarded $10.2 million in 2017 for reporting that CA had made false claims during negotiations for a U.S. federal contract (Thomson, 2017).

- Dr. Bijan Oughatiyan, a physician and former employee of IPC Healthcare, was awarded $11.4 million for reporting his employer's overbilling to Medicare, Medicaid, and other federal agencies. The firm had fraudulently reported it provided more costly services than it actually performed (Manson, 2017).

- Claudia Ponce de Leon, a Wells Fargo branch manager, reported her concerns about other employees opening accounts without customers' permission. She was fired in 2011 because Wells Fargo alleged she was a bad employee. Six years later, the Department of Labor ordered the bank to reinstate her and pay $577,500 in back wages, damages, and legal fees (Associated Press, 2017).

In the preceding examples, lie detection began only after a third party volunteered information, but sometimes information from others is deliberately sought in order to verify or dispute a suspected lie.

Finding Physical Evidence

The existence of physical evidence that seems to "prove" a lie is far from a guaranteed strategy for the successful confirmation of deception. The fundamental problem is that evidence can't confess—only people can. In the face of continued verbal denials, the best one can hope to do is weigh the evidence and try to determine guilt or innocence on the basis of reasonable doubt—just as jurors must do in a court case. The more physical evidence there is, the better your chances are of reducing any lingering doubt.

In practical terms, accumulated physical evidence should be considered as pieces of the puzzle rather than as final answers. You may wish to consider avoiding the temptation to confront some-

> ... physical evidence isn't always what it's purported to be.

one on the basis of the first physical evidence you find. Instead, keep your suspicions to yourself for as long as possible—and always remember that any given piece of apparently incriminating evidence can sometimes be reasonably explained. How reliable is the scent of someone else's cologne on your partner's clothes? A half-empty bottle of vodka found in your friend's backpack certainly raises doubts about his or her claim to have stopped drinking.

But it's important to remember that physical evidence isn't always what it's purported to be. In 2013, for example, the FBI admitted (QR) that some of its longstanding techniques for analyzing hairs found at crime scenes were scientifically invalid—which does little to help people like George Perrot. He was convicted of rape in 1992 and sentenced to 30 years in prison—on the basis of a single piece of hair and despite a complete lack of other physical evidence (Pilkington, 2015). In early 2016, Perrot was exonerated and released. For the record, even the victim of the crime had insisted at trial that Perrot could not have been her attacker (Innocence Project Staff, 2017). Physical evidence and scientific techniques for examining it can certainly help us detect deception and crime, but over-reliance could lead to errors in decision-making.

Receiving a Confession

The participants in the study by Park et al. (2002) said that lies are also uncovered when liars confess. There are three basic situations that may result in a confession:

- Direct confrontation of the liar
- Development of guilty feelings by the liar
- Inadvertent or indirect circumstances

Confronting a liar with information, evidence, and questions may result in a confession. It is possible that the liar has kept the lie bottled up and is eager to confess—if only someone would confront them and provide an opportunity to do so. When confronting a suspected liar, some experts advise asking questions that deliberately stoke emotions, such as "How did you feel when you took money out of my wallet?" Above all, keep in mind that the person you suspect of deception might actually be telling the truth, so proceed with caution. Psychologist Edward Geiselman recommends asking a series of open-ended "expansion" questions designed to draw out more and more details from the person being interviewed.

People who are telling the truth usually answer subsequent follow-up questions in more detail, but liars tend to repeat the same basic answer set each time so as to not provide any additional evidence that might betray them (Wollan, 2016).

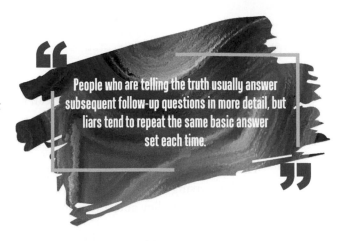

> "People who are telling the truth usually answer subsequent follow-up questions in more detail, but liars tend to repeat the same basic answer set each time."

Feelings of guilt on the part of the liar may also result in a confession. Such a confession can be totally unsolicited. This can happen when the lie has produced so much psychological pressure that the liar can no longer handle it. For example, a romantic partner who has repeatedly lied about working at a prestigious corporation decides one day to admit to his partner that he is a low-paid municipal employee. Was lie detection a part of a process that resulted in the confession? In one sense, no. But the lie detector may have indirectly facilitated the confession by creating a relationship where truth was valued, where guilt was emphasized, and where understanding was expected.

Confessions may also occur inadvertently. A liar may forget the story he or she told months earlier and accidentally tell what really happened during a casual conversation. Or they might not realize they're being recorded when saying something that appears to reveal their guilt. Consider the astonishing case of real estate heir Robert Durst (QR). He had long been suspected of murdering his wife in 1982, but her body was never found and he was never charged due to a lack of evidence (Gerber, 2018). In 2000, Susan Berman, who had supported Durst's alibi in his wife's disappearance, was found murdered, not long after Durst had paid her a total of $50,000. Less than a year later, Durst had moved to Galveston, Texas, where he was renting a room and pretending to be a mute woman (Viren, 2018). There he was charged with murdering and dismembering an elderly neighbor, Morris Black, but was eventually acquitted (Bagli, 2017). Intrigued by these events, HBO produced a documentary on Durst called *The Jinx: The Life and Deaths of Robert Durst* (2015). After taping the final scene, during which the producers surprised Durst with damning handwriting evidence relating to Berman's murder, he retreated to the bathroom. Unaware that his microphone was still recording, Durst said, "There it is. You're caught," and a moment later adds, "What the hell did I do? Killed them all, of course" (Yahr, 2015).

It turns out, however, that the documentary switched the order of those last two lines in the editing process. In the raw version, "Killed them all, of course," came several sentences before "What the hell did I do?" When the case goes to trial in 2020, only the unedited version is likely to be admitted as evidence, and Durst's defense is sure to make an issue out of the documentary maker's questionable editorial choices (Bagli, 2019).

Observing Behavior and Listening

Lie detection processes may involve evaluating the suspected liar's verbal and nonverbal behavior. As Vrij (2008) suggests, lying can be more cognitively complex than truth telling and this increases the strain on the liar's memory. As a result, liars *might* exhibit verbal and nonverbal behaviors that betray their deception, such as:

- **Blatant lies, easily refuted**: The suspect might tell a blatant lie that can be easily refuted (such as saying they did not need a company badge to enter a restricted area even though it is company policy and common practice).

- **Inconsistent statements**: The suspect's story may have inconsistencies. When first questioned, the suspect might say they arrived at work at 7:00 a.m. and no other car was in the parking lot. Later, they might say there were other cars parked nearby.

Having knowledge about facts relevant to the lie or familiarity with a particular context may aid in detecting lies.

Having knowledge about facts relevant to the lie or familiarity with a particular context may aid in detecting lies. As noted above, it can be beneficial to gather evidence about the suspected lie prior to confronting the liar. In the face of evidence, a liar may own up to his or her deception. Or, they may vehemently deny it. It is difficult to predict whether the liar will own it or choose to continue their deceit. If the suspected liar does not confess when presented with evidence of their lie, research suggests interviewers do have some viable choices to make about how to proceed:

- Taking what was said and fact-checking the information may increase the possibility of catching a liar. Blair, Levine, and Shaw (2010) call this process **content in context**. The online world in general (especially the vast amount of information people post to social media profiles) make information gathering for corroborating or disputing a story relatively easy to do.

- Expert knowledge of the subject matter, possessing factual information relevant to the lie, and having general familiarity can allow one to ask questions that are diagnostically strategic and context-sensitive (Levine, Blair, & Clare, 2014). Having a general plan but avoiding broad and irrelevant questions increases lie detection accuracy.

- According to Feeley and Young (1998), **global judgments** are by far the most frequent way of determining deceptive behavior—e.g., "His account just didn't seem plausible," or "She acted funny; something wasn't right." A meta-analytic study by DePaulo et al. (2003) found that *some* liars can be detected via global judgments such as the liar's vocal and verbal involvement (e.g., liars may be less forthcoming and tell less compelling stories).

- Relying on **unconscious processes** rather than traditional truth-or-lie judgments *may* more accurately reflect how lies are detected (ten Brinke, Stimson, & Carney, 2014). However, according to Bond, Levine, and Hartwig (2015) the majority of such indirect measures are inferior to direct judgments of truthfulness.

There are plenty of people who make the process of unassisted lie detection sound very easy. Well-known behaviorist David Lieberman (1998, p. 65), for example, promises readers a "series of questions which virtually guarantees that you will know (a) if you're being lied to and (b) what the truth is if it's not obvious from the lie." Unfortunately for all of us, and especially for the people who spend money on such books and other products, the results of actual scientific research on the ability of human beings to detect lies tell a different story.

CAN WE ACCURATELY DETECT LIES BY OBSERVING BEHAVIOR?

For decades, the process of examining another person's behavior for clues to deception was the most popular method used by academic researchers to determine how accurate people are in detecting deception. However, re-creating the conditions of everyday lie detection in research settings can be challenging (Vrij & Verschuere, 2013). Levine (2018) argues for deception study designs that are more ecologically valid. He and others believe that simulating deception detection in lab research falls short of how such detection works in the real world, in the following ways:

- **Passivity**: Most deception detection research is passive in nature. Participants are watching short clips of potential liars rather than interacting/conversing with real people.

- **Foreknowledge**: Participants are often aware that deception will be occurring so they go into the experiment with suspicions raised, primed to actively assess honesty and deceit.

- **Unfamiliarity**: Participants tend to view clips of strangers rather than people they know.

- **Brevity**: Exposure to potential deceivers is usually short, with clips often lasting no more than a minute in length.

- **Artificial base rates:** Most lie detection studies present participants with a 50/50 mix of lies and truth. This ratio is (hopefully) not the same as what the average person experiences in daily life.

The people in the sample clips may be addressing their opinion on a controversial topic, whether they like or dislike a person, whether they have just viewed a pleasant or emotionally disturbing video, or whether they have or have not just taken some money from somewhere nearby. In these experiments, the job of the human detectors is to accurately judge which recorded statements are true and which are false. But in the real world, there is no guarantee that deception is present in our interactions with other people, so we may not be actively tuned in to matters of truthfulness and deception (Levine, 2014). There may occasionally be, however, a few real-world situations that approximate these conditions—e.g., jurors listening to witnesses, law enforcement officers observing suspects while another officer interrogates them, or watching a salesperson interact with another customer while you are waiting.

> ... in the real world, there is no guarantee that deception is present in our interactions with other people, so we may not be actively tuned in to matters of truthfulness and deception.

Another problem with the design of these lie detection experiments is properly simulating the real-world motivation to lie. We know that the consequences of getting caught have to really matter to real-world liars, or they're unlikely to give us any behavioral clues that might help us detect their deception. Malone and DePaulo (2001) point out that the typical way of studying lie detection may fail to replicate high-stakes situations. When the stakes are not perceived as high, liars are not especially worried about getting caught and therefore fail to exhibit behaviors that are useful for detecting deception. This problem can occur when the lies being studied in the experiment are of little consequence or not well planned.

Aware of this deficiency, researchers in some experiments try to provide the human detector with either positive or negative incentives to do well (positive incentives are usually monetary and negative incentives could be the threat of being restricted to a physically unpleasant environment for long period of time). Knowing that detectors are more accurate at detecting high-stakes lies (Frank & Ekman, 1997), some experiments are designed to induce people to either lie or tell the truth about *actual* cheating and stealing they've participated in (see Chapter 7), but this is not typical.

Ways of Measuring Accuracy

As described previously, lie detectors in the research projects were shown an equal number of people who were honest and dishonest. Accuracy in such experiments is most often expressed as the percentage of correct judgments. If a person correctly identified 12 of 20 communicators, this person's lie detection accuracy would be 60%. Measuring accuracy in this way forces observers to make an unqualified decision regarding truth or deception.

But our real-life decisions about whether a person is lying can be ambiguous. We may be thinking, "Something makes me think this person is lying, but I'm not entirely sure." In fact, DePaulo and Morris (2004) found that a detector's *ambivalence* was a better way of distinguishing lies and truths than their actual lie/truth judgments. They found that people attempting to judge deception were far more ambivalent about lies than they were about truths. Of course, intuitive judgments are also subject to bias and inaccuracy (Myers, 2002), but listening to judges talk out loud as they go about deciding on lie/truth judgments may provide valuable information that the final lie/truth determination does not provide. Adopting tools like a seven-point rating scale (1=totally unsure to 7=very confident) would also allow judges to show how certain they are about their decision. Rating scales are not frequently used in experiments to measure lie detection accuracy, but they are informative when perceptual gradations involved in decision-making are important (see Griffin & Frank, 2018).

Lie Detection Accuracy: Nonprofessionals

How *accurate* are people at detecting lies? Some experts believe that we have about a 50/50 chance of correctly identifying lies:

- Vrij (2008) reviewed 39 studies and found an accuracy rate of 57%.

- Malone and DePaulo (2001) analyzed more than 100 studies with the average detection rate at 54%.

- DePaulo and Morris (2004) examined 253 samples, involving mostly students as lie detectors, with an average accurate rate of 53%.

These accuracy rates are consistent across a variety of settings (Bond & DePaulo, 2006). Such results seem to indicate that untrained observers are able to detect deception at rates that only slightly exceed chance. If you flipped a coin or randomly guessed on each trial, you would be competitive with those who based their judgments on what they perceived as reliable verbal or nonverbal cues.

Other researchers have determined there are many factors that contribute to the success of humans in identifying when they are being told lies. For example, ten Brinke et al. (2014) disagree about lie detection being no more accurate than chance. As mentioned earlier, results from their research indicate that the unconscious mind of humans can effectively identify cues to deception, but these accurate evaluations are overridden by conscious biases. However, it is worth noting that not everyone agrees with these views (e.g., see Levine & Bond, 2014).

Detecting deception in someone who is culturally distinct from us (e.g., different native languages) does not seem to have much effect on accuracy rates (Bond & Atoum, 2000; Bond & Rao, 2004). However, some research suggests that culture and language just might influence accuracy in deception detection. In one study, researchers actually found that native speakers were better at catching lies spoken in another language than they were at catching lies spoken in their own (Cheng & Broadhurst, 2005).

Are *groups* of people more accurate lie detectors than individuals? Individual perceptions of truth tellers and liars have been compared with the collective decisions of groups. Frank, Feeley, Paolantonio, and Servoss (2004) found that small groups containing six people were statistically more accurate than individuals in their judgments of deceptions, but not truthful statements. The accuracy rate of the individuals and small groups in another study found accuracy scores that slightly exceeded chance, which echo the findings of the extant literature on lie detection (Park, Levine, Harms, & Ferrara, 2002).

Lie Detection Accuracy: Professionals

The accuracy rates of professional lie detectors such as police officers, customs officers, federal polygraphers, robbery investigators, judges, lawyers, and psychiatrists are generally no better than that of the laypersons—within the 45–60% accuracy range (Ekman & O'Sullivan, 1991; Vrij, 2008).

> ... accuracy rates of professional lie detectors such as police officers, customs officers, federal polygraphers, robbery investigators, judges, lawyers, and psychiatrists are generally no better than that of the laypersons.

Historically, most of these studies have used low-stakes lies as the basis of their research. But a study published in 2015 had observers watch 36 videos of people (some truthful, some lying) in real-life, *high-stakes* situations. As expected, under these circumstances the liars were *somewhat* easier to spot. The police officers who participated in the study averaged

72% accuracy in detecting deception (the civilian participants averaged 68%). When it came to spotting the truth instead of lies, participants who worked as a group achieved an accuracy rate of 92% (Whelan, Wagstaff, & Wheatcroft, 2015).

Newer research designs allow professional participants to rely on techniques that more accurately reflect how they detect lies while on the job (e.g., detectives questioning a suspect). These studies have shown accuracy ceilings well above 90%. And in one study an interrogator was able to correctly distinguish truths from lies 100% of the time (Levine, 2015).

Lie Detection Accuracy in Close Relationships

As noted earlier, studies of lie detection accuracy are largely based on the behavior of people unknown to the evaluators who are conducting the research. Is lie detection accuracy helped or hindered when the person being judged is a close relationship partner? It can help in some respects and it can hinder in others (Knapp, 2006). Like so many things about relationships, the role and mechanics of deception are complicated. Summarizing years of research on the subject, Levine and Knapp (2018) offer the following four principles as a guide (pp. 334–335):

1. **People in close relationships are expected to recognize and respect the vulnerabilities that go with being in a close relationship.** Here, the operative word is vulnerabilities. In close relationships, lies are more likely to be evaluated on the basis of whether they protect the other's vulnerabilities or, in contrast, take advantage of them in a way that is perceived as unfair or harmful.

2. **People in close relationships feel sufficiently satisfied and emotionally invested in their relationships such that they want their relationships to continue.** In most cases, a key characteristic of a healthy relationship is that the partners don't imagine it ending—at least anytime soon. As this sense of "we-ness" grows, the "desire to maintain a future for the relationship increases." Against this backdrop, lies may be evaluated in terms of how they either help or hurt this future.

3. **People in close relationships have frequent opportunities to interact and mutually influence one another.** Any good relationship is a partnership, which means, among other things, that the parties have the power to persuade one another. This bi-directional flow of information means that, over time, conversations and topics recur (sometimes a lot, even taking on a life of their own). Great care must be taken, therefore, with both truths and deceptions, as they are likely to be around for a long time to come.

4. **People in close relationships believe they know and understand their partners well because they have acquired a great deal of general and personal information about each other**. Familiarity may not breed contempt, but it can create opportunities for misunderstanding or miscalculation. Partners may know each other better than they know themselves, or they may only *think* they do. Under these conditions, *overlooking or reinterpreting* behaviors of various kinds can occur, blinding us to the possibility of deception.

What are the implications of these principles? Once again, complicated. We would expect a person who is suspicious of deception to be more accurate when judging a close relationship partner than a stranger (Stiff, Kim, & Ramesh, 1992). And, sometimes, relationship closeness does indeed facilitate accurate lie detection:

- A close relationship partner may lie in transparent (obvious) ways.

- Behavioral signs of guilt or fear may overshadow any attempts at concealment of serious lies.

- The lack of practice with serious lies may also negatively affect the performance of those lies.

- There may even be a subconscious desire to get caught.

- The detector may be well aware of the liar's baseline behavior and is sensitive to any unusual changes in that behavior.

However, there are also forces working against lie detection accuracy in close relationships:

- Human lie detectors in close relationships know the problematic nature of suspicion. When a detector reveals suspicions, it has the potential to reduce trust and closeness. Thus, there may be hesitation to act on suspicions. In other words, lie detection may take a back seat to relationship maintenance even when lies are suspected.

- The liar is just as familiar with the target's behavior as the target is of the liar's. Therefore, inaccurate lie detection in close relationships may be due to the strategic reading and use of the target's behavior by the liar. About half the time, for example, the adolescents in Grady's (1997) study were able to identify strategies their parents used to detect their deception.

- The truth bias is even stronger in close relationships than it is in the general population, so serious lies are completely unexpected and the impulse to detect them isn't usually present.

- Low-stakes lies that support the close relationship partner and the relationship are expected, but in such cases detection is not an issue.

WHY HUMANS ARE INACCURATE LIE DETECTORS

It would not be practical to exhaustively list all the variables that can restrict the accurate identification of another person's deceptive behavior. However, brief discussions of the factors below make it easier to understand why humans aren't more accurate at lie detection. These discussions should also provide new appreciation for people who are quite competent at lie detection (these skilled detectors will be discussed later in the chapter). In the meantime, however, the news is more troubling for those who wish our lie detection skills exceeded the slightly better-than-chance levels reported in most studies. As explained below, most people's accuracy in detecting lies may actually be *much worse* than 50%.

The "Truth Bias"

A lie detector's accuracy score is typically derived from the number of correct identifications of both truth tellers and liars. However, human observers tend to perceive more messages as truthful than deceptive, which results in a greater accuracy for truthful messages and a lower accuracy for deceptive ones. This "truth bias," which negatively affects our ability to detect lies, is a result of both social and cognitive processes. DePaulo (1994) summed it up this way: "the empirical fact is that most people seem to believe most of what they hear most of the time" (p. 83).

Levine, Park, and McCornack (1999) have a similar concept, known as the "veracity effect." Part of Levine's Truth-Default Theory (TDT), the veracity effect suggests that we are much better at spotting truths than catching lies because our default setting is to presume that others are being honest (Levine, 2014). In situations (such as relationships) where the rate of truth telling is high and there is no reason to suspect lies, our ability to detect lies accurately may be much less than 50/50. When half the speakers being judged are telling the truth and half are lying, the truthful speakers are typically identified about 67% of the time, but our ability to identify the liars accurately is a dismal 34–37% (Levine, Kim, Park, & Hughes, 2006; Park, Levine, Harms, et al., 2002).

Socially, we assume people will usually tell us the truth, which leads us to perceive many more truths than lies. We get in the habit of generously treating messages that sound strange as truthful until more specific information is obtained. It's an efficient and social way to proceed when we interact with other people.

... "the empirical fact is that most people seem to believe most of what they hear most of the time."

In addition, the experiments conducted by Gilbert and colleagues (1990; 1993) remind us that incoming messages are initially—if only for an instant—accepted in our mind as true *prior to* a rational analysis of their veracity. Because of the nature of their work (a law enforcement professional, for example) or social environment, however, some people may treat incoming messages very differently. Instead of being biased toward the assuming the truth is being told, they have a lie bias (i.e., a tendency to assume the truth is not being told).

The "Lie Bias"

Having a general expectation that other people will lie is referred to as the "lie bias" effect. Prison seems to be a place where people are exposed to a lot of lies and can get almost immediate feedback on their accuracy in detecting them. The ability to detect lies accurately is a crucial part of adapting and surviving in this environment. It is not surprising, then, to find that prisoners have a lie bias. They are substantially more accurate than chance in detecting lies, but below 50% in detecting truths—the reverse of the veracity effect (Bond, Malloy, Arias, Nunn, & Thompson, 2005; Hartwig, Granhag, Strömwall, & Andersson, 2004).

A lie bias does not automatically mean lies will be detected more accurately. Without timely feedback on one's ability to detect lies, a lie bias can impede detection accuracy in the same way a truth bias does. Experienced law enforcement officers who were trained in observational lie detection also showed a lie bias and assumed too often that a suspect was lying (Meissner & Kassin, 2002). Elaad (2003) found that police interrogators often overestimated their ability to detect lies. In a situation where the expectation for lies is high, combined with human detectors who are confident they are good at detecting lies, there is likely to be a bias toward perceiving lies. If these interrogators do not receive timely information about the accuracy or inaccuracy of their lie judgments, we would not expect their lie detection ability to be high.

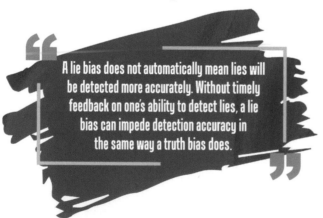

A lie bias does not automatically mean lies will be detected more accurately. Without timely feedback on one's ability to detect lies, a lie bias can impede detection accuracy in the same way a truth bias does.

Stereotypes

One of the most common problems associated with human lie detection is the disconnect between what people *think* liars look/act like and how they *really* look/act (Strömwall, Granhag, & Hartwig, 2004). Kaufmann, Drevland, Wessel, Goverskeid, and Magnussen (2003) found perceptions of credibility strongly influenced by social stereotypes regarding "appropriate" emotional expressions. Studies have shown that people who subscribe to popular stereotypes like "liars won't look at you" or "liars fidget a lot" are not likely to be good lie detectors (Feeley & Young, 1998; Vrij & Mann, 2001). Lie detectors who believe they are observing a liar are likely to see behaviors they associate with liars even though they aren't manifested by the speaker (Levine, Asada, & Park, 2006). Since liars are also familiar with common beliefs about liar behavior (e.g., fewer other-directed gazes), it is not surprising when liars don't manifest this behavior. Nevertheless, people maintain these beliefs because they often think back to a time when a liar they knew did look away or fidget a lot, ignoring all the other occasions when the liars they experienced did not manifest these characteristics. This is known as a *confirmation bias* (Nickerson, 1998).

The *Othello error* occurs when a questioner interprets certain behavioral signs as indicative of lying and not something else. A person's anger and/or nervousness, for example, might be the result of being falsely accused of lying rather than proof that someone is lying (Ekman, 2001). This error's curious name derives from events in Shakespeare's tragedy *Othello*. The title character (a powerful general) is tricked into believing that his wife Desdemona has been unfaithful to him. He convinces himself that she and her maidservant Emilia are clever liars, and interprets everything through this lens of presumed guilt. "Heaven truly knows that thou art false as hell," he tells his wife in Act 4, Scene 2.

We're not sure how Darth Maul got cast as Othello in this production, but it works.

Desdemona grows increasingly anxious as Othello continues to question her—which is understandable given that she knows he's already made up his mind and is probably going to kill her (spoiler alert: he does). As Inglis-Arkell (2014) describes it, "Her increasingly frantic attempts to correct the situation only make her look more guilty. She looks guilty because Othello suspects she's guilty. Once he starts looking at everything she does with suspicion, everything she does is suspicious."

People also have beliefs about what liars and truth tellers look like (Yamagishi, Tanida, Mashima, Shimoma, & Kanazawa, 2003; Zebrowitz, Voinescu, & Collins, 1996). But a person who is perceived to have an honest face (large eyes, facial symmetry, attractive) is not always telling the truth. The perceptual problem occurs because once we perceive someone as an honest or dishonest person, we are more likely to perceive their behavior in line with that perception. A negative or positive bias toward people from a given culture or ethnic group can work the same way (Bond & Atoum, 2000).

Stereotypes and biases are also linked to a common observational error called *the Brokaw hazard* (Ekman, 2001). The Brokaw hazard occurs when the human lie detector fails to acknowledge that a particular manifested behavior may just be that particular person's way of communicating and not a sign of deception. Good detectors try to base their judgments on *changes* in behavior (e.g., baseline) rather than the presence of a particular type of behavior—e.g., changes in hesitant speech rather than on the presence of hesitant speech.

Rightly or wrongly, lie detectors also seem to believe that aberrant or "weird" behavior (e.g., periodically raising one's voice without an apparent reason, occasional eye movements that follow a nonexistent flying insect, or doing intermittent stretching exercises with one's arms and legs) means a person is more likely to be dishonest (Bond, Omar, Pitre, & Lashley, 1992; Levine et al., 2000).

Overlooking or Incorrectly Using Behavioral Cues

Lie detection accuracy is also affected by the ways human lie detectors approach the behavioral cues manifested by the liar. As Ekman (1996) pointed out, parents don't teach their children what cues liars use and they often teach them to ignore them in order to facilitate effective social relations. As a result, poor human detectors (1) often base their judgment of deception on a single nonverbal cue even though they understand there may be many relevant cues and (2) overlook or minimize nonverbal cues and pay undue attention to verbal cues when judging deceptive messages (O'Sullivan, 2003). Ekman (2001, p. 165) also cautions: "the absence of a sign of deceit is not evidence of truth."

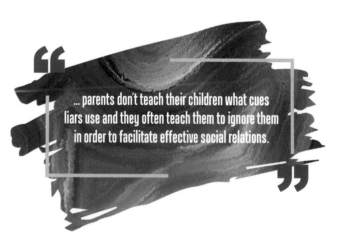

... parents don't teach their children what cues liars use and they often teach them to ignore them in order to facilitate effective social relations.

Making Judgments While Participating in Dialogue

Although deception detection experiments do not usually involve dialogue between the detector and the suspected liar, it is a common condition in everyday lie detection. Several factors detract from accurate lie detection during interaction (Burgoon, Buller, & Floyd, 2001; Dunbar, Ramirez, & Burgoon, 2003).

- **Lack of independence**: The behavior being observed by the lie detector is not independent of his or her own behavior. What is being observed, then, is the process of mutual influence—not an uncontaminated performance by a liar.

- **Probing effect**: The process of questioning or probing in order to detect deception seems to have a generally positive effect on perceptions of the target's honesty, but does not increase lie detection accuracy (Levine & McCornack, 2001). Surprisingly, this "probing effect" also occurs with prisoners who enter the encounter with a lie bias (Bond, Malloy, Thompson, Arias, & Nunn, 2004).

- **Distractions from nonverbal behavior**: Conversations require each interactant to pay attention to what is verbalized, making it more difficult to focus solely on nonverbal behavior. In addition, the verbal behavior is likely to be a mixture of truths, half-truths, and falsehoods (unlike a typical lie detection experiment) that may also make unambiguous perceptions of lying difficult. Lie detection experiments that involve viewing a videotape allow the observer to maintain a constant eye gaze with an unobstructed frontal view of the suspect's face and body. Politeness norms and movements that occur in conversations mean behavioral observations are often gleaned from short glances and some body features will be perceptually more accessible than others.

- **Lack of immediate feedback**: Finally, lie detectors in conversations do not usually obtain immediate feedback to validate or deny their inferences about deception. Such feedback is necessary in order to improve one's lie detection accuracy.

Characteristics and Behavior of the Liar

Some characteristics of liars also inhibit accurate lie detection. For example, the communication styles of extroverts make their lies harder to detect (Vrij, 2008). The demeanor of skilled liars, those with little concern for the truth, or with a lot at stake may mimic the behaviors of trustworthy and honest individuals. One of the biggest and most public lies was told by President Bill Clinton in January of 1998 when he stood in front of reporters in the Roosevelt Room of the White House and said, "I did not have sexual relations with that woman, Ms. Lewinsky." It was a lie designed to give voters who wanted to believe in him a reason to do so. Reportedly, in addition to the carefully crafted speech, Clinton even rehearsed his body language to make it stern and admonitory (Rothman, 2015).

Bill Clinton

Ironically, truth tellers who exhibit idiosyncratic or nervous behaviors can raise suspicion of being liars even though they are not. Levine et al. (2011) discuss how manipulating demeanor in deception judgment tasks drives accuracy scores. That is, there are those who look like liars, and others who come off as honest—regardless of the facts associated with their assertions. These performances play an important role in how they are judged by others.

Amanda Knox, an American exchange student, was found guilty of murdering her roommate, Meredith Kercher, in Italy in 2007. The murder case was subsequently dismissed by the Italian Supreme Court in 2015. When Knox returned home in 2011 and was interviewed on national television, some viewers thought she sounded guilty because she seemed evasive, looked blank and detached, and choked when answering some questions. Yet those very same behaviors were cited by others as reasons to think Knox was innocent. Knox has staunchly maintained her innocence since her arrest. Her case provides an excellent example of how some human detectors can use the same cues to reach opposite conclusions about lying or truth telling.

Characteristics and Behavior of the Detector

Despite the fact that lying and lie detection have been important features in human development over the past 5 to 6 million years, the ability to detect lies with a high degree of accuracy has not become a hard-wired ability (Ekman, 1996). People with poor memories or who do a poor job of monitoring their own behavior are likely to lack skills in lie detecting.

Learning lie detection skills is also problematic. Instead of learning to look for lying clues in someone else's demeanor, humans usually learn to politely ignore suspicious behavior, to be cautious about accusing someone of lying, and to rely on nonobservational types of information to validate another's lying behavior. Sometimes we ignore deception clues because we

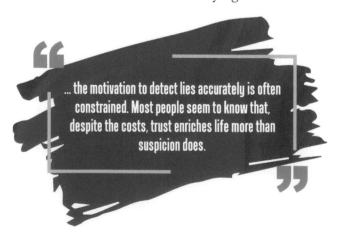

... the motivation to detect lies accurately is often constrained. Most people seem to know that, despite the costs, trust enriches life more than suspicion does.

want to be misled. In short, the motivation to detect lies accurately is often constrained. Most people seem to know that, despite the costs, trust enriches life more than suspicion does. Sometimes there are costs for people who are skilled at detecting subtle signs of covert behavior. In one research study, the skills necessary to be an effective human lie detector negatively affected students' popularity and social sensitivity ratings as well as their relationship satisfaction (DePaulo & Jordan, 1982).

Passive Observation vs. Active Questioning

Many research studies looking at the accuracy of human lie detection use passive observers. These observers generally are not interacting with the source (i.e., the possible liar), are not themselves asking any questions, and are relying on verbal and nonverbal responses to *scripted* contextual questions (e.g., Why didn't you steal the check?). This is not usually how determinations of veracity happen in everyday life. Interestingly, the act of observing a suspect being questioned can lead to enhanced source believability or a *probing effect* (Levine & McCornack, 2001). Levine notes this increases truth bias, but *not* accuracy about whether someone is lying. It may be counterintuitive, but his research indicates that given an identical answer from someone who was not questioned, the person who was questioned is more likely to be believed.

The circumstances during law enforcement interviews are unique in that questions are not overly scripted—as they often are in research studies. Also, there is prior knowledge or evidence that can be used to develop questioning relative to the lie. Any answers provided during the interview can be used in strategic follow-up questions. This type of *active questioning* reflects the methods of skilled lie detectors. Simply interacting and probing a source may result in lie detection accuracies that reflect those of passive observation studies (i.e., slightly above chance; Levine & McCornack, 2001). But more deliberate techniques like the *strategic use of evidence* (discussed later in this chapter) and prompting for diagnostically useful information can lead to higher judgment accuracy in both experts and laypersons (Levine et al., 2014). Levine (2015) summarized the findings of studies that examined various active questioning methods and found accuracy rates ranging from 69% to 100%.

ACCURACY OF PROFESSIONALS

As a result of confronting many more liars than truth tellers in their line of work, police officers typically overestimate their ability to detect lies (Elaad, 2003). Experience with liars is certainly an important part of learning to detect lies, but a comparable number of experiences with truth tellers, which those in law enforcement often don't have, are needed to create a better basis for comparison.

© Everett Collection/Shutterstock.com

The accuracy of professionals in detecting lies can also be adversely impacted because police interrogations are interactive and officers may pay less attention to nonverbal cues and more to verbal behavior. The motivation for police officers to detect any deceptive behavior is

> The motivation for police officers to detect any deceptive behavior is sometimes less important than obtaining evidence for a conviction.

sometimes less important than obtaining evidence for a conviction. Biases and invalid stereotypes applied to suspects during police interviews can be especially harmful. Cues that a suspect is lying may be ignored because investigators are more focused on getting a confession from the person being interviewed. If they are mistaken, they may not find out until after a trial—and that may take months if not years. Sometimes the belief that a truth teller is lying is so strong and so much time and energy have been invested in this belief by an officer that any information to the contrary, no matter when it is received, is unlikely to be taken into account.

Some of the factors that hinder accurate lie detection in the general public also affect professionals who are involved with lie detection as part of their work. For example, police training manuals sometimes provide questionable information about behavioral cues exhibited by liars—e.g., liars don't look at you, liars make unnatural posture changes, liars engage in nervous self-manipulations, liars place their hands over their mouth when speaking, etc. (Inbau, Reid, Buckley, & Jayne, 2001). As a result, police officers may have as many incorrect beliefs about deceptive behavior as do laypersons (Strömwall et al., 2004). In one study, those who were trained to use the invalid cues found in police manuals actually performed worse than those who had received no training (Kassin & Fong, 1999). Studies that examine the skills of professionals often do not allow them to interact with those being judged; therefore, they are unable to question subjects as they would in their professional line of work. When professionals are allowed to interview study participants without being constrained by a script, accuracy rates can be exceptionally high—in one case an expert was able to achieve 100% (Levine et al., 2014).

HIGHLY SKILLED DETECTORS

It turns out that not everyone is an average or below-average lie detector. Some people are highly skilled. Who are these people, and what is their secret for successful lie detection?

Some preliminary answers to these questions were proposed by Ekman and O'Sullivan (1991). They tested the lie detection ability of several different professional groups and noticed that the 34 Secret Service officers' accuracy rate of 65% exceeded that of all the other groups. More than half of these agents scored 70% or above. The researchers attributed their success to several factors: (1) detecting truthful and deceptive intent is central to their job in the Secret

Service and they are trained accordingly; (2) they learn to focus on nonverbal signals that might identify individuals who intend to harm the people they are protecting; (3) the importance of their job makes them highly motivated observers, and they get plenty of practice on the job; and (4) they also need to keep an open mind about a person's guilt and innocence that may put any tendency toward a truth or lie bias in check.

Subsequent studies by multiple researchers showed that highly skilled lie detectors weren't limited to Secret Service officers (Ekman, O'Sullivan, & Frank, 1999; Vrij & Mann, 2001; Vrij & Mann, 2005). Some clinical psychologists and law enforcement officers also showed exceptional skill at lie detection. The skilled lie detectors had several things in common:

- Highly motivated to detect deception
- Experienced in their job with liars
- Esteemed by others who knew their work as skillful lie detectors
- Attentive to nonverbal behavior, but did not rely on stereotypes of a liar's nonverbal behavior
- Observant of less-obvious verbal behavior involving ambiguous and contradictory statements
- Perceptive regarding subtle facial cues involved in the hiding of strong emotional reactions

There were somewhat unexpected results from another study in which brain-injured people were evaluated on their ability to identify liars. The brain-injured lie detectors had severe deficits in their ability to understand spoken sentences (aphasics), but were able to identify when someone was lying. Their ability to detect emotions associated with lies was significantly better than people without any language impairment (Etcoff, Ekman, Magee, & Frank, 2000).

Wizards

Based on research studies providing evidence that some people are highly skilled lie detectors, O'Sullivan and Ekman set out to find the best of the best or what they call "wizards" (O'Sullivan & Ekman, 2004; O'Sullivan, 2005). They tested more than 12,000 people on three different types of lies: lies about feelings, lies about opinions, and lies about committing a crime. The 14 people who scored 80% or better on each of these tests earned the wizards label. Another group of 15 *almost* wizards scored 90% on one type of lie and 80% or better on one of the other two types of lies. The wizards came from various occupational groups: therapists, law enforcement officers, judges, arbitrators, and artists. Most were between 40 and 60 years of age. They tended to be introverts, but also seemed to pay attention to their own behaviors. Overall, they understood that not all liars act the same way and they paid attention to both language and nonverbal communication.

As with much of the lie detection research, there are critics of the research on wizards. Bond and Uysal (2007) explain that the findings on wizards may be due to statistical chance. A meta-analytic study by Bond and DePaulo (2008) found that perception of a liar's credibility is the most important factor driving accuracy differences among judges rather than any ability inherent to the judges themselves.

Training

Is it possible to train people to be significantly better lie detectors? Maybe, but from the research that has been done on this topic we usually find that improvements in accuracy are negligible. While some training programs have increased accuracy rates dramatically (deTurck, Harzlak, Bodhorn, & Texter, 1990; Frank & Feeley, 2003), Vrij (2008) says the average accuracy of trained observers is 57% but the average rate for untrained observers is almost as good, at 54%. Few training programs achieve accuracy rates as high as 65%.

Obtaining higher results often depends on using training conditions that may not be present in the real world of lie detection: (1) grouping judges by background and professional experience (Hurley, Anker, Frank, Matsumoto, & Hwang, 2014; Shaw, Porter, & ten Brinke, 2013) and (2) pre-existing familiarity with the lie situation (e.g., being trained to spot lies in your own field; Reinhard, Sporer, Scharmach, & Marksteiner, 2011). Blair, Levine, and Vasquez (2015) provided judges with multiple opportunities to engage in a deception-detection task over a 6-week time period. They showed increases in accuracy rates from 69% to 89% during that timeframe. But, *changing the context* of the task

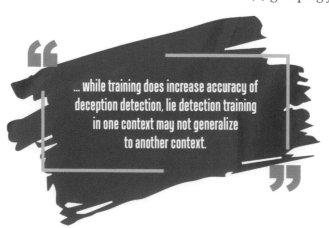

... while training does increase accuracy of deception detection, lie detection training in one context may not generalize to another context.

from a cheating scenario to a mock robbery *lowered* accuracy scores. This finding further supports the idea that, while training does increase accuracy of deception detection, lie detection training in one context may not generalize to another context.

Like a number of other training programs, Levine, Feeley, McCornack, Hughes, and Harms (2005) briefly trained people to look for certain nonverbal cues and compared the accuracy of those groups with groups that received no training. Consistent with the results of previous studies, this type of training produced modest improvements in lie detection accuracy. But the work of Levine and his colleagues also raises the possibility that these modest improvements might *not* be due to the training *per se* as much as to the content of the training because the training encourages more acute observation. Their experiments found, for example, that people trained to look for bogus nonverbal cues (unrelated to lying behavior) were significantly more accurate lie detectors than people who received no training and only slightly less accurate than those who were trained to look for nonverbal behavior typically associated with liars.

As previously mentioned, a major reason for the modest results associated with lie detection training seems to be related to the nature of the training itself (Frank & Feeley, 2003). Successful training programs need to be developed in accord with what we have learned from experts and effective lie detectors. Components of a successful lie detection training program should take the following considerations into account:

- Trainees need to be motivated to succeed and to see the relevance of the training to their personal and/or career goals.

- Trainees must be willing to give up old biases and stereotypes about liar behavior.

- Training materials need to focus on a variety of different truth tellers and liars.

- The stakes for the liars should be moderate to high.

- Trainees need to get immediate feedback on their performance and plenty of individual attention from the trainer.

- Trainees need to have plenty of time to practice.

- Trainees should be encouraged to talk about their lie/truth decisions so that trainers can use this information to guide future performance.

- Trainees should be taught the value of attending to both nonverbal and verbal behavior.

- Trainees should be exposed to different models of lie detection.

Any training program should emphasize skill in perceiving what Ekman and Friesen (1978) call micromomentary facial expressions (less than half a second in length); or include a model, based on research, that focuses on learning what behaviors or patterns of behavior typically distinguish liars and truth tellers (which is the subject of this 2014 FBI bulletin [QR]). This approach might involve a specific behavior like the presence of "distancing" words (fewer self-references) or something general like any behavior that doesn't seem to fit either the situation or the speaker's baseline behavior. Also, as we have seen from recent research by Levine (2015), lie detection training that focuses on the use of content in context and active/diagnostic questioning can substantially increase accuracy rates.

INTERVIEWS BY PROFESSIONALS

There are many professionals (other than police and military) who frequently conduct interviews as part of their job responsibilities. These include external auditors, internal auditors, fraud examiners, and special investigators who work in the corporate sector. The purpose of their interviews can be to gather information about whether a financial fraud or other crime against the employer has been committed with the possibility that criminal and/or civil charges may be filed against the alleged perpetrator. They interview witnesses who may have information about an incident, and they also interview suspects who may have committed an offense. Thus, their focus is on finding the truth. They must work diligently to identify when someone is lying to them.

Meeting with witnesses and suspected perpetrators may involve formal interviews during which the interviewee is asked a series of questions about the incident. One of the most important aspects of these types of interviews is for the interviewer to build and maintain rapport with the person being interviewed. Building rapport can also be beneficial in personal relationships, but professional interviewers generally will emphasize caution with regard to trying to use their techniques. In other words, "Don't try this at home."

The following list is not intended to be all-inclusive, but rather a sample of some of the planning that is required and utilized by professionals in order to detect lies so that they can get at the truth.

Recommended:

- Prepare a list of interview questions in advance with a focus on the information needed from this particular person.

- It can be helpful for the interviewer to have one of their coworkers in the interview room to serve as a scribe for taking notes. This person is only to take notes and not to participate in the interview.

- Identify where the interview will be conducted. It should be comfortable and quiet, preferably private so that other employees do not see who is being interviewed.

- There are advantages and disadvantages to interviewing a person in their own environment versus a room set up specifically for an interview. For example, a CEO could be interviewed in his/her office such that the interviewer could observe photographs and other memorabilia that might give clues about how embezzled assets were spent. However, there might be numerous interruptions in that kind of setting.

- Spend a few minutes building rapport with the person being interviewed. Simple topics such as the weather or traffic can help that person feel like they have something in common with the interviewer.

Not recommended:

- Do not say, "We're conducting an investigation." Wording should be more generic, such as "We're reviewing some procedures at your company."

- Do not close the door or block the exit. Interviewees must be allowed to leave at any time.

- Do not interrupt. Even if the interviewee is going a bit astray from the question asked, they may provide valuable information about the incident.

This section provides only a brief glimpse into the work that must be done by professionals for whom lie detection is an important aspect of their job. It takes years of specialized training and experience to conduct interviews successfully.

INTERROGATIONS BY LAW ENFORCEMENT

When lie detection is part of a person's job duties, as in the law enforcement arena, the process assumes special characteristics that are not present in everyday lie detection. "Interrogations" are special types of interviews designed *to obtain an admission of guilt* from the person being questioned. We will explore the unique characteristics of law enforcement and military interrogations in this section.

Pre-Interrogation Interview

In an interrogation, interviewers assume suspects are guilty, so their task is to persuade them to voluntarily confess (i.e., without the use of coercion, force, or threat). Some interrogations, however, are preceded by a pre-interrogation interview designed to gather information on someone's potential guilt or innocence (who, at this stage, is merely a "person of interest" rather than a suspect). If interviewers do not find reasons to suspect guilt, the person is sent home; if they suspect the interviewee is involved in the crime, then a formal interrogation is pursued (see next section).

There can be two major problems with pre-interrogation interviews:

- Interviewers may not always enter these interviews in a pure fact-finding state of mind. The interview is conducted with the belief that the interviewee had something to do with the crime. Adopting this "guilty" mindset can bias every aspect of the interview.

- What's worse, this biased mindset is too often accompanied by poor police training about behaviors associated with deception and a tendency by police officers to be overconfident about their ability to detect deception based on behavioral observation. As a result, interrogators may confidently perceive deceptive behavior at this stage when it simply isn't there—e.g., thinking a person shouldn't be as nervous as he or she appears (Elaad, 2003; Kassin, 2005).

Interrogating a Suspect

When a person of interest becomes a suspect, he or she is supposed to be presented with their "Miranda rights" before a formal interrogation can begin (*Miranda v. Arizona*, 1966). Thinking they have nothing to fear, 81% of people who later turn out to have been innocent waive these rights. The opposite is the case for those who turned out to be guilty; only 36% of them waived their Miranda rights (Kassin & Gudjonsson, 2004).

As we noted above, interrogations are typically conducted as though the suspect were guilty. Sometimes this triggers a self-fulfilling prophecy—i.e., the interrogator acting as if a person is guilty causes the suspect to act in ways that make them seem guilty. The presumption of guilt can be a powerful factor in blinding an interrogator to information that would normally cast doubt on the suspect's guilt. For example, when an innocent person falsely confesses to a crime, he or she may get key facts wrong that go unnoticed by the interrogator—even something as obvious as saying a victim who was known to have been shot once was shot multiple times (see "False Confessions" later in this chapter).

Bruce Boardman, a retired police interrogator in Austin, Texas, says that law enforcement officers need to consider the following when conducting an interrogation:

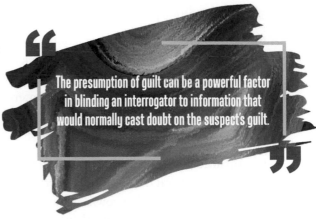

The presumption of guilt can be a powerful factor in blinding an interrogator to information that would normally cast doubt on the suspect's guilt.

- The goal or goals of the interrogation should be clear in the interrogator's mind. Not all questions will be directly related to these goals, but it is important to know what you want the questioning to produce.

- Start with easy questions. The first goal is to get the suspect used to talking.

- The lives that many suspects lead involve little recognition of their humanity. Sometimes interrogators can capitalize on this and obtain the information they desire by treating them in a compassionate manner.

- Make lying an issue. Tell the suspect that truth telling will make the interview go smoothly, but if you catch him or her lying about a small thing, you know they'll lie about bigger things and that won't be good.

- Different crimes may require different approaches. Burglars may not feel much guilt for their crime. *After all*, they might reason, *other people have more than I do so what's wrong with redistributing the wealth?* With this kind of crime, an interrogator may have to make the suspect believe that burglary is a serious offense. On the other hand, when a sex crime is involved, the guilt may already be so overwhelming for the suspect that the interrogator needs to play down the terrible nature of the crime in order to get the suspect to talk—e.g., "I can understand how a person who was subjected to as much child abuse as you were could do something like this. Under those same conditions, any of us might have done the same thing."

- Eliminate distractions in the interrogation room. Have the suspect face you with a blank wall behind you. Sometimes another officer is in the room. Sometimes it may be necessary to invade the suspect's personal space as part of the effort to break down his or her defenses.

- When the suspect begins to talk about the crime, do not interrupt. You can always go back later to flesh out details.

Interrogation Strategies

Interrogations involve isolation, confrontation, and other tactics—all designed to elicit a confession. The basic paradigm is to break down the suspect's defenses and then to build trust with the interrogator (Kassin, 1997; 2005; Kassin & Gudjonsson, 2004; Sargant, 1957/1997). There are numerous strategies used by interrogators to uncover lies and encourage a suspect to confess. Kalbfleisch (1994) identified 38 different strategies, but most of them can be distilled into the following broad categories:

- **Intimidation.** The aim of this tactic is to break down the suspect's defenses. It can be done in several different ways. Attacking the person and what they say is one way—e.g., "Don't lie to me, you coward!" Intimidation can also be accomplished by pointing out inconsistencies in a suspect's story and challenging the suspect to explain them. If the suspect omits or distorts any information, no matter how small, this can be used to charge him or her with lying about other things. After talking loudly to the suspect for a time, interrogators can also intimidate a suspect by suddenly staring at them in silence after a suspect's response. Sometimes interrogators will put pressure on a suspect by telling him or her that they are exhibiting deceptive behavior—e.g., "You're sweating" or "When I asked you about X you sure did take a long time to answer. Why was that?"

- **Persuasive appeals.** Interrogators also use various persuasive appeals to get suspects to tell the truth or confess to a crime. The following four appeals are common:

  1. A friendly approach is sometimes effective. The interrogator may express empathy ("I know what you're going through and it must be painful"), the desire to help ("I'm concerned about you. Confess and let me help you"), or praise ("I believe deep down you're a good guy; the kind of guy who wants to do the right thing").

  2. Sometimes the interrogator stresses the futility of resisting—e.g., "Don't make a bad situation worse. We're going to find out what happened with you or without you so why keep fighting it?"

  3. Making truth telling and/or confessing sound like a way to relieve the suspect's discomfort is another common appeal—e.g., "Believe me, confession is good for the soul. You'll feel better about yourself and you'll help your family get closure." The familiar "good cop/bad cop" routine is another method designed to give the suspect a way of relieving the discomfort created by the bad cop by confessing to the good cop.

  4. Sometimes interrogators try to minimize the severity of the crime in order to gain a confession. This can be done by telling the suspect that he or she was overwhelmed by circumstances (drugs, alcohol, peer pressure) and that others have done much worse. An interrogator may even hint that what happened might have been an accident.

- **Lies and deception**. Interrogators may say they have an eyewitness or a fingerprint when they don't; they may tell one of several suspects that he or she is the only one who is denying involvement in the crime when that isn't true; or they may test a suspect's truthfulness by distorting information in a question—e.g., Knowing that Person X had a broken *leg*, the interrogator may say, "You told us you saw Person X last week. Did she still have the cast on her arm at that time?" (The next section discusses deceptive strategies in detail).

Kassin (2007) and his colleagues surveyed more than 600 police interrogators to find out what techniques they used and how often, and what they believed about interrogation practices in general. If this is a topic that interests you, reviewing their findings (QR) would be a good way to educate yourself on the history of the various issues associated with it.

Deceptive Interrogation Strategies

Several strategies identified by Kassin and Kalbfleisch (above) as well as Leo (1996) show interrogators using deceit themselves as one of the means of uncovering a suspect's deception or to elicit a confession. This revelation comes as a shock to some people who often respond by asking if it's legal. In general, courts in the United States have answered "yes" to this question:

- *Lewis v. United States* (1966): "Misrepresentation by a police officer or agent concerning the identity of the purchaser of illegal narcotics is a practical necessity" (385 U.S. 206).

- *Frazier v. Cupp* (1969): The use of deception should be evaluated on the "totality of circumstances" and is generally acceptable unless it is done in such a way that would "be apt to make an innocent person confess" or "shock the conscience of the court or community" (394 U.S. 731).

- *United States v. Russell* (1973): "There are circumstances when the use of deceit is the only practicable law enforcement technique available" (411 U.S. 423).

A key example of the courts saying "no" to the permissibility of deception came in *Florida v. Cayward* (1989), in which law enforcement's use of deception clearly violated the practical guidelines set forth in the above rulings. In that particular case, the police produced fabricated laboratory reports—in other words, they manufactured evidence. That, said the court, was not the same as verbal deceit.

In the end, law enforcement officers would do well to study and learn the established case law in their particular jurisdictions (Van Brocklin, 2014). Because no two investigations are the same, what constitutes a coerced confession (illegal) versus a voluntary one (legal) is likely to vary from case to case.

Police manuals, according to Shuy (1998), advise against making promises or threats, but permit flattery, rough talk, trickery, accusations, and lies. So it would be *illegal* for a police interrogator to say, for example, "If you confess we'll make sure you get a lighter sentence," or "You wouldn't want cocaine found in your son's car would you?" It would, however, be perfectly legal for an interrogator to:

- Lie to a suspect about having evidence that does not actually exist—e.g., "We have your fingerprints on the murder weapon" or "The person you were with that night said you did it."

- Lie by saying that several other investigators have been working on this case and they have all concluded that the suspect is guilty.

- Falsely tell a male rape suspect that the victim was a prostitute with the expectation that the suspect will confess to what he now thinks is a lesser crime (Barker & Carter, 1990).

Other less obtrusive, but equally deceptive, information-gathering methods can be used to supplement the interrogation process:

- For example, the Israeli General Security Services has reportedly promised prisoners their freedom if they are able to obtain specific information from another prisoner that can be validated (Bowden, 2003).

- In another instance, several listening devices are planted in such a way that they are likely to be discovered by the prisoners while others that would record their conversations remain well hidden (Bowden, 2003).

- Another useful tactic is to deliberately omit information authorities already know. Research conducted by Granhag, Strömwall, Willén, and Hartwig (2013) showed how potentially deceptive techniques such as strategic use of evidence (SUE) and framing are advantageous to the interrogation process.

SUE concerns how and when interrogators choose to present the accused with the evidence against him or her. How evidence is presented is particularly important because it can directly affect how, when, or even if, a suspect confesses. As an interview/interrogation tactic, SUE was specifically developed as a way to help detect deception on the part of the accused

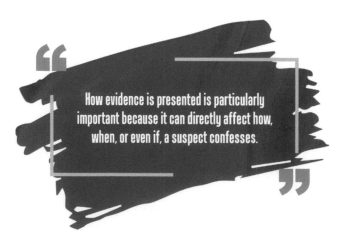

How evidence is presented is particularly important because it can directly affect how, when, or even if, a suspect confesses.

(Hartwig, Granhag, Strömwall, & Vrij, 2005). There are two basic methods of strategic disclosure: late and gradual (as opposed to the traditional, nonstrategic approach of presenting all the evidence up front).

The first premise underlying techniques like SUE is that would-be lie catchers who want to improve their accuracy have to take an active role in the detection process—creating situations that produce meaningful behavioral differences between liars and truth tellers (Levine, 2014). The second premise is that, under the right conditions, liars experience a heavier cognitive load than non-deceivers; therefore, their behaviors and/or verbal patterns may be different enough to allow interviewers to distinguish between them more accurately (Hartwig, Granhag, & Luke, 2014; Zuckerman, DePaulo, & Rosenthal, 1981).

Cognitive techniques like SUE are intended to get inside the heads of truth tellers and deceivers, putting cognitive obstacles in their way, and having investigators pay careful attention to how they choose to navigate around those obstacles. The theory suggests that a truth teller is likely to exhibit a different set of verbal behaviors in response to unexpected questions—such as asking them to retell the sequence of events in reverse order—since such inquiries are likely to be more difficult for liars to answer (Vrij, Fisher, & Blank, 2015).

© Lightspring/Shutterstock.com

There is some evidence that training in SUE can significantly improve an interviewer's accuracy in detecting deception. One study reported an accuracy rate of 65% for SUE-trained interviewers, compared to 43% for untrained interviewers (Luke et al., 2016).

Torture

The important question, of course, is whether torture, no matter what methods are included, gets a person to tell the truth or confess. Police and military interrogation experts do not think torture is always the best way to elicit truthful information. During World War II, the Nazis arrived at the same conclusion. Under torture, people will confess to anything and say whatever their captors want to hear. It is also a process that can have detrimental effects on the people doing it, and it provides a justification for one's enemies to also use torture. According to Bowden (2003), no law can be sufficiently nuanced to cover all situations in which torture might be appropriate. So he believes we should agree to ban torture, recognizing that military interrogators may sometimes engage in behavior

that could be labeled torture in certain cases. Under this scenario, a court would subsequently consider the circumstances of the case and determine whether such methods were called for or not.

What constitutes torture? Not everyone agrees. Extreme interrogation methods use physical, social, and psychological methods to break down the resistance of prisoners, make them feel they are no longer in control of their environment, instill fear, and then promise to help them out of their despair if they cooperate. Some believe these objectives can be achieved with "moderate physical pressure" that they do not consider "severe" enough to be torture. Those who subscribe to this "torture lite" regimen would not include the following as torture: sleep deprivation; isolation from human contact; questioning for 20 hours straight; exposure to extreme heat or cold; the use of drugs to cause confusion; rough treatment in the form of slapping, shoving, or shaking; and forcing a prisoner to stand or sit in uncomfortable positions for long periods of time. On the other hand, fewer disagree that such tactics as pulling out fingernails, maiming, burning, and sending electric shocks to a person's genitals constitute torture.

Confessions

A confession is a powerful form of evidence. For a jury, a confession of guilt will likely overshadow other strong evidence of a person's innocence.

Why Do People Confess?

Whether guilty or innocent, people make confessions for a variety of reasons (Kassin & Gudjonsson, 2004). Gudjonsson and Sigurdsson (1999) found confessions attributable to three sources. By far the most influential is the perceived *weight of the evidence* against the suspect. If the suspect is convinced that it is powerful, he or she is more likely to perceive the futility in professing innocence. They call the second factor *external pressure.* External pressure comes from

© igorstevanovic/Shutterstock.com

interrogation techniques and a suspect's fear of what the police might do if he or she doesn't confess. The third factor involves *internal pressure*. Internal pressure refers to guilt and other emotions experienced by the suspect and the extent to which these feelings can be alleviated by a confession. Internal pressure is illustrated in the first three examples below, whereas external pressure is exemplified by the last two examples:

- **Seeking notoriety.** There are always some people who voluntarily confess to crimes they did not commit. When there is a lot of publicity about the case, there are even more people willing to admit they committed the crime. Unmet needs for recognition or acceptance are behind some of these confessions; others may be related to some pathological need for self-punishment.

- **Individual personalities and dispositions.** The interrogation process is designed to persuade the suspect to confess and some people are more compliant and suggestible than others. This includes both guilty and innocent suspects. Their suggestibility is exacerbated by such things as sleep deprivation and isolation (Gudjonsson, 2003). Naïveté, anxiety, and diminished mental abilities may also make a person prone to confess. On the other hand, highly dogmatic people with strong beliefs may resist confessing for a long time. Confessions may also be difficult to obtain from people with fewer emotional attachments.

- **Trying to protect someone else.** Sometimes people who share the guilt with others will protect them by making a confession that excludes them. But an innocent person may also try to protect a person he or she thinks (or knows) is guilty by confessing to a crime.

- **Confusion and misunderstanding.** The process of being physically restrained and interrogated can be a chaotic process, calling for rapid decisions about a variety of unfamiliar matters. These are not ideal conditions for rational decision-making. In addition to facing a confusing and possibly unfamiliar situation, suspects are sometimes confronted with trickery and deceit by interrogators. Confused and anxious suspects may hear an interrogator say, "If you confess, we'll be done with you and you can get out of here." In the heat of the moment, the suspect may mistakenly think this means he or she can go home instead of to jail. When an interrogator falsely makes a suspect believe there is evidence that he or she committed the crime, both guilty and innocent people may confess. An innocent person may seriously question their own memory. Kassin and Gudjonsson (2004) tell of a 14-year-old boy who was falsely told that his hair was found in his dead sister's hand, that her blood was in his bedroom, and that he failed a polygraph exam. The boy thought he had a split personality and confessed to the crime.

- **Seeking relief.** People also confess because they are looking for a way to deal with a physically and mentally exhausting situation. A feeling of isolation and hopelessness brought on by the interrogation process can trigger confessions from both guilty and not guilty suspects. The innocent suspect realizes that repeated denials are not providing the desired relief so confession begins to look like a way to cope with the situation. When interrogators make a suspect believe that there is plenty of evidence to convict, an innocent suspect may think: "Even though I didn't do it, nobody will believe me so I might as well make a deal by confessing." Sometimes interrogators facilitate confessions by suggesting that confession will lead to more leniency. If the evidence against them is strong and there is, in fact, some leniency in exchange for a confession, suspects at the top of an organizational hierarchy are likely to jump at the chance rather than endure the strain of further interrogation.

False Confessions

People have confessed to murdering a person who was still alive and to crimes that occurred when there was strong evidence that they were nowhere near the scene of the crime when it was committed. Confessing to something we didn't do seems like an impossible scenario to most of us. However, it has happened to enough innocent people to justify asking if there are conditions under which any of us would do the same thing. As it turns out, under the right conditions almost anyone might make a false confession. Some people do it because they are sensation seekers, but the most vulnerable seem to be:

... under the right conditions almost anyone might make a false confession.

- Teenagers
- People who are easily persuaded
- People who reach a point where they think it is futile to declare their innocence any longer
- People who are afraid or have a low tolerance for confrontation and conflict
- People with mental disabilities

False confessions have been found to occur more frequently during interrogations of young, vulnerable suspects. In 2016, the *Los Angeles Times* reported on law professor James Duane's analysis of 125 proven false confessions in which he found that:

- 33% of the suspects were juveniles when they confessed, and
- 43% were mentally disabled or ill when they confessed.

The same article (QR) cited another study of 340 false admissions of guilt, 42% of which were done by juveniles (Duane, 2016). The article is based on Duane's book, *You Have the Right to Remain Innocent*. In it, he provides a particularly remarkable example of how an interrogation can lead to a false confession. A 16-year-old named Felix was interrogated by police late at night without an attorney or a parent present. After many hours of interrogation, Felix confessed on videotape to committing a murder. It was later found that he was incarcerated at a juvenile detention facility when the murder was committed. After that fact came to light, the murder charges were dismissed. This example shows the amount of pressure that can be placed on suspects by police interrogators.

Federal and local law enforcement agencies conduct their interrogations by relying on the structure of the *Reid technique* (Inbau et al., 2001) or the *behavioral analysis interview*. Using these methods, interrogators rely on accusations of guilt. Sympathy, crafting messages that morally justify the crime or explain how motives could justify one's actions, and rapport building are also used to instill a value in truth telling during the interrogation. These interrogation techniques may solicit false confessions because they are confrontational, potentially coercive, and highly suggestive (Kassin et al., 2010). In fact, Wright, Nash, and Wade (2015) found that the suggestive power of these interrogation techniques can even lead *witnesses* to corroborate false allegations.

With the advent of DNA testing, a number of convictions based on false confessions have been uncovered. Between 1971 and 2002, there have been 125 proven false confessions, 81% of them for murder (Kassin & Gudjonsson, 2004). A study of wrongful convictions for violent crimes in Illinois from 1989 to 2010 found 33 cases that involved false confessions (Anyaso, 2011).

> Between 1971 and 2002, there have been 125 proven false confessions, 81% of them for murder.

One of the most famous false confession cases involved five young men between the ages of 14 and 16 who confessed to the rape and brutal assault of a jogger in New York City's Central Park in 1989 (Kassin & Gudjonsson, 2004). The jogger was unable to identify her attacker(s), so the confessions were extremely influential in convicting the teens and sending them to jail—especially given that there was no physical evidence linking any of them to the crime. Four of the suspects each spent about 7 years in prison and the fifth approximately 13 years. They became known as the Central Park Five and were the subject of a documentary (QR) by Ken Burns in 2012.

In 2002, 13 years after their convictions, a man named Matias Reyes admitted that he alone raped the woman, and tests of his DNA confirmed it. The convictions of the Central Park Five were vacated and they sued the City of New York in 2003. In 2014, the city agreed to a $41 million settlement with the Five for wrongful incarceration, but would not admit to mishandling the case (Weiser, 2014).

Why did the Central Park Five confess to a crime they didn't commit? They initially denied the attack, but after many hours of being interrogated separately, denied of food, drink, and sleep, each boy eventually confessed. In theory, a true confession would contain information that the perpetrator alone would know. But sometimes interrogators, intentionally or not, provide information about the crime that suspects incorporate into their confession. There were many discrepancies in the teens' stories, but these were discounted by prosecutors:

- One of the teens initially tried to confess by saying the woman's head injuries were caused by punching. Later, when he was asked "Don't you remember somebody using a brick or stone?," he said the injuries were caused by a rock. Still later he indicated a brick was used.

- One said he remembered cutting the victim's clothes off with knife, but there were no knife cuts on the clothing.

- Two of the young men were taken to the park and each pointed in a different direction when asked where the crime took place.

- One said the victim wore blue shorts and a T-shirt. She was actually wearing long black tights and a long-sleeve jersey.

- Before his confession, another was taken to the crime scene and shown photos of the victim, making it difficult to know what he gleaned from this information and what he knew prior to that.

Back in 1989, when the Five were first accused, prominent New York City resident Donald J. Trump spent $85,000 to place full-page ads in four local newspapers. Referring to them as "muggers and murderers" (though not by name), Trump wrote that such people "should be forced to suffer and, when they kill, they should be executed for their crimes" (Hijazi, 2018). A month before the 2016 presidential election, Trump doubled-down on his original position, telling CNN, "They admitted they were guilty," and, "the police doing the original investigation say they were guilty. The fact that that case was settled with so much evidence against them is outrageous" (Burns, 2016). What evidence then-candidate Trump was referring to remains unclear.

Another well-known false confession case involved a 1997 murder of a woman in Norfolk, Virginia (Bennett, 2005). This case began with one sailor who said he was at home in bed with his wife when the crime occurred. The wife's account was not taken before she died of cancer three months later. During his interrogation, he was falsely told that the police had an eyewitness who saw him leave the victim's apartment. He took a polygraph test and was falsely told that he failed it. He began to question his own memory and was told that, unless he confessed, he'd face the death penalty. After 13 hours of interrogation, the sailor confessed. But his DNA was not a match, so the police proceeded on the assumption that he did not act alone. A friend of his who was described as "slow" and easily persuadable due to a previous head injury was then interrogated. His defense was that he was on duty—a claim that was not checked. After hours of questioning, the second sailor also confessed, but his DNA was not a match. This led to an interrogation of a third and fourth sailor, each of whom confessed, even though their DNA did not match that at the crime scene. In 1999, a convicted rapist admitted that he alone had committed the crime and his DNA was a match. However, after his initial confession he changed his story to include the other sailors. Later he said his inclusion of the other sailors was at the request of the police. In 2006, the case of Derek Tice, the fourth sailor convicted, was overturned because police continued to interrogate him after he invoked his Miranda right to remain silent and his lawyer did not object to the admission of his subsequent confession as evidence in court.

Reducing the Number of False Confessions

There are a number of changes in the way interrogations are conducted that could reduce the number of false confessions (Kassin & Gudjonsson, 2004). Most interrogations are between 2 and 4 hours in length, but false confessions often take much longer, averaging 16+ hours. This suggests that the physical and psychological toll associated with very long interrogations is high enough to lead to false confessions. The tactic of presenting false evidence and lying to the suspect substantially increases the number of false confessions and

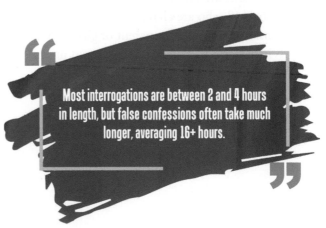

Most interrogations are between 2 and 4 hours in length, but false confessions often take much longer, averaging 16+ hours.

should be minimized. Some European law enforcement agencies do not permit this tactic. In addition, outright promises of leniency or implied leniency (e.g., telling the suspect that his crime was an accident or morally justified and that a jury will be lenient with him if he confesses) also cause innocent people to confess and courts will now reject confessions in which leniency was directly stated.

Video and/or audio recording of the interrogation process could also be a way of reducing false confessions. At the same time, it reduces the number of appeals, charges of misconduct, and increases the number of guilty pleas. Recording frees the interrogator from taking notes and provides an opportunity to view the video again in order to review key segments. Recorded interrogations can be beneficial for everyone involved—suspects, lawyers, juries, police officers, and judges. Over 20 states require recording during interrogations, and in 2014 the U.S. Department of Justice required all of its federal agencies to record interrogations. However, many of these mandates to require recording do not specify between audio and video formats. Great Britain and U.S. states such as Minnesota, Maine, Alaska, and Illinois require video recording of interrogations in capital cases. Police forces in some large U.S. cities also use video recording.

One area of controversy has to do with when the taping should begin—at the beginning of the interrogation or when the confession begins. If the confession is the only thing recorded, this likely will not decrease charges of coercion during the interrogation (Peres & Pallasch, 1998). When the interrogation is video recorded, researchers also say that the video should focus on both the interrogator and the suspect because observers (juries) tend to underestimate the amount of pressure exerted by the interrogator when the camera focuses entirely on the suspect (Lassiter, Slaw, Briggs, & Scanlan, 1992).

Very young children are especially susceptible to interrogation techniques designed to elicit a confession, and this has prompted new ways of dealing with such situations. Children younger than 13 who are charged with murder or sex crimes must be represented by a lawyer during interrogation, and a parent or guardian is required for felony cases. California enacted a statute in 2013 requiring interrogations of juveniles in homicide investigations to be video recorded.

SUMMARY

- People use various methods when attempting to determine if someone is deceiving them. One common method is to observe the target's nonverbal behavior and to listen to what he or she says. Research tells us that most people aren't particularly skilled at distinguishing liars and truth tellers simply by observing their behavior, with the majority scoring slightly better than chance (53–57%). Because judgments are usually affected by the truth bias, people may identify truth tellers at a much higher rate (67–68%) than liars (37–44%).

- In addition to the truth bias, there are many other reasons associated with our cognitions and perceptual processes that contribute to our lack of skill in identifying liars based on their behavior. Research indicates that relying on what sources say in context increases lie detection accuracy. For those people who engage in lie detection as part of their job, their accuracy rates are somewhat higher, but they too are plagued by problems that inhibit high rates of detection. Training may be able to improve a person's lie detection skills, but we won't know how much impact training has until further studies are conducted. There may be some people whose lie detection skills are extremely high. These "wizards" are at least 80% accurate in judging some types of lies, although their actual existence is regarded as doubtful by some researchers.

- Unassisted lie detection in police and military interrogations differs markedly from everyday lie detection. These interrogations often employ methods to break down a suspect's defenses as well as efforts to build trust. Questioning strategies typically involve intimidation, persuasive appeals, as well as lying and deception. Research shows that active questioning and the strategic use of information during interrogations significantly increase accuracy rates during lie detection. Legally, interrogators are allowed to tell suspects they have evidence against them that they do not have. Although the United States maintains it does not torture military detainees, there is evidence that it has occurred in recent years even though experts say it can elicit invalid information.

- For police and military interrogators, the observation of deceitful behavior is only important as it relates to a confession of guilt. As a result, an overly zealous interrogator can induce an innocent person to confess to a crime he or she didn't commit. Guilty or innocent, people may confess because they think the weight of evidence is against them, because the interrogation strategies have been persuasive, and/or because the suspect has certain personal characteristics and/or agendas that lead him or her to confess. False confessions might be reduced by not allowing interrogators to tell suspects they have evidence that they do not have, by eliminating marathon interrogation sessions, and by video recording both interrogator and suspect.

EXERCISES

1. Make a list of a few situations where someone lied to you about something meaningful. How did you discover the truth? Did you know they were lying to you at the time? How? Briefly describe how you discovered the truth and whether the method(s) were discussed in this chapter.

2. Do you believe there are any circumstances in which torturing a suspect in order to get him or her to tell the truth would be justified? What about an interviewer or interrogator lying to a suspect? If yes, what are those circumstances? If no, why not?

3. Do you think there are any conditions under which you would confess to a crime you did not commit? If you answered no, why not? If you answered yes, what are the conditions?

4. Would you like to be a wizard at lie detection? Why or why not? How accurate would you like to be in identifying liars by observing their nonverbal and verbal behavior? Why? How accurate would you like most people to be? Why? (Use a 1–100% scale for your answers, with 100% being completely accurate all the time.)

5. Ralph Waldo Emerson wrote in his Essay VII, "Prudence": "Every violation of truth is not only a sort of suicide in the liar, but a stab at the health of human society." Do you agree? Why or why not?

OF INTEREST

Noah Zandan's Ted-Ed lesson, "The Language of Lying" (QR), is premised on the notion (discussed in this chapter) that liars experience a greater cognitive load then truth tellers, and that this can create linguistic differences in their stories that can be discovered using certain techniques.

In this "Top-25" TED Talk (QR), Pamela Meyer summarizes deception detection techniques described in her 2010 book, *Liespotting*. Meyer draws on her own background as a certified fraud examiner and is the CEO of Calibrate, a company that specializes in deception detection training.

This link is the listing for James Duane's book (QR) *You Have the Right to Remain Innocent* (2016), referenced earlier in the chapter. Duane and his colleagues take a hard line against the commonly accepted idea that innocent people have nothing to lose by talking to investigators.

REFERENCES

Alford, C. F. (2001). *Whistleblowers: Broken lives and organizational power.* Ithaca, NY: Cornell University Press.

Anyaso, H. H. (2011, June 20). The high cost of wrongful convictions in Illinois. Dollars wasted, lives lost & ruined, justice run amok: A landmark investigation. *Northwestern University.* Retrieved from http://www.northwestern.edu/newscenter/stories/2011/

Associated Press. (2017, July 21). Wells Fargo ordered to reinstate whistleblower, pay $577,500. *The Seattle Times.* Retrieved from http://www.seattletimes.com

Bagli, C. V. (2017, September 1). If not for "The Jinx," Robert Durst may have avoided murder charges. *The New York Times.* Retrieved from http://www.nytimes.com

Bagli, C. V. (2019, April 24). As Durst murder case goes forward, HBO's film will also be on trial. *The New York Times.* Retrieved from http://www.nytimes.com

Barker, T., & Carter, D. (1990). "Fluffing up the evidence and covering your ASS": Some conceptual notes on police lying. *Deviant Behavior, 11,* 61–73. https://dx.doi.org/10.1080/01639625.1990.9967832

Barrera, M., & Hughes, J. (2014, May 20). Top 30 whistleblowing statutes—from Ralph Nader to Edward Snowden. *Global Workplace Insider.* Retrieved from https://www.globalworkplaceinsider.com

Bennett, B. (2005, December 12). True confessions? *Time Magazine,* pp. 45–46.

Blair, J. P., Levine, T. R., & Shaw, A. S. (2010). Content in context improves deception detection accuracy. *Human Communication Research, 36,* 423–442. https://dx.doi.org/10.1111/j.1468-2958.2010.01382.x

Blair, J. P., Levine, T. R., & Vasquez, B. E. (2015). Producing deception detection expertise. *Policing: An International Journal of Police Strategies & Management, 38,* 71–85. https://dx.doi.org/10.1108/pijpsm-09-2014-0092

Bond, C. F., Jr., & Atoum, A. O. (2000). International deception. *Personality and Social Psychology Bulletin, 26,* 385–395. https://dx.doi.org/10.1177/0146167200265010

Bond, C. F., Jr., & DePaulo, B. M. (2006). Accuracy of deception judgments. *Personality and Social Psychology Review 10,* 214–234. https://dx.doi.org/10.1207/s15327957pspr1003_2a

Bond, C. F., Jr., & DePaulo, B. M. (2008). Individual differences in judging deception: Accuracy and bias, *Psychological Bulletin, 134,* 477–492. https://dx.doi.org/10.1037/0033-2909.134.4.477

Bond, C. F., Jr., Levine, T. R., & Hartwig, M. (2015). New findings in nonverbal lie detection. In P. A. Granhag, A. Vrij, & B. Verschuere (Eds.), *Detection deception: Current challenges and cognitive approaches* (pp. 37–58). Hoboken, NJ: Wiley & Sons. https://dx.doi.org/10.1002/9781118510001.ch2

Bond, C. F., Jr., Omar, A., Pitre, U., & Lashley, B. R. (1992). Fishy-looking liars: Deception judgment from expectancy violation. *Journal of Personality and Social Psychology, 63,* 969–977. https://dx.doi.org/10.1037/0022-3514.63.6.969

Bond, C. F., Jr., & Uysal, A. (2007). On lie detection wizards. *Law and Human Behavior, 31,* 109–115. https://dx.doi.org/10.1007/s10979-006-9016-1

Bond, C. F., Jr., & Rao, S. R. (2004). Lies travel: Mendacity in a mobile world. In P. A. Granhag & L. A. Strömwall (Eds.), *The detection of deception in forensic contexts* (pp. 127–147). New York, NY: Cambridge University Press. https://dx.doi.org/10.1017/cbo9780511490071.006

Bond, G. D., Malloy, D. M., Thompson, L. A., Arias, E. A., & Nunn, S. N. (2004). Post-probe decision making in a prison context. *Communication Monographs, 71,* 269–285. https://dx.doi.org/10.1080/0363452042000288328

Bond, G. D., Malloy, D. M., Arias, E. A., Nunn, S. N., & Thompson, L. A. (2005). Lie-based decision making in prison. *Communication Reports, 18,* 9–19. https://dx.doi.org/10.1080/08934210500084180

Bowden, M. (2003, October). The dark art of interrogation. *The Atlantic Monthly, 292,* 51–76.

Burgoon, J. K., Buller, D. B., & Floyd, K. (2001). Does participation affect deception success? A test of the interactivity principle. *Human Communication Research, 27,* 503–534. https://dx.doi.org/10.1111/j.1468-2958.2001.tb00791.x

Burns, S. (2016, October 17). Why Trump doubled down on the Central Park Five. *The New York Times.* Retrieved from http://www.nytimes.com

Carnegie Council for Ethics in International Affairs. (2017, July 9). Jeffrey S. Wigand: Lecturer, expert witness, and consultant on tobacco issues. Retrieved from http://www.carnegiecouncil.org

Carr, R. (2005, December 11). In federal job: Blow whistle, get boot. *Austin American Statesman,* pp. A1, A6.

Cheng, K. H. W., & Broadhurst, R. (2005). The detection of deception: The effects of first and second language on lie detection ability. *Psychiatry, Psychology and Law, 12*(1), 107–118.

DePaulo, B. M. (1994). Spotting lies: Can humans learn to do better? *Current Directions in Psychological Science, 3*(3), 83–86. https://dx.doi.org/10.1111%2F1467-8721.ep10770433

DePaulo, B. M., & Jordan, A. (1982). Age changes in deceiving and detecting deceit. In R. S. Feldman (Ed.), *Development of nonverbal behavior in children* (pp. 151–180). New York, NY: Springer-Verlag. https://dx.doi.org/10.1007/978-1-4757-1761-7_6

DePaulo, B. M., Lindsay, J. J., Malone, B. E., Muhlenbruck, L., Charlton, K., & Cooper, H. (2003). Cues to deception. *Psychological Bulletin, 129,* 74–118. https://dx.doi.org/10.1037/0033-2909.129.1.74

DePaulo, B. M., & Morris, W. L. (2004). Discerning lies from truths: Behavioural cues to deception and the indirect pathway of intuition. In P. A. Granhag & L. A. Strömwall, (Eds.), *The detection*

of deception in forensic contexts (pp. 15–40). New York, NY: Cambridge University Press. https://dx.doi.org/10.1017/cbo9780511490071.002

deTurck, M. A., Harzlak, J. J., Bodhorn, D. J., & Texter, L. A. (1990). The effects of training social perceivers to detect deception from behavioral cues. *Communication Quarterly, 38,* 189–199. https://dx.doi.org/10.1080/01463379009369753

Duane, J. (2016, August 26). Innocent? Don't talk to the police. *Los Angeles Times.* Retrieved from http://www.latimes.com

Dunbar, N. E., Ramirez, A., Jr., & Burgoon, J. K. (2003). The effects of participation on the ability to judge deceit. *Communication Reports, 16,* 23–33. https://dx.doi.org/10.1080/08934210309384487

Ekman, P. (1996). Why don't we catch liars? *Social Research, 63,* 801–817. https://www.jstor.org/stable/40972316

Ekman, P. (2001). *Telling lies: Clues to deceit in the marketplace, politics, and marriage.* New York, NY: Norton.

Ekman, P., & Friesen, W. V. (1978). *Facial action coding system (FACS): A technique for the measurement of facial movement.* Palo Alto, CA: Consulting Psychologists Press.

Ekman, P., & O'Sullivan, M. (1991). Who can catch a liar? *American Psychologist, 46,* 913–920. https://dx.doi.org/10.1037//0003-066x.46.9.913

Ekman, P., O'Sullivan, M., & Frank, M. G. (1999). A few can catch a liar. *Psychological Science, 10,* 263–266. https://dx.doi.org/10.1111/1467-9280.00147

Elaad, E. (2003). Effects of feedback on the overestimated capacity to detect lies and the underestimated ability to tell lies. *Applied Cognitive Psychology, 17,* 349–363. https://dx.doi.org/10.1002/acp.871

Etcoff, N. L., Ekman, P., Magee, J. J., & Frank, M. G. (2000). Lie detection and language comprehension. *Nature, 405,* 139. https://dx.doi.org/10.1038/35012129

Feeley, T. H., & Young, M. J. (1998). Humans as lie detectors: Some more second thoughts. *Communication Quarterly, 46,* 109–126. https://dx.doi.org/10.1080/01463379809370090

Fischer, P., Krueger, J. I., Greitemeyer, T., Vogrincic, C., Kastenmüller, A., Frey, D., … Kainbacher, M. (2011). The bystander-effect: A meta-analytic review on bystander intervention in dangerous and non-dangerous emergencies. *Psychological Bulletin, 137*(4), 517–537. https://dx.doi.org/10.1037/a0023304

Florida v. Cayward, 552 So.2d 971 (1989) https://www.leagle.com/decision/19891523552so2d97111394

Frank, M. G., & Ekman, P. (1997). The ability to detect deceit generalizes across different types of high-stake lies. *Journal of Personality and Social Psychology, 72*(6), 1429–1439. https://dx.doi.org/10.1037//0022-3514.72.6.1429

Frank, M. G., & Feeley, T. H. (2003). To catch a liar: Challenges for research in lie detection training. *Journal of Applied Communication Research, 31,* 58–75. https://dx.doi.org/10.1080/00909880305377

Frank, M. G., Feeley, T. H., Paolantonio, N., & Servoss, T. J. (2004). Individual and small group accuracy in judging truthful and deceptive communication. *Group Decision and Negotiation, 13,* 45–59. https://dx.doi.org/10.1023/b:grup.0000011945.85141.af

Frazier v. Cupp, 394 U.S. 731 (1969) https://supreme.justia.com/cases/federal/us/394/731/

Gerber, M. (2018, April 16). Prosecutors lay out their case against Robert Durst, arguing he should stand trial for murder. *Los Angeles Times.* Retrieved from http://www.latimes.com

Gilbert, D. T., Krull, D. S., & Malone, P. S. (1990). Unbelieving the unbelievable: Some problems in the rejection of false information. *Journal of Personality and Social Psychology, 59,* 601–613. https://dx.doi.org/10.1037//0022-3514.59.4.601

Gilbert, D. T., Tafarodi, R. W., & Malone, P. S. (1993). You can't not believe everything you read. *Journal of Personality and Social Psychology, 65,* 221–233. https://dx.doi.org/10.1037//0022-3514.65.2.221

Glazer, M. P., & Glazer, P. M. (1989). *The whistleblowers.* New York, NY: Basic Books.

Grady, D. P. (1997). *Conversational strategies for detecting deception: An analysis of parent–adolescent child interactions.* Unpublished Ph.D. dissertation, University of Texas.

Granhag, P. A., Strömwall, L. A., Willén, R. M., & Hartwig, M. (2013). Eliciting cues to deception by tactical disclosure of evidence: The first test of the Evidence Framing Matrix. *Legal and Criminological Psychology, 18,* 341–355. https://dx.doi.org/10.1111/j.2044-8333.2012.02047.x

Griffin, D. J., & Frank, M. G. (2018). Intercultural communication schemas of deaf and hearing adults: Visuospatial decision-making during deception detection. *Journal of Intercultural Communication Research.* https://dx.doi.org/10.1080/17475759.2018.1507918

Gudjonsson, G. H. (2003). *The psychology of interrogations and conversions: A handbook.* New York, NY: Wiley.

Gudjonsson, G. H., & Sigurdsson, J. F. (1999). The Gudjonsson Confession Questionnaire-Revised (GCQ-R) factor structure and its relationship with personality. *Personality and Individual Differences, 27,* 953–968. https://dx.doi.org/10.1016/s0191-8869(98)00278-5

Harper, J. (2012, January 8). Hear the lonesome whistle blow: Workplace retaliation. *HuffPost.* Retrieved from http://www.huffpost.com

Hartwig, M., Granhag, P. A., & Luke, T. J. (2014). Strategic use of evidence during investigative interviews: The state of the science. In D. Raskin, C. Honts, & J. Kircher (Eds.), *Credibility Assessment,* (pp. 1–36). Cambridge, MA: Academic Press. https://dx.doi.org/10.1016/B978-0-12-394433-7.00001-4

Hartwig, M., Granhag, P. A., Strömwall, L. A., & Andersson, L. O. (2004). Suspicious minds: Criminals' ability to detect deception. *Psychology, Crime & Law, 10,* 83–95. https://dx.doi.org/10.1080/1068316031000095485

Hartwig, M. Granhag, P. A., Strömwall, L. A., & Vrij, A. (2005). Detecting deception via strategic disclosure of evidence. *Law and Human Behavior, 29*, 469–484. https://dx.doi.org/10.1007/s10979-005-5521-x

Hijazi, J. (2018, October 28). Trump wants to see the death penalty come "into vogue" again. He's wanted that for years. *Vox*. Retrieved from http://www.vox.com

Hurley, C. M., Anker, A. E., Frank, M. G., Matsumoto, D., & Hwang, H. C. (2014). Background factors predicting accuracy and improvement in micro expression recognition. *Motivation and Emotion, 38*, 700–714. https://dx.doi.org/10.1007/s11031-014-9410-9

Inbau, F. E., Reid, J. E., Buckley, J. P., & Jayne, B. P. (2001). *Criminal interrogation and confessions* (4th ed.). Gaithersburg, MD: Aspen.

Inglis-Arkell, E. (2014, May 16). The Othello error makes you sure everyone is lying. *Gizmodo*. Retrieved from http://www.io9.gizmodo.com

Innocence Project Staff. (2017, October 18). Massachusetts prosecutors dismiss indictment against George Perrot, concluding 30-year quest to prove his innocence. *The Innocence Project*. Retrieved from http://www.theinnocenceproject.org

Kassin, S. M. (1997). The psychology of confession evidence. *American Psychologist, 52*, 221–233. https://dx.doi.org/10.1037//0003-066x.52.3.221

Kassin, S. M. (2005). On the psychology of confessions: Does innocence put innocents at risk? *American Psychologist, 60*, 215–228. https://dx.doi.org/10.1037/0003-066x.60.3.215

Kassin, S. M., Drizin, S. A., Grisso, T., Gudjonsson, G. H., Leo, R. A., & Redlich, A. D. (2010). Police-induced confessions: Risk factors and recommendations. *Law and Human Behavior, 34*, 3–38. https://dx.doi.org/10.1007/s10979-009-9188-6

Kassin, S. M., & Fong, C. T. (1999). "I'm innocent!": Effects of training on judgments of truth and deception in the interrogation room. *Law and Human behavior, 23*, 499–516. https://dx.doi.org/10.1023/a:1022330011811

Kassin, S. M., & Gudjonsson, G. H. (2004). The psychology of confessions: A review of the literature and issues. *Psychological Science in the Public Interest, 5*(2), 33–67. https://dx.doi.org/10.1111/j.1529-1006.2004.00016.x

Kassin, S. M., Leo, R. A., Meissner, C. A., Richman, K. D., Colwell, L. H., Leach, A.-M., & La Fon, D. (2007). Police Interviewing and Interrogation: A Self-Report Survey of Police Practices and Beliefs. *Law and Human Behavior, 31*(4), 381-400. https://dx.doi.org/10.1007/s10979-006-9073-5

Kalbfleisch, P. J. (1994). The language of detecting deceit. *Journal of Language and Social Psychology, 13*, 469–496. https://dx.doi.org/10.1177/0261927x94134006

Kaufmann, G., Drevland, G. C. B., Wessel, E., Goverskeid, G., & Magnussen, S. (2003). The importance of being earnest: Displayed emotions and witness credibility. *Applied Cognitive Psychology, 17,* 21–34. https://dx.doi.org/10.1002/acp.842

Knapp, M. L. (2006). Lying and deception in close relationships. In A. L. Vangelisti & D. Perlman (Eds.), *Cambridge handbook of personal relationships* (pp. 517–532). New York, NY: Cambridge University Press.

Lacayo, R., & Ripley, A. (2002, December 30). Persons of the Year 2002: The whistleblowers. *Time*, pp. 30–60.

Lassiter, G. D., Slaw, R. D., Briggs, M. A., & Scanlan, C. R. (1992). The potential for bias in video-taped confessions. *Journal of Applied Social Psychology, 22,* 1838–1851. https://dx.doi.org/10.1111/j.1559-1816.1992.tb00980.x

Latané, B., & Darley, J. M. (1970). *The unresponsive bystander: Why doesn't he help?* Englewood Cliffs, NJ: Prentice Hall.

Leo, R. A. (1996). Inside the interrogation room. *The Journal of Criminal Law and Criminology, 86,* 266–303. https://scholarlycommons.law.northwestern.edu/jclc/vol86/iss2/2

Levine, T. R. (2014). Active deception detection. *Policy Insights from the Behavioral and Brain Sciences, 1*(1), 122–128. https://dx.doi.org/10.1177/2372732214548863

Levine, T. R. (2014). Truth-default theory (TDT): A theory of human deception and deception detection. *Journal of Language and Social Psychology, 33*(4), 378–392. https://dx.doi.org/10.1177/0261927x14535916

Levine, T. R. (2015). New and improved accuracy findings in deception detection research. *Current Opinion in Psychology, 6,* 1–5. https://dx.doi.org/10.1016/j.copsyc.2015.03.003

Levine, T. R. (2018). Ecological validity and deception detection research design. *Communication Methods and Measures, 12*(1), 45–54. https://dx.doi.org/10.1080/19312458.2017.1411471

Levine, T. R., Anders, L. N., Banas, J., Baum, K. L., Endo, K., Hu, A. D. S., & Wong, N. C. H. (2000). Norms, expectations, and deception: A norm violation model of veracity judgments. *Communication Monographs, 67,* 123–137. https://dx.doi.org/10.1080/03637750009376500

Levine, T. R., Asada, K. J. K, & Park, H. S. (2006). The lying chicken and the gaze avoidant egg: Eye contact, deception, and causal order. *Southern Communication Journal, 71,* 401–411. https://dx.doi.org/10.1080/10417940601000576

Levine, T. R., Blair, J. P., & Clare, D. D. (2014). Diagnostic utility: experimental demonstrations and replications of powerful question effects in high-stakes deception detection. *Human Communication Research, 40,* 262–289. https://dx.doi.org/10.1111/hcre.12021

Levine, T. R., & Bond, C. F. (2014). Direct and indirect measures of lie detection tell the same story: A reply to ten Brinke, Stimson, and Carney (2014). *Psychological Science, 25*(10), 1960–1961. https://dx.doi.org/10.1177/2F0956797614536740

Levine, T. R., Feeley, T. H., McCornack, S. A., Hughes, M., & Harms, C. M. (2005). Testing the effects of nonverbal behavior training on accuracy in deception detection with the inclusion of a bogus training control group. *Western Journal of Communication, 69,* 203–217. https://dx.doi.org/10.1080/10570310500202355

Levine, T. R., Kim, R. K., Park, H. S., & Hughes, M. (2006). Deception detection accuracy is a predictable linear function of message veracity base-rate: A formal test of Park and Levine's probability model. *Communication Monographs, 73,* 243–260. https://dx.doi.org/10.1080/03637750600873736

Levine, T. R., & Knapp, M. L. (2018). Lying and Deception in Close Relationships. In A. Vangelisti & D. Perlman (Eds.), *The Cambridge Handbook of Personal Relationships* (pp. 329–340). Cambridge, England: Cambridge University Press. https://dx.doi.org/10.1017/9781316417867.026

Levine, T. R., & McCornack, S. A. (2001). Behavioral adaptation, confidence and heuristic-based explanations of the probing effect. *Human Communication Research, 27,* 471–502. https://dx.doi.org/10.1093/hcr/27.4.471

Levine, T. R., Park, H. S., & McCornack, S. A. (1999). Accuracy in detecting truths and lies: Documenting the "veracity effect." *Communication Monographs, 66,* 125–144. https://dx.doi.org/10.1080/03637759909376468

Levine, T. R., Serota, K. B., Shulman, J., Clare, D. D., Park, H. S., Shaw, A. S., … Lee, J. H. (2011). Sender demeanor: Individual differences in sender believability have a powerful impact on deception detection judgments. *Human Communication Research, 37,* 377–403. https://dx.doi.org/10.1111/j.1468-2958.2011.01407.x

Lewis v. United States, 385 U.S. 206 (1966) https://supreme.justia.com/cases/federal/us/385/206/

Lieberman, D. J. (1998). *Never be lied to again.* New York, NY: St. Martin's Press.

Luke, T. J., Hartwig, M., Joseph, E., Brimbal, L., Chan, G., Dawson, E., … Granhag, P. A. (2016). Training in the Strategic Use of Evidence technique: Improving deception detection accuracy of American law enforcement officers. *Journal of Police and Criminal Psychology, 31*(4), 270–278. http://dx.doi.org/10.1007/s11896-015-9187-0

MacAskill, E. (2018, January 16). "Is whistleblowing worth prison or a life in exile?": Edward Snowden talks to Daniel Ellsberg. *The Guardian.* Retrieved from http://www.theguardian.com

Manson, P. (2017, February 7). Staffing firm settles fraud suit for $60M. *Chicago Daily Law Bulletin.* Retrieved from http://www.chicagolawbulletin.com

Malone, B. E., & DePaulo, B. M. (2001). Measuring sensitivity to deception. In J. A. Hall & F. J. Bernieri (Eds.), *Interpersonal sensitivity: Theory and measurement* (pp.103–124). Mahwah, NJ: Erlbaum.

Meissner, C. A., & Kassin, S. M. (2002). "He's guilty!": Investigator bias in judgments of truth and deception. *Law and Human Behavior, 26,* 469–480. https://dx.doi.org/10.1023/a:1020278620751

Miranda v. Arizona, 384 U. S. 336 (1966) https://supreme.justia.com/cases/federal/us/384/436/

Myers, D. G. (2002). *Intuition: Its powers and perils.* New Haven, CT: Yale University Press.

Nickerson, R. S. (1998). Confirmation bias: A ubiquitous phenomenon in many guises. *Review of General Psychology, 2*(2), 175–220. https://dx.doi.org/10.1037/1089-2680.2.2.175

O'Sullivan, M. (2003). The fundamental attribution error in detecting deception: The boy-who-cried-wolf effect. *Personality and Social Psychology Bulletin, 29,* 1316–1327. https://dx.doi.org/10.1177/0146167203254610

O'Sullivan, M. (2005). Emotional intelligence and deception detection: Why most people can't "read" others, but a few can. In R. E. Riggio & R. S. Feldman (Eds.), *Applications of nonverbal communication* (pp. 215–253). Mahwah, NJ: Erlbaum.

O'Sullivan, M., & Ekman, P. (2004). The wizards of deception detection. In P. A. Granhag & L. A. Strömwall (Eds.), *The detection of deception in forensic contexts* (pp. 269–286). New York, NY: Cambridge University Press.

Park, H. S., Levine, T. R., Harms, C. M., & Ferrara, M. H. (2002). Group and individual accuracy in deception detection. *Communication Research Reports, 19,* 99–106.

Park, H. S., Levine, T. R., McCornack, S. A., Morrison, K., & Ferrara, M. (2002). How people really detect lies. *Communication Monographs, 69,* 144–157. https://dx.doi.org/10.1080/714041710

Peffer, S. L., Bocheko, A., Del Valle, R. E., Osmani, A., Peyton, S., & Roman, E. (2015). Whistle where you work? The ineffectiveness of the Federal Whistleblower Protection Act of 1989 and the promise of the Whistleblower Protection Enhancement Act of 2012. *Review of Public Personnel Administration, 35*(1), 70–81. https://dx.doi.org/10.1177/0734371x13508414

Peres, J., & Pallasch, A. M. (1998, August 20). Confession debate: To tape or not? *Chicago Tribune.* Retrieved from http://www.chicagotribune.com

Pilkington, E. (2015, April 21). Thirty years in jail for a single hair: The FBI's "mass disaster" of false conviction. *The Guardian.* Retrieved from http://www.theguardian.com

Reinhard, M. A., Sporer, S. L., Scharmach, M., & Marksteiner, T. (2011). Listening, not watching: Situational familiarity and the ability to detect deception. *Journal of Personality and Social Psychology, 101,* 467–484. https://dx.doi.org/10.1037/a0023726

Rothman, L. (2015, January 26). The story behind Bill Clinton's infamous denial. *Time.* Retrieved from http://www.time.com

Sargant, W. (1997). *Battle for the mind: A physiology of conversion and brain-washing.* Cambridge, MA: ISHK. (Original work published 1957).

Shaw, J., Porter, S., & ten Brinke, L. (2013). Catching liars: Training mental health and legal professionals to detect high-stakes lies. *The Journal of Forensic Psychiatry & Psychology, 24,* 145–159. https://dx.doi.org/10.1080/14789949.2012.752025

Shuy, R. W. (1998). *The language of confession, interrogation, and deception.* Thousand Oaks, CA: Sage.

Stiff, J. B., Kim, H. J., & Ramesh, C. N. (1992). Truth biases and aroused suspicion in relational deception. *Communication Research, 19,* 326–345. https://dx.doi.org/10.1177/009365092019003002

Strömwall, L. A., Granhag, P. A., & Hartwig, M. (2004). Practitioners' beliefs about deception. In P. A. Granhag & L. A. Strömwall (Eds.), *The detection of deception in forensic contexts* (pp. 229–250). New York, NY: Cambridge University Press.

Swartz, M. (2016, December). Enron and on and on … Sherron Watkins, fifteen years later. *Texas Monthly.* Retrieved from http://www.texasmonthly.com

ten Brinke, L., Stimson, D., & Carney, D. R. (2014). Some evidence for unconscious lie detection. *Psychological Science, 25,* 1098–1105. https://dx.doi.org/10.1177/0956797614524421

Thomson, I. (2017, March 13). CA forks out $45m to make claims it screwed over US govt go away. *The Register.* Retrieved from http://www.theregister.co.uk

United States v. Russell, 411 U.S. 423 (1973) https://supreme.justia.com/cases/federal/us/411/423/

Van Brocklin, V. (2014, February 26). Case law on police deception. *PoliceOne.* Retrieved from http://www.policeone.com

Viren, S. (2018, July 3). I slept on Robert Durst's futon. *Houston Chronicle.* Retrieved from http://www.houstonchronicle.com

Vrij, A. (2008). *Detecting lies and deceit: The psychology of lying and the implications for professional practice* (2nd ed.). Cheshire, England: Wiley.

Vrij, A., Fisher, R. P., & Blank, H. (2015). A cognitive approach to lie detection: A meta-analysis. *Legal and Criminological Psychology, 22*(1), 1–21. https://dx.doi.org/10.1111/lcrp.12088

Vrij, A., & Mann, S. (2001). Telling and detecting lies in a high-stake situation: The case of a convicted murderer. *Applied Cognitive Psychology, 15,* 187–203. https://dx.doi.org/10.1002/1099-0720(200103/04)15:2%3C187::aid-acp696%3E3.3.co;2-1

Vrij, A., & Mann, S. (2005). Police use of nonverbal behavior as indicators of deception. In R. E. Riggio & R. S. Feldman (Eds.), *Applications of nonverbal communication* (pp. 63–94). Mahwah, NJ: Lawrence Erlbaum Associates, Inc.

Vrij, A., & Verschuere, B. (2013, January). Lie detection in a forensic context. *Oxford Bibliographies in Psychology.* https://dx.doi.org/10.1093/OBO/9780199828340-0122

Weiser, B. (2014, September 5). Settlement is approved in Central Park jogger case, but New York deflects blame. *The New York Times*: Retrieved from http://www.nytimes.com

Whelan, C. W., Wagstaff, G., & Wheatcroft, J. M. (2015). High stakes lies: Police and non-police accuracy in detecting deception. *Psychology, Crime & Law, 15*(2), 127–138. https://dx.doi.org/10.1080/1068316X.2014.935777

Whyall, J. (2018, June 20). Being a whistleblower: "I wouldn't do it again." *European Centre for Press & Media Freedom*. Retrieved from http://www.ecpmf.eu/

Wollan, M. (2016, April 22). How to interrogate someone. *The New York Times*. Retrieved from http://www.nytimes.com

Wright, D. S., Nash, R. A., & Wade, K. A. (2015). Encouraging eyewitnesses to falsely corroborate allegations: Effects of rapport-building and incriminating evidence. *Psychology, Crime & Law, 21*, 648–660. https://dx.doi.org/10.1080/1068316x.2015.1028543

Yamagishi, T., Tanida, S., Mashima, R., Shimoma, E., & Kanazawa, S. (2003). You can judge a book by its cover: Evidence that cheaters may look different from cooperators. *Evolution and Human Behavior, 24*, 290–301. https://dx.doi.org/10.1016/s1090-5138(03)00035-7

Yahr, E. (2015, March 16). "The Jinx" finale recap: Everything that led to Robert Durst saying "What … did I do? Killed them all, of course." *The Washington Post*. Retrieved from http://www.washingtonpost.com

Zebrowitz, L. A., Voinescu, L., & Collins, M. A. (1996). "Wide-eyed" and "crooked-faced": Determinants of perceived and real honesty across the life span. *Personality and Social Psychology Bulletin, 22*, 1258–1269. https://dx.doi.org/10.1177/01461672962212006

Zuckerman, M., DePaulo, B. M., & Rosenthal, R. (1981). Verbal and nonverbal communication of deception. In L. Berkowitz (Ed.), *Advances in experimental social psychology* (Vol. 14), pp. 1–57. New York, NY: Academic Press.

CHAPTER 10 Assisted Lie Detection

© Inked Pixels/Shutterstock.com

"I don't know anything about polygraphs, and I don't know how accurate they are, but I know they'll scare the hell out of people."

– Richard Nixon

"The polygraph works if most people who take the test think it will."

– Paul Ekman

"People have been deceived by a myth that a metal box in the hands of an investigator can detect truth or falsehood."

– United States Congress, House Report No. 198

Picture this: A criminal suspect sits in a police interrogation room with a kitchen colander on his head. Yes, a colander—the metal bowl full of holes used for washing lettuce or draining pasta. Wires run from the colander to a nearby copier machine. The suspect is told this is a "lie-detection machine." The police interrogators have already placed on the copier a piece of paper printed with the words, 'HE'S LYING.' When the suspect gives an answer the interrogators don't

believe, they press a button and the machine prints out the damning message. Convinced that the machine really is capable of detecting his lies, the suspect confesses.

This story first appeared in print in the June 22, 1977, edition of the *Philadelphia Inquirer* and was attributed to "a small police department in the county." But no police department in Pennsylvania or anywhere else has ever admitted using this colander-as-lie-detector strategy. Nevertheless, the story won't die. Versions of it have been widely circulated for many years on the Internet and reprinted in such places as the *Wall Street Journal, Playboy,* and advice columns. It was also depicted in an episode of the television series *Homicide* (Mikkelson, 2011). Jimmy Kimmel used a variation of this faux lie-detector machine on children in a series of skits called "Lie Detective" (QR) and "Naughty or Nice."

Part of the fascination with the colander legend is the stupidity of the criminal who believed such a ridiculous "machine" could actually tell he was lying. But just how "stupid" was he? Colanders aside, if the setup actually *looked and operated in a way that was credible* to most people, would their behavior differ all that much? In social sciences research, credible-looking-but-fake "lie detector" machines actually are used and are known as "bogus pipeline" devices. People who believe that technology can detect their true attitudes (as if it were a "pipeline" to the soul) are less likely to misrepresent those attitudes when connected to such a device (Roese & Jamieson, 1993). An FBI agent who had previously worked as a police officer told one of the authors of this textbook about an interrogation he had conducted. He informed the suspect that a "new technology" had been used to extract from the dead victim's brain the last images he saw before being murdered. Then the suspect was led to believe that these images included views of him. Convinced the police had these hard facts available, he confessed to the crime (apparently without asking to see the proof).

OUR FAITH IN MACHINES AS LIE DETECTORS

Many law enforcement and military organizations are obsessed with finding a machine that reliably detects lies. Dr. Paul Ekman found this out following the 9/11 attacks. Ekman knows as much about liar behavior and how to accurately observe it as anyone in the world. He has trained members of the FBI, Secret Service, police units, and military intelligence on the observation of liar behaviors. But when he inquired how he might help the CIA, Department of Defense, and other federal agencies, one representative told him, "I can't support anything unless it ends in a machine doing it" (Henig, 2006).

To date, there has never been a reliable lie-detection machine, much less an infallible one. Will there ever be? Some experts believe the odds are against it despite extraordinary amounts of money and effort directed toward its development. Part of the problem is that we give machines far more credit than they deserve. We are often quick to acknowledge human frailties in lie detection, but slow to acknowledge similar problems with lie-detection machines. Our misplaced faith in machines is propped up by a number of problematic assumptions about how machines operate. Specifically, that machines are:

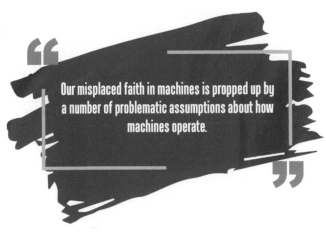

Our misplaced faith in machines is propped up by a number of problematic assumptions about how machines operate.

1. so reliable they will always perform the same way

2. capable of operating without error—i.e., they are 100% accurate

3. able to act independently of any biases or frailties human beings might have (never mind that humans build them, operate them, and interpret their output)

4. able to eliminate the inevitable ambiguities involved in any perceptual event

5. interpreters of bodily functions that can't even be controlled or manipulated by humans

6. actual lie detectors rather than mere readers of certain physiological and neurophysiological behavior that may or may not be linked to deception

The search for a machine to satisfy our need for an infallible and unambiguous lie detector is the primary focus of this chapter. We begin, of course, with what is probably the best known "lie detector" machine, the polygraph.

THE POLYGRAPH

The British novelist Daniel Defoe (of *Robinson Crusoe* fame) may have been the first to suggest that the truthfulness of a suspect could be determined by paying attention to physiological signs (Defoe, 1731). He reasoned that "guilt carries fear always about with it; there is a tremor in the blood of the thief, that, if attended to, would effectually discover him" (p. 34). By the late 19th and early 20th centuries, in the technological wake of the Industrial Revolution, various European scientists were exploring possible connections between physiological responses and deception. Then in 1915, Harvard graduate student William Marston built a machine that he claimed showed a link between systolic blood pressure readings and lying (National Research Council, 2003). He would later equip his more famous invention, Wonder Woman, with a Lasso of Truth, although some scholars claim that Marston never saw them as related concepts (Cronin, 2017). Building on these various efforts, a clunky prototype for today's polygraph was developed a few years later by a police officer named John Larson. By 1931, Larson protégé Leonarde Keeler had significantly refined the device into a streamlined, portable machine that measured multiple physiological responses (MacNeil, 2018).

With a few minor exceptions, the technology employed by today's polygraphs has remained basically unchanged for a century (MacAskill, 2015). And then as now, despite being an object of peculiar fascination in popular culture, its scientific and legal reviews were decidedly mixed. Marston himself was unable to get the polygraph admitted for use in court or accepted as a tool for ferreting out spies (Macdonald, 2016). And despite Keeler's enthusiasm

for his money-making device (patenting and mass-producing it, selling it to the FBI, opening the first polygraph school), his former mentor Larson utterly despaired of the invention, calling it "a Frankenstein's monster, which I have spent over 40 years in combating" (Grimes, 2007). Larson even went so far as to renounce Keeler and his methods (Carlsen, 2010). Curiously enough, Keeler seemed unable to use his polygraph (or any other method) to figure out that his wife was going to leave him for another man. According to Alder (2007), he died of a stroke at age 45, shattered and full of mistrust.

Even though the polygraph is often called a "lie detector," it does *not* detect lies or other forms of deception. In fact, it doesn't actually "detect" or otherwise uncover anything. Rather, it *measures physiological changes* in a person's body (heart rate, blood pressure, respiration, and skin conductivity) that result from things like cognition, arousal, anxiety, or stress. Proponents like Marston and Keeler believed these changes (or the lack thereof) were reliable physiological indicators of one's deceptiveness or truthfulness, but the scientific validity of these critical assumptions has never been firmly established (Synnott, Dietzel, & Ioannou, 2015).

Not surprisingly, therefore, *interpretation* of a polygraph examinee's responses is always necessary because—as we have pointed out elsewhere in this text—there is no known physiological response that is unique to liars and never exhibited by truth tellers (American Psychological Association, 2004). As a result, the responses to any given polygraph exam are always subject to *differing* interpretations. To attempt to compensate for this, government agencies often have more than one examiner who will review the results from the output of a polygraph exam, and some agencies have a centralized center where all results are sent for a final analysis. But such "safeguards" do nothing to bolster the reliability of a method that is more interpretive in nature than objectively scientific.

Those who promote the polygraph will often defend it by saying that not all interpretations are correct and not all examiners are experienced enough to make good interpretations. But in most cases, their arguments are premised on some version of the flawed underlying assumption that there is a direct and reliable bodily reaction to the lies we tell. For example, as the pro-polygraph website, LieDetectorTest.uk, confidently declares: "We know that when we tell a lie our bodies give us away—we start to sweat, our heart rate increases, and our breathing quickens." Many liars may indeed do these things, but as we will see, not all of them. And it is equally important to recognize that innocent people who don't respond well to machines, wires, and interrogations might, for example, sweat, experience increased heart rate, and breath more rapidly. Whether guilty or innocent, no one enjoys being treated as a suspect.

Who Administers and Takes Polygraph Exams?

Even though the use of the polygraph in criminal cases gets the most publicity, in the long, troubled history of the device, significantly more exams are administered by employers as a general screening tool, the task to which it is probably most poorly suited. During the Cold War, for example, the U.S. Department of State infamously used polygraphs to "weed out" from its own ranks suspected communists and homosexuals. Unsurprisingly, the results were dismal (Grimes, 2007).

In the 1980s, use of the polygraph to screen prospective employees had become so widespread and so problematic that Congress pressured President Reagan to sign the Employee Polygraph Protection Act in 1988, which prohibited private companies from using polygraphs to screen employees (although it permitted them to continue using polygraphs to investigate employees suspected of theft (Barnhorn & Pegram, 2011)).

Unlike Congress, Reagan himself had no reservations about the polygraph. In 1983, he issued a directive allowing federal agencies (including the military) to polygraph employees when investigating leaks of classified information (Hasson, 1983). The order proved so unpopular, however, that Reagan rescinded it in less than three months (Synnott et al., 2015). That same year, a skeptical Congress asked its Office of Technology Assessment (OTA) to assess the polygraph's scientific validity. Issued in November, the OTA's report painted a troubling portrait, noting that despite the government's polygraph use *tripling* in the preceding 10 years, there was simply no way to establish the instrument's validity based on the existing evidence. Moreover, their finding echoed those of previous governmental investigations in 1965 and 1976 (U.S. Congress, 1983). In the aftermath of 9/11, the U.S. Department of Energy greatly increased the use of the polygraph as a general screening tool. In response, the National Academy of Sciences and the National Research Council produced a report that once again declared the polygraph a scientifically unreliable instrument (Carlsen, 2010). And once again, government agencies paid little or no attention.

Despite these and other red flags raised over the years, U.S. government entities have continued to rely on the polygraph as a general screening device:

- People applying for positions with federal, state, and local government agencies are frequently asked to take a polygraph exam.

- Exams may also be given to certain nongovernmental employees who are engaged in work that is related to national security; a security service firm (e.g., armored car firms); or pharmaceutical manufacturers, distributors, and sellers.

- Polygraphs play a big role in who becomes a law enforcement officer, who has access to the most powerful weapons, and who can be entrusted with the nation's most closely guarded secrets.

The common characteristic of federal employees who can be asked to take a polygraph exam is their exposure to information, products, and services that affect the safety of many people. While many high-ranking government officials believe it is appropriate to use the polygraph in this way, not everyone agrees. In 1985, President Reagan believed information was being leaked by one or more of his cabinet members. He ordered polygraph tests, but exempted himself and Secretary of State George Shultz (Atlas, 1985). Shultz

Reagan and Shultz

© Consolidated News Pictures/Contributor/ Getty Images

had refused to take the test and threatened to resign, declaring, "management through fear and intimidation is not the way to promote honesty and protect security" (Kelly, 2004). Faced with a similar crisis of leaks more than 30 years later, President Trump reportedly considered using polygraph exams to weed out moles on his staff (Moss & Zaid, 2018).

Can Polygraph Results Be Entered as Evidence in Court?

Police agencies in the United Kingdom have only been using the polygraph exam since 2013, but it is not mandatory and can only be administered voluntarily with the explicit consent of a suspect or detainee (Marshall & Thomas, 2015). The public and private sectors in the United States, meanwhile, have long been enamored of the polygraph, where it is far more prevalent and has a variety of uses that include:

- pre-probation release of sex offenders and periodic tests thereafter
- suspected malingering
- on-the-job sexual harassment charges
- corporate theft
- contested divorces
- accusations of child abuse and rape

Despite this list, with very few exceptions the results of polygraph tests are not admissible as evidence in U.S. courts (Cummins, 2018). The U.S. Supreme Court does not support the results of polygraph tests as evidence. As one of eight justices who voted to uphold the military's ban on admitting polygraph evidence in court-martial cases, Justice Thomas said, "There is simply no way to know in a particular case whether a polygraph examiner's conclusion is accurate, because certain doubts and uncertainties plague even the best polygraph exams" (*United States v. Scheffer*, 1998).

> " The U.S. Supreme Court does not support the results of polygraph tests as evidence. "

Even the judicial uses described above are voluntary (or supposed to be) and the results are often used as a negotiating tool between parties. New Mexico is one of the rare exceptions, where courts will accept polygraph results as evidence so long as both the prosecution and the defense agree to do so (Kelly, 2004). Such agreement, however, is rarely reached (Howerton, 2016). For a state-by-state summary of current judicial policy on polygraph use in court, it's advisable to routinely check clearinghouse sites such as the one maintained by the National Sexual Violence Resource Center (QR).

Nevertheless, the polygraph can have powerful effects even if it is not admitted into court as evidence. For example, it can be used to induce confessions. When a suspect is told that he or she has failed a polygraph test and is subsequently interrogated, 30–40% of the suspects confess (Lykken, 1998). For a person who *strongly* believes in the accuracy of the polygraph, however, a failing result may make them think they are repressing information about their guilt. Under such conditions, some people have made false confessions (Eldeib, 2013).

Refusing to take a polygraph exam can increase the chances that a person will be a suspect or, at a minimum, perceived as someone who has something to hide (Tucker, 1985). Jon-Christopher Clark, who was not a person of interest in the August 2018 disappearance of girlfriend Kiera Bergman, says he was nevertheless strong-armed by Phoenix police pressuring him to take a polygraph test. He refused, stating, "I didn't want to do anything that would give the indication I was hiding anything but also didn't want anything on the record that would have them say I was doing anything or had any part in this" (Lohr, 2018). Wayne Cheney had been an early suspect in the murder of Iowa college student Mollie Tibbetts—and for good reason; he had a history of stalking arrests and guilty pleas. But Cheney maintained his innocence and repeatedly refused to take a lie detector test (Boroff, 2018). Weeks later, police arrested Cristhian Rivera after a resident's home security camera showed him following Tibbetts in his car the night she disappeared. After his arrest, Rivera confessed and took agents to the woman's body (Martinez, 2018).

Sometimes people who are being screened for security purposes will be given a polygraph exam periodically. These people have to pass multiple polygraph exams and no matter how many times they pass, one failure will have an adverse effect on their job. Without any formal charges being made, an innocent person's career can be ruined if he or she fails a polygraph exam. The case of career FBI agent Mark Mallah shows how this can happen. After "failing" a general screening polygraph test, he was subjected to a surprise raid of his home. All of his financial records were examined, and his personal notes and correspondence were analyzed. Even though he was returned to duty and no charges were ever filed, his career with the FBI was essentially over because the suspicion surrounding him would not disappear (Alexander, 2003). The polygraph examiner who implicated Mallah had a total of 10 weeks of training. By contrast, as the *Washington Post* observed when reporting this story, "In most states, barbers must have 26 weeks of training before earning a license to cut hair" (Zelicoff, 2002). Mallah's case and others were featured in a stinging *60 Minutes II* exposé of the U.S. Government's polygraph policy. The episode, titled "Final Exam," (QR) aired on December 12, 2001, and is still viewable on sites such as AntiPolygraph.org.

How Does the Polygraph Work?

Most polygraphs measure three types of physiological responses, recording each "channel" independently:

1. Pneumatic tubes are placed around the examinee's chest and stomach; these tubes measure **the depth and rate of breathing**.

2. An inflated blood pressure cuff wrapped around the examinee's arm gives an approximate mean of systolic and diastolic **blood pressure** as well as a measure of **heart rate**.

3. A clip containing metal electrodes is attached to the examinee's fingers to measure the skin's electrical resistance. Increased stress causes the hand to **sweat**, thereby causing electrical resistance to decrease.

Changes in these physiological responses in reaction to the examiner's questions were originally graphed on paper. Today, most are simply displayed on a monitor. Some exams also include the use of a movement pad that is placed on the chair where the subject sits. The pad measures general movements that might interfere with testing data, such as the use of countermeasures by examinees (American Polygraph Association, 2015).

The examiner tries to minimize any distractions that may influence the examinee's reactions. As a result, the examiner is often positioned behind the examinee and the examinee is told to maintain a steady position and give only yes or no answers. Needless to say, effective polygraph exams require subjects who are cooperative and believe in the polygraph's ability to detect their lies.

Procedures Followed in Polygraph Exams

Polygraph exams are used for several purposes, each necessitating different types of questions. For example:

- A criminal suspect can be asked a very specific question intended to differentiate truthful respondents from deceptive ones ("Did you take the turquoise necklace from the display case?").

- The questions asked to existing employees for security screening purposes are typically broader and the criteria for "passing" or "failing" any given question are not as clear ("Have you ever revealed classified information to an unauthorized person?").

- When polygraphs are used for employee selection during hiring, the examiner must decide if answers about a person's past ("Have you used marijuana in the last three years?") have any bearing on what the applicant's actual job will be. For example, if someone is applying for a national security job, does past use of recreational marijuana mean they're at risk of becoming an enemy spy?

Most polygraph exams last 60 to 90 minutes. Before the physiological monitors are attached to the suspect, the examiner talks with the examinee about the exam. During this phase, the examiner tries to build rapport and talks about the types of questions that will be asked. Discussing the questions in advance is designed to prevent any ambiguity the examinee might have about what they mean (and therefore how to answer them). But a critical part of this initial discussion is devoted to convincing the subject that the polygraph will unerringly detect lies.

For the exam to have *any* chance of being interpreted effectively, innocent people will need to be thinking along the lines of, "I am not going to lie, so I'm confident the machine will show I'm telling the truth." Guilty people, on the other hand, will need to have convinced themselves of something like, "Uh oh. I don't think I'm going to be able to lie without this machine picking it up." The examiner will also emphasize the need to tell the truth, but may add that too many admissions of inappropriate behavior will also be a concern.

The examiner may cite research findings and talk about his or her vast experience with an air of confidence in order to enhance the subject's belief in the accuracy of the polygraph exam. Since information about the polygraph's fallibility is now widely available, however, it is likely to be increasingly difficult to convince people otherwise.

Modern polygraphers use three primary techniques when it comes to questioning (Vennapoosa, 2010):

1. The relevant/irrelevant technique

2. The control (or comparison) question technique

3. The concealed information technique

We'll examine all of three of these categories below. Regardless of the particular technique being used, it is worth noting that the first question asked—no matter what it is—is considered to have no diagnostic value. Therefore, polygraph examiners will almost always place an unimportant question at the beginning of the sequence (National Research Council, 2003).

Relevant/Irrelevant Technique

The relevant/irrelevant (IR) technique is the oldest of the polygraph questioning techniques and was primarily used in criminal investigations, but modern polygraphers who are concerned about minimizing scientific inaccuracies generally disavow it. Unfortunately, that hasn't stopped it from still being used as a general screening tool in job interviews and other non-criminal settings (National Research Council, 2003).

As the name implies, IR is supposed to test the examinee's knowledge of whatever the investigation is focusing on (details of a crime, for example) by asking some questions that actually relate to the investigation and some that have nothing at all to do with it. The idea is that someone with knowledge of the actual events will, *overall, tend to respond differently* to relevant questions than irrelevant ones. Examples of relevant questions might include, "Do you know who committed the crime?" or asking about evidence found at the scene. An irrelevant (or neutral) question can be anything as long as it isn't relevant to the case and may even be completely random (e.g., "Is today Wednesday?"). More importantly, relevant questions are supposed to provoke an emotional response whereas irrelevant questions should not (unless, of course, someone just really has a thing for Wednesdays).

Control (or Comparison) Question Technique

Some innocent people might show a strong response to a relevant question (perhaps topics like violence and murder upset them), as in the following sequence of questions in a traditional IR approach:

1. **Is it afternoon?** (irrelevant)

2. **Is your name John Doe?** (irrelevant)

3. **Did you murder Ned Flanders by slicing open his intestines and chopping off his head**? (relevant)

Obviously, a truthful person's strong physiological response to this third question is hardly a fair test. So the "solution" to this glaring problem was the development of control questions (also known as comparison questions), and the control/comparison question technique (CQT) was born.

Irrelevant questions like one's name or time of day generally aren't going to bother anyone, but *comparison* questions are intended to be more alarming to non-deceptive people than even directly relevant questions—by creating *uncertainty* about their answers. A non-deceptive person (who believes a polygraph really works) will be far more certain about their answer to a relevant question ("Did you steal Matt Griffin's money?") than to a comparison question ("When you were a teenager, did you ever steal anything from anyone?").

Polygraph exams using the CQT typically ask three types of questions: neutral, control, and relevant. The questions are asked in this same sequence several times (adapted from Vrij, 2000, p. 176):

Neutral 1:	Do you live in the United States?
Control 1:	During the first 20 years of your life, did you ever take something that did not belong to you?
Relevant 1:	Did you take that camera?
Neutral 2:	Is your name Inigo Montoya?

Control 2:	Prior to 1987, did you ever do something dishonest or illegal?
Relevant 2:	Did you take that camera from the desk?
Neutral 3:	Were you born in the month of November?
Control 3:	Before age 21, did you ever lie to get out of trouble or to cause trouble for someone else?
Relevant 3:	Did you participate in any way in the theft of that camera?

Some modifications of the Control Question Test exist. *Probable-lie* CQT questions, for example, try to induce innocent people to lie on their own by choosing to answer "no." But in certain circumstances, *directed-lie* CQT questions might be used instead. In that case, examinees are told in advance to lie (by answering "no") rather than leaving it up to them to decide whether to lie or not (Honts, 1994; National Research Council, 2003; Raskin, Kircher, Horowitz, & Honts, 1989). The goal is to try to make sure the examinee is not telling the truth on the control questions, but critics such as Lykken (1998) say that such variations do little to improve the test.

In the *positive control* CQT scenario, examinees are told to answer a relevant question truthfully one time and deceptively the next—assuming that greater physiological arousal will occur with the lie. But Lykken (1998) points out that a rape victim might have similar levels of arousal for truthful and deceptive answers to questions like, "Did he use threats and force you to have intercourse?"

It is no surprise that the assumptions associated with the control question approach have been challenged:

- For one thing, people don't always react in predictable ways. A memory triggered by a word or phrase in a relevant question may heighten the arousal of an innocent person and make them seem guilty.

- As noted, the success of every polygraph exam is highly dependent on the skills of the examiner, who must be able to convince suspects that their lies *will* be exposed.

- The examiner must also be able to construct relevant questions that will elicit the responses liars and truth tellers are expected to give. In the question, "Did you pass the counterfeit money?" both liars and truth tellers can truthfully answer "yes." But it is likely that a "no" answer to the question, "Did you *know* the money you passed was counterfeit?" is not a true answer for both guilty and innocent examinees.

- Questions also need to be adapted to the person being tested—e.g., "Have you ever told a lie to avoid getting into trouble?" might be a useful control question for some examinees, but not for a person with a long criminal record.

As we have seen in exploring these various techniques, a polygraph exam is not a single, standardized test, so the influence (and skill and experience) of the examiner can have a profound effect on the results. Another one of the many possible exam types, the Concealed Information Technique, is discussed next.

Concealed Information Technique

More commonly known as the Guilty Knowledge Test (GKT), this polygraph exam technique is based on the assumption that the perpetrator of a crime will know things about the crime that innocent suspects will not. For example, assume the victim of a crime had been stabbed to death with a knife. Using the GKT technique, four knives are shown, one at a time, and the suspect is asked if the knife displayed is the one used in the killing. The suspect is instructed to say "no" each time, but the assumption is that the killer will show more physiological arousal when the knife actually used in the killing is displayed. The arousal level for innocent suspects, however, should be similar for each of the knives (Lykken, 1998).

It is best if the examiner does not know which alternative (in this case, which knife) is associated with the crime so that bias is not interjected into the way the questions are asked. A preliminary polygraph exam with people who are known to be innocent of the crime can provide insight on the equality of the alternatives and the extent to which any of them may inadvertently induce arousal in an innocent person.

For criminal cases, the Guilty Knowledge Test has advantages over the Control Question Test, but is not without its own problems. For example, a guilty person may not be aware of certain aspects of the crime or crime scene that might otherwise seem obvious to investigators. The perpetrator may not have perceptions and memories that investigators expect him or her to. On the other hand, an innocent person may have knowledge of the crime scene but not be the person who committed the crime. Guilty knowledge tests are not always easy to construct because they depend on using information known only to the guilty person and, in many cases, the details of a crime are already widely known because of media publicity.

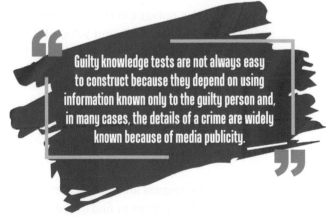

> Guilty knowledge tests are not always easy to construct because they depend on using information known only to the guilty person and, in many cases, the details of a crime are widely known because of media publicity.

Interpreting Polygraphs

There is no standard method of interpreting polygraphs, no standardized rules for determining what magnitude of arousal for any given channel equates to lying. How much breathing is too much? At what level does one's blood pressure and heart rate indicate deception?

No one knows. In short, there is no typical "lie response." Some polygraphers look at the general response trends and form a judgment; others will assign numerical values to differences in responses to control and relevant questions. Cutoff points for "inconclusive" tests are often arbitrary (never mind that there is no truly "conclusive" test). Many examiners score their own tests and are therefore subject to any biases associated with their view of the suspect—e.g., the knowledge that this person is a sex offender, the knowledge that the person is law enforcement's prime suspect, or even how they interpret the examinee's sullen facial expression. Forensic confirmation biases (Kassin, Dror, & Kukucka, 2013) or tunnel vision (Findley & Scott, 2006) may also lead to interpretation errors. Honts (1994) found that computer scoring is as good as human examiners, but still only about 70% accurate in classifying liars and truth tellers correctly.

The certainty of polygraph exams is anything but. Several cases vividly illustrate how polygraph interpretations can vary dramatically. Floyd "Buzz" Fay failed a polygraph exam and served two and a half years of a life sentence for a murder he did not commit. From prison, he sent the results of his polygraph exam to several experts. One said the charts indicated Fay was truthful and two others said the results should be interpreted as inconclusive (Kleinmuntz & Szucko, 1984a). Dr. Wen Ho Lee worked in nuclear weapons development at the Los Alamos National Laboratory and was suspected of espionage. He took a polygraph and passed. Later, an FBI polygraph examiner looked at the same data and concluded Lee had lied. Kleinmuntz and Szucko (1984b) examined the accuracy of six polygraph examiners who had similar experiences and who had taken the same polygraph training course. False positive error rates (identifying truth tellers as liars) varied between 18% and 50%, while false negative rates (identifying liars as truth tellers) ranged from 18% to 36%. Such numbers hardly inspire confidence.

In 1963 and 1974, Congressional committees recommended against the widespread use of polygraph exams. Sam Ervin, a U.S. senator from North Carolina, spoke against the polygraph during the 1974 committee and referred to the polygraph as *twentieth-century witchcraft* (Lykken, 1998). The work of the 2003 Committee to Review the Scientific Evidence on the Polygraph reinforced the shortcomings identified by earlier investigations.

Members of Congress are keenly aware of these shortcomings and typically refuse to take a polygraph exam. In an effort to find a security leak associated with 9/11, Congress called on the FBI. But when the FBI insisted that some members of Congress take a polygraph exam, they refused. Senator Richard Shelby said, "I don't know who among us would take a lie-detector test. First of all, they're not even admissible in court, and second of all, the leadership [of both parties] have told us not to do that" (Zelicoff, 2002). Nevertheless, in 1999 Senator Shelby was instrumental in authorizing the polygraphing of 15,000 scientists. The sweep was part of an effort to uncover spies who had been leaking information to China about nuclear weapons.

How Accurate Is the Polygraph?

As we have seen, there is no simple answer to questions about polygraph accuracy. Nevertheless, claims are made for the overall accuracy—and those claims vary dramatically. Not surprisingly, people who are trying to preserve the credibility of the polygraph often claim accuracy rates above 85%. But independent researchers often put the rate well below that. Saxe (1994) says the best controlled studies consistently produce wildly-varying error rates between 25% and 75%. Vrij (2000) insists that the error rates of both the Control Question Test and the Guilty Knowledge Test are substantial.

The difficulty in being more precise about the issue of accuracy is further compounded by the shortage of research that provides trustworthy data. Laboratory studies often lack the realism associated with actual polygraph exams while those based on actual polygraph exams often lack important controls—e.g., maintaining consistent procedures. And how should "inconclusive" results affect the accuracy rate? Some reports simply ignore them.

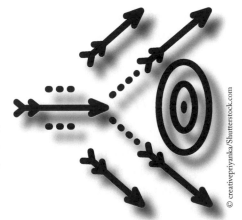

Scientists serving on the National Research Council's 2003 polygraph report concluded that, in the best case scenario:

> *In populations of examinees such as those represented in the polygraph research literature, untrained in counter-measures, specific-incident polygraph tests can discriminate lying from truth telling at rates well above chance, though well below perfection (p.4).*

"Well above chance, though well below perfection" is hardly a slam dunk. If you were innocent and failing a polygraph exam would send you to jail or ruin your career, you'd probably want a lot more assurance of the machine's accuracy before trusting your fate to it.

Innocent souls may be tempted to think, "I have nothing to hide, so I'll pass a polygraph test." But they should know that false positives are the most common mistake. Iacono and Patrick (1988) report a study in which 87% of the guilty test takers were correctly identified, but only 56% of the innocents. Lykken (1998) goes so far as to say, "an innocent suspect has nearly a 50:50 chance of failing a Control Question Test administered under adversarial circumstances…" (p. 277). While the error rate for false negatives (missing a guilty person) is lower, the effects can still be devastating when law enforcement relies solely on polygraph results to make their case for innocence. The infamous Green River killer (QR) murdered at least 48 women beginning in 1982. As a suspect in 1984, he took and passed a polygraph (Harden, 2003). He wouldn't be arrested for another 18 years.

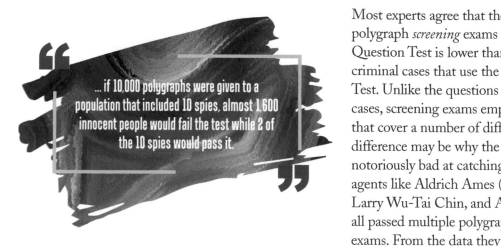

... if 10,000 polygraphs were given to a population that included 10 spies, almost 1,600 innocent people would fail the test while 2 of the 10 spies would pass it.

Most experts agree that the accuracy rate for polygraph *screening* exams that use the Control Question Test is lower than exams given in criminal cases that use the Guilty Knowledge Test. Unlike the questions used in criminal cases, screening exams employ *broad* questions that cover a number of different areas. This difference may be why the polygraph has been notoriously bad at catching spies. Double agents like Aldrich Ames (QR), Karl Koecher, Larry Wu-Tai Chin, and Ana Belen Montes all passed multiple polygraph exams. From the data they examined, the Committee to Review the Scientific Evidence on the Polygraph (2003) calculated that if 10,000 polygraphs were given to a population that included 10 spies, almost 1,600 innocent people would fail the test while 2 of the 10 spies would pass it. The committee's report concludes that the machine's accuracy:

> In distinguishing actual or potential security violators from innocent test takers is insufficient to justify reliance on its use in employee security screening in federal agencies (p.6).

In the end, the polygraph becomes more deterrent than detector. In 1983, a study by the Congressional Office of Technology Assessment concluded that the National Security Agency and the CIA "use the polygraph not to determine deception or truthfulness *per se*, but as a technique of interrogation to encourage admissions" (Kelly, 2004, p. 20). Saxe (1994) illustrated this self-fulfilling tendency in an experiment. He and his colleagues gave students the option of stealing money from a drawer. All the students were told they could keep the money if they passed a polygraph exam. One group was told that a new type of computer polygraph was being tested but there was some doubt about its accuracy. In a rigged demonstration of the machine's ability, it failed to detect a lie. Another group was told the new computer polygraph was virtually infallible (also confirmed by a rigged demonstration). Most of the students who had taken the money and believed the machine was infallible were identified as guilty, along with some of the innocent students. But this self-fulfilling tendency seemed to cut both ways. Of the students who were made to doubt the polygraph, *none of the ones who actually took the money were caught* and, once again, some of the innocent students were misidentified as guilty.

Can the Polygraph Be Beat?

As the above experiment—as well as the cases of the Green River killer and the spy Aldrich Ames—suggest, a guilty person can pass a polygraph exam. All they really have to do is believe they can. For his part, Ames dismissed the CIA's polygraph tests as "witch-doctory," telling the *Washington Post* that there was "no special magic" in beating the polygraph. "Confidence," he said, "is what does it. Confidence and a friendly relationship with the examiner. . .rapport, where you smile and you make him think that you like him" (Pincus, 1994).

A guilty person who wants to appear innocent on a polygraph exam that uses control/comparison questions would try to increase his or her arousal on those questions, hoping it would be greater than his or her arousal on the relevant questions. Common ways of doing this are biting one's tongue or pressing one's toes into the floor (or on a tack hidden in a shoe) in conjunction with the appropriate question. Waid, Orne, Cook, and Orne (1981) found the tranquilizer meprobamate to be effective in reducing arousal to relevant questions, but there is not a strong body of research on the effectiveness of drugs and/or alcohol in defeating the polygraph. Drugs that alter memory or one's sense of responsibility for a crime are likely to be the most effective. Some people may have the ability to alter their arousal levels by cognitively evoking emotional images or doing math problems, but this has not been carefully studied. There may be people who can beat polygraphs because they convince themselves they are not lying or don't care if they are (e.g., people with antisocial personality disorder), but to date there is little definitive research in this area.

Several studies have shown that, with training, half or more of the examinees who employ countermeasures can beat the polygraph (Honts & Hodes, 1982; Honts, Raskin & Kircher, 1983; Honts, Raskin & Kircher, 1994; Honts, Devitt, Winbush, & Kircher, 1996). While in prison, Floyd "Buzz" Fay learned how the control question polygraph test worked and trained 27 self-confessed convicts for 15–20 minutes resulting in 23 of the 27 being able to fool the machine's operators (Kleinmuntz & Szucko, 1984b; Lykken, 1998; Sullivan, 2001). In another case, liars who were accurately identified 80% of the time were given either biofeedback or relaxation training. With an increased ability to control their bodily responses, the accuracy of the polygraphs was reduced to about 20% (Corcoran, Lewis, & Garver, 1978). However, training people to beat the polygraph using countermeasures has gained the attention of federal prosecutors. In 2013, an Indiana man was sentenced to eight months in prison for obstructing justice—by teaching people countermeasures for polygraph exams. Elsewhere, Doug Williams, a retired Oklahoma City police officer, ran the website Polygraph.com, which provided instructional materials, DVDs, and personal training on how to beat federal polygraph exams. The object of a federal sting operation in 2015, he faced heavy fines and up to 20 years in prison (though was eventually sentenced to two years).

In response to countermeasures that remain readily available at sites like AntiPolygraph.org or wikiHow.com, some polygraphers rely on counter-countermeasures including close observation, asking examinees to remove their shoes so that they cannot use a tack to inflict pain, and movement detection devices.

As long as people crave a way of detecting lies and believe there is a machine capable of doing so, that device becomes a powerful force in society (Alder, 2007). The polygraph has hung around as long as it has, despite its many flaws, because we still seem to desperately need a lie-detecting machine. So far, at least, newer techniques such as functional magnetic resonance imaging (fMRI) have not gained enough widespread acceptance to replace the polygraph. But various other approaches are ongoing, as we discuss next.

MEASURING STRESS AS AN INDICATOR OF LYING

The polygraph is anchored to the assumption that liars will reveal themselves through physiological arousal. Several other efforts to build a lie detector are based on the similarly dubious assumption that all liars experience stress. As a result, devices measuring stress in the voice, eyes, stomach, and mouth have been linked to lie detection.

Stress in the Voice

The Psychological Stress Evaluator (PSE) first appeared in the 1970s. It was supposed to measure microtremors in the human voice that occur during times of stress. It was also marketed as a lie detector. During the next 35 years, the device changed its name to Voice Stress Analyzer (VSA) or Computer Voice Stress Analyzer (CVSA) but little else differed. Some companies have marketed a *new* product called Layered Voice Analysis (LVA) and claim that it works independent of previous VSA processes. Nemesysco is a company that advertises LVA on its website. It clearly states that LVA is not a voice stress technology and that it can detect "brain activity traces" using the voice as a medium (in any language). They also claim the tool uses algorithms to extract over 120 emotional parameters that can be reduced to 9 basic emotion categories.

In 1999, a Texas state representative introduced an unsuccessful bill that would have allowed licensed officers to use CVSA in criminal investigations. With the concern for screening airline passengers following 9/11, a form of the VSA that could fit into the eyeglasses of security personnel was also marketed at one point.

The fact that these lie and/or stress detectors have been around so long doesn't mean that they have been endorsed by the scientific community. On the contrary, numerous experiments cited by Hollien (1990) show that no version of the PSE/VSA adequately measures vocal microtremors, much less the variations in microtremors associated with different levels of stress. The most that can be said is that it can *sometimes* detect high stress levels. As for detecting deception, researchers conclude that voice stress analysis is about as accurate as flipping a coin (Hollien, 1990; Horvath, 1982). Damphousse's (2008) study conducted for the Department of Justice on VSA and LVA programs used over 300 recent arrestees who were randomly interviewed at a county jail about their drug usage. Urine tests were conducted after the interviews to determine how truthful their answers had been. On average, the two programs were 15% accurate in detecting lies and about 91% accurate in determining those who were nondeceptive. However, neither program was able to weed out lies with much confidence and the overall accuracy rates were reported as 50% in determining deception about recent drug use. One particularly sobering study on LVA used blind samples and provided the outputs of truth tellers and liars minus the voice recordings so that examiners could not use voices in their analyses (Harnsberger, Hollien, Martin, & Hollien, 2009). The outputs were provided to two instructors from the manufacturer of the LVA and two scientists trained by the manufacturer. Accuracy rates were between 42% and 56% and false positive rates (inaccurately judging a truth as a lie) were even higher—between 40% and 65%.

Smartphone apps are being developed to detect stress in the voice during real-life situations (Lu et al., 2012). Although such apps are likely to adopt VSA technology to provide users with decisions about others' veracity, these programs will also face many of the shortcomings mentioned previously.

Stress in the Eyes

A thermal-imaging camera can measure how much heat is emitted by various parts of the body at a distance of 10 or 12 feet. During a stressful fight/flight response, the blood flows to a region just inside each eye and the temperature in that region increases. This assumes of course that all liars suddenly feel the need to run away when lying and that no other cognitive, emotional, or physical activity (real or imagined) increases the temperature around the eyes. The Department of Defense conducted a study of the thermal-imaging camera's ability to detect lies (Pavlidis, Eberhardt, & Levine, 2002). Twenty soldiers at Fort Jackson, South Carolina, were tested in a simulated theft scenario that asked liars to stab a mannequin and rob it of $20. Six of the 8 liars (75%) and 11 of the 12 truth tellers (92%) were accurately identified. A traditional polygraph exam was also given to these soldiers and 75% of the liars and 67% of the truth tellers were accurately classified. The researchers concluded that more research is needed, but that the results of thermal-imaging are comparable to those of the polygraph. Given what we know about the polygraph, this is hardly a vigorous endorsement.

Stress in the Stomach

A team of gastroenterologists tested the idea that the gastrointestinal tract is sensitive to mental stress associated with lying (Pasricha, Sallam, Chen, & Pasricha, 2008). Stomach and heart measurements were taken of 16 liars and truth tellers who participated in a guilty task test using a deck of playing cards. Their heart and stomach activity was measured during the task using an EGG (electrogastrogram) and an EKG (electrocardiogram). The EGG was affected by lying, showing a significant decrease in the normal gastric slow waves. The heart rate of both liars and truth tellers increased significantly by participating in the task, but did not differ from one another. The researchers believe the EGG should be added to the standard polygraph in order to improve polygraph accuracy, and the medical school where the study was conducted has filed a patent for the use of the "gut-brain" relationship for lie detection.

Stress in the Mouth

If the preceding efforts don't offer enough proof that security agencies are willing to explore any and every avenue for that elusive key to identifying liars, Henig (2006) reports that the Department of Defense is supporting research on a "sniffer" test that measures stress hormones on one's breath. Similarly, some deception research has relied on saliva samples to detect levels of the hormone cortisol caused by the stress associated with lying (ten Brinke, Stimson, & Carney, 2014).

These and other tests that try to measure stress to detect lies are all based on the assumption that deceiving others invokes stress. While this is true in some instances, not all lies increase stress. Furthermore, some liars simply don't show physiological stress in situations where we would expect it to occur.

SCANNING THE BRAIN FOR LIES

Since 9/11, a lot of money and effort have been directed toward new lie-detection machines. Brain scans are based on the assumption that the ol' noggin will reveal a different pattern of activity during lying than during truth telling. One approach to mapping the brain uses an electroencephalograph and has often been referred to as "brain fingerprinting." The suspect wears a headband with electronic sensors that register his or her neurological responses (electrical activity) to words and images flashed on a screen. Like the polygraph's Guilty Knowledge Test, brain fingerprinting is based on the belief that

© MDGRPHCS/Shutterstock.com

certain words and images will produce very different brain activity within the perpetrator of a crime than in an innocent suspect. A brain wave called a P300 indicates a person has recognized something familiar (Farwell & Donchin, 1991).

Peer-reviewed, scientific research on brain fingerprinting is minimal and critics have pointed out numerous problems with the procedure. Farwell and Donchin's original study (1991) claimed a 100% accuracy rate for classifying liars and truth tellers, but 12.5% of those tested were classified as "inconclusive" (meaning it wasn't clear if they were lying or telling the truth). Rosenfeld, Soskins, Bosh, and Ryan (2004) were able to teach people how to reduce the rate of identifying guilty suspects from 82% to 18% using simple countermeasures. They also claimed that a replication of Farwell and Donchin's original study detected concealed information at a rate of only 48% (Feder, 2001). Hu, Hegeman, Landry, and Rosenfeld (2012) were able to overcome examinees' use of countermeasures by increasing the number of irrelevant stimuli in the test. They found detection rates from 71% to 92% using this method.

Federal law enforcement agencies point out that brain fingerprinting is not an effective method for screening purposes and that its validity is heavily dependent on the examiner's skill in selecting appropriate questions based on information about the crime (U.S. General Accounting Office, 2001). For example, an innocent person may be familiar with certain aspects of the crime and not be the perpetrator; similarly, the perpetrator of the crime may not remember the color of his murder victim's dress. All of life's experiences are not stored in memory forever or with the same accessibility. Drugs, alcohol, brain damage, and anxiety (or other mental states) while perpetrating the crime can all affect the ability to detect guilty knowledge.

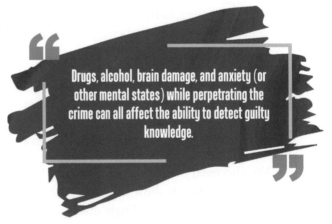

> Drugs, alcohol, brain damage, and anxiety (or other mental states) while perpetrating the crime can all affect the ability to detect guilty knowledge.

As noted above, scientists and companies in the private sector are also using a brain mapping technique called functional magnetic resonance imaging (fMRI) to distinguish liars from truth tellers. The machine claims to measure blood flow to activated areas of the brain during lying and truth telling. A person lies flat on his or her back in a heavy, tube-like machine with the head immobilized. Suspects give yes and no answers using a response mechanism attached to their fingers. Bodily movement may negatively affect the scan and the presence of any metal in the body will render a subject untestable. These machines are also very expensive—some costing as much as $3 million (Talbot, 2007).

A number of studies, ranging in accuracy from 77% to 90%, have found specific regions of the brain that are activated during deception (Ganis, Kosslyn, Stose, Thompson, & Yurgelun-Todd, 2003; Kozel et al., 2004; Kozel, Padgett, & George, 2004; Langleben et al., 2002; Lee et al., 2002; Phan et al., 2005; and Spence et al., 2001). Private companies such as No Lie MRI and Cephos Corporation promote the technology for legal, employment, and national security screenings and they advertise the technology's accuracy rating at 90%. Different types of lies sometimes reveal more regions of activation, but most studies find brain activation during lying in the anterior cingulate cortex (three inches behind the middle of the forehead) and the prefrontal cortex (a few inches inside the skull near the left ear).

These brain areas are activated during a wide range of other mental functions as well, but their association with response inhibition and higher order decision making suggests how they might be associated with a lie response. Nancy Kanwisher, a cognitive scientist at the Massachusetts Institute of Technology, doesn't think the current brain-mapping for lies is very specific. She argues, "Saying 'You have activation in the anterior cingulate' is like saying, 'You have activation in Massachusetts'" (cited by Talbot, 2007, p. 61). Researchers readily admit that there is much to learn about using fMRI for the purposes of deception detection. The legal system has also recognized issues surrounding the use of fMRI in courtrooms, and although attempts have been made, U.S. courts do not allow results from these tests as evidence (Rusconi & Mitchener-Nissen, 2013).

There may be several unique neural pathways for different types of lies. For example, patterns of brain activity may be different for half-truths, denials, and exaggerations. Patterns for lies that include some truth may be different than those that are strictly lies. Kosslyn believes there are differences between spontaneous and well-rehearsed lies as well (Henig, 2006). Lee et al. (2002) focused on feigned memory impairment, and Phan et al. (2005) examined lies involving increased anxiety.

We also need to know more about the responses of different types of individuals, especially those who do not show the expected pattern (Ganis et al., 2003). Ultimately any machine should be able to unfailingly distinguish truth tellers from liars when their motivations and reactions are consistent with a real, high-stakes situation.

We know relatively little about the effectiveness of fMRI countermeasures, but one study found altered breathing, delayed responses, and mentally imaging a specific place to be ineffective (Kozel et al., 2005). However, a more recent study showed it was quite simple to train participants in fMRI-specific countermeasures that actually did lower accuracy rates (Ganis, Rosenfeld, Meixner, Kievit, & Schendan, 2011). Examinees who are noncompliant (e.g., delaying responses or moving their head) can also be problematic for the test. Kosslyn emphasized the work that needs to be done when he said, "Searching for a 'lie zone' of the brain as a counterterrorism strategy is like trying to get to the moon by climbing a tree" (Henig, 2006).

Despite its theoretical, ethical, legal, procedural, and accuracy problems, fMRI has often received unbounded praise from media sources. CNBC described it as a "sure-fire way to identify a liar." Just the words "brain scans indicate…" are enough to make many people believe what would otherwise be labeled a "bad explanation" (Talbot citing Weisberg, p. 58). The apparently unquenchable desire to discover a machine that will identify lies means there will continue to be a huge market for such products. As a result, companies continue to push fMRIs as a sure-fire way of uncovering deceptive behavior (Ritter, 2006). Websites like Brains on Trial provide an extensive look into fMRI technology for use in deception detection.

Despite the theoretical, ethical, legal, procedural, and accuracy problems, fMRI has often received unbounded praise from media sources.

DO "TRUTH" SERUMS WORK?

Movies and television shows have frequently shown a prisoner who is injected with sodium pentothal or sodium amytal and whose secrets subsequently come flying out. It is true that sodium pentothal and sodium amytal may induce a state of relaxation and/or drowsiness. It is also true that a person may lose some inhibitions and talk more, but it does not follow that people in this state will then tell the truth and nothing but the truth. In a case involving a confession to a murder obtained after a police physician administered a so-called truth serum, the U.S. Supreme Court ruled that the conviction was unconstitutional (*Townsend v. Sain*, 1963). A federal appeals court made little distinction between alcohol intoxication and truth serums, saying:

> *The intravenous injection of a drug by a physician in a hospital may appear more scientific than the drinking of large amounts of bourbon in a tavern, but the end result displayed in the subject's speech may be no more reliable (Lindsey v. United States, 1956).*

A stronger dose of sodium pentothal is commonly used as a sedative, an anesthetic during surgery, and it is the first of three drugs administered during execution by lethal injection. The use of barbiturates to elicit repressed and suppressed information from patients has long been used in psychotherapy but does not provide a reliable way to deal with, for example, suspected malingering (Rogers & Wettstein, 1988). In fact, these so-called truth serums also make a patient more susceptible to suggestion, so psychiatrists sometimes inadvertently bias the feelings and/or memories the patient reveals.

Furthermore, these drugs can lead a person to confuse truth and illusion (Sullivan, 2001), so it is no surprise that some state courts treat confessions and testimony induced by these drugs as inadmissible. Some researchers are finding that oxytocin, a hormone also used as a drug, may increase honesty and cooperation (Arueti et al., 2013). But, as we have seen with other truth serums, it is not likely to be used in real applications or allowed in legal proceedings.

INTEGRITY TESTS: PAPER LIE DETECTORS?

Each year millions of integrity tests, also known as honesty tests, are given to people—primarily as a pre-employment screening procedure. The tests are designed to reduce the effects of illegal and counterproductive behavior in the workplace such as theft and absenteeism. Some tests focus on the identification of certain personality characteristics—e.g., hostility, dependability, conscientiousness, and trouble with authority. Other tests probe an applicant's attitudes toward honesty and previous involvement with counterproductive work behavior. These tests, then, seem better designed to detect honesty than deception.

Even though the socially desirable answer to such questions may seem obvious, the creators of the test normally have ways to offset "faking good" responses (Miner & Capps, 1996). Sometimes special scales are used that were derived by asking people to answer questions based on what they *think* is the desired response. Items with a high degree of social desirability are eliminated or given less weight in scoring. Or the consistency or inconsistency associated with several items may be used to indicate fake-good responses. When test takers are suspected of faking good answers, their results are invalidated.

The question of whether honesty tests actually measure honesty has been controversial (O'Bannon, Goldinger, & Appleby, 1989; Ones, Viswesvaran, & Schmidt, 1993; Sackett, Burris, & Callahan, 1989; U.S. Congress, 1990). In a perfect world, the employee's honest and dishonest behavior on the job would be compared with his or her test score in order to determine the validity of the test. But, as is readily obvious, the honesty criterion is not easy to establish. For example:

1. the data from a person who would have been honest on the job may not be included because he or she was denied employment due to an honest admission of stealing something as a child

2. a lot of dishonest (and honest) employee behavior is unknown to the employer

3. a person may be treated as a dishonest employee for lying about something trivial, but that same person might be honest about a matter with serious consequences

lying and deception in HUMAN INTERACTION

A meta-analysis of the results of 300 integrity test studies found that their validity is low for job and training performance, counterproductive work behaviors, and turnover (Van Iddekinge, Roth, Raymark, & Odle-Dusseau, 2012). Self-reported attitudes are a poor predictor of actual behavior. Almost everyone believes they are generally honest and will honestly report that as they answer items on an integrity test. But it does not necessarily follow that their behavior in an actual situation will mirror their response to an item on a test.

> Almost everyone believes they are generally honest and will honestly report that as they answer items on an honesty test. But it does not necessarily follow that their behavior in an actual situation will mirror their response to an item on a test.

A number of studies do report positive correlations between the results of integrity tests and (1) counterproductive workplace behavior (e.g., job turnover, absenteeism) and (2) supervisor ratings of employees. But critics argue that too many of the studies supporting the validity of these tests were conducted by people associated with the development of the tests.

Honesty tests, like other methods of assisted deception detection, are subject to a certain amount of error. It is therefore inevitable that such techniques will eliminate some people with integrity who would have been upstanding employees and support the hiring of others who turn out to be disasters. Many agree that honesty tests should not be the sole basis for an employment decision, but that they are likely to be a screening measure that is as good, if not better, than the alternatives—e.g., references, a background check, a drug test, or an integrity-focused, in-person interview.

ANALYZING VERBAL CLUES

In everyday interaction, people can listen for verbal clues to deception, but computers provide a way of rapidly analyzing the speech of a suspected liar. What language patterns do these methods attribute to liars and how accurate are they?

- Pennebaker, Booth, and Francis (2007) developed a computer program that searches 2,300 words and word stems, each of which can be put in several different categories—e.g., the word "cried" could be classified as "sadness," "negative emotion," "overall affect," and a "past tense verb." Their system, *Linguistic Inquiry and Word Count (LIWC)*, has identified the following linguistic features as occurring significantly more among liars than truth tellers: fewer first person singular pronouns (*I, me, my*); more negative emotion words; and fewer "exclusive" words—i.e., prepositions and conjunctions such as *but, except, without* used by speakers to distinguish one thing from another (Pennebaker, 2011).

- *Statement Validity Analysis (SVA)* was originally developed as a way of testing the veracity of testimony by child witnesses and victims in cases of sexual abuse (Undeutsch, 1982). Courts in several European countries allow the results of SVA to be introduced as evidence. SVA involves three steps: a structured interview with the target, an analysis of the verbal content contained in a transcript of the initial interview, and an interpretation of the content analysis using a standard set of questions (Köhnken, 2004). But the problems associated with SVA are plentiful. The content analysis is dependent on a single person, and laboratory studies indicate that SVA is inaccurate 25–35% of the time (Vrij, 2000). And Bull (2004) said that attempts to train police and social workers to perform the analysis were problematic.

- Another approach is called *Scientific Content Analysis (SCAN)* (Sapir, 1987). This system for deception detection is based on assumptions about the nature of truthful statements versus untruthful statements. Unfortunately, individual differences in personality, gender, and culture are not taken into consideration (Shearer, 1999). McClish (2008) developed his own method of statement analysis by combining information from methods like SCAN with what he intuitively derived from his own experience at the U.S. Marshall's Service Training Academy. His website, StatementAnalysis.com, features a program built into the domain where users can upload a text statement and receive an analysis of deception—but a subscription is required.

- *Reality Monitoring (RM)* is a method of analyzing language use that is based on the belief that true memories are encoded differently than created ones (Johnson & Raye, 1981; Sporer, 2004). True memories are believed to contain more representations attributed to the senses and more contextual information—e.g., remembered feelings and precise story details. Vrij (2014) cites various studies that show RM is able to identify liars from 63% to 72% of the time. Overall, he claims the tool achieves 70% accuracy.

In an effort to test several of the preceding methods, Porter and Yuille (1996) conducted an experiment. They told university students to steal money from a folder in a professor's office while others were given permission to retrieve the same folder (without the money in it). In a subsequent interview, some students were told to confess the truth, others were told to create a truthful alibi, still others were told to mix some true statements with some lies, and the last group was told to invent a completely false alibi. All of the students were given a small monetary payment to increase their motivation. Each student was interrogated with the same structured interview and their responses were transcribed for analysis. The verbal behavior on the transcript was analyzed with SVA, RM, SCAN, and similar methods. Only 3 of 18 language features showed any significant differences between liars and truth tellers. These three, all from SVA, identify the verbal behavior of truth tellers as containing *more details,* being *twice as coherent,* and having more *admissions of memory loss.*

Using computer programs and other linguistic analysis tools to examine various kinds of verbal behavior does provide a quicker and more systematic way of analyzing a complex data set, but as we have seen with all of the mechanisms in this chapter, achieving a very high rate of distinguishing liars from truth tellers is difficult. Reliably detecting veracity using certain patterns of verbal behavior and lexical patterns will require more research and further advances in technology. We still have a long way to go.

ANALYZING FACIAL CLUES

Feelings are reflected in facial expressions, so the facial expression (or some part of it) reflecting a liar's true feelings may "leak" and appear in a fleeting facial microexpression. These microexpressions are often missed by untrained human observers (Ekman, 2001), but with training or video records, they can be identified. The Facial Affect Coding System (FACS) enables researchers to code virtually any facial movement (Ekman & Friesen, 1978).

© Rvector/Shutterstock.com

FACS has been used in conjunction with computers that study video of faces in order to identify the type of facial expression, its intensity, and the onset/offset time (Bartlett, Hager, Ekman, & Sejnowski, 1999; Cohen, Zlochower, Lien, & Kanade, 1999). The computer-assisted analysis of facial expressions is faster and more accurate than human observers. Bartlett, Littlewort, Frank, and Lee (2014) found that trained human observers were 55% accurate in discriminating between actual and faked facial expressions of pain; the computer was 85% accurate on the same task.

But as discussed elsewhere in the book, faces may not always be the best place to look for lies. All of us get a lot of social feedback on our faces, and this facilitates a proficiency at facial deception. Practiced liars or those with a high level of motivation to succeed in a deception may show exceptional masking skills. In addition, the face may be a good place to look for some kinds of deception and not others. For example, Ekman, Friesen, and O'Sullivan (2005) had nurses tell an interviewer they were watching a pleasant film when, in fact, the film graphically portrayed amputations and burns. In this study, the researchers specifically focused on the extent to which nurses (who were highly motivated based on their career ambitions) manifested their true feelings in the way they smiled. Only about half of the nurses who were lying about the film they were watching were correctly identified. But a subsequent laboratory study involving lies about a theft or about political beliefs accurately classified 80% of both liars and truth tellers relying on FACS to measure micro-expressions (Frank & Ekman, 1997). Context, motivation, and the type of lie being told (e.g., false smiles versus opinion lies) all seem to influence the degree to which the face may betray liars.

AUTOMATED COMPUTER PROGRAMS

Recently, researchers at the University of Arizona began testing the Automated Virtual Agent for Truth Assessments in Real-Time (AVATAR) with U.S. Customs and Border Protection. The machine has a screen that displays an animated talking face asking yes or no questions to travelers crossing the border who have been pre-screened. The system monitors vocalics, eye movement, pupil dilation, and facial expressions and analyzes these cues to make a determination of veracity. Although published research is lacking on the success of this type of system, the researchers claim that the system reached up to 90% accuracy during its development in the lab (Border Patrol Kiosk Detects Liars, 2012). Burgoon, Schuetzler, and Wilson (2015) examined how computer programs are able to examine patterns or global trends in nonverbal cues during deception. The presence of rigidity in the body during concealed knowledge tests is also being examined with computer kiosks that interact with humans (Twyman, Elkins, Burgoon, & Nunamaker, 2014).

As more of our communication continues to take place via the Internet and through social media, deception detection via computer-mediated channels becomes increasingly important. Scientists are creating tools to detect fake Facebook profiles, spam product reviews (Ott, Cardie, & Hancock, 2012), and fake tweets (Gupta, Lamba, & Kumaraguru, 2013). Even research communities are seeking out computer-assisted tools to detect researchers who submit publications containing faked data (Konnikova, 2015).

Some basic questions remain when dealing with automated computer-assisted deception detection:

- Are the correct cues being measured?

- Is the measurement process effective and appropriate to the situation?

- Is the accuracy in identifying lies high enough to warrant further research with the system?

Also, we must recognize that there may be effects of avatar/human interactions that we do not yet understand. For example, some people may not like talking to a non-human during an interview that contains suspicious questioning. Although people are often enamored with the idea of finding a fool-proof way to detect lies, and the use of new technologies in everyday communication is becoming very common, the presence of some of the factors discussed in this chapter may mean that many of these will turn out to be frivolous pursuits.

SUMMARY

This chapter, like the preceding one, focused on lie detection. The central question addressed this time was whether machines, drugs, questionnaires, or computers provide accurate lie detection. The inescapable conclusion is that all known methods of lie detection are fallible and subject to substantial error rates, often 25% or more. These are terrifying odds for an innocent person and a poor way for a society to catch would-be criminals.

The polygraph is known as a lie-detection machine, but all it really detects are changes in a person's physiological arousal, measured by breathing, blood pressure, heart rate, and skin conductance. It is the *interpretation* of these changes that occur in response to certain questions that determines whether a lie is judged to have occurred or not. Because of the possibility of different interpretations given to the same data, and a sufficiently high error rate, polygraph results are not admissible as evidence in most court cases. The polygraph is least accurate when it is used to screen employees and more accurate when testing a suspect's knowledge of a specific crime. The most common polygraph error is identifying truth tellers as liars. Several studies indicate examinees can artificially alter their arousal in order to create a false polygraph reading. Despite numerous problems associated with the use of polygraphs as lie detectors, they are still widely used by law enforcement agencies.

Functional magnetic resonance imaging (fMRI) is an attempt to show which areas of the brain are activated when people lie. Some regions of the brain are stimulated for certain types of lies, but there may be more than one "lie response." Law enforcement and security agencies are hopeful that brain mapping will replace the polygraph as a more accurate method of detecting lies. Currently, the procedure is too expensive and faces too many limitations to experience widespread usage.

Mechanisms that show little likelihood of replacing the polygraph include those based on the assumption that liars will always manifest stress. Measuring stress in the voice, eyes, stomach, and the mouth are all ways that have been explored in the quest to find a better lie detector. Truth serums do not detect lies or truth. They make a person less inhibited and more talkative, but can't guarantee truth telling. Integrity questionnaires are designed to measure the honesty of prospective employees. Their validity is poor and often difficult to measure, and their questions are strongly affected by social desirability.

This chapter also discussed attempts to use computers to analyze the verbal and facial behavior of liars and truth tellers in an effort to identify distinguishing characteristics. It concluded by examining attempts to use computers that can interact with humans to catch lies and by touching on attempts to detect deception via online and social media communication.

So far our belief that machines will provide us with an infallible lie detector is unwarranted. We have examined physiological, psychological, and neurological data associated with liars and have yet to uncover a clearly identifiable pattern that occurs every time a person lies. Given the different types of lies, individual differences, and the inevitable use of countermeasures, the future identification of such a lie response is doubtful. As a consequence, we will have to treat lie detection as we do other predictions about human behavior—in terms of probabilities and as only one piece of information relative to the likelihood that a person has lied. It is especially important that the public be aware of the potential for error and invasion of privacy associated with any so-called lie detector marketed to consumers.

EXERCISES

1. Why do you think it is so hard to develop a machine that will identify liars and truth tellers with a high degree of accuracy? In your answer, consider the nature of language, the nature of lies, and the nature of human beings.

2. Do you think the fascination with machines as lie detection is peculiar to our own cultural history and values?

3. You are an inventor and have just designed the perfect lie detection instrument. What does it look like, how does it work, and what is it capable of doing?

4. You have just been approached by a person who has invented the perfect lie detection instrument. It can be held in one's hand, it is 100% accurate, and it can detect lies 100 feet away. The inventor wants to begin manufacturing and selling these devices to anyone who will buy them. They aren't cheap, but most people can afford one. You have the power to decide whether this product is marketed or destroyed. Make a list of the advantages and disadvantages you foresee and decide whether to approve it or not.

5. Do the Internet and social media make it easier or more difficult to catch lies? If there were ways to ensure that everyone could detect deception via social media, do you think people would continue to use these channels as a way to interact or might they fall out of favor?

OF INTEREST

On his YouTube channel, leading polygraph critic Doug Williams features the original *60 Minutes* interview that first propelled him to notoriety. He eventually served two years in prison as the result of a controversial federal sting operation.

Netflix's wildly popular *Making a Murderer* documentary generated renewed interest in Dr. Larry Farwell's brain fingerprinting technology after he was featured in Part 2 of the show. *Newsweek* summarizes the role Farwell played in helping Steven Avery's legal team formulate a new defense.

Despite its horrific track record as a general employment screening device, government agencies at various levels continue to (mis)place their faith in the polygraph. As a result, perfectly qualified candidates can be turned away in error. WIRED recounts the long, sad history of the polygraph in public life.

REFERENCES

Alder, K. (2007). *The lie detectors: The history of an American obsession.* New York, NY: Free Press.

Alexander, J. B. (2003). *Winning the war: Advanced weapons, strategies, and concepts for the post-9/11 world.* New York, NY: St. Martin's Press.

American Polygraph Association. (2015). Retrieved from http://www.polygraph.org/section/resources/frequently-asked-questions

American Psychological Association. (2004, August 5). The truth about lie detectors (aka polygraph tests). Retrieved from http://www.apa.org

Arueti, M., Perach-Barzilay, N., Tsoory, M. M., Berger, B., Getter, N., & Shamay-Tsoory, S. G. (2013). When two become one: The role of oxytocin in interpersonal coordination and cooperation. *Journal of Cognitive Neuroscience, 25,* 1418–1427. https://dx.doi.org/10.1162/jocn_a_00400

Atlas, T. (1985, December 21). Reagan lets Shultz, himself off the lie-test hook. *Chicago Tribune.* Retrieved from http://www.chicagotribune.com

Barnhorn, D., & Pegram, J. E. (2011). Speak the truth and tell no lies: An update for the Employee Polygraph Protection Act. *Hofstra Labor and Employment Law Journal, 29,* 141–187.

Bartlett, M. S., Littlewort, G. C., Frank, M. G., & Lee, K. (2014). Automatic decoding of facial movements reveals deceptive pain expressions. *Current Biology, 24,* 738–743. https://dx.doi.org/10.1016/j.cub.2014.02.009

Bartlett, M. S., Hager, J. C., Ekman, P., & Sejnowski, T. J. (1999). Measuring facial expressions by computer image analysis. *Psychophysiology, 36,* 253–263. https://dx.doi.org/10.1017/s0048577299971664

Border Patrol Kiosk Detects Liars. (2012). *Emergency Management.* Retrieved from http://www.emergencymgmt.com/safety/Border-Patrol-Kiosk-Detects-Liars.html

Boroff, D. (2018, August 5). Pig farmer with history of stalking arrests questioned again about Mollie Tibbetts, refuses to take polygraph. *New York Daily News.* Retrieved from http://www.nydailynews.com

Bull, R. (2004). Training to detect deception from behavioural cues: Attempts and problems. In P. A. Granhag & L. A. Strömwall (Eds.), *The detection of deception in forensic contexts* (pp. 251–268). New York, NY: Cambridge University Press. https://dx.doi.org/10.1017/cbo9780511490071.011

Burgoon, J.K., Schuetzler, R., & Wilson, D.W. (2015). Kinesic patterning in deceptive and truthful interactions. *Journal of Nonverbal Behavior, 39,* 1–24. https://dx.doi.org/10.1007/s10919-014-0190-4

Carlsen, E. (2010, Spring). Truth in the machine: Three Berkeley men converged to create the lie detector. *California.* Retrieved from http:// https://alumni.berkeley.edu/california-magazine

Cohen, J. F., Zlochower, A. J., Lien, J. J., & Kanade, T. (1999). Automated face analysis by feature point tracking has high concurrent validity with manual FACS coding. *Psychophysiology, 36*, 35–43. https://dx.doi.org/10.1017/s0048577299971184

Corcoran, J. F. T., Lewis, M. D., & Garver, R. B. (1978). Biofeedback—conditioned galvanic skin response and hypnotic suppression of arousal: A pilot study of their relation to deception. *Journal of Forensic Sciences, 23*, 155–162. https://dx.doi.org/10.1520/jfs10665j

Cronin, B. (2017, May 30). When did Wonder Woman's lasso become a weapon of truth? *Comic Book Resources*. Retrieved from http://www.cbr.com

Cummins, E. (2018, September 20). Polygraph tests don't work as lie detectors and they never have. *Popular Science*. Retrieved from http://www.popsci.com

Damphousse, K.R. (2008). Voice stress analysis: Only 15 percent of lies about drug use detected in field test. *National Institute of Justice Journal, 259*, 8–12. https://dx.doi.org/10.1037/e444972008-003

Defoe, D. (1731). An effectual scheme for the immediate preventing of street robberies and suppressing all other disorders of the night: With a brief history of the night-houses, and an appendix relating to those sons of hell, call'd incendiaries. London: Printed for J. Wilford. Retrieved from https://catalog.hathitrust.org/Record/100577418

Ekman, P. (2001). *Telling lies: Clues to deceit in the marketplace, politics, and marriage.* New York, NY: Norton.

Ekman, P., & Friesen, W. V. (1978). *Facial action coding system: A technique for the measurement of facial movement.* Palo Alto, CA: Consulting Psychologists Press. https://dx.doi.org/10.1037/t27734-000

Ekman, P., Friesen, W. V., & O'Sullivan, M. (2005). Smiles when lying. In P. Ekman & E. Rosenberg (Eds.), *What the face reveals* (pp. 201–216). New York, NY: Oxford University Press. https://dx.doi.org/10.1093/acprof:oso/9780195179644.003.0010

Eldeib, D. (2013, March 10). Polygraphs and false confessions in Chicago. *Chicago Tribune*. Retrieved from http://www.chicagotribune.com

Farwell, L. A., & Donchin, E. (1991). The truth will out: Interrogative polygraphy ("lie detection") with event-related brain potentials. *Psychophysiology, 28*, 531–547. https://dx.doi.org/10.1111/j.1469-8986.1991.tb01990.x

Feder, B. J. (2001, October 9). Truth and justice, by the blip of a brain wave. *New York Times*, p. D3.

Findley, K. A., & Scott, M. S. (2006). The multiple dimensions of tunnel vision in criminal cases. *Wisconsin Law Review, 2*, 291–397.

Frank, M. G., & Ekman, P. (1997). The ability to detect deceit generalizes across different types of high stake lies. *Journal of Personality and Social Psychology, 72*, 1429–1439. https://dx.doi.org/10.1037//0022-3514.72.6.1429

Ganis, G., Kosslyn, S. M., Stose, S., Thompson, W. L., & Yurgelun-Todd, D.A. (2003). Neural correlates of different types of deception: An fMRI investigation. *Cerebral Cortex, 13,* 830–836. https://dx.doi.org/10.1093/cercor/13.8.830

Ganis, G., Rosenfeld, J. P., Meixner, J., Kievit, R. A., & Schendan, H. E. (2011). Lying in the scanner: Covert countermeasures disrupt deception detection by functional magnetic resonance imaging. *Neuroimage, 55,* 312–319. https://dx.doi.org/10.1016/j.neuroimage.2010.11.025

Grimes, W. (2007, March 2). The tangled web of the truth machine. *New York Times.* Retrieved from http://www.nytimes.com

Gupta, A., Lamba, H., & Kumaraguru, P. (2013). $1.00 per rt# bostonmarathon# prayforboston: Analyzing fake content on Twitter. In *eCrime Researchers Summit* (pp. 1–12). IEEE. https://dx.doi.org/10.1109/ecrs.2013.6805772

Harden, B. (2003, November 6). Killer of 48 women makes deal to avoid death penalty. *Austin American Statesman,* pp. Al, 9.

Harnsberger, J. D., Hollien, H., Martin, C. A., & Hollien, K. A. (2009). Stress and deception in speech: Evaluating layered voice analysis. *Journal of Forensic Sciences, 54,* 642–650. https://dx.doi.org/10.1111/j.1556-4029.2009.01026.x

Hasson, J. (1983, March 11). Reagan cracks down on leaks. *UPI.* Retrieved from http://www.upi.com/archives

Henig, R.M. (2006, February 5). Looking for the lie. *New York Times Magazine,* Section 6, pp. 47–57.

Hollien, H. (1990). *The Acoustics of crime: The new science of forensic phonetics.* New York, NY: Plenum.

Honts, C.R. (1994). Psychophysiological detection of deception. *Current Directions in Psychological Science, 3,* 77–82. https://dx.doi.org/10.1111/1467-8721.ep10770427

Honts, C. R., & Hodes, R. L. (1982). The effect of multiple physical countermeasures on the detection of deception. *Psychophysiology, 19,* 564–565. (Abstract).

Honts, C. R., Raskin, D. C., & Kircher, J. C. (1983). Detection of deception: Effectiveness of physical countermeasures under high motivation conditions. *Psychophysiology, 20,* 446–447. https://dx.doi.org/10.1111/j.1469-8986.1983.tb00923.x

Honts, C. R., Raskin, D. C., & Kircher, J. C. (1994). Mental and physical countermeasures reduce the accuracy of polygraph tests. *Journal of Applied Psychology, 79,* 252–259. https://dx.doi.org/10.1037//0021-9010.79.2.252

Honts, C. R., Devitt, M. K., Winbush, M., & Kircher, J. C. (1996). Mental and physical countermeasures reduce the accuracy of the concealed knowledge test. *Psychophysiology, 33,* 84–92. https://dx.doi.org/10.1111/j.1469-8986.1996.tb02111.x

Horvath, F. (1982). Detecting deception: The promise and reality of voice stress analysis. *Journal of Forensic Sciences, 27,* 340–352. https://dx.doi.org/10.1520/jfs11488j

Howerton, M. (2016, November 4). Rare NM Law allows polygraph results in criminal trials. *KOAT Action 7 News.* Retrieved from http://www.koat.com

Hu, X., Hegeman, D., Landry, E., & Rosenfeld, J.P. (2012). Increasing the number of irrelevant stimuli increases ability to detect countermeasures to the P300-based complex trial protocol for concealed information detection. *Psychophysiology, 49,* 85–95. https://dx.doi.org/10.1111/j.1469-8986.2011.01286.x

Iacono, W. G., & Patrick, C. J. (1988). Assessing deception: Polygraph techniques. In Rogers, R. (Ed.), *Clinical assessment of malingering and deception* (pp. 205–233). New York, NY: Guilford.

Johnson, M. K., & Raye, C. L. (1981). Reality monitoring. *Psychological Bulletin, 88,* 67–85. https://dx.doi.org/10.1037/0033-295x.88.1.67

Kassin, S. M., Dror, I. E., & Kukucka, J. (2013). The forensic confirmation bias: Problems, perspectives, and proposed solutions. *Journal of Applied Research in Memory and Cognition, 2,* 42–52. https://dx.doi.org/10.1016/j.jarmac.2013.01.001

Kelly, J. (2004). The truth about the lie detector. *Invention and Technology, 19,* 14–20.

Kleinmuntz, B., & Szucko, J. J. (1984a). Lie detection in ancient and modern times: A call for contemporary scientific study. *American Psychologist, 39,* 766–776. https://dx.doi.org/10.1037//0003-066x.39.7.766

Kleinmuntz, B., & Szucko, J. J. (1984b). A field study of the fallibility of polygraphic lie detection. *Nature, 308,* 449–450. https://dx.doi.org/10.1038/308449a0

Köhnken, G. (2004). Statement validity analysis and the 'detection of the truth.' In P. A. Granhag & L. A. Strömwall (Eds.), *The detection of deception in forensic contexts* (pp. 41–63). New York, NY: Cambridge University Press. https://dx.doi.org/10.1017/cbo9780511490071.003

Konnikova, M. (2015, May 22). How a gay-marriage study went wrong. *The New Yorker.* Retrieved from http://www.newyorker.com/science/

Kozel, F. A., Johnson, K. A., Mu, Q., Grenesko, E. L., Laken, S. J., & George, M. S. (2005). Detecting deception using functional magnetic resonance imaging. *Biological Psychiatry, 58,* 605–613. https://dx.doi.org/10.1016/j.biopsych.2005.07.040

Kozel, F. A., Padgett, T. M., & George, M. S. (2004). A replication of the neural correlates of deception. *Behavioral Neuroscience, 118,* 852–856. https://dx.doi.org/10.1037/0735-7044.118.4.852

Kozel, F. A., Revell, L. J., Lorberbaum, J. P., Shastri, A., Elhai, J. D., Horner, M. D., ... George, M.S. (2004). A pilot study of functional magnetic resonance imaging brain correlates of deception in healthy young men. *Journal of Neuropsychiatry and Clinical Neurosciences, 16,* 295–305. https://dx.doi.org/10.1176/jnp.16.3.295

Langleben, D.D., Schroeder, L., Maldjian, J. A., Gur, R. C., McDonald, S., Rangland, J. D., … Childress, A. R. (2002). Brain activity during simulated deception: An event-related functional magnetic resonance study. *NeuroImage, 15,* 727–732. https://dx.doi.org/10.1006/nimg.2001.1003

Lee, T. M. C., Liu, H. L., Tan, L. H., Chan, C. C. H., Mahankali, S., Feng, C. M., … Gao, J. H. (2002). Lie detection by functional magnetic resonance imaging. *Human Brain Mapping, 15,* 157–164. https://dx.doi.org/10.1002/hbm.10020

Lindsey v. United States, 237 F.2d 893 (9th Cir. 1956).

Lohr, D. (2018, August 17). Boyfriend of missing Phoenix teen Kiera Bergman refuses polygraph test. *HuffPost.* Retrieved from http://www.huffingtonpost.com

Lu, H., Frauendorfer, D., Rabbi, M., Mast, M. S., Chittaranjan, G. T., Campbell, A. T., … Choudhury, T. (2012). StressSense: Detecting stress in unconstrained acoustic environments using smart-phones. *In Proceedings of the 2012 ACM conference on ubiquitous computing,* 351–360. https://dx.doi.org/10.1145/2370216.2370270

Lykken, D.T. (1998). *A tremor in the blood: Uses and abuses of the lie detector.* New York, NY: Plenum.

MacAskill, E. (2015, January 4). British and Dutch researchers develop new form of lie-detector test. *The Guardian.* Retrieved from http://www.theguardian.com

Macdonald, J. V. (2016, July 8). William Moulton Marston, the psychologist who created Wonder Woman. *Mental Floss.* Retrieved from http://www.mentalfloss.com

MacNeil, J. (2018, February 2). Polygraph first used to get a conviction, February 2, 1935. *EDN Network.* Retrieved from http://www.edn.com

Marshall, D., & Thomas, T. (2015). Polygraphs and sex offenders: The truth is out there. *Probation Journal, 62,* 128–139. https://dx.doi.org/10.1177/0264550515571395

Martinez, G. (2018, August 22). Neighbor's security footage helped detectives crack Mollie Tibbetts case, investigator says. *Time.* Retrieved from http://www.time.com

McClish, M. (2008). *I know you are lying* (7th ed.). Winterville, NC: PoliceEmployment.com.

Mikkelson, B. (2011, July 4). Colander lie detector. Retrieved from http://www.snopes.com

Miner, J. B., & Capps, M. N. (1996). *How honesty testing works.* Westport, CT: Quorum.

Moss, B. P., & Zaid, M. (2018, September 7). Trump wants to polygraph his own staff. That's nuts. *Politico Magazine.* Retrieved from http://www.politico.com

National Research Council. (2003). *The polygraph and lie detection.* Washington, DC: The National Academies Press. https://dx.doi.org/10.17226/10420

O'Bannon, R. M., Goldinger, L., & Appleby, G. S. (1989). *Honesty and integrity testing: A practical guide.* Atlanta, GA: Applied Information Resources.

Ones, D. S., Viswesvaran, C., & Schmidt, F. L. (1993). Comprehensive meta-analysis of integrity test validities: Findings and implications for personnel selection and theories of job performance. *Journal of Applied Psychology, 78,* 679–703. https://dx.doi.org/10.1037//0021-9010.78.4.679

Ott, M., Cardie, C., & Hancock, J. (2012). Estimating the prevalence of deception in online review communities. *In Proceedings of the 21st international conference on World Wide Web* (pp. 201–210). ACM. https://dx.doi.org/10.1145/2187836.2187864

Pasricha, T., Sallam, H., Chen, J., & Pasricha, P. J. (2008). The moment of truth: Stress, lying and the GI tract. *Expert Review, Gastroenterol Hepatol, 2,* 291–293. https://dx.doi.org/10.1586/17474124.2.3.291

Pavlidis, I., Eberhardt, N. L., & Levine, J. (2002). Seeing through the face of deception. *Nature, 415,* 35. https://dx.doi.org/10.1038/415035a

Pennebaker, J. W. (2011). *The secret life of pronouns: What our words say about us.* New York, NY: Bloomsbury Press.

Pennebaker, J. W., Booth, R. J., & Francis, M. E. (2007). Linguistic Inquiry and Word Count (LIWC 2001). Austin, TX: Liwc.net.

Phan, K. L., Magalhaes, A., Ziemlewicz, T. J., Fitzgerald, D. A., Green, C., & Smith, W. (2005). Neural correlates of telling lies: A functional magnetic resonance imaging study at 4 Tesla. *Academic Radiology, 12,* 164–172. https://dx.doi.org/10.1016/j.acra.2004.11.023

Pincus, W. (1994, April 29). Ames pleads guilty to spying, gets life term. *Washington Post.* Retrieved from http://www.washingtonpost.com

Porter, S., & Yuille, J. C. (1996). The language of deceit: An investigation of the verbal clues to deception in the interrogation context. *Law and Human Behavior, 20,* 443–457. https://dx.doi.org/10.1007/bf01498980

Raskin, D. C., Kircher, J. C., Horowitz, W. W., & Honts, C. R. (1989). Recent laboratory and field research on polygraph techniques. In J. C. Yuille (Ed.), *Credibility assessment* (pp. 1–24). Dordrecht, The Netherlands: Kluwer Academic Publishers. https://dx.doi.org/10.1007/978-94-015-7856-1_1

Ritter, M. (January 29, 2006). Brain scans may be used as lie detectors. *Associated Press.*

Roese, N. J., & Jamieson, D. W. (1993). Twenty years of bogus pipeline research: A critical review and meta-analysis. *Psychological Bulletin, 114,* 363–375. https://dx.doi.org/10.1037/0033-2909.114.2.363

Rogers, R., & Wettstein, R. M. (1988). Drug-assisted interviews to detect malingering and deception. In Rogers, R. (Ed.), *Clinical assessment of malingering and deception* (pp. 105–204). New York, NY: Guilford.

Rosenfeld, J. P., Soskins, M., Bosh, G., & Ryan, A. (2004). Simple, effective countermeasures to P300-based tests of detection of concealed information. *Psychophysiology, 41,* 205–219. https://dx.doi.org/10.1111/j.1469-8986.2004.00158.x

Rusconi, E., & Mitchener-Nissen, T. (2013). Prospects of functional magnetic resonance imaging as lie detector. *Frontiers in Human Neuroscience, 7.* https://dx.doi.org/10.3389/fnhum.2013.00594

Sackett, P. R., Burris, L. R., & Callahan, C. (1989). Integrity testing for personnel selection: An update. *Personnel Psychology, 42,* 491–529. https://doi.org/10.1111/j.1744-6570.1989.tb00666.x

Sapir, A. (1987). *The LSI course on scientific content analysis* (SCAN). Phoenix, AZ: Laboratory for Scientific Interrogation.

Saxe, L. (1994). Detection of deception: Polygraph and integrity tests. *Current Directions in Psychological Science, 3,* 69–73. https://dx.doi.org/10.1111/1467-8721.ep10770416

Shearer, R. A. (1999). Statement analysis: SCAN or scam? *Skeptical Inquirer, 23,* 40–43.

Spence, S. A., Farrow, T. F., Herford, A. E., Wilkinson, I. D., Zheng, Y., & Woodruff, P. W. (2001). Behavioural and functional anatomical correlates of deception in humans. *Neuroreport, 12,* 2849–2853. https://dx.doi.org/10.1097/00001756-200109170-00019

Sporer, L. S. (2004). Reality monitoring and detection of deception. In P. A. Granhag & L. A. Strömwall (Eds.), *The detection of deception in forensic contexts* (pp. 64–102). New York, NY: Cambridge University Press. https://dx.doi.org/10.1017/cbo9780511490071.004

Sullivan, E. (2001). *The concise book of lying.* New York, NY: Farrar, Straus & Giroux.

Synnott, J., Dietzel, D., & Ioannou, M. (2015). A review of the polygraph: History, methodology and current status. *Crime Psychology Review, 1*(1), 59–83. https://dx.doi.org/10.1080/23744006.2015.1060080

Talbot, M. (2007, July 2) Duped. *The New Yorker,* 52–61.

ten Brinke, L., Stimson, D., & Carney, D. R. (2014). Some evidence for unconscious lie detection. *Psychological Science, 25,* 1098–1105. https://dx.doi.org/10.1177/0956797614524421

Townsend v. Sain, 327 U.S. 293 (U.S. Supreme Court, 1963).

Tucker, E. (1985, November 18). Refusal to take polygraph test leads to Md. court contest. *The Washington Post.* Retrieved from http://www.washingtonpost.com

Twyman, N. W., Elkins, A. C., Burgoon, J. K., & Nunamaker, J. F. (2014). A rigidity detection system for automated credibility assessment. *Journal of Management Information Systems, 31,* 173–202. https://dx.doi.org/10.2753/mis0742-1222310108

Undeutsch, U. (1982). Statement reality analysis. In A. Trankell (Ed.), *Reconstructing the past: The role of psychologists in criminal trials* (pp. 27–56). Deventer, The Netherlands: Kluwer.

United States v. Scheffer, 523 US 303 (1998).

U.S. Congress, Office of Technology Assessment. (1983). *Scientific validity of polygraph testing* (OTA-TM-H-15). Washington, DC: U.S. Government Printing Office.

U.S. Congress, Office of Technology Assessment. (1990). *The use of integrity tests for pre-employment screening* (OTA-SET-442). Washington, DC: U.S. Government Printing Office.

U.S. General Accounting Office (2001). *Investigative techniques federal agency views on the potential application of "brain fingerprinting."* Washington, DC: U.S. Government Printing Office.

Van Iddekinge, C.H., Roth, P.L., Raymark, P.H., & Odle-Dusseau, H.N. (2012). The criterion-related validity of integrity tests: An updated meta-analysis. *Journal of Applied Psychology, 97,* 499–530. https://dx.doi.org/10.1037/a0021196

Vennapoosa, C. (2010, January 4). Polygraph questioning techniques. *Exforsys, Inc.* Retrieved from http://www.exforsys.com

Vrij, A. (2000). *Detecting lies and deceit: The psychology of lying and the implications for professional practice.* New York, NY: Wiley.

Vrij, A. (2014). Verbal lie detection tools: Statement Validity Analysis, Reality Monitoring and Scientific Content Analysis. In P. A. Granhag, A. Vrij, & B. Verschuere (Eds.), *Detecting deception: Current challenges and cognitive approaches* (pp. 3–36). West Sussex, England: Wiley & Sons. https://dx.doi.org/10.1002/9781118510001.ch1

Waid, W. M., Orne, E. C., Cook, M. R., & Orne, M. T. (1981). Meprobamate reduces accuracy of physiological detection of deception. *Science, 212,* 71–73. https://dx.doi.org/10.1126/science.7209522

Zelicoff, A. P. (2002, August 9). Polygraph hypocrisy. *Washington Post,* p. A23.

PART IV

ying and deception for the masses

PART IV lying and deception for the masses

The previous chapters have portrayed lying and deception primarily from the standpoint of interpersonal communication. In these final chapters, the context for our discussion is the public arena. Chapter 11 focuses primarily on spoken messages delivered by political leaders to mass audiences and addresses questions like how much honesty people really want from their leaders and how much deception they are willing to tolerate. In Chapter 12, we turn our attention to written messages that reach the masses, examining lying and deception by journalists, historians, and others. Chapter 13 is devoted to the deceptive nature of visual messages seen by the public and delivered via a variety of media.

CHAPTER 11 Public Lies and Political Leadership

"The political arena is second only to warfare as a domain where lies are expected, do in fact occur, and to a substantial extent are tolerated."
– J. A. Barnes

"Political language. . .is designed to make lies sound truthful and murder respectable."
– George Orwell

"Controlling stories is power indeed. And who could benefit most from such a power?"
– Kelly Barnhill

Despite their grand scale, public lies do have some characteristics in common with lies told between individuals:

- The *reasons* for lying are not all that different even though the language may be—e.g., "I didn't tell you in order to protect our marriage" vs. "Withholding that information from the public is in the interest of national security."

- *Self-deception* is another quality found in both interpersonal and public acts of deception. The need for makers of a failed public policy to convince themselves that their policy is sound is not all that different from what a spouse may do in response to a failing marriage.

- The types of lies in both public and interpersonal spheres range from relatively unimportant (low stakes) to serious (high stakes).

- Messages designed for public consumption, like those targeted at a specific individual, may also use linguistic constructions that leave the question of intentional deceit ambiguous (see deception's "blood relatives" in Chapter 7).

- The mutual influence of liar and target is also a feature that interpersonal and public lies share. By the expectations they espouse and their response to deceptive messages, the public exerts an influence on the construction of messages directed its way by leaders; similarly, leaders influence public responses by the way they choose to publicly communicate.

But public lies are also distinguished by certain characteristics that make them decidedly unique from lies told between individuals.

SPECIAL CHARACTERISTICS OF PUBLIC LIES

The special nature of public lies can be understood by examining a few distinguishing features:

1. Adapting to multiple audiences
2. Information control
3. Message distribution and responsibility
4. Detection responsibility

Adapting to Multiple Audiences

The target of public lies sounds like a single entity, *the* public, but *the* public is composed of many audiences, each with its own needs and goals. Inevitably, groups with incompatible interests will seek favor from the same political leader. In a democracy, a leader needs as many votes as possible from each of these audiences in order to get (and stay) elected. How do politicians—whose own beliefs are bound to be at odds with some of the many audiences whose support they need—communicate in ways that gain widespread support? Certainly not by telling the unvarnished truth.

In an effort to gain the votes of audiences with competing views, the temptation may be great for leaders to pretend to support goals and positions that they do not. Put another way, deception can be a useful mechanism for mobilizing various sources of power needed by politicians. But Rue (1994) cautions that the process of building social coherence ". . . is achievable only within certain optimal limits of deception. That is, if there is too little or too much of it, then the social order will break down" (p. 215).

Information Control

You may have heard the expression "information is power." And in the information economy of the 21st century, such sayings have never been more fitting. Leaders realize that their ability to create and access information is a crucial factor in gaining and maintaining power:

- Sometimes pertinent information can be made even less accessible to the public when a deceiver classifies it for national security reasons.

- Individuals and/or groups loyal to the public liar may receive and use relevant information (whether true or false) that is not provided to other groups. For example, politicians often have media outlets they favor and others they ignore.

- Public lies may also be shaped and structured in elaborate ways, using a variety of resources at the command of the leader. The goal is to influence when an issue is discussed and how the public should think about it. When he was a presidential candidate, Richard Nixon was televised while he pretended to be taking phone calls from the public (Pratkanis & Aronson, 2001). "Astroturfing" is the term used to describe when public events are staged using paid participants, and the practice is common in modern politics (Schneider, 2015).

- Access to and control of information also allow presidents to falsely report or interpret events so that they fit a predetermined policy. During the presidential campaign of 1964, Lyndon Johnson repeatedly stated that he would not escalate the war in Vietnam by bombing North Vietnam. The Pentagon Papers later revealed that plans for bombing were being discussed while he was making these public assurances. Johnson's Republican opponent called him "soft" on bombing so the president was eager to counter that perception. The Gulf of Tonkin incident provided such an opportunity. On August 2, 1964, three North Vietnamese boats closed rapidly on two U.S. destroyers in the Tonkin Gulf. One of the destroyers fired first and one machine gun bullet from the boats struck a destroyer. No one was injured. Two nights later, a sonar operator supposedly reported a "continuous torpedo attack" resulting in the destroyers firing for hours at nothing. Johnson and Secretary of Defense Robert McNamara reported these events as vicious attacks on American troops that justified escalating the war by

© Stan Wayman/Contributor/Getty Images

Defense Secretary Robert McNamara

bombing North Vietnam. Almost 40 years later, in an interview for the documentary *The Fog of War* (Morris, 2003), an aging McNamara finally admitted what many journalists and critics of the Johnson administration had expected all along. He acknowledged the alleged torpedo attack never even happened. With Johnson's approval, the secretary had fabricated the story as a pretense for escalating the war against North Vietnam. But the revelation was merely the icing on the cake for a man who in some ways defined the art of the modern political lie. Journalists like David Halberstam were decrying McNamara's systematic pattern of deception as early as 1972. The secretary saw himself as a loyalist serving a greater good (the president, not the people), and that made him an especially effective deceiver. After all, what better way is there to control information than to make it up?

> *It was part of his sense of service. He believed in what he did, and thus the morality of it was assured, and everything else fell into place. It was all right to lie and dissemble for the right causes. It was part of service, loyalty to the President, not to the nation, not to colleagues, it was a very special bureaucratic-corporate definition of integrity; you could do almost anything you wanted as long as it served your superior. (p.581)*

- Two of the primary justifications George W. Bush gave the American public for the invasion of Iraq in 2003 were that: (1) Iraq had weapons of mass destruction (WMDs) and planned to use them against the United States, and (2) Iraq was working with Al Qaeda terrorists. The evidence supporting these claims was severely lacking and some key information that contradicted the claims was not revealed to the public (Rampton & Stauber, 2003).

- Barack Obama surged from his status as an idealistic but inexperienced first-term Illinois senator to winning the presidency by promising a new era of "hope and change."

This slogan was a deliberate jab at the outgoing Bush administration, whose credibility with the American public deteriorated after revelations about the false pretenses for the invasion of Iraq, its botched response to Hurricane Katrina, and a reluctance to police Wall Street that fueled the 2008

economic meltdown. During the course of his first presidential campaign, Obama pledged among other things to comprehensively reform America's health care system, in a way that would "bend the cost curve downward" while expanding insurance coverage to all Americans. When Republican opponents countered that federal control of the health insurance market would create higher costs and push millions of Americans out of their current plans, Obama reassured voters that "if you like your plan, you can keep your plan." He continued to make this promise repeatedly after being elected, through the legislative fight to pass the Affordable Care Act (ACA) of 2010, and during the 2012 campaign when Republican rival Mitt Romney warned voters that insurers might have to cancel many plans. Obama's promise was exposed as false in 2013, when insurers canceled millions of individual-market health insurance policies to replace them with ACA-compliant plans. Although some in his administration argued Obama's promise was based on "incomplete data" (resembling the "faulty intelligence" excuse Bush claimed as the impetus for invading Iraq), it came to light that officials from the Department of Health and Human Services had provided the president with a report in 2010 explicitly stating it was unlikely his promise could be kept. White House officials reportedly put the "sensitive" report on lockdown until after Obama's re-election (Griffin & Frates, 2013).

Leaders may have legitimate reasons for not revealing certain sources of information, but saying their sources are classified or "sensitive" is a tactic also used by those who do not want their claims to be closely scrutinized (in the Trump era, this would seem to be the default approach). As Wise (1973) points out, "One of the most damaging aspects of government lying is that even if the truth later emerges, it seldom does so in time to influence public opinion or public policy" (p. 345).

Message Distribution and Responsibility

Leaders in the modern world often have others who deliver deceptive messages on their behalf (another strategy that has surged in popularity under Trump). There are plenty of staff members, friends, family, supporters—even media outlets—who assume this responsibility, with or without explicit instructions from the top. The actions on behalf of the president by cabinet members, other government agencies, public relations firms, and political supporters often buffer his or her responsibility for deceptive intent. This is why a leader's accountability for deception is often difficult to prove. John Poindexter, President Reagan's National Security Advisor, used a much-maligned strategy known as *plausible deniability*, designed to shield the president from responsibility for direct knowledge of illegal actions that occurred during the Iran-Contra affair (Walton, 1996).

Nevertheless, outright deception occurs when government sources try to *manipulate* information that is disseminated to the public. This can occur in a variety of ways but usually involves attempts to influence news reports. Three common strategies are: (1) event staging, (2) pseudo-events, and (3) planting prepackaged and unidentified news reports with the media.

Staged Events

Both major political parties have a long history of creating props, planting audience questions, scripting the president's behavior, and in other ways manipulating events to ensure they cast an impression of a leader who is positive, confident, and in control. In 2005, a satellite television feed accidentally captured these preparations for a reportedly "spontaneous" give-and-take videoconference President Bush scheduled with American troops in Iraq. It was billed as a chance for the president to hear directly from the troops and White House reporters were summoned to witness the event. The participating soldiers were handpicked and coached for 45 minutes prior to the interaction on what questions the president would ask, what answers they should give, and how best to express their answers. Even with the preparation, there were awkward moments when the answers didn't match the questions. At first, the existence of any rehearsal was denied by the White House and Pentagon. Later, a White House spokesman said the prepping was done in order to make the soldiers feel at ease (VandeHei, 2005).

Pseudo-Events

A "pseudo-event" is an event that occurs solely for the purpose of generating media and public attention. The term was coined by historian Daniel Boorstin (1992) to describe a tactic perfected by Edward Bernays, who founded the field of public relations and also happened to be a nephew of psychoanalysis pioneer Sigmund Freud. A crucial element of Bernays' strategy was to create pseudo-events, which on their surface appeared to have a purpose different from their true goal. For example, consider a famous pseudo-event Bernays created in 1929 during the Easter Parade in New York City. A group of well-dressed women led by Bertha Hunt started a scandal by walking into a crowded Fifth Avenue during the height of the parade and lighting up cigarettes.

At the time, smoking tobacco was chiefly a habit for men in the United States. Women who smoked were stigmatized as being "of low character" and occasionally arrested for engaging in what most people thought should be a strictly male activity (Segrave, 2005). Bernays informed several newspapers in advance that this "protest act" was going to happen, saying the women were smoking in a public place to display their "liberation" from outdated sexist mores. And that's how the press covered it—the *New York Times* ran a story about it titled "Group of Girls Puff at Cigarettes as a Gesture of Freedom" (Tye, 1998). Coverage of what came to be known as the "Torches of Freedom March" quickly spread to newspapers across the country.

In reality, the women were not smoking in public as a protest. Bertha Hunt (Bernays' secretary) and several of her friends had been paid to do it by George Washington Hill, President of the American Tobacco Company. Hill was an opportunist, not a feminist. "If I can crack the women's market, it will be like opening a new gold mine right in our front yard," he told Bernays (Brandt, 2009, p. 82). Public attention to the "march" made Hill's wish come true— women's use of tobacco in public increased dramatically across the country. The impact of this pseudo-event on women's smoking stems in part from its masquerade as something other than an ad campaign; previous campaigns that explicitly encouraged women to buy cigarettes had failed miserably (Segrave, 2005).

This tactic has been used by several presidential administrations to manage public relations. The aforementioned second Tonkin Gulf attack on U.S. ships claimed by the Johnson Administration could be counted as a pseudo-event, although technically there was no "event" in the first place. A more canonical but equally deceptive example occurred during the George H.W. Bush Administration in 1990. A 15-year-old Kuwaiti girl identified only as Nayirah appeared before the "Congressional Human Rights Caucus" in Washington, DC to describe war atrocities she witnessed when her country was invaded months earlier by Iraqi troops led by President Saddam Hussein. Her oral testimony lasted only minutes, but received extensive news coverage that shocked the American public. Nayirah claimed to have been present when Iraqi soldiers forced their way into a hospital in Kuwait City and burst into the nursery where she worked as a volunteer. She reported watching in horror as the soldiers "took the babies out of incubators, took the incubators, and left the children to die on the cold floor. It was horrifying." President Bush quoted Nayirah's testimony numerous times in the weeks that followed as he made a case to the American public for why the United States should intervene. Public sentiment toward getting involved in the "crisis in the Persian Gulf" was initially quite negative, but Americans gradually came to accept Bush's case, thanks in part to Nayirah's heart-wrenching testimony. But two years after the United States entered the "Gulf War," it came to light that Nayirah's account was a complete fabrication. She had not observed soldiers entering the hospital, nor had she ever volunteered in the hospital, nor was she even in Kuwait during the Iraqi occupation. At the time, she was attending a private boarding school in Maryland, a privilege she enjoyed as the daughter of the Kuwaiti Ambassador to the United States. And despite its official sounding title, the "caucus" she testified before was not technically a government-sponsored event, but a publicity stunt created by the PR firm Hill & Knowlton with funding from the Kuwaiti government and quiet encouragement from the Bush Administration (MacArthur, 1992).

Prepackaged News

In 1983, Jamieson and Campbell made an observation that might easily have been made today: "There is considerable evidence of the power of government to manipulate press coverage. Government agencies spend huge sums of money to disseminate their messages through the mass media" (p. 103). This can be done through news "leaks" or newspaper editorials, but a controversial method that briefly gained popularity in the mid-2000s was the video news release (VNR). These professionally produced video segments were designed to present a particular point of view while appearing to be just another news story produced by a television network or local station. Thousands of VNRs were distributed and broadcast—many without acknowledgment of the government's role in their production (Barstow & Stein, 2005; Nelson & Park, 2014). They were typically produced by public relations firms hired by federal agencies although some federal agencies produced their own.

Despite the fact that many messages from leaders emanate from sources other than their own mouth, presidential candidates and presidents do speak directly to the public on occasion—e.g., presidential debates, press conferences, and formal televised speeches. But rehearsals and scripting of behavior are very much at play in these appearances, so the behaviors typically associated with liars in more spontaneous contexts (see Chapter 7) may not be useful indicators of deception. When leaders have such a high degree of control over the dissemination and delivery of their messages, the methods of deception detection need to be adapted accordingly.

Detection Responsibility

When a leader communicates a deceptive message to the public, he or she has the advantage of special access to and control over information relevant to the issue. In addition, the question of whether the leader initiated the deceptive message can be hidden in a complex network of people and organizations that distribute the message. However, the sheer number of possible lie detectors representing the public interest can offset these advantages. Broadcast and print reporters, bloggers, whistleblowers, and special interest organizations are some of those who take on the responsibility for detecting deceptive public messages. The Annenberg School of Communication at the University of Pennsylvania maintains FactCheck, a system that monitors the factual accuracy of claims made by politicians in TV ads, debates, speeches, interviews, and news releases. PR Watch, a project of the Center for Media and Democracy, specifically focuses on deceptive and misleading public relations campaigns. The quantity and diversity of these watchdogs mean that there may be differing views on what is deceptive, the seriousness of the deception, and the source of the deception. But it is public participation in and discussion of these issues that enables consensus to occur if there is to be any.

Ultimately, it seems that the public is responsible for detecting lies directed its way. Some states have laws against political lying, but they are ineffective because:

1. they often conflict with the First Amendment right to free speech

2. they require proof the lie was done knowingly and with malice

3. they often cannot be enforced quickly enough in political campaigns to offset any damaging effects the lie may have had

In 1997, voters in the state of Washington were asked to consider implementing physician-assisted suicide. Opponents of the initiative distributed a leaflet that said, in part, that this proposal would "let doctors end patients' lives without benefit of safeguards" and a person with "no special qualifications" could terminate a life, including "your eye doctor." The State brought suit against the opponents of Initiative 119, saying they had violated a state law against making false statements in political advertising. In a 5–4 vote, the Washington State Supreme Court argued that the responsibility for determining the truth or falsity of political speech did not rest with the State, but with the people (Jackson, 2007).

DOES THE PUBLIC WANT HONESTY FROM LEADERS?

The answer to this question is more complicated than one might think. On one hand, the American public does not maintain a high level of trust in the truthfulness of political and governmental leaders. The public is aware of many lies perpetrated by elected officials. As a result, the public regularly calls for its leaders and prospective leaders to exhibit greater honesty. At the same time, however, many don't expect leaders will ever exhibit the high level of honesty often called for. There may even be an implicit understanding that certain kinds of deception are a necessary part of any leader's behavior. In addition, it is clear that the public doesn't always want to hear the truth. On several occasions,

... it is clear that the public doesn't always want to hear the truth.

they have cast their presidential votes for the candidate they felt was more dishonest and voted against candidates who were explicitly forthright (e.g., in the 1984 campaign, when Mondale said he would raise taxes, his lead against Reagan eroded and never recovered). And given the quantity of leader behavior that is or might be deceptive, leaders are held accountable for relatively few falsehoods and punished for even fewer. In short, the public says they want more honesty from their leaders, but they don't expect or want them to be totally honest.

DIMINISHING TRUST AND THE DEMAND FOR TRUTH

Even though probably all U.S. presidents have lied to the American public, philosopher and cultural critic Sissela Bok (1978) believes that in 1960 when President Eisenhower lied about sending planes to spy on the Soviet Union, "it was one of the crucial turning points in the spiraling loss of confidence by U.S. citizens in the word of their leaders" (p. 142). Shortly thereafter, lies told to the American public about the conduct of the Vietnam War were revealed in the Pentagon Papers and President Nixon resigned after it was discovered he authorized and lied about a burglary of the Democratic Party's national headquarters. As a result, says Bok (1978) citing a 1975/76 Cambridge Survey Research poll that found 69% of Americans agreeing that "over the last ten years, this country's leaders have consistently lied to the people" (p. xviii).

The passage of time has done little to change the public trust in its leaders. An October 1992 Time/CNN poll found 63% of the respondents saying they had little confidence that government leaders talk straight and 75% believed there was less honesty in government in 1992 than there was in 1982. Nearly 40% said neither of the 1992 candidates for President (Bush and Clinton) usually told the truth. Gallup polls conducted over the last 40 years show a scalloped but overall consistent decline in American's trust of all three branches of the federal government (see Figure 11.1; numbers represent the percentage with a "great deal" or "fair amount" of trust in the branch).

A familiar charge by public deception detectors is that presidential candidates do not keep their campaign promises after they are elected. However, Fishel (1985) examined concrete promises by Presidents Kennedy, Johnson, Nixon, Carter, and Reagan and found serious, good faith efforts to keep roughly two thirds of their promises. A study of Clinton's promises came to the same conclusion (Jamieson, 2000).

The problem, of course, is that there is little or no effort devoted to about 33% of their promises, and some important promises are not kept despite a president's best efforts to do so. Furthermore, the public is not likely to remember many promises that are kept when ones of special significance are not—e.g., keeping the country out of war, ending a war, reducing the deficit, balancing the budget, providing adequate medical care. People may not remember the promises Barack Obama has kept, but many will remember losing health insurance

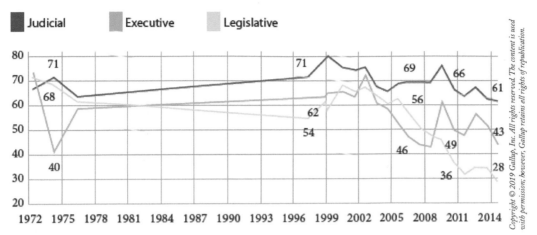

Figure 11.1: Americans' Trust in the Three Branches of Federal Government, 1972–2014 (Jones, 2014)

plans they liked after he said "if you like your plan, you can keep your plan." Donald Trump may well be remembered for utterly eclipsing his predecessors when it comes to making false or misleading claims. As of April 2019—just over two years into presidency—the *Washington Post*'s Fact Checker service had documented more than 10,000 such instances.

THE CONSEQUENCES OF DISTRUST

The negative fallout from this distrust is cynicism and a sense of helplessness within the public. Voters may find it hard to punish a candidate for deceptive behavior when all candidates appear to be deceptive. Some don't vote; others become cynical. The public's sense of futility in the face of lying leaders was ironically captured by President Nixon, who reportedly had no compunction about lying to anyone—the press, the public, or his closest staff members (Gergen, 2000; Rceves, 2001):

> . . .*when information which properly belongs to the public is systematically withheld by those in power, the people soon become ignorant of their own affairs, distrustful of those who manage them, and—eventually—incapable of determining their own destinies (Wise, 1973, p. 339).*

A healthy society could not exist if no one ever trusted what politicians say, but a certain level of distrust may actually be functional in a democratic society. Barnes (1994) put it this way: "one argument in favour of democracy is that it prompts us to treat all statements by politicians with caution" (p. 33).

Wariness, however, is usually not sufficient and is often accompanied by a public outcry for greater honesty. In 1987, *U.S. News & World Report* found that 72% of the people they polled felt a president should *never* lie to the American public and 59% said a president should *never* lie to a foreign government (*U.S. News & World Report*). Not as many of today's savvy citizens are likely to subscribe to these extremes, but they still demand leaders with a greater sense of integrity and honesty. Or do they?

TELL US THE TRUTH AND WHAT WE WANT TO HEAR

> The public does not often respond favorably to a leader who dwells too long on the complexity of an issue, admits to being conflicted about a position, or confesses to being puzzled about how to solve a problem.

Many political analysts agree that presidential candidate Walter Mondale made a mistake that severely damaged his campaign when he said he might have to increase taxes in order to deal with the growing national debt. Former Governor of California Gray Davis was roundly criticized as an alarmist by the citizens of his state when he said there was credible evidence that terrorists were planning to bomb certain bridges and nothing happened. Political truth tellers don't always fare well (Garcia, 2004; Keller, 2001). The public does not often respond favorably to a leader who dwells too long on the complexity of an issue, admits to being conflicted about a position, or confesses to being puzzled about how to solve a problem. Garrett and Penny (1998) attribute this to the fact that "absolutism sells" so politicians seek to make complex issues deceptively simple and identify solutions as bipolar—either good or bad.

Leaders who receive public support are not only expected to have answers, they should have *feel-good* answers. When the public responds in this way, it is sure to play an influential role in any deceptive, inconsistent, or ambiguous messages from their leaders. Boorstin (1992) leaves little doubt about the role the public plays in structuring the messages it receives: "By harboring, nourishing, and ever enlarging our extravagant expectations we

© Yayayoyo/Shutterstock.com

create the demand for the illusions with which we deceive ourselves. And which we pay others to make to deceive us" (p. 5). Linking the phenomenon to the master of public illusion and manipulation, P. T. Barnum, Boorstin adds, "Barnum's great discovery was not how easy it was to deceive the public, but rather how much the public enjoyed being deceived"(p. 209).

DOES THE PUBLIC FAVOR DISHONESTY?

A month prior to the 1988 Presidential election and again in 1992, voters were asked by pollsters to rate the candidates' honesty on a scale of 1–10 with 10 being the most honest. In both years, the candidate who rated highest lost the election. In 1988, Bush won with a 6.4 rating while Dukakis had 6.9; in 1992, Clinton won with a 5.8 rating with Perot at 6.7 and Bush at 6.2. In 1996, 58% of those polled rated Dole having the most honesty and integrity, but Clinton was elected even though only 40% said he had the most honesty and integrity (Gallup Poll, 1996; Louis Harris Poll, 1988; Princeton Survey Research, 1992). How can we explain the public's call for honest leaders with their election of candidates who are rated less honest?

The answer, in a word, may be ideology, at least according to several recent studies. Dishonesty is unlikely to dissuade voters who are driven primary by ideology. In other words, a candidate or politician may be a prolific liar, but at least he or she is "my liar" (Healy, 2018). When politicians tell the public what they want to hear, make them feel comfortable, and demonstrate control of the situation, they become more likeable. Bailey (1988) says effective leaders engender a public trust that is based on something more akin to the kind of love you might have for a family member coupled with certain heroic virtues like courage, endurance, and a vision for the future. You believe in them, even though you may not always believe what they say. Once this kind of relationship has been achieved, it tends to diminish the desire for the close scrutiny and accounting of leader behavior. It would certainly help explain endorsements like this one by Jonathan Chait (2006) of the *New Republic*. After noting several instances of deceptive behavior by Senator John McCain, he explained his preference for McCain as President: "I think McCain has a genuine desire to transform his party and his country, and he's willing to say things he doesn't agree with in order to be able to do it."

There may even be an unspoken public awareness that getting things done and effectively communicating are not necessarily characteristic of the person who can always be counted on to be honest. Honesty, then, is a vital part of leadership, but leadership encompasses a great deal more than honesty alone. In at least one study, for example, leader characteristics like benevolence—even trust—mattered more than outright honesty (Yakowicz, 2014).

Occasionally, public officials are held accountable for their lies—in court or at the ballot box. But the public typically does not hold leaders accountable for much of their deceptive behavior.

This is particularly true when the leader is popular and the lives of the voting public are reasonably happy. But Jamieson (2000) points out that this is a perilous stance to take. Tolerance for deceptive discourse, she observes, makes the public a partner to the leader's deception, diminishes the value of the voter, and sets an inappropriate standard for those who govern.

LYING AND DECEPTION: THE LEADER'S PERSPECTIVE

Given the public's repeated call for honest political leaders, it is no surprise that politicians respond by saying they will be honest. Richard Nixon, one of our most deceptive presidents, told Republican delegates in 1968, "Truth will become the hallmark of the Nixon administration." Following Nixon's Watergate scandal, President Carter told voters he would never lie to the American public. U.S. Senator John McCain dubbed his 2000 bid for the Republican presidential nomination "The Straight Talk Express." President Reagan frequently told a story about his confessing to a personal foul that referees missed in a high school football game to illustrate how telling the truth had been firmly instilled in him. However, the story itself turned out to be not true (Pfiffner, 2004). Unlike his predecessors in office and on the campaign trail, President Trump gave what may be the most accurate answer to date on the honesty question: "I do try, and I always want to tell the truth. When I can, I tell the truth," he explained to an ABC News reporter (Cole, 2018). One thing is certain: If a leader believes that truth is a commodity that only one person can possess, this ironically requires characterizing one's opponents as falling short in this area—charging that they distort information, change their position on an issue, etc. A 48-hour fact-check of Trump on the campaign trail found that he did exactly that–being far less accurate when attacking the press or his opponents (Cohen, 2018).

Deception Plays a Role in the Political Process

Even as politicians trumpet their commitment to truth telling, they know that deception is also a part of the leader's communicative repertoire. In 2000, McCain's "Straight Talk Express" quickly derailed in South Carolina when he lied about his true feelings concerning the flying of the Confederate flag over the state's Capitol. The cause, he later said, was to keep from losing the South Carolina primary. Gearing up for a run at the Republican presidential nomination in 2008, McCain cultivated a friendship with televangelist Jerry Falwell whom he called an "evil influence on the Republican Party" only a few years earlier. He also praised President Bush's leadership

on the war on terror even though he had previously criticized many of Bush's decisions associated with it.

Politicians must make themselves and their accomplishments look good while undermining their opponents; members of their own party may require support they don't deserve; members of the opposition party may have to be cajoled in order to pass legislation; diverse groups of contributors and voters may want promises of future support; etc. Each of these circumstances may create difficult choices and deception is not an uncommon response. As Garrett and Penny (1998) observed: "If speaking the truth means losing the battle, political calculations often call for a lie" (p. 2). Rue believes some deception is an integral part of the political process:

> *If democracy were truly inconsistent with deception, then how does it come to pass, one wonders, that election campaigns are dominated by it? It comes to pass because the political system rewards it. (1994, p. 246)*

Leaders Are Likely to Be Skilled Deceivers

If politicians do decide to respond to certain situations with deceptive messages, they are likely to do so with considerable skill. This is particularly true for those at the top of the political food chain as they have the most experience. Deception is one manifestation of the many ways successful people manipulate their social environment. Being an effective communicator requires manipulation and may require deception in order to achieve a wide range of goals, including the establishment of reciprocal alliances, moving up in an organizational hierarchy, and acquiring resources (Buss, Gomes, Higgins, & Lauterbach, 1987). Deception, like truth telling (as noted in Chapter 1), is a way of accomplishing things.

Keating and Heltman (1994) offered some direct support for the belief that male leaders can be good deceivers if they choose to be. First, males were videotaped lying and telling the truth about their opinion of a distasteful drink. The degree to which each man was thought to be acting truthfully was rated without hearing the words they spoke. Later, the men participated in a group decision-making project without an appointed leader. The men who emerged as leaders in the decision-making groups were also the men whose deceptive messages were rated as most truthful. This pattern was also observed with children, but not adult females.

The Political Downside of Deception

Even though political leaders may become skilled deceivers who learn to use lies to accomplish worthwhile (and not so worthwhile) goals, they always run the risk of suffering the negative consequences that can accompany this behavior.

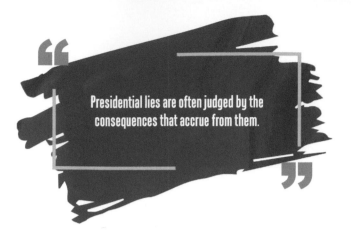

> Presidential lies are often judged by the consequences that accrue from them.

Presidential lies are often judged by the consequences that accrue from them. Positive consequences stemming from a policy that involved lies by a president may render the lies less consequential; negative consequences, however, are likely to magnify the outrage over the lies. Alterman (2004), however, cites several cases in which presidential lies to Congress and the American public about matters of war and peace seemed to have had minor consequences in the short term, but had major negative consequences for American policies in the long run—e.g., how Franklin Roosevelt's lies about agreements he made with Stalin at the Yalta conference set in motion more than four decades of a "cold war" with the Soviet Union.

Negative consequences may also take the form of voter disapproval or the disintegration of the deceiver's character. The risk to the deceiver's character is greater as deception becomes a less conscious and habitual response. When lying becomes an easy response and any sanctions associated with it are far from the deceiver's mind, deception may lose the strategic value it may have had. The deceiver has put aside the public's right to know and thinks he or she is the best judge of what the public needs. The goal of serving others takes a permanent back seat to the deceiver's own political desires. And the deceiver's reality becomes distorted by a belief in his or her own lies, which may lead to a sense of invulnerability and righteousness. Bok (1978, p. 173) addresses the issue in this way:

> As political leaders become accustomed to making such excuses, they grow insensitive to fairness and to veracity. Some come to believe that any lie can be told so long as they can convince themselves that people will be better off in the long run. From there, it is a short step to the conclusion that, even if people will not be better off from a particular lie, they will benefit by all maneuvers to keep the right people in office.

DECEPTION'S BLOOD RELATIVES REVISITED

Without information bearing on a speaker's intention to deceive, we run the risk of attributing deceptive intent to those who have none. For example, Ekman (2001) points out that a broken promise is not a lie unless the promise-maker did not intend to keep it; a false account may occur because the speaker believed it to be true or was unaware of contrary information; an exaggeration may not have been intended to be taken literally. At the same time, however, there are some linguistic and message constructions that seem more likely to stir within us the possibility of deception.

In Chapter 7 we introduced the concept of deception's blood relatives. The idea is that there are certain ways of constructing messages that increase the possibility that people will make attributions of deception—without any knowledge of the speaker's intent. Deceivers use these constructions, but they are also constructions that occur in everyday speech without any intention to mislead (Bavelas, Black, Chovil, & Mullett, 1990). Imprecision, ambiguity, and indirectness are but a few examples. Without clear proof of deceptive intent, the most that can be said is that these messages sometimes accentuate a close kinship to deception. Because these constructions are closely associated with deception, the presence of any contextual indicators of deception (e.g., the situation calls for it or rewards it) will quickly lead to an attribution of deception. Deception's blood relatives, according to Rue (1994, p. 246), comprise a useful part of the political leader's communicative repertoire.

> *There are many honest and truthful ways to elicit positive responses from voters, but it has long been recognized that they are less effective than deceptive means. Exaggeration, distortion, quoting out of context, innuendo, false promises, pandering, scare tactics, and flat-out-lies have become the standard fare of political campaigns.*

The way political speakers treat language, facts, and sources helps us understand why the blood relatives of deception bear such a close resemblance to deception itself. These constructions also help a speaker who is so inclined to deflect intent, responsibility, and previous knowledge.

Language

There are many ways to use language to deceive while simultaneously providing a reasonable defense against those who say deception has occurred. Some of these include:

- implying something but not asserting it
- using abstract terminology to create ambiguity rather than clarity
- being imprecise rather than precise
- addressing an issue indirectly rather than directly

For example, a politician may *imply* action, if not policy, by saying: "Our cars should get better gas mileage and we should not be dependent on oil. We need to use more ethanol." On the other hand, no action or policy was asserted so the intent to mislead can be denied. When a politician knows his or her message will be heard by multiple audiences, he or she may use *abstract and/or coded terminology* like "family values" to communicate with supporters while denying that there was any intent to mislead other audiences (Fleming, Darley, Hilton, & Kojetin, 1990).

Euphemisms are a way of *avoiding precise language* without admitting any intent to mislead—e.g., President Reagan's use of the phrase "tax reform" instead of "tax increase." Luntz (2007), a pollster for the Republican Party, advises candidates on the positive and negative power of certain words. He would have recommended "tax simplification" instead of "tax reform." To be positive, he advises, use "electronic intercepts" instead of "wiretapping," "opportunity scholarships" instead of "vouchers," and "exploring for energy" instead of "digging for oil." "Prosperity" can be counted on to deliver a positive reaction, whereas labeling an opponent as a product of "Washington" is likely to produce a less positive one.

Indirect speech is tangential, relating to one aspect of a question but not to its direct purpose ("Did you smoke marijuana?"—*"I never broke the laws of my country."*) or a non-sequitur ("How do you explain Bush's low approval ratings in the polls?"—*"Remember, these are only snapshots in time."*).

While such responses may be considered evasive and not the response preferred, labeling them as lies will be difficult to prove. Deceivers pay close attention to language and those who wish to expose them must listen carefully. When a politician says (as Clinton did), "I have authorized more new law enforcement officers to ensure the safety of our citizens than the previous two administrations combined," a listener would do well to focus on the word "authorized." There is no indication whether this authorization was approved and authorization does not have anything to do with keeping citizens safer.

Facts

Attention to potentially deceptive messages may also be linked to the way a speaker uses facts. Attributions of half-truths occur when listeners are aware of **pertinent omissions** and think they should have been included. Marro (1985) gives this example:

> "Question: Has the Assistant Secretary of State been invited to China? Answer: No. (Meaning: He will go to China as an adviser to the vice president. It is the vice president who has been invited. Therefore, I am not lying. Rationale: I have to say this because protocol requires that the Chinese must publicly extend the invitation.)"

In some instances, the speaker can argue that the omission was not pertinent or that he or she was unaware of the information. When a speaker does intend to mislead his audience, it is safer if the audience is unaware of the omission—e.g., a politician who accuses his opponent of proposing 2.2 trillion dollars in new spending without also saying that his or her own proposal contains 2.5 trillion in new spending.

The use of **inaccurate facts** is often the basis for accusing a person of a deliberately misleading message. But the speaker may respond by saying he or she was only repeating information they were given or that it was what he or she believed to be true at the time it was said. Cannon (2007), for example, argues that President George W. Bush believed he told the truth and that any statements he made that turned out to be false were made with the belief that they were true. Critics, however, point out that his initial lack of diligence in seeking out and weighing a diversity of facts bearing on a decision and his subsequent refusal to admit factual errors can turn attributions of "mistakes" into "deception" and "self-deception."

Unique interpretations of facts may also be a part of the deceiv-er's communicative bag of tricks. His or her defense is that the interpretation is not deliberately deceptive, and merely his or her own perception. But efforts to mislead can be transparent if they run counter to popular belief and/or other known facts. President Clinton's special interpretations were viewed within the situational demands for lying and other factual information. He denied having an "affair" with Monica Lewinsky because he felt the term "affair" implied romance and that was not the case; he also denied having a "sexual relationship" with Lewin-sky because he said he believed this phrase meant "intercourse," which was not part of their relationship. It was equally diffi-cult for Jim Oberweis in the 2006 Illinois GOP gubernatorial  campaign to defend his interpretations when he ran ads with selected news stories written about his opponent but altered the headlines to reflect negatively on his opponent (FactCheck, 2006). Political candidates are notorious for interpreting the same data in very different ways. For exam-ple, in the 2004 Presidential campaign, Bush said Kerry voted over 350 times for higher taxes on the American people during his 20-year Senate career. The Bush campaign included votes Kerry cast to leave taxes unchanged (when Republicans proposed cuts) and also votes he cast in favor of tax cuts proposed by Democrats that Bush aides viewed as watered down (Jackson, 2004).

Inconsistent statements legitimately occur when politicians face circumstances that alter their views. But incongruent position and policy statements may also be used deceptively. This can occur when audience support is sought by telling them what they want to hear, not what the politician believes. Thus, politicians often con-sider their own inconsistency as a modification of their position or a reversal, but their opponent's inconsistencies are "waffling," "indecisiveness," and "flip-flopping." If their language is carefully crafted or the inconsistency not well publicized, a politician may be able to argue that the seem-ingly inconsistent message is not inconsistent at all. If the inconsistency was not recorded, the politician may say he or she doesn't even remem-ber having made the statement.

> If their language is carefully crafted or the inconsistency not well publicized, a politician may be able to argue that the seemingly inconsistent message is not inconsistent at all.

Finally, deceivers sometimes use ***irrelevant facts*** to bolster the case for their political position or to attack others. Consider the compelling and factual story of Sarah McKinley told by gun rights advocate Gayle Trotter during a U.S. Senate hearing on gun violence in 2013:

> *Home alone with her baby, Sarah McKinley called 911 when two violent intruders began to break down her front door. Before police could arrive and while Ms. McKinley was still on the phone with 911, these violent intruders broke down her door. One of the men had a foot-long hunting knife. As the intruders force their way into her home, Ms. McKinley fired her weapon, fatally wounding one of the violent attackers. The other fled.*

Trotter told this story to support her case for why senators should vote against renewing the U.S. Assault Weapons Ban of 1994, which had expired in 2004. Efforts to renew the ban began shortly after the 2012 tragedy at Sandy Hook Elementary School in Newtown, Connecticut, when Adam Lanza murdered 20 young students and 6 adult staff members with an assault weapon before turning it on himself (Barron, 2012). Trotter's purpose in relating the story was clear—guns may be used to harm innocent people, but innocent people can also use them to defend themselves when police are slow to respond to a call for help. However, the Remington 870 Express 12-gauge shotgun Ms. McKinley used to fend off her attackers did not count as an assault weapon under the proposed legislation and thus would not have been banned by it (Weiner, 2013). As an informed and experienced gun rights advocate, it is difficult to believe Trotter was not aware of this; it is more plausible that she intended to create a misleading impression with a frightening but irrelevant narrative.

Sources

Speakers have ways of deflecting accountability for their own statements by attributing what they say to other sources. Sometimes the speaker claims that the source of information must remain *anonymous* for fear of retribution or because the information has implications for national security—e.g., "a 'highly placed' source in X country." Sometimes sources are identified in an effort to state the politician's position without taking full responsibility for it—e.g., "The think tank, Completely Unbiased, Inc., said my opponent's positions represent a danger to our democratic system."

PRESIDENTIAL LIES

Jody Powell, President Carter's press secretary, said that the government has the right and sometimes an obligation to lie to the American public in "certain circumstances." This is not a new idea. More than 2,300 years ago, Plato described what he called "the noble lie." These were lies told by government leaders for their perception of the public good—to maintain order and keep society functioning in a productive manner (Jowett, 1982). The fact that U.S. presidents and other government officials have lied to the American people throughout the nation's history is hardly debatable (Polman, 2003). But whether these lies can be justified by "certain circumstances" is debatable. Pfiffner (1999; 2004) identified five common types of presidential lies that vary in the amount of damage they are likely to do to society. Only one type of lie is justified by the circumstances.

Justified Lies

Most people believe our leaders are justified in lying to our country's enemies, particularly in a time of war. In World War II, the U. S. Army had a special unit whose primary duty was to deceive and trick the enemy (Gerard, 2002). However, not everyone is equally approving of lies to an enemy that also require deceiving the American public. So when presidents lie to their own citizens, the criterion for acceptability is directly linked to whether it was necessary in order to protect American lives.

An example of a justified lie was when Carter told reporters in 1980 that a military mission to save 52 American hostages held in Iran would definitely fail and was not being planned. In fact, a military rescue plan had been in effect for several months. By telling the truth, Carter would have jeopardized the mission and the lives of those involved.

President Jimmy Carter

Minor Lies

It is difficult to understand why presidents tell some lies. They are lies about matters that have little or no relevance to their ability to govern and give them no apparent political advantage. Since some people suspect minor lies lead to major lies, telling minor lies have the potential to be damaging to the politician. Consider the following examples (Perry & Cummings, 2000):

- President Johnson repeatedly told the story about how his great-great grandfather had died at the Alamo. Later, when the story was challenged, he said it was a slip of the tongue and that Johnson's elderly relative had actually died at the battle of San Jacinto. But historians found no evidence of the modified claim either.

- President Reagan claimed to have photographed Nazi death camps at the end of World War II. But he never left California during World War II. As a member of the First Motion Picture Unit of the Army Air Corps, Reagan had spent a lot of time showing films of the death camps, so perhaps in his memory it seemed as if he'd been there in person.

- President Kennedy is widely believed to have completed a speed reading course that left him capable of reading 1,200 words per minute. This assertion was especially curious since he was able to read about 700 words per minute, which is twice as fast as most people. According to biographer Richard Reeves, Kennedy had signed up for a speed reading course, but never went. The myth was started by JFK's sister, Eunice Shriver, who bragged to a white house reporter that her brother could read 1,500 words per minute. The reporter, Hugh Sidey, actually tested Kennedy and arrived at the 700 words per minute number. But Kennedy persuaded him to print 1,200 as a compromise (Lamb, 1993/n.d.).

Lies to Prevent Embarrassment

These lies are commonly expected from political figures. They are not justified, but they are generally not seen as egregious as lies that cover up important facts or policies. This type of lie is clearly motivated by the self-interest of the politician—but motivated by their belief that such lies are necessary in order to gain or maintain a position from which they could help the American people:

- President Kennedy lied about having Addison's disease and his physicians also lied about it. For Kennedy, this was a painful and debilitating disease that required painkillers for his back, steroids, antispasmodics for colitis, antibiotics for urinary tract infections, and other medicines. Kennedy feared public knowledge of this would ruin his chance to become president.

- As Vice President, Gerald Ford discussed the possible resignation and pardon of President Nixon with White House Chief of Staff Alexander Haig in 1974. Ford admitted meeting with Haig but lied about the subjects discussed at the meeting. Ford's full and unconditional pardon of former president Nixon just one month into his own presidency seemed so suspicious that Congress took the highly unusual move of asking the new president to testify publicly.

- President George W. Bush didn't disclose his 1976 arrest and conviction for driving under the influence of alcohol until growing evidence forced him to in the closing days of the 2000 presidential campaign.

- President Obama has spoken candidly about his struggles with smoking, but claimed to have kicked the habit entirely when he began his first term in 2008. Nevertheless, several sources have disputed this claim, most notably Dr. Jeffrey Kuhlman, his assigned White House physician (Altman & Zeleny, 2010).

Lies to Cover Up or Omit Key Facts

Presidents sometimes lie about events that have a major impact on the American people—facts they have a right to know. These lies represent a serious breach of trust and represent the kind of lies that impugn the government's credibility and debase the democratic system.

President Eisenhower's 1960 denial that America was sending U-2 spy planes (pictured) over the Soviet Union is often cited as the beginning of an era in which the public's trust in the truthfulness of public officials began to erode. Although Eisenhower did not want anything to jeopardize the signing of a nuclear test ban treaty with the Soviet Union, he was sending spy planes over their territory. The Soviets knew about the spy planes, but

© KPG_Payless/Shutterstock.com

Congress and the American public did not. When the Soviet Union said they had shot one down, Eisenhower said this would be impossible since we weren't engaged in spying on the Soviet Union. Then the Soviets showed photos of the plane's wreckage and the pilot who had safely ejected.

In 1962, President Kennedy said there were no American troops engaged in combat in Vietnam. He did not say that American pilots were flying helicopters for South Vietnamese combatants.

President Nixon repeatedly lied when he said he had nothing to do with the burglary of the Democratic National Committee headquarters in the Watergate office complex. At one point he told the CIA to tell the FBI to stop their investigation because it would reveal a CIA covert operation. His role in this burglary and cover-up was a criminal act and led to his resignation (contrary to popular belief, Nixon was never impeached; he resigned to avoid the increasingly likely possibility that he would be impeached (charged) by the House, tried and convicted by the Senate, and removed from office).

Vice President George H. W. Bush said he was "out of the loop" on discussions involving the selling of arms to Iran (considered an enemy) for hostages. He claimed he had no foreknowledge of this plan and must have been deliberately excluded from these meetings to protect him. However, testimony by his Secretary of State and Secretary of Defense pointed out that he was at several meetings in which they objected to the plan and Bush supported it (Walsh, 1994).

According to the evidence gathered by Woodward (2006), the George W. Bush administration repeatedly avoided telling the truth about the war in Iraq to the American public, Congress, and themselves.

Lies of Policy Deception

The most serious lies, according to Pfiffner (2004), occur when the president says the government is following one policy when, in fact, they are following another. This, he argues, is an abuse of power and negates the role of the people in the governing process.

During the presidential campaign of 1964, President Johnson said he would not send American "boys" to Vietnam to fight battles that Vietnamese "boys" should be fighting. Nevertheless, he continued to send American troops to Vietnam and withheld information about the extent to which our troops were involved in the fighting. He thought that negative information about the war would be detrimental to his "great society" domestic programs so he continued to present optimistic views of the war despite military reports to the contrary. To Congress, he understated the cost of the war and the true number of troops requested by his generals. As the war continued, his military commanders learned that Johnson only wanted to hear good news, which further distorted the information about the war.

The bombing of Cambodia in 1969 involved falsified reports and lies. President Nixon sent a message to the ambassador to South Vietnam indicating that there would be no more bombing in Cambodia. But he told his military commanders to continue the bombing. He told them to say they were only providing support to the South Vietnamese soldiers. North Vietnam, South Vietnam, and Cambodia knew of the bombing, but Congress and the American public did not.

The policy of the United States during the mid-1980s was to make no concessions to terrorists for the return of hostages. Iran wanted weapons for the release of American hostages held in Lebanon. In addition, Congress voted to shut off funds for the support Contra rebels in Nicaragua and President Reagan signed it. Despite these policies, arms were sold to Iran and the money for these weapons was diverted to the Contras. At different points in the investigation, Reagan said he didn't approve these transactions, that he couldn't remember whether he approved these transactions, and that he did approve these transactions.

In 2013, former National Security Agency (NSA) contractor Edward Snowden began leaking classified material documenting the immense powers the NSA possesses to surveil Americans' telephone and electronic communications. For years, the intelligence agency swept up the telephone data of virtually every American and maintained the ability to spy on virtually anyone's Internet activity with a keystroke. These revelations contradicted the testimony of James Clapper, the Director of National Intelligence who months earlier had told Congress the NSA did not collect information "in bulk" on American citizens. He later apologized with the Orwellian excuse that his blatant lie was the "least untruthful" answer he could think of (Kessler, 2013). The Obama administration and several members of Congress then went on the defensive, consistently telling the American people the NSA surveillance programs were legal, constitutional, and checked by thorough congressional oversight. But then new documents leaked by Snowden contradicted these claims. These documents revealed that members of Congress who are supposed to be able to provide oversight were systematically denied basic information about surveillance capabilities by the NSA. They also revealed that in 2011, a secret ruling from the Foreign Intelligence Surveillance Court found significant parts of the NSA's domestic spying activities to be in violation of the Fourth Amendment to the U.S. Constitution prohibiting unreasonable searches and seizures. Sources within the intelligence community (unnamed, of course) have said President Obama was made aware of the ruling as soon as it was rendered by the court, but took no action to remedy the problem (Ackerman, 2015).

© bahagiyo/Shutterstock.com

Of the 10,000 documented misstatements in his first two-plus years in office, Donald Trump's most repeated deceptions appear designed to rally his base around core policy issues he campaigned on—505 lies about immigration, including 160 specifically claiming that his much-touted southern border wall with Mexico was already being built (Rosenberg, 2019).

MAINTAINING PUBLIC VIGILANCE

How can the public be alert to the deceptive behavior of political leaders? Given the leader's skill with language, their control of information, and their various options for disseminating information, public lie detection is a formidable task. The press, bloggers, and various concerned organizations are likely to continue investigating the factual accuracy of statements by these leaders. But citizens also need to practice critical listening skills. Listening closely to what a political leader says and how it is said will not automatically reveal the deceivers and the truth tellers. It may, however, cause a listener to suspend his or her judgment about the truthfulness of a speaker's remarks until further information can be obtained. If enough listeners from different political parties demand more responsible rhetoric, then such discourse has a better chance of occurring. The following questions represent only a few of the standards that citizen-listeners could employ to address concerns about deception.

- **Does the speaker cite an accessible source for his or her claim?** When an accessible source is cited, it can be checked. When sources are unidentified or inaccessible to others, the credibility of the claim rests entirely on the credibility of the speaker.

- **Does the speaker compare his or her own efforts to those of his or her opponent?** When speakers criticize something their opponents have done, listeners will profit by hearing how the speaker's own behavior compares with his or her opponent's. This gives the listener more tangible information to check out, serves as a preventative measure for selective omissions, and tends to reduce an "attack only" form of discourse.

- **Does the speaker provide sufficient detail and contextual information?** Like interpersonal deception, lies to the public are often short on specifics. Details not only provide more things to check, but show the speaker's desire to fully inform the listener. Ambiguity and high level abstractions may be called for on occasion, but they also increase the zone of the unknown. It is interesting to note that in the 2020 Democratic presidential primary campaign, Elizabeth Warren distinguished herself from other candidates by deliberately focusing on specific, detailed policy proposals. Her approach was so unique that it earned her the cover of TIME on May 20, 2019. Next to her photo was the caption, "I HAVE A PLAN FOR THAT" (Edwards, 2019).

- **Does the speaker address the issue or question directly?** There may be good reasons for a speaker to evade or ignore an issue. When listeners are unaware of these reasons, however, they are likely to wonder if the speaker has something to hide.

- **Is the speaker responsible for what he or she says?** When speakers attribute information or claims they make to others, without formally acknowledging it as their position, they also set the stage for negating responsibility for the claim at a later time. Listeners have the right to know what the speaker is willing to be accountable for.

- **Does the speaker show an understanding of a complex world and an appreciation for the limitations of certainty?** Political leaders need to convince listeners that they know what they are doing while simultaneously acknowledging the probabilistic nature of the issues we all face. The likelihood of future deception increases when leaders are extremely absolute or extremely conditional in their behavior.

- **Does the speaker develop an argument?** Claims alone do not show the way a person thinks. However, the development of an argument gives a listener a chance to understand and evaluate the speaker's reasoning, how different ideas were brought together, and how he or she developed their attitudes and opinions.

Jamieson (2000, p. 56) says that a citizen's judgment is facilitated when candidates are unambiguous, fair, consistent, accurate, unbiased, and tell the full story. She summarizes her position this way:

> *The likelihood that the public will be misled is minimized if the competing views are available and tested by advocates, audiences, and the press, if all sides engage in warranted argument, and if they accept responsibility for defending their own claims and the claims others offer on their behalf. This concept sounds idealistic, but unless a certain critical degree of substantive interchange is preserved among candidates, the people, and the media that control their encounters, the possibility of a critical information deficit will exist.*

SUMMARY

Public lies have some special characteristics. They have to be adapted to multiple audiences. The deceiver has a great deal more control over the relevant information than the target. Associates of the deceiver often deliver his or her message, making responsibility for the deception elusive. The responsibility for detecting public deception is clearly up to the nation's press, its citizens, and special interest groups.

The public typically calls for more honesty from its political leaders, but they also want them to say what they want to hear. This means leaders and prospective leaders respond by saying they will be honest and forthright with the public, but deceptive behavior often occurs. In this sense, then, the public's mixed message to political leaders makes them a party to the deception. Since the middle of the 20th century, public trust in American political leaders has waned considerably. Many citizens have a cynical view of truth telling as practiced by politicians, and expect them to deceive. Curiously, however, many political lies go unpunished and sometimes voters even choose to vote for the politician they believe is less than honest, especially if they see themselves as aligned ideologically with that candidate.

Leaders are good communicators and can be skilled deceivers if they choose to be. They understand that there are many opportunities for deception in the life of a politician. Ironically, many see deception as a way to remain politically viable. Although some deception of the public by political leaders may be necessary, their deceptive behavior can and does have negative consequences as well—for the deceiver, the public, and the democratic process.

Proof of political lies requires evidence of the speaker's intention to deceive. This is often very difficult to obtain—especially since the same language can be used to tell the truth and a lie. The blood relatives of deception are messages that have features that commonly elicit suspicion or attributions of deception—e.g., ambiguity, lack of detail, indirectness, etc. The skillful use of language, facts, and sources allows a leader to be deceptive while simultaneously allowing him or her to deny it. Nevertheless, enough evidence for presidential lies exists to identify various types according to their degree of acceptability. Public lies about governmental policies are the most egregious, but lies about matters of national security can be justified.

The chapter concluded with some guidelines for listening critically to messages of political leaders—not with the intent of invariably highlighting deceptive behavior, but as a way of remaining alert to the possibility of deception.

1. Do you think the public is in any way accountable for lies told by political leaders? If not, why not? If so, in what ways and to what extent? Use specific examples.

2. This chapter focused on deceptive behavior by political leaders directed toward the general public. Select another leadership category—e.g., religious, business, scientific, legal, labor, volunteers—and compare it to the material in this chapter. Discuss similarities and differences.

3. In the 1960 presidential debates, Kennedy proposed supporting U.S. intervention in Cuba by supporting the anti-Castro exiles. He claimed that the exiles were receiving no support from the administration. Vice President Nixon, his opponent, knew exiles were being trained for a possible invasion of Cuba, but felt he could not reveal this. So he chose to attack Kennedy's proposal as reckless and irresponsible—exactly the opposite of what he believed. Was this lie justified? If not, why? If so, on what grounds? Name any other ways you think Nixon could have handled this situation.

OF INTEREST

From the archives of the 2016 presidential campaign, the PBS broadcast *NewsHour* takes an in-depth look at lies and misstatements as the primary campaigns were in full swing. The video is embedded in an article that chronicles additional examples, going back to the eras of Kennedy and Nixon—entitled "The History of Lies on the Campaign Trail."

Deception researcher Bella DePaulo tackles the phenomenon of presidential lies in the era of Donald Trump. Her conclusion is that we are indeed in unique territory, arguing that never in the history of the republic has a president lied so easily, so frequently, or so cruelly. This article was written in 2017, a little less than a year after Trump took office.

lying and deception in HUMAN INTERACTION

REFERENCES

Ackerman, S. (2015, June 9). Obama lawyers asked secret court to ignore public court's decision on spying. *The Guardian*. Retrieved from http://www.theguardian.com

Alterman, E. (2004). *When presidents lie: A history of official deception and its consequences.* New York, NY: Viking.

Altman, L. K., & Zeleny, J. (2010, February 28). Obama passes checkup but still struggles with smoking habit. *New York Times.* Retrieved from http://www.nytimes.com

Bailey, F. G. (1988). *Humbuggery and manipulation: The art of leadership.* Ithaca, NY: Cornell University Press.

Barnes, J. A. (1994). *A pack of lies.* New York, NY: Cambridge University Press.

Barron, J. (2012, December 12). Nation reels after gunman massacres 20 children at school in Connecticut. *New York Times.* Retrieved from http://www.nytimes.com

Barstow, D., & Stein, R. (March 13, 2005). The message machine: How the government makes news; Under Bush, a new age of prepackaged television news. *New York Times,* Section 1, 1.

Bavelas, J. B., Black, A., Chovil, N., & Mullett, J. (1990). *Equivocal communication.* Newbury Park, CA: Sage.

Bok, S. (1978). *Lying: Moral choice in public and private life.* New York, NY: Pantheon Books.

Boorstin, D. J. (1992). *The image: A guide to pseudo-events in America.* New York, NY: Vintage Books.

Brandt, A. (2009). *The cigarette century.* New York, NY: Perseus.

Buss, D. M., Gomes, M., Higgins, D. S., & Lauterbach, K. (1987). Tactics of manipulation. *Journal of Personality and Social Psychology, 52,* 1219–1229. https://dx.doi.org/10.1037//0022-3514.52.6.1219

Cannon, C. M. (January/February, 2007). Untruth and consequences. *Atlantic, 299,* 56–61.

Chait, J. (April 30, 2006). McCain's a weasel, but he's my weasel. *Austin American Statesman,* H3.

Cohen, M. (2018, October 27). 48 hours fact checking Trump. *CNN.* Retrieved from http://www.cnn.com

Cole, D. (2018, November 1). Trump: 'When I can, I tell the truth'. *CNN.* Retrieved from http://www.cnn.com

Edwards, H. S. (2019, May 9). 'I have a plan for that.' Elizabeth Warren Is betting that Americans are ready for her big ideas. *TIME.* Retrieved from http://www.time.com

Ekman, P. (2001). *Telling lies: Clues to deceit in the marketplace, politics, and marriage.* New York, NY: Norton.

FactCheck.org. (March 3, 2006). Faking news in the Illinois governor race. Retrieved from http://www.factcheck.org

Fishel, J. (1985). *Presidents and promises: From campaign pledge to presidential performance.* Washington, DC: CQ Press.

Fleming, J. H., Darley, J. M., Hilton, J. L., & Kojetin, B. A. (1990). Multiple audience problem: A strategic communication perspective on social perception. *Journal of Personality and Social Psychology, 58,* 593–609. https://dx.doi.org/10.1037//0022-3514.58.4.593

Gallup Poll for CNN/*USA Today,* June 18–19, 1996.

Garcia, A. Jr. (September 4, 2004). We demand the truth, then punish the politicians who speak it. *Austin American Statesman,* A19.

Garrett, M., & Penny, T. J. (1998). The fifteen biggest lies in politics. New York, NY: St. Martin's Press.

Gerard, P. (2002). Secret soldiers: The story of World War II's heroic army of deception. New York, NY: Dutton.

Gergen, D. R. (2000). *Eyewitness to power.* New York, NY: Simon & Schuster.

Griffin, D., & Frates, C. (2013, October 30). Sources: White House told insurance execs to keep quiet on Obamacare. *CNN Politics.* Retrieved from http://www.cnn.com

Halberstam, D. (1993). *The Best and the Brightest* (Anniversary Edition). New York, NY: Ballantine Books.

Healy, M. (2018, December 20). Voters have high tolerance for politicians who lie, even those caught doing it. *Los Angeles Times.* Retrieved from http://www.latimes.com

Jackson, B. (March 23, 2004). Bush accuses Kerry of 350 votes for "higher taxes." Higher than what? *FactCheck.org.* Retrieved from http://www.factcheck.org

Jackson, B. (2007, May 10). False ads: There oughta be a law!—Or maybe not. *FactCheck.org.* Retrieved from http://www.factcheck.org

Jamieson, K. H. (2000). *Everything you think you know about politics. . .and why you're wrong.* New York, NY: Basic Books.

Jamieson, K. H., & Campbell, K. K. (1983). *The interplay of influence.* Belmont, CA: Wadsworth.

Jones, J. M. (2014, September 15). Americans' trust in executive, legislative branches down. *Gallup.* Retrieved from http://www.news.gallup.com

Jowett, B. (trans., 1982). *Plato's Republic.* New York, NY: Modern Library.

Keating, C. F., & Heltman, K. R. (1994). Dominance and deception in children and adults: Are leaders the best misleaders? *Personality and Social Psychology Bulletin, 20,* 312–321.

Keller, J. (November 18, 2001). It's true: We can't handle the truth. *Austin American Statesman,* L8.

Kessler, G. (2013, June 12). Clapper's least untruthful statement to the Senate. *Washington Post*. Retrieved from http://www.washingtonpost.com

Lamb, B. (n.d.). President Kennedy: Profile of power (12/12/93). *Booknotes*. Retrieved from http://www.booknotes.org (Original work broadcast December 12, 1993)

Louis Harris Poll, October 18–November 4, 1988.

Luntz, F. (2007). *Words that work: It's not what you say, it's what people hear*. New York, NY: Hyperion.

MacArthur, J. (1992, January 6). Remember Nayirah, witness for Kuwait? *New York Times*. Retrieved from http://www.nytimes.com

Marro, A. (March/April, 1985). When the government tells lies. *Columbia Journalism Review, 23*, 29–41.

Morris, E. (2003). *The fog of war*. New York, NY: Sony Pictures Classics.

Nelson, M. R., & Park, J. (2014). Publicity as covert marketing? The role of persuasion knowledge and ethical perceptions on belies and credibility in a video news release story. *Journal of Business Ethics*. http://dx.doi/10.1007/s10551-014-2227-3.

Perry, J. M., & Cummings, J. (2000, October 11). History has shown politicians can't resist a little embroidery. *The Wall Street Journal*. Retrieved from http://www.wsj.com

Pfiffner, J. P. (2004). *The character factor: How we judge America's presidents*. College Station, TX: Texas A & M Press.

Pfiffner, J. P. (1999). The contemporary presidency: Presidential lies. *Presidential Studies Quarterly, 29*, 903–917.

Polman, D. (June 29, 2003). To tell the truth. *Austin American Statesman*, H1, H5.

Pratkanis, A., & Aronson, E. (2001). *Age of propaganda: The everyday use and abuse of persuasion*. New York: W. H. Freeman.

Princeton Survey Research, October 20–November 2, 1992.

Rampton, S., & Stauber, J. (2003). *Weapons of mass deception*. New York, NY: Jeremy P. Tarcher/ Penguin.

Reeves. R. (2001). *President Nixon: Alone in the White House*. New York, NY: Simon & Schuster.

Rosenberg, P. (2019, May 12). What's behind Donald Trump's bewildering avalanche of lies? Nothing good. Part 1 of 2. *Salon*. Retrieved from http://www.salon.com

Rue, L.D. (1994). *By the grace of guile*. New York, NY: Oxford University Press.

Schneider, D. (2015, July 22). 1-800-HIRE-A-CROWD. *The Atlantic*. Retrieved from http://www.theatlantic.com

Segrave, K. (2005). *Women and smoking in America, 1880–1950*. New York, NY: McFarland & Co.

U.S. News & World Report (February 23, 1987) p. 54.

Tye, L. (1998). *The father of Spin: Edward L. Bernays and the birth of public relations*. New York, NY: Henry Holt and Co.

VandeHei, J. (2005, October 14). Troops put in a good word to Bush about Iraq. *The Washington Post*. Retrieved from http://www.washingtonpost.com

Walsh, L. E. (1994). *Iran-Contra: The final report*. New York, NY: Three Rivers Press.

Walton, D. (1996). Plausible deniability and evasion of burden of proof. *Argumentation, 10,* 47–58. https://dx.doi.org/10.1007/bf00126158

Weiner, R. (2013, January 30). Gayle Trotter: Guns make women safer. *Washington Post*. Retrieved from http://www.washingtonpost.com

Wise, D. (1973). *The politics of lying: Government deception, secrecy, and power*. New York, NY: Random House.

Woodward, B. (2006). *State of denial*. New York, NY: Simon & Schuster.

Yakowicz, W. (2014, September 19). Why honesty is not always the best policy at work. *Inc.* Retrieved from http://www.inc.com

CHAPTER 12 Deceptive Writing

© nito/Shutterstock.com

"History is the version of past events that people have decided to agree upon."
— *Napoleon Bonaparte*

"There is nothing to fear except the persistent refusal to find out the truth."
— *Dorothy Thompson*

Deceptive writing is a phenomenon that occurs in a variety of venues common to daily life. This chapter examines four of these arenas. The first two concern deceptive authors who are writing about other people and events:

- gathering and reporting the news

- writing history

In the other two variants, the subject of the deception are the authors themselves:

- writing memoirs

- résumé writing

Each of these domains has gained more than a little notoriety in recent years as a fairly consistent source of distortion, misinformation, and misrepresentation.

GATHERING AND REPORTING THE NEWS

The framers of the U.S. Constitution knew it was important to have a press that was not controlled or operated by any branch of government. In fact, the First Amendment to the Constitution places freedom of the press on par with such bedrock rights as freedom of speech and religious liberty. The founders believed that those who control information control people's decisions (and thus their lives). Those who gather and report information, therefore, should be as independent of the government as possible.

This vision of a free press is one that allows the gathering and reporting of information without the kind of censorship and manipulation characteristic of totalitarian societies. A free press can provide opportunities for the voicing of various perspectives, no matter how unpopular. A free press can also assume responsibility for uncovering vital information that would otherwise remain hidden from a public that has a right to know (e.g., Watergate in the 1970s and NSA wiretapping in the 2010s). In short, an independent press is the agent of a free citizenry—serving as a source of reliable information, a forum for discussion, and a defense against demagoguery.

Despite this noble design, the reality is more complicated. While the public continues to maintain belief in the important role of a free press in American society, it is also a source of persistent criticism in opinion polls. A Pew Research Center poll conducted in 2013 found 68% of respondents (of all political stripes and demographic backgrounds) agreeing that the press does a good job of preventing leaders from "doing things that shouldn't be done," a double-digit increase from two years earlier.

Aside from this "watchdog" role, however, Americans tend to view other core functions of the press with much greater skepticism. In the same 2013 survey, 67% of Americans felt that news organizations were inaccurate in their reporting (up from about 50% in 2001). Elsewhere in the 2013 data, clear majorities denigrated the press for being uncaring, politically biased, too focused on unimportant stories, and unduly influenced by power. The Gallup organization summed up the overall attitudinal trend this way: "Americans' trust in mass media has generally been edging downward from higher levels in the late 1990s and the early 2000s" (McCarthy, 2014).

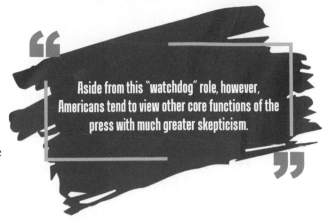

Aside from this "watchdog" role, however, Americans tend to view other core functions of the press with much greater skepticism.

There are likely many reasons for this erosion of public trust. One possibility is that the decay is structural in nature, paralleling the overall decline in reliance on traditional news sources in favor of social media sites and other digital sources (Rupp, 2014). Yet Gallup has found little confidence in news sources of *any* kind, old or new, regardless of platform. Faith in traditional newspapers stands at 22%, news from the Internet at 19%, and television news at 18%. Of the 16 American institutions Gallup asked the public to evaluate, only Congress ranked lower (Newport, 2015).

Deceptive News Reporting

In the end, the simplest explanation for the causes of this ongoing decline may be the numerous high-profile examples of deceptive journalism that continue to plague the industry. Journalists who make up, plagiarize, or exaggerate the stories they report are not numerous when compared to the total number of reporters or the total number of stories. But when deception occurs, a great deal of public attention ensues and the impact on a news organization's credibility can be devastating, potentially calling into question the veracity of all its reporting, be it past, present, or future. No caliber of organization seems immune to this phenomenon, nor does the experience level of the journalist appear to have much to do with the practice. The examples of such lapses are too numerous to list in their entirety, but the following are representative:

- **1981**—*Washington Post* reporter Janet Cooke was fired and had to return a Pulitzer Prize for a story about an 8-year-old heroin addict who didn't exist. He was, she said, a composite of many young addicts she had uncovered (Schudel & Langer, 2016).

- **1998**—Veteran reporter for the *Boston Globe*, Mike Barnicle, was fired for writing a story that could not be verified about two cancer patients who became friends. He also published George Carlin jokes without acknowledging the comedian. Patricia Smith, also with the *Boston Globe*, was fired when she admitted occasionally making up a colorful quote when she felt it would make a better story. She said the basic ideas in her stories were honest even though the characters were sometimes fictional. This was also the year Stephen Glass, who wrote for the *New Republic*, admitted he made up all or parts of dozens of stories. He even made fake documents that were designed to provide verification of his stories (QR).

- **1999**—A reporter for the Owensboro Kentucky *Messenger-Inquirer* fabricated five columns about her life-and-death struggle with cancer when, in fact, she had AIDS.

- **2000**—Three interns at the *San Jose Mercury News* were suspended for plagiarizing and using unverified quotes and sources. A political reporter at the *Sacramento Bee* admitted to fabricating and plagiarizing stories.

- **2003**—Over the course of 4 years, in 36 of 73 stories, reporter Jayson Blair of the *New York Times* plagiarized, invented quotes, and lied about his reporting location. Another *Times* reporter, Rick Bragg, was suspended and later quit after it was discovered that he used the work of researchers, interns, and strangers in his own stories and did not give them credit.

- **2004**—Veteran reporter Jack Kelley of *USA Today* and his editor resigned in response to revelations of fabricated stories and other deceptive behavior. Kelley reportedly asked his friends to act like they were the sources of information for certain stories and wrote scripts for them to follow (Steinberg, 2004).

- **2008**—Lobbyist Vicki Iseman sued the *New York Times* for libel after the prestigious "paper of record" published a tabloid-like article on its front page in February 2008. The article intimated that she and then-presidential candidate John McCain had an affair in the late 1990s (Orey, 2009). Other news organizations publicly excoriated the *Times* for publishing a piece that was little more than hearsay (Kinsley, 2008). A year after the article was published, Iseman dropped her lawsuit. In exchange, the *Times* agreed to publish a retraction of sorts, in which its editors stated that the newspaper "did not intend to conclude . . . that Ms. Iseman had engaged in a romantic affair with Senator McCain or an unethical relationship" (Kurtz, 2009).

- **2012**—Despite an already successful career as a monologist and cultural critic, Mike Daisey decided to fabricate key elements of his 2010 performance "The Agony and the Ecstasy of Steve Jobs," which purported to describe horrific working conditions at Apple factories in China. But it wasn't until excerpts of the monologue were aired to the scrutiny of a wider audience on public radio's *This American Life* in January of 2012 that things began to unravel. Initially insisting that they had spent weeks fact-checking Daisey's chilling details (such as gun-toting factory guards and the use of underaged workers), *This American Life* retracted the story two months later (Isherwood, 2012). (QR).

- **2014**—*Rolling Stone* was forced to admit that their trust in reporter Sabrina Rudin Erdely was "misplaced" after key details of her article "A Rape on Campus" were called into question by *The Washington Post* (Shapiro, 2014). Erdely's original story purported to describe the brutal gang rape of a female student at a fraternity house on the campus of the University of Virginia. Perhaps to its credit, *Rolling Stone* ultimately asked the dean of the Columbia School of Journalism for an independent investigation of the failure. His formal report was published by the magazine in April 2015, along with a full and formal retraction of the rape story (Coronel, Coll, & Kravitz, 2015).

- **2015**—Ending the reign of television's most popular anchor, *NBC Nightly News'* Brian Williams (pictured) was suspended for several months (then permanently removed) when it came to light that he had repeatedly said, in his own words, "things that weren't true" (Calamur, 2015). Over the years, whenever he would recount details of his experiences as an embedded journalist during the Iraq War, Williams maintained that he had been in a helicopter that was hit by enemy fire (Bauder, 2015). In a testament to the perhaps-unintentional but ever-growing journalistic power of social media, it was a simple Facebook comment by a veteran who was present during Williams' Iraq tour that caused everything to unravel. In early February 2015, *NBC Nightly News* showed Williams taking a soldier to a New York Rangers game.

At the event, the announcer told the crowd that the veteran, Sergeant Major Tim Terpak, "was responsible for the safety of Brian Williams and his NBC News team after their Chinook helicopter was hit and crippled by enemy fire." When NBC posted this footage on Facebook, Lance Reynolds, a crew member from the actual helicopter struck in Iraq that day (which was not Williams'), felt compelled to comment. "Sorry dude," he wrote, "I don't remember you being on my aircraft." With that, the proverbial floodgates opened and other service members present at the Iraq incident joined in repudiating Mr. Williams' version of events (Somaiya, 2015). Williams' initial apologies online and on-air did little to silence his critics. He admitted he knew it was the helicopter in front of him that had been hit, but that "constant viewing of the video showing us inspecting the impact area" and "the fog of memory over 12 years" made him "conflate" the two copters (Tritten, 2015). "This was a bungled attempt by me to thank one special veteran," he added (Mahler, Somaiya, & Steel, 2015). It didn't help matters that two years earlier Williams had regaled David Letterman with an unhesitatingly clear, vivid, and detailed description of the events he would later attribute to a faulty memory.

- **2015**—Having been accused by *Mother Jones* magazine of multiple instances of journalistic deception, Fox News personality Bill O'Reilly seemed to be made of Teflon. Unlike Williams, the far more serious accusations against O'Reilly didn't appear to stick—despite evidence that directly contradicted his statements (Rothkopf, 2015). Among other things, he was accused of exaggerating his record as a war correspondent and fabricating certain aspects of his assignments—e.g., trips to Northern Ireland and the Falklands that never happened (Corn & Schulman, 2015). O'Reilly never admitted any wrongdoing, casting aspersions on his accusers instead (Waldman, 2015). His journalistic career was ultimately brought down by his sexual advances to coworkers (Fox News settled at least six sexual harassment lawsuits against O'Reilly between 2000 and 2017), not by his numerous, demonstrably deceptive reporting habits (QR).

- **2018**—As part of a broader campaign to influence the 2016 election, the Russian government used social media trolls and state-run outlets to peddle fake news stories alleging that candidate Hillary Clinton was deathly ill, that she was collaborating with wealthy financiers to overthrow the U.S. government, that the United States was on the brink of war with Russia, and other topics intended to sow concern and confusion among voters. Department of Justice Special Counsel Robert Mueller indicted 13 Russians over the stories, alleging an elaborate plot to use social media to spread divisive political and cultural content. The extent to which Russia's activity influenced the outcome of the election has been a source of fierce debate. President Trump and members of his administration insisted Russia's efforts did not have any impact on the outcome of the election. In order to quantify the impact of fake news on the election, Ohio State University researchers Gunther, Beck, and Nisbet (2018) conducted a survey in late 2016 and early 2017 of voters who supported Obama in 2012. The researchers found a significant correlation between belief in the fake news statements and vote choice. Specifically, a much larger percentage of those Obama voters who did not believe any of the fake news statements voted for Hillary Clinton in 2016 (89%) than those who believed one of the statements (61%) and those who believed two or three of them (17%). The researchers concluded that "former Obama voters who believed one or more of these fake news stories were 3.9 times more likely to defect from the Democratic ticket in 2016 than those who did not believe any of the false claims." However, the researchers also emphasized that one cannot conclude from the survey that fake news caused Obama voters to defect from Clinton in 2016. For example, it is possible some voters first decided not to vote for Clinton, and then in turn cited false stories in order to rationalize their vote.

Deceptive News Gathering

Some reporters find it necessary to use deceptive tactics to get the information they need to report a story truthfully. For example, a reporter may pretend not to be one or lie about the real point of the story on which they're working. Some news organizations prohibit their reporters from misrepresenting themselves and many journalists point out that they would not like someone doing it to them. Nevertheless, the use of deception to get a story was established long ago. In 1887, Nellie Bly (pictured) of the *New York World* got herself admitted to the New York City Women's Lunatic Asylum in order to expose the horrible practices occurring within its walls.

Undercover journalism continues today and in some instances is considered prize-worthy. About 22% of the journalists in one survey said that pretending to be somebody else to get a story may be justified (Weaver & Wilhoit, 1996). The most common justifications are linked to: (1) the belief that the reporters are merely lying to bad people who are doing harmful things and, (2) the inability to get the information using non-deceptive methods. Undercover segments by television reporters also tend to get good audience ratings, although "good ratings" is not likely to be used as a justification for deceptive news gathering.

Since the 1960s, television news has presented numerous reports in which reporters gathered information using hidden cameras. They have exposed car repair scams, physical abuse in orphanages and nursing homes, discriminatory behavior toward African-American customers and job applicants, and more. In 1992, ABC News reporters used hidden cameras to expose unsanitary food handling procedures at the Food Lion grocery chain. Food Lion sued ABC and a national dialogue about the ethics of deceptive news gathering ensued. Following the statement that journalistic deception is generally wrong, the Poynter Institute, a school specifically devoted to journalism, said it may be justified if it meets the following criteria:

1. The story is of profound importance and vital to the public interest—e.g., when great harm is being done to people.

2. All other alternatives to get the story have been exhausted.

3. The reporter and employer are willing to reveal publicly how the deception was used to get the story and the reasons for it.

4. The reporter and employer are willing to provide the time, funding, and resources in order to pursue the story fully.

5. The harm prevented as a result of the story outweighs any harm caused by acts of deception.

6. Prior to the deception, the reporter and employer should thoroughly discuss and weigh the short- and long-range consequences of their deception, its impact on journalistic credibility, their motivations, the deceptive act relative to their editorial mission, and the legal implications of the action.

Guidelines like these encourage reflection and discussion, but still allow considerable latitude in decision making. For example, what is of "profound importance" to one news organization may not be to another. The harm prevented versus the harm done is also a judgment that may garner widely different views. As a response to Food Lion's charges that ABC had inaccurately presented information by the way they edited the 45 hours of undercover videotape, a seventh guideline has been suggested (Davidson, 1998; Meyer, 1997):

7. The whole data set gathered by the reporter(s) must be available for examination as a check on accuracy and any misleading ideas resulting from the editing process.

Attributions of Deception and "Fake News"

In the above examples of reporters who deliberately falsified stories and lied to gain access to information, the intent to deceive is pretty clear. However, there are numerous characteristics and practices associated with the gathering, writing, and presenting of the news that serve as a lightning rod for accusations of deception within the news media—whether deceptive intent is involved or not. The story may be accurately perceived as misleading, distorted, incomplete, or biased, but deceptive intent may not be involved. Deliberately deceptive or not, the following factors may be perceived as deceptive and negatively impact the credibility of the news media.

Poor Journalism

Journalistic errors tend to be highly visible. When they occur, some people are bound to see them as a deliberate attempt to mislead the public, as a sign that journalists can't be trusted, as proof that the news media outlets are incompetent—or all of the above. But journalists, like everyone

"Journalistic errors tend to be highly visible."

else, don't always do their jobs perfectly—and this opens the door to potential charges of deception.

One problem that can occur is the reliance on limited or biased sources of information. A reporter may rely too often on the same sources (Lee & Solomon, 1990). Helen Thomas (2006), a White House correspondent for more than 40 years, believes the White House press corps does not adequately keep the public informed when they assume information put out by the administration is the complete story.

Boehlert (2006) and Rich (2006) believe the same could be said about the press in general. The press often dismissed the need to develop stories based on evidence that President Bush knowingly misled the nation in making the case to go to war in Iraq. They argued that the public was well aware that Bush made false claims about Saddam Hussein's link to Al Qaeda and the presence of weapons of mass destruction in Iraq. A July 2006 Harris poll, however, revealed that 50% of the Americans polled believed that Iraq had weapons of mass destruction and 64% believed that Saddam had a strong connection to Al Qaeda. Critics of the press point to such findings as a sign that the press abdicated its responsibility to keep American citizens accurately informed.

The need to verify information is at the heart of good reporting. When a quote or story is printed and/or broadcast that turns out to be false, accusations of deception are likely to be forthcoming even though there may not have been any intent to deceive. In May 2005, *Newsweek* said that a forthcoming military report would attest to the fact that American interrogators had flushed a copy of the Quran down a toilet to unnerve detainees. A reliable, but anonymous, government source was cited. After a number of people died in Muslim riots in several cities around the world, *Newsweek* said their source would not stand by the original report so they were retracting the story. Even though their government source would not verify the report, detainees released from Guantanamo Bay had been complaining about copies of the Quran being thrown in the toilet for two years (Seelye & Lewis, 2005). Far less serious, but also unverified, was the story that women with blonde hair would be extinct within 200 years. CBS, ABC, CNN, and numerous other news media reported the article without checking with the World Health Organization (WHO), the supposed source of the information (QR). In 2002, the story was traced to a German women's magazine that cited the work of a nonexistent anthropologist at WHO. The false story, however, continued to circulate into 2006.

News stories are inevitably incomplete, but when information deemed critical and highly relevant to the story is omitted, the question of deceptive intent may be raised. In October 2002, Pribble et al. (2006) analyzed 1,799 health news stories and found 75% of them did not include an interview with a health professional or have specific recommendations on how to prevent or ameliorate a medical condition. Only 12% noted the prevalence of a disease, which is important in assessing risk. The West Nile Virus was the second most frequently reported topic even though only about 1% of the American TV audience faced the possibility of contracting it. When stories about new drugs omit potentially harmful side effects or fail to examine possible ties between drug researchers and drug companies, the public may understandably feel deceived.

Employer Constraints

Newspapers, magazines, and television news are part of a money-making business. Can a free press corps devoted to reporting truthfully and accurately coexist effectively within an organization whose primary goal is to make a financial profit? The reporter's target audience, advertisers, and parent company all have vested interests in the content of their reporting. Auletta (2003, p. xii) put it this way:

> I worry about the owners of journalistic properties making business decisions that harm journalism. . .As a reporter, I've learned it's the nature of corporate executives to extol the virtues of synergy, profit margins, the stock price, cost cutting, extending the brand, demographics, ratings, and getting on the team. Journalists rarely share these concerns. . .

One cost-cutting measure that has affected some news organizations is a reduction in the number of fact-checkers. This is a business decision with potentially direct consequences on the accuracy of reporting (Featherstone, 1997). In 1984, there were 50 companies in the United States with controlling interests in the news media. In 2005, there were just six. People associated with these companies and the companies themselves are often active in shaping the events that become news. Lee and Solomon (1990, p. xiv) ask the obvious question about reporters who work for these companies, "Will they bite the hand that feeds them?" Thomas (2006) points out that "the hand that feeds them" may extend beyond the corporation itself because some aspects of the corporation's business may be dependent on maintaining a positive relationship with certain highly placed people in the U.S. government or possibly the government of another country.

This doesn't necessarily mean a reporter's story will be censored or that he or she will be told what to write. But some influence is inevitable. In order to make money, stories have to be timely and interesting, but corporate concerns may make certain stories less of a priority. The news may be inextricably linked to their employer's other products. The ownership may also influence the way news is presented.

For example, some believe news should be easy to understand and full of familiar images with minimal space and time given to the complexities and uncertainties that often accompany life's stories. The fear that a competitor will print or air a story first can affect both the depth of a report and the source verification process. News bureaus also engage in copycat reporting in an effort to match their competitors. This process can lead to distortion. After one story about President Ford being "accident prone" occurred, reporters looked for other instances of this behavior. After several more stories, Ford's image as a "bumbler" was secure (Cohen, 1997). So much so, in fact, that *Saturday Night Live* turned it into comedy gold, featuring Chevy Chase as the hapless leader (QR). Any time a person is characterized by repeatedly emphasizing one aspect of his or her behavior, distortion is a legitimate complaint.

Competition can also lead to problems. If one newspaper gets a quote wrong, it is likely to be repeated many times by competing news services before it is corrected. Tate (1984) illustrates the absurdity of "copycat" reporting in the story of an early 20th-century reporter who was asked why so many stories of shipwrecks featured a cat that survived. The reporter explained:

> *One of those wrecked ships carried a cat, and the crew went back to save it. I made the cat the feature of my story, while other reporters failed to mention the cat, and were called down by their city editors for being beaten. The next time there was a shipwreck there was no cat; but the other ship news reporters did not wish to take chances, and put the cat in. I wrote a true report, leaving out the cat, and then I was severely chided for being beaten. Now when there is a shipwreck all of us always put in a cat. (p. 37)*

Story Production

Various decisions about how much space to devote to a story, where to position the story relative to other stories, and the reporter's choice of words are all potential sources of perceived or actual deception. Even the decision about what stories should be reported is one that affects the public's perception of how accurately reality is being presented. For example, an editor may not want to do a story detailing malnutrition, homelessness, disease, and abuse occurring among thousands of children in a foreign country. The story is depressing, costly, and difficult to obtain. During the late 1930s and early 1940s, American newspapers, including the *New York Times* (owned by Jews of German descent), consciously ignored or downplayed the mass murders that were taking place in Nazi Germany (Leff, 2005; Lipstadt, 1986). Yet, somehow, the heroic struggle to retrieve a single child ("Baby Jessica") who fell down a well in the United States can be a headline story for weeks (QR).

"Hyping" a story can also distort reality. National news stories are frequently the driving force behind a local story on the same issue. This is a practice that runs the risk of magnifying the importance of the story or the frequency of the event being reported. Shark attacks on human beings are rare and the frequency remains fairly constant, but in the absence of other headline-grabbing stories, a few prominent and fear-provoking stories can make shark attacks seem like an epidemic. In 2002, news stories about child abductions were plentiful even though the number of child abductions by strangers had been between three and five thousand per year since the 1980s (Gándara, 2002; Kirn, 2002). Crime reporting, says Penny (2005), "has more than doubled since the eighties, even though the overall crime rate has steadily declined." Based on stories in the press, the American Automobile Association (AAA) issued a publication saying road rage was increasing. The press then cited the AAA report as the source of information that road rage was a national problem.

Reporter Biases

Reporters, like every other human being, are subject to their own personal, perceptual, and memory biases that can influence actual or perceived distortions in their stories. Attitudinal biases encompass such things as political party preference and stereotypes about certain groups. A reporter may, for example, interview more people with attitudes known to be similar to his or her own than people whose opinions are different. Some journalists believe that the most influential bias is not political, but professional—i.e., the bias toward getting a provocative or sensational story that will build their reputations as skilled reporters.

Observational biases include all the difficulties experienced by eyewitnesses—missing parts of the story that *are* there while seeing other parts that aren't. Sometimes reporters will start with an idea of how a story will develop and then find information that confirms it (Nickerson, 1998). The strong belief, for example, that obesity in young children is a major problem may cause a reporter to miss key evidence to the contrary.

Consumer Biases

Sometimes it doesn't matter how hard journalists try to present the news in an unbiased and balanced manner. Highly partisan readers and viewers on both sides of an issue are not likely to want or to perceive any news as "fair" unless it unequivocally favors their point of view. When the other side of the issue in question is presented, it is, by definition, a sign of bias in their minds. Even news consumers whose views on an issue are not extreme are likely to have a similar reaction if they are convinced the media is biased (Giner-Sorolla & Chaiken, 1994). Research by Vallone, Ross, and Lepper (1985) and Perloff (1989) confirms this "hostile media" phenomenon. Vallone and his colleagues recruited 144 pro-Israeli and pro-Arab observers who were shown six

> Highly partisan readers and viewers on both sides of an issue are not likely to want or to perceive any news as "fair" unless it unequivocally favors their point of view.

American news clips from the 1982 Israeli war with Lebanese Arab militants. Both were certain the coverage was heavily biased in favor of the other side. The pro-Arab viewers heard 42 references that painted Israel in a positive light while the pro-Israeli viewers heard only 16; the pro-Israeli viewers heard 57 references that painted Israel in a negative light and the pro-Arab viewers heard only 26. For highly partisan viewers, whether they represent a country or a political party, the mainstream news media is often perceived as hostile. The cognitive road from hostile to deceptive may not be a long one.

lying and deception in **HUMAN INTERACTION**

President Trump has claimed that he invented the term "fake news" to describe news coverage he deems unfairly critical of himself or his administration. He didn't—the term was coined by journalists in the 1890s—but he certainly has popularized it. By one estimate (QR), he had uttered the word "fake" more than 1,000 times since being elected, usually applied to stories, journalists, or news organizations. Over the course of his presidency, the range of sources he has declared as "fake" continues to grow—he decries "fake books," "the fake dossier," "fake CNN," and even "fake search engines," claiming that Google search results are "rigged" to mostly show only negative stories about him (Gold, 2018).

Trump is far from the first president to grouse about the way the press covers him. However, as presidential historian Michael Beschloss has argued, Trump doesn't seem to share his predecessors' appreciation of the necessity of a free press as contemplated by the country's founders. Trump also has the ability to deliver his complaints directly to the public via friendly hosts on Fox News and through his social media streams. "He's got social media that reaches perhaps 100 million people," noted Beschloss. "We've never seen a president before with that kind of weapon" (Keith, 2018).

More often than not, when Trump says a news story is fake, it isn't actually false. Instead, it means he just doesn't like it. Decrying negative news coverage of his administration, Trump claimed, "They [journalists] don't cover stories the way they're supposed to be. They don't even report them in many cases, if they're positive." While running for president, Trump used to say the monthly unemployment figures reported by the Obama administration were fake. "Because the number is a phony number, five percent," then-candidate Trump said in August 2016 during a speech in Florida. "It's not down to five percent. It's probably 20 or 21 per-cent. Some people think it's higher." (For the record, an unemployment rate of 20% or more would rival that of the Great Depression.)

But all of that was before the election. Now that Trump is president, he no longer calls the unemployment rate phony. In fact, he touts low unemployment as one of his great achievements and complains the "fake news" media doesn't cover it enough (Levin, 2019).

About "Objectivity"

Beginning in the 1920s, the idea of objectivity began to grow roots in American journalism. It was an idea designed to temper a reporter's subjectivity and bias that, in turn, was expected to broaden the consumer base for the news organizations (Kaplan, 2002; Schudson, 1990; 2001).

But there has never been widespread agreement on exactly what objective journalism means. Normally, it implies one, several, or all of the following: *fairness*, *balance*, *truth*, and *accuracy*. Martin (1997) identifies three common interpretations of the term:

1. being nonpartisan by not advocating a position on a controversial issue
2. maintaining value neutrality by stating facts without making value judgments
3. not distorting facts and understanding.

Many journalists think of objectivity as a way of describing their *method* of reporting rather than a personal trait. It is something one should always strive for—knowing that it can never be fully realized. Kovach and Rosensteil (2001) say journalistic truth is similar to scientific and historical truth. They call it *functional truth*—the best truth at the time, but subject to further investigation and change. In this view, truthful reporting is a process. It is more than the accuracy of a single story.

What processes will promote greater objectivity in a reporter's work? Schudson (1990), drawing on principles associated with the scientific method, suggests the following:

1. Stories and statements can be subjected to independent observation and verification.

2. Reporters and employers should be personally committed to public interest journalism and minimizing bias; reporters should be forthright about their biases and methods, admit mistakes, and be honest about what they know and don't know.

3. Reporters should submit their work to a process of intersubjective consensus involving editors, sources, and others.

4. A skeptical mindset for both reporters and editors should be maintained. It is important to point out, however, that in everyday practice, the guidelines for being "objective" can be complex.

For example, the idea of trying to avoid value judgments may be a worthy aspiration in many cases, but even neutrality can be viewed as a type of value statement. Furthermore, writing in a value-free manner is being less than entirely truthful if the story is based on information solely from sources the reporter knew were biased (Kovach & Rosensteil, 2001). Even if true value neutrality could be achieved, it might not always be in the public's best interest. Edward R. Murrow (pictured) was the kind of reporter others are told to emulate, but much of his reputation as a journalist is linked to *advocacy*, not neutrality—e.g., his critical exposure of Senator Joseph McCarthy's demagoguery and his appeals on behalf of America's migrant farm workers.

In contrast to the calls for objectivity in the 1930s, MacDougall (1972) said reporters needed to ". . .crusade more" and use interpretation "to explain why bad situations exist" (p. vi). William Randolph Hearst and Joseph Pulitzer claimed they were advocating for the public interest when they exaggerated atrocities in Cuba that led to the Spanish-American War. Hearst also worked with the U.S. government to enact legislation against marijuana by exaggerating its harmful effects. The problem with advocacy, of course, is that the line between advocating for personal interests or causes and advocating for the public interest is not always clear.

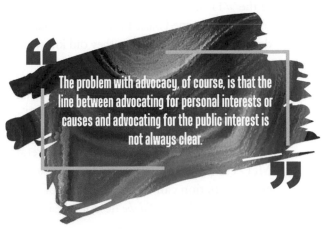

The problem with advocacy, of course, is that the line between advocating for personal interests or causes and advocating for the public interest is not always clear.

A reporter's personal value judgments can be troublesome even when they are not part of his or her official reports. *Wall Street Journal* reporter Farnaz Fassihi practiced value neutrality in her official reports from Iraq, but her personal email to 40 of her friends was filled with value judgments that were contrary to the positive images of the war maintained by the president and his administration. It wasn't long before her email was widely circulated on the Internet. Her reporting on Iraq was terminated because her biases, although originally expressed privately, had become part of her public record as a reporter (Read, 2004).

Another fundamental precept of objective reporting is to "stick to the facts." But which facts? Every happening can be reported with different facts, thereby creating a situation in which a factually accurate story may be perceived by some people as hiding the truth. Furthermore, different types of facts may be considered news in one generation and not in another. In the 1950s, sports reporter Bud Collins told his editor at the *Boston Herald* about some heated exchanges he had had with one of baseball's greatest players, Ted Williams. His editor told him that the readers of the *Herald* weren't interested in his problems with ballplayers—only what happened in the game (Bianchi, 2002). Today, it would not be surprising to find the reverse happening—that facts associated with a game take a back seat to those associated with a player's personality.

But reporters at a sporting event might also avoid seeking facts about a "streaker" or people demonstrating for a cause because doing so would only give them the publicity they seek. In that case, people who attended the game and people who read or heard about it from the press would have experienced a different set of facts. Correcting factual inaccuracy may also be put aside when related facts are plentiful and important. Jamieson and Waldman (2002) tell the story about how the Bush Administration told reporters that Osama Bin Laden admitted on a videotape that some of the 9/11 hijackers did not even know they were on a suicide mission. But journalists who later saw the videotaped basis for this "fact" found Bin Laden saying that not all the hijackers knew the details of the operation, but they did know they were on a "martyrdom operation."

Sometimes facts need a journalist's interpretation to make sense of them. For example, a reporter may need to supplement the fact that the Giants won a game by pointing out that the win was likely to be a psychological relief for the team since it ended a 14-game losing streak. Interpreting the facts is a necessary part of the reporter's job and not inconsistent with an objective approach. But journalistic interpretation, unlike that of fiction writers, is constrained. McLeese (1998) contends that the pressure on journalists to write stories that are as interesting as fiction can lead to an abuse of factual interpretation, as was the case with Patricia Smith at the *Boston Globe* described earlier. In McLeese's words:

> . . .*the lines distinguishing fact from fiction, let alone fact from truth, have become increasingly blurred. The most ambitious feature stories are expected to emulate the best short stories—with the same sharply etched characterization, psychological motivation, evocative description, narrative momentum and moral purpose.*

"Balanced" reporting is another guideline often associated with objectivity. The process of seeking both sides of a controversial issue will presumably offset any tendency to slant the news toward one point of view. However, some issues have many slightly different points of view. Do all of them need to be represented? Does balance mean that all points of view should be given equal weight or credibility? A reporter may try to be fair and balanced with regard to the facts of a story, but this may also mean that not all the people who provided information to the reporter will play an equal role in the story. Most scientists, for example, believe the planet is experiencing climate change caused by humans, but there are a handful who don't. Would a reporter be rewarded for his or her objectivity and reporting in the public interest by giving both points of view equal weight in the story?

While it may be productive to aspire to objectivity, most reporters are savvy enough to realize they can never fully achieve it. Despite their best efforts, they will occasionally produce inaccurate and/or unintentionally deceptive news reports. Sometimes the perception of deceptive and/or biased news reports has less to do with a reporter's behavior and more to do with the nature of the audience's knowledge and attitudes. So the credibility of the news is partly dependent on reporters' commitment to serving the public interest and partly on the public's understanding and acceptance of the various constraints under which the news is produced and perceived.

WRITING HISTORY

News journalists write about current events whereas historians write about news events that took place in the past. Both are "reporters" in this sense, so it is not surprising that their plight is similar when it comes to matters of truthfulness and deception.

Historical events, like current events, are happenings that can be reported in different ways. Some aspects of an event are selected for telling and others are not. The past "as it actually happened" is subject to revision and reinterpretation. Santayana (1905–06/1998, p. 397) put it this way: "History is always written wrong, and so always needs to be rewritten." But, as Popper (1950) said, "this does not mean, of course, that all interpretations are of equal merit" (p. 450). Shermer and Grobman (2000) believe the best interpretations of history use a method they call "historical science." Among other things, this method:

> Historical events, like current events, are happenings that can be reported in different ways. Some aspects of an event are selected for telling and others are not.

- makes use of a formal peer review process

- strives for objectivity in an effort to control bias and/or forthrightly acknowledges biases

- couches claims in terms of probabilities and the likelihood of error

- builds arguments on the convergence of multiple forms of evidence—e.g., written documents, eyewitness testimony, photographs, and physical evidence.

A number of well-known and respected historians have admitted plagiarizing material and publishing inaccurate quotes (Italie, 2002). In one case, Stephen Ambrose, World War II historian and author of commercial blockbusters like *Band of Brothers*, referenced material taken from other sources using footnotes, but failed to indicate that it was verbatim (and therefore plagiarism). It later came to light that he likely made up entire interviews that he claimed to have conducted with former president Eisenhower (Harris, 2010). Producing intentionally false historical accounts may be motivated by money, political or religious biases, or a desire to enhance one's professional reputation. Deception of a less intentional sort may occur when an author is careless or inaccurate in labeling notes taken from other sources. Over time, these notes may come to be viewed by the author as his or her own words.

Many believed British historian David Irving was unfairly rewriting history when he claimed that the gas chambers at Auschwitz did not exist and that no Jew was gassed there during

World War II. He said that documents do not show Hitler was out to annihilate the Jews or that he issued orders to that effect. In general, he was denying that the Holocaust ever occurred. The denial of the Holocaust had been espoused by a handful of speakers and authors since World War II, but because Irving had written a number of historical accounts of World War II, Sherman and Grobman (2000, p. 49) say he was "arguably the most historically sophisticated of the deniers." After historian Deborah Lipstadt called him out in her book, *Denying the Holocaust: The Growing Assault on Truth and Memory* (1993), Irving sued her for libel. In 2000, a British court denied his charge and made him pay $3.1 million to cover costs Lipstadt had incurred. In 2006, he was sentenced to three years in an Austrian prison because the country's law prohibits anyone from denying or diminishing the reality of the Holocaust. Irving was convicted of breaking this law by what he said in two speeches given to Austrian audiences in 1989.

Lipstadt's battle with Irving was dramatized in the 2016 film *Denial*. In 2017, she gave a TED Talk about her experiences (QR).

Factors Leading to Distortion and Deception

Like the process of producing the news, historical accounts are subject to possible distortion during the information gathering, analyzing, and/or writing phases. There are, for example:

- historians who make mistakes because they don't do their job well

- historical accounts that are influenced by the wishes of publishers and community groups that constrain and/or change them

- historians whose writing style and choice of words seem to slant the interpretation of an event

- personal biases through which historians and public audiences view past events

Each of these factors could be part of an intentionally deceptive act or simply one that is perceived that way. Historians are not always aware of the biases that may lead them to produce an inaccurate historical account. But even when history writers freely acknowledge their biases, they seldom link their biases to an *intentional* desire to produce an inaccurate historical account. The following factors are some common sources of distortion and inaccuracy in the writing of history (Ayres, 2000; Loewen,1995; 1999; Ravitch, 2003).

Creating Heroes and Glorifying the Past

Keyes (2004) points out that America, like other cultures, has its heroes, legends, and stirring quotes, but he goes on to say:

A striking number of America's historical legends are apocryphal in whole or in part. Many of our most stirring quotations—'Give me liberty or give me death,' 'No taxation without representation,' 'I have not yet begun to fight!'—were never uttered in the form they're remembered, at the time they were supposed to have been said, or by the person who was supposed to have said them. (p. 49)

Sometimes the history we learn is about people and events that fulfill the images we wish for, a history of "wartless stereotypes," a "Disney" version of history (Loewen, 1995). Leaders, community members, and authors who prefer this type of history are happy to keep repeating the same old myths. Accuracy becomes less of an issue than the maintenance of unblemished and inspiring tales. There is often little interest in revealing any imperfect or repugnant aspects for fear the person or event in question will no longer be considered worthy. Yet a person's status as a role model might also be enhanced by the knowledge that he or she experienced frailties common to all human beings and still achieved great things. Students of history may also learn some important lessons from a history presented with all its imperfections. Consider the following:

- Columbus is credited with discovering America. A holiday is named in his honor. Historians use his name as a way of dividing historical epochs (e.g., pre-Columbian). But many Europeans and Africans reached different parts of North America long before Columbus and Columbus' ships did not reach what is now the United States. There is little evidence that Columbus or his crew believed the world was flat. Columbus wanted to find gold and, when he didn't, he returned to Spain with 500 of the nearly 5,000 slaves he would eventually transport to Europe. In 1499, he found gold on Haiti and brutally forced the native Arawaks to mine it for him (Loewen, 1995).

- George Washington is called the "father of our country." He was America's first president and his face adorns the one-dollar bill and Mount Rushmore. Early in his life he was a slave owner. He is remembered as a great military general, but his career included some important military defeats—enough that the Continental Congress considered firing him more than once. He was not eager to go to war with the British and argued against separation from Great Britain as a member of the Virginia House of Commons (Ayres, 2000). Fleming (2005) says the winter Washington spent at Valley Forge with his troops was not severe, as is often reported, but relatively mild. The story that Washington told his father he had chopped down a cherry tree because he could not tell a lie *is a lie*. A biographer (who was formerly a minister) made it up in order to enhance Washington's image (Weems, 1806/1968).

- Abraham Lincoln is often said to have been America's greatest president. His face is on the five-dollar bill and rises six stories high on Mt. Rushmore. He is well known for signing the Emancipation Proclamation and freeing America's slaves. At the same time, Bennett (2000) says he liked "darky" jokes, habitually used the "N" word, and supported the Fugitive Slave Act, which compelled the return of escaped slaves to their owners. In debates he emphasized whites should remain in a "superior" position to blacks and that blacks should not have the right to vote, serve on juries, marry whites, or hold public office. As president, he opposed the spread of slavery, but in 1862 he wrote to the *New York Times* that if he could save the Union without freeing any slaves, he would (Lind, 2005). Pfiffner (2004) points out that effective politicians work within the political realities they face and that Lincoln could not have been elected president and subsequently been in a position to sign the Emancipation Proclamation if he had positioned himself as an abolitionist.

- Helen Keller is known for her extraordinary achievements in the face of her disabilities. She was blind and deaf but learned to read and write. She couldn't speak, but later learned to speak in a whisper. She graduated from college, wrote many books, and received a Pulitzer Prize for her autobiography. She helped found the American Civil Liberties Union, supported the NAACP (the premier civil rights organization for African Americans), and led suffrage marches. She was also a radical socialist who supported the communist revolution in Russia (Rosenthal, n.d.).

- Woodrow Wilson was governor of New Jersey and president of the United States. He played a primary role in the founding of the League of Nations, an international organization dedicated to avoiding war. He abolished child labor, established the Federal Trade Commission, and limited railroad workers to 8-hour work days. But he also sent more American troops to fight in Latin America than at any other time in our country's history. He was a racist who would not appoint African Americans to political office and vetoed a racial equality clause in the League of Nations charter (Matthews, 2015).

- The Puritans are often thought of as dreary, pleasure-hating people. Calling a person "Puritanical" implies they have a stern, rigid morality, believe in self-control and hard work, and consider pleasure as wrong or unnecessary. But Norton (2002) says Puritans liked to drink, play games, and enjoyed sex. She says they often wore colorful outfits and consumed large quantities of beer, rum, ale, and alcoholic cider.

- America would not have won the race to the Moon without Wernher von Braun (pictured). Yet the architect of America's space program had been a member of the Nazi Party in Germany, an officer in the SS, and chief designer of the V2 rocket that killed thousands in Europe. Thousands more died building the V2 as slave laborers brought in from the nearby Dora concentration camp. Over the years, Von Braun himself gave conflicting answers about these details of his pre-American life. Today more than ever, historians remain bitterly divided over how to view his legacy (Couronne, 2019).

© Bachrach/Contributor/Getty Images

Larger-than-life heroes (especially flawed ones) and villains (and complex villains in particular) are a vital part of any society's history. Learning how their images were created and how those images evolve and change over time is an act of truth-seeking.

Political Biases

Both right-wing and left-wing political groups have tried to influence the content of public school history textbooks. Each group wants to make the writing of history comport with their values.

In one case, the Texas State Board of Education stated that J. M. Faragher's history textbook *Out of Many: A History of the American People* (1994) could not be used in the state because it contained information about prostitution that was inappropriate for high school students (Associated Press, 2002). In a section called "Cowboys and Prostitutes," the book says that 50,000 women west of the Mississippi worked as prostitutes during the second half of the 19th century. It reads:

> *In cattle towns, many women worked as prostitutes. Like most cowboys, most prostitutes were unmarried and in their teens and 20s.*

Both right-wing and left-wing political groups have tried to influence the content of public school history textbooks. Each group wants to make the writing of history comport with their values.

Often fed up with underpaid jobs in dressmaking or domestic service, they found few alternatives to prostitution in cattle towns.

The board thought this was an unflattering depiction of the West, an exaggeration of the practice of prostitution, an implication that all cowboys went to prostitutes, and a failure to acknowledge that prostitution was not limited to the area west of the Mississippi. Ravitch (2003) believes that underlying the desire to exclude scandalous or morally offensive behavior from textbooks is the worry that textbook content will have a powerful influence on a student's values and behavior. Some teachers, of course, can only wish that were the case.

According to Ravitch (2003), it is the influence of political pressure groups that has led to a portrayal in '90s-era world history books of all civilizations as equally advanced and equally humane. She points out that this "cultural equivalence" is not likely to help students understand why some civilizations flourished and others didn't, why some populations seem forever trapped in poverty, and why democracy and human rights are important in multiethnic and multireligious societies.

In Texas and elsewhere, meanwhile, textbook controversies are ongoing—including debate over the use of titles that appear to call for a "balanced" view of slavery (QR).

Religious Biases

Various translations of the Bible sometimes tell different stories. This may be due to competing judgments/biases made by the authors, translators, or religious groups who want a text consistent with their beliefs. Sometimes changes are made to reflect current linguistic and/or political preferences (as in changing "sons" of God to "children" of God). The New International Version of the Bible provides a footnoted alternative for the translation of

© Lincoln Rogers/Shutterstock.com

"Red Sea" as "sea of reeds" or marshy area. Such translations open up the possibility that the Red Sea did not have to be miraculously parted for people to pass through as in the common Exodus story. The King James Version omits this alternative translation (Avalos, 2006).

People who believe that the Bible is an accurate historical account can simply believe that the authors were infallible reporters; for them, no corroborating evidence is necessary. Others, however, seek archeological verification of Biblical accounts (Laughlin, 2000). Archeologists have been searching for evidence to support the story of Exodus for more than a century. Many now believe that there is no conclusive proof that the Israelites were in Egypt, enslaved, lost in the desert for years, or that they conquered the land of Canaan (Watanabe, 2001). Finkelstein and Silberman (2001) say the book of Exodus was written 600 years after it supposedly happened and was likely intended as a political manifesto to unite various Israelite factions against rival Egyptians.

But for some Jews and Christians, the historical truth is less important than the powerful effect of a story about freedom. Carol Meyers, a professor of religion at Duke University, says the writers of the Bible did not set out to write history using the same standards for accuracy and truth that we apply today. "People who try to find scientific explanations for the splitting of the Red Sea are missing the boat in understanding how ancient literature often mixed mythic ideas with historical recollections," she said. "That wasn't considered lying or deceit; it was a way to get ideas across" (Watanabe, 2001). Among religious studies scholars, there is an old expression that aptly describes this mixture of truth, history, and storytelling: "All of these stories are true—and some of them actually happened."

Publisher Constraints

Publishers are interested in historical accuracy, but the strength of this commitment may waver when the choice is between accuracy and sales. All high schools in Texas use the same history textbook; the same is true of California. Thus, if a publisher's book is adopted in one or both states, it is a major source of income. As a result, they want very much to please the textbook decision-making boards in these and other large-market states. Companies have admitted that state education boards may dictate content. Such demand can lead to changes they (and the authors) think are erroneous in order to appease some board members (Bahadur, 2001; Ravitch, 2003).

Writing Decisions

Attributions of deception and/or distortion in history textbooks may also emanate from the author's language and writing style. Among other things, this may involve the extent of coverage given to a historical event, the extent to which the event is shown to be interdependent with other events, the certainty with which information is presented, and the use of words that communicate a positive or negative affect.

Loewen (1995) says authors of high school history texts too often try to write in a way that will not offend anyone. One illustration of how difficult the achievement of this goal might be is found in the offense taken by some to the phrase "founding fathers" (Ravitch, 2003). In the process of trying to produce a history book that doesn't offend anyone, writers may produce a history that is not only less accurate, but one that students find uninteresting, superficial, and at odds with the goal of creating a citizenry knowledgeable about their country's past.

The information in these texts that is relevant to any particular event is too often gleaned from familiar sources, including competing textbooks. Without a skeptical stance or a desire to look for a new perspective, the standard stories are repeated over and over. We are taught that:

© Morphart Creation/Shutterstock.com

- evolution was the work of Charles Darwin and fail to learn that Alfred Russell Wallace (pictured) is considered to be the co-discoverer of the theory of natural selection (Shermer, 2002)

- Charles Lindbergh was the first to fly *solo* across the Atlantic Ocean, but fail to learn that 80 others had made the flight before him (Ayres, 2000)

- an engineer who worked for RCA invented television when, in fact, it was a teenage Idaho farm boy named Philo T. Farnsworth (Schatzkin, 2002)

- Edison invented the electrical current, but not that Nikola Tesla developed the alternating electrical current (AC) that powers our homes and businesses and that it was also Tesla, not Marconi, who invented radio (Cheney, 2001)

- Betsy Ross sewed the first American flag, but fail to learn that this claim, made by her grandson, cannot be supported by other evidence (Ayres, 2000)

- the Wright brothers were the first to engage an airplane in sustained flight, but do not learn about the others who may have flown an airplane before the Wright brothers (Ayres, 2000; Shulman, 2002).

WRITING MEMOIRS

In theory, a memoir or autobiography is a written account of thoughts, emotions, people, and events that the author actually experienced. It is one person's truth—the author's. But as controversial cultural critic H.L. Mencken (1924) observed: "Honest autobiography is. . .a contradiction in terms" (p. 270). Any given event experienced by the memoirist was probably also experienced by others who may not have perceived it the same way.

Unlike journalists, however, memoirists are not always obligated to account for different perspectives in their story. Given the imperfect nature of memory, some discrepancies with the memories and perceptions of others are expected and viewed as natural. Many authors believe memoirs should be considered creative literature and released from a factual standard. But memoirs by public figures written today may be the basis of future historical accounts and the extent to which they are valid is an important issue. The public is often willing to overlook some exaggerations and, on occasion, grant plenty of dramatic license. This is particularly true when the memoir is especially well written, the author is not a public figure, or the story depicts something the public has a strong desire to believe.

When a memoir is based on a person's life experiences, but the author creatively blends in fictional elements in order to make a good story, it can be truthfully labeled as such. In 1968, Exley called his book, *A Fan's Notes*, a "fictional memoir." After Frey's *A Million Little Pieces* (2003) was widely criticized for its inaccuracies, subsequent editions carried a disclaimer. When disclaimers accompany memoirs, they typically mention one or more of the following: that the time sequence of events has been altered, that composite characters have been created, that names have been changed, and/or that other details have been made up. Stephen Glass, the journalist who admitted faking dozens of stories when he worked for *The New Republic*, took no chances with his memoir, *The Fabulist* (2003). Even though the book is about a character named Stephen Glass who experiences the same journalistic rise and fall that the author did, the book is clearly labeled "fiction."

Fiction can infiltrate memoirs in many ways—none of which, Goodman (2006) believes, is good for public consumption:

> The morphing of truth and fiction promotes a world in which facts are 'subjective' and reality 'flexible.' It feeds an indifference to honesty and a belief that every truth is up for grabs. At its most extreme it lends credibility—street cred—to such frauds as the Holocaust denial.

Some memoirs are deliberately deceptive and, like news reports and the writing of history, some are either unintentionally misleading or perceived as deceptive when they aren't.

Deceptive Memoirs

The purported Holocaust memoir *Fragments: Memories of a Wartime Childhood* by Wilkomirski (1996) won the National Jewish Book Award. But when so many facts alluded to in the memoir could not be verified, it was determined to be a completely fraudulent account that qualified more as a novel than a memoir (Maechler, 2001).

More commonly, the deceptiveness in memoirs is limited to a specific event or events that the author may have exaggerated or changed in order to make a more interesting or dramatic story. Rigoberta Menchú, who won the Nobel Peace Prize in 1992, authored an autobiography about Mayan peasants and the horrors of war in Guatemala. Stoll's (1999) research, however, indicates that certain events in the book could not have happened in the way they were depicted and others could not have been recalled from the author's memory. *A Million Little Pieces* (noted above), a memoir about the James Frey's drug addiction and recovery, became a best seller. When some of the facts in the book were disputed, the author acknowledged that his life and the book were not a perfect match (Martelle & Collins, 2006).

When memoirs focus on growing up with dysfunctional family members, it is not surprising if charges of deception are made against the author by relatives. Some of Helget's family members and neighbors flatly deny events recounted in her widely praised *A Summer of Ordinary Ways* (2005). And members of Augusten Burroughs' family actually sued him over his memoir, *Running with Scissors* (2002).

Factors Leading to Distortion and Deception

Memoirs, like other forms of public writing we've addressed in this chapter, are affected by various factors that either lead to deception or produce an account that is perceived as slanted or deceptive. The following influences are common:

Poor Memory

Memoirists depend on their personal recall of events and remembered happenings are not always accurate. Readers recognize the imperfect nature of memory and often grant memoirists a certain margin of error in recall. This is not the case, however, when documentary evidence can be produced that is contrary to the facts recalled by the memoirist. This happened with Robert Reich's 1997 memoir, *Locked in the Cabinet*, an account of his tenure as a member of President Clinton's cabinet.

Subjective Perceptions

In *The Summer of Ordinary Ways*, the author says she saw her father kill a cow with a pitchfork when she was a child. Her father says this never happened, but admits she may have seen him trying to move an already dead cow with a pitchfork (Tevlin & Williams, 2005). Memoirists don't always perceive things the way others do, particularly when recalling events from childhood.

Although counter-perceptions expressed by numerous people may cast doubt on the truthfulness of a memoir, memoirists' perceptions (of actual events, at least) are normally accepted as an inherent part of writing one.

Advocacy

When memoirs are written with the goal of advocating for a cause, the desire to be persuasive may supersede the desire to adhere to actual events in one's life story. The aforementioned biography of Rigoberta Menchú (1984) mixed fact and fiction in an effort to call the world's attention to the tragic happenings in Guatemala. Some of the happenings that Menchú made up may actually have occurred, but they could not have been drawn from her personal experience. Some have described this work as a "biomythography"—meaning that a life story is supplemented with fictional material in order to portray a "greater truth." The cause in *Fragments* is the Holocaust—depicted from a child's perspective. It is a stirring and often believable account, but it is fiction. The author of *A Million Little Pieces* (2003), wanted to inspire others to help those addicted to drugs and give hope to addicts in the recovery. A completely true account of the author's life may also have been a best seller, but James Frey felt that his story needed a more persuasive punch in certain places than the truth alone could deliver.

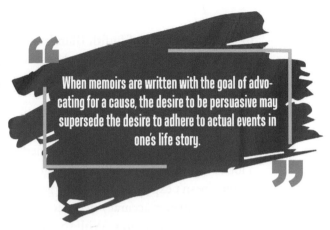

> When memoirs are written with the goal of advocating for a cause, the desire to be persuasive may supersede the desire to adhere to actual events in one's life story.

In similar fashion, Peggy Seltzer, a white suburbanite educated at private schools, justified writing *Love and Consequences* (2008) in literary blackface—posing as biracial gang member Margaret B. Jones and writing in her own form of Ebonics—because she was "giving a voice to people who people don't listen to" (Listverse, 2010). Before being exposed, early reviewers had been overwhelmingly positive. But, says writer David Mills, "all they know about the black world is what they've read in other media," referring not only to Seltzer but also to the mostly white, mostly middle- and upper-class editors who approved the manuscript in the first place. Her publisher recalled the book, offering refunds to anyone who had already purchased a copy (Bates, 2008).

Making a Better Story

As noted earlier, the public often permits memoirists a certain amount of embellishment. And if they write a terrific story, there will always be some readers who simply do not care how much of it is untrue. For example, one Amazon.com reviewer of *The Summer of Ordinary Ways* said:

> *Who among us hasn't been absolutely certain about the way an event transpired, only to be unequivocally told that's not how it happened? And if there is some fiction*

or wishful thinking thrown into this story, well—life isn't often very exciting, and I bet you can't show me ANY memoir that is without embellishment. . .If I were to later find out that this entire book was in fact a novel and not a work of non-fiction, I wouldn't appreciate it any less—it is that well-written.

In the front matter of Judith Blunt's memoir, *Breaking Clean* (2002), she says, "I want to acknowledge those who might choose a different version of the story than the one I tell. . .I've long since made my peace with the variety of fiction we call truth."

Publisher Needs

Most publishers are primarily concerned about publishing memoirs that will sell well and make a lot of money. They don't want to get sued, but they also count on the idea that the reading public doesn't expect works in this genre to be 100% factual and accurate. Because of possible lawsuits, however accuracy may become more of an issue for publishers when the memoirs are written by public figures. With so much at stake, however, it remains a curiosity that, unlike newspapers and magazines, many book publishers do not have fact checkers.

WRITING RÉSUMÉS

Résumés are not technically "written for the public," but they may be viewed by a wide spectrum of people. If the résumé belongs to a public figure, it is scrutinized by an even larger audience. To what extent do people include deceptive information on their résumés? In one study, 473 out of 1,100 résumés contained one or more significant inaccuracies (Koeppel, 2006). The hundreds of firms that now do résumé checking operate on the assumption that about 25% will have some major misrepresentation in them.

"Everything on your resume is true ... right?"

© Cartoon Resource/Shutterstock.com

Deceptive Résumés

The most frequent résumé lies deal with education, and unearned college degrees top that list. Even fraudulent medical degrees and medical board certifications are not unusual. Keyes (2004, p. 65) says that an investigation by the Government Accountability Office found 28 senior federal employees with bogus college degrees. Other common résumé lies include: place of birth, dates of employment, descriptions of job responsibilities, inflated salary figures of previously held jobs, and fake references.

Putting false information on résumés is not limited to any particular industry, gender, job, or salary level. Executives from Oracle, Lotus Development Corp., Radio Shack, Bausch & Lomb, Veritas Software, and the U. S. Olympic Committee have all done it. A former athletic director at Dartmouth University and a former Poet Laureate of California also did it (Cullen, 2006; Keyes, 2004). In 1979, Marilee Jones misrepresented her college degrees when she applied for a job at the Massachusetts Institute of Technology (MIT). Eventually, she coauthored an important book about college admissions and became the dean of admissions at MIT. But she never changed her false résumé and was asked to resign in 2007 when the fabrications were uncovered. It is not without irony to note that her well-received book on the college admissions process urged students not to try to be perfect.

The website FakeResume even gives advice on how to be more strategic in putting false information on one's résumé—e.g., rent your own post office box as an address for references or use your friends to act as references; don't leave gaps in employment history, and if you do, attribute it to a tragic death in the family; order or make fake degrees and transcripts; and have a ready and believable story to tell about anything you fabricate.

Factors Leading to Distorted and Deceptive Résumés

Some people believe the practice of falsifying résumés is so widespread that they must do the same in order to compete. Some rationalize that the lies are not going to hurt anyone; others reason, for example, that saying you have a college degree when you're only six hours short is a small lie. From the employer's perspective, it is this faulty reasoning process—resulting in the decision to lie—that makes such a person an undesirable employee. With this precedent set, what's to keep them from using this same flawed reasoning once he or she is on the job? Use whatever justification you want if you're thinking about padding or otherwise deceiving on your résumé. Just recognize that most people don't do it and that employers are more savvy than ever when it comes to spotting such lies.

The line between a résumé that emphasizes a person's strengths and one that deceives about them is not hard to see. There's a big difference between a college student who lies about her grade point average and one who honestly reports that she had a 3.2 grade point average in her major but omits the fact that her overall grade point average was 2.6. If the question of her overall GPA arises in a job interview, she can be forthright about it and provide valid reasons to explain why it is lower.

The negative impact of a deceptive résumé is sometimes years in the making. Bill Richardson, former governor of New Mexico, said he was drafted to play pro baseball by the Kansas City Athletics when he was a young man. Thirty-eight years later he admitted this information was not correct (Smith, 2005). Successful football coach George O'Leary left false information on his résumé for years, but it was only after he was hired to coach at Notre Dame that these facts were checked and he was fired after only a week on the job. Keyes (2004) uses O'Leary's situation to address the question of why an old résumé lie still matters when the perpetrator has repeatedly demonstrated successful performance on the job. He says:

> . . .*many wondered if this punishment fit the crime. The phony athletic achievements and spurious master's degree he claimed were merely youthful indiscretions, they said. O'Leary's successful decades as a high school and college football coach more than compensated. That left an important question unanswered, however: What happened to the truthful job applicants who competed with O'Leary for the many jobs he'd won on the basis of phony credentials? This question must be posed to anyone who uses an embellished résumé to win a position. (p. 67)*

Job site Monster.com recommends resisting such deceptive temptations entirely when it comes to telling one's story on a résumé. Its site lists common lies told by job-seekers, how such lies are likely to be discovered by potential employers, and general strategies for avoiding résumé deception altogether (QR).

SUMMARY

News reports, historical accounts, memoirs, and résumés are all documents written for public consumption. Some writers in each venue have deliberately fabricated information in these documents. In addition, there are factors associated with the production of each document that can influence unintentionally deceptive writing and truthful accounts that others perceived as deceptive.

Acts of intentionally deceptive news writing are not frequent, but they have a profoundly adverse effect on the credibility of news organizations. In addition, reporters sometimes use deception to gain access to information and must contend with various factors that may influence actual or perceived slanting of the news. Some sources of news bias emanate from the reporter's methods of news gathering and the way he or she writes the story. The reporter's employer is another potential source of news bias. But sometimes the perception of biased news is rooted in the biases of the news consumers—e.g., the perceptions of a particular news event by those who have a highly partisan view about that event, known as the "hostile media effect." Although some news organizations are content to be known by their biases, most try to reduce sources of bias and perceived bias by adopting methods to ensure greater objectivity and emphasizing their commitment to producing news in the public's interest.

There are many similarities in the writing of history and the writing of news. Each deals with an evolving truth, each has experienced intentionally deceptive writers, and each has to cope with a variety of factors that may inject bias into its writing. The writing of history may be influenced not only by a writer's own needs and biases, but also by the preferences of his or her publisher. Sometimes political and/or religious groups also try to influence the way history is written.

Even though memoirists also face factors that can lead to slanting and bias in their writing, these authors often receive less sanctioning for inaccuracies and biases. Embellishment and dramatic license are often tolerated, but when the author is a public figure and/or documentary evidence is found that refutes the author's account, the author is held accountable. Although memoirs are usually thought of as personal truths, they are sometimes written with the intent of being a more general truth.

Résumé writers try to emphasize their strengths, but they are not encouraged to lie. Nevertheless, firms that check résumés report that about 25% of the time people provide inaccurate information about some significant aspect of their background and experience. These résumé lies are primarily about the person's education, but lies about previous employment and salary are also common.

EXERCISES

1. This chapter dealt with the writing of news, history, memoirs, and résumés. Consider another venue in which there is writing for the public: science. As an initial reference, see *Voodoo Science: The Road From Foolishness to Fraud* (2000). Identify any known acts of deception (e.g., the cloning experiments reported by Hwang Woo-Suk from South Korea) and the factors that may lead to perceived or actual deception in scientific writing.

2. Cut out and sort into two piles several newspaper articles that you think are: (1) deceptive and/or greatly distorted/slanted and (2) several that you think exhibit little distortion/slanting. Mix up the two piles and have another person read the articles and sort them into the same two piles. Discuss why you agree and/or why you disagree with the way the other person sorted the articles. Pro tip: You might want to do this twice. Once with a person who is similar to you in terms of worldview and again with someone whose worldview is very different from yours.

3. When it comes to the American tradition of Thanksgiving and the history it is supposedly based on, can you separate fact from fiction? Consider giving the following quiz to your friends and family, and definitely your other professors:

   a. **True or false? The Plymouth colony was the first European settlement in what is now the United States of America.**

      False. There were many settlements in the area that is now the United States prior to 1620, but the Plymouth colony was not a quest for gold or an attempt to claim land for a foreign government. Instead, there were individuals and families seeking religious freedom—an appealing way to begin the history of America. It is often necessary, however, to sanitize this "feel good" beginning—downplaying or omitting unpleasantries like the settlers' treatment of Native Americans, which involved killing and enslaving them, stealing their crops, spreading disease among them, and robbing their graves (Loewen, 1995; Philbrick, 2006).

   b. **True or false? Only 35 of the 102 people aboard the Mayflower were Pilgrims.**
      True.

   c. **True or false? The modern version of celebrating Thanksgiving was not introduced until 1863, a full 242 years after the first Pilgrim celebration.**
      True.

d. **The Pilgrims were not inpart of the modern Thanksgiving celebration until the 1890s—nearly 40 years after it became an annual celebration in the United States.**

True.

e. **True or false? The reason for the Thanksgiving celebration of 1621 was to give thanks for surviving the first harsh winter.**

Likely false. The Thanksgiving feast of 1621 was probably a traditional English celebration of a successful harvest.

4. Identify passages in this textbook that you think are deceptive and/or distorted/slanted. List the reasons for your perceptions. Ask others if they agree with you.

OF INTEREST

As this chapter notes, writing history can be a fraught process, even for the scholar who is genuinely interesting in simply finding out what happened. But when such writing is agenda-driven, readers should be especially skeptical. David Barton has made a career out of spinning American history so that it fits with his theocratic, fundamentalist Christian worldview. In 2012, his suspect methods finally caught up with him.

In this short essay, the non-profit American Press Institute explains how "objectivity" in journalism is a myth that has taken on a life of its own. As we note elsewhere in this chapter, objectivity is perhaps best understand as a method rather than an attitude—and one that we are more in need of than ever before.

REFERENCES

Associated Press (2002, July 8). Education board's decision draws fire from co-author. *Austin American Statesman*.

Auletta, K. (2003). Backstory: Inside the business of the news. New York, NY: Penguin Press.

Avalos, H. (2006, February/March). Twisting scripture. *Free Inquiry, 26*, 38–44.

Ayres, T. (2000). *That's not my American history book: A compilation of little-known events and forgotten heroes.* Dallas, TX: Taylor Trade Publishing.

Bahadur, G. (2001, November 10). Board accepts book with changes. *Austin American Statesman*, pp. B1, 5.

Bates, K. G. (2008, March 21). Writers respond to a 'faux memoir' of gang life. *National Public Radio*. Retrieved from http://www.npr.org

Bauder, D. (2015, June 19). Williams loses 'Nightly News' anchor job. *Austin American Statesman*, p. A4.

Bennett, Jr., L. (2000). *Forced into glory: Abraham Lincoln's white dream.* Chicago, IL: Johnson Publishing Co.

Bianchi, M. (2002, July 10). Dysfunctional stars are nothing new. *Austin American Statesman*, p. D2.

Blunt, J. (2002). *Breaking clean.* New York, NY: Knopf.

Boehlert, E. (2006). *Lapdogs: How the press rolled over for Bush.* New York, NY: Free Press.

Burroughs, A. X. (2002). *Running with scissors.* New York, NY: Picador.

Calamur, K. (2015, June 18). It's official: Brian Williams out as 'NBC Nightly News' anchor. *National Public Radio*. Retrieved from http://www.npr.org/

Cheney, M. (2001). *Tesla: Man out of time.* New York, NY: Touchstone.

Cohen, E. D. (1997). Forms of news bias. In E. D. Cohen & D. Elliott (Eds.), *Contemporary ethical issues* (pp. 58–64). Santa Barbara, CA: ABC-CLIO.

Corn, D., & Schulman, D. (2015, February 19). Bill O'Reilly has his own Brian Williams problem. *Mother Jones.* Retrieved from http://www.motherjones.com

Coronel, S., Coll, S., & Kravitz, D. (2015, April 5). Rolling Stone and UVA: The Columbia University Graduate School of Journalism Report. *Rolling Stone.* Retrieved from http://www.rollingstone.com/

Couronne, I. (2019, July 20). Wernher Von Braun: From rocket builder for Hitler to Apollo hero. The *Times of Israel.* Retrieved from http://www.timesofisrael.com

Cullen, L.T. (2006, May 1). Getting wise to lies. *Time*, p. 59.

Davidson, S. (1998, November/December). Food lyin' and other Buttafuocos. *IRE Journal, 21*, 6–10.

Faragher, J. M. (1994). *Out of many: A history of the American people*. New York, NY: Prentice-Hall.

Featherstone, L. (1997, July/August). Chucking the checkers. *Columbia Journalism Review, 36*, 12–13.

Finkelstein, I., & Silberman, N. A. (2001). *The Bible unearthed: Archaeology's new vision of ancient Israel and the origin of its sacred texts*. New York, NY: Free Press.

Fleming, T. (2005). Myth and truth at Valley Forge. *American History, 40*, 42–50.

Frey, J. (2003). *A million little pieces*. New York, NY: Doubleday.

Gándara, R. (2002, August 17). Despite all the headlines, abductions by strangers are rare. *Austin American Statesman*, p. D3.

Giner-Sorolla, R., & Chaiken, S. (1994). The causes of hostile media judgments. *Journal of Experimental Social Psychology, 30*, 165–180. https://doi.org/10.1006/jesp.1994.1008

Glass, S. (2003). *The fabulist: A novel*. New York, NY: Simon & Schuster.

Gold, H. (2018, August 28). Trump slams Google search as 'rigged'—but it's not. *CNN*. Retrieved from http://www.cnn.com

Goodman, E. (2006, January 20). Fuzzing the line between fact and fiction. *Austin American Statesman*, p. A11.

Gunther R., Beck, P. A., & Nisbet, E. C. (2018). Fake news may have contributed to Trump's 2016 victory. Retrieved April 26, 2019, from https://assets.documentcloud.org/documents/4429952/Fake-News-May-Have-Contributed-to-Trump-s-2016.pdf

Harris, P. (2010, April 25). Band Of Brothers author accused of fabrication for Eisenhower biography. *The Guardian*. Retrieved from http://www.theguardian.com

Helget, N.L. (2005). *The summer of ordinary ways: A memoir*. St. Paul, MN: Borealis Books.

Isherwood, C. (2012, March 18). Speaking less than truth to power. *The New York Times*. Retrieved from http://www.nytimes.com/

Italie, H. (2002, January 24). Slips, accusations bedevil several popular historians. *Austin American Statesman*, pp. A1, 12.

Jamieson, K. H., & Waldman, P. (2002). *The press effect: Politicians, journalists, and the stories that shape the political world*. New York, NY: Oxford University Press.

Kaplan, R. L. (2002). *Politics and the American press: The rise of objectivity, 1865–1920*. New York, NY: Cambridge University Press.

Keith, T. (2018, September 2). President Trump's description of what is "fake" is expanding. *National Public Radio*. Retrieved from http://www.npr.org

Keyes, R. (2004). *The post-truth era: Dishonesty and deception in everyday life*. New York, NY: St. Martin's Press.

Kirn, W. (2002, August 26). Invasion of the baby snatchers. *Time Magazine*, p. 38.

Kinsley, M. (2008, February 25). McCain and the *Times*: The real questions. Retrieved from http:/www.slate.com

Koeppel, D. (2006, April 23). Fudging the facts on a résumé is common, and also a big risk. *The New York Times*. Retrieved from http://www.nytimes.com

Kovach, B., & Rosenstiel, T. (2001). *The elements of journalism: What newspeople should know and the public should expect*. New York, NY: Crown.

Kurtz, H. (2009, February 20). Lobbyist Vicki Iseman settles libel suit over *N.Y. Times* story linking her to McCain. *The Washington Post*. Retrieved from http://www.washingtonpost.com

Laughlin, J. C. H. (2000). *Archaeology and the Bible*. New York, NY: Routledge.

Lee, M. A., & Solomon, N. (1990). *Unreliable sources: A guide to detecting bias in the news media*. New York, NY: Lyle Stuart.

Leff, L. (2005). *Buried by the Times: The Holocaust and America's most important newspaper*. New York, NY: Cambridge University Press.

Levin, B. (2019, March 8). White House: Jobs numbers that make us look bad are fake news. *Vanity Fair*. Retrieved from http://www.vanityfair.com

Lind, M. (2005). *What Lincoln believed: The values and convictions of America's greatest president*. New York, NY: Doubleday.

Lipstadt, D. E. (1986). *Beyond belief: The American press and the coming of the Holocaust*, 1933–1945. New York, NY: Free Press.

Lipstadt, D. E. (1993). *Denying the Holocaust: The growing assault on truth and memory*. New York, NY: Free Press.

Listverse. (2010, March 6). Top 10 infamous fake memoirs. Retrieved from http://www.listverse.com/

Loewen, J. W. (1995). *Lies my teacher told me: Everything your American history textbook got wrong*. New York, NY: The New Press.

Loewen, J. W. (1999). *Lies across America. What our historic sites get wrong*. New York, NY: The New Press.

MacDougall, C. D. (1972). *Interpretative reporting*. 8th ed. New York, NY: Macmillan.

Maechler, S. (2001). *The Wilkomirski affair: A study in biographical truth*. New York, NY: Random House.

Mahler, J., Somaiya, R., & Steel, E. (2015, February 5). With an apology, Brian Williams digs himself in deeper with copter tale. *The New York Times*. Retrieved from http://www.nytimes.com/

Martelle, S., & Collins, S. (2006, January 11). Memoir might need reshelving under 'hoax.' *Austin American Statesman*, pp. A1, 12.

Martin, M. (1997). Objectivity and news bias. In E. D. Cohen & D. Elliott (Eds.), *Journalism ethics: A reference handbook* (pp. 54–57). Santa Barbara, CA: ABC-CLIO.

Matthews, D. (2015, November 20). Woodrow Wilson was extremely racist—even by the standards of his time. *Vox*. Retrieved from http://www.vox.com

McCarthy, J. (2014, September 17). Trust in mass media returns to all-time low. Retrieved from http://www.gallup.com

McLeese, D. (1998, June 23). When truth gets tweaked by journalists. *Austin American Statesman*.

Menchú, R. (1984). *I, Rigoberta Menchú: An Indian woman in Guatemala*. London, UK: Verso.

Mencken, H. L. (1924). *Prejudices* (fourth series). New York, NY: Knopf.

Meyer, P. (1997, February 17). Food Lion case shows that cameras, indeed, can lie. *USA Today*, p. 15A.

Newport, F. (2015, February 11). Brian Williams situation plays out in context of already low trust in mass media. Retrieved from http://www.gallup.com

Nickerson, R. S. (1998). Confirmation bias: A ubiquitous phenomenon in many guises. *Review of General Psychology*, 2, 175–220. https://dx.doi.org/10.1037//1089-2680.2.2.175

Norton, M. B. (2002). *In the devil's snare: The Salem witchcraft crisis of 1672*. New York, NY: Knopf.

Orey, M. (2009, January 5). The lobbyist v. the New York Times. *BusinessWeek Online*. Retrieved from http://www.ebscohost.com. (Accession number 36005845)

Penny, L. (2005). *Your call is important to us: The truth about bullshit*. New York, NY: Crown.

Perloff, R. M. (1989). Ego-involvement and the third person effect of televised news coverage. *Communication research*, 16, 236–262.

Pew Research Center (2013, August 8). Amid criticism, support for media's 'watchdog role' stands out. Retrieved from http://www.people-press.org

Pfiffner, J. P. (2004). *The character factor: How we judge America's presidents*. College Station, TX: Texas A&M Press.

Philbrick, N. (2006). *Mayflower: A story of courage, community, and war*. New York, NY: Viking.

Popper, K. R. (1950). *The open society and its enemies*. Princeton, NJ: Princeton University Press.

Pribble, J. M., Goldstein, K. M., Fowler, E. F., Greenberg, M. J., Noel, S. K., & Howell, J. D. (2006). Medical news for the public to use? What's on local TV news. *The American Journal of Managed Care, 12,* 170–176.

Ravitch, D. (2003). *The language police: How pressure groups restrict what students learn.* New York, NY: Knopf.

Read, R. (2004, October 3). Reporters feelings on Iraq highlights perils of e-mail. *The Oregonian,* Northwest Section, p. A13.

Reich, R.L (1997). *Locked in the cabinet.* New York, NY: Knopf.

Rich, F. (2006). *The greatest story ever sold: The decline and fall of truth from 9/11 to Katrina.* New York, NY: Penguin Press.

Rosenthal, K. (n.d.). The politics of Helen Keller. *International Socialist Review.* Retrieved from http://www.isreview.org

Rothkopf, J. (2015, March 2). Fox News finally stops pretending the Bill O'Reilly scandal is a liberal conspiracy. *Salon.* Retrieved from http://www.salon.com/

Rupp, K. L. (2014, September 19). Confidence lost. *U.S. News & World Report.* Retrieved from http://www.usnews.com

Santayana, G. (1905–06/1998). *The life of reason.* Amherst, NY: Prometheus Books.

Schatzkin, P. (2002). *The boy who invented television: A story of inspiration, persistence, and quiet passion.* Burtonsville, MD: TeamComBooks.

Schudel, M., & Langer, E. (2016, March 30). Bill Green, Post ombudsman who investigated fabricated Janet Cooke story, dies at 91. *The Washington Post.* Retrieved from http://www.washingtonpost.com

Schudson, M. (1990). *Origins of the ideal of objectivity in the professions.* New York, NY: Garland.

Schudson, M. (2001). The objectivity norm in American journalism*. *Journalism: Theory, Practice & Criticism, 2,* 149–170. https://dx.doi.org/10.1177/146488490100200201

Seelye, K., & Lewis, N. A. (2005, May 17). Newsweek says it is retracting Quran report. *The New York Times,* p. A-1.

Shapiro, T. R. (2014, December 5). Key elements of Rolling Stone's U-Va. gang rape allegations in doubt. *The Washington Post.* Retrieved from http://www.washingtonpost.com/

Shermer, M. (2002). *In Darwin's shadow: The life and science of Alfred Russell Wallace: A biographical study on the psychology of history.* New York, NY: Oxford University Press.

Shermer, M., & Grobman, A. (2000). *Denying history: Who says the Holocaust never happened and why do they say it?* Berkeley, CA: University of California Press.

Shulman, S. (2002). *Unlocking the sky: Glenn Hammond Curtiss and the race to invent the airplane*. New York, NY: HarperCollins.

Smith, T. (2005, November 24). Billy ball: One-time prospect acknowledges draft info wrong. *Albuquerque Journal*.

Somaiya, R. (2015, February 4). Brian Williams admits he wasn't on copter shot down in Iraq. *The New York Times*. Retrieved from http://www.nytimes.com/

Steinberg, J. (2004, March 20). USA Today finds top writer lied. *The New York Times*. Retrieved from http://www.nytimes.com

Stoll, D. (1999). *Rigoberta Menchú and the story of all poor Guatemalans*. Boulder, CO: Westview Press.

Tate, C. (1984). "What do ombudsmen do?" *Columbia Journalism Review, 23*, 37–41.

Tevlin, J., & Williams, S. T. (December 15, 2005). Dark and stormy memoir creates family rift: A Minnesota writer is lauded—and accused of betraying the truth. *Minneapolis Star Tribune*, p. 1A.

Thomas, H. (2006). *Watchdogs of democracy? The waning Washington press corps and how it has failed the public*. New York, NY: Simon & Schuster.

Tritten, T. (2015, February 4). NBC's Brian Williams recants Iraq story after soldiers protest. *Stars & Stripes*. Retrieved from http://www.stripes.com/

Vallone, R. P., Ross, L., & Lepper, M. R. (1985). The hostile media phenomenon: Biased perception and perceptions of media bias in coverage of the Beirut massacre. *Journal of Personality and Social Psychology, 49*, 577–585. https://dx.doi.org/10.1037//0022-3514.49.3.577

Waldman, P. (2015, February 24). The Bill O'Reilly scandal, made simple. *The Washington Post*. Retrieved from http://www.washingtonpost.com

Watanabe, T. (2001, April 22). Faiths defend Exodus story as science offers new history. *Austin American Statesman*, pp. H1, 5.

Weaver, D. H., & Wilhoit, G. C. (1996). *The American journalist in the 1990s*. Mahwah, NJ: Erlbaum.

Weems, M. L. (1806/1968). *The life of George Washington*. 5th ed. Augusta, GA: Geo. P. Randolph.

Wilkomirski, B. (1996). *Fragments: Memories of a wartime childhood*. New York, NY: Schocken.

CHAPTER 13 Visual Deception

© Oleg Belov/Shutterstock.com

© Slaven/Shutterstock.com

© Elzbieta Sekowska/Shutterstock.com

"In a very real sense, believing is seeing."
– *Steven Novella*

"We don't see things as they are, we see them as we are."
– *Anonymous*

"We need for people to know what's possible, and to think before they believe."
– *YouTube user Ctrl Shift Face, creator of the Bill Hader/Schwarzenegger deepfake*

Could a fake video start a real war? In the 21st century, the answer may be yes. Imagine the following scenario: A fake (but completely convincing) video of the President of the United States appears on social media and instantly spreads around the world like wildfire. In it, he or she announces, "I've just launched a pre-emptive nuclear strike against Iran." If you're Iran or one of its allies (Russia, for example), what do you do? You don't have hours or days to determine whether the video is real or not. Do you retaliate or just hold your breath and hope the sun keeps shining?

If you think this scenario sounds far-fetched, you're right. But if you think it's impossible, you're naïve. Security experts even have a name for it—"false flag." A false flag operation is when a third-party tries to trigger a conflict between two enemies by staging an attack that appears to be the work of one side or the other (Benjamin & Simon, 2019).

But it isn't just in the arena of armed conflict that the presence of false flag videos threaten to upend accuracy and reliability. In May of 2019, without checking its validity, Fox Business Network tweeted what it thought was a real video of House Speaker Nancy Pelosi stammering and staggering through a press conference (QR). The Speaker had actually given a press conference, but the clip Fox tweeted was heavily edited to make her appear impaired. Some even thought she was drunk. President Trump, who is famous for believing everything he sees on Fox, retweeted the fake clip with the headline, "PELOSI STAMMERS THROUGH NEWS CONFERENCE." YouTube removed the video (except news stories that revealed it as fake) but Facebook only reduced its visibility because the company has no policy that stipulates the information that someone posts has to be true (Waterson, 2019).

Such visual deception has become so prevalent—and potentially malevolent—that we considered moving this chapter to the beginning of the book. After all, the use of visual images is as old as humanity itself. Whether intentionally deceptive or not, from the beginning they certainly seem to have been fanciful and imaginative, like this cave painting found in Argentina. Such art is exactly that—*art*—and therefore not expected to be literal re-creations of reality. We understand and accept them as abstract representations rather than a faithful form of visual recordkeeping. We expect artists to challenge the way we see things—even if some find their work distasteful (QR). In fact, the only truly "bad" art may be the kind that doesn't move us in any way at all.

Historically, we have tended to perceive photographs and videos, unlike paintings, as inherently believable—to be credible captures of reality, a kind of visual truth. But the days of assuming that videos and photos are inherently accurate and truthful are over.

We must now accept that this longstanding difference from non-digital forms of representation (including magic and illusion) no longer exists, and that deception accomplished via video and photos should cease to surprise us (Lester and Yambor, 2019).

A CULTURE OF RECORDABILITY

Other than arts like painting and drawing, visual recordability advanced very little over time before suddenly exploding in the last half-century. And now in the Digital Age, we live in a culture utterly defined by recordability. Consider:

- 1.2 trillion digital photos were taken in 2017 alone, 85% of them using smartphones (Richter, 2017)

- In 2018, 84% of all marketing communications were expected to be visual (Cummings, 2016)

- The human brain processes images 60,000 times faster than it does text (Pant, 2015)

And with every new visual platform comes new forms of deception—so much so that the expectation of recordability as visual truth seems to be declining (Rothman, 2018). Whereas in the past it could be difficult to doctor film and photographs—and only a small group of experts could accomplish edits that would fool the public—today almost anyone can, and without much effort.

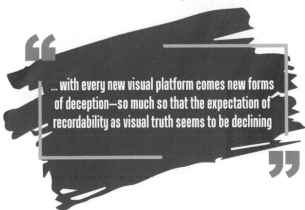

> ... with every new visual platform comes new forms of deception—so much so that the expectation of recordability as visual truth seems to be declining

Instead of assuming a visual record is realistic or accurate, we are now (or at least ought to be) learning to doubt what we see. Some edits made to visual images are more entertaining (e.g., app filters) than concerning, but increasingly there are ways to edit visuals that hold chilling implications (QR).

The Internet and our many devices allow us to post and distribute images and videos rapidly and often with a lack of caution. As expected, rates of online use are growing:

• In 2018, the Pew Research Center reported that 95% of Americans own a cell phone (77% of which are smartphones)

• Only 8% of adults used social media sites in 2005; by 2019 that number had ballooned to 73% of all adults, and to 93% of adults aged 25–29 (Perrin & Anderson, 2019)

• In 2016, Pew found that the stigma associated with online dating had waned and that approximately 27% of adults aged 18–24 were using dating apps. However, eHarmony (QR) claims that fully 40% of Americans are using online dating (of course, such claims are no doubt good for their business model).

• Social media sites and apps now rely primarily on visual sharing; theoretically, this is an easy way for users to cast themselves in a positive light or make a specific statement of some kind. But users should beware—opening oneself to a mass audience can bring unintended critiques, especially on Reddit (QR).

THE CREDIBILITY OF VISUAL IMAGES

Why do mediated visual images play such a dominant role in our society? To a large extent, the development of our visual culture is the result of two widespread (but fallacious) beliefs. One myth is that our eyes see things as they "really" are—that they will not deceive us. Underlying this belief is the sense that if our eyes can't be trusted to see the world as it really is, our very survival as a species is threatened. It is worth noting, however, that visual perception by our species has always been subject to cognitive and emotional sources of distortion. The second false belief is that cameras are able to fully capture reality, when in fact they can only show a portion of what took place (and that's assuming that they have in no way been altered).

Myth #1: We See Things as They Really Are

Even though our eyes are subject to some of the same distortions that affect cameras (e.g., lighting and viewing location), we don't view our world in the way that cameras capture information. Unlike cameras, our eyes are connected to a brain (presumably our own, for now at least). As a result, what we see is affected by other sensory and cognitive processes—each of which has the power to distort perception. Memories, expectations, biases, heightened emotions—even our cultural background (Köster, Itakura, Yovsi, & Kärtner, 2018)—may all affect our visual sensemaking. Such factors work together in a process that researchers call *priming*—when we're processing something that is visually ambiguous, we tend to go with what we already know (or at least what we think we know). If you're looking for Bigfoot, the black blob in the forest that's actually a tree trunk might look like Bigfoot. But if you're looking for a black bear, that same tree trunk might look like a black bear (Novella, 2018).

© Antilo/Shutterstock.com

Myth #2: Cameras See Things as They Really Are

The erroneous belief that our eyes are capable of capturing an unbiased image of reality is compounded by the belief that cameras do. But they don't. The simple fact is that cameras capture data, not reality. To be sure, cameras are continuously getting better at capturing data, but even the newest 360-degree devices have solved some limitations (like restricted viewing angle) but not others (like distance, size distortion, and object quality).

HISTORY OF PHOTOGRAPHS

The first photographic technology was developed by Joseph Nicéphore Niépce and in 1826 his camera captured what is considered the earliest surviving photograph of the real world, the "View from the Window at Le Gras."

Soon after the photographic process was developed, people began experimenting with ways to alter photos (Brugioni, 1999; Kobre, 1995; Lester, 1988). In the 1860s, "spirit photographers" would pre-expose a part of a negative plate with an image of a client's deceased loved

© ullstein bild Dtl./Contributor/Getty Images

one and then use the same plate to photograph the client. This was sufficient evidence for many to believe that the spirits of their relatives were hovering around them.

Edited photos quickly took on a rich history in politics and popular culture:

- Consider the curious (and hotly-debated) case of the "Lincoln/Calhoun Composite Photoprint." Depending on which version of the story you believe, it goes kind of like this:

  - Thomas Hicks once painted a portrait of John C. Calhoun, the former vice-president and senator, based on a photograph by Mathew Brady.

  - In 1852, after Calhoun was dead, A.H. Ritchie made an engraving of the Calhoun portrait.

  - After Lincoln died in 1865, there weren't many truly presidential portraits of the famously unattractive president floating around (Waters, 2017). So printmaker William Pate came up with the idea of superimposing Lincoln's head (from another Brady photograph) onto Calhoun's body to create the heroic-looking print of Lincoln.

  Remarkably, the deception stood for nearly 100 years, not being discovered until someone realized that Lincoln's mole was on the wrong cheek (Selwyn-Holmes, 2010). Regardless— or perhaps *because of* the controversy—today the Calhoun version costs about $65 whereas the Lincoln composite will set you back $1,200. Perhaps the whole thing is helped by the ironic fact that Lincoln and Calhoun were political opposites.

- Lincoln himself knew a thing or two about photographic manipulation. He asked Mathew Brady to retouch his photos to do things like make his neck appear shorter (Vallely, 2004). Lincoln would later credit Brady with helping him get elected (Waters, 2017).

- Doctored photos of Germany's Kaiser Wilhelm supposedly cutting off the hands of babies were used as propaganda in World War I (Vallely, 2004). Stalin's communist Russia was notorious for editing photos (King, 1997) and the alteration of photos in American political campaigns occurred as early as 1928.

- In 1917, two girls in England were able to pull off a photographic hoax that ended up gaining public notoriety because it duped even Sir Arthur Conan Doyle, creator of the otherwise unfoolable detective Sherlock Holmes. Originally a joke aimed at their father, the photos of the "Cottingley fairies" were created using simple staging—but the women didn't admit the hoax until 1983. At a recent auction, the images were expected to fetch nearly £70,000 (Press Association, 2019)(QR).

HISTORY OF FILM/VIDEO

In 1874, French astronomer Pierre Janssen captured photos of Venus eclipsing in front of the Sun and was able to put them together in cinematic style. In 1878, Eadweard Muybridge took a series of photographs that could be put together in animation style to show a horse in motion. By the late 1880s and early 1890s, Louis Le Prince, Thomas Edison, and the Lumière brothers all developed separate (and competing) techniques for producing video. Edison prevailed and built the first film studio in 1893.

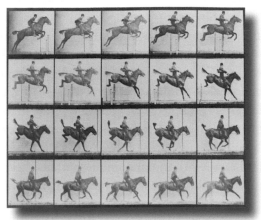

© Everett Histoical/Shutterstock.com

Silent films like Edison's were the first medium to use techniques like angles, timing, cropping, and editing to *set the scene* (discussed later in the chapter). Early special effects in cinematography were accomplished during filming (rather than after) and included increasing the frame rate, use of double-exposure, reverse motion, and stitching together different negatives to create an illusion. Fast forward to current times and the majority of film manipulations and special effects have moved to post-production and use computers and computer-generated imagery (CGI) to set up that which is not possible in real life.

... now we're entering the era of the "deepfake" (deep learning plus fake), powered by artificial intelligence (AI).

For more than 20 years already, even casual users have had access to software and systems that made *editing* video relatively easy. Until recently, however, it was considerably more challenging to alter the image content within a video (removing or adding visuals from/to the original), but now we're entering the era of the "deepfake" (*deep learning* plus *fake*), powered by artificial intelligence (AI)—where one or more of the original faces in the video are convincingly replaced with others. Since 2017, actresses Daisy Ridley, Gal Gadot, Emma Watson, Taylor Swift, and Scarlett Johansson have all been the subject of deepfake celebrity pornographic videos (Roettgers, 2018). Another variant of the deepfake phenomenon is to alter the words someone in the video is speaking by substituting someone else's voice (Vincent, 2018). Filmmaker Jordan Peele even created a short PSA video to demonstrate the potential of deepfakes by altering a Barack Obama clip coupled with his own vocal impersonation of the former president (QR).

These techniques are still in their infancy, but there's already been "an app for that" when it comes to making deepfakes (on Reddit, of course), so the genie is officially out of the bottle. Within a short time, political manipulation, mass panic, false advertising, and character assassination will have found a potent new tool du jour—one that makes the results all but impossible to distinguish from yesterday's fakes. One wonders, nearly a century after the Mercury Theatre on the Air famously (but unintentionally) panicked radio listeners with its uber-realistic dramatization of *The War of the Worlds*, what will the next (and, this time, deliberately deceptive) Orson Welles be able to accomplish? Or just imagine if a hoaxer today were to successfully disseminate something similar to this famous "found footage" scene from *Signs* (2002) (QR). What the announcer in the film says—"All initial opinions are this is genuine. What you're about to see may disturb you"—would be putting it mildly.

SEEING AND BELIEVING IN THE DIGITAL AGE

The dinosaurs of *Jurassic World* and concert holograms of Tupac and Biggie and Kanye are entertaining and powerful, of course, but they're not meant to fool anyone. And for much of digital history, even when the intention was to fool, spotting digital fakes remained relatively easy.

But not anymore.

The "uncanny valley"—the eeriness we feel at seeing something we recognize as almost-but-not-quite human (as in the rendering shown here)—may soon be a thing of the past. Actor Peter Cushing had been dead for more than 20 years when he appeared once again as Grand Moff Tarkin in the Star Wars prequel *Rogue One* (2016). Unlike previous CGI attempts, observed *The Guardian*, the effect was thrilling, remarkable, and breathtaking—and only a *little* uncanny (Walsh, 2016). Samuel L. Jackson's digital transformation into a much younger Nick Fury for 2019's *Captain Marvel* was even more convincing. "Wow," Jackson himself tweeted when the first trailer was released, "this Marvel de-aging thing is doper than I thought" (Sharf, 2018). By most accounts, the tipping point for this "new realism" began with Paul Walker's posthumous appearance in *Furious 7* (Patterson, 2015). Video games are also entering a new phase of ultra-realistic human characters, with the potential to surpass the uncanny valley once and for all (QR).

Social media sites like Twitter aid in the distribution and prevalence of deceptive visuals. After Superstorm Sandy in 2012, for example, researchers used an automated system to detect over 10,000 unique tweets containing fake images—such as sharks swimming down the street (Gupta, Lamba, Kumaraguru, & Joshi, 2013). Many of the same images got recycled after subsequent hurricanes like Harvey, Irma, and Michael.

As a result of such high-profile exposés of doctored images and video, we would expect a heightened vigilance in examining the nature of these visuals. But that doesn't appear to have happened. Why do visual images tend to retain their credibility when we know they can be so easily manipulated? Perhaps the relationship of visual images to deception is similar to that of words to deception. Like spoken deception, its visual cousin can be accomplished in many ways—e.g., through omissions, additions, half-truths, material presented out of context, etc. Despite the widespread knowledge that words can be used to manipulate narratives, numerous studies show that we still maintain a *truth bias* for verbal behavior. We expect people to tell us the truth unless we have reason to believe otherwise. The truth bias applied to visual materials would suggest that most people believe most of what they see most of the time. Perhaps our affinity for visual truth is like that of verbal truth in that it is preferable to the alternatives—widespread distrust, suspicion, paranoia, and ultimately a dysfunctional society. Plus, who has the time to diligently verify everything?

Still, for everyday citizens, understanding how visual images are faked and being vigilant for harmful fakes is part of being an effective consumer of visual information. Doing so may sometimes require visiting websites like Snopes to check out the validity of an image that seems suspicious, but more often we have to rely on our knowledge of how people deceive others visually. Scholars refer to these skills as *media literacy* or *new literacy*. That is, the idea that we must be literate and able to accurately decipher information from a wide range of media channels (not just print and books). In other words, we need to know what to look for.

This literacy begins with understanding how visual images can be manipulated in the first place.

MANIPULATING VISUAL IMAGES

What techniques are used to fake visual images? There are about as many ways to deceive with recorded visual images as there are with words, but the most common are as follows:

1. Setting the scene in a recording so that it communicates a particular message

2. Using the camera or other recording device in ways that make the recording communicate the desired message

3. Modifying the recorded image so that it tells the story desired by the image-maker

4. Falsely labeling the recorded image

Setting the Scene

Like theatrical performances, visual artifacts can be "staged" with the use of props, costumes, and actors. The photographer or producer may also tell the people being recorded where and how to position themselves and how to act— e.g., "speak with less fluency so it seems more realistic." Amateur photographers do this when they look for the most desirable background for a shot or tell people to falsely display an emotion (often a forced smile). Although it is common to smile or "say cheese" when being photographed, this was not always a standard part of photography in the United States (as you can see from this old photograph) and it is still not practiced in every country throughout the world. To sell more cameras, the Eastman Kodak company began an advertising campaign that started in 1893 and lasted for decades (Kotchemidova, 2010). Their goal was to show how personal photography could be fun, so the images of people being photographed in their ads looked happy and were smiling. By the 1940s, the idea that smiling was an expected part of having your photo taken was firmly entrenched in America's culture (Kotchemidova, 2006). Not that it's a bad thing.

© Everett Historical/Shutterstock.com

> Even some animal documentaries are less than honest in how they establish a realistic scene.

Even some animal documentaries are less than honest in how they establish a realistic scene. At one time, Marty Stouffer was known for his stoic-sounding voiceovers and the elegant footage of animals on his show *Wild America*. However, he was eventually accused of deceptive techniques, including tying down a rabbit with fishing string so that a raccoon could catch it, moving larvae from their natural resting place so that fish would eat them,

lying and deception in **HUMAN INTERACTION**

and using fences to keep (sometimes farm-raised) animals in the shot (Palmer, 2010). After several allegations of unethical behavior and accompanying lawsuits, PBS canceled the show. Stouffer defended himself at the time by saying, among other things, "Film costs $125 a roll. We don't have eight or ten or one hundred hours of film to leave rolling until one of these fish grabs a bug" (Boboltz, 2015).

Staging hard-to-film natural behavior is certainly a more acceptable deception than staging an animal's behavior that would not normally occur in nature—such as starting fights between animals that would otherwise avoid each other or provoking animals to attack and then showing them being shot by human actors in "self defense" (Bousé, 2003).

A particularly infamous case of staging was part of the Oscar-winning documentary *White Wilderness* in 1958. A Disney film crew photographed a few dozen lemmings in staged suicide (QR) where the animals were shown jumping off a cliff into water (Douglas, 1992). This single portrayal created the now-commonplace myth about the self-destructive behavior of these rodents (calling masses of people "lemmings" is often used as an insult).

Even today, staged animal fights show up as click-bait on YouTube and other sites.

Ways of Recording the Visual Image

Schwartz (2003) points out that a photographer is always making decisions when creating a visual image that will affect what it portrays, from the choice of lens to the use of light. Thus, different types of information are represented depending on the method used to capture the image. Color photographs provide hues that black-and-white photos do not. Symbolically, black-and-white photography may also communicate a temporal dimension—i.e., the past. Three-dimensional visual images provide information that is not contained in two-dimensional images. With built-in filters and entire apps designed specifically for the purpose of altering images, it is now easier than ever to distort and deceive viewers by using a method of creating that bears little resemblance to the original subject of the image.

Once the type of image-recording is selected, the image-maker must decide what to shoot. Out of all the possible images to record, which should be selected? Sometimes individual shots will accurately represent the reality they capture, but inaccurately reflect the "big picture."

For example, a politician might be touring a poverty-stricken section of town for several hours and soberly contemplating the obvious problems. She smiles for a split second when her host makes a joke, but that's when a news photographer snaps her picture—seeming to laugh in the face of poverty—making her look insensitive to the obvious problems and inaccurately representing 99.5% of her behavior in this situation.

Abraham (2003) showed how stereotypes of African Americans can be perpetuated with visual images that depict them primarily in the context of stories about violence, poverty, and drugs. Such visual stereotyping, he says, can be particularly insidious because it doesn't proclaim itself openly. And when reporters use hidden cameras, they may seek out only those images that verify their expectations and ignore contrary images. In drone strikes targeted at militants and leaders of the Taliban and Al Qaeda, pictures are often shown of the unmanned aircraft and a headshot of the leader who has been killed. The American government releases these images in an effort to appeal to the use of precision bombing and reduced civilian casualties. But reports reveal that between 2004 and 2011, drones also killed approximately 2,900 *civilians*. It has taken up to eight drone strikes to kill a militant target and up to 15 civilians die for every militant killed (Benjamin, 2013). Photos of the wider aftermath of drone attacks are generally not shown to the public.

After selecting the image-making device and the image to be recorded, the image-maker chooses the kind of shot that will best communicate the desired message. Camera shots are like words in the sense that each type of shot has a multi-meaning potential and context plays a crucial role in determining its meaning. In Hitchcock's *North by Northwest*, the hero (Cary Grant) lurks on a balcony above a room that contains the heroine and the villains she doesn't know are planning to murder her. He tries to warn her with a message on a book of matches that he drops into the room (QR—with apologies for the dubbed music). Normally, close-ups of the matchbook and/or the heroine's face would be used to draw the viewer's attention, but instead, the shot is taken from Grant's perspective far above. This unusual point of view heightens the audience's sense of involvement and shared apprehension.

Still photography, video, and film share the ability to alter meanings through the use of distance, focus, point of view, color, lighting, balance, angle, density, contrast, and a host of other features. But unlike still photographs, films and videos can follow a moving target and make an uninterrupted visual record. The resulting array of possible shots would fill a sizeable dictionary, although the purpose of most shots is to elicit varying degrees of attention and emotion (Langford, 1998; 2000; Messaris, 1994; 1997; Monaco, 2000). To illustrate a few of the ways different meanings can be conveyed using different camera shots, consider the following variables.

Shot Location

Cameras are often used to capture what would be a viewer's normal way of seeing something. But since things can be seen from many angles and in many different ways, the location or angle in which the image is captured plays an important role in how the message is interpreted. Britain's Prince William was captured in a photo that would appear to show him flipping off a group of people. Viewing other photographs of the same moment reveal a completely different story (QR).

Shot Clarity

Indistinct images may mean less importance and cause your eyes to focus on something else. Indistinct shots of Bigfoot and the Loch Ness Monster can add to (or, we hope, detract from) believability because they prohibit close scrutiny. Fuzzy images allow viewers to read into a photo whatever they want. Blurry shots may also be used to indicate speed when something is actually stationary.

© Bettmann/Contributor/Getty Images

Focusing and Close-Ups

The word "focus" may refer to the clarity with which a shot is taken or to the tight framing of the shot's target. "Soft" focus can be used to create a more ambiguous or even romantic mood while a sharp focus is associated with clarity. Close-ups are used to signal greater intimacy, involvement, and/or more importance while distant shots commonly provide the context and set the scene. Close-ups make things stand out and, when something or someone is noticeable, it is also perceived to have influence in that situation. For example, when a camera focuses on one person in a conversation, that individual is more likely to be perceived as a causal agent. When the camera focuses solely on a person confessing to a crime, mock jurors are more likely to judge the confession as voluntary and perceive the suspect as guilty than if both suspect and interrogator are videotaped (Lassiter, 2002).

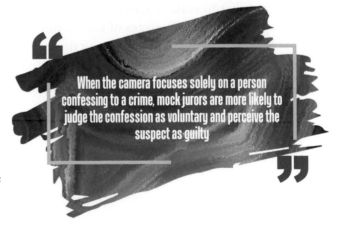

> When the camera focuses solely on a person confessing to a crime, mock jurors are more likely to judge the confession as voluntary and perceive the suspect as guilty

Modifying the Recorded Image

Once the image is recorded, it can be modified in many ways, including, but not limited to, the following: (1) rearranging, (2) retouching, (3) inserting, and (4) deleting.

Rearranging

Rearranging takes the visual subjects and rearranges or repositions them in order to tell a different and/or more dramatic story (see Mitchell's *The Reconfigured Eye*, 1992). For example, parades and golf matches would be much less interesting to the viewer if they were presented in real time and space. Instead, shots taken at different times and/ or places become part of a coherent narrative. In interviews and debates, the reaction shots are not always expressions that immediately followed the previous comment. If this shot of the space shuttle looks too perfect, that's because it is. All of the elements are real, but they've been rearranged for dramatic impact.

One of the most infamous examples of rearranging occurred in 1982 when editors at *National Geographic* digitally moved two pyramids closer together to make a better looking image for the cover. Given the magazine's reputation for producing "true" images of nature, this technically minor manipulation was viewed by many as scandalous. It's worth noting that the photographer, who was upset that his iconic image had been altered, had no qualms about paying the men in the picture to ride their camels back and forth until he was able to get the shot he wanted (Nickle, 2017).

Photo rearrangement is also used to make politicians look foolish. George W. Bush was once shown reading to a group of schoolchildren—but the photograph was altered so that it appeared he was holding the book upside down (Jaffe, 2002).

Retouching

Retouching is usually done to make the visual image look more pristine or to alter perceptions of attractiveness. Among other changes, it is not unusual for images of movie and television personalities, models, public figures, and people appearing in advertisements to have their skin tone altered; the thickness of their eyebrows or hips reduced; their wrinkles, stray hairs, and skin blemishes removed; their teeth and eyes whitened; and their pupils, breasts, and buttocks enlarged. In 2015, Kim Kardashian famously "broke the Internet" with a photo of her nude backside. The public response was overwhelming, but a lot of it had to do with the blatant retouching of her back, waist, and buttocks.

There is no shortage of videos and photos showing "before and after" retouches of people. In 2014, a Utah school was accused of selectively removing items from female students' yearbook photos (such as tattoos and nose rings). They also added sleeves and undershirts if students lacked them. The following year, a high school senior attending a private school used Reddit to communicate dismay at administrators for (re)issuing student IDs that had been manipulated in ways that included face thinning, skin smoothing, skin and lip recoloring, and eyebrow recoloring and shaping.

Photos of criminals and others who have been missing for years can be retouched in order to show what changes the passing of time has likely brought about. In June 1994, O. J. Simpson's photo appeared on both *Time* and *Newsweek* magazines but *Time's* photo was darkened (QR). *Time* said it was done for dramatic effect, but it was viewed by many readers as an attempt to make Simpson appear more sinister.

© nito/Shutterstock.com

Retouching is also done with nature scenes—e.g., when an editor wants greener grass or a "cleaner" image of the planet Venus.

Inserting

By definition, inserting part of one photo into another or combining two separate photos is an act of fiction. If the audience is unaware of the insertion, then it becomes an act of deception as well. In an official photo taken at the 1999 wedding of England's Prince Edward, his nephew, Prince William, did not smile. So William's smiling face from another photo was digitally inserted into the official photo and all was well in the royal household. The same process of insertion is used to "bring back" deceased friends and family members by digitally including them in current photos.

As mentioned previously, movies often insert living actors into films with deceased people or insert deceased actors into new films (from *Forrest Gump* to *Rogue One*). Since movies are designed to be entertaining, the intent of these insertions is rarely considered deceptive. But attributions of deception can still happen—even if the creator considered it a humorous act rather than a primarily deceptive one (e.g., a 1989 cover of *TV Guide* placed Oprah Winfrey's head on the body of movie actress Ann-Margret in what was intended by the artist as a lighthearted illustration; it didn't help that "Oprah" was sitting provocatively on a pile of cash). As a general practice, circulating images with the heads of female celebrities on the bodies of other women has become so common that it requires special websites whose purpose it is to catalog the fakes.

The University of Wisconsin tried to make the school seem more diverse by inserting the face of an African-American student into a brochure photo showing a group of football fans. A lawsuit brought by the student edited into the photo resulted in a $10 million "budgetary apology" to be used for recruitment of minority students and diversity initiatives (Paul, 2014). Such diversifying of universities (in photography, at least) is widespread. Pippert, Essenburg, and Matchett (2013) analyzed over 10,000 photos from 165 institutions of higher education in the United States and found that the majority of schools portray diversity in marketing materials that differs significantly from the actual student population. The modern trend by universities is to use student actors in photos and videos who are "racially ambiguous" or who appear multi-ethnic (as in this stock photo). That is, instead of risking the perception or claims that they are inflating the proportion of students in their advertising materials who are non-Caucasian, schools are increasingly using images of people who are not easily regarded as any particular ethnicity.

© Harbucks/Shutterstock.com

In 2003, *Los Angeles Times* photographer Brian Walski combined two photographs captured moments apart of a British soldier directing Iraqi civilians to take cover during combat. But when an employee of the *Hartford Courant* (which had used the photo) noticed that the image appeared altered, an investigation ensued and Walski was soon dismissed from the *Times* (Irby, 2003). Apparently, Walski preferred the blending of the two photographs better than either one of them and didn't feel that it significantly changed the story behind the event. But, the *Times* and other newspapers depend on strict policies about altered photographs in order to maintain their credibility as sources of news. When news photos are altered for any reason, it raises questions about the extent to which other reported information might also be altered to tell a better story.

Even though some degree of damage may have occurred in the preceding examples, the originators would claim that harm was not their intent. There are, however, other examples of insertions that were created explicitly for the purpose of hurting others—too many to count, in fact. But for a fairly up-to-date listing at any point in time, check out the "Fauxtography" feature at Snopes. There you'll find the good, the bad, and the truly ugly sides of digital fakery.

Deleting

Visual images can also be altered by taking something away from the original—a person, an object, a sound, etc. Cherished photos of yourself that also happen to have hated in-laws or an ex-partner in them can be realistically preserved with the offending parties removed. All prisoners in the New York State prison system are required to have their photograph taken when they are clean shaven. But Rabbi Shlomo Helbrans, who was sentenced to 12 years for kidnapping, requested an exemption on religious grounds. Eventually, the case was settled by sending a photo of the bearded Rabbi to a company that digitally eliminated the beard (James, 1994).

In Stalin's Russia, the deletion of personal and political rivals from photos was a common practice (King, 1997), but it has been done by other political leaders including Hitler and China's Mao Zedong. The hope was that these deletions would permanently alter the historical record of the country. Benito Mussolini had the handler removed from a photo so that he and his sword could look more heroic posing on the handler's horse. The iconic photo of the Kent State Massacre by John Filo shows a woman mourning over a body lying face down in the street. In the original (Google it), a fence post was very awkwardly positioned behind her head. The distracting piece of hardware was conveniently deleted before the image was published in numerous magazines. The altered version won the Pulitzer and is considered one of the iconic photos of 20th century American history.

Labeling the Image

Labeling a visual image requires little effort since the visual image itself is left intact. Mislabeling for deceptive purposes can be a relatively straightforward and uncomplicated act. For example, the "Surgeon's Photo" of a toy submarine with a model of a serpent's head attached was labeled "Loch Ness Monster" and induced many people to believe the myth. Only after 60 years was this intentional lie revealed (Hallemann, 2017).

In 2015, a local Fox affiliate in Memphis posted a photo on its social media page showing a massive urban fire. The comment read "Baltimore in flames," but the photo was from a fire in Venezuela the previous year—the image spread rapidly before someone pointed out that it was not Baltimore. The station quickly removed it and issued an apology.

Today, images and videos can go viral astonishingly fast. In 2014, Abdel Aziz Al-Atibi posted a photo he took of his young nephew and two piles of rocks he constructed to resemble shallow graves (Hooton, 2014). The Internet took over and the photo was quickly mislabeled as an image of an orphaned child from Syria lying near shallow graves of his parents who were killed in war. When the artist realized his image was being misconstrued as genuine journalism, he released shots of his happy (and living) nephew from their photo shoot (QR).

Sometimes the content of the visual image is not disputed, but it is labeled in a deceptive way by the message accompanying the image. For example:

> Sometimes the content of the visual image is not disputed, but it is labeled in a deceptive way by the message accompanying the image.

- Email phishing scams often use the actual logos of legitimate banks and businesses in order to deceive their victims. (best advice: Never log in to any of your accounts using a link contained in an email; always go directly to the site and log in from there).

- In 1999, Fox aired a show featuring an archaeologist uncovering various artifacts in an Egyptian tomb as if he didn't know what it was he might find. Actually, one of the tombs was discovered in the 1800s and the archaeologist had discovered another tomb a month before the broadcast. The archaeologist and crew knew everything that would be "found" before the show began (Moore, 2000).

- Wise (1990) recounts ABC News broadcasting an unlabeled simulation of an actor resembling accused American spy Felix Bloch handing over a briefcase to another man in the context of a story about the Bloch spy case. Many viewers believed they were seeing an actual transaction between a spy and a Soviet agent.

- In 2009, a video of Barack Obama's trip to Russia circulated with a description about how Russian officials snubbed him. With the help of a little deceptive labeling, the video created the impression that the Russians refused to shake the president's hand. However, in the video Obama was actually introducing a Russian politician to U.S. officials (and thus gesturing with his arm as he made the introductions). Watching the video with the proper information alters the interpretation entirely (QR).

Another possible source of misleading labeling occurs when a visual image is labeled solely according to its genre—e.g., movie, documentary, advertisement, news, science, art, etc.

The viewer must then must choose the degree of truthfulness or fiction to assign to the genre. However, truth and fiction are increasingly melded together in every genre. The labels are less effective than they used to be in delineating whether a viewer is seeing truth or fiction:

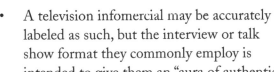

" ... genre labels are less effective than they used to be in delineating whether a viewer is seeing truth or fiction. "

- A television infomercial may be accurately labeled as such, but the interview or talk show format they commonly employ is intended to give them an "aura of authenticity" (Messaris, 1997, p. 143). *Intended* is the operative word here. In the early 1990s, Cher's career nearly imploded after she appeared in a series of much-maligned infomercials. The ultimate proof of how poorly they were received came when *Saturday Night Live* spoofed them (Klara, 2019).

- A television program devoted to an alien autopsy or questioning whether United States astronauts actually landed on the moon may begin with the necessary disclaimer, but viewers who miss the beginning may find the content credible. This is exactly what happened with the Discovery Channel's "documentary-style" special "Megalodon: The Monster Shark Lives" (it was, after all, Shark Week 2013). Many viewers missed the brief opening disclaimer and thought they were watching a horrible new reality unfolding. "It was presented in such a way that you could very easily watch it and not know it was fictional," one shark expert told NPR (Yahr, 2018).

- In the 1991 movie *JFK*, fictional new material was seamlessly blended into some old, grainy, black-and-white film from the 1960s. Since movies are made for the viewers' entertainment, they are generally considered fiction, but the segment in *JFK* combined grainy, black-and-white footage of the actual Kennedy assassination with similar-looking fictional footage. The intent was to make this segment of the film look authentic and support the theme developed in the rest of the movie (which was in color). Despite these controversies, director Oliver Stone had as many supporters as detractors when it came to his unorthodox storytelling style. "Doesn't Oliver Stone have the right to speculate on American history?" asked film critic Gene Siskel (1991) in his review for the *Chicago Tribune*. His colleague Roger Ebert agreed: "*JFK* is a brilliant reflection of our unease and paranoia, our restless dissatisfaction. On that level, it is completely factual" (Keeling, 2017).

- *The Path to 9/11*, a television miniseries about the events leading up to the attack on the World Trade Center, was based on interviews and documents from the 9/11 Commission's report. It was presented in the style of a documentary. But the show itself contained fictional scenes, composite characters and dialogue, as well as time compression. Former Secretary of State Madeline Albright and former National Security Advisor Sandy Berger argued that they were portrayed in fictional and defamatory ways (SPIN, 2006).

Such problems will likely occur whenever attempts are made to "dramatize" historical events. Audiences, not to mention any central characters who may still be living, had their own view of how these events actually unfolded, but strict adherence to these perceptions may not provide the drama and entertainment the producers wish to achieve. This disconnect between reality and its retelling as art is especially common in blockbuster Hollywood biopics. Despite winning Oscars in four out of five nominated categories, *Bohemian Rhapsody* (2018) was roundly criticized for taking creative license with the timeline of key events and its use of overly-sanitized plotlines (Huff & Shanley, 2018).

Participants on reality TV are often coached to say things that will make a good story. Their actual behavior is often heavily edited for the same purpose. Staged scenes, reenactments, and altered dialogue are commonplace:

- On *The Dating Experiment*, a female participant did not like a suitor who the producers wanted her to like. So, they interviewed her and asked her about her favorite celebrity. She said she really loved Adam Sandler. For the show, Sandler's name was edited out, and the male suitor's name was inserted.

- When a couple on *Joe Millionaire* went for a walk behind some trees, the following statement that the woman had made earlier in the day in a completely different context was dubbed in: "It's better if we're lying down" (Poniewozik, 2006).

- In 1999, paid actors rented a house in Idaho pretending to be deranged new homeowners who mud wrestled in their front yard and covered the rest of the yard with 52 pink flamingos. This was to be part of a "hidden camera" special called *World's Nastiest Neighbors* (Lowry, 1999).

- A colleague of ours was a participant on a reality TV show, *Elimidate*, when he was in college. He told us some lies may even begin before participants are selected. In order to be selected, prospective participants make up stories to make themselves look like an energetic, outgoing, and slightly outrageous person who has the potential to generate a good story line. Once the show begins filming, participants are coached on how to produce conflict and action by confronting and challenging the other participants. The producers helped select the participants' clothes for the images they wanted to portray. They even told our colleague which players should be eliminated and which ones should be selected.

Reality shows have evolved to take on other (sometimes inappropriate) elements of deception in their plots. For example, *Undercover Boss* has the CEO of a company act as a normal customer or entry-level worker to interact with the organization's employees. A few other guises used for "reality" entertainment were a millionaire on a dating show who was really a construction worker, and a dating show where the male participants were (unknowingly) competing to court a transgender female.

SPOTTING FAKE VISUAL IMAGES

Besides using our awareness and own beliefs about what is true or false, there are tools that can be used to detect fake images. For example, digital photos can be masked with an invisible watermark to detect alterations of the image. Digital watermarks are useful because the watermark cannot be seen without a known algorithm. If a watermarked image is altered, it can be detected via programs that rely on statistical schemes (Ohkita, Yoshida, Kitamura, & Fujiwara, 2009). Although some manufacturers sell digital cameras with watermarking capabilities, the technology has yet to gain wide acceptance (Meerwald & Uhl, 2009). Researchers are developing software that anyone can use on their own computer to detect manipulated images (Sutardja, Ramadan, & Zhao, 2015). In the meantime, you should, at a minimum, adopt the following three practices:

1. Be Alert to the Possibility of Deceptive Visual Images

Most of the photos or videos we view are not intentionally manipulated (for now at least), but the availability of software and phone apps that make the altering of images easy should cause consumers of these messages to be wary. If a particular visual image is worth the time to question, the first area of concern should be the source of the image. Is the image-maker identified? Is there any reason to question the motives of the source relative to this image, whether identified or not? Political campaigns, social issues, and scientific debates all feature players who have something to win or lose.

Case in point: The infamous photo purporting to show John Kerry protesting with Jane Fonda was widely circulated on the Internet during Kerry's 2004 presidential campaign in an effort to depict him as "soft" on dealing with terrorists (QR). A photo of Jane Fonda taken in 1972 was inserted into a 1971 photo of Kerry. The two were not appearing together as the photo indicates (Hafner, 2004; Light, 2004). But the damage was done, fooling many Americans and even some newspapers in Britain (Vallely, 2004).

2. Examine the Visual Image

You don't have to be an expert in the detection of visual manipulation in order to look for some obvious signs of deception. Knowing the techniques used by people who create deceptive visuals can enhance our ability to detect when an image has been altered.

Sometimes inconsistencies are derived from one's knowledge of how things normally work. They may also be found within the visual image or video itself. If the background is not consistent, it may mean something has been inserted; if the focus of images nearest the camera and those furthest from it are similar, tampering should be suspected. Computer-generated images sometimes stand out because they are ridiculously sharp/clear and feature well-defined edges that traditional photography is less likely to capture.

Smith (2018) recommends using the following strategies to sniff out fakes:

- Do a reverse image search using Google Image or sites like TinEye

- Check debunking sites like Snopes to see if the photo has already been outed as fake

- Because most people, including most fakers, are not cognizant of the physics of light and shadow, use this to your advantage. Get a ruler, select objects in the photo, and draw lines from points on those objects to the corresponding points in their shadows. Do as many of these as you can. The lines should appear to *converge on a single light source*. If some of the lines appear to be aiming elsewhere, then that object or objects may have been digitally added (as in the image at right).

© Andrey_I/Shutterstock.com

- Use photo or image editing software to wildly adjust settings like brightness, contrast, and exposure. If *solid blocks of color appear* after those extreme manipulations are done, it suggests something was digitally removed. In real life, even patches of black contain a wide range of brightness and therefore different color values.

- Automatically assume that almost any shark image posted after a storm is fake

When it comes to digital sleuthing, the above list is a good starting point. But if you really, *really* want to get into the weeds when it comes to investigating photo fakery, we recommend articles like this case study by van Ess (2017), "Inside the Trenches of an Information War" (QR).

While you're at it, you might also consider following Twitter and other social media accounts dedicated to unmasking instances of digital deception worldwide (it is, after all, a worldwide phenomenon). As of this writing, current Twitter accounts devoted to such services include **@PicPedant**, **@HoaxofFame**, and **@FakeAstroPix**. There are dozens more, many of them genre-specific.

One last general observation: Skilled fakers may also do some old-fashioned "smudging" to cover their tracks. For example, a few years ago the National Rifle Association (NRA) used the addition of a bright sun glare to try to cover up their editing tracks (Mathis-Lilley, 2015). They posted a photo on their website showing a diverse group of citizens at a pro-gun rally. But it was a readily available commercial stock photo. The original image did not show the people holding pro-NRA signage, and the addition of the glare was an obvious attempt to cover up evidence of editing.

3. Use Qualifiers When Talking About Visual Image Authenticity

Most of us have developed a sense of caution about what other people tell us. When we suspect they may not be telling us the truth, we are reluctant to accept it unequivocally. We say things like, "Well, he said he wasn't the one who did it, but I sure wouldn't be surprised to find out he did do it." Now more than ever, visual images deserve the same kind of healthy skepticism and caution. You might, for example, say: "I know what it looked like in the video, but videos and photos can be altered. Let's find out if the video is authentic first." Then do a little homework to see if you can find information about whether the image was altered. Of course, you should be prepared to face some serious blowback if the person you're challenging is highly partisan or otherwise heavily invested in their need to believe the image.

SUMMARY

Our everyday experience is filled with mediated visual images. Photos and videos exert a strong influence on what we know and believe about our world. The power of social media is undeniable. As people often do, they first believe before they disbelieve; that is, there is a visual truth bias. The belief that our eyes and cameras see things as they "really are" is a strongly held belief by many—despite the widespread knowledge that our eyes can deceive us, that recorded visual images can be faked, and that visual manipulation is increasingly accomplished with considerable expertise by everyday citizens. Today, apps and other software make it easy to skip the step of producing a one-to-one image of reality before taking on the alteration process. Instead the modifications are increasingly built-in.

The doctoring of visual images has a long history. Photographs were faked soon after photography was invented, and altering film and staging techniques were common in creating storylines in early silent films. But the digital revolution has made it possible to manipulate visual images and videos almost seamlessly, and to create computer-generated beings that can satisfy our curiosity more than live human actors. Our visual world is rapidly and dramatically changing and that requires each citizen to increase his or her visual intelligence. Some doctored visual images are funny or inconsequential, the equivalent of a white lie, but others can be catastrophic when they throw into question serious matters of science, law, religion, journalism, or politics. Look up some deepfake videos—do they bother you? Anyone who isn't gravely concerned about the implications of this kind of technology simply isn't paying attention.

Some of the many ways visual images can be manipulated were identified in this chapter. They included: (1) setting or staging a scene in order to convey a particular message; (2) using a camera in ways that promote a particular message—e.g., the length, angle, and clarity of the shot and/or the distance and location of the camera; (3) modifying the visual image after it is recorded—e.g., rearranging, retouching, inserting, and/or deleting the content; and (4) labeling the recorded image in ways that lead to the desired interpretation.

We concluded with some specific recommendations for citizens as they process and experience mediated visual images. Without altogether abandoning our visual truth bias, we need to be alert to the possibility that a photo or video has been manipulated. We also need to learn some basic ways to detect alterations ourselves and make use of resources whose business it is to detect fake visual images. The way we talk about visual images should also be subject to the same kind of qualifiers that we use when evaluating verbal behavior.

EXERCISES

1. The "truth bias" is a powerful effect and is well documented in the deception detection literature (see Levine, 2019). It seems that it occurs both in what we hear and what we see. Its effects influence our judgments for both verbal behavior and mediated visual images. There are also deceptive visual images that could be classified as "low-stakes" and "high-stakes" lies, as with verbal behavior in Chapter 7. Can you identify other similarities in the production and detection of deceptive visual images that are similar to spoken and written deception?

2. Why do you think people tend to trust visual images as inherently authentic (the visual truth bias) when they know it is so easy to alter these images? Simply adding a particular label can make a major impact on how the same image is otherwise received. Try it yourself: Take a photo and make two versions of it. In one version put a truthful label, and in the other put a deceptive label. Show it to your friends and family and see if they can detect the falsely-labeled version. Why were they good or bad at this task?

OF INTEREST

Welcome to the game-changer. YouTube user Ctrl Shift Face deliberately created this sophisticated deepfake of comedian Bill Hader's face replaced with that of Arnold Schwarzenegger. His purpose was to educate the public about the realities and dangers of what's possible, and he even shared examples of his data sets and techniques with NBC News. It only took two days to create, and he did it using free software called DeepFaceLab.

Not to be missed: The Bronx Documentary Center's online exhibit detailing some of the more egregious manipulations from the first 150 years of photography. Included: OJ's *Time* magazine cover, *National Geographic*'s moving pyramids, North Korean propaganda, and many more. The other linked features on the site are also worth a visit.

Speaking of *National Geographic*'s pyramids, in this 2016 op-ed, the publication's editors explain how they learned their lesson and offer recommendations for keeping the field of photography honest in the Digital Age and the era of Photoshop.

In this digital archeology of how the modern myth of the Loch Ness Monster came to be, the *New York Times* traces its own frantic coverage of Nessie in the mid-1930s. It's hard not to be amused when reading these articles, but modern media are no less immune to such flights of fancy.

REFERENCES

Abraham, L. (2003). Media stereotypes of African Americans. In P. M. Lester & S. D. Ross (Eds.), *Images that injure* (2nd ed., pp. 87–92). Westport, CT: Praeger.

Benjamin, M. (2013). *Drone warfare: Killing by remote control.* New York, NY: Verso.

Benjamin, D., & Simon, S. (2019, July 5). How fake news could lead to real war. *Politico*. Retrieved from http://www.politico.com

Boboltz, S. (2015, May 13). These are some of the sketchy ways nature documentaries are actually filmed. *Huffpost*. http://www.huffpost.com

Bousé, D. (2003). Computer-generated images: Wildlife and natural history films. In L. Gross, J. S. Katz, & J. Ruby (Eds.), *Image ethics in the digital age* (pp. 217–245). Minneapolis, MN: University of Minnesota Press.

Brugioni, D. A. (1999). *Photo fakery.* Dulles, VA: Brassey's.

Cummings, C. (2016, November 28). Infographic: What consumers really want from your video content. *Adweek*. Retrieved from http://www.adweek.com

Douglas, S. (1992, February 21). Scientists demolish lemming legends. *The Vancouver Sun*, p. D2.

Gupta, A., Lamba, H., Kumaraguru, P., & Joshi, A. (2013). Faking Sandy: Characterizing and identifying fake images on Twitter during Hurricane Sandy. *WWW 2013 Companion: Proceedings of the 22nd International Conference on World Wide Web*, 729–736. http://dx.doi.org/10.1145/2487788.2488033

Hafner, K. (2004, March 11). The camera never lies, but the software can. *The New York Times*. Retrieved from http://www.nytimes.com

Hallemann, C. (2017, April 21). How the Daily Mail created the modern myth of the Loch Ness Monster. *Town & Country*. Retrieved from http://townandcountrymag.com

Hooton, C. (2014, January 17). 'Heartbreaking' Syria orphan photo wasn't taken in Syria and not of orphan. *Independent*. Retrieved from http://www.independent.co.uk

Huff, L., & Shanley, P. (2018, October 23). 'Bohemian Rhapsody': What the critics are saying. *The Hollywood Reporter*. Retrieved from http://www.hollywoodreporter.com

Irby, K. (2003, April 2). *L.A. Times* photographer fired over altered image. *Poynter*. Retrieved from http://www.poynter.org

Jaffe, J. (2002, November 16). Dubya, willya turn the book over? *WIRED*. Retrieved from http://www.wired.com

James, G. (1994, December 29). Computer replaces razor for rabbi's prison picture. *The New York Times*. Retrieved from http://www.nytimes.com

Keeling, R. (2017, April 19). Oliver Stone's JFK: A masterful blend of fact and fiction. *Den of Geek!* Retrieved from http://www.denofgeek.com

King, D. (1997). *The commissar vanishes: The falsification of photographs and art in Stalin's Russia.* New York, NY: Metropolitan.

Klara, R. (2019, February 11). How informercials almost ruined Cher's career. *ADWEEK.* Retrieved from http://www.adweek.com

Kobre, K. (1995). The long tradition of doctoring photos. *Visual Communication Quarterly, 2,* 14–15.

Köster, M., Itakura, S., Yovsi, R., & Kärtner, J. (2018). Visual attention in 5-year-olds from three different cultures. *PloS one, 13*(7), e0200239.

Kotchemidova, C. (2006). Why we say "cheese": Producing the smile in snapshot photography. *Critical Studies in Media Communication, 22,* 2–25.

Kotchemidova, C. (2010). Emotion culture and cognitive constructions of reality. *Communication Quarterly, 58,* 207–234.

Langford, M. (1998). *Advanced photography.* 6th ed. Boston, MA: Focal Press.

Langford, M. (2000). *Basic photography.* 7th ed. Boston, MA: Focal Press.

Lassiter, G. D. (2002). Illusory causation in the courtroom. *Current Directions in Psychological Science, 11,* 204–208.

Lester, P. M. (1988). Faking images in photojournalism. *Media Development, 1,* 41–42.

Lester, P. M., & Yambor, M. (2019). Visual deception: From camo to Cameron. In Docan-Morgan, T. (Ed.), *The Palgrave handbook of deceptive communication* (pp. 857–875). New York, NY: Palgrave Macmillan.

Levine T. R. (2019). An overview of detecting deceptive communication. In Docan-Morgan, T. (Ed.), *The Palgrave handbook of deceptive communication* (pp. 289–301). New York, NY: Palgrave Macmillan.

Light, K. (2004, February 28). Fonda, Kerry and photo fakery. *Washington Post,* p. A21.

Lowry, B. (1999, May 16). "Inside Edition" vs. Fox: When reality attacks! *Austin American Statesman,* pp. E6–7.

Mathis-Lilley, B. (2015, January 14). NRA picture of diverse gun rights rally appears to be photo-shopped from stock image. *Slate.* Retrieved from http://www.slate.com

Meerwald, P., & Uhl, A. (2009). Watermarking of raw digital images in camera firmware: Embedding and detection. In T. Wada, F. Huang, & S. Lin (Eds.), *Advances in image and video technology* (pp. 340–348). Berlin, Germany: Springer.

Messaris, P. (1994). *Visual literacy: Image, mind, and reality.* Boulder, CO: Westview.

Messaris, P. (1997). *Visual persuasion: The role of images in advertising*. Thousand Oaks, CA: Sage.

Mitchell, W. J. (1992). *The reconfigured eye: Visual truth in the post-photographic era*. Cambridge, MA: MIT Press.

Monaco, J. (2000). *How to read a film*. New York, NY: Oxford University Press.

Moore, F. (2000, November 13). Fox buried truth on 'Lost Tombs'. *The Journal Times*. Retrieved from http://www.journaltimes.com

Nickle, R. (2017, February 28). Visual deceptions: National Geographic and the pyramids of Giza. *Medium*. Retrieved from http://www.medium.com

Novella, S. (2018, August 2). Prior exposure influences what we see. *Neurologica Blog*. Retrieved from https://theness.com/neurologicablog

Ohkita, K., Yoshida, M., Kitamura, I., & Fujiwara, T. (2009). Improving capability of locating tampered pixels of statistical fragile watermarking. In A. Ho, Y. Shi, H. Kim, & M. Barni (Eds.), *Digital watermarking* (pp. 279–293). Berlin, Germany: Springer.

Palmer, C. (2010). *Shooting in the wild: An insider's account of making movies in the animal kingdom*. San Francisco, CA: Sierra Club Books.

Pant, R. (2015, January 16). Visual marketing: A picture's worth 60,000 words. Business2Community. Retrieved from http://www.business2community.com

Patterson, J. (2015, March 27). CGI Friday: A brief history of computer-generated actors. *The Guardian*. Retrieved from http://www.theguardian.com

Paul, A. M. (2014, March 15). When images of diversity don't match reality. *The Epoch Times*. Retrieved from http://www.theepochtimes.com

Perrin, A., & Anderson, M. (2019, April 10). Share of U.S. adults using social media, including Facebook, is mostly unchanged since 2018. *Pew Research Center*. Retrieved from http://www.pewresearch.org

Pippert, T. D., Essenburg, L. J., & Matchett, E. J. (2013). We've got minorities, yes we do: Visual representations of racial and ethnic diversity in college recruitment materials. *Journal of Marketing for Higher Education, 23*, 258–282.

Poniewozik, J. (2006, February 6). How reality TV fakes it. *Time Magazine, 167*, 60–62.

Press Association. (2019, March 31). Cottingley Fairies fake photos to go under the hammer. *The Guardian*. Retrieved from http://www.theguardian.com

Richter, F. (2017, August 31). Smartphones cause photography boom. *Statista*. Retrieved from http://www.statista.com

Roettgers, J. (2018, February 21). Porn producers offer to help Hollywood take down deepfake videos. *Variety*. Retrieved from http://www.variety.com

Rothman, J. (2018, November 5). In the age of A.I., is seeing still believing? *The New Yorker*. Retrieved from http://www.newyorker.com

Schwartz, D. (2003). Professional oversight: Policing the credibility of photojournalism. In L. Gross, J. S. Katz, & J. Ruby (Eds.), *Image ethics in the digital age* (pp. 27–51). Minneapolis, MN: University of Minnesota Press.

Selwyn-Holmes, A. (April 24, 2010). Lincoln-Calhoun composite. *Iconic Photos*. Retrieved from http://www.iconicphotos.wordpress.com

Sharf, Z. (2018, September 5). 'Captain Marvel' de-Aged Samuel L. Jackson to look years younger, and even he's shocked by the end result. *IndieWire*. Retrieved from http://www.indiewire.com

Siskel, G. (1991, December 20). Oliver Stone's 'JFK' is remarkable moviemaking. *Chicago Tribune*. Retrieved from http://www.chicagotribune.com

Smith, B. (2018, July 24). Fake news, hoax images: How to spot a digitally altered photo from the real deal. Australian Broadcasting Corporation. Retrieved from http://abc.net.au

SPIN Staff. (2006, September 11). Controversial new 9/11 miniseries. *SPIN*. Retrieved from http://www.spin.com

Sutardja, A., Ramadan, O., & Zhao, Y. (2015). *Forensic methods for detecting image manipulation-copy move* (Technical Report No. UCB/EECS-2015-84). University of California at Berkeley.

Vallely, P. (2004, February 18). Lies, damned lies and photography: How the camera can distort the truth. *Independent*. Retrieved from http://www.independent.co.uk

van Ess, H. (2017, February 22). Inside the trenches of an information war. *Medium*. Retrieved from http://www.medium.com

Vincent, J. (2018, April 17). Watch Jordan Peele use AI to make Barack Obama deliver a PSA about fake news. *The Verge*. Retrieved from http://www.theverge.com

Walsh, J. (2016, December 16). Rogue One: The CGI resurrection of Peter Cushing is thrilling—but is it right? *The Guardian*. Retrieved from http://www.theguardian.com

Waters, M. (2017, July 12). The great lengths taken to make Abraham Lincoln look good in portraits. *Atlas Obscura*. Retrieved from http://www.atlasobscura.com

Waterson, J. (2019, May 24). Facebook refuses to delete fake Pelosi video spread by Trump supporters. *The Guardian*. Retrieved from http://www.theguardian.com

Wise, D. (1990, May 13). The Felix Bloch affair. *The New York Times Magazine, 42*.

Yahr, E. (2018, July 26). A fake Shark Week documentary about megalodons caused controversy, so why is Discovery bringing it up again? *Washington Post*. Retrieved from http://www.washingtonpost.com

INDEX

N

Nader, Ralph (whistleblower), 323
Narcissistic personality disorder, 262–266
Narrative, visual, 500
Nathaniel Borenstein, 31
National Academy of Sciences, 378
National Business Ethics Survey, 82
National Geographic, 500, 511
National Research Council, 378
National Rifle Association (NRA), 509
National Security Agency (NSA), 79, 388, 438
NATURE, 121
Nazi Germany, 61
   news coverage of, 457
NBA (National Basketball Association), 178–179
NBC Nightly News, 451
Negative affect, 232
Negative feelings, 234
Negative reactions, 236
Negativity, 233
Negotiations, 206, 239
Nervous mannerisms, 203
Nervousness, 232
Neuroscience, 85
New literacy, 495
New Republic, 450
Newspapers, 238
Newsweek, 455
New York Times, 450, 512
Nielsen, Kirstjen, 13
Nigerian letter scam, 290
Nilsen, T.R., 78
Nixon, Richard, 12, 417, 424, 425, 437
Noble lies, 61, 187, 434–435
Nonprofessionals, accuracy of, 331–332
Nontrivial lies, 206
Nonverbal behavior, 11, 131, 231, 339
Nonverbal concealment behaviors, 131
North, Oliver, 12
North by Northwest (1959 film), 498
Nostalgia, 58, 175

NSA wiretapping, 448
Nyberg, David, 8–9, 26, 45, 61, 65, 71, 78, 179

O

Obama, Barack, 62, 79, 418, 424, 436, 493, 504
Obama administration, 438
Oberweis, Jim, 433
Objectivity, 459–462
Observation, 34–42, 341
   behavioral, 328–334
   independent, 460
Observation conditions, 38–39
Observer characteristics, 36–38
Obsessive-compulsive personality disorder, 267
Office of Technology Assessment (Congress), 378, 388
Older siblings, 130
O'Leary, George, 476
Omissions
   journalistic, 455
   lies of, 436–437
Online behavior, 134
Online dating services, 221
Online deception, 209, 216, 221, 246
Online scams, 290–292
Open-ended question, 152
Opinion leaders, 30
Opossums, 109
Optimism, 172, 177
Orchids, 99
O'Reilly, Bill, 191, 274, 452
Othello error, 337
Other minds problem, 135
Other people, 30
Out of Many (1994 book), 467–468
Overconfidence, 191
Overlooking, 334
Overlooking behavioral cues, 338
Owls, 118

P

Packer, George, 57
Paltering, 238–239, 246

Paradox, 143
Paranormal phenomena, 295–296
Parasites, 113
Parental lies, 143
Parents, 82–83, 131–132, 139, 140–143
Parker, George C. (con artist), 288
Partisanship, 458
Pathogens, 97
Pathological lying, 258–260
The Path to 9/11 (TV miniseries), 505–506
Patternicity, 179–180
Patterson, Robert (Bigfoot hoax), 302
Pecard, David (impostor), 278–279
Peeking experiments, 130
Peele, Jordan, 493
Peer groups, 140, 207
Peer pressure, 150
Peer review, 463
Pelosi, Nancy, 488
Pentagon papers, 418, 424
Perception, 472–473
Performers, 190
Perrott, George (wrongful conviction), 326
Persian Gulf War, 421–422
Personal beliefs, 33, 170
Personality, 355
Personality disorders, 259–267
Person of interest, 348
Perspective-taking, 130, 135–136
Persuasive appeals, 350
Pertinent omissions, 432
Perversive deception among animals, 103–109
Peter the Adequate, 227
Pew Research Center, 448, 490
Phishing, 31, 290–291, 504
Photography, 222
   history of, 491–492
Photo lineup, 41
Physical affliction, 189–190
Physical appearance, 220, 221
Physical appearance (animals), 110–112
Physical well-being, 189–190
Physics, 166, 298